Requirements Engineering

Requirements Engineering

From System Goals to UML Models to Software Specifications

Axel van Lamsweerde

A John Wiley and Sons, Ltd., Publication

Other Wiley Editorial Offices

John Wiley & Sons Inc., 111 River Street, Hoboken, NJ 07030, USA

Jossey-Bass, 989 Market Street, San Francisco, CA 94103-1741, USA

Wiley-VCH Verlag GmbH, Boschstr. 12, D-69469 Weinheim, Germany

John Wiley & Sons Australia Ltd, 42 McDougall Street, Milton, Queensland 4064, Australia

John Wiley & Sons (Asia) Pte Ltd, 2 Clementi Loop #02-01, Jin Xing Distripark, Singapore 129809

John Wiley & Sons Canada Ltd, 6045 Freemont Blvd, Mississauga, Ontario, L5R 4J3, Canada

Wiley also publishes its books in a variety of electronic formats. Some content that appears in print may not be available in electronic books.

Library of Congress Cataloging-in-Publication Data:

Lamsweerde, A. van (Axel)
  Requirements engineering : from system goals to UML models to software specifications / Axel van Lamsweerde.
    p. cm.
  Includes bibliographical references and index.
  ISBN 978-0-470-01270-3 (pbk.)
  1. Software engineering. 2. Systems engineering. I. Title.
  QA76.758.L28 2009
  005.1 – dc22

                                                                                2008036187

Credit for cover image: Kunsthistorisches Museum
Vienna/Bridgeman Art Library; Bruegel/Tower of Babel, 1563

British Library Cataloguing in Publication Data

A catalogue record for this book is available from the British Library

ISBN 978-0-470-01270-3

Typeset in 10/13pt Sabon by Laserwords Private Limited, Chennai, India
Printed and bound in Great Britain by Bell & Bain, Glasgow

Pour Dominique
Avant tout, et pour tout

Contents

Foreword   **xvii**

Preface   **xxi**

Part I   Fundamentals of Requirements Engineering   **1**

1   Setting the Scene   **3**
   1.1   What is requirements engineering?   3
       1.1.1   The problem world and the machine solution   4
       1.1.2   Introducing our running case studies   6
       1.1.3   The WHY, WHAT and WHO dimensions of requirements engineering   12
       1.1.4   Types of statements involved in requirements engineering   17
       1.1.5   Categories of requirements   23
       1.1.6   The requirements lifecycle: Processes, actors and products   30
       1.1.7   Target qualities and defects to avoid   35
       1.1.8   Types of software projects   40
       1.1.9   Requirements in the software lifecycle   42
       1.1.10   The relationship of requirements engineering to other disciplines   45
   1.2   Why engineer requirements?   47
       1.2.1   Facts, data and citations about the requirements problem   47
       1.2.2   The role and stakes of requirements engineering   51
   1.3   Obstacles to good requirements engineering practice   52
   1.4   Agile development processes and requirements engineering   53
       Summary   55
       Notes and Further Reading   56
       Exercises   58

2   Domain Understanding and Requirements Elicitation   **61**

2.1   Identifying stakeholders and interacting with them   62
2.2   Artefact-driven elicitation techniques   64
       2.2.1   Background study   64
       2.2.2   Data collection   65
       2.2.3   Questionnaires   65
       2.2.4   Repertory grids and card sorts for concept-driven acquisition   66
       2.2.5   Storyboards and scenarios for problem world exploration   67
       2.2.6   Mock-ups and prototypes for early feedback   70
       2.2.7   Knowledge reuse   72
2.3   Stakeholder-driven elicitation techniques   76
       2.3.1   Interviews   77
       2.3.2   Observation and ethnographic studies   79
       2.3.3   Group sessions   80
2.4   Conclusion   81
       Summary   82
       Notes and Further Reading   84
       Exercises   85

3   Requirements Evaluation   **87**

3.1   Inconsistency management   88
       3.1.1   Types of inconsistency   88
       3.1.2   Handling inconsistencies   89
       3.1.3   Managing conflicts: A systematic process   90
3.2   Risk analysis   93
       3.2.1   Types of risk   94
       3.2.2   Risk management   95
       3.2.3   Risk documentation   101
       3.2.4   Integrating risk management in the requirements lifecycle   102
3.3   Evaluating alternative options for decision making   105
3.4   Requirements prioritization   108
3.5   Conclusion   112
       Summary   113
       Notes and Further Reading   114
       Exercises   116

4   Requirements Specification and Documentation   **119**

4.1   Free documentation in unrestricted natural language   120
4.2   Disciplined documentation in structured natural language   121
       4.2.1   Local rules on writing statements   121
       4.2.2   Global rules on organizing the requirements document   124

Contents ix

4.3	Use of diagrammatic notations		127
	4.3.1	System scope: context, problem and frame diagrams	127
	4.3.2	Conceptual structures: entity–relationship diagrams	130
	4.3.3	Activities and data: SADT diagrams	133
	4.3.4	Information flows: dataflow diagrams	134
	4.3.5	System operations: use case diagrams	136
	4.3.6	Interaction scenarios: event trace diagrams	136
	4.3.7	System behaviours: state machine diagrams	138
	4.3.8	Stimuli and responses: R-net diagrams	142
	4.3.9	Integrating multiple system views and multiview specification in UML	142
	4.3.10	Diagrammatic notations: Strengths and limitations	144
4.4	Formal specification		145
	4.4.1	Logic as a basis for formalizing statements	146
	4.4.2	History-based specification	151
	4.4.3	State-based specification	155
	4.4.4	Event-based specification	163
	4.4.5	Algebraic specification	167
	4.4.6	Other specification paradigms	172
	4.4.7	Formal specification: strengths and limitations	173
4.5	Conclusion		174
	Summary		176
	Notes and Further Reading		179
	Exercises		183
5	**Requirements Quality Assurance**		**187**
5.1	Requirements inspections and reviews		188
	5.1.1	The requirements inspection process	188
	5.1.2	Inspection guidelines	190
	5.1.3	Requirements inspection checklists	191
	5.1.4	Conclusion	195
5.2	Queries on a requirements database		196
5.3	Requirements validation by specification animation		198
	5.3.1	Extracting an executable model from the specification	199
	5.3.2	Simulating the model	199
	5.3.3	Visualizing the simulation	200
	5.3.4	Conclusion	200
5.4	Requirements verification through formal checks		202
	5.4.1	Language checks	202
	5.4.2	Dedicated consistency and completeness checks	203
	5.4.3	Model checking	205
	5.4.4	Theorem proving	208

	5.5	Conclusion	211
		Summary	213
		Notes and Further Reading	214
		Exercises	217

6   Requirements Evolution   **219**

	6.1	The time–space dimensions of evolution: Revisions and variants	220
	6.2	Change anticipation	223
	6.3	Traceability management for evolution support	225
		6.3.1 Traceability links	226
		6.3.2 The traceability management process, its benefits and cost	233
		6.3.3 Traceability management techniques	237
		6.3.4 Determining an adequate cost–benefit trade-off for traceability management	244
	6.4	Change control	246
		6.4.1 Change initiation	247
		6.4.2 Change evaluation and prioritization	248
		6.4.3 Change consolidation	249
	6.5	Runtime monitoring of requirements and assumptions for dynamic change	249
	6.6	Conclusion	251
		Summary	252
		Notes and Further Reading	254
		Exercises	256

7   Goal Orientation in Requirements Engineering   **259**

	7.1	What are goals?	260
	7.2	The granularity of goals and their relationship to requirements and assumptions	261
	7.3	Goal types and categories	265
		7.3.1 Types of goal: behavioural goals vs soft goals	265
		7.3.2 Goal categories: Functional vs non-functional goals	269
	7.4	The central role of goals in the requirements engineering process	272
	7.5	Where are goals coming from?	275
	7.6	The relationship of goals to other requirements-related products and processes	276
		7.6.1 Goals and scenarios	276
		7.6.2 Intentional and operational specifications	277
		7.6.3 Goals and use cases	277
		7.6.4 Goals and model-checked properties	277
		7.6.5 Goal orientation and agent orientation	278
		7.6.6 Goal orientation and object orientation	278
		7.6.7 Goal orientation and top-down analysis	279

	Summary	279
	Notes and Further Reading	280
	Exercises	283

Part II   Building System Models for Requirements Engineering   **287**

8   Modelling System Objectives with Goal Diagrams   **293**
8.1   Goal features as model annotations   294
8.2   Goal refinement   297
8.3   Representing conflicts among goals   301
8.4   Connecting the goal model with other system views   302
8.5   Modelling alternative options   303
    8.5.1   Alternative goal refinements   304
    8.5.2   Alternative responsibility assignments   305
8.6   Goal diagrams as AND/OR graphs   307
8.7   Documenting goal refinements and assignments with annotations   308
8.8   Building goal models: Heuristic rules and reusable patterns   309
    8.8.1   Eliciting preliminary goals   309
    8.8.2   Identifying goals along refinement branches   311
    8.8.3   Delimiting the scope of the goal model   316
    8.8.4   Avoiding common pitfalls   317
    8.8.5   Reusing refinement patterns   319
    8.8.6   Reusing refinement trees associated with goal categories   326
    Summary   328
    Notes and Further Reading   329
    Exercises   331

9   Anticipating What Could Go Wrong: Risk Analysis on Goal Models   **335**
9.1   Goal obstruction by obstacles   336
    9.1.1   What are obstacles?   336
    9.1.2   Completeness of a set of obstacles   337
    9.1.3   Obstacle categories   338
9.2   Modelling obstacles   339
    9.2.1   Obstacle diagrams   339
    9.2.2   Conditions on obstacle refinement   341
    9.2.3   Bottom-up propagation of obstructions in goal AND-refinements   342
    9.2.4   Annotating obstacle diagrams   343
9.3   Obstacle analysis for a more robust goal model   344
    9.3.1   Identifying obstacles   344
    9.3.2   Evaluating obstacles   349
    9.3.3   Resolving obstacles in a modified goal model   349
    Summary   353

Notes and Further Reading   355
Exercises   356

10 Modelling Conceptual Objects with Class Diagrams   **359**
  10.1   Representing domain concepts by conceptual objects   360
         10.1.1   What are conceptual objects?   360
         10.1.2   Object instantiation: classes and current instances 361
         10.1.3   Types of conceptual object   362
         10.1.4   Object models as UML class diagrams   363
         10.1.5   Object features as model annotations   364
  10.2   Entities   366
  10.3   Associations   366
  10.4   Attributes   371
  10.5   Built-in associations for structuring object models   373
         10.5.1   Object specialization   373
         10.5.2   Object aggregation   376
  10.6   More on class diagrams   377
         10.6.1   Derived attributes and associations   377
         10.6.2   OR-associations   378
         10.6.3   Ordered associations   379
         10.6.4   Associations of associations   379
  10.7   Heuristic rules for building object models   380
         10.7.1   Deriving pertinent and complete class diagrams from goal diagrams 380
         10.7.2   Object or attribute?   384
         10.7.3   Entity, association, agent or event?   384
         10.7.4   Attribute of a linked object or of the linking association? 385
         10.7.5   Aggregation or association?   386
         10.7.6   Specializing and generalizing concepts   386
         10.7.7   Avoiding common pitfalls   387
         Summary   389
         Notes and Further Reading   391
         Exercises   392

11 Modelling System Agents and Responsibilities   **395**
  11.1   What are agents?   396
  11.2   Characterizing system agents   397
         11.2.1   Basic features   397
         11.2.2   Agent capabilities   397
         11.2.3   Agent responsibilities and goal realizability   399
         11.2.4   Agents as operation performers   401
         11.2.5   Agent wishes and beliefs   402
         11.2.6   Agent dependencies   403

11.3   Representing agent models   405
        11.3.1   Agent diagrams and instance declarations   405
        11.3.2   Context diagrams   406
        11.3.3   Dependency diagrams   407
11.4   Refinement of abstract agents   408
11.5   Building agent models   411
        11.5.1   Heuristics for building agent diagrams from goal models   411
        11.5.2   Generating context diagrams from goal models   413
        Summary   415
        Notes and Further Reading   417
        Exercises   418

12   Modelling System Operations   421
12.1   What are operations?   422
12.2   Characterizing system operations   425
        12.2.1   Basic features   425
        12.2.2   Operation signature   425
        12.2.3   Domain pre- and post-conditions   426
        12.2.4   Operation performer   427
12.3   Goal operationalization   427
        12.3.1   Required pre-, post- and trigger conditions for goal satisfaction   427
        12.3.2   Agent commitments   430
        12.3.3   Goal operationalization and satisfaction arguments   432
12.4   Goals, agents, objects and operations: The semantic picture   434
12.5   Representing operation models   435
        12.5.1   Operationalization diagrams   435
        12.5.2   UML use case diagrams   435
12.6   Building operation models   437
        12.6.1   Heuristics for building operationalization diagrams   437
        12.6.2   Generating use case diagrams from operationalization diagrams   442
        Summary   442
        Notes and Further Reading   444
        Exercises   445

13   Modelling System Behaviours   449
13.1   Modelling instance behaviours   450
        13.1.1   Scenarios as UML sequence diagrams   450
        13.1.2   Scenario refinement: Episodes and agent decomposition   452
13.2   Modelling class behaviours   454
        13.2.1   State machines as UML state diagrams   455
        13.2.2   State machine refinement: Sequential and concurrent sub-states   459
13.3   Building behaviour models   463
        13.3.1   Elaborating relevant scenarios for good coverage   465

13.3.2   Decorating scenarios with state conditions   467

13.3.3   From scenarios to state machines   469

13.3.4   From scenarios to goals   473

13.3.5   From operationalized goals to state machines   475

Summary   477

Notes and Further Reading   480

Exercises   481

14   Integrating Multiple System Views   **485**

14.1   A meta-model for view integration   485

14.1.1   Overall structure of the meta-model   487

14.1.2   The goal meta-model   488

14.1.3   The object meta-model   489

14.1.4   The agent meta-model   490

14.1.5   The operation meta-model   491

14.1.6   The behaviour meta-model   492

14.2   Inter-view consistency rules   493

14.3   Grouping related view fragments into packages   496

Summary   498

Notes and Further Reading   498

Exercises   499

15   A Goal-Oriented Model-Building Method in Action **501**

15.1   Modelling the system-as-is   503

15.1.1   Step 1: Build a preliminary goal model illustrated by scenarios   503

15.1.2   Step 2: Derive a preliminary object model   506

15.2   Modelling the system-to-be   507

15.2.1   Step 3: Update the goal model with new goals illustrated by scenarios   507

15.2.2   Step 4: Derive the updated object model   510

15.2.3   Step 5: Analyse obstacles, threats and conflicts   512

15.2.4   Step 6: Analyse responsibilities and build the agent model   515

15.2.5   Step 7: Make choices among alternative options   517

15.2.6   Step 8: Operationalize goals in the operation model   518

15.2.7   Step 9: Build and analyse the behaviour model   521

15.3   Handling model variants for product lines   524

Summary   528

Notes and Further Reading   529

Exercises   529

Part III   Reasoning About System Models   **535**

16   Semi-Formal Reasoning for Model Analysis and Exploitation   **537**

16.1   Query-based analysis of the model database   538

16.1.1 Checking the structural consistency and completeness of the model 538

16.1.2 Generation of other views for dedicated analyses 540

16.1.3 Traceability management 540

16.1.4 Analogical model reuse 541

16.2 Semi-formal analysis of goal-oriented models 544

16.2.1 Conflict analysis 544

16.2.2 Heuristic identification of obstacles 549

16.2.3 Threat analysis: From goal models to anti-goal models 551

16.3 Reasoning about alternative options 557

16.3.1 Qualitative reasoning about alternatives 557

16.3.2 Quantitative reasoning about alternatives 560

16.4 Model-driven generation of the requirements document 562

16.5 Beyond RE: From goal-oriented requirements to software architecture 566

16.5.1 Deriving a software data architecture from the object model 567

16.5.2 Deriving an abstract dataflow architecture from the agent and operation models 568

16.5.3 Selecting an architectural style from architectural requirements 570

16.5.4 Architectural refinement from quality requirements 571

Summary 574

Notes and Further Reading 576

Exercises 578

17 Formal Specification of System Models **583**

17.1 A real-time temporal logic for specifying model annotations 584

17.1.1 State assertions 584

17.1.2 Temporal assertions 585

17.1.3 Real-time temporal constructs 586

17.2 Specifying goals in the goal model 588

17.3 Specifying descriptive properties in the object model 592

17.4 Specifying operationalizations in the operation model 594

17.5 Back to the system's semantic picture 596

Summary 598

Notes and Further Reading 599

Exercises 599

18 Formal Reasoning for Specification Construction and Analysis **603**

18.1 Checking goal refinements 604

18.1.1 Using a theorem prover 604

18.1.2 Formal refinement patterns 604

18.1.3 Using bounded SAT solvers 608

18.2 Deriving goal operationalizations 609

18.2.1 Using bounded SAT solvers 610

18.2.2 Formal operationalization patterns   610

18.3 Generating obstacles for risk analysis   613

     18.3.1 Regressing obstructions through domain properties   614

     18.3.2 Using formal obstruction patterns   617

18.4 Generating anti-goals for security analysis   618

     18.4.1 Specifying security goals   618

     18.4.2 Identifying security goals and initial anti-goals   620

     18.4.3 Refining anti-goals   621

18.5 Formal conflict analysis   622

     18.5.1 Deriving boundary conditions for conflict   623

     18.5.2 Formal resolution of divergences   625

18.6 Synthesizing behaviour models for animation and model checking   627

     18.6.1 Goal-driven model synthesis   628

     18.6.2 Scenario-driven model synthesis   628

     Summary   635

     Notes and Further Reading   636

     Exercises   637

Bibliography   **641**

Index   **669**

Foreword

During the past 60 years of software development for digital computers, development technique, in one of its dimensions, has evolved in a cyclical pattern. At each successive stage, developers recognize that their task has been too narrowly conceived: the heart of the problem is further from the computer hardware than they had thought. Machine code programming led to Fortran, Cobol and Algol, languages aimed at a more problem-oriented way of programming. Then, as program size grew with increasing machine capacities, mere program writing led to notions of program design, software architecture, and software function specification in the large. In a culminating step, functional specification led to a more explicit focus on system requirements – the needs and purposes that the system must serve.

As a wider range of applications embraced more ambitious systems, it gradually became apparent that identifying and capturing system requirements was not an easy task. Published surveys showed that many systems failed because their requirements had not been accurately identified and analysed. Requirements defects proved enormously costly to repair at later stages. By the mid-1980s *requirements engineering* became recognized as an inchoate discipline, or sub-discipline, in its own right. Since the early 1990s it has had its own conferences and a growing literature. It embraces a large spectrum of activities, from discovering the needs and purposes of stakeholders – everyone who would be in any substantial way touched by the proposed system – and resolving the inevitable conflicts, to devising detailed human and computer processes to satisfy the identified system requirements. Requirements engineering must therefore include investigation and analysis of the world in which the requirements have their meaning, because it is in, and through, that world that the computer, executing the developed software, must bring about the desired effects.

Requirements engineering is hard. It is hard to elicit human needs and purposes and to bring them into harmony. Furthermore, there is an inherent dissonance between the quasi-formal world of computer programs – defining the programmed *machine* in each system – and the non-formal *problem world* of the system requirements. Programs can be treated as formal mathematical objects, capable of being proved to satisfy a given formal specification. The world of system requirements, by contrast, may comprise parts drawn from the natural world, from human participants, from engineered devices, from the built environment, and from every context with which the system interacts directly or indirectly. The problem world is typically heterogeneous and inherently non-formal. We implant the machine in this world, and we program the machine to monitor and control the world through the narrow interface of states and events that it can sense and affect directly. To the extent that the system aims at automation, we are handing to a formally programmed machine a degree of control over a complex and non-formal reality. The common sense and everyday practical knowledge with which human beings can deal with the world is replaced by the formal rules embodied in the software. Even if a system is adaptive, or intelligent or self-healing, its abilities are rigidly bounded by the machine's programmed behaviour, and by the narrow interface which provides it with its sole window on the problem world.

Requirements engineers, then, must be at home in both formal and non-formal worlds, and must be able to bring them together into an effective system. Axel van Lamsweerde has been among the leaders of the requirements engineering discipline since the 1980s, well qualified for this role by a strong background in formal computer science – his early publications were formal papers on concurrency – and an intense practical interest in all aspects of the engineering of computer-based systems. This splendid book represents the culmination of nearly two decades of his research and practical experience. He and his colleagues have developed the KAOS method associated with his name, and have accumulated much practical experience in developing solutions to realistic problems for its customers and users.

As we might expect, the book does what a book on requirements engineering must ideally do. The conceptual basis of the book and the KAOS method is the notion of a *goal*. A goal is a desirable state or effect or property of the system or of any part of it. This notion is flexible enough to apply through many levels of analysis and decomposition, from the largest ambitions of the organization to the detailed specification of a small software module. This book brings together the most formal and the most non-formal concerns, and forms a bridge between them. Its subject matter ranges from techniques for eliciting and resolving conflicting requirements of stakeholders, through the structuring of system goals and their allocation to agents in the machine and the problem world, to the definition and use of a temporal logic by which requirements can be formally analysed and the necessary software functionality derived from the analysis results.

The explanations are copious. Three excellent running examples, drawn from very different kinds of system, illuminate detailed points at every level. Each chapter includes exercises to help the reader check that what has been read has also been understood, and often to stimulate further thought about deeper issues that the chapter has recognized and discussed. Readers who are practising requirements engineers will find the book an excellent source for learning or recapitulating effective approaches to particular concerns. To take one example, there is an incisive discussion – to be found in a section of Chapter 16 – of the task of evaluating alternative architectures and how to set about it. Another example is the crisp account of temporal logic, given in a few pages in the following chapter. This account is so clear and well judged that it can act as both an introduction and a reference tool for all developers who recognize the power and utility of the formalism and want to use it. The comprehensive bibliographical commentaries in every chapter map out the terrain of what has by now become a substantial literature of the requirements engineering discipline.

The author's friends and colleagues, who know him well, have been waiting for this book with high expectations. These expectations have been amply fulfilled. Readers who have not yet acquainted themselves deeply with the author's work should begin here, immediately. They will not be disappointed.

Michael Jackson,
The Open University and Newcastle University
February 2008

Preface

Requirements Engineering (RE) is concerned with the elicitation, evaluation, specification, analysis and evolution of the objectives, functionalities, qualities and constraints to be achieved by a software-intensive system within some organizational or physical environment.

The requirements problem has been with us for a long time. In their 1976 empirical study, Bell and Thayer observed that inadequate, incomplete, inconsistent or ambiguous requirements are numerous and have a critical impact on the quality of the resulting software. Noting this for different kinds of projects, they concluded that 'the requirements for a system do not arise naturally; instead, they need to be engineered and have continuing review and revision'. Some 20 years later, different surveys over a wide variety of organizations and projects in the United States and in Europe have confirmed the requirements problem on a much larger scale. Poor requirements have been consistently recognized to be the major cause of software problems such as cost overruns, delivery delays, failures to meet expectations or degradations in the environment controlled by the software.

Numerous initiatives and actions have been taken to address the requirements problem. Process improvement models, standards and quality norms have put better requirements engineering practices in the foreground. An active research community has emerged with dedicated conferences, workshops, working groups, networks and journals. Requirements engineering courses have become integral parts of software engineering curricula.

The topic has also been addressed in multiple textbooks. These fall basically into two classes. Some books introduce the requirements engineering process and discuss general principles, guidelines and documentation formats. In general they remain at a fairly high level of coverage. Other books address the use of modelling notations but are generally more focused on modelling software designs. Where are such models coming from? How are they built? What are their underlying requirements? How are such requirements elaborated, organized and analysed? Design modelling books do not address such issues.

In contrast, this book is aimed at presenting a systematic approach to the engineering of high-quality requirements documents. The approach covers the entire requirements lifecycle and integrates state-of-the-art techniques for requirements elicitation, evaluation, specification, analysis and evolution. *Modelling* plays a central role in this approach. Rich models provide a common interface to the various requirements engineering activities. Such models capture the multiple facets of the system as it is before the software project starts *and* as it should be after project completion. Such a system generally comprises both software components, pre-existing or to be developed, external devices and people playing specific roles. The book's main emphasis is on the *technical* aspects of the requirements engineering process; the socio-psychological issues involved in that process are merely introduced together, with references to dedicated books where such issues are covered in greater depth.

Organization and content

The book is structured in three parts:

- A comprehensive introduction to the fundamentals of requirements engineering (Chapters 1–7).

- A thorough treatment of system modelling in the specific context of engineering requirements (Chapters 8–15).

- A presentation of various forms of reasoning about system models for model building, analysis and exploitation, from semi-formal to qualitative to formal reasoning (Chapters 6–18).

Part I of the book introduces the fundamental concepts, principles and techniques for requirements engineering. It discusses the aim and scope of requirements engineering, the products and processes involved, requirements qualities to aim at and flaws to avoid, the critical role of requirements engineering in system and software engineering, and obstacles to good requirements engineering practices. Key notions such as 'requirement', 'domain property' and 'assumption' are precisely defined. State-of-the-art techniques for supporting the various activities in the requirements lifecycle are reviewed next.

- For *requirements elicitation*, techniques such as interviews, observation or group sessions are based on different forms of interaction with system stakeholders. Other techniques such as scenarios, prototypes or knowledge reuse are based on artefacts to help acquire relevant information.

- For *requirements evaluation*, various techniques may help us manage conflicting concerns, analyse potential risks, evaluate alternative options and prioritize requirements.

- For *requirements documentation*, a wide variety of techniques may help us specify and structure large sets of requirements, from the use of structured natural language to diagrammatic notations to formal specifications.

- For *requirements quality assurance*, we may conduct inspections and reviews, submit queries to a requirements database, validate requirements through animation or verify requirements through formal checks.

- For *requirements evolution*, various techniques are available for change anticipation, traceability management, change control and on-the-fly change at system runtime.

To conclude the first part of the book and introduce the next parts, goal orientation is put forward as a basic paradigm for requirements engineering. Key elements such as goals, agents and scenarios are defined precisely and related to each other.

Part II is devoted to system modelling in the specific context of engineering requirements. It presents a goal-oriented, multiview modelling framework integrating complementary techniques for modelling the system-as-is and the system-to-be.

- AND/OR goal diagrams are used for capturing alternative refinements of functional and non-functional objectives, requirements and assumptions about the system.

- AND/OR obstacle diagrams are used for modelling what could go wrong with the system as modelled, with the aim of deriving new requirements for a more robust system. This view is especially important for mission-critical systems where safety or security concerns are essential.

- UML class diagrams are used for defining and structuring the conceptual objects manipulated by the system and referred to in goal formulations.

- Agent diagrams are used for modelling active system components, such as people playing specific roles, devices and software components, together with their responsibilities and interfaces.

- Operationalization diagrams and UML use cases are used for modelling and specifying the system's operations so as to meet the system's goals.

- UML sequence diagrams and state diagrams are used for modelling the desired system behaviours in terms of scenarios and state machines, respectively.

Each modelling technique is explained separately first, with a strong emphasis on well-grounded heuristics for *model building*. The full system model is obtained from those various views through mechanisms for view integration.

To conclude the second part of the book, a constructive method is presented for elaborating a full, robust and consistent system model through incremental integration of the goal, object, agent, operation and behaviour sub-models. Goals and scenarios drive the elaboration and integration of these sub-models. The elaboration proceeds both top down, from strategic objectives, and bottom up, from operational material available. The requirements document is then generated systematically by mapping the resulting model into some textual format annotated with figures. The document produced preserves the goal-oriented structure and content of the model, and fits prescribed standards if required.

The model-based requirements engineering approach described in Part II, known as *KAOS*, has been developed and refined over more than 15 years of research, tool development and experience in multiple industrial projects. KAOS stands for '**K**eep **A**ll **O**bjectives **S**atisfied'. (*Kaos* happens to be the name of an allegorical movie by the Taviani brothers based on Luigi Pirandello's five tales on the multiple facets of our world.)

Part III reviews goal-based reasoning techniques that support the various steps of this requirements engineering approach. The transition from requirements to software architecture is discussed as well. The analysis techniques fall into three complementary classes:

- Query-based techniques can be used for checking model well-formedness, for managing traceability among model items, and for retrieving reusable model fragments.

- Qualitative and quantitative techniques help evaluate alternative options arising during the requirements engineering process. Such options correspond to alternative goal refinements, responsibility assignments, conflict resolutions or countermeasures to the identified hazards or threats. The evaluation of options is based on the non-functional goals identified in the goal model.

- Formal techniques can be used incrementally and locally, where and when needed, to support goal refinement and operationalization, conflict management, analysis of obstacles to goal achievement, analysis of security threats for countermeasure exploration, synthesis of behaviour models, and goal-oriented model checking and animation. Such techniques require the corresponding goals, operations and domain properties to be specified formally.

Approach

The book presents both a comprehensive state of the art in requirements engineering (Part I) *and* a systematic method for engineering high-quality requirements (Parts II and III), anchored on this state of the art.

Like the method and supporting tools, this book is 'two-button' in nature. The material covering formal methods for requirements engineering is optional and is concentrated near the end of the book; the 'formal button' is mostly pressed in Chapters 17 and 18. Formal techniques are useful in requirements engineering to enforce higher precision in specifications and to support much richer forms of analysis for requirements quality assurance. They turn out to be essential for reasoning about critical goals concerning system safety and security. Formal techniques are, however, mostly hidden from Chapters 1 to 16, even though they are to some extent involved at different places here and there. The aim is to make solid modelling techniques more accessible to a much wider audience. For example, formal refinement patterns are seen in Chapter 18 to produce goal refinements that are provably correct and complete (Section 18.1). They are introduced informally in Chapter 8 to support the critical task of refining goals in a systematic way (see the model-building heuristics in Section 8.8). Similarly, obstacle analysis is handled formally in Chapter 18 but introduced informally in Chapter 9. Extensive experience with students, tutorial attendees and practitioners over the years shows that this way of hiding the underlying mathematical apparatus works remarkably well. Like Molière's Monsieur Jourdain, who is writing prose without being aware of it, they are using temporal logic without really knowing it.

On the other hand, other readers with some background in formal methods might be interested in a more formal treatment of model-based RE from the beginning. Such readers can press the 'formal button' earlier, as they will have no difficulty in making the hidden formal apparatus visible. The semi-formal techniques and numerous examples presented in Parts II and III can easily be translated into the simple formalism based on temporal logic introduced in Section 4.4.2 and further detailed in Chapter 17.

Unlike many books consisting of a mere exposition of a catalogue of notations and illustrations of their use, this book puts a strong emphasis on *constructive* techniques for building high-quality system models using a coherent subset of notations. A rich variety of heuristic rules is provided that combines model-building strategies, tactics and patterns, common pitfalls and bad smells. Much more than specific notations, what matters here is the quality and usefulness of the models and documents elaborated, and the process according to which such artefacts are built. Experience in teaching modelling for more than 20 years to students and practitioners has convinced us that effective guidance in model building is what is needed most – in the same way as good programming methods, techniques and patterns are known to be much more important than the use of a specific programming language.

Speaking of notations, we will use standard ones wherever we can. In particular, we will see how UML class diagrams, use cases, sequence diagrams and state diagrams can be systematically derived from goal models, and vice versa. The only new notations introduced in the book refer to abstractions that are crucially missing in the UML for requirements engineering; namely, goal diagrams, obstacle diagrams and context diagrams.

The concepts, principles and techniques throughout the book are illustrated by numerous examples from *case studies* to give the reader more concrete insights into how they can be used in practical settings. The wide applicability of the techniques is demonstrated through running examples from completely different domains: an information system, an embedded control system and a distributed collaborative application to be developed as a product family. These running examples arise from simplifications of real systems for library management, train control and meeting scheduling, respectively. The method is also shown in action in the stepwise elaboration of an entire multi-view model of a mine safety control system. The requirements document generated semi-automatically from the latter model is shown in the book's accompanying website.

For more active reading, each chapter ends with a series of exercises, problems and bibliographical notes. Some of the exercises provide additional case studies for more substantial experimentation, in particular in student projects. The bibliographical notes are intended to open the window on past achievements in the field and directions for further study.

A professional modelling tool that supports the goal-oriented RE method in this book is freely accessible to the reader for building limited-size models and requirements documents (http://www.objectiver.com). The tool includes, among other components, a graphical model editor, an HTML generator for navigation and zooming in/out through large models, a model database query engine with pre-defined model consistency checks, and a requirements document generator. The book does not assume that the reader will use this tool. However, playing with it for building models involved in the book's exercises and case studies, and generating requirements documents semi-automatically from the models, will result in more active and enjoyable learning. As a side effect, further insight will be gained on the benefits of using tools for requirements engineering.

Readership

The book is primarily intended for two categories of reader:

- Students in computing science, information systems or system engineering who need a solid background in techniques for requirements engineering and system modelling – typically, final-year undergraduate or first-year graduate students who take a course on software engineering or a more dedicated course on requirements engineering or system modelling. The book can be used as a supplement to other textbooks for a course on software engineering, or as main support for a one-term course on requirements engineering or system modelling.

- Professional engineers, business analysts, system analysts, consultants or project leaders who, beyond general guidelines, need systematic guidance for elaborating and analysing high-quality requirements.

Parts I and II, covering the fundamentals of requirements engineering and model building, have no real prerequisite. The more advanced techniques in Part III, and Chapters 17 and 18 in particular, assume some elementary background in the logical foundations of computing science together with more analytical reasoning skills.

How to use the book

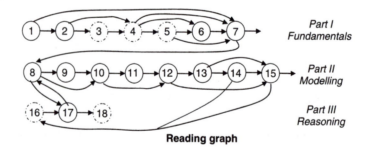

Part I
Fundamentals

Part II
Modelling

Part III
Reasoning

Reading graph

The material in the book has been organised to meet different needs. Multiple tracks can therefore be followed corresponding to different selections of topics and levels of study. Such tracks define specific paths in the book's reading graph. Arrows in this graph denote reading precedence, whereas dotted circles indicate partial reading of the corresponding chapter by skipping some sections.

- *Track 1: Model-free introduction to RE.* Part I of the book can be used for an RE course with very little modelling. Along this track, students are expected to follow or have followed another course on system modelling. Section 4.3 is provided to summarize popular modelling notations for RE, defining each of them concisely, highlighting their complementarity and illustrating their use in the running case studies. Optionally, Section 4.4 on formal specification and Section 5.4 on formal verification may be skipped for shorter courses or students with no background in the logical foundations of computing.

- *Track 2: Model-based introduction to RE.* This track is intended for an RE course with substantial coverage of modelling techniques. The material in Part I up to Section 4.2 is taken. Section 4.3 is provided as a contextual entry point to subsequent chapters emphasizing model construction. Section 4.4 (formal specification), Chapter 5 (requirements inspection, validation and verification) and/or Chapter 6 (requirements evolution) are skipped depending on course length or reader focus. The track then proceeds with Chapter 7 and key chapters from Part II; namely, Chapter 8 on goal modelling, Chapter 10 on object modelling, Chapter 12 on operation modelling and Chapter 15 showing how the techniques introduced in these chapters fit together to form a systematic model-building method. Ideally, Chapters 9, 11 and 13 should be included as well to cover risk, responsibility and behaviour models.

- *Track 3: Introduction to early model building for model-driven software engineering.* This track is intended for the RE part of a software engineering course. (I used to follow it for the first third of my SE course.) It consists of Chapter 1, introducing the basics of RE, Chapter 7, introducing system modeling from a RE perspective, and then Chapters 8–13 on model building, concluded by Chapter 15 showing a fully worked-out case study. For shorter coverage, Chapter 11 may be skipped, as key material there is briefly introduced in Chapters 7, 8 and 10 and briefly recalled in Chapter 12.

- *Tracks 4.n: Hybrid RE tracks.* Depending on student profile, teacher interests and course length, multiple selections can be made out of Parts I and II so as to cover essential aspects of RE and model-based RE. Chapter 1 is required in any selection. Typical combinations include Chapter 1, Chapter 2, [Chapter 3], Chapter 4 limited to Sections 4.1 and 4.2, [Chapter 5], [Chapter 6], Chapter 7, Chapter 8, [Chapter 9], Chapter 10, Chapter 12, [Chapter 13] and Chapter 15, where brackets indicate optional chapters. (I have used such combinations on several occasions.)

- *Track 5: The look-ahead formal track.* Students with some background in formal methods do not necessarily have to wait until Part III to see formal modelling and analysis in action. They will have no difficulty making the material in Part II more formal by expressing the specifications and patterns there in the temporal logic language introduced in Section 4.4 and detailed in Chapter 17.

- *Track 6: The advanced track.* A more advanced course on RE, for students who have had an introductory course before, can put more emphasis on analysis and evolution by in-depth coverage of the material in Chapter 3, Section 4.4 in Chapter 4, Chapter 5, Chapter 6, Chapter 9 (if not covered before), Chapter 14, Chapter 16, Chapter 17 and Chapter 18. This track obviously has prerequisites from preceding chapters.

Additional resources

Lecture slides, additional case studies, solutions to exercises and model-driven requirements documents from real projects will gradually be made available on the book's Web site.

Acknowledgement

I have wanted (and tried) to write this book for a long time. This means that quite a few people have been involved in some way or another in the project.

My first thanks go to Emmanuel Letier. The book owes much to our joint work over 10 years. Emmanuel contributed significantly to some of the techniques described in Parts II and III, notably the techniques for agent-based refinement and goal operationalization. In addition to that, he created initial models and specifications for several case studies, examples and exercises in the book. Emmanuel was also instrumental in making some of the pillars of the modelling framework more solid.

Robert Darimont deserves special thanks too. He initiated the refinement pattern idea and provided initial insights on goal conflicts. Later he gave lots of feedback from his daily use of the method and supporting tools in industry. This feedback had a large influence on enhancements, notably through considerable simplification and polishing of the original framework.

Speaking of the original framework, Steve Fickas and Martin Feather had a strong influence on it through their work on composite system design. I still believe that Martin's simple but precise semantics for agent responsibility is the one to rely on.

Many people joined the research staff in the KAOS project and contributed in some way or another. I wish to thank in particular Christophe Damas, Anne Dardenne, Renaud De Landtsheer, Bruno Delcourt, Emmanuelle Delor, Françoise Dubisy, Bernard Lambeau, Philippe Massonet, Cédric Nève, Christophe Ponsard, André Rifaut, Jean-Luc Roussel, Marie-Claire Schayes, Hung Tran Van and Laurent Willemet.

Quite a few students provided valuable feedback from using some of the techniques in their MS thesis or from studying draft chapters. I would like to acknowledge in particular Nicolas Accardo, Pierre-Jean Fontaine, Olivier Haine, Laurent Hermoye, Jonathan Lewis, Florence Massen, Junior F. Monfils, Alessandra de Schrynmakers and Damien Vanderveken.

Many thanks are also due to all those who provided helpful comments and suggestions on earlier drafts of the book, including Alistair Suttcliffe, Klaus Pohl, Steve Fickas, Bill Robinson and the Wiley reviewers. Martin Feather gave substantial feedback on my attempts to integrate his DDP approach in the section on risk analysis. I am also very much indebted to Michael Jackson for taking time to read the manuscript and write such a nice foreword.

Earlier colleagues at Philips Research Labs provided lifetime stimulation for technical precision, highly needed in RE, including Michel Sintzoff, Philippe Delsarte and Pierre-Jacques Courtois. François Bodart at the University of Namur opened a window on the area for me and excited my attraction to real-world case studies.

Writing a book that in places tries to reconcile requirements engineering (RE) and formal methods (FM) is quite a challenge. I am indebted to the many RE researchers and practitioners I met for their scepticism about formal methods, and to the many FM researchers I met for their scepticism about RE as a respectable area of work. Their combined scepticism contributed a great deal to the never-ending quest for the Holy Grail.

Besides the multiple laptops and typesetting systems I used during the painful process of book writing, I would like to acknowledge my cellos and Johann Sebastian Bach's genial suites, which helped me a great deal in recovering from that pain.

Last but not least, the *real* thanks go to Dominique for her unbounded patience and endurance through years and years – she would most probably have written this sort of book three times faster; to Nicolas, Florence and Céline for making me look ahead and for joking about book completion on every occasion; and to Agathe, Inès, Jeanne, Nathan, Louis and Nina for reminding me constantly that the main thing in life cannot be found in books.

Part I

Fundamentals of Requirements Engineering

The purpose of this part of the book is twofold:

- **To introduce the motivation, conceptual background and terminology on which the rest of the book will rely.**

- **To provide a comprehensive account of state-of-the-art techniques for requirements engineering.**

Chapter 1 defines what requirements engineering (RE) is about, its aim and scope, its critical role in system and software engineering, and its relationship to other disciplines. We will see there what requirements are, what they are not, and what are 'good' requirements. The chapter reviews the different categories of requirements found in a project, and the different types of projects in which such requirements may need to be engineered. The requirements lifecycle is also discussed together with the various products, activities and actors involved in the RE process.

The next chapters explain the main techniques available for supporting this process. The presentation is structured by the activity that such techniques support in the requirements lifecycle; namely, domain understanding and requirements elicitation, requirements evaluation and agreement, requirements specification and documentation, requirements quality assurance and requirements evolution management. For each technique we will see what it consists of, its strengths and limitations, and guidelines for using it.

Chapter 2 reviews a variety of techniques that we may use for understanding the domain in which the software project takes place and for eliciting the right requirements for a new system. Some techniques are based on artefacts to help acquire relevant information, such as questionnaires, scenarios, prototypes or reusable knowledge sources. Other techniques are based on specific kinds of interaction with system stakeholders to drive the acquisition process, such as interviews, observations or group sessions.

Chapter 3 addresses the process of evaluating the elicited objectives, requirements and assumptions about the new system. The evaluation techniques discussed there may help us manage conflicting concerns, analyse potential risks with the envisaged system, evaluate alternative options for decision making and prioritize requirements for incremental development under limited resources.

Once the system objectives, requirements and assumptions have been elicited and evaluated, we must make them fully precise and organize them into some coherent structure to produce the requirements document. **Chapter 4** overviews specification techniques that may help us in this task, such as templates in structured natural language, diagrammatic notations for capturing specific aspects of the system, and formal specification of critical aspects for more sophisticated analysis.

Chapter 5 reviews the main techniques available for requirements quality assurance. Such techniques may help us check the requirements document for desired qualities such as completeness, consistency, adequacy or measurability of statements. They range from informal to semi-formal to formal techniques. The chapter discusses inspections and reviews, queries we may submit on a requirements database, requirements validation through specification animation and requirements verification through formal checks.

Chapter 6 addresses the important problem of managing requirements evolution. As the world keeps changing, the system objectives, requirements and assumptions may need to be frequently revised or adapted. The chapter discusses evolution along revisions and variants, and reviews a variety of techniques for change anticipation, traceability management, change control and dynamic adaptation at system runtime.

To conclude this first part of the book and introduce the second part, **Chapter 7** introduces goal orientation as a basic paradigm for RE. It defines what goals are and explains why goals are so important in the RE process. The chapter also relates goals to other key ingredients of this process, such as requirements regarding the software to be developed, assumptions about its environment, domain properties, scenarios of interaction between the software and the environment, and agents involved in such interactions.

This first part of the book provides a framework on which the model-driven techniques detailed in Parts II and III will be anchored.

1

Setting the Scene

This chapter introduces requirements engineering (RE) as a specific discipline in relation to others. It defines the scope of RE and the basic concepts, activities, actors and artefacts involved in the RE process. In particular, it explains what requirements there are with respect to other key RE notions such as domain properties and environment assumptions. Functional and non-functional requirements will be seen to play specific roles in the RE process. The quality criteria according to which requirements documents should be elaborated and evaluated will be detailed. We will also see why a careful elaboration of requirements and assumptions in the early stages of the software lifecycle is so important, and what obstacles may impinge on good RE practice.

The chapter also introduces three case studies from which running examples will be taken throughout the book. These case studies will additionally provide a basis for many exercises at the end of chapters. They are taken from quite different domains to demonstrate the wide applicability of the concepts and techniques. Although representative of real-world systems, the case study descriptions have been simplified to make our examples easily understandable without significant domain expertise. The first case study is a typical instance of an information system. The second captures the typical flavour of a system partly controlled by software. The third raises issues that are typical of distributed collaborative applications and product families.

1.1 What is requirements engineering?

To make sure that a software solution correctly solves a particular problem, we must first correctly understand and define what problem needs to be solved. This seems common sense at first sight. However, as we shall see, figuring out what the right problem is can be surprisingly difficult. We need to discover, understand, formulate, analyse and agree on *what* problem should be solved, *why* such a problem needs to be solved and *who* should be involved in the responsibility of solving that problem. Broadly, this is what requirements engineering is all about.

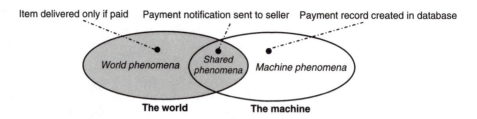

Figure 1.1   *The problem world and the machine solution*

1.1.1 The problem world and the machine solution

The problem to be solved arises within some broader context. It is in general rooted in a complex organizational, technical or physical *world*. The aim of a software project is to improve this world by building some *machine* expected to solve the problem. The machine consists of software to be developed and installed on some computer platform, possibly together with some input/output devices.

The problem world and the machine solution have their own phenomena while sharing others (Jackson, 1995b). The shared phenomena define the interface through which the machine interacts with the world. The machine monitors some of the shared phenomena while controlling others in order to implement the requirements.

Figure 1.1 illustrates this for a simple e-commerce world. In this example, the world owns the phenomena of items being delivered to buyers only once they have been paid; the machine owns the phenomena of payment records being created in the machine's database. The phenomena of payment notifications being sent to sellers are shared, as the machine can control them whereas the world can monitor them.

Requirements engineering is concerned with the machine's effect on the surrounding world and the assumptions we make about that world. As a consequence, it is solely concerned with world phenomena, including shared ones. Requirements and assumptions have their meaning in the problem world. In contrast, software design is concerned with machine phenomena.

The system-as-is and the system-to-be

In the system engineering tradition, the word *system* will be used throughout the book to denote a set of components interacting with each other to satisfy some global objectives. While being intrinsically composite, a system can be seen as a whole through the global properties emerging from component interactions. Such properties include the objectives underpinning component interactions and laws regulating such interactions.

- *Example 1.* Consider an e-auction system on the Internet. This system is made up of components such as sellers, buyers, shipping companies, an independent e-payment subsystem, e-mail systems, and the software to be developed or extended for inserting and advertising items, handling bids, billing highest bidders, recording evaluations of sellers and buyers, securing transactions and so forth. Global properties emerging from component interactions include the satisfaction of buyers getting wider access to interesting items, the satisfaction of sellers getting wider access to potential buyers, auction rules regulating the system, trustworthiness relationships and so on.

- *Example 2.* A flight management system includes components such as pilots, air traffic controllers, on-board and on-ground instruments, the autopilot software to be developed, an independent collision-avoidance subsystem and so forth. Global properties emerging from component interactions include the objectives of rapid and safe transportation of passengers, regulating laws about wind directions, aircraft speed, minimal distance between aircrafts and so forth.

In a machine-building project, our business as requirements engineers is to investigate the problem world. This leads us to consider two versions of the same system:

- The *system-as-is*, the system as it exists before the machine is built into it.

- The *system-to-be*, the system as it should be when the machine will be built and operated in it.

In the previous example of an auction world, the system-as-is is a standard auction system with no support for electronic bidding. The system-to-be is intended to provide such support in order to make items biddable from anywhere at any time. In a flight management world, the system-as-is might include some autopilot software with limited capabilities; the system-to-be would then include autopilot software with extended capabilities. In the former example the system-to-be is the outcome of a new software project, whereas in the latter example it results from a software evolution project.

Note that there is always a system-as-is. Consider a project aimed at developing control software for a MP4 player, for example. The system-as-is is the conventional system allowing you to listen to your favourite music on a standard hi-fi subsystem. The system-to-be is intended to mimic the listening conditions of the system-as-is while providing convenient, anywhere and any-time access to your music.

The software-to-be and its environment

The machine's software to be developed or modified is just one component of the system-to-be. We will refer to it as the *software-to-be*. Other components will in general pertain to the machine's surrounding world. They will form the *environment* of the software-to-be. Such components may include:

- People or business units playing specific roles according to organizational policies.

- Physical devices operating under specific rules in conformance with physical laws – for example sensors, actuators, measurement instruments or communication media.

- Legacy, off-the-shelf or foreign software components with which the software-to-be needs to interact.

As we are concerned with the problem world, we need to consider both the system-*as-is*, to understand its objectives, regulating laws, deficiencies and limitations, and the system-*to-be*, to elaborate the requirements on the software-to-be accordingly together with assumptions on the environment.

The systems-to-be-next

If we want to build an evolvable machine in our problem world, we need to anticipate likely changes at RE time. During software development or after deployment of the system-to-be, new problems and limitations may arise. New opportunities may emerge as the world keeps changing. We may then even need to consider more than two system versions and foresee what the next system versions are likely to be. Beyond the system-as-is and the system-to-be, there are *systems-to-be-next*. Requirements evolution management is an important aspect of the RE process that will be discussed at length in Chapter 6.

Requirements engineering: A preliminary definition

In this setting, we may apprehend requirements engineering more precisely as a coordinated set of activities for exploring, evaluating, documenting, consolidating, revising and adapting the objectives, capabilities, qualities, constraints and assumptions that the system-to-be should meet based on problems raised by the system-as-is and opportunities provided by new technologies. We will come back to those various activities in Section 1.1.6 and will have a much closer look at them in subsequent chapters.

1.1.2 Introducing our running case studies

To make the nature of RE more apparent and more concrete, we will consider a variety of case studies. The following descriptions are intended to set up the context in which our running examples will be used throughout the book. They will also provide further insights into the scope and dimensions of the problem world. We should not consider them as problem statements, but rather as fragmentary material collected from preliminary investigations of the problem world (perhaps by use of the elicitation techniques discussed in Chapter 2).

Case study 1: Library Management

The University of Wonderland (UWON) wants to convert its library system into a new system to ensure more effective access to state-of-the-art books, periodicals and proceedings while reducing operational costs. The current system consists of multiple unconnected library subsystems, one for each UWON department. Each department subsystem is responsible for its own library according to department-specific procedures for book acquisition, user registration, loan management, bibliographical search and access to library resources. Such services are essentially manual in most UWON libraries. They rely on card indexes maintained by library staff according to some keyword-based classification scheme. Such schemes are specific to each department. A few departments are using rudimentary file-based software written by their members.

Some of the complaints about the current system as reported by university authorities, library staff, department members or students include the following:

- Unnecessary duplicate acquisition, by several departments, of infrequently accessed copies of books or proceedings that are relevant to more than one department.

- Unnecessary subscription, by several departments, to expensive journals that are relevant to more than one department.

- Acquisition of books or proceedings of marginal interest to the university, which could be borrowed from other universities with which UWON has an agreement.

- Subscription to journals of marginal interest to the university, which could be accessed in other universities with which UWON has an agreement.

- Unavailability of requested books, for a variety of reasons such as department budget restrictions, excessive borrowing by the same user, lack of enforcement of rules limiting loan periods, loss or stealing of book copies and so on.

- Unavailability of journal issues while they are being bound into yearly volumes.

- Lack of traceability to previous borrowers when books, proceedings or journal volumes are found to be damaged.

- Inaccuracy of card indexes, e.g. a book is stated as being available whereas it is not found at the appropriate place in the shelves.

- Bibliographical search restricted to library opening hours.

- Slow, tedious bibliographical search due to manipulation of card indexes.

- Inaccurate search results, due to poor classification of books, journals or proceedings within departments.

- Incomplete or ineffective search results, due to relevant books, journals or proceedings being indexed in other UWON department libraries, or unavailable at UWON.

The new UWON library system should address such problems through a software-based solution integrating all department libraries. The new system should interoperate with library systems from partner universities.

It should provide interactive online facilities for book acquisition, user registration, loan management, bibliographical search and book reservation. Access to such facilities should be restricted to specific user categories, according to authorization rules specific to each facility.

The new system should take advantage of opportunities provided by new technologies. In particular, it should support subscriptions to e-journals, provide access to foreign digital libraries (under specific conditions), support e-mail communication between staff and users, enable bibliographical search from anywhere at any time, and provide a Web-based interface for book e-seller comparison, selection, and order submission.

Case study 2: Train Control

Traffic at Wonderland airport (WAX) has increased drastically over the past few years. The increase in the number of companies and flights calls for the building of new terminals. The increase in the number of passengers calls for a new transportation system between all terminals, and between the main terminal and Wonderland City. The current bus transportation system has reached its limits in terms of transportation capacity and quality of service. Buses are slow and often late due to traffic jams; passengers need to stand in long queues, sometimes for an unacceptably long time, which may cause them to miss flight connections, and so on.

The government of Wonderland has decided to replace bus transportation by a train-based system. The envisaged system is aimed at increasing transportation capacity, speed and quality of service. The decision is also motivated by recent regulations for reducing greenhouse gas production.

Preliminary investigations suggest that software-controlled movement of trains will allow for better punctuality, higher frequency and better information to passengers.

A consortium has been set up to undertake this project. It brings together government representatives, airport authorities, Wonderland Railways and the engineering company selected to implement the project. The latter is subcontracting the software part of it to a software house.

In the new system, all terminals will be interconnected through an underground circular, one-track railway. The main terminal and city terminal will be interconnected by a two-track line (one for each direction). The main terminal also has parking tracks for inactive trains, servicing and so on. Each track is divided into track segments of a fixed size called blocks. Each terminal holds one block called a station block. Each block is equipped with an entry signal (or 'virtual gate') and multiple sensors to detect the presence of trains, identify trains and their speed and so on.

The envisioned software is expected to control the acceleration of trains, the opening of train doors, the block signals and the display of information about the current/next station on information panels inside trains. The railway company would also like to reduce operational costs. A fully automated, driverless option is envisaged as an alternative to the standard option. In this standard option, train drivers have to follow recommendations issued by the software and respond to regular stimuli issued by the software to check driver responsiveness. The driverless option is currently being discussed with the unions.

Various concerns about the new system have already emerged at this preliminary stage:

- In order to ensure rapid transportation of passengers, trains should run fast, without unnecessary delays, and at high frequency, during rush hours at least.

- In order to guarantee safe transportation of passengers, the probability of accidents must fall below the threshold imposed by safety regulations. In particular, the distance between two trains following each other must always be sufficient to prevent the back train from hitting the front train in case the latter stops suddenly. The speed of a train on a particular block may never exceed the limit associated with that block. Trains may never enter a block whose entry signal is set to 'stop'. Train doors must always be kept closed while a train is moving.

- In order to ensure comfortable transportation, trains should accelerate/decelerate smoothly. Passengers at a station should be informed in time about trains arriving. Passengers inside a train should be informed in time that the train is departing, which companies are being served by the next stop and so on.

Case study 3: Meeting Scheduling*

With the advent of globalization, companies and organizations are increasingly distributed over multiple sites and countries. Wonderland Software

---

* *Source*: Adapted from S. Fickas, A. Finkelstein, M. Feather and A. Van Lamsweerde, 1997, with kind permission of Springer Science and Business Media.

Services (WSS) has identified a large potential market for meeting-scheduling software that would exploit Internet-based communication technologies. Scheduling meetings with busy people is generally a nightmare. It is hard to find a date and a place that suit everyone's constraints; meeting organizers need to pester people to get their availability; other people are unnecessarily inconvenienced by messages that do not concern them; when the meeting is scheduled some constraints have changed in the meantime; new scheduling cycles need to be repeated when no date/location is found in a reasonably short period; and so forth. As a result, meetings tend to be organized poorly and late; important people sometimes do not show up; and there is a significant, unnecessary overhead in the scheduling process.

Meetings are typically scheduled as follows. A meeting initiator informs potential participants about the need for a meeting and specifies a date range within which the meeting should take place, asking people to return their availability constraints within that time interval. Constraints are typically expressed as two sets: an exclusion set specifying dates within the date range when the participant could not attend, and an optional preference set specifying dates within the date range on which the participant would prefer the meeting to take place (a date may refer to a full day or a period in a day). In some cases, the initiator may also ask participants who will play an active role in the meeting for specific requirements regarding the meeting room (e.g. projector, laptop, network connection, videoconferencing facilities etc.). 'Important' participants may optionally be asked to state preferences for meeting locations.

The scheduled meeting date should belong to the stated date range and to none of the exclusion sets; it should ideally belong to as many preference sets as possible. The meeting venue should ideally fit the preferences of important participants. A date conflict occurs when no date can be found outside all exclusion sets. A room conflict occurs when no room can be found, at any date outside all exclusion sets, which meets the room requirements. Conflicts can be resolved in several ways: the initiator may extend the date range, some participants may remove dates from their exclusion set, or some participants may decline the invitation to attend. A new scheduling cycle may thus be required in case of conflict.

The envisioned meeting scheduler software should reflect as closely as possible the way meetings are typically managed. It should be useable by administrative staff and provide major improvements in several respects:

- Average participant attendance should increase thanks to the selection of meeting dates and locations that are the most convenient to potential participants.

- Meetings should be scheduled as quickly as possible once they are initiated.

- Meeting dates and locations should be notified as quickly as possible to all potential participants once they are scheduled. In all cases, there should be sufficient time between notification and the meeting date.

- The organizational overhead should be kept as low as possible on the initiator's side. In particular, the meeting scheduler should support all required interactions with participants, for example to communicate requests, get replies (even from participants not reacting promptly), assist in negotiation and conflict-resolution processes, and inform participants on request about the state of the scheduling process.

- The amount of interaction with potential participants for meeting scheduling, in number and length of messages, should be kept as small as possible.

The new meeting scheduler must be able to handle multiple meeting requests in parallel. Meeting requests can be competing by overlapping in time or space. Concurrency must thus be managed under physical constraints; a person may not be at two different places at the same time, and a meeting room may not be allocated to more than one meeting at a time.

To allow as much flexibility as possible, dynamic replanning of meetings should be supported. On the one hand, participants should be allowed to modify their exclusion set, preference set and/or preferred location until the meeting is scheduled. On the other hand, exceptional constraints should be accommodated after a meeting is scheduled, such as the need to schedule an urgent, more important meeting. The original meeting date or location may then need to be changed; sometimes it may even be cancelled. In all cases some way of replanning should be set up.

The system should be flexible enough to accommodate different data formats (e.g. date or address formats) and evolving data (e.g. the set of concerned participants may vary during the scheduling process, and the address at which a participant can be reached may change).

There are also security concerns to be taken into account, such as the following:

- Meeting initiation should be restricted to authorized personnel.

- Confidentiality rules should be enforced, for instance a non-privileged participant should not be aware of constraints stated by other participants, or of other meetings to which the latter are invited.

Rather than a single product, WSS is thinking of a product family. The customization space should cover the following variations:

- Professional meetings, private meetings.

- Single-site meetings, meetings where the target site needs to be determined as well, electronic meetings.

- Regular meetings (e.g. for a university course), occasional meetings.

- Single-level meetings or multi-level meetings where the importance of a person attending a specific meeting is higher or lower with respect to other meetings.

- Single-level participation or multi-level participation where the importance of a meeting getting a specific attendee is higher or lower with respect to other attendees.

- Single-level participants or multi-level participants where some participants are hierarchically more important than others (regardless of a specific meeting) or have less flexibility in changing their constraints.

- Variations on what participating in a meeting means, e.g. full attendance, partial attendance, participation through delegation.

- Variations on what constraints are about, e.g. no preference set, unordered preferences, ordered preferences, date availability dependent on meeting location.

- Parameterizability on explicit conflict-resolution rules that are tunable by the client, e.g. 'best meeting dates and locations should be determined by considering participants with higher importance first', 'in case of date conflict the scheduler will propose a person of lower importance to withdraw from the meeting', 'in case of date conflict the meeting scheduler will propose a participant to withdraw from another meeting of lower importance', 'a date within some exclusion set will be considered if the corresponding participant has high flexibility'.

- Mono-lingual, multi-lingual communication with participants.

- Variations on additional features such as support for elaborating the meeting agenda or the meeting minutes.

1.1.3 The WHY, WHAT and WHO dimensions of requirements engineering

The preceding case-study descriptions give us a preliminary idea of the wide range of issues we need to consider in the RE process.

As noted before, the investigation of the problem world leads us to consider two versions of the system. The system-*as-is* has problems, deficiencies and limitations. For example, money is wasted in the UWON library system-as-is by the acquisition of duplicate or rarely used resources; access to bibliographical search facilities is severely limited in both time and location. In the WAX transportation system-as-is, flight connections are missed due to slow bus transportation and poor information to passengers. In the meeting scheduling system-as-is, meeting initiators are overloaded and meeting dates are not chosen well enough, which sometimes results in poor meeting attendance.

The system-*to-be* is intended to address those problems based on technology opportunities. It will do so only if the software-to-be and the organizational and physical components defining the environment are able to cooperate effectively. In the UWON library system-to-be, the new software has to cooperate effectively with environmental components such as patrons, staff, anti-theft devices, digital libraries and external library systems. In the WAX train system-to-be, the train-control software has to operate in conjunction with environmental components such as track sensors, train actuators, passengers, information panel devices and so forth. In the meeting scheduling system-to-be, the scheduler software has to cooperate effectively with environmental components such as meeting initiators and participants, e-mail systems, e-agenda managers, the communications network and so on. In the end, what really matters is the satisfactory working of the software–environment pair.

The problem world may thus be structured along three dimensions. We need to figure out *why* a system-to-be is needed, *what* needs must be addressed by it, and *who* in this system will take part in fulfilling such needs (see Figure 1.2).

The WHY dimension

The contextual reasons for a new version of a system must be made explicit in terms of objectives to be satisfied by it. Such objectives must be identified with regard to the limitations of the system-as-is and the opportunities to be exploited. This requires some careful analysis. What are those objectives precisely? What are their ramifications? How do they interact? How do they align with business objectives?

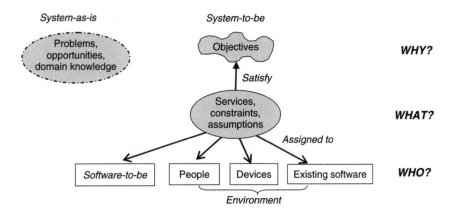

Figure 1.2 *Three dimensions of requirements engineering*

As we will see more thoroughly in subsequent chapters, such analysis along the WHY dimension is generally far from simple.

Acquiring domain knowledge   We need to get a thorough understanding of the domain in which the problem world is rooted. This domain might be quite complex in terms of concepts, regulating laws, procedures and terminology. If you are not sufficiently convinced by the complexity of library management or meeting scheduling, think of domains such as air traffic control, proton therapy, power plants or stock exchanges. (Chapter 2 will present techniques to help us acquire domain knowledge.)

Evaluating alternative options in the problem world   There can be alternative ways of satisfying the same identified objective. We need to assess the pros and cons of such alternatives in order to select the most preferable one. (Chapters 3 and 16 will present techniques to support this task.)

- *Example: Library management.* We could satisfy the objective of extensive coverage of the literature through a non-selective journal subscription policy or, alternatively, through access to digital libraries. The two alternatives need to be evaluated in relation to their pros and cons.

- *Example: Train control.* We could satisfy the objective of avoiding train collisions by ensuring that there will never be two trains on the same block or, alternatively, by ensuring that trains on the same block will always be separated by some worst-case stopping distance. The pros and cons of each alternative must be assessed carefully.

- *Example: Meeting scheduling.* The objective of knowing the time constraints of invited participants could be satisfied by asking them their constraints via e-mail or, alternatively, by accessing their electronic agenda directly.

Evaluating technology opportunities   We also need to acquire a thorough understanding of the oppportunities provided by technologies emerging in the domain under consideration, together with their implications and risks. For example, what are the strengths, implications and risks associated with digital libraries, driverless trains or e-agendas?

Handling conflicts   The objectives that the system-to-be should satisfy are generally identified from multiple sources which have conflicting viewpoints and interests. As a result, there may be different perceptions of what the problems and opportunities are; and there may be different views on how the perceived problems should be addressed. In the end, a coherent set of objectives needs to emerge from agreed trade-offs. (Chapters 3, 16 and 18 will present techniques to support that task.)

- *Example: Library management.* All parties concerned with the library system-to-be will certainly agree that access to state-of-the-art books and journals should be made more effective. There were sufficient complaints reported about this in the system-as-is.

Conflicts are likely to arise, though, when this global objective is refined into more concrete objectives in order to achieve it. Everyone will acclaim the objective of improving the effectiveness of bibliographical search. However, university authorities are likely to emphasize the objective of cost reduction through integration of department libraries. Departments might be reluctant to accede to the implications of this, such as losing their autonomy. On the other hand, library staff might be concerned by strict enforcement of rules limiting library opening periods, the length of loan periods or the number of loans to the same patron. In contrast, library patrons might want much more flexible usage rules.

- *Example: Train control.* All parties will agree on the objectives of faster and safer transportation. Conflicts will, however, appear between the railway company management and the unions while exploring the pros and cons of alternative options with or without drivers, respectively.

The WHAT dimension

This RE dimension is concerned with the *functional services* that the system-to-be should provide to satisfy the objectives identified along the WHY-dimension (see Figure 1.2). Such services often rely on specific system *assumptions* to work properly. They need to meet *constraints* related to performance, security, usability, interoperability and cost – among others. Some of the services will be implemented by the software-to-be whereas others will be realized through manual procedures or device operations.

The system services, constraints and assumptions may be identified from the agreed system objectives, from usage scenarios envisioned in the system-to-be, or from other elicitation vehicles discussed in Chapter 2. They must be formulated in precise terms and in a language that all parties concerned understand to enable their validation and realization. They should be traceable back to system objectives so that we can argue that the latter will be satisfied. The formulation of software services must also be mapped to precise specifications for use by software developers (the nature of this mapping will become clearer in Section 1.1.4).

This analysis of the required services, constraints and assumptions is in general far from simple, as we will see in greater detail in subsequent chapters. Some might be missing; others might be inadequate with respect to objectives stated explicitly or left implicit; others might be formulated ambiguously or inconsistently.

- *Example: Library management.* We might envision a bibliographical query facility as a desirable software service in the UWON library system-to-be. To enable validation, we should define this service in terms that are comprehensible by library staff or by the students who would use it. The definition should make it possible to argue that the objectives of increased coverage, information accuracy and wider accessibility will be achieved through that service. One assumption to meet the objective of anywhere/anytime accessibility is that library users do have Web access outside library opening hours. Constraints on the bibliographical query service might refer to the average response time to a query, the interaction mode and query/answer format for useability by non-experts, and user privacy (e.g. non-staff users should not be able to figure out what other users have borrowed).

- *Example: Train control.* For the WAX train system-to-be, we must define the service of computing train accelerations in terms that allow domain experts to establish that the objective of avoiding collisions of successive trains will be guaranteed. There should be critical constraints on maximum delays in transmitting acceleration commands to trains, on the readability of such commands by train drivers so as to avoid confusion and so forth. Assumptions about the train-tracking subsystem should be made explicit and validated.

The WHO dimension

This RE dimension addresses the assignment of responsibilities for achieving the objectives, services and constraints among the components of the system-to-be – humans, devices or software. Decisions about responsibility assignments are often critical; an important objective, service or constraint might not be achieved if the system component responsible for it fails to behave accordingly.

- *Example: Library management.* The objective of accurate book classification will not be achieved if department faculty members, who might be made responsible for it, do not provide accurate keywords when books are acquired in their area. The objective of limited loan periods for increased availability of book copies will not be achieved if borrowers do not respond to warnings or threatening reminders, or if the software that might be responsible for issuing such reminders in time fails to do so.

- *Example: Train control.* The objective of safe train acceleration will not be achieved if the software responsible for computing accelerations produces values outside the safety range, or if the driver responsible for following the safe instructions issued by the software fails to do so.

Responsibility assignments may also require the evaluation of alternative options. The same responsibility might be assignable to different system components, each alternative assignment having its pros and cons. The selected assignment should keep the risks of not achieving important system objectives, services or constraints as small as possible.

- *Example: Library management.* The objective of accurate book classification might be assigned to the software-to-be; the latter would retrieve relevant keywords from electronic abstracts supplied by publishers, and classify books accordingly. The downsides of such an assignment are increased development costs and the risk of sometimes bizarre classifications. The same objective might alternatively be assigned to the relevant department, at the risk of piles of books waiting for overloaded faculty members to classify them.

- *Example: Train control.* The objective of safe train accelerations might be under the direct responsibility of the software-to-be, in a driverless alternative, or under the responsibility of train drivers who would follow indications issued by the software-to-be. Each alternative has associated strengths and risks that need to be analysed carefully.

Elaborating the software-environment boundary As illustrated by the previous examples, alternative responsibility assignments generally yield different system proposals in which more or less functionality is automated. When we select responsibility assignments from multiple alternatives, we make decisions on what is going to be automated in the system-to-be and what is not. The boundary between the software-to-be and its environment thus emerges from such decisions. This boundary is rarely fixed a priori when the RE process starts. Assessing alternative boundaries and deciding on a specific one is an important aspect of the RE process along the WHO dimension.

1.1.4 Types of statements involved in requirements engineering

Throughout the RE process we need to collect, elaborate, correct or adapt statements that may differ in mood and in scope (Jackson, 1995a; Parnas & Madey, 1995).

Descriptive vs prescriptive statements

Descriptive statements state properties about the system that hold regardless of how the system behaves. Such properties hold typically because of some natural law or physical constraint. Descriptive statements are in the indicative mood. For example, the following statements are descriptive:

- If train doors are open, they are not closed.
- The same book copy cannot be borrowed by two different people at the same time.
- A person cannot physically attend two meetings on different continents on the same day.

Prescriptive statements state desirable properties about the system that may hold or not depending on how the system behaves. Such statements need to be enforced by system components. They are in the optative mood. For example, the following statements are prescriptive:

- Train doors shall always remain closed when the train is moving.
- A patron may not borrow more than three books at the same time.
- The meeting date must fit the constraints of all important participants.

The distinction between descriptive and prescriptive statements is essential to make in the context of engineering requirements. We may need to negotiate, weaken, change or find alternatives to prescriptive statements. We cannot negotiate, weaken, change or find alternatives to descriptive statements.

Statement scope

Section 1.1.1 introduced a partition of phenomena into world, machine and shared phenomena to make the point that RE is concerned with the problem world only. If we focus our attention on the software part of the machine we want to build, we obtain a similar

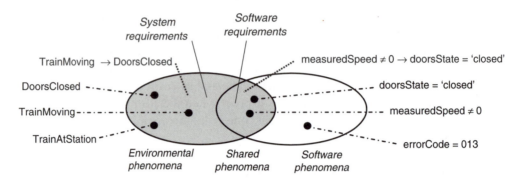

Figure 1.3   *Phenomena and statements about the environment and the software-to-be*

partition. A phenomenon is owned by the software-to-be, by its environment, or shared among them. The environment includes the machine's input/output devices such as sensors and actuators.

For example, the phenomenon of a train physically moving is owned by the environment (see Figure 1.3); the software controller cannot directly observe whether the train is moving or not. The phenomenon of a train's measured speed being non-null is shared by the software and the environment; it is controlled by a speedometer in the environment and observed by the software. The phenomenon of an error variable taking a particular value under a particular condition is owned by the software; the environment cannot directly observe the state of this variable.

The RE process involves statements about the system-to-be that differ in scope. Some statements may refer to phenomena owned by the environment without necessarily being shared with the software-to-be. Other statements may refer to phenomena shared between the environment and the software-to-be; that is, controlled by the software and observed by the environment, or vice versa.

In view of those differences in mood and scope, we can now more precisely define the various types of statement involved in the RE process. Their interrelationships will be discussed next.

Requirements, domain properties, assumptions and definitions

A *system requirement* is a prescriptive statement to be enforced by the software-to-be, possibly in cooperation with other system components, and formulated in terms of environmental phenomena. For example:

- All train doors shall always remain closed while a train is moving.
- Patrons may not borrow more than three books at a time.
- The constraints of a participant invited to a meeting should be known as soon as possible.

Satisfying system requirements may require the cooperation of other system components in addition to the software-to-be. In the first example above, the software train controller might be in charge of the safe control of doors; the cooperation of door actuators is also needed, however (passengers should also be required to refrain from opening doors unsafely).

As we will see in Section 1.1.6, the system requirements are to be understood and agreed by all parties concerned with the system-to-be. Their formulation in terms of environmental phenomena, in the vocabulary used by such parties, will make this possible.

A *software requirement* is a prescriptive statement to be enforced solely by the software-to-be and formulated only in terms of phenomena shared between the software and the environment. For example:

- The doorsState output variable shall always have the value 'closed' when the measuredSpeed input variable has a non-null value.
- The recorded number of loans by a patron may never exceed a maximum number x.
- A request for constraints shall be e-mailed to the address of every participant on the meeting invitee list.

A software requirement constrains the observable behaviours of the software-to-be in its environment; any such behaviour must satisfy it. For example, any software behaviour where *measuredSpeed* $\neq 0$ and *doorsState* = 'open' is ruled out according to the first software requirement in the above list.

Software requirements are to be used by developers; they are formulated in the vocabulary of developers, in terms of software input/output variables.

Note that a software requirement is a system requirement by definition, while the converse is not true (see Figure 1.3). When no ambiguity arises, we will often use the term *requirement* as a shorthand for 'system requirement'.

The notion of system requirement is sometimes referred as 'user requirement' or 'customer requirement' in the literature or in descriptions of good practice. The notion of software requirement is sometimes referred as 'product requirement', 'specification' or even, misleadingly, 'system requirement'. We will avoid those phrases in view of possible confusion. For example, many 'user requirements' do not come from any software user; a 'system' does not merely consist of software; a 'specification' may refer in the software engineering literature both to a process and to a variety of different products along the software lifecycle (requirement specification, design specification, module specification, test case specification etc.).

A *domain property* is a descriptive statement about the problem world. It is expected to hold invariably regardless of how the system will behave – and even regardless of whether there will be any software-to-be or not. Domain properties typically correspond to physical laws that cannot be broken. For example:

- A train is moving if and only if its physical speed is non-null.
- A book may not be borrowed and available at the same time.
- A participant cannot attend multiple meetings at the same time.

An *assumption* is a statement to be satisfied by the environment and formulated in terms of environmental phenomena. For example:

- A train's measured speed is non-null if and only if its physical speed is non-null.
- The recorded number of loans by a borrower is equal to the actual number of book copies physically borrowed by him or her.
- Borrowers who receive threatening reminders after the loan deadline has expired will return books promptly.
- Participants will promptly respond to e-mail requests for constraints.
- A participant is on the invitee list for a meeting if and only if he or she is invited to that meeting.

Assumptions are generally prescriptive, as they constrain the behaviour of specific environmental components. For example, the first assumption in the previous list constrains speedometers in our train control system.

The formulation of requirements, domain properties and assumptions might be adequate or not. We will come back to this throughout the book. The important point here is their difference in mood and scope.

Definitions are the last type of statement involved in the RE process. They allow domain concepts and auxiliary terms to be given a precise, complete and agreed meaning – the same meaning for everyone. For example:

- TrainMoving is the name for a phenomenon in the environment that accounts for the fact that the train being considered is physically moving on a block.
- A patron is any person who has registered at the corresponding library for the corresponding period of time.
- A person participates in a meeting if he or she attends that meeting from beginning to end.

Unlike statements of other types, definitions have no truth value. It makes no sense to say that a definition is satisfied or not. However, we need to check definitions for accuracy, completeness and adequacy. For example, we might question the above definition of what it means for a person to participate in a meeting; as a result, we might refine the concept of participation into two more specialized concepts instead – namely, full participation and partial participation.

In view of their difference in mood and scope, the statements emerging from the RE process should be 'typed' when we document them (we will come back to this in Section 4.2.1). Anyone using the documentation can then directly figure out whether a statement is a requirement, a domain property, an assumption or a definition.

Relating software requirements to system requirements

The link between the notions of system requirement and software requirement can be made more precise by introducing the following types of variables:

- *Monitored variables* are environmental quantities that the software monitors through input devices such as sensors.

- *Controlled variables* are environmental quantities that the software controls through output devices such as actuators.

- *Input variables* are data items that the software needs as input.

- *Output variables* are quantities that the software produces as output.

These different types of variable yield a more explicit framework for control systems, known as the *four-variable model* (Parnas and Madey, 1995); see Figure 1.4. As we can see there, input/output devices are highlighted as special interface components between the control software and its environment.

In this framework, we can define system requirements and software requirements as distinct mathematical relations. Let us use the standard notations $\subseteq$ and $\times$ for set inclusion and set Cartesian product, respectively.

- A system requirement *SysReq* is a relation between a set M of monitored variables and a corresponding set C of controlled variables:

$$SysReq \subseteq M \times C$$

- A software requirement *SofReq* is a relation between a set I of input variables and a corresponding set O of output variables:

$$SofReq \subseteq I \times O$$

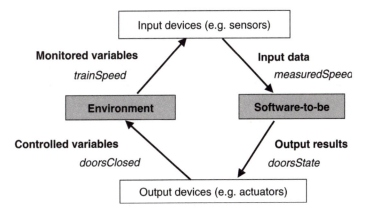

Figure 1.4 *Four-variable model*

A software requirement *SofReq* 'translates' the corresponding system requirement *SysReq* in the vocabulary of the software's input/output variables.

Satisfaction arguments

Such translation of a system requirement into a software requirement is not a mere reformulation obtained by mapping the environment's vocabulary into the software's one. Domain properties and assumptions are often required to ensure the 'correctness' of the translation; that is, the *satisfaction* of the system requirement when the corresponding software requirement holds.

Let us illustrate this very important point. We first introduce some shorthand notations:

$$A \rightarrow B \text{ for '} if \text{ A } then \text{ B'}, \quad A \leftrightarrow B \text{ for 'A } if \text{ and } only \text{ if B'}.$$

We may express the above examples of system requirement, software requirement, domain property and assumption for our train system in the shorter form:

(*SysReq:*)	TrainMoving → DoorsClosed
(*SofReq:*)	measuredSpeed ≠ 0 → doorsState = 'closed'
(*Dom:*)	TrainMoving ↔ trainSpeed ≠ 0
(*Asm:*)	measuredSpeed ≠ 0 ↔ trainSpeed ≠ 0
	DoorsState = 'closed' ↔ DoorsClosed

To ensure that the software requirement *SofReq* correctly translates the system requirement *SysReq* in this simple example, we need to identify the domain property *Dom* and the assumptions *Asm*, and make sure that those statements are actually satisfied. If this is the case, we can obtain *SysReq* from *SofReq* by the following rewriting: (a) we replace measuredSpeed ≠ 0 in *SofReq* by TrainMoving, thanks to the first equivalence in the assumptions *Asm* and then the equivalence in the domain property *Dom*; and (b) we replace doorsState = 'closed' in *SofReq* by DoorsClosed thanks to the second equivalence in *Asm*.

The assumptions in *Asm* are examples of *accuracy* statements, to be enforced here by the speedometer and door actuator, respectively. Accuracy requirements and assumptions form an important class of non-functional statements to be considered in the RE process (see Section 1.1.5). Overlooking them or formulating wrong ones has sometimes been the cause of major software disasters. We will come back to this throughout the book.

Our job as requirements engineers is to elicit, make precise and consolidate requirements, assumptions and domain properties. Then we need to provide *satisfaction arguments* taking the following form:

$$\{SOFREQ, ASM, DOM\} \models SysReq$$

which reads:

> if the software requirements in set *SOFREQ* are satisfied by the software, the assumptions in set *ASM* are satisfied by the environment, the domain properties in set *DOM* hold and all those statements are consistent with each other,
>
> then the system requirements *SysReq* are satisfied by the system.

Such a satisfaction argument could not be provided in our train example without the statements *Asm* and *Dom* previously mentioned. Satisfaction arguments require environmental assumptions and domain properties to be elicited, specified and validated. For example, is it the case that the speedometer and door actuator will always enforce the first and second assumptions in *Asm*, respectively?

In Chapter 6, we will see that satisfaction arguments play an important role in managing the traceability among requirements and assumptions for requirements evolution. In Part II of this book, we will extend them to higher-level arguments for goal satisfaction by requirements and assumptions.

1.1.5 Categories of requirements

In the above typology of statements, the requirements themselves are of different kinds. Roughly, functional requirements refer to services that the software-to-be should provide, whereas non-functional requirements constrain how such services should be provided.

Functional requirements

Functional requirements define the functional effects that the software-to-be is required to have on its environment. They address the 'WHAT' aspects depicted in Figure 1.2. Here are some examples:

- The bibliographical search engine shall provide a list of all library books on a given subject.
- The train control sofware shall control the acceleration of all the system's trains.
- The meeting scheduler shall determine schedules that fit the diary constraints of all invited participants.

The effects characterized by such requirements result from *operations* to be automated by the software. Functional requirements may also refer to environmental conditions under which such operations should be applied. For example:

- Train doors may be opened only when the train is stopped.
- The meeting scheduler shall issue a warning when the constraints entered by a participant are not valid.

Functional requirements characterize units of functionality that we may want to group into coarser-grained functionalities that the software should support. For example, bibliographical search, loan management and acquisition management are overall functionalities of the library software-to-be. Units of functionality are sometimes called *features* in some problem worlds; for example, call forwarding and call reactivation are features generally provided in telephony systems.

Non-functional requirements

Non-functional requirements define constraints on the way the software-to-be should satisfy its functional requirements or on the way it should be developed. For example:

- The format for submitting bibliographical queries and displaying answers shall be accessible to students who have no computer expertise.
- Acceleration commands shall be sent to every train every 3 seconds.
- The diary constraints of a participant may not be disclosed to any other invited participant.

The wide range of such constraints makes it helpful to classify them in a taxonomy (Davis, 1993; Robertson & Robertson, 1999; Chung *et al.*, 2000). Specific classes can then be characterized more precisely. Browsing through the taxonomy may help us acquire instances of the corresponding classes that might have been overlooked (Section 2.2.7 will come back to this).

Figure 1.5 outlines one typical classification. The taxonomy there is not meant to be exhaustive, although it covers the main classes of non-functional requirements.

Quality requirements

Quality requirements state additional, quality-related properties that the functional effects of the software should have. They are sometimes called 'quality attributes' in the software engineering literature. Such requirements complement the 'WHAT' aspects with 'HOW WELL' aspects. They appear on the left-hand side in Figure 1.5.

Safety requirements are quality requirements that rule out software effects that might result in accidents, degradations or losses in the environment. For example:

- The controlled accelerations of trains shall always guarantee that a worst-case stopping distance is maintained between successive trains.

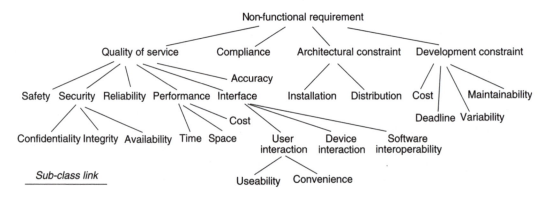

Figure 1.5 *A taxonomy of non-functional requirements*

Security requirements are quality requirements that prescribe the protection of system assets against undesirable environment behaviours. This increasingly critical class of requirements is traditionally split into subcategories such as the following (Amoroso, 1994; Pfleeger, 1997).

Confidentiality requirements state that some sensitive information may never be disclosed to unauthorized parties. For example:

- A non-staff patron may never know which books have been borrowed by others.

Among these, *privacy requirements* state that some private information may never be disclosed without the consent of the owner of the information. For example:

- The diary constraints of a participant may never be disclosed to other invited participants without his or her consent.

Integrity requirements state that some information may be modified only if correctly done and with authorization. For example:

- The return of book copies shall be encoded correctly and by library staff only.

Availability requirements state that some information or resource can be used at any point in time when it is needed and its usage is authorized. For example:

- A blacklist of bad patrons shall be made available at any time to library staff.
- Information about train positions shall be available at any time to the vital station computer.

Reliability requirements constrain the software to operate as expected over long periods of time. Its services must be provided in a correct and robust way in spite of exceptional circumstances. For example:

- The train acceleration control software shall have a mean time between failures of the order of 10^9 hours.

Accuracy requirements are quality requirements that constrain the state of the information processed by the software to reflect the state of the corresponding physical information in the environment accurately. For example:

- A copy of a book shall be stated as available by the loan software if and only if it is actually available on the library shelves.
- The information about train positions used by the train controller shall accurately reflect the actual position of trains up to X metres at most.

- The constraints used by the meeting scheduler should accurately reflect the real constraints of invited participants.

Performance requirements are quality requirements that constrain the software's operational conditions, such as the time or space required by operations, the frequency of their activation, their throughput, the size of their input or output and so forth. For example:

- Responses to bibliographical queries shall take less than 2 seconds.
- Acceleration commands shall be issued to every train every 3 seconds.
- The meeting scheduler shall be able to accommodate up to X requests in parallel.

Performance requirements may concern other resources in addition to time or space, such as money spent in operational costs. For example:

- The new e-subscription facility should ensure a 30% cost saving.

Interface requirements are quality requirements that constrain the phenomena shared by the software-to-be and the environment (see Figure 1.3). They refer to the static and dynamic aspects of software-environment interactions; input/output formats and interaction sequences should be compatible with what the environment expects. Interface requirements cover a wide range of concerns depending on which environmental component the software is interacting with.

For human interaction, *useability requirements* prescribe input/output formats and user dialogues to fit the abstractions, abilities and expectations of the target users. For example:

- The format for bibliographical queries and answers shall be accessible to students from any department.

Other human interaction requirements may constrain software effects so that users feel them to be 'convenient' in some system-specific sense. For example:

- To ensure smooth and comfortable train moves, the difference between the accelerations in two successive commands sent to a train should be at most X.
- To avoid disturbing busy people unduly, the amount of interaction with invited participants for organizing meetings should be kept as low as possible.

For interaction with devices or existing software components, *interoperability requirements* prescribe input/output formats and interaction protocols that enable effective cooperation with those environmental components. For example:

- The meeting scheduling software should be interoperable with the WSS Agenda Manager product.

Figure 1.5 covers other categories of non-functional requirements in addition to quality requirements.

Compliance requirements

Compliance requirements prescribe software effects on the environment to conform to national laws, international regulations, social norms, cultural or political constraints, standards and the like. For example:

- The value for the worst-case stopping distance between successive trains shall be compliant with international railways regulations.
- The meeting scheduler shall by default exclude official holidays associated with the target market.

Architectural requirements

Architectural requirements impose structural constraints on the software-to-be to fit its environment, typically:

- *Distribution constraints* on software components to fit the geographically distributed structure of the host organization, the distribution of data to be processed, or the distribution of devices to be controlled.
- *Installation constraints* to ensure that the software-to-be will run smoothly on the target implementation platform.

Here are some examples of architectural requirements:

- The on-board train controllers shall handle the reception and proper execution of acceleration commands sent by the station computer.
- The meeting scheduling software should cooperate with email systems and e-agenda managers of participants distributed worldwide.
- The meeting scheduling software should run on Windows version X.x and Linux version Y.y.

Architectural requirements reduce the space of possible software architectures. They may guide developers in the selection of an appropriate architectural style, for example an event-based style. We will come back to this in Section 16.5.

Development requirements

Development requirements are non-functional requirements that do not constrain the way the software should satisfy its functional requirements but rather the way it should be developed (see the right-hand part of Figure 1.5). These include requirements on development costs, delivery schedules, variability of features, maintainability, reusability, portability and the like. For example:

- The overall cost of the new UWON library software should not exceed X.
- The train control software should be operational within two years.
- The software should provide customized solutions according to variations in type of meeting (professional or private, regular or occasional), type of meeting location (fixed, variable) and type of participant (same or different degrees of importance).

Possible overlaps between categories of requirements

The distinction between *functional* and *non-functional* requirements should not be taken in a strict, clear-cut sense. The boundary between those two categories is not always clear. For example, consider the following requirement in a safety injection system for a nuclear power plant (Courtois & Parnas, 1993):

- The safety injection signal shall be on whenever there is a loss of coolant except during normal start-up or cool down.

Is this a functional or a safety requirement? Both, we might be inclined to say. Similarly, many functional requirements for a firewall management software are likely to be security requirements as well. Call screening is traditionally considered as a functional feature in telephony software, even though it is about keeping the caller's phone number confidential.

Likewise, some of the non-functional requirements categories in Figure 1.5 may overlap in specific situations. Consider, for example, a denial-of-service attack on a patient's file that prevents surgeons from accessing critical patient data during surgery. Does this violate a security or a safety requirement? Similarly, the requirement to send acceleration commands to trains at very high frequency is related to both performance and safety. More generally, availability requirements often contribute to both security and reliability.

Uses of requirements taxonomies

In spite of possible overlaps in specific situations, what matters in the end are the roles and benefits of a requirements taxonomy in the RE process.

a. *More specific characterization of requirements.* Requirements categories allow us to characterize more explicitly what requirements refer to, beyond our general definition as prescriptive statements to be enforced by the software and formulated in terms of environmental phenomena.

b. *More semantic characterization of requirements.* The distinction between requirements categories allows for a more semantic characterization of requirements in terms of prescribed *behaviours.*

- There are requirements that prescribe *desired* behaviours. For example, scheduler behaviours should result in a meeting being scheduled every time a corresponding request has been submitted. Many functional requirements are of this kind.

- There are requirements that rule out *unacceptable* behaviours. For example, any train controller behaviour that results in trains being too close to each other must be avoided. Many safety, security and accuracy requirements are of this kind.

- There are requirements that indicate *preferred* behaviours. For example, the requirement that *'participants shall be notified of the scheduled meeting date as soon as possible'* states a preference for scheduler behaviours where notification is sooner over behaviours where notification is later. Likewise, the requirement that *'interactions with participants should be kept as limited as possible'* states a preference for scheduler behaviours where there are fewer interactions (e.g. through e-agenda access) over behaviours where there are more interactions (e.g. through e-mail requests and pestering). Many performance and '-ility' requirements are of this kind, for example useability, reuseability, portability or maintainability requirements. When alternative options are raised in the RE process, we will use such requirements to discard alternatives and select preferred ones (see Chapters 8 and 16).

c. *Differentiation between confined and cross-cutting concerns.* Functional requirements tend to address single points of functionality. In contrast, non-functional requirements tend to address cross-cutting concerns; the same requirement may constrain multiple units of functionality. In the library system, for example, the useability requirement on accessibility of input/output formats to non-expert users constrains the bibliographical search functionality. It may, however, constrain other functionalities as well, for example user registration or book reservation. Similarly, the non-disclosure of participant constraints might affect multiple points of functionality such as meeting notification, information on the current status of planning, replanning and so on.

d. *Basis for RE heuristics.* The characterization of categories in a requirements taxonomy yields helpful heuristics for the RE process. Some heuristics may help elicit requirements that were overlooked, for example:

  - Is there any accuracy requirement on information X in my system?
  - Is there any confidentiality requirement on information Y in my system?

Other heuristics may help discover conflicts among instances of requirements categories known to be potentially conflicting, for example:

  - Is there any conflict in my system between hiding information on display for better useability and showing critical information for safety reasons?
  - Is there any conflict in my system between password-based authentication and useability requirements?
  - Is there any conflict in my system between confidentiality and accountability requirements?

We will come back to such heuristics in Chapters 2 and 3 while reviewing techniques for requirements elicitation and evaluation. As we will see there, conflict detection is a prerequisite for the elaboration of new requirements for conflict resolution.

1.1.6 The requirements lifecycle: Processes, actors and products

As already introduced briefly, the requirements engineering process is composed of different activities yielding various products and involving various types of actors.

A *stakeholder* is a group or individual affected by the system-to-be, who may influence the way this system is shaped and has some responsibility in its acceptance. As we will see, stakeholders play an important role in the RE process. They may include strategic decision makers, managers of operational units, domain experts, operators, end-users, developers, subcontractors, customers, and certification authorities.

For example in our library management system, stakeholders might include the UWON board of management, department chairs, library staff from the various departments and from partner universities, ordinary users and software consultants. In the WAX transportation system, stakeholders might include airport authorities, government representatives, airline companies, Wonderland Railways, passengers, union representatives and software subcontractors. In the meeting scheduling system, stakeholders might include a variety of people who schedule meetings (local, international, intra- or inter-organization meetings), a variety of people who attend such meetings under different positions, secretaries and software consultants.

Note that the set of stakeholders may vary slightly from the system-as-is to the system-to-be. In the WAX transportation system-to-be, for example, bus drivers will no longer be involved whereas railways personnel will.

In spite of their difference in aim and supporting techniques, the activities composing the RE process are highly intertwined. We review them individually first and then discuss their interaction.

Domain understanding

This activity consists of studying the system-as-is within its organizational and technical context. The aim is to acquire a good understanding of:

- The domain in which the problem world is rooted.

- What the roots of the problem are.

More specifically, we need to get an accurate and comprehensive picture of the following aspects:

- The organization within which the system-as-is takes place: its structure, strategic objectives, business policies, roles played by organizational units and actors, and dependencies among them.

- The scope of the system-as-is: its underlying objectives, the components forming it, the concepts on which it relies, the tasks involved in it, the information flowing through it, and the constraints and regulations to which the system is subject.

- The set of stakeholders to be involved in the RE process.

- The strengths and weaknesses of the system-as-is, as perceived by the identified stakeholders.

The product of this activity typically consists of the initial sections in a preliminary draft proposal that describe those contextual aspects. This proposal will be expanded during the elicitation activity and then used by the evaluation activity that comes after.

In particular, a *glossary of terms* should be established to provide definitions of key concepts on which everyone should agree. For example, in the library system-as-is, what precisely is a patron? What does it mean to say that a requested book is being reserved? In the train system, what precisely is a block? What does it mean to say that a train is at a station? In the meeting scheduling system, what is referred to by the term 'participant'? What does it mean to say that a person is invited to a meeting or participates in it? What precisely are participant constraints?

A glossary of terms will be used throughout the RE process, and even beyond, to ensure that the same term does not refer to different concepts and the same concept is not referred to under different terms.

Domain understanding is typically performed by studying key documents, investigating similar systems and interviewing or observing the identified stakeholders. The cooperation of the latter is obviously essential for our understanding to be correct. Chapter 2 will review techniques that may help us in this task.

Requirements elicitation

This activity consists of discovering candidate requirements and assumptions that will shape the system-to-be, based on the weaknesses of the system-as-is as they emerge from domain understanding. What are the symptoms, causes and consequences of the identified deficiencies and limitations of the system-as-is? How are they likely to evolve? How could they be addressed in the light of new opportunities? What new business objectives could be achieved then?

The aim is thus to explore the problem world with stakeholders and acquire the following information:

- The opportunities arising from the evolution of technologies and market conditions that could address the weaknesses of the system-as-is while preserving its strengths.

- The improvement objectives that the system-to-be should meet with respect to such weaknesses and opportunities, together with alternative options for satisfying them.

- The organizational and technical constraints that this system should take into account.

- Alternative boundaries that we might consider between what will be automated by the software-to-be and what will be left under the responsibility of the environment.

- Typical scenarios illustrating desired interactions between the software-to-be and its environment.

- The domain properties and assumptions about the environment that are necessary for the software-to-be to work properly.

- The requirements that the software-to-be should meet in order to conform to all of the above.

The requirements are by no means there when the project starts. We need to discover them incrementally, in relation to higher-level concerns, through exploration of the problem world. Elicitation is a *cooperative learning* process in which the requirements engineer and the system stakeholders work in close collaboration to acquire the right requirements. This activity is obviously critical. If done wrong, it will result in poor requirements and, consequently in poor software.

The product of the elicitation activity typically consists of additional sections in the preliminary draft proposal initiated during the domain understanding activity. These sections document the items listed above. The resulting draft proposal will be used as input to the evaluation activity coming next.

The elicitation process can be supported by a variety of techniques, such as knowledge reuse, scenarios, prototyping, interviews, observation and the like. Chapter 2 will discuss these.

Evaluation and agreement

The aim of this activity is to make informed decisions about issues raised during the elicitation process. Such decisions are often based on 'best' trade-offs on which the involved parties should agree. Negotiation may be required in order to reach a consensus.

- *Conflicting concerns* must be identified and resolved. These often arise from multiple viewpoints and different expectations.

- There are *risks* associated with the system that is being shaped. They must be assessed and resolved.

- The *alternative options* identified during elicitation must be compared with regard to quality objectives and risks, and best options must be selected on that basis.

- Requirements *prioritization* is often necessary for a number of reasons:

  a. Favouring higher-priority requirements is a standard way of resolving conflicts.

  b. Dropping lower-priority requirements provides a way of integrating multiple wishlists that would together exceed budgets and deadlines.

  c. Priorities make it easier to plan an incremental development process, and to replan the project during development as new constraints arise such as unanticipated delays, budget restrictions, deadline contractions etc.

The product of this activity typically consists of final sections in the preliminary draft proposal initiated during the preceding activities. These sections document the decisions made after assessment and negotiation. They highlight the agreed requirements and assumptions about the selected system-to-be. The system proposal thereby obtained will serve as input to the specification activity coming next.

The evaluation process can be supported by a variety of qualitative and quantitative techniques. Chapters 3 and 16 will provide a comprehensive sample of these.

Specification and documentation

This activity consists of detailing, structuring and documenting the agreed characteristics of the system-to-be as they emerge from the evaluation activity.

The resulting product is the *requirements document* (RD). In this document, the objectives, concept definitions, relevant domain properties, responsibilities, system requirements, software requirements and environmental assumptions are specified precisely and organized into a coherent structure. These specifications form the core of the RD. Satisfaction arguments should appear there as well (see Section 1.1.4.). Other sections in the RD may include a description of likely variants and revisions, acceptance test data and cost figures. The RD may also be complemented by annexes such as the preliminary system proposal after domain understanding, elicitation and evaluation, to provide the context and rationale for decisions taken, as well as technical annexes about the domain.

The requirements document will be used for a variety of purposes throughout the software lifecycle, as we will see in Section 1.1.9 (see Figure 1.7). To enable validation and commitment, any RD portion that concerns specific parties, such as customers, domain experts, (sub)contractors, developers or users, must be specified in a form understandable by them.

A wide range of techniques can be used to support the specification and documentation process, including structured natural language templates, diagrammatic notations and formal specifications. Chapter 4 will discuss these.

Requirements consolidation

The purpose of this activity is quality assurance. The specifications resulting from the preceding activity must be carefully analysed. They should be *validated* with stakeholders in order to pinpoint inadequacies with respect to actual needs. They should also be *verified* against each other in order to find inconsistencies and omissions before the software requirements are transmitted to developers. Any error found must be fixed. The sooner an error is found, the cheaper the fix will be.

The main product of this activity is a consolidated requirements document, where the detected errors and flaws have been fixed throughout the document. Other products may include a prototype or mock-up built for requirements validation, additional test data coming out of verification, a proposed development plan, the contract linking the client and the software developer, and a call for tenders in the case of development subcontracting.

Section 1.1.7 will detail the quality criteria addressed by this activity more precisely, together with the various types of errors and flaws that may need to be fixed. Section 1.2 will discuss the consequences of not fixing them. Chapter 5 will present techniques for requirements quality assurance.

Requirements engineering: A spiral process

The above activities are sometimes called *phases* of the RE process. There are, of course, *data dependencies* among them. Consolidation requires input from specification; specification requires input from evaluation; evaluation requires input from elicitation; and elicitation requires input from domain understanding. We should not think of these phases as being applied in a strict sequence, however. They are generally intertwined, they may overlap, and backtracking from one phase to preceding ones may be required.

Overall, the RE process can be viewed as an iteration on successive increments according to a spiral model (Boehm, 1988; Kotonya & Sommerville, 1997). Figure 1.6 shows such process model for the activities previously discussed in this section.

Each iteration in Figure 1.6 is triggered by the need to revise, adapt or extend the requirements document through addition, removal or modification of statements such as requirements, assumptions or domain properties.

A new iteration may take place at different stages of the software lifecycle:

- Within the RE process itself, as such statements are found during consolidation to be missing, inadequate or inconsistent with others.

- During software development, as such statements turn out to be missing, unfeasible or too costly to implement, incompatible with new implementation constraints, or no longer adequate as the problem world has evolved in the meantime.

- After software deployment, as the problem world has evolved or must be customized to specific contexts.

'Late' iterations of the RE process will be further discussed in Chapter 6 on evolution management and in Section 16.5 where the interplay between RE and architectural design will appear more clearly.

The spiral process model depicted in Figure 1.6 is fairly general and flexible. It may need to be specialized and adapted to the specificities of the problem world and to the standards

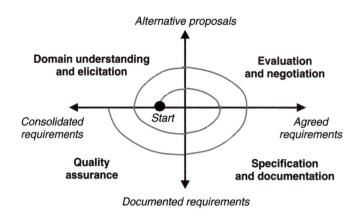

Figure 1.6 *The requirements engineering process*

of the host organization, for example by further defining the nature of each increment or the intertwining with software development cycles. The important points, though, are the range of issues to consider, the complementarity and difference among RE activities, their data dependencies and the iterative nature of the RE process.

1.1.7 Target qualities and defects to avoid

Elaborating a good requirements document is difficult. We need to cater for multiple and diverse quality factors. Each of these may be hard to reach.

Quality factors define the goals of the RE process. They provide the basis for evaluating successive versions of the requirements document. This section defines them precisely together with their opposite, that is, the requirements defects that we must avoid. References to those qualities and defects will appear throughout the book. In particular, Chapter 5 and Parts II and III will detail a variety of techniques for checking them. Let us start with the qualities first.

- *Completeness.* The requirements, assumptions and domain properties, when taken together, must be sufficient to ensure that the system-to-be will satisfy all its objectives. These objectives must themselves be fully identified, including quality-related ones. In other words, the needs addressed by the new system must be fully covered, without any undesirable outcomes. In particular, we must have anticipated incidental or malicious behaviours of environmental components so that undesirable software effects are ruled out through dedicated requirements. A requirement on software behaviour must prescribe a desired output for all possible inputs. The specification of requirements and assumptions must also be sufficiently detailed to enable subsequent software development.

- *Consistency.* The requirements, assumptions and domain properties must be satisfiable when taken together. In other words, they must be compatible with each other.

- *Adequacy.* The requirements must address the *actual* needs for a new system – explicitly expressed by stakeholders or left implicit. The software requirements must be adequate translations of the system requirements (see Section 1.1.4). The domain properties must correctly describe laws in the problem world. The environmental assumptions must be realistic.

- *Unambiguity.* The requirements, assumptions and domain properties must be formulated in a way that precludes different interpretations. Every term must be defined and used consistently.

- *Measureability.* The requirements must be formulated at a level of precision that enables analysts to evaluate alternative options against them, developers to test or verify whether an implementation satisfies them, and users to determine whether they are met or not in the system under operation. The assumptions must be observable in the environment.

- *Pertinence.* The requirements and assumptions must all contribute to the satisfaction of one or several objectives underpinning the system-to-be. They must capture elements of the problem world rather than elements of the machine solution.

- *Feasibility.* The requirements must be realizable in view of the budget, schedule and technology constraints.

- *Comprehensibility.* The formulation of requirements, assumptions and domain properties must be comprehensible by the people who need to use them.

- *Good structuring.* The requirements document should be organized in a way that highlights the structural links among its elements – refinement or specialization links, dependency links, cause–effect links, definition–use links and so forth. The definition of a term must precede its use.

- *Modifiability.* It should be possible to revise, adapt, extend or contract the requirements document through modifications that are as local as possible.

- *Traceability.* The *context* in which an item of the requirements document was created, modified or used should be easy to retrieve. This context should include the rationale for creation, modification or use. The *impact* of creating, modifying or deleting that item should be easy to assess. The impact may refer to dependent items in the requirements document and to dependent artefacts subsequently developed – architectural descriptions, test data, user manuals, source code etc. (Traceability management will be discussed at length in Section 6.3.)

Note that critical qualities such as completeness, adequacy and pertinence are not defined in an absolute sense; they are *relative* to the underlying objectives and needs of a new system. The latter may themselves be implicit, unclear or even unidentified. Those qualities can therefore be especially hard to enforce.

Section 1.2.1 will review some facts and figures about project failures that are due to poor-quality requirements. Elaborating a requirements document that meets all of the above qualities is essential for the success of a software project. The techniques described in this book are aimed at supporting this task. As a prerequisite, we should be aware of the corresponding types of defect to avoid.

Requirements errors and flaws

Table 1.1 lists various types of defects frequently found in requirements documents. Each entry in Table 1.1 corresponds to the opposite of one of the preceding qualities. Table 1.2 and Table 1.3 suggest examples of defects that we might find in requirements documents for our case studies.

The defect types in Table 1.1 can be divided into two classes according to the potential severity of their consequences.

There are *errors* whose occurrence may have fatal effects on the quality of the software-to-be:

- Omissions may result in the software failing to implement an unstated critical requirement, or failing to take into account an unstated critical assumption or domain property.

- We cannot produce a correct implementation from a set of requirements, assumptions and domain properties that contradict each other.

Omission	Problem world feature not stated by any RD item – e.g. missing objective, requirement or assumption; unstated software response to some input.
Contradiction	RD items defining a problem world feature in an incompatible way.
Inadequacy	RD item not adequately stating a problem world feature.
Ambiguity	RD item allowing a problem world feature to be interpreted in different ways – e.g. ambiguous term or statement.
Unmeasurability	RD item stating a problem world feature in a way that cannot be precisely compared with alternative options, or cannot be tested or verified in machine solutions.
Noise	RD item yielding no information on any problem world feature.
Overspecification	RD item stating a feature not pertaining to the problem world but to the machine solution.
Unfeasibility	RD item that cannot be realistically implemented within the assigned budget, schedule or development platform.
Unintelligibility	RD item stated in an incomprehensible way for those who need to use it.
Poor structuring	RD items not organized according to any sensible and visible structuring rule.
Forward reference	RD item making use of problem world features that are not defined yet.
Remorse	RD item stating a problem world feature too late or incidentally.
Poor modifiability	RD items whose modification may need to be globally propagated throughout the RD.
Opacity	RD item whose rationale, authoring or dependencies are invisible.

Table 1.1   *Defects in a requirements document (RD)*

- Inadequacies may result in a software implementation that meets requirements, assumptions or domain properties that are not the right ones.

- Ambiguous and unmeasurable statements may result in a software implementation built from interpretations of requirements, assumptions or domain properties that are different from the intended ones.

In addition to errors, there are *flaws* whose consequences are in general less severe. In the best cases they result in a waste of effort and associated risks:

- Useless effort in finding out that some noisy or overspecified aspects are not needed – with the risk of sticking to overspecified aspects that may prevent better solutions from being taken.

- Useless effort in determining what requirements to stick to in unfeasible situations – with the risk of dropping important requirements.

Omission	No requirement about the expected state of train doors in case of emergency stop.
Contradiction	Train doors must always be kept closed between stations.
	And elsewhere:
	Train doors must be opened once a train is stopped after an emergency signal.
Inadequacy	If a book copy has not been returned one week after the third reminder has been issued, the negligent borrower shall be notified that he or she has to pay a fine of £*X*.
	Rather than
	If a book has not been returned one week after the third reminder has been issued, a fine of £*x* shall be retained from the borrower's registration deposit and a notification will be sent to the borrower.
Ambiguity	Train doors shall be opened as soon as the train is stopped at a platform.
	(Possible interpretations:)
	The front of the train is (stopped) at a platform *or* The whole train is (stopped) at a platform?
Unmeasurability	Information panels inside trains shall be user-friendly.

Table 1.2   *Errors in a requirements document: Examples*

- Useless effort in the understanding or reverse engineering of unintelligible, poorly defined, poorly structured or poorly traceable aspects – with the risk of wrong understanding or wrong reverse engineering.

- Excessive effort in revising or adapting a poorly modifiable RD – with the risk of incorrect change propagation.

The various types of defect in Table 1.1 may originate from any RE activity – from elicitation to evaluation to documentation to consolidation (see Figure 1.6). Omissions, which are the hardest errors to detect, may happen at any time. Contradictions often originate from conflicting viewpoints that emerged during elicitation and were left unresolved at the end of the RE process. Inadequacies often result from analyst–stakeholder mismatch during elicitation and negotiation. Some flaws are more likely to happen during documentation phases – such as noise, unintelligibility, forward reference and remorse, poor structuring, poor modifiability and opacity.

Overspecifications are frequently introduced in requirements documents written by developers or people who want to jump promptly to technical solutions. They may take the form of

Noise	Every train car will be equipped with a software-controlled information panel together with non-smoking signs posted on every window.
Overspecification	The setAlarm method must be invoked on receipt of a stopAlarm message.
Unfeasibility	The meeting scheduler will also make travel arrangements such as flight, car and hotel reservations for every participant who needs to travel to attend the meeting.
Unintelligibility	A requirement statement containing five acronyms.
Poor structuring	Intertwining of book acquisition and loan management aspects.
Forward reference	Multiple uses of the concept of 'participating in a meeting' in the requirements document and then, several pages later, the definition: A person *participates* in a meeting if he or she attends that meeting from beginning to end.
Remorse	After multiple uses of the undefined concept of 'participating in a meeting', the last one is directly followed by an incidental definition between brackets such as: (a person *participates* in a meeting if he or she attends that meeting from beginning to end).
Poor modifiability	Use of fixed numerical values for quantities throughout the requirements document (e.g. for *maximum loan period, meeting notification deadline* or *train speed thresholds*), when such values are subject to change over time or from one variant to another.
Opacity	A requirement such as: the commanded speed of a train must always be at least 7 mph above its physical speed, without any contextual information about the origin of and rationale for this requirement, and its impact on other requirements.

Table 1.3 *Flaws in a requirements document: Examples*

flowcharts, variables that are internal to the software (rather than shared with the environment, cf. Figure 1.3), statements formulated in terms of programming constructs such as sequential composition, iterations or go-tos. 'Algorithmic requirements' implement declarative requirements that are left implicit. They might incorrectly implement these hidden requirements. They cannot be verified or tested against them. They may preclude some alternative 'implementation' of the hidden requirements that might prove more effective with respect to other quality requirements.

In view of their potentially harmful consequences, requirements errors and flaws should be detected and fixed in the requirements document. Chapter 5 will review a variety of techniques for requirements quality assurance. In particular, Table 1.1 may be used as a basis for requirements inspection checklists (see Section 5.1.3). Model-based quality assurance will be discussed at length in Parts II and III.

1.1.8 Types of software projects

There are different types of projects for which requirements need to be elaborated. As we will see, different project types may entail variations in the RE process discussed in Section 1.1.6.

Greenfield vs brownfield projects

In a *greenfield* project, a brand new software solution is built from scratch to address problems with the system-as-is and exploit new opportunities from technology evolution or market conditions. In a *brownfield* project, the system-as-is already offers software solutions; the software-to-be needs to integrate, improve, adapt or extend such solutions. Note that a greenfield project may become brownfield as the software evolves after deployment. As examples:

- The WAX train transportation system is a greenfield project.

- The UWON library project would be brownfield if we needed to integrate legacy software from some departments.

Greenfield projects are sometimes specialized further into *normal design* vs *radical design* projects (Vicenti, 1993). In a normal design project, engineers solve problems by making improvements to existing technologies or by using them in new ways. They have a good idea of what features the target artefact will provide. In contrast, radical design projects result in fundamentally new technologies. The creators of the target artefact have little idea at the beginning of how this artefact will work and how its components should be arranged. Radical design projects are much less common. They are exploratory by nature.

Customer-driven vs market-driven projects

In a *customer-driven* project, a software solution is developed to address the actual needs of one specific customer in the context of one specific organization. In a *market-driven* project, a software solution is developed to address the potential needs of a whole market segment. There are projects lying between those extremes where the software-to-be is aimed at a specific class of customers within a specific domain. As examples:

- The WAX train transportation system is a customer-driven project.

- The meeting scheduler system is a market-driven project.

- The UWON library project lies somewhere in between, as other universities might be potentially interested in such software to integrate and manage their libraries.

In-house vs outsourced projects

In an *in-house* project, the same company or consortium is carrying out all project phases. In an *outsourced* project, the development is carried out by subcontractors – usually once the project requirements have been established. In general, the contractor is selected by evaluating proposals in response to a call for tenders. There are again projects lying in between, where only specific development phases are being subcontracted. As examples:

- The meeting scheduler is a WSS in-house project.

- The WAX train transportation project is likely to be an outsourced one.

Single-product project vs product-line projects

In a *single-product* project, a single product version is developed for the target customer(s). In a *product-line* project, a product family is developed to cover multiple variants. Each variant customizes the product to a specific class of users or a specific class of items to be managed or controlled. It usually shares commonalities with other variants while differing at specific variation points. Note that a greenfield, single-product project may evolve into a brownfield, product-line one where the single product initially delivered evolves into multiple variants. As examples:

- The WAX train transportation system is a single-product project (at least at inception).

- The meeting scheduler is a product-line project. Variability might refer to the type of customer or the type of meeting.

- If we consider the in-car light-control software for a car manufacturer, variability might refer to different car categories where the software should be installed.

A software project is generally multi-type along the above dimensions. For example, the meeting scheduler might be a greenfield, market-driven, in-house, product-line project.

As far as RE is concerned, these project types have commonalities and differences. On the commonality side, they all need to be based on some form of requirements document at some development stage or another. For example, there is no way of developing a high-quality software product in a brownfield, market-driven, in-house, product-line project without any formulation of the requirements for the software and the assumptions on the environment. Differences from one project type to the other may lie in the following aspects of the RE process:

- *Respective weights of requirements elicitation, evaluation, documentation, consolidation and evolution.* Documentation has been observed to be more prominent in customer-driven projects, whereas prioritization is more prominent in market-driven projects (Lubars *et al.*, 1993). Consolidation is likely to be more prominent in greenfield, customer-driven, mission-critical projects.

- *Use of specific techniques to support RE activities.* For example, greenfield projects may require prototyping techniques for requirements elicitation and risk-based evaluation techniques for decision making (see Chapters 2 and 3). Product-line projects may require feature diagrams for capturing multiple system variants (see Chapter 6).

- *Intertwining between requirements engineering and product design.* In greenfield projects, and in radical design projects in particular, requirements might emerge only once critical design decisions have been made or a product prototype is available.

- *Respective weights of functional and non-functional requirements.* Brownfield projects are often concerned with improving product quality. Non-functional requirements are therefore prominent in such projects.

- *Types of stakeholder involved in the process.* A market-driven project might involve specific types of stakeholder such as technology providers, service providers, retailers, consumers, legislator and the like.

- *Types of developer involved.* The skills required in an outsourced project might be limited to implementation skills, whereas an in-house, greenfield project might require advanced analysis skills.

- *Specific uses of the requirements document.* In an outsourced project, the RD is often used as an annex to the call for tenders, as a reference for evaluating submitted proposals and as a basis for progress monitoring and product evaluation.

1.1.9 Requirements in the software lifecycle

As we saw before, the requirements document is the main product of the RE process. It defines the system-to-be in terms of its objectives, constraints, referenced concepts, responsibility assignments, requirements, assumptions and relevant domain properties. It may also describe system variants and likely evolutions.

Requirements engineering is traditionally considered as the preliminary phase of a software project. The requirements document may indeed be used subsequently in a variety of contexts throughout the software lifecycle. Figure 1.7 summarizes the impact of the requirements document on various software engineering artefacts. The arrows there indicate impact links (which may be bidirectional). Let us briefly review lifecycle activities where the requirements document may be used.

Software prototyping   In development processes that integrate a prototyping phase, the requirements already elicited provide input for building an initial prototype or mock-up.

Architectural design   A software architecture defines the organization of the software in terms of configurations of components, connectors capturing the interactions among components, and constraints on the components, connectors and configurations (Shaw & Garlan, 1996; Bosch, 2000). The architecture designed must obviously meet the software requirements. In

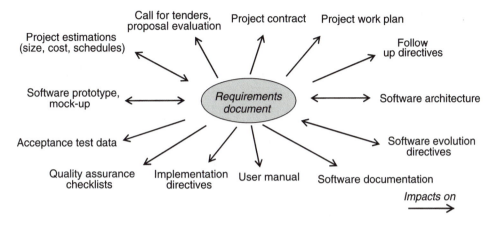

Figure 1.7 *Requirements in the software lifecycle*

particular, architectural choices may have a deep impact on non-functional requirements (Perry & Wolf, 1992). The requirements document is therefore an essential input for architectural design activities such as:

- The identification of architectural components and connectors.
- Their specification to meet the requirements.
- The selection of appropriate architectural styles.
- The evaluation of architectural options against non-functional requirements.

Software quality assurance   The requirements document provides the ultimate reference for quality assurance activities. In particular:

- Requirements provide the basis for elaborating acceptance test data that cover them.
- They are used to define checklists for software inspections and reviews.

Implementation and integration   These later steps of the software lifecycle must take non-functional requirements such as interface and installation requirements into account.

Documentation   The requirements document, possibly in summarized form, is an important component of the software documentation. Parts of it may be used for writing user manuals.

Maintenance   The requirements document, together with problem reports and approved modification requests, provides the input material for revising, adapting, extending or contracting the software product.

Project management   The requirements provide a solid basis for project management tasks such as:

- Estimating project size, cost and schedules, e.g. through function points (Low & Jeffery, 1990).
- Planning development activities.
- Writing a call for tenders and evaluating proposals (for outsourced projects).
- Writing the contract linking the developer and the customer.
- Reviewing progress during an incremental development.
- Assessing development team productivity.
- Evaluating the final product.

Many software process models and development methodologies recognize the important role of requirements throughout the software lifecycle. For example, the diagrams summarizing the RUP Unified Process show how the requirements document permeates all project phases from inception to elaboration to construction to transition (Jacobson *et al.*, 1999).

The inevitable intertwining of RE, system design and software architecture design

We might think of RE and design ideally as two completely separate processes coming one after the other in a waterfall-like fashion. This is rarely the case in practice. A complex problem is solved by identifying subproblems, specifying them and solving them, which recursively yields new subproblems (Nilsson, 1971). The recursive nature of problem solving makes the problem and solution spaces intertwined. This applies, in particular, when we elaborate requirements, a corresponding system-to-be and a corresponding software architecture.

Such intertwining occurs at places where we need to make decisions among alternative options based on quality requirements, in particular:

- When we have elicited a system objective and want to decompose it into sub-objectives – different decompositions might be envisioned, and we need to select a preferred one.
- When we have identified a likely and critical risk – different countermeasures might be envisioned, and we need to select a preferred one.
- When we have detected a conflict between requirements and want to resolve it – different resolutions might be envisioned, and we need to select a preferred one.
- When we realize a system objective through a combination of functional services, constraints and assumptions – different combinations might be envisioned, and we need to select a preferred one.

- When we consider alternative assignments of responsibilities among components of the system-to-be – a more suitable one must eventually be selected. In this process, we might consider alternative component granularities as well.

All these situations involve *system* design decisions. Once such a decision has been made, we need to recursively elicit, evaluate, document and consolidate new requirements and assumptions based on it. Different decisions may result in different proposals for the system-to-be, which, in turn, are likely to result in different *software* architectures. Conversely, while elaborating the software architecture we might discover new requirements or assumptions that had been overlooked thus far.

Let us illustrate this intertwining of RE and design in our case studies.

In the meeting scheduler, the objective of knowing the constraints of invited participants might be decomposed into a sub-objective of knowing them through e-mail requests or, alternatively, a sub-objective of knowing them through access to their electronic agenda. The architecture of a meeting scheduler based on e-mail communication for getting constraints will be different in places from one based on e-agendas. Likewise, there will be architectural differences between an alternative where meeting initiators are taking responsibility for handling constraint requests and a more automated version where a software component is responsible for this.

In our train control system, the computation of train accelerations and the transmission of acceleration commands to trains might be under responsibility of software components located at specific stations. Alternatively, this responsibility might be assigned, for the acceleration of a specific train, to the on-board software of the train preceding it. These are *system* design options that we need to evaluate while engineering the system requirements, so that preferred options can be selected for further requirements elaboration. Those two alternatives result in very different software architectures – a semi-centralized architecture and a fully distributed one. The alternative with an ultra-reliable component at specific stations is likely to be selected in order to better meet safety requirements.

1.1.10 The relationship of requirements engineering to other disciplines

Section 1.1.3 discussed how wide the scope of RE is. Section 1.1.6 showed how diverse its activities and actors are. It is therefore not surprising that some areas of RE are connected to other disciplines and research communities.

The discipline of RE has a primary interaction with, of course, *software engineering* (SE). As frequently said, the former is about getting the right system whereas the latter is about getting the software right in this system. The previous section discussed numerous interactions between RE and SE processes and products. In addition, RE benefits from SE technology for designing tools to support its activities – such as smart editors, prototyping tools, analysers, documentation tools, configuration managers and the like.

There are other disciplines to which RE is connected. We just mention the connections here; they will appear more clearly as we discuss RE techniques, by activity, in Chapters 2 to 6.

Domain understanding and requirements elicitation

Analysing system objectives, tasks and roles is a concern shared with *systems engineering*, sometimes called systems analysis in the business application domain.

For control systems, *control theory* provides techniques for modelling controllers and controlled processes. These techniques can be used to analyse the environment and the interactions that the software should have with it.

The system-as-is and the system-to-be are generally grounded within an organization. The structure, business objectives, policies and operational procedures of this organization need to be understood and analysed. Effective techniques for doing so are found in *management science* and *organization theory*.

The quality of communication between requirements engineers and stakeholders is a necessary condition for the effectiveness of domain understanding and requirements elicitation. Principles and guidelines can be borrowed from *behavioural psychology* here. Some of the techniques used for elicitation originate in *sociological theories* of human groups; others are grounded on ethnographical principles from *anthropology* (see Section 2.3.2).

Requirements elicitation amounts to a form of knowledge acquisition for which techniques have been developed in *artificial intelligence*.

The elicitation and analysis of specific categories of non-functional requirements may be supported by dedicated techniques found in other disciplines, for example *reliability theory* for safety requirements, *security engineering* for security requirements, probabilistic *performance evaluation* for performance requirements, *cognitive psychology* and *human-computer interaction* (HCI) for useability requirements. In particular, the HCI literature contains a significant number of dedicated techniques for eliciting, evaluating, specifying and validating user interface requirements based on user models and task models.

Requirements evaluation and agreement

The assessment of alternative options against qualities and risks is a general issue addressed by *decision theory* and the literature on *risk management*. Specific techniques such as multicriteria analysis are highly relevant in this context.

Management science also provides principles and theories on the art of *negotiation* and *conflict management*. These issues are addressed from a different perspective in *artificial intelligence* in the context of multi-agent planning.

Requirements specification, documentation and consolidation

There is some partial overlap between the techniques available to support these activities and the languages, structuring mechanisms and analysis tools found in the software engineering literature on *software specification*. Some of the software design notations can be lifted up to RE, including a subset of the UML, as we will see in Part II. *Formal methods* provide technological solutions for analysing requirements when the latter are available in fully formalized, machine-processable form. They will be introduced in Sections 4.4 and 5.4 and further discussed in Chapters 17 and 18.

Requirements evolution

From a managerial perspective, this area intersects with the area of *change management* in management science. From a technical perspective, it intersects with the area of version control and *configuration management* in software engineering.

Modelling as a transversal activity

Parts II and III of this book will present a model-driven approach to requirements engineering where multifaceted models of the system-as-is and the system-to-be are built as a common interface to the various RE activities. Requirements modelling is connected to other disciplines in computing science where models are used, notably:

- Conceptual models in *databases* and *management information systems*.

- Task models in *human–computer interaction*.

- Models for representing domain knowledge and structuring problem spaces in *artificial intelligence*.

1.2 Why engineer requirements?

Now that we have a better idea of what RE is about, we could ask ourselves whether it is worth the effort. This section discusses why and to what extent the engineering of high-quality requirements is an essential precondition for the success of a software project. We first review some citations and facts that provide anecdotal evidence about the importance of RE and the consequences of poor RE. Then we discuss the role and critical impact of RE in the software lifecycle from a more general perspective.

1.2.1 Facts, data and citations about the requirements problem

The phrase 'requirements problem' refers to software project failures that have been attributed to poor or non-existent requirements.

An old problem

The requirements problem is among the oldest in software engineering. An early empirical study of a variety of software projects revealed that incomplete, inadequate, inconsistent or ambiguous requirements are numerous and have a critical impact on the quality of the resulting software (Bell & Thayer, 1976). These authors concluded that 'the requirements for a system do not arise naturally; instead, they need to be engineered and have continuing review and revision'. This was probably the first reference to the phrase 'requirements engineering', suggesting the need for systematic, repeatable procedures for building high-quality artefacts.

A consensus has been rapidly growing that such engineering is difficult. As Brooks noted in his landmark paper on the essence and accidents of software engineering, 'the hardest single part of building a sofware system is deciding precisely what to build ... Therefore, the most important function that the software builder performs for the client is the iterative extraction and refinement of the product requirements' (Brooks, 1987).

Requirements errors are the most expensive software errors

Lots of time and money can be saved if requirements errors and flaws are detected and fixed at the RE stage rather than later. Boehm and Papaccio reported that it costs 5 times more to detect and fix requirements defects during design, 10 times more during implementation, 20 times more during unit testing and up to 200 times more after system delivery (Boehm & Papaccio, 1988).

Requirements errors are numerous and persistent

Requirements errors are not only usually costly; they are numerous and persistent over the software lifecycle. Jones states that US companies average one requirements error per function point (Jones, 1995). According to an earlier study, for management information systems 55% of software faults can be traced to the requirements and design phases; the figure is 50% for military software and 45% for systems software. The overall figure, weighted by occurrences, is 52%, with 25% from the requirements phase and 27% from the design phase (Jones, 1991). In her study of software errors in NASA Voyager and Galileo programs, Lutz consistently reported that the primary cause of safety-related faults was errors in functional and interface requirements (Lutz, 1993).

Other studies have confirmed the requirements problem on a much larger scale. A survey over 8000 projects undertaken by 350 US companies suggested that only 16% of them were considered to be successful; 33% of them failed without having ever been completed; and 51% succeeded only partially; that is, with partial functionalities, major cost overruns and significant delays (Standish Group, 1995). When asked about the main reasons for this, about 50% of the project managers identified requirements-related problems as the primary cause; specifically, the lack of user involvement (13%), requirements incompleteness (13%), changing requirements (11%), unrealistic expectations (9%) and unclear objectives (5%). An independent survey of 3800 European organizations in 17 countries led to parallel conclusions. When asked where their main software problems were, more than half of the managers ranked requirements specification and management in first position (Ibanez & Rempp, 1996).

The requirements problem has been echoed in various business reports about the lack of alignment between business problems and IT solutions. An Accenture study in 2003 pointed out the mismatch between IT investments and business objectives. A Giga Group report in 2001 consistently recommended that IT projects be prioritized according to their contribution to business objectives. Another report by Meta Group in 2003 claimed that 60–70% of IT project failures are to be attributed to poor requirements gathering, analysis and management.

Other studies led independently to the consistent conclusion that many software problems and failures are to be attributed to poor RE, for example Lyytinen and Hirscheim, 1987 and Jones, 1996.

Requirements errors are the most dangerous software errors

The requirements problem gets even worse in the case of mission-critical systems such as safety-critical or security-critical systems. Many harmful and sometimes tragic software failures were recognized to be traceable back to defective requirements (Leveson, 1995; Neumann, 1995; Knight, 2002).

For example, 290 people were killed when a civil IranAir A300 Airbus was confused with a hostile F-14 aircraft and shot by the US *Vincennes* warship in July 1988. Investigations revealed that the origins of this tragedy were a mix of threatening conditions and missing requirements on the AEGIS combat software. Some timing requirements for successive input events to be threatening were missing. Furthermore, critical information on aircraft displays to allow pilots to assess threats correctly was missing, such as current altitude and ascending/descending mode of 'target' aircraft (US Department of Defense, 1988).

Neumann reports on several cases in the London underground system where people were killed due to doors opening or closing in unexpected circumstances without alarm notification to the train driver (Neumann, 1995).

As noted before, omissions and inadequacies do not refer to requirements only. Many reported problems originate in missing, inadequate, inaccurate or changing assumptions and properties about the environment in which the software operates. An early study of software engineering practice already made that point (Curtis *et al.*, 1988). Sadly enough, its conclusions remained valid. Let us first mention a few cases of inadequate assumptions or domain properties.

The first version of the London ambulance despatching system was based on a series of assumptions about the environment, for example that radio communication would work in all circumstances, that the ambulance localization system would always work properly, that crews would always select the ambulance being allocated to them by the software, that they would always go to the incident assigned to them by the software, that they would always press ambulance availability buttons correctly and when needed, that no incident data could be lost and so forth. The two tragic failures of this system from October to November 1992 resulted from a combination of circumstances that violated many such assumptions (LAS, 1993).

Hooks and Farry mention an aerospace project where 49% of requirements errors were due to incorrect facts about the problem world (Hooks & Farry, 2000).

An inadequate assumption about the environment of the flight guidance system may have contributed to the tragic crash of an American Airlines Boeing 757 in Cali (Colombia) in December 1995 (Modugno *et al.*, 1997). The information about the point in space where the pilot was expected to initiate the flap extension was assumed to arrive before the plane actually reached that point in space. The aircraft landing in Cali had already passed that point, which resulted in the guidance software ordering the plane to turn around towards a mountain.

Domain properties, used explicitly or implicitly for elaborating requirements, may be wrong as well. A famous example is the Lufthansa A320 Airbus flight to Warsaw, in which the plane ran off the end of the runway, resulting in injuries and loss of life. The reverse thrust was disabled for up to nine seconds after landing on a waterlogged runway (Ladkin, 1995). In terms of the satisfaction argument discussed in Section 1.1.4, the problem might be recollected in simplified form as follows (Jackson, 1995a). The autopilot had the system requirement that reverse thrust be enabled if and only if the plane is moving on the runway:

(*SysReq*:)   ReverseThrustEnabled ↔ MovingOnRunway

The software requirement given to developers in terms of software input/output variables was:

(*SofReq*:)   reverse = 'on' ↔ WheelPulses = 'on'

An argument that this software requirement entails the corresponding system requirement had to rely on assumptions on the wheels sensor and reverse thrust actuator, respectively:

(*Asm*:)   WheelPulses = 'on' ↔ WheelsTurning
            reverse = 'on' ↔ ReverseThrustEnabled,

together with the following domain property:

(*Dom*:)   MovingOnRunway ↔ WheelsTurning

This domain property proved to be inadequate on the waterlogged Warsaw runway. Due to aquaplaning, the plane there was moving on the runway without wheels turning.

A similar case occurred recently where a car driver was run over by his luxurious computerized car while opening a gate in front of it. The software controlling the handbrake release had the system requirement:

'The handbrake shall be released if and only if the driver wants to start.'

The software requirement was:

'The handbrake control shall be "off" if and only if the normal running of the motor is raised.'

The assumption that

'The driver wants to start if and only if he presses the acceleration pedal'

is adequate; but the domain property stating:

'The normal running of the motor is raised if and only if the acceleration pedal is pressed'

proved to be inadequate on a hot summer's day. The car's air conditioner started automatically, due to the car's door being open while the driver was opening the gate in front, which resulted in the normal running of the motor being raised and the handbrake being released.

In addition to cases of wrong assumptions or wrong domain properties, there are cases where failure originates from environmental *changes* that render the original assumptions no longer adequate. A concrete example showing the problems with changing environments, in the context of our train control case study, is the June 1995 New York subway crash. The investigation revealed that the distance between signals was shorter than the worst-case stopping distance of trains; the assumption that a train could stop in the space allowed after the signal was adequate for 1918 trains but inadequate for the faster, longer and heavier trains running in 1995 (16 June 1995 *New York Times* report, cited in Hammond *et al.*, 2001).

The well-known *Ariane 5* rocket failure is another example where environmental assumptions, set for requirements satisfaction, were no longer valid. Software components were reused from the *Ariane 4* rocket with ranges of input values that were different from the expected ones due to changes in rocket features (Lions, 1996). In the same vein, the Patriot anti-missile system that hit US military barracks during the first Gulf War had been used for more than 100 hours. The system was assuming missions of 14 hours at most (Neumann, 1995).

Missing or inadequate requirements/assumptions may have harmful consequences in security-critical systems as well. For example, a Web banking service was reported to have no adequate requirements about how the software should behave when a malicious user is searching for all bank accounts that match some given 4-digit PIN number (dos Santos *et al.*, 2000).

As we will see in Chapter 5, there are fortunately techniques for spotting errors in requirements and assumptions. For example, such techniques uncovered several dangerous omissions and ambiguities in TCAS II, a widely used aircraft collision-avoidance system (Heimdahl & Leveson, 1996). This important topic will be covered in depth in Chapters 5, 9, 16 and 18.

1.2.2 The role and stakes of requirements engineering

The bottom line of the previous section is that engineering high-quality requirements is essential, as errors in requirements, assumptions and domain properties tend to be numerous, persistent, costly and dangerous. To support that conclusion, we may also observe the prominent role that RE plays with respect to multiple stakes.

Technical stakes   As we saw in Section 1.1.9, the requirements document (RD) provides a basis for:

- Deriving acceptance test data.

- Designing the software architecture and specifying its components/connectors.

- Defining quality-assurance checklists.

- Writing the documentation and user manuals.

- Handling requests for software evolution.

Communication stakes   The RD provides the main reference through which the various parties involved in a software project can communicate with each other.

Project management stakes   The RD provides a basis for determining the project costs, required resources, development steps, milestones, review points and delivery schedules.

Legal stakes   The RD forms the core of the contract linking the software provider, customers and subcontractors (if any).

Certification stakes   Quality norms are increasingly enforced by law or regulations on projects in specific domains such as medical, transportation, aerospace or nuclear. They may also be requested by specific customers in other domains. Such norms constrain the development process and products. At the *process* level, maturity models such as CMMI, SPICE or ISO9001 require RE to be taken seriously. For example, CMMI Maturity Level 2 imposes a requirements management activity as a necessary condition for process repeatability; Level 3 requires a repeatable requirements development process (Ahern *et al.*, 2003). At the *product* level, standards such as IEEE-STD-830 or ESA PSS-05 impose a fairly elaborate structure on the requirements document (see Section 4.2.2).

Economic stakes   The consequences of numerous, persistent and dangerous errors related to requirements can be economically devastating.

Social stakes   When not sufficiently user centred, the RE process may overlook important needs and constraints. This may cause severe deteriorations in working conditions, and a wide range of reactions from partial or diverted use of the software to mere rejection of it. Such reactions may have severe consequences beyond user dissatisfaction. For example, in the London ambulance system mentioned in the previous section, misuse and rejection of the new system by ambulance drivers were reported to be among the main causes of failure.

1.3 Obstacles to good requirements engineering practice

Many practitioners have heard about the requirements problem and may have experienced it. The critical role of RE in the success of a software project is widely recognized. Process maturity models promote spending effort in RE activities. A recent large-scale study has confirmed that almost any project includes some RE activity, whatever its type and size (Jones, 2003).

In spite of all this, the current state of RE practice is still, by and large, fairly limited in terms of effort spent on this activity and technology used to support it (Glass, 2003). Practitioners are in a sense like cigarette smokers who know that smoking is pretty unhealthy but keep smoking. The reasons for this may be in the following *obstacles* to spending effort and money in the RE process:

- Such effort generally needs to be spent before the project contract is signed, without a guarantee that a contract will be signed.

- There might be stronger concerns and pressure on tight schedules, short-term costs and catching up on the latest technology advances.

- Too little research work has been devoted to RE economics. On one hand, the benefits and cost saving from using RE technology have not been quantified. They are hard to measure and not enough evidence has been gained from large-scale empirical studies. On the other hand, progress in RE activities is harder to measure than in design or implementation activities.

- Practitioners sometimes feel that the requirements document is exceedingly big and complex (Lethbridge *et al.*, 2003). In such cases it might not be maintained as the project evolves, and an outdated document is no longer of any use.

- The requirements document may be felt to be too far away from the executable product for which the customer is paying. In fact, the quality of requirements does not indicate much about the quality of the executable product.

- RE technology is sometimes felt to be too heavyweight by some practitioners, and too vague by others.

- Beyond general guidelines, the transfer of effective RE techniques through courses, textbooks and pilot studies has been much more limited than in other areas of software engineering.

We need to be aware of such obstacles to find ways of overcoming them. Chapters 2–6 will review standard techniques to support the RE process more effectively. In this framework, the next parts of the book will detail a systematic method for building a multifaceted system model from which a well-structured requirements document can be generated. This method will make the elicitation, evaluation, documentation, consolidation and evolution efforts more focused and more effective.

1.4 Agile development processes and requirements engineering

More agility in the RE process might address some of the previously mentioned obstacles in some software projects.

Agile processes are aimed at *early* and *continuous* provision of functionality of value to the customer by reducing both the RE effort and the requirements-to-code distance.

To achieve this, the spiral RE process in Figure 1.6 iterates on very short cycles, where each cycle is directly followed by a short implementation cycle:

- A RE cycle is shortened by eliciting some useful functional increment directly from the user, and by shortcutting the evaluation, specification and consolidation phases; or by making these very rudimentary to expedite them. For example, the specification phase may amount to the definition of test cases that the implementation must pass.

- The implementation cycle next to a RE cycle is shortened as (a) the functional increment from this RE cycle is expected to be small; and (b) this increment is implemented by a small team of programmers working at the same location, following strict programming rules, doing their own unit testing and staying close to the user to get instant feedback for the next RE cycle.

The functional increment elicited at a RE cycle is sometimes called *user story*. It captures some unit of functionality of direct value that the user can write and deliver easily to the programming team.

Agile processes have emerged in certain development communities and projects as a reaction against overly heavyweight practices, sometimes resulting from the misinterpretation of process models and the amount of 'ceremony' and reporting they require. However, it is important to highlight the underlying *assumptions* that a project must fulfil for an agile process to work successfully. Such assumptions delimit the applicability of agile processes:

- All stakeholder roles, including the customer and user roles, can be reduced to one single role.

- The project is sufficiently small to be assignable to a single, small-size, single-location development team.

- The user can be made available at the development site or can interact promptly and effectively.

- The project is sufficiently simple and non-critical to disregard or give little consideration to non-functional aspects, environmental assumptions, underlying objectives, alternative options and risks.

- The user can provide functional increments quickly, consistently (so that no conflict management is required) and gradually from essential to less important requirements (so that no prioritization is required).

- The project requires little documentation for work coordination and subsequent product maintenance. Precise requirements specification before coding is not an issue.

- Requirements verification before coding is less important than early release.

- New or changing requirements are not likely to require major code refactoring and rewrite, and the people in charge of product maintenance are likely to be the product developers.

These assumptions are quite strong. Many projects obviously do not meet them all, if any – in particular, projects for mission-critical systems. We would obviously not like our air traffic control, transportation, power plant, medical operation or e-banking systems to be obtained through agile development of critical parts of the software.

Agility is not a binary notion, however. Depending on which of the preceding assumptions can be fulfilled and which cannot, we can achieve more or less agility by paying more or less attention to the elicitation, evaluation, specification and consolidation phases of an RE cycle, making it longer or shorter.

From this perspective, the approach discussed in Parts II and III is intended to make RE cycles shorter by:

- Supporting functional goals and scenarios as units of value to stakeholders.

- Focusing on declarative formulations for incremental elaboration, and incremental analysis only when and where needed.

- Providing constructive guidance in model-based RE through a variety of heuristics and patterns.

- Integrating tool support for effort reduction by elimination of clerical work.

Summary

- The focus of RE is the investigation, delineation and precise definition of the *problem world* that a machine solution is intended to improve. The scope of investigation is broad. It involves two system versions. Next to the system-as-is, the system-to-be comprises the software to be developed and its environment. The latter may comprise people playing specific roles, physical devices operating under physical laws, and pre-existing software. The questions to be addressed about the system-to-be include WHY, WHAT, HOW WELL and WHO questions. Such questions can be answered in a variety of ways, leading to a range of alternative options to consider, each having associated strengths and risks.

- Requirements engineers are faced with multiple transitions to handle: from the problem world to the machine interface with it; from a partial set of conflicting concerns to a complete set of consistent statements; from imprecise formulations to precise specifications; from unstructured material to a structured document; from informal wishes to a contractual document. There are multiple levels of abstraction to consider, with strategic objectives at the top and technical requirements at the bottom. Multiple abstraction levels call for satisfaction arguments, as we need to show that the higher-level concerns are satisfied by the lower-level ones.

- The RE process is an iteration of intertwined activities for eliciting, evaluating, documenting, consolidating and changing the objectives, functionalities, assumptions, qualities and constraints that the system-to-be should meet based on the opportunities and capabilities provided by new technologies. Those activities involve multiple stakeholders that may have conflicting interests. The relative weight of each activity may depend on the type of project.

- The RE process involves different types of statements. Requirements are prescriptive statements about software functionalities, qualities and development constraints. They are expressed in the vocabulary of the problem world. Domain properties are descriptive statements about this world. Assumptions are statements about expected behaviours of environmental components. We need to make appropriate assumptions and identify correct domain properties to elaborate the right requirements.

- These different types of statements have to be specified and structured in the requirements document. Their specification must meet multiple qualities, among which completeness and adequacy are most critical. The requirements document is a core artefact in the software lifecycle, as many software engineering activities rely on it. Its quality has a strong impact on the software project – notably, its successful completion, the development and maintenance costs, the rate of user acceptance and satisfaction, system security and safety. Studies on the requirements problem have consistently shown that requirements errors are numerous, persistent, costly and dangerous. Wrong hidden assumptions can be the source of major problems.

- There are a few misconceptions and confusions about RE to avoid:

  a. The target of investigation is not the software but a system of which the software is one component.

  b. RE does not amount to some translation of pre-existing problem formulations.

  c. RE and design are not sequentially composed in a waterfall-like fashion. RE involves system design. In view of the alternative options arising in the RE process, we need to make decisions that may subsequently influence software design. Conversely, some requirements might sometimes emerge only in the later stages of software design.

  d. Unlike domain properties, requirements may need to be negotiated, weakened or changed.

  e. 'Precise' does not mean 'formal'. Every statement must have a unique, accurate interpretation without necessarily being machine processable.

  f. A set of notations may be a necessary condition for a RE method but certainly not a sufficient one. A method should provide systematic guidance for building complex requirements documents.

Notes and Further Reading

The grounding of machine requirements in the problem world is amply discussed in Jackson (1995b). One of the first characterizations of RE as investigation of WHY, WHAT and HOW issues appeared in Ross and Schoman (1977a). This seminal paper emphasized the importance of analysing the contextual objectives that the system-to-be needs to address. It introduced viewpoints as a composition mechanism for RE. Twenty years later, Zave consistently argued that the relationship between objectives, functionalities, constraints and software requirements is a key aspect of the RE process (Zave, 1997). Requirements evolution along variants and revisions is also discussed there.

The important distinction between descriptive and prescriptive statements appeared first in Jackson & Zave (1993) and was echoed in Jackson (1995a) and Zave and Jackson (1997). The differentiation between system requirements and software requirements is discussed in Jackson (1995a), where the latter are called 'specifications'. Similar distinctions were made in the more explicit setting of the four-variable model in Parnas and Madey (1995).

Satisfaction arguments have been known for a long time in programming methodology. When we build a program P in some environment E the program has to satisfy its specification S. Therefore we need to argue that $P, E \models S$. Such argumentation was first lifted up to the RE phase in Yue (1987). The need for satisfaction arguments at RE time is discussed in Jackson (1995a) and convincingly illustrated in Hammond *et al.* (2001) in the context of the REVEAL methodology for requirements engineering. Such arguments were made explicit in terms of goal refinement and goal operationalization in Dardenne *et al.* (1991), Dardenne *et al.* (1993) and van Lamsweerde (2000b).

The spiral model of software development is described in Boehm (1988). An adaptation to requirements development was suggested first in Kotonya & Sommerville (1997). Agile processes in the context of RE are briefly introduced in Leffingwell and Widrig (2003). The need for early delivery of useful subsystems was recognized in Parnas (1979).

Numerous books and papers propose requirements taxonomies, notably Thayer and Dorfman (1990), Davis (1993), Robertson and Robertson (1999) and Chung *et al.* (2000).

A thorough discussion of specification errors will be found in Meyer's paper on the specifier's "seven sins" (Meyer, 1985). Those 'sins' are illustrated there on a published specification of a text formatting problem, where most defects are found in a few lines! Yue was probably the first to define requirements completeness and pertinence with respect to underlying objectives (Yue, 1987). The best discussion on requirements measurability is in Robertson and Robertson (1999), which proposes so-called fit criteria as a way of checking whether a requirement is measurable (we come back to this in Sections 4.2 and 5.1). Some of the qualities expected for a requirements document are also presented in Davis (1993).

The distinction between customer-specific and market-driven projects is discussed from an RE perspective in Lubars *et al.* (1993). Radical design projects are contrasted with normal design ones from an engineering perspective in Vicenti (1993).

The view of RE as a composite system design activity is elaborated technically in Feather (1987) and Fickas and Helm (1992). The inevitable intertwining of RE and architectural design is argued in Nuseibeh (2001). To some extent it is a transposition, to the earlier phases of the software lifecycle, of an argument made before for specification and implementation (Swartout & Balzer, 1982).

Stories and analyses of poor RE in mission-critical systems can be found in Leveson (1995) and Neumann (1995). For regular updates check the RISKS Digest Forum Web site, moderated by P. G. Neumann under the auspices of the ACM Committee on Computers and Public Policy.

An obvious indication of the vitality of RE as an autonomous discipline is the number of introductory textbooks on the subject. They cover general insights, principles, guidelines and modelling notations for RE. A sample of these includes Gause and Weinberg (1989). Davis (1993), Loucopoulos and Karakostas (1995), Kotonya and Sommerville (1997), Kovitz (1999), Robertson and Robertson (1999), Maciaszek (2001), Lauesen (2002) and Bray (2003). Among these, Davis (1993) contains an extensive annotated bibliography on early work. A good overview of requirements capture within the software lifecycle is provided in Pfleeger (2001).

The running case studies in this book have some origins in the literature. The library system significantly expands on a toy specification benchmark (Wing, 1988), to address RE issues based on a real library system in a large university environment. The train control system is partially inspired by the BART system (Winter *et al.*, 1999), the old-time McGean train system (Feather, 1994) and the author's experience of missing flight connections in large airports due to poor local transportation facilities. The meeting scheduling system expands on an earlier version (van Lamsweerde *et al.*, 1993), partially published in Feather *et al.* (1998), based on personal experience in organizing international meetings.

Exercises

- Consider the library world suggested by the case study description in Section 1.1.2. Draw a world-and-machine diagram similar to Figure 1.1 showing where the following phenomena are located: BookCopyReturned (the return of a book by a patron); ReturnEncoded (the encoding of a returned book by library staff at a terminal); LoanRecordUpdated (the corresponding database update); BookCopyInShelves (the physical availability of a book copy in library shelves); BookAvailabilityDisplayed (the displaying at a terminal of a book's availability status); BookCoversThisTopic (the fact that a book covers such or such topic); BookKeywordsEncoded; DatabaseSearched; and QueryAnswerDisplayed.

- Distribute the list of complaints, reported in the case study description of the library system in Section 1.1.2, among different viewpoints associated with specific stakeholders.

- From the case study description of the library system, elaborate alternative options to meet the objective of reduced book stealing at UWON. Assess each alternative against its risks.

- Consider the case study description of the train control system. Discuss the respective strengths and risks associated with alternative responsibility assignments of the prescriptive statement *TrainDoorsClosedWhileMoving*; namely, to the train driver, to a dedicated clerk, to passengers or to an on-board software controller.

- Identify a sample of strategic objectives, functional services and environmental assumptions from the case study descriptions of the library, train control and meeting scheduling systems.

- Draw a diagram similar to Figure 1.3 for the meeting scheduling case study. Make your diagram more precise by depicting a four-variable model of it.

- Repeat the previous exercise on your favourite cashpoint machine (ATM).

- Provide a sample of descriptive statements and a sample of prescriptive statements from the case study descriptions of the library, train control and meeting scheduling systems, respectively.

- Consider a simple traffic light system to regulate safe pedestrian crossing on a busy lane. Consider the following system requirement:

  (*SysReq*:)   The traffic lights shall allow pedestrians to safely cross the lane by stopping cars

  together with the following software requirements:

  (*SofReq1*:)   The light switch for pedestrians will be set to 'green' within x seconds after the pedestrian button has been pressed.
  (*SofReq2*:)   The light switch for cars will be set to 'red' at least y seconds before the light switch for pedestrians is set to 'green'.

  Find missing environment assumptions and domain properties that are necessary to build the following satisfaction argument:

  $$\{SofReq1,\ SofReq2,\ assumptions?,\ domain\ properties?\} \models SysReq$$

  Are the missing domain properties adequate? Are the missing assumptions realistic?

- Find out where such a satisfaction argument fails in the car handbrake control story reported in Section 1.2.1.

- Section 1.1.4 gives a few examples of non-functional requirements for our running case studies. Identify additional non-functional requirements mentioned in the case study descriptions, and classify them according to the taxonomy in Figure 1.5. For example, to what class does the following requirement belong?

  The meeting date and location should be notified to participants x weeks before the meeting at latest.

- Extend the case study descriptions in Section 1.1.2 with other non-functional require-ments that might be worth considering. To elicit them, browse through the requirements taxonomy in Figure 1.5 and look for system-specific instances of the various categories.

- Find or invent other examples of requirement/assumption defects in the case study descriptions, in addition to those in Tables 1.2 and 1.3.

- Imagine that you need to convince your manager that the project budget has to cover X person-months for the RE task. Prepare a full argument for this.

Domain Understanding and Requirements Elicitation

2

This chapter provides an overview of the techniques we may use for the first phase in the spiral model of the RE process introduced in Chapter 1 (see Figure 1.6). Domain understanding and requirements elicitation are highly intertwined processes. Their objectives are the following:

- Understand the system-as-is and its context.

- Identify the problems and opportunities calling for a new system.

- Discover the *real* needs of stakeholders with respect to the new system.

- Explore alternative ways in which the new system could address those needs.

This preliminary phase of the RE process involves a great deal of *knowledge acquisition*. We need to acquire the contextual knowledge under which the system-to-be will be elaborated. This knowledge generally covers the following:

- Knowledge about the *organization* – its structure, business objectives, policies, roles and responsibilities.

- Knowledge about the *domain* in which the problem world is rooted – the concepts involved in this domain, the objectives specific to it, the regulations that may be imposed in it.

- Knowledge about the *system-as-is* – its objectives, the actors and resources involved, the tasks and workflows, and the problems raised in this context.

The output of the understanding and elicitation phase typically consists of a preliminary draft proposal report describing the system-as-is, its surrounding organization, the underlying domain, the problems identified in it, the opportunities to be exploited, and alternative ways in which the problems might be addressed in view of such opportunities. This draft proposal will be used as input to the evaluation phase coming next. A glossary of terms should be appended to it.

An effective process for domain understanding and requirements elicitation combines different techniques that vary by their degree of interaction with stakeholders:

- *Artefact-driven* techniques rely more on specific types of artefact to support the elicitation process. They are described in Section 2.2.

- *Stakeholder-driven* techniques rely more on specific types of interaction with stakeholders. They are described in Section 2.3.

As a prerequisite, we must identify the right stakeholders for effective knowledge acquisition.

2.1 Identifying stakeholders and interacting with them

Stakeholder cooperation is essential for building a shared understanding of the problems to be addressed by the system-to-be. Such cooperative learning is a critical path to obtaining complete, adequate and realistic requirements. We should therefore select the right sample of stakeholders and define a modus operandi to overcome multiple difficulties along this path.

Stakeholder analysis

For comprehensive understanding and exploration of the problem world, the determination of a representative sample of stakeholders should be based on their respective roles, stakes, interests and type of knowledge they can contribute. The following criteria may be used for this:

- Relevant position in the organization.

- Effective role in making decisions about the system-to-be.

- Level of domain expertise.

- Exposure to perceived problems.

- Influence in system acceptance.

- Personal objectives and conflicts of interest.

The set of stakeholders may need to be updated during the RE process as new perspectives emerge.

Handling obstacles to effective knowledge acquisition

There are many difficulties inherent in the understanding and elicitation process. We need to be aware of them in order to find ways of overcoming them.

- *Distributed and conflicting knowledge sources.* There are in general many different sources to consider – multiple stakeholders and large volumes of documents and data. Such sources are often spread out. They may conflict with each other for a variety of reasons: competition among representatives of different departments, diverging interests and perceptions, different priorities and concerns, outdated documents and the like.

- *Difficult access to sources.* Knowledge sources may not be easily available. Key people are generally very busy. They may not be convinced that it is worth spending time on the elicitation process. Others are sometimes reluctant to provide important information as they feel not free to do so, or are suspicious about the consequences of moving from one system to another. Relevant data may be hard to collect.

- *Obstacles to good communication.* There may be significant communication barriers originating from people with different backgrounds, terminology and cultures.

- *Tacit knowledge and hidden needs.* Getting key information from stakeholders may be quite hard. Knowledge is often tacit; it is implicit in the stakeholder's mind or felt to be common sense. For example, expert people might not explain details or connections among particular elements as they assume that we know what they are. People involved in routine tasks may have a hard time explaining things from a distance. On the other hand, stakeholders often don't know what they really want, or have difficulties expressing what they want and why they want it. They may jump straight into solutions without being able to make explicit what the underlying problems are. They may be unable to distinguish between essential aspects and subsidiary details. They may find it difficult to map hypothetical descriptions of the system-to-be onto real working conditions in the future. They may also have unrealistic expectations.

- *Sociopolitical factors.* External factors may interfere significantly with the process, such as politics, competition, resistance to change, time/cost pressures etc.

- *Unstable conditions.* The surrounding world may be volatile. The structure of the organization may change, people may appear or disappear, the perceived needs or priorities may change and so forth.

Interacting with stakeholders

These difficulties call for general skills and initiatives on the part of the requirements engineer:

- *Communication skills.* The ability for effective interaction with a variety of people is essential. We must be able to address the right issues for the people we interact with, in view of their specific role in the knowledge-acquisition process. We need to use the right terminology for them in view of their specific background. We must be able to listen carefully and ferret out the key points. We should be able to form trusting interpersonal relationships in order to be accepted by stakeholders and appear as a partner.

- *Knowledge reformulation.* Review meetings must be organized where the relevant knowledge about the problem world, acquired from multiple sources, is presented in an integrated, structured way. This is essential for validating and refining such knowledge, for keeping stakeholders involved and for increasing their confidence in the way the system-to-be is shaping up. Review meetings should take place at appropriate milestones during the elicitation process in order to redirect it if necessary.

2.2 Artefact-driven elicitation techniques

To support the acquisition process, there are techniques that rely more on specific types of artefact. Such artefacts include pre-existing documentation about the system-as-is, data samples, questionnaires, conceptual grids and cards, scenarios of interactions among system components, system prototypes and bodies of reuseable knowledge. Let us look at each of these in greater detail.

2.2.1 Background study

If we are unfamiliar with the system-as-is, we may acquire knowledge about the system, its surrounding organization and the underlying domain by collecting, reading and synthesizing relevant documentation:

- To learn about the *organization*, we may study documents such as organizational charts, business plans, policy manuals, financial reports, minutes of important meetings, job descriptions, business forms and the like.

- To learn about the *domain*, we may study books, surveys and published articles. We should study regulations enforced within the domain, if any. We may also look at reports on similar systems in that domain.

- To learn about the *system-as-is* specifically, we may study reports that document information flows, work procedures, business rules, forms exchanged between organizational units and so forth. When available, reports about defects, complaints and change requests are especially helpful in spotting problems with the system-as-is. If the system is already software based, relevant software documentation such as user manuals should be considered as well.

Background study is sometimes called content analysis. An obvious strength of this technique is that it supplies basic information that will be needed afterwards, in particular the terminology used, the objectives and policies to be taken into account, the distribution of responsibilities among stakeholders and so forth. This technique allows us to prepare before meeting stakeholders. It therefore appears as a prerequisite to other elicitation techniques.

The main problem with background study is the amount of documentation that we may need to consider. There can be many documents, some of which can be quite voluminous. Key information has to be extracted from a mass of irrelevant details. Some documents can also be inaccurate or outdated.

To address this data-mining problem, we should first acquire some *meta-knowledge* for guiding the background reading process; that is, we should first know what we need to know and what we don't need to know. We may then use such meta-knowledge to prune the documentation space and focus on relevant aspects only. As we will see later on, a model-driven approach provides a solution to this problem. When we know what kind of model should emerge from the elicitation process, we may use that information to drive the process accordingly.

2.2.2 Data collection

We may complement our background study by collecting relevant facts and figures that are not explicitly available in documents, such as marketing data, usage statistics, performance figures, average costs and so forth. We can achieve this by selecting representative data sets from available populations, or through some experimental study.

Data collection can be helpful for eliciting non-functional requirements related to useability, performance and costs. The price to pay is the time it might take to obtain representative and reasonably accurate data. To reach reliable conclusions, we need to deploy statistical sampling methods. The data collected must then be *interpreted* correctly if we want to derive adequate requirements from it.

2.2.3 Questionnaires

This technique consists of submitting a list of specific questions to selected stakeholders. Each question may be given a brief context and requires a short, standardized answer from a pre-established list of possible answers. Stakeholders just need to return the questionnaire marked with the answers that they feel are most appropriate. There can be different types of question (Whitten & Bentley, 1998):

- A *multiple-choice* question merely requires selecting one answer from the associated list of possible answers.

- A *weighting* question provides a list of statements that need to be weighted by the respondent to express the perceived importance, preference or risk of the corresponding statement. Weights may be *qualitative* values (such as 'very high', 'high', 'low' etc.) or *quantitative* values (such as percentages).

On the plus side, questionnaires may allow us to acquire subjective information promptly, at low cost (in terms of elicitation time), remotely and from a large number of people.

On the minus side, the acquired information is likely to be biased on several grounds: the sample of people to whom the questionnaire was sent, the subset of people who were willing to respond, the set of questions and the set of predetermined answers. There is no direct interaction with respondents and little room for providing context underlying the questions. Respondents may not comprehend the implication of their answers. Different respondents may interpret the same question or answer in different ways. As a consequence, some answers may provide inaccurate, inadequate or inconsistent information.

The bottom line is that we need to design our questionnaires very carefully. We have to validate them prior to their use in order to make sure that such pitfalls are avoided or mitigated. Validation criteria include:

- Representativeness and statistical significance of the target sample of respondents.

- Coverage of the list of questions and possible answers.

- Absence of bias in questions and possible answers, and in their presentation.

- Non-ambiguity of question/answer formulations.

We may use some tricks to discard inconsistent answers, such as the use of implicitly redundant questions that a respondent might answer differently. We should favour closed-ended questions with accurate answers to ensure reliable input from respondents.

High-quality questionnaires are generally considered as a useful complement to interviews. They are typically used prior to interviews to prepare for them. The factual information and perceptions acquired through questionnaires may allow us to better target subsequent interviews (see Section 2.3.1).

2.2.4 Repertory grids and card sorts for concept-driven acquisition

These techniques are sometimes used for knowledge acquisition in expert system development. The idea is to acquire further information from available domain concepts by asking stakeholders to characterize these concepts or categorize them.

Repertory grids

In this technique, stakeholders are given a set of domain concepts that have already been elicited. They are asked to further characterize each of them through attributes and corresponding value ranges, to be provided in a concept-attribute matrix.

For example, a grid associated with the concept of Meeting might be filled in with attributes such as Date, Location and Attendees together with corresponding value ranges, e.g. Mon–Fri for Date.

Card sorts

Stakeholders are given a set of cards. Each card is associated with a specific domain concept. The card may represent this concept textually (by a word or phrase), graphically (by a picture), or a mix of these. Each stakeholder is asked to partition the set of cards into subsets based on his or her own criteria. For each subset, he or she is then asked the reason for grouping the cards together in this subset. We may thereby obtain implicit properties as classification criteria. For each of these we may further ask whether the property is descriptive or prescriptive in order to consider it as a candidate domain property or requirement, respectively (see Section 1.1.4). The process may be repeated with the same cards, yielding new groupings resulting in new properties explaining them.

For example, a stakeholder might group the Meeting and Participant cards together. The elicited reason for such grouping might be, on the first iteration, the underlying property that participants need to be invited to a meeting; this property would be classified as prescriptive. On the second iteration, we might obtain another reason for the Meeting and Participant cards to be again grouped together; namely, the prescriptive property that the scheduler must know the constraints of invited participants to attend the meeting.

Conceptual laddering

To complement the previous techniques, we may also ask stakeholders to arrange some of the concepts submitted into taxonomical trees. For example, the RegularMeeting and Sporadic Meeting concepts might be categorized as subclasses of the Meeting concept.

These three concept-acquisition techniques are simple, cheap, easy to use and sometimes effective in prompt elicitation of missing information about domain concepts. However, they may produce subjective results with no guarantee of accuracy and relevance to the problem world. They may also become fairly complex to manage for large sets of concepts.

2.2.5 Storyboards and scenarios for problem world exploration

The use of *narratives* proves very effective in the early stages of the RE process to elicit or validate useful information from concrete examples of how things are running in the system-as-is, or how they should be running in the system-to-be.

In their loosest form, such narratives are called *storyboards*. They tell a story about the system-as-is or the system-to-be in terms of a sequence of snapshots. Each snapshot may be represented in a suggestive form for quick, easy understanding, for example a sentence, sketch, picture, slide, screenshot and so on. A storyboard can be passive or active:

- In *passive* mode, stakeholders are told the story. The storyboard is used for explanation or validation.

- In *active* mode, stakeholders contribute to the story. The storyboard is used for joint exploration.

A storyboard can be made more structured by making the following aspects explicit alongside the story:

- *Who* the players are.
- *What* happens to them.
- *How* it happens through specific episodes.
- *Why* this happens.
- *What if* such and such an event occurs.
- What could go wrong as a consequence.

This kind of question-based structuring provides complementary dimensions for exploring the problem world.

A *scenario* illustrates a typical sequence of interactions among system components that meets an implicit objective. It amounts to a structured form of storyboard covering the *who, what* and *how* dimensions.

Scenarios are widely used throughout the software lifecycle (Weidenhaupt *et al.*, 1998). In requirements engineering there are two main uses:

- Explaining how the system-*as-is* is running is often made simpler through concrete examples of real-life interaction sequences.

- Exploring how the system-*to-be* should be running is often made easier through concrete examples of hypothetical interaction sequences. Such examples provide a good basis for further elicitation:

  a. We may ask specific questions about them.

  b. We may in particular elicit the underlying objectives.

  c. We may generalize them into models of desired system behaviour (as we will see it in Chapters 13 and 18).

Let us consider our meeting scheduling case study. One typical scenario for organizing a meeting in the system-to-be might involve the following interactions between a meeting initiator, the software scheduler and meeting participants:

1. The initiator asks the scheduler to plan a meeting within a particular date range. The request includes a list of desired participants.

2. The scheduler checks that the initiator is entitled to do so and that the request is valid. It confirms to the initiator that the requested meeting is initiated.

3. The scheduler asks all participants in the submitted list to send their date and location constraints back within the prescribed date range.

4. When a participant returns his or her constraints, the scheduler validates them (e.g. with respect to the prescribed date range). It confirms to the participant that the constraints have been safely received.

5. Once all valid constraints are received, the scheduler determines a meeting date and location that fit them.

6. The scheduled meeting date and location are notified to the initiator and to all invited participants.

There are different types of scenario.

- *Positive vs negative* scenarios. A positive scenario illustrates what should happen in terms of one behaviour that the system should cover. A negative scenario is a counter-example: it illustrates what may not happen in terms of one behaviour that the system should exclude. For example, the previous scenario is a positive one. A negative scenario might be the following:

1. A participant returns a list of constraints covering all dates within the prescribed date range.

2. The scheduler forwards this message to all participants asking them for alternative constraints within an extended date range.

Note that the reason for this scenario to be a negative one is kept implicit – in this case, the scenario illustrates the implicit requirement that information about participant behaviours and constraints should not be disclosed to others.

- *Normal vs abnormal* scenarios. A normal scenario captures a course of interaction where everything proceeds as normally expected. Abnormal scenarios capture desired interaction sequences under exceptional circumstances that depart from the normal course of interaction. Normal and abnormal scenarios are positive. For example, the previous six-step scenario is a normal one. There should be abnormal scenarios to cover cases such as the following:

  - The meeting initiator is not among the authorized ones.

  - A participant's constraints are not valid (in some sense to be made precise).

  - The participant constraints are not all received in due time.

Scenarios have strengths and limitations as elicitation vehicles. On the positive side, they are concrete and support a narrative style of description. Examples of desired or undesired behaviour naturally arise during the elicitation process. Scenarios can be used easily by stakeholders with different backgrounds to build a shared understanding of how components do interact in the system-as-is or how they should or should not interact in the system-to-be. Moreover, their usage extends beyond the elicitation phase – in particular, as animation sequences when we validate requirements, as counter-examples when we verify behavioural requirements, and as test cases when we define acceptance tests from the requirements (see Chapter 5).

On the downside, scenarios are inherently partial. As they are just examples, they do not cover all possible system behaviours under all possible circumstances. This is somewhat similar to the coverage problem for test cases. A reasonably comprehensive set of scenarios requires us to enumerate multiple combinations of individual component behaviours; this inevitably results in a combinatorial explosion problem. On the other hand, multiple stakeholders may state their scenarios at different levels of granularity, which raises integration problems. Such scenarios may contain details that are irrelevant to the point the scenario is trying to make. Complex scenarios may also be hard to comprehend for lack of structure. Moreover, too early use of scenarios may introduce some risk of overspecification; the sequencing of some interactions might not be strictly required, or the allocation of responsibilities among interacting components might be premature. Last but not least, scenarios keep properties about the system implicit. They capture interaction sequences, but not the reasons why such sequences should or should not take place; that is, the requirements underlying them (see the preceding negative scenario example). In the end, implicit properties need to be made explicit to support negotiation, analysis, implementation and evolution.

Despite these numerous limitations, we cannot live without scenarios. They spontaneously jump in during elicitation and provide useful information that we might perhaps not obtain otherwise. Easy-to-use notations are therefore required to express scenarios unambiguously, together with dedicated techniques for infering useful properties and models from them. We will come back to this in Chapters 4, 8, 13, 15 and 18.

2.2.6 Mock-ups and prototypes for early feedback

As mentioned at the beginning of this chapter, stakeholders often find it difficult to project textual system descriptions onto future working conditions. To overcome this difficulty, we may show them a 'reduced' sketch of the product to help visualize what the latter will look like. This principle has been successfully used in civil engineering for many years. Showing a reduced sketch of a software product in action may help understand some of its features, clarify others and reveal inadequate or missing features.

A *software prototype* is a quick implementation of some aspects of the system-to-be. Its aim is to get early feedback from stakeholders and prompt further elicitation. The focus in general is on requirements that are unclear, hard to formulate or hard to understand.

There are different kinds of prototype depending on which aspects are being prototyped:

- A *functional prototype* shows aspects related to software functionalities. For example, a meeting scheduler prototype might show a tentative process for initiating a meeting and asking participants' constraints, without considering the requirements constraining the search for optimal schedules. The aim would be to validate that process and elicit further requirements related to it.

- A *user interface prototype* shows static and dynamic aspects of user-software interaction; that is, formats for data entry and output display, and dialogue patterns. For our case study, the prototype might show the format and dialogue required for submitting participant constraints to the scheduler. User interface prototyping is very common. Useability requirements are much easier to elicit and validate through a prototype than through textual descriptions.

For prototyping to be cost effective, we must be able to build prototypes very quickly. To achieve this we may use executable specification languages, very high-level programming languages (such as functional or logic programming languages), program generators (such as simulation generators or user interface generators), generic services and the like.

The prototyping process is generally iterative and combines requirements validation and elicitation as follows:

```
repeat
     build next prototype version from selected requirements;
     show prototype executions;
     get feedback from stakeholders;
     update requirements from feedback
until prototype gets full agreement from stakeholders
```

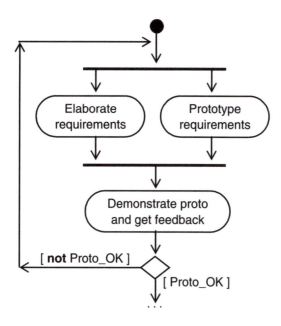

Figure 2.1 *Requirements prototyping*

Figure 2.1 gives a pictorial representation of this process as a UML activity diagram. Requirements elaboration and prototyping are shown there as parallel activities. The process terminates on an agreed prototype together with a corresponding set of requirements. Some of the requirements may have been revised during the process; others may have been elicited from stakeholder feedback.

The resulting set of requirements is the primary target of prototyping. In general, it is the only product kept for subsequent development. The prototype is then called *mock-up* or *throwaway prototype*. Alternatively, the prototype may be converted into a final software product through a series of semantics-preserving optimizations (Balzer *et al.*, 1982). The term *evolutionary prototype* is used in such a case.

Prototyping as an elicitation vehicle has a built-in advantage: experimenting with some concrete flavour of what the system might look like helps us understand the implications of some requirements, clarify others, turn inadequate requirements into adequate ones, and elicit requirements that are hidden in the stakeholder's mind. We can use the prototype for other purposes beyond elicitation and validation, such as user training before the final product is available and simulation of stubb components during integration testing.

Prototyping has limitations too. By definition, a prototype does not cover all aspects of the software-to-be. Most often it leaves some functionalities aside and restricts itself to a few non-functional requirements (such as useability requirements). Requirements about performance, cost, reliability, real-time constraints or interoperability with other software are ignored. Prototypes can therefore be misleading and set stakeholder expectations too high. Moreover, throwaway prototypes are often built through 'quick and dirty' means; the resulting code is generally inefficient and poorly structured. Converting throwaway prototypes into evolutionary ones may therefore be quite hard. Conversely, evolutionary prototypes are costly and may take too much time to develop with regard to the primary concern of eliciting adequate requirements promptly. In all cases, there can be inconsistencies between the updated requirements and the prototype code; the confidence in the results obtained through prototyping will be decreased in case of requirements–code mismatch.

2.2.7 Knowledge reuse

Systems are rarely conceived from scratch. Requirements engineers and stakeholders tend to reuse knowledge from past experience with related systems. Such knowledge may refer to the host organization, to the domain in which the problem world is rooted, to the kind of problems that were experienced with similar systems, and to the kind of requirements that need to be considered for addressing such problems.

Systematic reuse of knowledge can significantly speed up the elicitation process. The reuse-based parts of the process then combine the following steps:

---

1. Retrieve relevant knowledge fragments from other systems.

2. Transpose them to the target system.

3. Validate the transposed fragments, adapt them as necessary, and integrate them with the other knowledge fragments being elicited.

Transposition can be achieved through various mechanisms such as instantiation, specialization or translation of the retrieved knowledge fragments into the vocabulary of the target system (see below). Adaptation may require further elicitation.

There are different types of reuse depending on whether the reused knowledge is domain independent or domain specific.

Reuse of domain-independent knowledge

Section 1.1.5 already introduced requirements taxonomies. Knowledge of such taxonomies may prompt questions to elicit system-specific instances of requirements classes in the taxonomy, such as: 'Is there any requirement from this class in my system?'

For example, consider the taxonomy of performance requirements shown in Figure 2.2. This taxonomy extends the one given in Figure 1.5. For our train control case study, we might observe that no performance-related requirements were elicited so far. Browsing through the taxonomy in Figure 2.2, we might ask questions about numbers of trains to be handled at airport peak times. For the meeting scheduling system, we might look at all points in the system where responses are required in reaction to input stimuli and, for each of them, ask

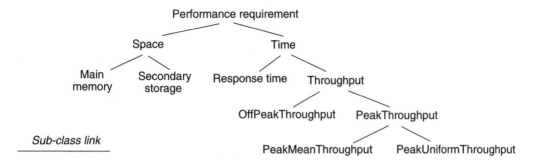

Figure 2.2 *Performance requirements classes in a reusable catalogue*
Source: Adapted from Chung, L., Nixon, B., Yu E. and Mylopoulos, J. 2000, with kind permission of Springer Science and Business Media.

what the corresponding average response time should be. This might result in assumptions about expected response time for participants to send back their constraints, or requirements on the deadline before which the meeting schedule should be notified.

Here are a few more examples of taxonomy-based questions to elicit requirements or assumptions that might have been overlooked:

- (From Information subclass of FunctionalRequirement:) Is there any requirement in my system about keeping specific classes of users informed about specific classes of states?

- (From Privacy subclass of SecurityRequirement:) Is there any private information manipulated by the system? If so, what are the corresponding privacy requirements?

- (From Availability subclass of SecurityRequirement:) Is there any system service or resource whose access is critical under certain conditions? If so, what are the corresponding availability requirements?

Requirements taxonomies can be expanded with domain-independent knowledge on how specific requirements classes should be refined (Chung *et al.*, 2000) or on which requirements class is likely to conflict with which other (van Lamsweerde *et al.*, 1998).

Reuse of a *meta-model* is another form of domain-independent reuse. In this case we are acquiring knowledge about the organization or about the target system as instantiation of elements of the meta-model according to which the organization or system is modelled. Such a meta-model is the domain-independent artefact being reused. It helps us figure out what questions to ask and when.

For example, if the organization is modelled in terms of actors, tasks, resources and dependencies, the meta-model will contain meta-classes such as *Actor*, *Task*, *Resource* and *Dependency*, inter-related through links that are specific to the meta-model. If the system is modelled in terms of goals, objects, agents and operations, the meta-model will contain meta-classes such as *Goal*, *Object*, *Agent* and *Operation*, inter-related through links that are specific to the meta-model (see Figure 2.3).

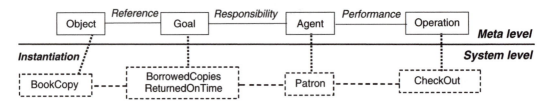

Figure 2.3 Reusing a meta-model to drive elicitation

Elicitation then proceeds by traversing the meta-model, in an order prescribed by the modelling method, in order to acquire corresponding meta-class instances (Dardenne *et al.*, 1993). We just state the principle here as we will come back to this in detail in Chapter 14.

Reuse of domain-specific knowledge

The idea here is to reuse some abstraction of the domain. We consider an abstract domain consisting of abstract concepts, tasks, actors, objectives, requirements and domain properties. These elements of the abstract domain are defined once and for all. We then elicit portions of our system as specializations of those abstract elements to our target domain, with inheritance and domain-specific renaming of inherited features.

Let us provide a simple illustration of this principle for our library management case study. An abstraction of it would be the domain of *resource management*. This domain might be structured in terms of the following abstract elements:

- *Concepts* such as 'resource', 'resource unit', 'resource directory', 'repository', 'resource request', 'resource usage', 'resource availability', 'resource reservation' etc.

- *Tasks* such as 'managing the acquisition of resource units', 'handling resource requests', 'tracking the history of resource usage' etc.

- *Actors* such as 'resource user', 'resource manager' etc.

- *Objectives* such as 'ensuring wide accessibility of resource units to users', 'ensuring appropriate resource localization in the repository for easy retrieval' etc.

- *Requirements* on the usage of resource units such as imposing some precondition on its usage (e.g. payment or reservation) and limiting usage time or simultaneous use of multiple units (e.g. 'a user may not use more than x resource units at a time').

- *Domain properties* such as 'a resource may have multiple units', 'a resource unit is a unit of one single resource only', 'a resource unit is no longer in the repository when it is used' etc.

For our target library system, we can specialize abstract elements such as:

resource, resource unit, repository, user, manager

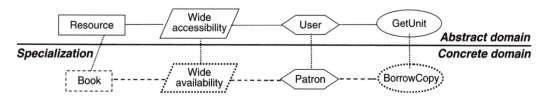

Figure 2.4 *Reusing an abstract domain to drive elicitation*

into the notions of:

book, book copy, library shelves, patron, library staff

respectively (see Figure 2.4). It is indeed the case that any instance of a book copy that can be borrowed is an instance of a useable resource unit, for example. When the proposed specializations are agreed, we select the features attached to the abstract counterpart for inheritance and library-specific renaming. The abstract specifications of tasks, objectives, requirements and domain properties on resources are thereby transposed to the library domain, for example:

'A patron may not borrow more than *x* book copies at a time.'

We must then validate the transposed specifications for adequacy and adapt them where necessary. Only those features that are relevant to our target domain need to be retrieved, transposed and adapted, of course.

An abstract domain can thereby be reused for multiple target domains. In the previous example, we might retrieve, specialize and adapt relevant abstract elements for different systems such as a CD/DVD loan management system, seat allocation in a flight reservation system, seat allocation in a concert booking system and so forth.

To increase the adequacy of reused knowledge, the abstract domain should be made more structured and more accurate. For example, suppose that the resource management domain is structured in terms of multiple specializations of the resource concept. We might distinguish between *returnable* and *consumable* resource units, *sharable* and *non-sharable* resource units and so forth. Each abstract specialization would have specific tasks, objectives, requirements and domain descriptions associated with it. The reusable features for one specific target domain are then likely be more accurate and more adequate.

For example, a copy of a book turns out to be a *returnable* and *non-sharable* resource unit. We would then get a specific domain property stating that 'a copy of a book can be borrowed by at most one patron at a time'. In a stock management system, stock items turn out to be *consumable* resources; no requirement about limiting item usage time would then be considered.

We can also increase the effectiveness of reuse by considering different parts of our target domain as specializations of different abstract domains. Multiple inheritance of appropriate features from different domains is then supported.

For example, the library domain includes parts such as:

book acquisition, user registration, loan management, library querying

that are specializations of abstract domains such as:

e-shopping, group membership management, resource management, data management

respectively. The accuracy requirement stating:

'The library database must accurately reflect the library shelves'

would then be inherited, after appropriate renaming, from a requirement in the *data management* domain stating:

'The managed database must accurately reflect the state of the corresponding environment data.'

Reuse-based elicitation has strengths and limitations. On the plus side, the elicitation effort may be considerably reduced when the target system is sufficiently 'close' to the known systems being reused, where 'close' refers to some conceptual, intentional or behavioural distance. Arguments about the benefits of design patterns apply equally here (Gamma *et al.*, 1995; Buschmann *et al.*, 1996). In particular, the reused knowledge fragments may codify high-quality RE done in the past. The result is therefore likely to be of better quality and obtained through a more guided process. Reuse-based elicitation also encourages abstraction and a common terminology for recurring patterns of organizations, concepts, objectives, tasks, behaviours and problems.

On the downside, it may be sometimes hard to identify the right abstractions, to structure them and to specify them appropriately for significant reusability. It may also be hard to determine whether a candidate fragment is worth reusing; similarity distances are not easy to define and measure. The composition of fragments from multiple domains and their integration in the target system may raise problems of consistency and compatibility, especially in the case of a complex domain. Too much time might be spent in validation of inappropriate features and tricky adaptations. Last but not least, the scaleability of reuse-based techniques is bound by the availability of effective tool support.

Section 16.1 will further discuss the analogical reuse of models along the lines introduced here.

2.3 Stakeholder-driven elicitation techniques

The techniques in this section rely more on specific types of interaction with stakeholders. To obtain adequate and relevant information about the organization, the domain and the problems with the system-as-is, direct interactions with the owners of such information prove to be invaluable. Such interactions may be organized according to a specific protocol. The techniques reviewed here include interviews, observation and group sessions.

2.3.1 Interviews

Interviews are generally considered as a primary technique for requirements elicitation. They typically proceed as follows.

---

1. We select a specific stakeholder with regard to the target information we want to acquire. Depending on the type of information, the selected person might be a domain expert, a manager, a salesperson, a consultant, an operator, an end-user etc.

2. We organize a meeting with the interviewee where we ask questions and record answers in some form.

3. We write a report from interview transcripts.

4. We submit the report to the interviewee for validation and refinement.

The three case study descriptions in Section 1.1.2 illustrate the kind of report that might summarize a first series of stakeholder interviews for the library, train control and meeting scheduling systems, respectively.

Two kinds of interview are traditionally distinguished:

- In a *structured interview*, we have prepared a pre-established set of questions. This set is structured according to a specific purpose associated with the interview. Some of the questions may be open-ended, others may ask for a choice among several answers provided.

- In an *unstructured interview*, there is no pre-established set of questions. The interview consists of a free, informal discussion with the stakeholder about the system-as-is, how it is working, what are the problems perceived by the interviewee, and how he or she would like such problems to be addressed in a new system.

Structured and unstructured interviews have their respective merits. A structured interview supports more focused discussion and avoids rambling among unrelated issues. An unstructured interview allows for exploration of issues that might otherwise be overlooked. Effective interviews should therefore mix the two modes, starting with structured parts, followed by unstructured ones.

The effectiveness of an interview can be measured by a weighted ratio between:

- the *utility* and *coverage* of the acquired knowledge; and

- the *time* taken to acquire it.

Interviews sometimes involve multiple stakeholders. This may help save people's time. Multistakeholder interviews are, however, likely to be less effective due to weaker interpersonal communication, more limited involvement of individuals and potential barriers on speaking freely.

Interviews have strengths and limitations. On the plus side, they support the elicitation of potentially important information that cannot be obtained through background study – typically, descriptions of how things proceed *really* in practice, personal complaints, suggestions for improvement, perceptions and feelings and the like. Interviews also allow for a direct, flexible, on-the-fly search for relevant information through new questions triggered from answers to previous ones.

On the downside, it is sometimes hard to compare what different interviewees are saying and integrate their input into a coherent body of knowledge. Subjective information has to be interpreted, and the borderline between subjective and objective information is not necessarily obvious to establish. Last but not least, the effectiveness of an interview is fairly dependent on the interviewer's attitude and the appropriateness of questions.

Interviewing guidelines

Some practical rules can therefore be followed to increase the effectiveness of interviews:

- Identify the right sample of people to interview, in order to build a complete and reliable picture – people with different responsibilities, expertise, tasks and exposure to potential problems.

- Come prepared to the interview so that you can focus on the right issue for that interviewee at the right time. Keep control over the interview – without making it too obvious in order to avoid the impression of everything being preset.

- Make the interviewee feel comfortable from the very beginning. The starting point is especially critical. Find an appropriate trick to break the ice; consider the person first rather than the role; ask permission to record. Introduce context and motivation. Ask easy questions first.

- Do appear as a partner at all times.

- Centre your interview on the interviewee's work, concerns and problems.

- Be focused and keep open-ended questions for the end.

- Be open-minded. Be ready to follow another course of action from interesting, unexpected answers.

- Ask *why* questions about decisions already made, about pre-established 'solutions' or any other questionable aspect – without appearing to offend.

- In view of the goal of acquiring as much useful information as possible from the interviewee, there are some types of questions to be banished:

  a. Avoid opiniated or biased questions, in which you express your opinion or bias on an issue.

  b. Avoid affirmative questions in which you implicitly impose some answer.

    c. Avoid questions that can be anticipated as unanswerable by that interviewee.

    d. Avoid questions perceived as 'stupid' by the interviewee in view of domain knowledge. (You can do this by prior acquisition of domain knowledge through background study.)

- Edit interview transcripts and structure them promptly as contextual information is still fresh in your mind, including interviewee's attitude, tone, gestures etc.

- Plan for a retrospective account of the interview in order to consolidate the acquired information with the interviewee and keep him or her in the loop.

One big question still remains: how should the structured parts of an interview actually be structured? As we will see in Part II of the book, a *model-driven* approach may provide an answer to this question. When the target of the elicitation process is a comprehensive, multifaceted model of the *system-as-is* and the *system-to-be*, we can structure our interviews according to the structure of the underlying meta-model; that is, the model in terms of which the system model has to be built.

2.3.2 Observation and ethnographic studies

This technique is based on the premise that understanding a task by observing it while it is carried out may be easier than by letting someone explain it to us (Suchman, 1987). A classic example of this is the task of tying one's shoelaces (Goguen & Linde, 1993). The point especially applies to business processes or work procedures involving multiple people who may not realize what the others are doing, or have a hard time explaining it.

    Task observation can be passive or active:

- In the case of *passive observation*, the requirements engineer does not interfere with the people involved in the task. He or she is just watching from outside and recording what is going on through notes, video cameras etc. As in data collection, these records must then be sorted out and interpreted correctly.

    a. *Protocol analysis* is a particular case of passive observation where a subject is performing a task and concurrently explaining it.

    b. *Ethnographic studies* are another particular case of passive observation where the requirements engineer tries, over long periods, to discover emergent properties of the social group involved in the observed process (Hughes *et al.*, 1995). The observation does not only refer to task performance but also to attitudes of task participants, their reactions in specific situations, their gestures, conversations, jokes etc.

- In the case of *active observation*, the requirements engineer gets involved in the task, sometimes to the point where he or she becomes a member of the work team.

The main strength of observation techniques is their ability to reveal tacit knowledge that would not emerge through other techniques. (The *tacit knowledge* problem was discussed in Section 2.1.) There has been limited experience to substantiate this argument, notably in the air traffic control domain. Ethnography-based observation was applied there to analyse how controllers handle paper strips representing flight plans. The observation revealed an implicit mental model of air traffic that an automated version of the system needed to preserve (Bentley *et al.*, 1992). More generally, the anthropological roots of ethnographic techniques make them especially suited to complex organizational systems where tacit, culture-specific features need to be discovered and taken into account. Another obvious strength of such techniques is their contextualization of the acquired information.

However, observation-based techniques have serious limitations. First of all, they are costly to deploy. To reach meaningful conclusions, observation must take place over significant periods, at different times and under different workload conditions. Even so, the conclusions can be inaccurate, as people tend to behave differently when they are being observed. The observer must be accepted by the group of observed people, which may be difficult and require extra time. Analysing records to infer emerging features may also be quite hard. Pointing out relevant features from a mass of irrelevant details may be far from trivial and subject to interpretation errors. Last but not least, observation-based techniques are by essence oriented towards the understanding of how the *system-as-is* is working. They are weaker at pointing out problems and opportunities to be addressed by the *system-to-be*.

Some of the guidelines for interviewing people apply here as well, in particular:

- Establish a trusting relationship.

- Organize debriefing meetings to hand the material back to the observed people and validate it with them.

Looking at tricky ways of doing things may also result in discovering problems that the working person is trying to overcome.

2.3.3 Group sessions

This technique is based on the premise that there is more space for perception, judgement and invention in a group of people, thanks to the diversity of its members and the interactions among them. Elicitation takes place during a series of group workshops, each typically taking a few days, separated by individual follow-up activities. Wall charts and other audiovisual aids are used to help foster discussions and collect the material emerging from group interactions.

Group sessions can be structured or unstructured:

- In *structured group sessions*, the role of each participant is clearly defined, for example leader, moderator, reporter, user, manager or developer. Each participant has to contribute to the joint elaboration of requirements according to his or her specific role and viewpoint. Such elaboration is generally focused on high-level features of the target product. Group synergies are expected to emerge at some point. Techniques such as *focus groups, JAD* (Joint Application Development) or *QFD* (Quality Function Deployment) are variants of this approach that differ by the definition of the roles and document templates used to support and document the joint elaboration process (Wood & Silver, 1995; Macaulay, 1996).

- In *unstructured group sessions*, also called *brainstorming* sessions, the respective roles of participants are less clearly established:

  a. In the first stage, each participant must spontaneously generate as many ideas as possible to improve a task or address a recognized problem. Idea generation must be free from prejudice, censorship or criticism by others.

  b. In the second stage, the participants need jointly to evaluate each idea with respect to agreed criteria such as effectiveness, feasibility and cost, in order to prune out some of the ideas and prioritize the others according to these criteria (Robertson & Robertson, 1999).

Group sessions have several benefits. Their less formal style of interaction can reveal aspects of the *system-as-is* or issues about the *system-to-be* that might remain hidden under formal interactions during interviews. Synergies in structured groups may result in better and much easier resolution of conflicting viewpoints. Freedom of thought in brainstorming sessions may result in more inventive ways of addressing the problems recognized. A broad range of ideas may also be rapidly collected.

Group-based techniques raise problems and difficulties as well. The composition of the group is critical. Key actors need to be involved. Such people in general are very busy and may be unable to spend significant time in successive workshops. The leader must have a high profile, both technically and in terms of communication skills. There are risks associated with group dynamics that may result in biased, inadequate or incomplete information being elicited – in particular, dominance by some individuals and difficulty for others in communicating. A lack of focus and structure in sessions may result in a paucity of concrete results and a waste of time. Last but not least, more technical issues are likely to be addressed only superficially in view of the time allotted and the average level of expertise of the group in such issues.

2.4 Conclusion

Getting the right system-to-be is critically dependent on domain understanding and requirements elicitation. The more support that can be provided for these intertwined activities, the better.

One single technique does not do the job. Each was seen to have strengths and limitations. A combination of techniques based on their respective strengths is therefore needed to get a complete, adequate and accurate picture. Which combination to consider may depend on the organization, the domain and the specific project. In any case we should use a mix of artefact-driven and stakeholder-driven techniques in view of their complementarity.

Some reported examples of such combinations include the following:

- *Contextual inquiry* combines observation of the workplace, open-ended interviews and prototyping (Beyer & Holtzblatt, 1998).

- We may similarly combine ethnographic observation techniques and prototyping (Kotonya & Sommerville, 1997).

- RAD (Rapid Application Development) combines JAD group sessions, where the reporter role is played by the software development team, evolutionary prototyping and code-generation tools (Wood & Silver, 1995).

Stakeholder-driven techniques assume a target set of stakeholders to interview, observe or involve in group sessions. This may not always be the case, notably in market-driven or product line projects (cf. Section 1.1.8). Alternative techniques such as *market studies* may be more suitable in such projects. We can then identify practices, problems, trends and opportunities on a much larger scale.

Domain understanding and requirements elicitation form just one phase in the spiral RE process introduced in Chapter 1 (see Figure 1.6). The next phases of evaluation, specification and consolidation may raise new problems, such as conflicts among requirements, overexposure to risks, missing or inadequate features and so forth. The resolution of such problems is a source of further elicitation of new requirements or modified ones. Specific techniques for supporting such resolutions will be reviewed in the next chapters associated with those phases.

The various elicitation techniques reviewed in this chapter raised a recurring issue of *structure*. How should background study and data collection be organized and focused? Is there any way to anchor scenarios on more structured artefacts? Can prototyping be organized stepwise on functional or non-functional increments? How should reusable knowledge fragments be structured? How should questionnaires and interviews be structured? How can we extract relevant features from the mass of details in observation records? How should group sessions be organized to avoid rambling discussions?

Model-driven elicitation provides an answer to those questions. The systematic construction of 'rich' models allows for more structured and focused applications of the elicitation techniques discussed in this chapter. By 'rich' we mean models that inter-relate multiple system facets – the concepts involved in the *system-as-is* and the *system-to-be*, their objectives, actors, tasks, behaviours, requirements, assumptions and domain properties. Part II of the book will focus on the systematic elaboration of such models.

Summary

- Domain understanding and requirements elicitation are intertwined activities whose aim is to understand the system-as-is in context, identify the problems with it in the light of new opportunities, and explore the objectives, requirements and assumptions regarding the system-to-be. This preliminary phase of the RE process involves a great deal of knowledge acquisition about the surrounding organization, the domain in which the problem world is rooted and the problem world itself. This RE phase is critical; if done wrong, it may result in incomplete and inadequate system requirements and assumptions. It often needs to be repeated as the subsequent evaluation, documentation, analysis and evolution phases may raise new issues to be explored.

- Eliciting the right objectives, requirements and assumptions is inherently difficult. There are multiple sources of elicitation to consider, including documents and people playing specific roles in the organization. Such sources are partial and often inconsistent with each other. There are access and communication problems. We need to identify the right stakeholders and take the right attitude with them. Harmonious cooperation between requirements engineers and stakeholders is essential. Difference in backgrounds may result in important information being kept implicit or overwhelmed with irrelevant details.

- There are different types of artefacts that we may use to help us understand the domain and elicit the right requirements. The study of relevant documentation about the organization, the domain and the *system-as-is* is a prerequisite to other elicitation techniques. The acquisition of non-functional requirements may be facilitated by collecting data that are not available from existing documents. Unbiased questionnaires may reach a larger number of people and help us better target subsequent interviews. Repertory grids and card sorts are sometimes helpful for acquiring implicit information about domain concepts. Concrete scenarios of interaction among system components help explain the system-as-is or explore the system-to-be. Prototypes we can build quickly, show to stakeholders and revise or extend incrementally may help us obtain more adequate requirements about expected functionalities and user interface aspects. We may also reuse domain-independent knowledge about the kind of requirement and assumption we need to acquire, or domain-specific knowledge about a relevant class of similar systems. Reuse consists of retrieving relevant knowledge, transposing it to the specifics of the target system, validating the result and adapting it if necessary.

- There are different interaction techniques we may use for knowledge acquisition from stakeholders. Interviews are the primary means for obtaining information from selected stakeholders. To be effective, they must be driven by a carefully designed set of issues to address through structured and unstructured questioning. Passive or active observation may sometimes help us acquire in a more straightforward way knowledge of how things are being done. Observation may reveal tacit knowledge that might be hard to acquire through other techniques. Group sessions may reveal important system aspects from free or structured interactions among a diverse, carefully selected set of people.

- The various techniques we may use for requirements elicitation have specific strengths and weaknesses, some of which may be mitigated by the use of technique-specific guidelines. An effective elicitation process should combine multiple techniques whose strengths complement each other. The best combination should ensure an optimal balance between the utility of the acquired knowledge and the cost of the acquisition process. Which combination works best may depend on the organization, on the target system and on project constraints.

- A model-based approach to RE should provide a comprehensive structure for what needs to be elicited, thereby making the use of the elicitation techniques in this chapter more effective.

Notes and Further Reading

Requirements elicitation is fairly close to knowledge acquisition as studied in artificial intelligence for expert system development (Byrd *et al.*, 1992). Similar principles and techniques for knowledge acquisition are discussed in Carlisle Scott *et al.* (1991) and Hart (1992). Conceptual laddering and card sort techniques are detailed in Rugg and McGeorge (1995, 1997). An application of card sorts to the elicitation of quality requirements is described in Upchurch *et al.* (2001).

The effectiveness of scenarios for requirements elicitation and validation is widely recognized among practitioners (Sommerville & Sawyer, 1997; Haumer *et al.*, 1998; Weidenhaupt *et al.*, 1998). Scenarios were first introduced in software design method- ologies (Rumbaugh *et al.*, 1991; Rubin & Goldberg, 1992; Jacobson *et al.*, 1993). Many RE methodologies recommend using them for eliciting requirements and exploring their implications. They often propose heuristics and guidelines for scenario elaboration and scenario-based analysis (Hsia *et al.*, 1994; Potts *et al.*, 1994; Potts, 1995; Regnell *et al.*, 1995; Leite *et al.*, 1997; Rolland & Ben Achour, 1998; Sutcliffe, 1998). Scenarios are also a good vehicle for exploring useability issues (Carroll & Rosson, 1995). They can be used as positive/negative examples for inductive synthesis of their underlying objectives (van Lamsweerde & Willemet, 1998) or of behaviour models generalizing them (Whittle & Schumann, 2000; Uchitel *et al.*, 2003; Damas *et al.*, 2005). A good account of the use of scenarios in RE and software engineering, with convincing illustrations in various domains, will be found in Alexander and Maiden (2004). The use of storyboards in conjunction with use cases is suggested in Leffingwell and Widrig (2003).

Prototyping as a means of requirements elicitation and validation is a fairly old idea. Gomaa and Scott discuss the benefits of a throwaway protoype system that used the APL programming language for prototyping (Gomaa & Scott, 1981). Balzer and colleagues argue for an evolutionary prototyping approach based on the use of the GIST executable specification language (Balzer *et al.*, 1982). Requirements prototyping is discussed further in RE textbooks such as Davis (1993), Loucopoulos and Karakostas (1995) and Kotonya and Sommerville (1997). Technical approaches to prototyping are described in greater detail in Budde (1984) and Hekmatpour and Ince (1988) based on the use of PROLOG and VDM as prototyping languages, respectively.

There have been numerous efforts to apply the principles explained in this chapter for reuse-based elicitation. Multiple terminologies have been used for domain-specific abstractions to be reused, for example requirements clichés (Reubenstein & Waters, 1991), analysis patterns (Fowler, 1997b), or problem frames (Jackson, 2001). The variations essentially concern the kind of abstraction being reused, the sophistication of reuse mechanisms, and the availability of tool support. The *abstractions* may cover structural models of domain concepts (Reubenstein & Waters, 1991; Ryan & Mathews, 1993; Fowler, 1997b; Sutcliffe & Maiden, 1998); intentional models of domain goals and ways of achieving them (Dardenne *et al.*, 1993; Darimont, 1995); or task models for solving specific classes of problems in the domain (Reubenstein & Waters, 1991; Jackson, 2001). The *reuse mechanisms* may include specialization with single or multiple inheritance (Reubenstein & Waters, 1991), traversal of a specialization hierarchy of domains (Sutcliffe & Maiden, 1998); or structural and semantic matching based on analogical reasoning techniques (Maiden & Sutcliffe, 1993; Massonet & van Lamsweerde, 1997). Knowledge reuse is closely related to analogical reasoning, an area studied extensively in artificial intelligence (Prieditis, 1988; Hall, 1989).

Gause and Weinberg provide a comprehensive coverage of issues related to stakeholder-based elicitation techniques (Gause & Weinberg, 1989).

Principles and guidelines for effective interviews are discussed extensively in textbooks on user-centred system analysis (Beyer & Holtzblatt, 1998; Whitten & Bentley, 1998) and knowledge acquisition (Carlisle Scott *et al.*, 1991; Hart, 1992).

Observation-based approaches to task understanding for requirements elicitation are discussed in greater detail in Goguen and Linde (1993), Goguen and Jirotka (1994), Hughes *et al.* (1995) and Kotonya and Sommerville (1997).

Macaulay provides a thorough coverage of requirements elicitation from group sessions (Macaulay, 1996), including focus groups, workshops and approaches such as Joint Application Design (JAD), Quality Function Deployment (QFD) and Cooperative Requirements Capture (CRC). Guidelines for effective brainstorming are proposed in Robertson and Robertson (1999). A detailed account of the process of designing and running effective workshops for requirements elicitation will be found in Gottesdiener (2002).

The ACRE framework is intended to assist requirements engineers in the selection of the most appropriate combinations of elicitation techniques (Maiden & Rugg, 1996). The selection there is based on a series of questions driven by a set of facets associated with the strengths and weaknesses of each technique.

Exercises

- Section 2.1 lists a series of obstacles to effective knowledge acquisition for domain understanding and requirements elicitation. Illustrate each of these in the library, train control and meeting scheduling case studies described in Section 1.1.2.

- Consider the library, train control and meeting scheduling case studies. For each of them, identify the types of document that would be worth considering for background study prior to the use of other elicitation techniques.

- Extend the normal scenario for meeting scheduling in Section 2.2.3 with a reasonably comprehensive set of associated abnormal scenarios.

- Identify normal and abnormal scenarios for the library system-as-is. Identify normal, abnormal and negative scenarios for the train control system-to-be.

- Analyse similarities and differences between an *ambulance despatching* service and an on-line *taxi call* service in order to build an abstract domain that would cover related concepts, tasks, actors, objectives, requirements and domain properties. Then show how some of the requirements for the on-line taxi call service could be elicited through knowledge reuse.

- Repeat the previous exercise for a system that allocates berths to tankers in an oil terminal and a system that assigns gates to landing aircrafts in an airport, respectively.

- Prepare a set of interviews for acquiring knowledge about the library *system-as-is* and for eliciting requirements on the library *system-to-be*. To achieve this, (a) identify the set of stakeholders to be interviewed and explain why each of them is relevant to the elicitation process; (b) for each interviewee, determine the purpose of the interview and the type of information to be acquired; (c) design a structured set of questions for that purpose and that interviewee; and (d) identify open tracks that might be worth exploring at the end of the interview.

- Repeat the previous exercise on the train control system and on the meeting scheduling system.

- Section 2.3.1 reviews some types of question to be banished from interviews. Illustrate each of them in the library, train control and meeting scheduling case studies.

- Identify some tasks in the library system-as-is and in the meeting scheduling system-as-is that would be most amenable to observation, and explain why you believe so.

- Imagine yourself as a leader of structured group sessions to elicit requirements for the library system-to-be. Identify participants you would like in your group and explain why. Based on the objectives and outputs of the elicitation process recalled at the beginning of this chapter, imagine some document templates that might be worth using to foster discussions and document the results of the joint elicitation process.

Requirements Evaluation

The techniques discussed in the previous chapter help us identify stakeholder needs together with alternative ways of addressing these in the system-to-be. Following the spiral model of the RE process introduced in Chapter 1 (see Figure 1.6), we now need to evaluate the elicited requirements and assumptions on several grounds:

- Some of them can be inconsistent with each other, especially in cases where they originate from multiple stakeholders having their own focus and concerns. We need to detect and resolve such inconsistencies. Conflicting viewpoints must be managed in order to reach a compromise agreed by all parties.

- Some requirements or assumptions can be overexposed to risks, in particular safety hazards, security threats or development risks. We need to analyse such risks carefully and, when they are likely and critical, overcome or mitigate them through more realistic and robust versions of requirements or assumptions.

- The alternative options we may have identified must be compared in order to select the 'best' options for our system. As introduced in Chapter 1, alternative options may arise from different ways of satisfying the same objective or from different responsibility assignments in which more or less functionality is automated. They may also arise from different ways of resolving conflicts or managing risks. Alternative options should be evaluated in terms of their contribution to non-functional requirements and their reduction of risks and conflicts.

- In the selected alternatives, the requirements might not all be able to be implemented in the first place in view of development constraints such as budgets, project phasing and the like. We need to prioritize requirements in such cases.

The target of requirements evaluation is a set of low-risk, conflict-free requirements and assumptions that stakeholders agree on. Negotiation may often be required to reach such a target. As we already saw in Section 1.1.6, requirements evaluation is intertwined with requirements elicitation. It may start as soon as some elicited material is ready for evaluation and negotiation. This chapter provides an overview of the techniques we may use for requirements evaluation. It successively discusses inconsistency management (Section 3.1), risk analysis (Section 3.2), evaluation of alternative options (Section 3.3) and requirements prioritization (Section 3.4).

3.1 Inconsistency management

Requirements engineers live in a world where inconsistencies are the rule, not the exception. Inconsistencies generally arise from multiple viewpoints and concerns. They must be detected and eventually resolved, even though they prove temporarily useful for eliciting further information within single viewpoints.

This section defines the different types of inconsistencies we may find in an RE project and introduces principles and techniques for handling them. Conflicts are an important type of inconsistency that deserves special attention. We will discuss them in greater detail by reviewing the various steps of a systematic process for conflict management.

3.1.1 Types of inconsistency

Generally speaking, inconsistent statements violate a *consistency rule* that links them explicitly or implicitly. Different types of consistency rule define different types of inconsistency:

- *Terminology clash*. The same concept is given different names in different statements. For example, one statement states some condition for '*participating*' in a meeting whereas another statement states an apparently similar or related condition for '*attending*' a meeting.

- *Designation clash*. The same name designates different concepts in different statements. For example, one stakeholder interprets '*meeting participation*' as full participation until the meeting ends, whereas another interprets it as partial participation.

- *Structure clash*. The same concept is given different structures in different statements. For example, one statement speaks of a participant's excluded dates as '*a set of time points*', whereas another speaks of it as '*a set of time intervals*'.

- *Strong conflict*. There are statements that cannot be satisfied when taken together; their logical conjunction evaluates to **false** in all circumstances. This amounts to classical inconsistency in logic. In our meeting scheduler, there would be a strong conflict between one statement stating that '*the constraints of a participant may not be disclosed to anyone else*' and another stating that '*the meeting initiator should know the participants' constraints*'. (Those statements might originate from stakeholders having the participant's and initiator's viewpoint, respectively.)

- *Weak conflict or divergence*. There are statements that are not satisfiable together under some condition. This condition, called a *boundary condition*, captures a particular combination of circumstances that makes the statements strongly conflicting when it becomes true. The boundary condition must be feasible; that is, it can be made true through possible system behaviours. Divergence thus amounts to potential conflict. It is a weaker form of conflict that occurs more frequently in RE. For example, a stakeholder having the staff's viewpoint in our library system might state, '*a borrower should return a borrowed book copy within two weeks*'. A stakeholder having the borrower's viewpoint might state, '*a borrower should keep a borrowed book copy as long as he or she needs it*'. Those two statements are *not* strongly conflicting as long as the borrower does not need the borrowed book copy for more than two weeks. A feasible boundary condition making the three statements logically inconsistent when taken together is '*Needing the borrowed book copy for more than two weeks*'.

3.1.2 Handling inconsistencies

Clashes in terminology, designation and structure are most effectively countered by careful elaboration of a *glossary of terms* that everyone agrees and sticks to. Such a glossary should provide a precise, intelligible definition of all terms used and, for some of them, a list of *accepted synonyms*. Glossary elaboration takes place during domain understanding and requirements elicitation (see Section 1.1.6).

Handling strong and weak conflicts is more difficult. Beyond the symptoms of conflicts, we need to act on their causes. Conflicts are generally rooted in two kinds of problems:

- Multiple stakeholders have different objectives and priorities. Such objectives are sometimes incompatible. Conflicts between requirements should therefore be analysed in terms of differences between their underlying objectives. Once such differences are resolved, the resolution is to be propagated down to the requirements level (Robinson, 1989).

- In addition to incompatibilities between multiple viewpoints, there are inherent incompatibilities between non-functional requirements, or between functional and non-functional requirements. For example:

  - Password-based authentication for increased security often conflicts with useability requirements.

  - Confidentiality and accountability requirements tend to conflict.

  - Performance requirements about system throughput may conflict with safety requirements.

  - Increasing system maintainability may result in increasing development costs.

Conflict resolution often includes some form of *negotiation*. The resolution process may then proceed iteratively as follows (Boehm *et al.*, 1995):

- Stakeholders are identified together with their personal objectives with regard to the system-to-be (these are called *win* conditions).

- Differences between these win conditions are captured together with their associated risks and uncertainties.

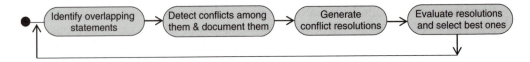

Figure 3.1 Conflict management

- The differences are reconciled through negotiation to reach a mutually agreed set of objectives, constraints and alternatives to be considered at the next iteration.

3.1.3 Managing conflicts: A systematic process

The more systematic the techniques for handling conflicts are, the more effective the outcome is likely to be. Conflict management can be made more systematic through a number of steps with dedicated techniques for each step (Robinson *et al.*, 2003). Figure 3.1 shows these various steps. Let us have a closer look at each of them.

Identifying overlapping statements

Intuitively, statements overlap each other if they refer to some common or inter-related phenomena. For example, the phenomena of acquiring, borrowing and returning book copies are inter-related as they refer to the common concept of 'book copy'. So are the phenomena of opening and closing train doors, or the phenomena of gathering meeting constraints and determining meeting schedules.

Overlaps can be identified on purely syntactic grounds, such as referring to common terms. On more semantic grounds, we may identify overlapping statements as they involve inter-related concepts or behaviours (Spanoudakis *et al.*, 1999).

Detecting and documenting conflicts among overlapping statements

Conflicts can be detected in several ways:

- *Informal detection.* We may informally determine whether the overlapping statements are satisfiable together and under what conditions they are not.

- *Heuristic detection.* We may use detection heuristics based on predetermined categories of requirements and conflicts (van Lamsweerde *et al.*, 1998; Chung *et al.*, 2000). Section 1.1.5 already introduced this principle through a few examples. Here are a few more detection heuristics.

  - Check *information* requirements vs *confidentiality* requirements that refer to related objects, for example the requirement 'Allow users to be informed about the loan status of books' vs the requirement 'Do not allow students to know which user has borrowed what'.

  - Check requirements on *decreasing* some quantity vs requirements on *increasing* a related quantity. For example, 'Increase coverage of journal subscriptions' vs 'Decrease operational costs'.

  – Check *satisfaction* requirements that can be instantiated to multiple competing system components. For example, two instantiations of the requirement 'Achieve meeting scheduled within prescribed date range' can be conflicting when there are multiple competing initiator requests and short, overlapping date ranges.

- *Formal detection.* We may detect conflicts between statements using formal techniques based on inconsistency checking, theorem proving or derivation of boundary conditions (Manna & Pnueli, 1992; Owre *et al.*, 1995; van Lamsweerde *et al.*, 1998). Formal conflict detection requires overlapping statements to be formalized in a logic-based specification language; see Sections 4.4 and 18.5.

- *Lightweight detection.* To overcome the difficulty of such formalization, we may use lightweight versions of formal techniques. For example, we may check whether overlapping statements match some assertion templates that were proved once for all to be conflicting with each other. This technique, based on conflict patterns, will be discussed in Section 18.5. Informal versions of it can be used as well, as we will see in Section 16.2.

Documenting conflicts Once they have been detected, conflicts should be documented for later resolution. Documentation tools can record conflicts and point out statements involved in multiple conflicts, most conflicting statements, non-conflicting statements, overlapping statements and so on. This may be useful for impact analysis.

A standard documentation technique consists of building an *interaction matrix* (Kotonya & Sommerville, 1997). Each row/column in the matrix is associated with a single statement. The matrix element S_{ij} has a value *1* if statement S_i conflicts with statement Sj, *0* if these statements are distinct and do not overlap, and *1000* (say) if they overlap without conflicting.

A simple spreadsheet can then count the *number of non-conflicting overlaps* and the *number of conflicts* involving a single statement, by:

- Summing down the corresponding column, and

- Computing the quotient and remainder of the integer division of the total by 1000, respectively.

If we now consider all statements together, the overall number of non-conflicting overlaps and conflicts is obtained by a similar division on the sum across the bottom total line. Table 3.1 shows an interaction matrix. The total number of non-conflicting overlaps and conflicts is given

Statement	S1	S2	S3	S4	Total
S1	0	1000	1	1	1002
S2	1000	0	0	0	1000
S3	1	0	0	1	2
S4	1	0	1	0	2
Total	1002	1000	2	2	2006

Table 3.1 *An interaction matrix*

by the quotient and remainder of the integer division of 2006 by 1000, respectively; that is, 2 and 6.

A more scaleable technique can be used when the statements are recorded as objectives, requirements and assumptions in a *requirements database*. Conflict links are then created between conflicting items, and the previous type of analysis is performed through a standard database query engine. This kind of use of a requirements database will be detailed in Sections 5.2 and 16.1.

Yet another approach consists of using specific notations for recording multiple stakeholder viewpoints and inter-viewpoint consistency rules. Conflicts are then documented by marking the rules being violated (Nuseibeh *et al.*, 1994).

Generating conflict resolutions

Following the process in Figure 3.1, we must sooner or later resolve the detected conflicts:

- Not too late – that is, before software development starts – otherwise we could develop anything from inconsistent statements.

- Not too soon, to allow for further elicitation of useful information within individual viewpoints in spite of their inconsistency with others (Hunter & Nuseibeh, 1998).

Instead of jumping straight on to one specific resolution, it is generally better to explore multiple alternative resolutions so that the best one can be selected, according to specific evaluation criteria, and possibly reconsidered later on as the system evolves (Easterbrook, 1994). Several approaches can be followed to explore the space of possible resolutions.

Using elicitation techniques   We may use the techniques reviewed in Chapter 2 to elicit alternative conflict resolutions with stakeholders – notably, stakeholder-based techniques such as interviews and group sessions (see Section 2.3). The target resolutions should capture a reasonable compromise for all parties involved in the conflict. One extreme alternative to consider in the resolution space is the appeal to some appropriate authority.

Using resolution tactics   We may also produce resolutions systematically by use of operators that encode conflict-resolution tactics. Some operators transform the conflicting statements or the objects involved in such statements. Other operators introduce new requirements (Robinson & Volkov, 1997; van Lamsweerde *et al.*, 1998). Let us give a sample of such operators:

- *Avoid boundary condition.* Ensure in some way or another that the boundary condition for conflict can never become true. For example, consider again the divergence between the statements 'A borrower should return a borrowed book copy within two weeks' and 'A borrower should keep a borrowed book copy as long as he or she needs it'. The boundary condition for strong conflict was seen to be 'Needing the borrowed book copy for more than two weeks'. Avoiding this boundary condition might be achieved by keeping some copies of popular books always unable to be borrowed; such copies are available for direct use in the library at any time when needed (this tactic is often implemented in university libraries).

- *Restore conflicting statements.* Ensure in some way or another that the conflicting statements become together satisfiable again reasonably soon after the boundary condition has occurred. This might be achieved in the previous example by forcing borrowers to return book copies even if they are still needed and then allowing them to borrow the required book copies again soon after.

- *Weaken conflicting statements.* Make one or several of the conflicting statements less restrictive so that the conflict no longer exists. This tactic is frequently used. In general, the statements being weakened are those that have lower priority. For example, the statement 'A borrower should return a borrowed book copy within two weeks' might be weakened into 'A borrower should return a borrowed book copy within two weeks unless he or she gets explicit permission to keep it longer for some good reason'. The divergence would then disappear.

- *Drop lower-priority statements.* This is an extreme case of the previous tactic where one or several lower-priority statements involved in the conflict are weakened to the point that they are universally true.

- *Specialize conflict source or target.* Identify the source (or target) objects involved in conflicting statements and specialize these so that the conflict disappears. For example, let us come back to the conflict between the statements 'Allow users to be informed about the loan status of books' and 'Do not allow students to know which user has borrowed what'. This conflict can be resolved by specializing the conflict source object 'user' into 'staff user' so that the first statement is transformed into the conflict-free version 'Allow staff users to be informed about the loan status of books'. Alternatively, the conflict target object 'loan' can be specialized into an anonymized version in which status information no longer covers the identity of borrowers.

Evaluating conflict resolutions to select a best one

Once alternative conflict resolutions have been explored, we need to make a decision on which 'best' resolution to select (see Figure 3.1). The basis for this decision is provided by evaluation criteria such as the degree of contribution of the resolutions to critical non-functional requirements, and the reduction of other risks and conflicts. Techniques for this will be discussed in Section 3.3. The selection may also call for negotiation with stakeholders (Robinson, 1990).

Conflict management is an important aspect of RE. Based on the introductory material in this section, the goal-based models detailed in Part II will allow for more in-depth coverage in Chapters 16 and 18.

3.2 Risk analysis

Many software failures originate from our natural inclination to conceive over-ideal systems (see Section 1.2.1). In the early phases of wild enthusiasm about their project, requirements engineers and stakeholders tend to make unrealistic assumptions – the environment and the software will behave as expected, the development project will run as planned. However, moving from the system-as-is to the system-to-be inevitably raises several types of risk. If risks go unrecognized or underestimated, the requirements will be incomplete or inadequate as they will not take such risks into account.

This section presents principles and techniques for early risk management at RE time. Section 3.2.1 defines the notion of risk and introduces the various types of risk found in an RE project. Section 3.2.2 reviews techniques that may help us along the various steps of risk management; namely, risk identification, risk assessment and risk control. Risk documentation is briefly discussed in Section 3.2.3. A systematic method integrating risk identification, assessment and control in the RE process is presented in Section 3.2.4.

3.2.1 Types of risk

A *risk* is an uncertain factor whose occurrence may result in a loss of satisfaction of a corresponding objective. The risk is said to *negatively impact* on this objective.

A risk has a *likelihood of occurrence* and one or several undesirable *consequences* associated with it. Each consequence is uncertain as well; it has a likelihood of occurrence if the risk does occur. Each consequence has a *severity* in terms of degree of loss of satisfaction of the corresponding objective.

In our train control system, the risk of passengers manually forcing train door opening may negatively impact on the objective of keeping doors closed while the train is moving; severe accidents were reported where this risk did occur (Neumann, 1995). In our library system, the risk of book copies being lost or stolen may negatively impact on the objective of regular availability of book copies. In our meeting scheduling system, the risk of participants not checking their e-mail regularly may negatively impact on the objective of scheduling convenient meeting dates, as e-mail requests for constraints could be missed.

The likelihood of a risk should not be confused with the likelihood of a consequence of this risk. For example, the risk of train doors opening while the train is moving has some likelihood; the consequence of passengers falling out of the train when the train is moving with open doors has some other likelihood.

As risks may have a negative impact on corresponding objectives, risk types correspond to types of objectives that could be missed in the system-to-be:

- *Product-related risks* negatively impact on functional or non-functional objectives of the target product (see Section 1.1.5). Functional risks may result in the product's inability to deliver the required services. Non-functional risks may result in the product's inability to deliver the required qualities of service. These notably include safety hazards and security threats.

- *Process-related risks* negatively impact on objectives of the development process. They may result in delayed product delivery, cost overruns, deterioration of project team morale and so forth.

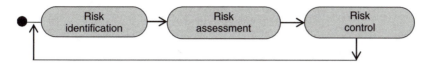

Figure 3.2 Risk management

3.2.2 Risk management

Risk management is an essential part of requirements evaluation. Some requirements or assumptions might not take risks sufficiently into account. When this is the case, we must identify new requirements as *countermeasures* to risks that are too likely or whose possible consequences are too severe. We should then evaluate such countermeasures in turn as they might involve new risks or conflicts with other important requirements.

Risk management is thus an iterative process. Figure 3.2 shows the three steps involved at each cycle (Boehm, 1991; Jones, 1994). Let us have a closer look at each of them.

Risk identification

An obvious prerequisite to risk control is the awareness of possible risks impacting negatively on the objectives of our project. We can use several techniques for this.

Risk checklists We may consider checklists of common risks for instantiation to the project's specifics. Such checklists can be built from risk categories that negatively impact on corresponding requirements categories introduced in Section 1.1.5:

- For product-related risks, the checklists refer to missing or inadequate functionalities, wrong assumptions about the environment, safety hazards, security threats and vulnerabilities, reliability gaps concerning critical features, information inaccuracy, poor performance, unusability of features or feature rejection by users. Those risk categories can be specialized further along the taxonomy depicted in Section 1.1.5; see Figure 1.5. In our train control system, for example, instantiating the generic risk of information inaccuracy to the inaccuracy of train position/speed information would result in identifying a potential risk of train accelerations being computed from inaccurate estimates of locations and speeds of successive trains.

- For process-related risks, the checklists refer to requirements volatility, personnel shortfalls, dependencies on external sources, unrealistic schedules or budgets, or poor risk management. For example, lack of experienced personnel or excessive turnover in the company subcontracting the software part of the new train-based transportation system is a process-related risk to be seriously considered.

The product- and process-related risk categories listed here cover Boehm's list of top ten risks (Boehm, 1989). In a similar spirit, the Software Engineering Institute has elaborated a process-oriented risk taxonomy together with a comprehensive list of questions to help in spotting project-specific risks along this taxonomy (Carr *et al.*, 1993). Note that poor risk management is the most important risk as it results in all other types of risks.

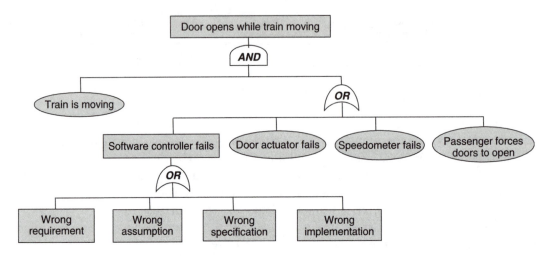

Figure 3.3   *Portion of fault tree for train door control system*

Component inspection   Another risk-identification technique for product-related risks consists of reviewing the various components of the system-to-be. For each component, we may determine what its possible failures are together with their respective causes and consequences.

For example, our train control system includes components such as the on-board train controller, the station computer, the train tracking system and the communication infrastructure; or finer-grained components such as the acceleration controller, the doors controller, track sensors and so on. For each of these we might investigate the nature, causes and consequences of possible failures.

Risk trees   The identification of risks through component inspection can be made more systematic by the use of risk trees. Such trees organize failures, causes and consequences along causal links. They are sometimes called *fault trees* when the failures relate to safety hazards (Leveson, 1995) or *threat trees* when they relate to security threats (Amoroso, 1994). Figure 3.3 shows a simple fault tree for our train control system.

Risk trees have two kinds of node. *Failure nodes* capture independent failure events or conditions. They are represented by circles or rectangles depending on whether they are basic or decomposed further into causes. *Logical nodes* are AND or OR nodes that capture causal links. In the case of an AND node, the causing child nodes must all occur for the parent node to possibly occur as a consequence. In the case of an OR node, only one of them needs to occur.

Such trees may be used to capture process-related risks as well. In the most general case, they are directed acyclic graphs where one child failure node may be causally linked to multiple parent failure nodes.

To identify failure nodes in a risk tree, we may use risk checklists and guidewords (Jaffe *et al.*, 1991; Leveson, 1995; Pfleeger, 2001). *Guidewords* capture patterns of failure through specific words such as:

- *NO*: 'something is missing'

- *MORE*: 'there are more things than expected'; *LESS*: 'there are fewer things than expected'

- *BEFORE*: 'something occurs earlier than expected'; *AFTER*: 'something occurs later than expected'

Once a risk tree has been built, we can enumerate all minimal AND combinations of leaf events or conditions, each of which is sufficient for causing the root failure node. The set of such combinations is called the *cut set* of the risk tree. This set is obtained by taking all leaf nodes of another tree, called the *cut-set tree*, derived top down from the risk tree as follows:

- The top node of the cut-set tree is the top logical node of the risk tree.

- If the current node in the cut-set tree is an *OR* node, it is expanded in as many child nodes as there are alternative child nodes in the risk tree; if it is an *AND* node, it is expanded into one single aggregation node composed of all conjoined child nodes in the risk tree.

- The process terminates when the child nodes obtained are all basic events or conditions or aggregations of basic events or conditions.

Figure 3.4 shows a fault tree together with its associated cut-set tree. The fault tree corresponds to the one given in Figure 3.3, where all leaves are assumed to represent basic conditions. The cut set is given by the set of leaf nodes of the cut-set tree; that is, the set

$$\{\{TM, WR\}, \{TM, WA\}, \{TM, WS\}, \{TM, WI\}, \{TM, DAF\}, \{TM, SF\}, \{TM, PFDO\}\}.$$

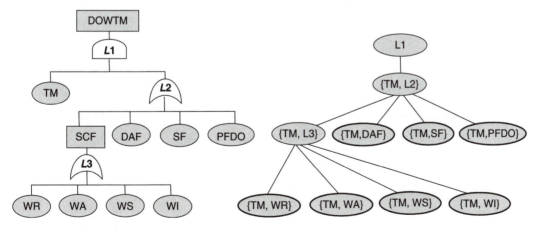

Figure 3.4 *Fault tree and its cut-set tree*

Using elicitation techniques   The elicitation techniques reviewed in Chapter 2 can also be used to identify system-specific risks:

- *Scenarios* may be used to raise *WHAT IF* questions and point out failure situations. For some given scenario, we may systematically explore potential deviations, for example expected interactions that do not occur, that occur too late, that occur under different conditions and so forth.

- *Knowledge reuse* techniques may be applied to risks previously experienced with similar systems or within the same organization.

- *Group sessions* may be specifically dedicated to the identification of project-specific risks.

Risk assessment

The identified risks should be assessed in terms of the likelihood of their occurrence and the severity of their possible consequences (see Figure 3.2). We need to do this in order to *prioritize* the risks and determine an appropriate response for likely risks that have severe consequences.

Qualitative assessment   In general it is hard to estimate the likelihood and severity of a risk in a precise way. *Risk levels* based on qualitative estimations are therefore often used. Such estimations typically range over qualitative scales, for example:

- From 'very unlikely' to 'very likely' for the likelihood of a risk or consequence.

- From 'low' to 'catastrophic' for the severity of a consequence.

We may then elaborate a risk assessment table for each identified risk to support the subsequent risk control step. For example, the result of assessing the risk 'Doors open while train is moving' in Figure 3.3 might be captured by the assessment table in Table 3.2.

Risk assessment tables provide the basis for a rough prioritization of risks. Having defined one such table for every identified risk, we may compare them and give higher consideration to risks that have higher severity levels.

	Risk likelihood		
Consequences	**Likely**	**Possible**	**Unlikely**
Loss of life	*Catastrophic*	*Catastrophic*	*Severe*
Serious injuries	*Catastrophic*	*Severe*	*High*
Train car damaged	*High*	*Moderate*	*Low*
No. of passengers decreased	*High*	*High*	*Low*
Airport reputation damaged	*Moderate*	*Low*	*Low*

Table 3.2   *Severity of consequences by risk likelihood levels for 'Doors open while train moving'*

This technique is quite easy to use, but its conclusions are limited. The severity values are coarse-grained and may be subjective; the likelihood of consequences is not taken into account.

Quantitative assessment   Alternatively, we may use numerical scales for risk estimation and comparison:

- The likelihood of a risk and the likelihood of a consequence are estimated in a discrete range of probability *values*, such as (0.1, 0.2, ..., 0.9, 1.0), or in a discrete range of probability *intervals*, such as (0–0.3, 0.3–0.5, 0.5–0.7, 0.7–1.0).

- The severity of a consequence is estimated on a scale of *1* to *10*, say.

We may then estimate the *risk exposure* for a risk r with independent consequences c as follows:

$$Exp(r) = \sum_c L(c) \times S(c),$$

where $L(c)$ and $S(c)$ are the likelihood and severity of consequence c, respectively. We may then compare the exposures of the various identified risks, possibly weighted by their likelihood of occurrence, and give higher consideration to risks with higher exposure.

Qualitative and quantitative scales share a common weakness: the scores used for risk assessment and comparison may be inaccurate, because they are based on subjective values. Such values cannot be measured and validated in terms of physical phenomena in the environment. What does it really mean to say that the risk 'Doors open while train moving' has a likelihood of 0.3, that the likelihood of the consequence 'Serious injuries' is 0.4, or that the severity of the consequence 'no. of airport passengers decreased' is 6 on a 1–10 scale? For comparison purposes, however, the problem is attenuated as long as the scores are assigned *consistently* from one risk being compared to the other.

Still, the question remains of where such scores are coming from. The elicitation techniques reviewed in Chapter 2 might be used to obtain them from domain experts. A historical database of accumulated measurements might be helpful as well. Even though the accuracy of score values may remain questionable, risk-based decision making based on such expert estimates will be much more effective than decision making without any basis.

Risk control

Once we have identified and assessed product- and process-related risks, we need to address these in some way or another (see Figure 3.2). High-exposure risks must be reduced through countermeasures. This reduction should be cost-effective.

Countermeasures yield new requirements or modified versions of elicited requirements. For product-related risks, the effectiveness of countermeasures should ideally be monitored at system runtime. If alternative countermeasures are anticipated at RE time, the system can then shift from one countermeasure to the other at runtime in case the currently selected one appears ineffective (see Section 6.5).

Similarly to conflict management, it is thus better to explore alternative countermeasures first and then make a selection based on evaluation criteria.

Exploring countermeasures

We may identify countermeasures through several means.

Using elicitation techniques   The techniques in Chapter 2 can be applied for eliciting countermeasures as well; in particular, stakeholder-based techniques such as interviews or group sessions.

Reusing known countermeasures   We may also instantiate generic countermeasures to the specific context of our project. For example, Boehm's list of top ten risks comes with alternative countermeasures for each of them (Boehm, 1989), such as:

- Simulations or targeted analysis to counter risks of poor performance.

- Prototyping or task analysis to counter risks of poor usability.

- Use of cost models or multisource estimation to counter risks of unrealistic budgets or schedules.

Using risk-reduction tactics   Such tactics allow us to produce alternative countermeasures in a systematic way. Here is a sample:

- *Reduce risk likelihood.*   Introduce new requirements to ensure that the likelihood of occurrence of the risk is significantly reduced. For example, let us assume that train drivers were assigned the responsibility of executing the acceleration commands generated by the software controller. Consider the risk of drivers failing to do so, for example because they fall asleep or are unduly distracted by some other activity. The likelihood of occurrence of this risk might be reduced by requiring prompts for driver reaction to be generated regularly by the software.

- *Avoid risk.* Introduce new requirements ensuring that this specific risk may never occur. This is a boundary case of the previous strategy, where the likelihood is reduced to zero. For example, the risk of passengers forcing doors to open might be avoided by requiring that (a) the doors actuator reacts to the software controller exclusively, and (b) the software controller checks the train's speed before responding to any opening request from passengers.

- *Reduce consequence likelihood.* Introduce new requirements ensuring that the likelihood of occurrence of this consequence of the risk is significantly reduced. For example, the likelihood of severe injuries or loss of life in the case of unexpected door opening might be reduced by requiring that the software controller generates an alarm within train cars in the case of door opening during train moves.

- *Avoid risk consequence.* Introduce new requirements prescribing that a severe consequence of this tolerated risk may never occur. For example, new requirements might be introduced to ensure specifically that train collisions cannot occur in case the risk of inaccurate train position or speed information does occur.

- *Mitigate risk consequence.* Introduce new requirements to reduce the severity of consequences of this tolerated risk. For example, consider the risk of important meeting participants having a last-minute impediment. The absence of such participants can be mitigated in the system by integrating new facilities such as videoconferencing, appointment of proxies and the like.

Selecting the most appropriate countermeasures

Once countermeasures have been explored, we need to select the most appropriate ones. The selection criteria include the cost-effectiveness of countermeasures and their contribution to other, non-functional requirements.

For a risk r with exposure $Exp(r)$, the cost-effectiveness of a countermeasure cm can be measured in terms of *risk-reduction leverage*, defined as follows:

$$RRL(r, cm) = (Exp(r) - Exp(r|cm))/\text{cost}(cm)$$

where $Exp(r|cm)$ denotes the new risk exposure if the countermeasure cm is selected.

The countermeasures with highest risk-reduction leverages should then normally be selected.

The comparison of countermeasures can be refined by considering:

- Cumulative countermeasures in the preceding definition of *RRL*, to account for the fact that the same risk may be reduced by multiple countermeasures.

- Cumulative *RRLs*, to account for the fact that the same countermeasure may reduce multiple risks.

3.2.3 Risk documentation

As noted before, the *Identify–Assess–Control* cycle in Figure 3.2 may need to be repeated as countermeasures can introduce new risks in their turn; risk management is an iterative process. This process should be documented in the requirements document to provide the rationale for countermeasure requirements and to support requirements evolution – changes in requirements may entail changes in risks and the need for different countermeasures. The documentation is also needed for risk monitoring at system runtime and dynamic selection of more appropriate countermeasures.

Risk documentation should ideally include, for each identified risk:

- The conditions or events characterizing its occurrence.

- Its estimated likelihood of occurrence.

- Its possible causes and consequences.

- The estimated likelihood and severity of each possible consequence.

- The countermeasures that were identified together with their respective risk-reduction leverage.

- The selected subset of countermeasures.

This documentation can be organized around risk trees. We will come back to this in Chapter 9.

3.2.4 Integrating risk management in the requirements lifecycle

NASA's *Defect Detection Prevention* approach (*DDP*) is a notable effort to systematize the *Identify–Assess–Control* cycle and integrate risk management in the RE process (Feather and Cornford, 2003; Feather *et al.*, 2005). The approach is supported by a quantitative reasoning tool with rich visualization facilities. It handles multiple risks in parallel and explicitly considers risk consequences as loss of attainment of the corresponding objective.

In DDP, objectives, risks and countermeasures are called requirements, failure modes and PACTs, respectively. There is a coarser counterpart of the notion of risk-reduction leverage, called *effectiveness*, defined as the proportion by which a countermeasure reduces a risk.

The likelihood of risks, the severity of consequences and the effectiveness of countermeasures must be estimated quantitatively by elicitation from domain experts or from accumulated measurements.

As Figure 3.5 shows, the DDP approach consists of three steps.

Step 1: Elaborate the impact matrix

We first need to build a *risk–consequence table* with domain experts. This table captures the estimated severity of the consequences of each risk. For each pair of objective *obj* and associated risk *r*, it specifies an estimated loss of proportion of attainment of the objective if the risk occurs – from *0* (no loss) to *1* (total loss). The last line of the table yields the overall criticality of each risk, obtained by summing down the corresponding column in the following weighted way:

$$Criticality\ (r) = Likelihood\ (r) \times \sum_{obj} (Impact\ (r, obj) \times Weight\ (obj))$$

Risks are thereby prioritized by critical impact on all objectives. The last column of the impact matrix yields the overall loss of proportion of attainment of each objective, obtained by

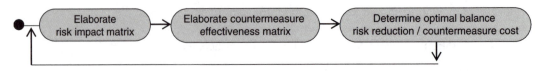

Figure 3.5   *Risk management with DDP*

Objectives	Risks				Loss of objective
	Late returns (likelihood: 0.7)	Stolen copies (likelihood: 0.3)	Lost copies (likelihood: 0.1)	Long loan by staff (likelihood: 0.5)	
Regular availability of books copies (weight: 0.4)	*0.30*	*0.60*	*0.60*	*0.20*	**0.22**
Comprehensive coverage of library (weight: 0.3)	*0*	*0.20*	*0.20*	*0*	**0.02**
Staff load reduced (weight: 0.1)	*0.30*	*0.50*	*0.40*	*0.10*	**0.04**
Operational costs decreased (weight: 0.2)	*0.10*	*0.30*	*0.30*	*0.10*	**0.05**
Risk criticality	**0.12**	**0.12**	**0.04**	**0.06**	

Table 3.3   A DDP risk–consequence table for the library management case study. Internal cells give the severity of consequences measured in proportion of objective being lost if the risk occurs

summing across the corresponding line in the following weighted way:

$$Loss\,(obj) = Weight\,(obj) \times \sum_{r} (Impact\,(r, obj) \times Likelihood\,(r))$$

The most risk-driving objectives are thereby highlighted.

Table 3.3 shows an impact matrix for our library management case study (the values in the last line/column were rounded to two significant digits). Note again that the numbers taken individually have no accurate meaning; they are to be considered in a relative sense for pairwise comparison. Also note that we might play with such tables in a spreadsheet-like fashion to see how criticalities and losses are affected by modifications of weights, likelihoods and loss of proportion of attainment. From this table the DDP tool produces a bar chart visualizing the critical impact, by decreasing order, of the various risks on all objectives.

Step 2: Elaborate the effectiveness matrix

We need to build a *risk–countermeasure table* with domain experts. This table captures estimated risk reductions by alternative countermeasures. For each pair of countermeasure *cm* and weighted risk *r*, it specifies an estimation of the fractional reduction of the risk if the countermeasure is applied – from *0* (no reduction) to *1* (risk elimination). The last line of the table yields the cumulative reduction of each risk through the combined effect of countermeasures. It is obtained by multiplicative combination of individual reductions down the corresponding column, according to the following formula:

$$combinedReduction\ (r) = 1 - \Pi_{cm}\ (1 - Reduction\ (cm, r))$$

The terms $1 - Reduction(cm, r)$ in the above product represent reduction rates of the likelihood that the risk r still occurs in spite of the corresponding countermeasure cm. Risks are thereby compared by their global reduction through the combined application of countermeasures. The last column of the effectiveness matrix yields the overall single effect of each countermeasure. It is obtained by multiplications across the corresponding row, according to the following formula:

$$overallEffect\ (cm) = \sum_{r} (Reduction\ (cm, r) \times Criticality\ (r))$$

The most globally effective countermeasures are thereby highlighted. In this calculation of single effect, risk criticality is determined in terms of the risk's initial likelihood, as if no other countermeasure were applied that could reduce this likelihood. DDP offers a more refined option for overall effect of a countermeasure based on risks with their likelihoods as already reduced by whichever of the other countermeasures have already been selected. It also allows for the possibility that a countermeasure, while reducing some risks, increases others. Those more refined calculations are detailed in Feather and Cornford, 2003.

Table 3.4 shows an effectiveness matrix for the risks in Table 3.3.

Counter-measures	Weighted risks				
	Late returns (likelihood: 0.7)	Stolen copies (likelihood: 0.3)	Lost copies (likelihood: 0.1)	Long loan by staff (likelihood: 0.5)	Overall single effect of counter-measure
E-mail reminder sent	0.70	0	0.10	0.60	0.12
Fine subtracted from registration deposit	0.80	0	0.60	0	0.12
Borrower deregistration & addition to black list	0.90	0.20	0.80	0	0.16
Anti-theft device	0	1	0	0	0.12
Combined risk reduction	**0.99**	**1**	**0.93**	**0.60**	

Table 3.4   *A DDP risk–countermeasure table for the library management case study. Internal cells give the fractional reduction of risk likelihood*

Step 3: Determine an optimal balance between risk reduction and cost of countermeasure
Each countermeasure has a benefit in terms of risk reduction, but also some cost associated
with it (as introduced before). We need to estimate costs with domain experts. The DDP tool
may then visualize the effectiveness of each countermeasure together with its cost. A risk
balance chart shows the residual impact of each risk on all objectives if the corresponding
countermeasure is selected. We can then explore optimal combinations of countermeasures
that achieve risk balance with respect to cost constraints. In general it may be worth considering
an 'optimal' combination of countermeasures to select. In the simple example of Table 3.4,
there would be 16 possible combinations to explore (ranging from none to all four). DDP has
a simulated annealing optimization procedure to find near-optimal selections. The optimality
citerion can be set by the user, for example 'maximize the total expected attainment of
objectives under some given cost threshold' or 'minimize the total cost for remaining above
some given level of attainment'.

The DDP approach provides a good illustration of the kind of technology supporting
the risk *Identify–Assess–Control* cycle during requirements evaluation. It covers most of the
risk management concepts discussed in this section; links risks explicitly to objectives and
requirements; exhibits typical quantitative reasoning schemes that are available for requirements
evaluation; and has convenient tool support for carrying out such reasoning and for visualizing
the results.

Risk management is an essential aspect of RE. The goal-based models in Part II of the book
will allow for more in-depth coverage of this topic in Chapters 9, 16 and 18.

3.3 Evaluating alternative options for decision making

As already introduced in Chapter 1 and earlier in this chapter, the requirements engineer is
moving through a range of alternative options where decisions need to be made repeatedly
with stakeholders:

- A system objective might be satisfiable through alternative combinations of sub-objectives,
  functional features and assumptions.

- There might be alternative responsibility assignments among system components, resulting in different software–environment boundaries.

- A conflict between statements might be resolved by alternative resolutions.

- A risk might be reduced through alternative combinations of countermeasures.

For each type of alternative option, we need to make decisions based on specific evaluation
criteria.

The main criterion for comparing options is their respective degree of contribution to
the various non-functional requirements that were elicited (see Section 1.1.5, Figure 1.5) or,
equivalently, their degree of reduction of the risks of not meeting such requirements. Other
criteria may need to be considered, such as the degree of resolution of identified conflicts.

Options	Non-functional requirements		
	Fast response	Reliable response	Minimal inconvenience
Get constraints by e-mail	−	+	−
Get constraints from e-agenda	++	−−	++

Table 3.5 *Qualitative contributions of options to non-functional requirements*

Once the evaluation criteria have been set up, we need to compare the various options in order to select the most preferred one.

Qualitative reasoning techniques

The evaluation of multiple options can be based on some form of qualitative reasoning. The NFR framework provides a typical example of what can be done (Chung *et al.*, 2000). The technique is merely introduced here, as it will be detailed in Section 16.3 after goal models have been thoroughly discussed.

The general idea is to expose the positive or negative influence of alternative options on non-functional requirements. Consider our meeting scheduler case study. Suppose we have to choose between two alternative options for knowing the participant's constraints: obtaining them by e-mail requests or by accessing the participant's electronic agenda. Table 3.5 shows the qualitative contribution of the two options to three important non-functional requirements for our meeting scheduler. Getting the participant's constraints by e-mail might contribute negatively to a fast response (as the invited participant might be non-responsive), positively to a reliable response (as the participant is likely to know his or her exact constraints) and negatively to minimal inconvenience (as the participant might get multiple e-mail reminders). On the other hand, getting the participant's constraints by accessing his or her elecronic agenda might contribute very positively to a fast response, very negatively to a reliable response (as the participant's e-agenda is very likely to reflect her actual availabilities inaccurately) and very positively to minimal inconvenience (as no participant interaction is required).

The question, of course, is where qualitative labels such as '+', '−', '++' and '−−' are coming from and how they are used for decision making:

- The NFR framework assumes a structured model like the ones we will introduce in Part II of the book. A goal model captures, among other things, alternative ways of refining the system objectives into sub-objectives and requirements. The resulting AND/OR graph can also represent degrees of satisfaction of objectives and degrees of contribution, positive or negative, of lower-level objectives to higher-level ones.

- Rules for propagating the qualitative labels along the contribution paths in this graph allow us to qualitatively evaluate the degree to which the higher-level goals are satisfied in each alternative option. The option where the critical higher-level objectives are better satisfied is then selected.

Quantitative reasoning techniques

The evaluation of multiple options can also be based on some form of quantitative reasoning. *Weighted matrices* are a standard system engineering technique for quantitative decision support. Such matrices are somewhat similar to those introduced in the preceding section for risk management. They capture estimated scores of each option with respect to the various evaluation criteria.

Each criterion is assigned some weighting that represents its significance relatively to others – typically, a numerical proportion. A matrix cell associated with an option *opt* and a criterion *crit* represents the estimated score percentage of the option with respect to the criterion; a value *x* means that the option satisfies the criterion in *x*% of the cases. The last line of the matrix gives the total score of each option as a weighted summation of its scores with respect to the various criteria:

$$totalScore\,(opt) = \sum_{crit} (Scores\,(opt, crit) \times Weight\,(crit))$$

We can thereby compare options by their overall score with respect to all criteria. The best-score option may then be considered for selection.

Table 3.6 shows a weighted matrix for two alternative ways of getting a participant's constraints in our meeting scheduling system. Three non-functional requirements are used as evaluation criteria:

- A *time performance* requirement ('fast response').

- An *accuracy* requirement ('reliable response').

- A *convenience* requirement ('minimal inconvenience').

See Figure 1.5 in Chapter 1. In Table 3.6, the e-agenda alternative is estimated to satisfy the *Minimal inconvenience* requirement perfectly, whereas it appears fairly poor with respect to the *Reliable response* requirement; it is felt that e-agendas may not be perfectly up to date in 70% of the cases. The option of asking participants' constraints through e-mail is seen to emerge according to such estimates. As in the previous section, an objective comparative conclusion is reached from subjective estimates of weights and contributions. The latter may be tuned up in a spreadsheet-like manner.

Evaluation criteria (non-functional requirements)	Significance weighting	Option scores	
		Get constraints by e-mail	Get constraints from e-agenda
Fast response	0.30	0.50	0.90
Reliable response	0.60	0.90	0.30
Minimal inconvenience	0.10	0.50	1.00
TOTAL	**1.00**	**0.74**	**0.55**

Table 3.6 *Weighted matrix for evaluating alternative options in the meeting scheduler*

3.4 Requirements prioritization

The requirements emerging from the elicitation and evaluation phases often need to be prioritized. There are several reasons for this:

- The development of all the features desired by stakeholders may exceed resource limitations in terms of available budget, manpower or time to delivery.

- The development may need to be planned by successive increments and releases, and replanned in the case of unexpected circumstances arising during development, such as unanticipated delays, budget restrictions, personnel shortages or pressure on time to deliver.

- Priority information may be used in conflict management to weaken or even drop lower-priority requirements (see Section 3.1.3).

In such cases, we need to decide which requirements are *mandatory*, which are *superfluous* (at least in the first project phase) and which would be *nice to have* if resource constraints allow.

Constraints for effective prioritization

To make comparisons and decisions more effective, prioritization should rely on several premises:

a. Priorities should be ordered by levels, each level containing requirements of equal priority. For easier prioritization, the number of such levels should be kept small.

b. The characterization of levels should be qualitative rather than quantitative, and relative rather than absolute, e.g. 'higher than' rather than 'high', 'medium' or 'low'.

c. The requirements being compared should be comparable. They should refer to the same level of granularity and abstraction.

d. The requirements being compared should be independent, or at least not mutually dependent, so that one requirement can be kept while the other is discarded or deferred.

e. The classification of requirements by priority level should be negotiated with stakeholders so that everyone agrees on it.

Premises (c) and (d) are satisfied when a goal-based model is used to support the prioritization process. We can then select nodes with a common parent node in the goal refinement graph, or at least at the same refinement level, as candidate items for comparison (see Chapters 7 and 8).

Prioritization techniques

A simple, straightforward way of setting priorities among requirements is to gather key players in the decision process and ask them to rank requirements under the above constraints.

The result of this ranking might be highly subjective and produce arbitrary, inadequate or inconsistent results in some cases. The *value–cost comparison* method provides a more systematic approach for requirements prioritization (Karlsson & Ryan, 1997). This method meets premises (a) to (c) and globally works as follows:

- We calculate the relative contribution of each requirement to the project's overall *value*.

- We calculate the relative contribution of each requirement to the project's overall *cost*.

- We plot the result on a value–cost diagram partitioned into subareas associated with priority levels. In this diagram, the x axis represents cost percentage whereas the y axis represents value percentage (see Figure 3.6).

To calculate the relative contribution of each requirement to the project's overall value and cost, we use a standard technique in decision theory (Saati, 1980). This technique, known as *Analytic Hierarchy Process (AHP)*, is applied twice – once for the case where the comparison criterion is *value*, once for the case where it is *cost*.

Given the comparison criterion and a set of requirements $R_1, R_2, \ldots, R_n$ contributing to it, the *AHP* procedure determines in what proportion each requirement contributes to the criterion. The procedure has two basic steps.

Step 1: Compare requirements pairwise according to the criterion
We build a $n \times n$ matrix in which the element R_{ij} estimates how R_i's contribution to the criterion compares to

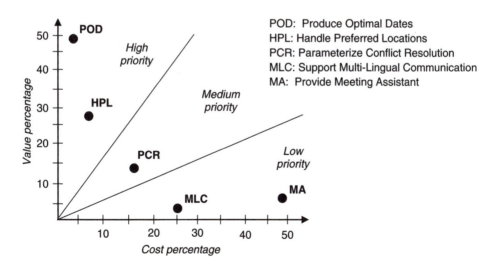

Figure 3.6 *Value-cost requirements prioritization for the meeting scheduler: outcome of the AHP process*

R_j's contribution on the following scale:

1 contributes equally   *7 contributes very strongly more*
3 contributes slightly more   *9 contributes extremely more*
5 contributes strongly more

In this comparison matrix, the symmetrical element R_{ji} is thus the reciprocal $1/R_{ij}$.

Step 2: Estimate how the criterion distributes among all requirements The criterion distribution is given by the eigenvalues of the comparison matrix. These eigenvalues are estimated by averaging over normalized columns as follows:

- *Normalize columns of the comparison matrix.* Each element of the comparison matrix is replaced by the result of dividing this element by the sum of the elements in its column.

- *Average across lines.* The estimated proportion in which R_i contributes to the criterion is then obtained by taking the sum of elements on the ith line of the normalized matrix, divided by the number of elements along the line.

Table 3.7 shows a comparison matrix resulting from Step 1 applied to our meeting scheduler case study. The criterion there is instantiated to the project's overall *value*. For example, the requirement of determining a best possible schedule fitting the excluded/preferred dates of invited participants is estimated to contribute *very strongly more* to the project's overall value than the requirement of providing a meeting assistant that would help manage the meeting agenda, minutes, attendance list and so on.

Table 3.8 shows the result of Step 2 applied to the comparison matrix in Table 3.7 (the values were rounded to two significant digits). The last column appended to the normalized

	Produce optimal date	Handle preferred locations	Parameterize conflict resolution strategy	Multilingual communication	Meeting assistant
Produce optimal date	1	3	5	9	7
Handle preferred locations	1/3	1	3	7	7
Parameterize conflict resolution strategy	1/5	1/3	1	5	3
Multilingual communication	1/9	1/7	1/5	1	1/3
Meeting assistant	1/7	1/7	1/3	3	1

Table 3.7 *AHP comparison matrix with relative values of requirements on the meeting scheduler*

	Produce optimal date	Handle preferred locations	Parameterize conflict resolution strategy	Multilingual communication	Meeting assistant	**Relative value**
Produce optimal date	0.56	0.65	0.52	0.36	0.38	**0.49**
Handle preferred locations	0.19	0.22	0.31	0.28	0.38	**0.28**
Parameterize conflict resolution strategy	0.11	0.07	0.10	0.20	0.16	**0.13**
Multilingual communication	0.06	0.03	0.02	0.04	0.02	**0.03**
Meeting assistant	0.08	0.03	0.03	0.12	0.05	**0.07**

Table 3.8 *AHP normalized matrix and relative contributions of requirements to the project's overall value*

	Produce optimal date	Handle preferred locations	Parameterize conflict resolution strategy	Multilingual communication	Meeting assistant
Produce optimal date	1	1/3	1/5	1/5	1/7
Handle preferred locations	3	1	1/5	1/5	1/7
Parameterize conflict resolution strategy	5	5	1	1/3	1/5
Multilingual communication	5	5	3	1	1/3
Meeting assistant	7	7	5	3	1

Table 3.9 *AHP comparison matrix with relative costs of requirements on the meeting scheduler*

matrix shows each requirement's relative contribution to the overall value of the project. For example, the requirement of determining a best possible schedule is seen to account for 49% of the project's overall value, whereas the requirement of providing a meeting assistant accounts for 7% of it.

Replaying now Step 1 and Step 2 of the *AHP* process for the case where the criterion is requirements *cost* – that is, the cost for implementing the corresponding requirement – we obtain Tables 3.9 and 3.10, respectively.

The resulting relative contributions to the project's *value* and *cost* may now be plotted on a *value–cost diagram* partitioned in three priority levels, say. Figure 3.6 shows how the five

	Produce optimal date	Handle preferred locations	Parameterize conflict resolution strategy	Multilingual communication	Meeting assistant	**Relative cost**
Produce optimal date	0.05	0.02	0.02	0.04	0.08	**0.04**
Handle preferred locations	0.14	0.05	0.02	0.04	0.08	**0.07**
Parameterize conflict resolution strategy	0.24	0.27	0.11	0.07	0.11	**0.16**
Multilingual communication	0.24	0.27	0.32	0.21	0.18	**0.25**
Meeting assistant	0.33	0.38	0.53	0.63	0.55	**0.48**

Table 3.10 *AHP normalized matrix and relative contributions of requirements to the project's overall cost*

requirements on the meeting scheduler are prioritized accordingly. The requirements 'Produce optimal dates' and 'Handle preferred locations' are seen to emerge at the higher-priority level, the requirement 'Parameterize conflict resolution strategy' is of medium priority, whereas the requirements 'Support multilingual communication' and 'Provide a meeting assistant' are relegated to the lower-priority level.

One difficulty with this prioritization technique is the potential for inconsistent estimations in the comparison matrix built at Step 1 of the AHP process. For consistent comparison, the pairwise requirements ordering must be transitive; that is, if R_1 is estimated to contribute to the criterion x more than R_2 and R_2 is estimated to contribute to it y more than R_3, then R_1 must contribute z more than R_3, with x, y, z in the ordered set {slightly, strongly, very strongly, extremely} and $x \leqslant y \leqslant z$. The AHP process also provides means for assessing consistency ratios and comparing them with acceptability thresholds (Saati, 1980).

3.5 Conclusion

The evaluation techniques in this chapter support the early identification of potential problems with elicited material, the exploration of alternative options to address them, and the selection of best options. To determine the relative value of the options being compared, the techniques often involve some form of qualitative or quantitative assessment. An objective conclusion is reached from subjective estimates of weighted contributions of options to evaluation criteria.

The adequacy and accuracy of such estimates are critical. Their determination requires judgement and experience. We need to obtain them from domain experts, and may therefore use some of the elicitation techniques reviewed in Chapter 2 to get adequate and accurate estimates. Such estimates should ideally be cross-checked by other stakeholders and validated from empirical data. In any case, the outcome of the evaluation process should be discussed with stakeholders to reach a common agreement.

One recurring issue raised by evaluation techniques is the identification and comparability of the items to be evaluated. These items should be overlapping (in the case of conflict management) or independent (in the case of option assessment or requirements prioritization). They should pertain to the same level of abstraction and granularity. As Part II and Part III will show, *models* facilitate the use of evaluation techniques by providing refinement structures in which comparable items are highlighted.

Summary

- The objectives, requirements and assumptions elicited from multiple concerns and viewpoints must be evaluated on several grounds. They might be formulated in terms of inconsistent terminologies or incompatible structures. Their formulation might be interpreted in inconsistent ways. Some of them might not be satisfiable when taken together under specific conditions. Some requirements or assumptions might be overexposed to different types of risks. Alternative options may arise during elicitation. In view of resource limitations, the requirements might not all be implementable in the first development cycle. All such problematic situations need to be identified and resolved. Their resolution yields new requirements or modified ones.

- Inconsistent terminologies, structures and interpretations are better addressed through the elaboration of a glossary of terms to which every party agrees and sticks.

- Conflict management comprises the identification of overlapping statements, the detection and documentation of conflicts among them, the generation of conflict resolutions and the selection of the best resolutions. Divergence is the most frequent form of conflict where the statements become logically inconsistent when some boundary condition holds. Conflicts can be detected more systematically using formal methods or heuristics based on categories of requirements and conflicts. They can be documented using interaction matrices or conflict links in a requirements database. Alternative resolutions can be explored by the use of elicitation techniques or resolution operators that capture different tactics for conflict resolution.

- We have a natural tendency to envision over-ideal systems where everything will work fine. Empirical evidence shows that this is a big mistake. Systems are highly exposed to different types of risk. A risk is an uncertain factor that may result in loss of attainment of objectives of the development product or process. New requirements for a more realistic and more robust system are obtained through risk management.

- Risk management is an iteration of risk identification, assessment and control. Risk identification is critical and can be supported by risk checklists, component inspection, risk tree analysis and elicitation techniques. Risk assessment can be supported by qualitative or quantitative techniques for estimating risk exposure based on risk likelihood and severity of consequences. The adequacy and accuracy of such estimates are crucial and depend on expert judgement and empirical data. Risk control consists of exploring alternative countermeasures to reduce high-exposure risks in a cost-effective way. Such countermeasures can be obtained by use of elicitation techniques, reuse of generic countermeasures to known risk classes, or operators that capture different strategies for risk reduction. The countermeasures with the highest risk-reduction leverages should then be selected. Risks should be documented to provide the rationale for countermeasures introduced in the requirements document and to support their evolution. DDP is a tool-supported approach that integrates risk *Identify–Assess–Control* cycles within the RE process.

- Development resources are generally limited. Development processes may be phased in successive increments. Therefore, requirements often need to be prioritized. The prioritization process should rank comparable and independent requirements by qualitative priority levels. Such a process can be supported by an AHP-based cost–value comparison technique to rank requirements by levels according to their relative contribution to the project's overall value and cost.

- A recurring principle in RE is to consider alternative options before selecting those that best meet specific evaluation criteria. Options include different ways of resolving conflicts, reducing risks and prioritizing requirements. Non-functional requirements play a decisive role in selecting the best options. They provide evaluation criteria that can be weighted by importance to score options qualitatively or quantitatively. Option selection may require negotiation with stakeholders to reach agreement on final choices.

- The evaluation techniques in this chapter are critically dependent on the identification and comparability of the items to be evaluated. Models for RE should provide abstractions and structures to support this.

Notes and Further Reading

A comprehensive survey on requirements conflict management can be found in Robinson *et al.* (2003). This paper discusses the various steps of conflict management further and gives an overview of a representative sample of RE research projects on the topic. It provides additional perspectives from other areas such as database view integration, knowledge acquisition, distributed artificial intelligence and negotiation support systems. The paper includes an extensive bibliography with more than 250 references on the topic.

The view that inconsistency is inevitable in software engineering and should be tolerated through specific mechanisms was first introduced in Balzer (1991) and elaborated further in the context of requirements in Finkelstein *et al.* (1994). Inconsistency as a violation of consistency rules linking multiple viewpoints is introduced in Nuseibeh *et al.* (1994). This paper describes a mechanism for integrating multiple views on a specification through such rules.

The different types of inconsistencies found in RE are discussed further in van Lamsweerde *et al.* (1998). This paper introduces the notion of divergence and describes techniques for conflict detection and resolution. Various conflict-resolution strategies are discussed there that complement the ones introduced in Robinson and Volkov (1997). The notion of requirements overlap as a precondition for conflict is studied in Spanoudakis and Finkelstein (1997). The principle of generating conflict resolutions first before selecting a preferred one is advocated in Easterbrook (1994). Conflicts should not be resolved too prematurely in order to allow for further elicitation from conflicting views. Formal frameworks allowing for inconsistency tracking and reasoning in spite of inconsistency are discussed in Hunter and Nuseibeh (1998).

Several of the requirements evaluation techniques in this chapter involve negotiation with stakeholders and decision makers. A general treatment of negotiation techniques falls outside the scope of this book. The interested reader may refer to Pruitt (1981) and Raiffa (1982). Negotiation-based resolution of conflicts is discussed in Robinson (1990), Easterbrook (1994) and Boehm *et al.* (1995).

Good introductions to software risk management can be found in Boehm (1989), Charette (1989) and Jones (1994) or in introductory textbooks on software engineering such as Blum (1992). The May/June 1997 issue of *IEEE Software* magazine has a good selection of papers on the topic. A more dedicated literature is available for specific types of risks such as safety risks (Jaffe *et al.*, 1991; Leveson, 1995) or security risks (Amoroso, 1994; Anderson, 2001; Viega & McGraw, 2001). In particular, fault trees, guidewords and safety checklists are thoroughly covered in Leveson (1995). Threat trees are discussed in greater depth in Schneier (2000) under the name of attack trees. The principle of runtime monitoring of risks in order to shift to better design alternatives at system runtime was first introduced in Fickas and Feather (1995) and studied further in Feather *et al.* (1998). Several RE methodologies integrate risk analysis as a significant phase of the RE process (Anton & Potts, 1998; van Lamsweerde & Letier, 1998; Leveson, 2002). Risks are explicitly handled as conditions causing the loss of attainment of corresponding objectives in van Lamsweerde and Letier (2000) and Feather *et al.* (2005). Formal and heuristic techniques for the identification and control of such risks, called *obstacles* to goal satisfaction, are described in van Lamsweerde and Letier (2000).

The use of a weighted matrix for evaluating alternative options is illustrated in Lejk and Deeks (2002). A more systematic treatment of multicriteria analysis can be found in Vincke (1992). Qualitative techniques for evaluating RE options are further discussed in Chung *et al.* (2000) and Mylopoulos *et al.* (2001).

More details on the value–cost prioritization of requirements and the Analytic Hierarchy Process will be found in Karlsson and Ryan (1997) and Saati (1980).

Exercises

- Find the boundary condition that makes the following two requirements strongly conflicting in an ambulance despatching system. (Patient's viewpoint:) 'The free ambulance nearest to the incident scene should be despatched'; (driver's viewpoint:) 'Ambulances should keep close to their station'. Explore alternative resolutions for this divergence using the resolution-generation operators from Section 3.1.

- Find the boundary condition that makes the two following driving rules, enforced by the State of California, strongly conflicting: (a) 'Drivers may not exceed the speed limit of 55 m.p.h.' and (b) 'Drivers may not slow down traffic'. Explore alternative resolutions for this divergence using the resolution-generation operators from Section 3.1.

- Consider a Web-based hotel reservation system in which the full deposit is kept in case of late cancellation (regardless of whether the room is eventually occupied or not). Do a rational rederivation of this countermeasure following the risk *Identification–Assessment–Control* cycle discussed in Section 3.2. Estimate the risk-reduction leverage for this countermeasure and compare it with the one associated with alternative countermeasures of your choice.

- Identify safety hazards as potential failures in the following simplified version of a patient monitoring system. For each of them, build a fault tree, together with its cut-set tree, showing how those failures can be caused from basic events.

    Each patient in the emergency service of Wonderland City Hospital is monitored by an analog device that measures factors such as pulse, temperature, blood pressure and skin resistance. The software monitors these factors on a periodic basis, customized to each patient, and keeps them in a database for patient history tracking. For each patient, safe ranges are specified for each factor. If a factor falls outside of a patient's safe range, the nurse's station is notified.

- Build a security threat tree for the risk of denial of service incurred by your favourite e-mail server. Compute the cut set of this tree.

- Perform a DDP-style risk analysis for the meeting scheduling case study described in Section 1.1.2.

- Build a weighted matrix for evaluating the following alternative options in the library management case study: (a) keep the current journal subscription system where journals relevant to one department are subscribed to on the department's budget and journal issues are mailed to the department; (b) shift to an e-subscription system where the university subscribes to electronic versions of all journals relevant to all departments and journal issues are electronically available to all members of the university.

- Consider the case study description for the library management system in Section 1.1.2. Extract five requirements that might need to be prioritized in view of resource limitations. Perform a cost–value prioritization using the AHP process.

4

Requirements Specification and Documentation

Following the spiral model of the RE process introduced in Chapter 1, we reach the phase where the results of the elicitation and evaluation phases need to be precisely specified and documented (see Figure 1.6). This phase is generally intertwined with the previous ones; it may start as soon as some elicited material has been evaluated and agreed.

The *input* of the specification and documentation phase is a bunch of agreed statements of different types: general objectives, system requirements, software requirements, environmental assumptions, relevant domain properties and concept definitions (see Section 1.1.4). These statements refer to the system-to-be; some of the domain properties and definitions may arise from the system-as-is.

The *output* of the specification and documentation phase is the first version of the requirements document (RD). As we saw in Chapter 1, the RD provides a precise *specification* of all those statements, organized according to some coherent structure, so as to meet the various qualities defined in Section 1.1.7.

- The structure of the RD should make it easy to understand it, retrieve and analyze its items, follow dependency links, trace items back to their rationale and make appropriate changes.

- Each RD statement should be precisely specified in an appropriate *specification language*. This language should support communication with stakeholders and software engineers. Parts of it should ideally be amenable to analysis by software tools for specification validation and verification in the next phase of the RE process (see Chapter 5).

This chapter reviews the wide range of techniques that we may use for requirements specification and documentation, from informal to semi-formal to formal.

The semi-formal and formal techniques will provide a basis for the techniques detailed in Parts II and III, respectively. The focus here is on the notations and constructs that we can use in the specification process, whereas in the next parts of the book we will see how we can use these to build and analyse useful models for RE.

4.1 Free documentation in unrestricted natural language

The first obvious option is to document all the agreed statements through prose in natural language. This practice has several advantages. There are no limitations in expressiveness on what we can specify in natural language. There is no communication barrier either; free text in natural language can be understood by all parties. No special training is required.

On the downside, unstructured prose in natural language is prone to several of the defect types discussed in Section 1.1.7 (see Table 1.1), notably ambiguities, noises, forward references, remorse, unmeasurable statements and opacity.

Ambiguities are inherent to natural language. They can be especially harmful as different parties may interpret the same sentence in different ways. Consider the following sentence that might be produced in our train control case study:

> 'Full braking shall be activated by any train that receives an outdated acceleration command or that enters a station block at a speed higher than X m.p.h. and to which the preceding train is closer than Y metres.'

This safety-critical requirement might be interpreted in two ways. In the case of a train entering a station block too fast:

- The first interpretation requires full braking to be activated when an outdated command is received *or* when the preceding train is too close.

- The second interpretation requires full braking only in the case where the preceding train is too close.

Whatever the right interpretation might be, taking the wrong one is clearly harmful in this example.

There are other frequent problems with poor use of natural language, notably confusion between the '*and*' and '*or*' connectives. A frequent mistake arises in case analysis situations where people write:

If Case1 **then** <Statement1>
or if Case2 **then** <Statement2>   (F1)

instead of:

If Case1 **then** <Statement1>
***and* if** Case2 **then** <Statement2>   (F2)

Assuming that the two cases do not overlap and cover all possible cases, we can easily see that formulation (F1) does not require anything as it reduces to universal truth. By standard manipulations in propositional logic, formulation (F1) reduces to

(not Case1 **or** Statement1) **or** (**not** Case2 **or** Statement2), that is,

> **not** (Case1 **and** Case2) **or** Statement1 **or** Statement2,

that is,

> **not false or** Statement1 **or** Statement2, that is, **true or** Statement1 **or** Statement2,

which reduces to **true**. Similar manipulations show that formulation (F2) is what we want as it amounts to:

> (Case1 **and** Statement1) **or** (Case2 **and** Statement2).

In addition to such problems with natural language, there are problems with unstructured prose. Forward references and remorse are frequent. Specific information is hard to localize. There is no guidance for organizing the requirements document. Last but not least, the absence of formalization precludes any form of automated analysis.

4.2 Disciplined documentation in structured natural language

To overcome the problems with free documentation in unrestricted natural language, we may follow *local* rules on how statements should be written in natural language, and *global* rules on how the requirements document should be organized.

4.2.1 Local rules on writing statements

A more disciplined use of natural language may rely on stylistic rules for technical writing, decision tables for complex combinations of *if–then* conditions and predefined statement templates.

Using stylistic rules for natural language specification

Standard principles of technical writing may be adapted to the context of writing a requirements document. Here are some helpful ones:

- Identify who will read this and write accordingly.
- Say what you are going to do before doing it.
- Motivate first, summarize after.
- Make sure that every concept is defined before its use.
- Keep asking yourself questions such as: *Is this comprehensible to my reader? Can he or she get lost at this point? Is this the appropriate level of detail? Is this relevant, here or elsewhere? Is this enough for that? Can it be interpreted in different ways? Can it be expressed in a simpler way?*

- Never include more than one requirement, assumption or domain property in a single sentence.

- Keep sentences short.

- Use '*shall*' for prescriptive statements that are mandatory and '*should*' for desirable ones.

- Avoid unnecessary jargon and acronyms.

- Use suggestive examples to clarify abstract statements.

- Use bulleted lists for explaining related items that detail a preceding statement.

- Annotate text with diagrams to express complex relationships among items.

- Introduce figures to provide visual overviews and emphasize key points.

- Use tables to collect related facts.

- Use equations to relate quantitative information.

- Avoid complex combinations of conditions with nested or ambiguously associated conditions.

Using decision tables for complex combinations of conditions

Decision tables are a standard technique for structuring complex *if–then* conditions (Pollack & Hicks, 1971). Consider the ambiguous natural language requirement about train braking introduced in Section 4.1, for example. The following decision table may be used instead:

(input conditions)	Train receives outdated acceleration command	T	T	T	T	F	F	F	F
	Train enters station block at speed $\geq X$ mph	T	T	F	F	T	T	F	F
	Preceding train is closer than Y metres	T	F	T	F	T	F	T	F
(output conditions)	Full braking activated	X		X		X			
	Alarm generated to station computer	X	X	X	X				

The upper and lower parts of a decision table are associated with atomic input and output conditions, respectively. The upper part of columns is filled in with truth values (*T* or *F*) for the corresponding input conditions; the filling is made systematic through binary decomposition of groups of adjacent cells. The lower part of the table indicates which output conditions must hold in the corresponding case. Cases are combined through conjunction down a column and disjunction across columns.

In general, the table can be reduced through two kinds of simplification:

- A column has to be eliminated when the AND combination of its input conditions turns out to be impossible in view of known domain properties.

- Two columns may be merged when their input conditions result in the same combination of output conditions. For example, the first and third columns above may be merged, with the truth value for the second input condition becoming '–', meaning 'T or F'.

In addition to ambiguity reduction, decision tables provide other benefits:

- The tables can be checked for completeness and redundancy. We can easily detect missing or redundant cases just by counting columns before the table is simplified and reduced. Assuming N input conditions, there are missing cases if the number of columns with truth values is less than 2^N. Detecting such incompleteness at specification time is obviously beneficial. If this number is greater than 2^N, there are redundant cases. (We will come back to this in Section 5.1.)

- Decision tables provide acceptance test data almost for free. Each column defines a class of input–output test data. Selecting representatives for each such class ensures a satisfactory coverage criterion known as *cause–effect* coverage in the literature on black-box testing (Myers, 1979).

Using predefined statement templates

Templates may be helpful for presenting various types of statements in standardized form and for managing their traceability. A statement template provides named fields such as the following:

- Statement *identifier* for unique reference throughout the RD; it might be a suggestive name or a hierarchically numbered identifier to express the decomposition of statement S_i into statements S_{ij}.

- Statement *category*, to make it clear whether the statement is a functional requirement, a quality requirement, an assumption, a domain property, a definition, a scenario and so forth.

- *Specification* of the statement itself, written according to the preceding stylistic rules.

- *Fit criterion* according to which analysts, developers, testers and users can determine whether the statement is satisfactorily satisfied in the system-to-be.

- *Source* from which the statement was elicited (e.g. a stakeholder or report), for statement traceability (see Section 6.3).

- *Rationale* of the statement, for better understanding and traceability (see Section 6.3).

- Positive or negative *interaction* with other statements (see Section 3.1.3).

- *Priority* level, for comparison with other statements and prioritization (see Section 3.4).

- *Stability* and/or *commonality* levels, for change management (see Section 6.2).

Complementing some statements with a fit criterion ensures that they are measurable (Robertson & Robertson, 1999). The importance of making requirements, assumptions and domain properties measurable was introduced in Section 1.1.7. A *fit criterion* associated with a statement quantifies the extent to which this statement must be satisfied. It is often associated with non-functional requirements but can complement other types of statements as well. A fit criterion can be used for assessing alternative options against it, and for checking whether the associated statement is adequately satisfied by the implementation. Here are a few examples for our running case studies:

Specification:	The bibliographical search facility shall deliver prompt responses to queries.
Fit criterion:	Responses to bibliographical queries should take less than 2 seconds in 90% of cases and no more than 5 seconds in other cases.
Specification:	Information displays inside trains shall be informative and easy to understand.
Fit criterion:	A survey after 3 months of use should reveal that at least 75% of travellers experienced in-train information displays as helpful for finding their connection.
Specification:	The scheduled meeting dates shall be convenient to invited participants.
Fit criterion:	Scheduled dates should fit the diary constraints of at least 90% of invited participants in at least 80% of cases.
Specification:	The meeting scheduling system shall be easy for secretaries to learn.
Fit criterion:	X% of secretaries shall successfully complete a meeting organization after a Y-day training.

4.2.2 Global rules on organizing the requirements document

In addition to the preceding rules constraining the use of natural language, we may also follow more global rules that constrain the organization of the requirements document (RD). These include rules for grouping related items and global templates for standardizing the RD structure.

Grouping rules

For greater document cohesion, RD items that directly relate to a common factor should be grouped within the same section (Davis, 1993). A common factor might be, for example:

- a system objective

- a conceptual object

- a task

- a subsystem

- a system component

- an environmental condition

- a software feature

Requirements document templates

Templates may also be used for imposing a standard structure on RDs. Figure 4.1 shows a well-known example of such a template (IEEE, 1998).

```
1. Introduction

    1.1 Purpose of the requirements document

    1.2 Scope of the product

    1.3 Definitions, acronyms and abbreviations

    1.4 References

    1.5 Overview of the remainder of the document

2. General description

    2.1 Product perspective

    2.2 Product functions

    2.3 User characteristics

    2.4 General constraints

    2.5 Assumptions and dependencies

    2.6 Apportioning of requirements

3. Specific requirements

    3.1 Functional requirements

    3.2 External interface requirements

    3.3 Performance requirements

    3.4 Design constraints

    3.5 Software quality attributes

    3.6 Other requirements

    Appendices

    Index
```

Figure 4.1 *The IEEE Std-830 standard template for organizing a requirements document*

To build a requirements document according to the IEEE Std-830 template, we first need to write an *Introduction* to the document (Section 1.1 and Section 1.5) and to the system-to-be: its domain, scope and purpose (Section 1.2). We need to make the terminology precise and define all domain-specific concepts (Section 1.3). The elicitation sources have to be listed as well (Section 1.4).

In the *General description* part, the relationship of the software-to-be to its environment has to be specified in terms of interfaces and modes of interaction with users, devices and other software (Section 2.1). Then we need to overview the expected functionalities of the software-to-be (Section 2.2). The assumptions about expected software users must be made explicit, for example in terms of experience and expertise (Section 2.3). The next section must overview constraints that will restrict development options, such as hardware limitations, implementation platform, critical concerns, regulations and the like (Section 2.4). Then we need to document environmental factors that might affect the requirements if they change (Section 2.5). This *General description* part ends by identifying which requirements are optional and might be delayed until future versions (Section 2.6).

Next comes the core of the RD; all requirements are to be detailed there (Section 3). The IEEE Std-830 standard provides alternative templates for this section. The specifier may select the one felt most appropriate for the domain and type of system. Figure 4.1 shows one of those. Note the structuring in terms of functional requirements (Section 3.1) and various categories of non-functional requirements (Section 3.2 - Section 3.6); see Figure 1.5 in Chapter 1. The last section gathers quality requirements related to security, availability, reliability and maintainability (Section 3.6).

Numerous similar templates are used by practitioners. They are usually specific to companies, government agencies (e.g. MIL-STD-498) or international organizations (e.g. NASA's SMAP-DID-P200-SW or ESA's PSS-05).

The VOLERE documentation template is another variant of the IEEE Std-830 structure for organizing requirements documents (Robertson & Robertson, 1999). It makes an explicit distinction between users, clients and other stakeholders. It also proposes additional sections for other relevant RD items such as:

- domain properties (called 'facts')

- costs

- risks

- development work plan

- procedures for moving from the *system-as-is* to the *system-to-be*

The combined use of strict rules on natural language usage and RD organization addresses some of the problems with free documentation in unrestricted natural language while preserving expressive power and high accessibility. Ambiguities and noise may be reduced. Fit criteria increase measureability. A predefined RD structure provides some guidance in writing the documentation and ensures document standardization. It also makes it easier to localize specific RD items. However, the absence of formalized information still precludes any form of automated analysis.

4.3 Use of diagrammatic notations

As a substitute to natural language prose or to complement it, we may document specific system aspects in the RD using a semi-formal specification language. *Semi-formal* means that the items under consideration and their inter-relationships are declared formally, whereas the statements that describe or prescribe their properties are informally specified in natural language. *Formal* means 'in some machine-processable form', thanks to a well-defined language syntax and semantics. The declaration sub-language is generally graphical, for easier communication with stakeholders, but formal, for surface-level analysis by automated tools. In the same way as compilers can detect variables that are used but not declared, such tools can pinpoint specification items that are used but not declared.

This section reviews a sample of semi-formal notations that we can use for documenting specific aspects of the system-to-be in the RD. Among the myriad diagrammatic notations found in the software engineering literature, the ones presented here have been selected for several reasons: they support abstractions that are relevant to RE; they cover complementary aspects to be documented in the RD; they are fairly standard and widely used; and a significant portion of them is standardized in the UML subset that we will further study in Part II of the book.

The aim here is to introduce and compare specification notations and constructs. The next parts of the book will show how we can use these effectively to construct and analyse useful models for RE in a systematic, goal-oriented way. The presentation hereafter is structured according to the complementary aspects that the notations capture.

4.3.1 System scope: context, problem and frame diagrams

The first type of diagram allows us to delimit the problem world by declaring its components and their shared phenomena (see Section 1.1.1). We can also annotate components with natural language specifications of requirements that constrain them or refer to them.

The components may include business units or people playing specific roles, physical devices including sensors and actuators, software components, data repositories, communication infrastructures and so forth. The phenomena at their interface can be events, messages, transmitted data and the like. They are *controlled* by some component and *monitored* by others.

Context diagrams

As shown in Figure 4.2, a *context diagram* is a simple graph where nodes represent system components and edges represent connections through shared phenomena declared by the labels (DeMarco, 1978; Jackson, 2001). For example, the Initiator component in Figure 4.2 controls the meetingRequest event, whereas the Scheduler component monitors it; the Scheduler component controls the constraintsRequest event, whereas the Participant component controls the constraintsSent event.

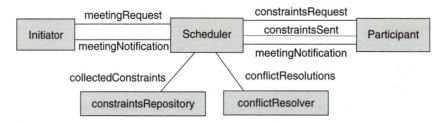

Figure 4.2 *Context diagram for the meeting scheduling system*

A component in general does not interact with all other components. A context diagram provides a simple visualization of the direct environment of each component; that is, the set of 'neighbour' components with which it interacts, together with their respective interfaces.

Problem diagrams

A context diagram can be further detailed by indicating explicitly which component controls a shared phenomenon, which component constitutes the machine we need to build, and which components are affected by which requirements. The resulting diagram is called a *problem diagram* (Jackson, 2001).

Figure 4.3 shows a problem diagram excerpt for the meeting scheduling system. A rectangle with a double vertical stripe represents the machine we need to build. A rectangle with a single stripe represents a component to be designed. An interface can be declared separately; the exclamation mark after a component name prefixing a declaration indicates that this component controls the phenomena in the declared set. For example, the *f* label declaration in Figure 4.3 states that the *Scheduler* machine controls the phenomena *determineDate* and *determineLocation*.

A dashed oval represents a requirement. It may be connected to a component through a dashed line, to indicate that the requirement *refers* to it, or by a dashed arrow, to indicate that the requirement *constrains* it. Such connections may be labelled as well to indicate which corresponding phenomena are referenced or constrained by the requirement. For example, the

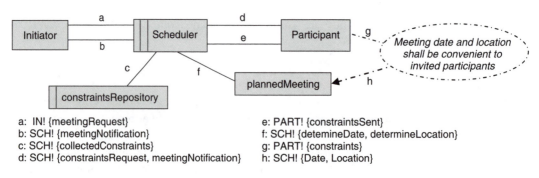

a: IN! {meetingRequest}
b: SCH! {meetingNotification}
c: SCH! {collectedConstraints}
d: SCH! {constraintsRequest, meetingNotification}

e: PART! {constraintsSent}
f: SCH! {detemineDate, determineLocation}
g: PART! {constraints}
h: SCH! {Date, Location}

Figure 4.3 *Problem diagram for the meeting scheduling system*

h label declaration in Figure 4.3 indicates that the requirement appearing there constrains the phenomena *Date* and *Location* controlled by the *Scheduler* machine.

Frame diagrams

Instead of writing problem diagrams from scratch for every problem world we need to delimit, we might predefine a number of frequent problem patterns. A specific problem diagram can then be obtained in matching situations by instantiating the corresponding pattern (Jackson, 2001). This is another illustration of the knowledge reuse technique discussed in Section 2.2.7.

A *frame diagram* is a generic problem diagram capturing such a problem pattern (called a *frame*). The interface labels are now typed parameters; they are prefixed by 'C', 'E' or 'Y', depending on whether they are to be instantiated to causal, event or sympbolic phenomena, respectively. A generic component in a frame diagram can be further annotated by its type:

- A *causal* component, marked by a 'C', has some internal causality that can be enforced, e.g. it reacts predictably in response to external stimuli. A machine component is intrinsically causal.

- A *biddable* component, marked by a 'B', has no such enforceable causality, e.g. it consists of people.

- A *lexical* component, marked by an 'X', is a symbolic representation of data.

The upper part of Figure 4.4 shows two frame diagrams. The one on the left-hand side represents the *Simple Workpieces* frame. It captures a problem class where the machine is a tool allowing a user to generate information that can be analysed and used for other purposes. The frame diagram on the right-hand side represents the *Information Display* frame. It captures a problem class where the machine must present information in a required form to environment components. The frame diagram specifies that the InformationMachine component monitors a causal phenomenon *C1* from the RealWorld component and produces an event phenomenon *E2* for a Display component as a result. The requirement constraining the latter component is a generic accuracy requirement, as indicated by the ' ~' symbol; it prescribes that the information displayed should accurately reflect a causal phenomenon *C3* from the RealWorld component. (Accuracy requirements were introduced in Section 1.1.5.)

The lower part of Figure 4.4 shows corresponding frame instantiations yielding problem diagrams. The phenomenon instantiations, compatible with the corresponding parameter type, are shown on the bottom. The component instantiations, compatible with the corresponding component type, are annotated with the name of the generic component to indicate their role in the frame instantiation. For example, the instantiated right-hand side requirement states that the notified meeting date and location must be the one determined by the Scheduler component.

Other frames can be similarly defined and instantiated, for example for problems where the environment behaviours must be controlled by the machine in accordance with commands issued by an operator, or for problems where the machine must transform intput data into output data (Jackson, 2001).

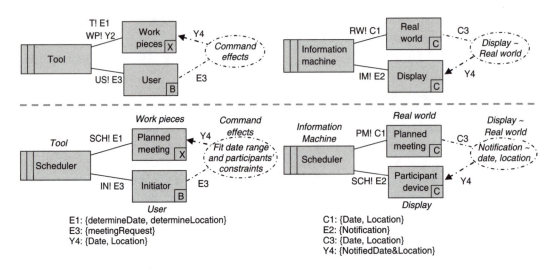

E1: {determineDate, determineLocation}
E3: {meetingRequest}
Y4: {Date, Location}

C1: {Date, Location}
E2: {Notification}
C3: {Date, Location}
Y4: {NotifiedDate&Location}

Figure 4.4 *Frame diagrams and their instantiation*

Context and problem diagrams provide a simple, convenient notation for delimiting the scope of the system-to-be in terms of components relevant to the problem world and their static interconnections. There is a price to pay for such simplicity. The properties of the interaction among pairs of components are not made precise. The granularity of components and the criteria for a component to appear in a diagram are not very clear either. For example, a Network component might be part of the problem world of scheduling meetings involving participants who are geographically distributed. According to which precise criteria should this component appear or not in Figure 4.3? Problem diagrams may also become clumsy for large sets of requirements. How do we compose or decompose them? What properties must be preserved under composition or decomposition? Chapter 11 will come back to those issues. A more precise semantics will be given for components and connections, providing criteria for identifying and refining components and interconnections. We will also see there how the useful view offered by context and problem diagrams can be derived systematically from goal diagrams.

4.3.2 Conceptual structures: entity–relationship diagrams

The *system-as-is* and *system-to-be* involve conceptual items that are generally structured from finer items and inter-related with each other. Entity–relationship diagrams (ER) are a classical notation for declaring conceptual items and their structural properties (Chen, 1976). Numerous variants and extensions of ER diagrams have been proposed over the years, culminating in the class diagram notation found in the UML standard (Rumbaugh *et al.*, 1999). This section introduces a basic form of ER diagram suitable for RE. Chapter 10 will detail techniques for building such diagrams systematically.

An *ER diagram* is made from three core constructs: entities, attributes and relationships.

Entities

An *entity* is a class of concept instances that have distinct identities and share common features. Such features may be attributes or relationships (as defined below). In an ER diagram, entities are represented by rectangles. For example, the Meeting concept is captured as an entity in Figure 4.5; each Meeting instance has a distinct identity, and like any other instance it is characterized by a *Date*.

An informal but precise *definition* should annotate every entity in a diagram. For example, consider the Participant entity in Figure 4.5 that captures the set of all possible participant instances. We should make it clear what the concept of 'meeting participant' really means, for example:

> Person expected to attend the meeting, at least partially, in a specific role. Appears in the system when the meeting is initiated and disappears when the meeting is no longer relevant to the system.

Attributes

An *attribute* is an intrinsic feature of an entity regardless of other entities. It has a name and a range of values. For example, *Date* appears as an attribute of *Meeting* in Figure 4.5. The Participant entity is characterized by the attributes Name, Address and Email.

Relationships

A *relationship* is a feature that conceptually links several entities together. Each entity plays a specific *role* in the conceptual link. The *arity* of the relationship is the number of entities linked by it. Binary relationships are represented by plain lines labelled by their name. For example, the *Invitation* concept appears as a binary relationship in Figure 4.5; it links *Participant*, playing the role *invitedTo*, and *Meeting*, playing the role *Invites*.

Relationships can be characterized by attributes as well. For example, the constraints a participant may have on meeting dates and locations are captured in Figure 4.5 through the *Constraints* relationship linking the Participant and Meeting entities. This relationship is characterized by two attributes; namely, excludedDates and preferredDates. The range of those attributes might be declared as a set of time intervals (not represented there). In the UML

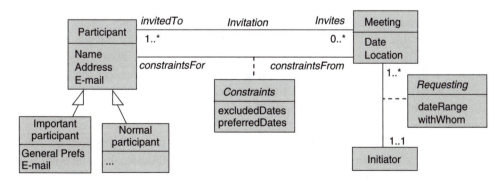

Figure 4.5 *Portion of an entity-relationship diagram for the meeting scheduler*

syntax, the attributes of a relationship are represented inside a rectangle hanging on the relationship.

A *multiplicity* on one side of a relationship specifies the minimum and maximum number of entity instances on this side that may be linked at the same time to a given single subtuple of entity instances on the other sides. For example, the *0..** multiplicity on the Meeting side of the *Invitation* relationship states that a Participant instance may at any time be invited to zero up to an arbitrary number of different meetings. Conversely, a Meeting instance expects at least one participant, as specified by the *1..** multiplicity on the Participant side.

Specialization and inheritance

In the semantic network tradition, entities can be specialized into subclasses (Quillian, 1968; Brodie *et al.*, 1984). Any instance of a subclass must be an instance of the superclass; the subclass then by default inherits all attributes and relationships attached to the superclass. For example, the two arrows in Figure 4.5 specify that the Participant entity is specialized in two subclasses; important participants are distinguished from normal ones. Both subclasses by default inherit the Name, Address and Email attributes of Participant together with the *Invitation* and *Constraints* relationships. The subclasses may be further characterized through distinguishing attributes and relationships; for example, important participants are further characterized in Figure 4.5 by general preferences that they might have regardless of any specific meeting.

Attaching the Email attribute to the ImportantParticipant subclass inhibits the default inheritance of this attribute from the Participant superclass – we might want the contact e-mail for important participants to refer to another person. The general principle is that more specific features override more general ones.

ER diagrams are a simple graphical notation for structuring and relating domain concepts. In comparison with flat lists of definitions found in a glossary of terms, they provide a more structured overview of such concepts. ER diagrams are also more structured than relational tables; specific attribute–value pairs cannot be attached to single tuples in a table. Multiplicities allow simple statement patterns to be formalized. Specialization with inheritance makes it possible to factor out structural commonalities in superclasses, reuse general features in multiple subclasses, and enhance the modifiability of concept documentation by propagating changes in features from superclass to subclasses.

On the downside, multiplicities in ER diagrams do not make the important distinction between requirements and domain descriptions (see Section 1.1.4). Consider, for example, the *Loan* relationship between the Patron and bookCopy entities in our library system. A *0..max* multiplicity on the bookCopy side would capture the *prescriptive* statement that a patron may not borrow more than *max* books at a time, whereas a *0..1* multiplicity on the Patron side would capture the *descriptive* statement that a book cannot physically be borrowed by more than one patron at a time.

The practical difficulty of building adequate ER diagrams for complex applications is another serious problem. Which conceptual items should appear in an ER diagram, which ones should not and why? When a conceptual item is felt necessary, should it be represented as an entity, a relationship or an attribute? What are the criteria for making choices? Chapter 10 will provide comprehensive answers to these questions. The semantics of ER diagrams will be made further precise; heuristics and guidelines will be provided for building adequate ER models systematically from models of the objectives to be accomplished by the system.

4.3.3 Activities and data: SADT diagrams

In the system-as-is or system-to-be, activities take place that process data. SADT diagrams allow these activities and data to be documented in a graphical way (Ross & Schoman, 1977a). SADT stands for 'Structured Analysis and Design Technique'. It provides two kinds of diagrams that are inter-related:

- *Actigrams* declare activities by their input/output data and interconnect them through data dependency links.

- *Datagrams* declare system data by their producing/consuming activities and interconnect them through control dependency links.

- A data–activity duality principle requires actigram items to have some counterpart in a datagram, and vice versa.

The SADT actigram in Figure 4.6 specifies the activity of HandlingConstraints in our meeting scheduling system. The concept of meetingConstraints, appearing as an output there, is specified by the datagram in Figure 4.7.

An *actigram* specifies system activities. The latter can be refined into sub-activities. For example, the HandlingConstraints activity is decomposed in Figure 4.6 into three sub-activities; namely, AskConstraints, ReturnConstraints and MergeConstraints. Each activity may be characterized by four types of labelled arrows: 'west' and 'east' arrows declare input and output data, respectively; 'north' arrows declare data or events that control the activity; 'south' arrows denote system components that process it. For example, the ReturnConstraints sub-activity has constraintRequest as input, individualConstraints as output, dateRange and Deadline as controlling data and Participant as processing component.

In a similar way, *datagrams* specify system data through four types of labelled arrows: 'west' and 'east' arrows declare activities that produce and consume the data, respectively; 'north' arrows declare activities that control data integrity; 'south' arrows denote resources needed for processing the data. For example, the meetingConstraints data in Figure 4.7 have MergeConstraints as producing activity, PlanMeeting as consuming activity, CheckValidity as controlling activity and constraintsRepository as memory support. Datagrams are refinable as well.

Tools can analyse the specifications produced in the SADT graphical language. They check rules of consistency and completeness such as the following:

- The input/output data of an activity must appear as input/output data of sub-activities for the refinement to be consistent (see meetingRequest and meetingConstraints in Figure 4.6).

- Any activity (or data) must have an input and an output (or a producer and a consumer).

- A controlling activity in a datagram must be defined in an actigram.

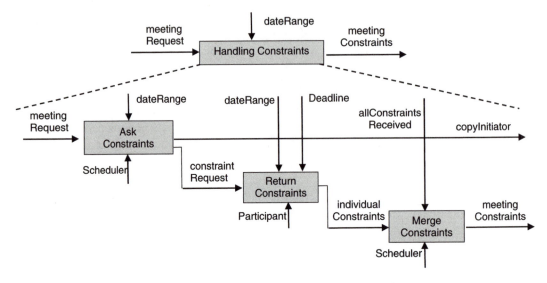

Figure 4.6 *SADT actigram for the meeting scheduler*

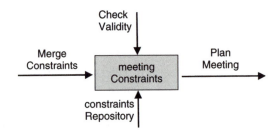

Figure 4.7 *SADT datagram for the meeting scheduler*

These tools would detect that a CheckValidity activity is missing in the refining actigram of Figure 4.6, as the latter rule is violated when checking the diagrams in Figures 4.6 and 4.7.

The SADT specification technique was a precursor of others in many respects. It supports multiple views that are linked through consistency rules. The language is conceptually richer for RE than many of the semi-formal notations that were developed afterwards. In addition to data and activities, it supports some rudimentary representation of events, triggers and responsibility assignments to system components. SADT also supports stepwise refinement of global specifications into more detailed ones – an essential feature for complex specifications.

4.3.4 Information flows: dataflow diagrams

Dataflow diagrams (DFD) are a simpler though less expressive form of actigram. The DFD notation has been popular among practitioners for quite a long time. It was adopted by diagrammatic specification techniques such as *SA* (DeMarco, 1978) and *OMT* (Rumbaugh *et al.*, 1991). The items we can specify with DFDs are operations in the system-as-is or system-to-be, together with their data dependencies:

- DFD operations are activities that transform data. They are declared and linked together through their respective input/output data flows.

- The origin and termination of a flow can be specified as a system component or a data repository in which operations can put or get data.

- The rules according to which an operation transforms input data into output data are specified either by another DFD refining the operation or by an annotation in free or structured natural language.

Figure 4.8 shows a DFD diagram for the meeting scheduling system-to-be. Some of the constraint-handling operations there correspond to those introduced with the same name in Figure 4.6.

Bubbles in a DFD represent operations that are processed by an implicit system component associated with the DFD (here, the scheduler). The arrows capture the incoming/outgoing flows of the data labelling them. Boxes denote system components originating or terminating a flow. Double bars denote data repositories.

The semantics of a bubble with incoming and outgoing arrows is simply that the operation needs the data flowing in to produce the data flowing out. There is no control flow implied by this; DFD diagrams capture data dependencies among operations without prescribing any ordering of events or sequencing of operations. Making DFD specifications executable requires a precise operational semantics for the dataflow language, including rules for firing and synchronizing data transformations within the same operation and among different operations. It also requires an executable formalization of the informal rules for transforming input data into output data.

The simplicity of DFD diagrams explains their popularity for the communication and documentation of operational aspects of the system in a structured, summarized way. DFD tools can check the graphical declarations against some forms of consistency and completeness – in much the same way as SADT tools or static semantics checkers in compilers. The price to pay

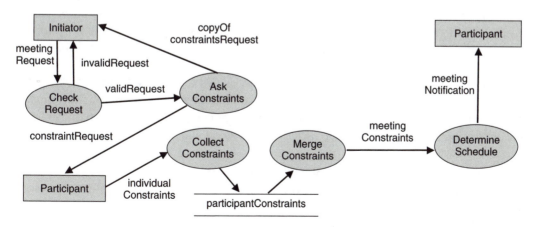

Figure 4.8 *Dataflow diagram refining the operation "schedule meeting"*

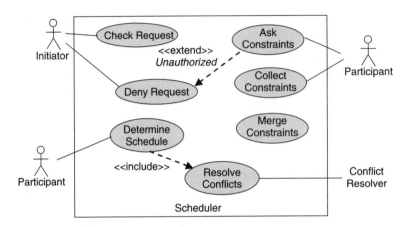

Figure 4.9 *Use case diagram for the meeting scheduler*

for simplicity is of course the limitation in which requirements-related aspects we can really capture and analyse automatically. We come back to this in Section 4.3.10.

4.3.5 System operations: use case diagrams

Further simplicity can be achieved by further sacrificing precision. A *use case diagram* collects all the operations that an active system component has to perform within a rectangle associated with it (Rumbaugh *et al.*, 1999). For each operation interacting in one way or another with another system component, a line between the operation and this component is drawn to capture the interaction. The active system components are called *actors*. Those marked with a 'fellow' icon represent environment components. For example, the AskConstraints operation in the use case diagram for the software actor named Scheduler in Figure 4.9 interacts with the environment actor named Participant. The actor ConflictResolver is another component of the software-to-be that interacts with the scheduler's ResolveConflicts operation.

An operation may *include* finer-grained ones. For example, ResolveConflicts is a 'sub-operation' of DetermineSchedule. We can thereby factor out common sub-operations of multiple operations. An *extend* link associates a 'variant' operation with a normal one; the variant is to be applied in some exceptional situation characterized by a condition name labelling the link. For example, DenyRequest is an alternative course of action to be taken, instead of asking participants for their constraints, when the condition named *Unauthorized* holds.

Use case diagrams provide a simple functional outline of the system-to-be. They are fairly vague though. Operations and components are just captured by their name; what interactions consist of is unclear; the semantics of 'include' and 'extend' links is not very clear either.

4.3.6 Interaction scenarios: event trace diagrams

To complement the outline view provided by a use case diagram and bring more precision, we may provide an event trace diagram that details what bubbles and interaction lines convey. Such a diagram shows typical interaction sequences among the interacting components. Section 2.2.5 introduced scenarios as interaction sequences among components and discussed the role of scenarios for explaining the system-as-is and exploring the system-to-be. Positive/negative scenarios provide examples and counter-examples of desired behaviour; normal/abnormal scenarios illustrate normal/abnormal course of interaction.

Event trace diagrams (ET) are an easy-to-use notation for specifying positive scenarios. Numerous variants and extensions have been proposed over the years, notably the *message sequence charts* (MSCs) used as a standard notation in the telecommunications industry (ITU, 1996) and *sequence diagrams* found in the UML standards (Rumbaugh *et al.*, 1999). ET diagram here, and will come back to the UML notation in Chapter 13.

An *ET diagram* represents a parallel composition of timelines. Each timeline is associated with the behaviour of a component instance in the scenario. It is represented by a vertical line labelled by the name of the corresponding component; time progresses down the line. Horizontal arrows represent directed interactions between component instances. Each arrow is labelled by an interaction event. The event is controlled by the source component instance and monitored by the target component instance. Attributes may be attached to an event to capture information transmission during interaction from source to target.

An interaction event is synchronously controlled by the source and monitored by the target. An ET timeline defines a total order on incoming/outgoing events according to event precedence. An entire ET diagram defines a partial order on all events; events along non-interacting timelines are not comparable according to precedence.

Figure 4.10 shows an ET diagram specifying a meeting scheduling scenario. (This scenario was introduced in Section 2.2.5 as an informal narrative.) The first event in the temporal sequence of interactions is *meetingRequest*, controlled by an Initiator instance and monitored by a Scheduler instance. To allow for transmission of the information required for organizing the meeting, the *meetingRequest* event carries two attributes: dateRange and withWhom. The event named *?constraints* captures the interaction where the Scheduler instance asks a Participant instance for his or her constraints within a dateRange. The two *notification* events, with attributes date and location, are simultaneously produced by the Scheduler for synchronous consumption by the corresponding targets.

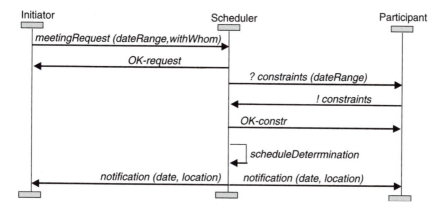

Figure 4.10   *A normal scenario for scheduling a meeting*

The MSC and UML variants of ET diagrams have more sophisticated features. The limited form considered here is simple enough to be used by scenario specifiers and to be understood by stakeholders. As in the case of the other semi-formal notations reviewed in this section, we need to annotate the diagrams with informal statements to provide full details on the scenarios.

ET diagrams provide a natural, straightforward way of declaring scenarios. The strengths and limitations of ET scenarios are those discussed in Section 2.2.5.

4.3.7 System behaviours: state machine diagrams

ET diagrams can represent the dynamics of system components but only very partially. An ET timeline specifies a particular behaviour of a specific component instance along a partial sequence of interactions. For example, the ET diagram in Figure 4.10 does not tell us what should happen if the meeting request is invalid. This diagram refers to a specific Participant instance; it does not tell us that the constraints of all Participant instances invited to the meeting should be available before the meeting date is determined, nor what should happen in the case of conflicting constraints among multiple Participant instances. Moreover, state information is left implicit in ET diagrams.

State machine diagrams (SM) are a classic technique for specifying entire sets of behaviours. Numerous variants and extensions of SM diagrams have been proposed in the literature (see the bibliographical notes at the end of this chapter). We introduce a basic form of SM diagram here; SM models will be further discussed in Chapter 5, in the context of model checking and animation, and in Chapter 13, in the context of goal-oriented modelling of system behaviours.

An SM diagram represents the admissible behaviours of an arbitrary instance of some component of the system-as-is or system-to-be. A *behaviour* is captured by a sequence of state transitions for the system items that the component controls. State transitions result from the occurrence of events. Figure 4.11 shows an SM diagram specifying the admissible behaviours of a meeting scheduler in terms of possible state transitions for a meeting that it controls.

Graphically, a SM diagram looks like a directed graph where nodes represent states and arrows represent transitions. Nodes are labelled by state names, whereas transitions are labelled by event names. The graph is a pictorial view of the *transition relation* defining possible state transitions for a controlled item. This relation maps pairs (*state, event*) to successor states. It is a function in a case of deterministic behaviour; the same pair then cannot be mapped to multiple successor states. The semantics of a single transition from state $s1$ to state $s2$, labelled by event ev, is the following:

if the controlled item is in state $s1$ and event ev occurs **then** this item moves to state $s2$.

States

A SM *state* captures the set of all situations where some variable characterizing the controlled item always has the same value regardless of other characterizing variables, whose values may differ from one situation in this set to the other. These variables may correspond to attributes or relationships controlled by the component and declared in an associated entity–relationship diagram. For example, the state *MeetingScheduled* in Figure 4.11 corresponds to the set of all situations where the meeting has a determined value for its attributes *Date* and *Location* (see Figure 4.5), regardless of other characterizing variables, such as who is invited to that meeting. Similarly, the state *doorsOpen* for a train controlled by a train controller corresponds to the set of all situations where the controlled attribute DoorsState has the value 'open' regardless of other train attributes such as Speed, which might be '0 m.p.h.' in one situation of this set and '30 m.p.h.' in another.

Two particular states can be introduced in an SM diagram. The initial state, represented by a black circle in Figure 4.11, corresponds to the state of the controlled item when it appears in the system. Symmetrically, the final state, represented by a bull's eye in Figure 4.11, corresponds to the state of the controlled item when it disappears from the system.

Transitions and guards

An SM *transition* captures a state change caused by the occurrence of an associated event. As opposed to states that have some duration, events are instantaneous phenomena. They may correspond to external stimuli from the component's environment (e.g. the meetingRe- quest event in Figure 4.11) or to applications of some operation by the component. For example, the scheduleDetermination event in Figure 4.11 corresponds to an application of the determineSchedule operation in Figure 4.9.

A transition may be *guarded* by some condition, represented by a condition name or an expression enclosed in brackets. For example, the guard [All available] in Figure 4.11 expresses that all participant constraints are available. A guarded transition to a target state fires *if* the associated event occurs while the controlled item is in the source state and *only if* the guard condition is true. The event thus has no effect if the guard is false. Note that event occurrence is a *sufficient* condition for transition firing, whereas a guard is a *necessary* condition for firing.

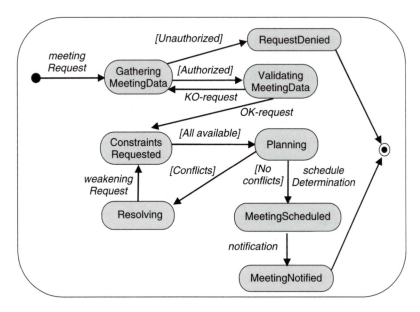

Figure 4.11 *State machine diagram for a meeting controlled by the meeting scheduler*

A transition without an event label fires automatically. A guarded, label-free transition is thus fired as soon as the guard condition becomes true.

Traces and scenario generalization

An SM *trace* is a sequence of successive states in the SM diagram up to some point. For example,

    <GatheringMeetingData; RequestDenied>

and

    <GatheringMeetingData; ValidatingMeetingData; GatheringMeetingData; ValidatingMeetingData; ConstraintsRequested>

are two traces in the SM diagram shown in Figure 4.11. An SM diagram may have infinitely many traces, whereas a trace by definition is always finite.

If we annotate the Scheduler timeline in the scenario of Figure 4.10 with explicit state information about the meeting it controls, we notice that this timeline corresponds to a trace

    <ValidatingMeetingData; ConstraintsRequested; Planning; MeetingScheduled; MeetingNotified>.

This trace is a subtrace of an SM trace in Figure 4.11. The scenario is *covered* by a path in the SM graph in Figure 4.11. A SM diagram *generalizes* ET diagrams along two dimensions: it refers to any instance of a system component, not just a specific one, and it covers more traces.

Non-deterministic behaviours

As introduced earlier, a non-deterministic behaviour is captured in an SM diagram by multiple outgoing transitions labelled with the same event name. Figure 4.12 illustrates this on part of an SM diagram for a train controlled by our train controller. In many safety-critical and security-critical systems, this kind of source of uncertainty has to be ruled out. Tools can check for deterministic SM behaviour automatically (see Section 5.4).

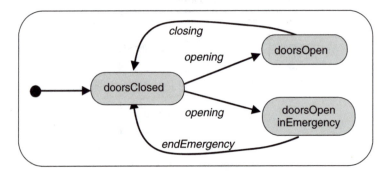

Figure 4.12   *Non-determinstic behaviour in a SM diagram*

Concurrent behaviours and statecharts

In general, a component controls multiple variables that evolve in parallel. For example, our train controller might control the variables *DoorsState* and *MovementState* in parallel. Representing this in a single, monolithic diagram would lead to a combinatorial explosion of states to be represented explicitly. Suppose, in our example, that the possible values for the variable *DoorsState* are 'open', 'openInEmergency' and 'closed', whereas the possible values for the variable MovementState are 'stopped', 'accelerating' and 'decelerating'. Within a single diagram we would in principle need nine states to represent all possible combinations of values. For a component having N variables each having M possible values, we would need M^N states! Moreover, a single SM state would mix up values from different variables.

To represent concurrent behaviours we need to define SM diagrams as parallel compositions of other SM diagrams – typically, one per variable evolving in parallel. Instead of M^N states we only need to represent $M \times N$ states explicitly; the M^N states are still there, but they are kept implicit. We can then also represent real concurrency as it naturally occurs in the system. Extending SM diagrams with concurrent sub-states leads us to the *statechart* notation (Harel, 1987, 1996). Figure 4.13 shows a statechart composed of two parallel SM diagrams. For the sake of simplicity, we assume two possible states in each sub-diagram. The dashed line between the two sub-diagrams captures their parallel composition.

A trace in an SM diagram defined as a parallel composition of other SM diagrams is now a sequence of successive aggregated states up to some point. For example, the following trace is among the traces of the SM diagram in Figure 4.13:

<(doorsClosed, trainStopped); (doorsClosed, trainMoving); (doorsClosed, trainStopped); (doorsOpen, trainStopped)>

When parallel SM diagrams are fully formalized, tools can automatically check desired properties on them and generate counterexample traces in case of property violation (see Sections 4.4.4 and 5.4). The semantics usually taken by tools for concurrency is an *interleaving semantics*; in the case of two transitions being fired in the same state, one is taken after the other according to a non-deterministic choice.

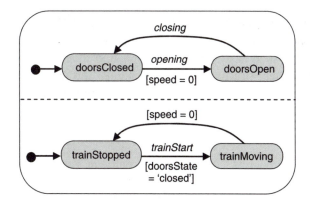

Figure 4.13 *Parallel composition of SM diagrams for* DoorsState *and* MovementState

SM diagrams are frequently used for specifying reactive systems and user interfaces. They provide a convenient notation for specifying the system's dynamics. Identifying the right states and the right level of granularity for states and transitions can, however, be difficult. Another problem is the diversity of semantics of different SM notations – even sometimes of the same notation! For example, labelled transition systems assume that no other event can occur, when a component is in a particular state, than those labelling outgoing transitions; many other SM notations assume that other events can occur, leaving the component in the same state.

In addition to a simple semantics for concurrent behaviours, we need heuristics for identifying the right states and transitions, and techniques for building SM diagrams incrementally and systematically. Chapters 13 and 18 will come back to those issues.

4.3.8 Stimuli and responses: R-net diagrams

It is sometimes desirable to document in a diagram all the required responses to a single stimulus. The R-net notation was introduced for that purpose (Alford, 1977). It makes it easy to visualize answers to *WHAT IF?* questions that stakeholders might ask about external stimuli.

An R-net diagram specifies all the operations that a system component is required to perform, possibly under a particular condition, in response to a particular input stimulus.

Figure 4.14 shows an R-net diagram for the input stimulus of requesting a new meeting to be scheduled. Graphically, an R-net looks like a directed tree where arrows indicate precedence. Non-delimiter nodes can be of three types. The root hexagon represents the input stimulus. Boxes indicate operations needing to be applied as responses to the stimulus. Circles represent decision points, with outgoing arrows labelled by the corresponding condition. Operations may evaluate data or conditions, produce an output, or generate events to be considered as stimuli in R-nets for other components.

Note that the R-net in Figure 4.14 provides another view of the information contained in the upper portion of the state machine in Figure 4.11. The input stimulus corresponds to an incoming event, the application of R-net operations results in successor states in the state machine, and R-net conditions appear as guards on SM transitions. An R-net provides a partial, operational view of a full SM; it focuses on the required responses to one specific input stimulus.

4.3.9 Integrating multiple system views and multiview specification in UML

The semi-formal constructs in this chapter allow a variety of system aspects to be specified in the requirements document, such as system components and their constrained interconnections, domain concepts and their structural links, operations and information flows, interaction scenarios and component behaviours. Each type of diagram is dedicated to a specific *view* of the system.

View integration

For comprehensive and coherent coverage, these different views should be complementary and integrated. *Inter-view consistency rules* are a standard mechanism for integrating diagrams of different types (Rumbaugh *et al.*, 1991; Nuseibeh *et al.*, 1994). They prescribe constraints that the specifier should enforce to ensure view compatibility and complementarity.

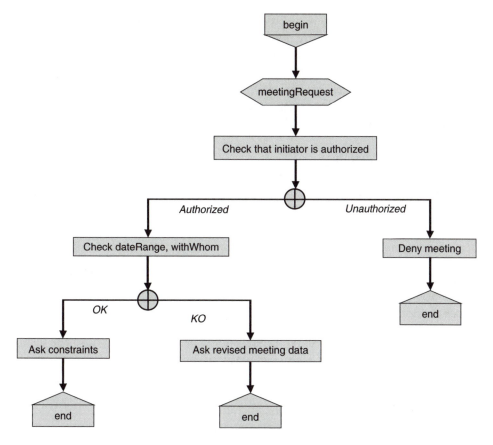

Figure 4.14 *R-net for a meeting request stimulus*

Here is a typical sample of inter-view consistency rules that we might consider for the specification constructs introduced in this section.

Every component and interconnection in a problem diagram must be further specified in an ET diagram.

Every shared phenomenon in a problem diagram must appear as an event in an ET diagram or as an entity, attribute or relationship in an ER diagram.

Every data item in a flow or repository of a DFD diagram must be declared as an entity, attribute or relationship in an ER diagram.

Every state in an SM diagram must correspond to a value for an attribute or relationship in an ER diagram.

Every attribute carried by an interaction event in an ET scenario must be declared in an ER diagram.

Every interaction event in an ET scenario must appear in a corresponding SM diagram.

Events in an SM diagram that are not external stimuli to the component must correspond to operations performed by the component and declared in a DFD diagram.

Such rules may be included in requirements inspection checklists (see Section 5.1.3). They can also be checked automatically by query tools on a multiview specification database (see Section 5.2). They are a specification counterpart of the static semantics checks automated by programming language compilers.

Inter-view consistency rules are also helpful for requirements evolution. They provide explicit constraints that are to be maintained when changes are made to items to which they refer. Section 6.3 will come back to this.

Multiview specification in UML

Among the multiple types of diagrams standardized in the Unified Modeling Language, several are relevant to the RE process:

- *Class diagrams* provide a structural, entity-relationship view of the system.
- *Use case diagrams* are used for outlining an operational view.
- *Sequence diagrams* complement such a view through interaction scenarios.
- *State diagrams* provide a behavioural view through statecharts generalizing the event traces in scenarios.

These different types of diagram will be further studied in Part II of the book. The techniques there will help us build models in a systematic way using UML notations together with other, RE-dedicated ones.

4.3.10 Diagrammatic notations: Strengths and limitations

A semi-formal specification comprises formal and informal parts. The formal part declares different system aspects that we need to take into account and provides a placeholder for descriptive and prescriptive statements about them. These statements are left informal as they are formulated in (structured) natural language. 'Informal' does not mean 'imprecise', of course, and the specifier must strive to avoid the defects discussed in Section 1.1.7.

The formal part of a semi-formal specification is generally expressed in a graphical language. A 'box-and-arrow' style of expression highlights important system aspects by abstracting them from details. It is generally easy to use and easy to communicate to stakeholders. A textual counterpart of graphical specifications may also be considered for analysis and reporting of large-scale specifications (Teichroew & Hershey, 1977).

Semi-formal specifications can be processed by software tools for graphical editing and surface-level analysis. They are then generally maintained in a *requirements database*. This database is structured according to the constructs of the formalism. It can be checked through queries, as we will see in greater detail in Section 5.2. In addition to inter-view queries like those suggested in the preceding section, a query tool may handle intra-view queries to check some form of internal consistency and completeness. An intra-view query might be, for example:

'Is there any SM state other than the final state with no outgoing transition?'

Those benefits of semi-formal notations, combined with recent standardization efforts, explain the growing popularity of some specific subsets of the UML language (Dobing & Parsons, 2006).

On the other hand, semi-formal notations have limitations. By their nature, they allow us to specify surface-level features of RD items without paying too much attention to the properties of such items. For example, what are the invariant properties of an entity or a relationship? What is the precise effect of the application of an operation? What is the precise meaning of an SM state beyond its name and incoming/outgoing event labels? The deep semantics of RD items has to be stated informally, with all the problems incurred by natural language. As a consequence, semi-formal notations are only amenable to fairly limited forms of analysis.

The 'box-and-arrow' semantics of graphical notations often lacks precision. It is therefore easy to use such notations in the wrong way. The same specification can also be interpreted in different ways by different people.

The semi-formal constructs in this chapter address mainly functional and structural aspects. There are other important aspects that we need to consider in a requirements document, notably system objectives, non-functional requirements and assumptions about the environment. Part II of the book will introduce other semi-formal constructs for such aspects, together with a variety of techniques for building semi-formal, multiview system models.

4.4 Formal specification*

A semi-formal specification declares some items of the requirements document (RD) formally, but leaves the descriptive and prescriptive statements about those items informal. Formal specification goes one step further by formalizing such statements as well. The benefits expected from formalization are a higher degree of precision in the formulation of statements, precise rules for their interpretation and much more sophisticated forms of validation and verification than can be automated by tools.

As the collection of statements we may want to specify formally can be large, the formalism in general provides mechanisms for organizing the specification into *units* linked through *structuring relationships*, such as unit instantiation, specialization, import or enrichment. Each unit has a declaration part, where the variables of interest are declared, and an assertion part, where the intended properties of the declared variables are formalized.

This section overviews the main paradigms available for specifying some aspects of the requirements document formally. (Remember that *formal* means 'in some machine-processable form'.) This will provide a basis for some of the specification analysis techniques reviewed in Chapter 5 and for the more advanced requirements analysis techniques studied in Chapters 17–18.

As the various paradigms for formal specification are grounded in logic, we start by briefly reviewing some necessary rudiments of classical logic.

---

* This section is provided here for comprehensive coverage of the topic of this chapter. It may be skipped by fast-track readers only interested in a general overview of RE fundamentals or with no background in rudimentary discrete mathematics. Its material is, however, a prerequisite for Chapters 17–18.

4.4.1 Logic as a basis for formalizing statements

Like any formal system, logic is made up of three components: a syntax, a semantics and a proof theory:

- The *syntax* is a set of rules that defines the grammatically well-formed statements.

- The *semantics* is a set of rules that defines the precise meaning of such statements.

- The *proof theory* is a set of inference rules that allows new statements to be derived from given ones.

Propositional logic

This logical system is the simplest one. It allows us to compose propositions recursively through logical connectives such as $\wedge$ ('and'), $\vee$ ('or'), $\neg$ ('not'), $\rightarrow$ ('implies') and $\leftrightarrow$ ('equivalent to'). For example, we may write a propositional statement such as

trainMoving $\rightarrow$ doorsClosed

where trainMoving and doorsClosed are non-decomposable propositions called proposition symbols.

The *syntax* of propositional logic can be recursively defined by two simple rules over a vocabulary of proposition symbols:

<atomicProposition> ::= **true** | **false** | <propositionSymbol>
<statement> ::=<atomicProposition>| ($\neg$ <statement>)
         |(<statement> $\wedge$ <statement>) | (<statement> $\vee$ <statement>)
         |(<statement> $\rightarrow$ <statement>) |(<statement> $\leftrightarrow$<statement>)

In the preceding rules, '<s>' in the definition meta-language means 'any instance of syntactic category *s*', '::=' is the definition meta-symbol, and '|' denotes an alternative choice.

Semantic rules tell us how to evaluate the meaning of a statement for a given way of interpreting its atomic elements. In propositional logic this is quite simple. An *interpretation* of a set of statements assigns truth values to all their proposition symbols. The meaning of a statement under that interpretation is its truth value.

Let val_I be the interpretation function that assigns truth values T (for *true*) or F (for *false*) to every proposition symbol of a statement under interpretation I. (The truth values T and V in the definition meta-language should not be confused with the symbols **true** and **false** in the defined language, respectively.) Let VAL_I be the semantic evaluation function that returns the truth value of the entire statement under interpretation I. The semantics of propositional logic is recursively defined through the following rules, where $S, S1$ and $S2$ denote arbitrary propositional statements.

VAL_I (**true**) $=$ T, VAL_I (**false**) $= F$, VAL_I (P) $= val_I$ (P) for any propositional symbol P

VAL_I (¬S) $=$ T if VAL_I (S) $= F$

   F if VAL_I (S) $= T$

VAL_I (S1 ∧ S2) $= T$ if VAL_I (S1) $= T$ and VAL_I (S2) $= T$

   F otherwise

VAL_I (S1 ∨ S2) $= T$ if VAL_I (S1) $= T$ or VAL_I (S2) $= T$

   F otherwise

VAL_I (S1 → S2) $= T$ if VAL_I (S1) $= F$ or VAL_I (S2) $= T$

   F otherwise

VAL_I (S1 ↔ S2) $= T$ if VAL_I (S1) $= VAL_I$ (S2)

   F otherwise

For example, consider the preceding statement 'trainMoving → doorsClosed' and an interpretation *I* that assigns the following truth values to its proposition symbols:

val_I (trainMoving) $= F$, val_I (doorsClosed) $= F$.

According to the semantic rule for implications, the propositional semantics of that statement is:

VAL_I (trainMoving → DoorsClosed) $= T$.

The *inference rules* from a proof theory enable us to derive new statements from given ones systematically. For each rule, the given statements are called the *premise* and the new derived statement is called the *conclusion*. A *sound* rule guarantees that the conclusion is true in all the interpretations that make the premise true. To analyse statements or derive their consequences (e.g. for adequacy checking), a tool can perform derivations automatically by repeated application of sound inference rules. No semantic evaluation of the conclusions is then necessary if the initial statements are accepted as being true in the interpretations of interest.

Here are a few sound rules of inference in propositional logic (the upper and lower parts of the rule are the premise and conclusion, respectively):

$$\frac{P \to Q, \; P}{Q} \; modus\ ponens \qquad \frac{P \to Q, \; Q \to R}{P \to R} \; chaining \qquad \frac{P \lor Q, \; \neg P \lor R}{Q \lor R} \; resolution$$

Let us provide a simple example of derivation using the resolution rule. From the premise

¬ trainMoving ∨ doorsClosed,   trainStopped ∨ trainMoving

we derive the following conclusion in one step:

doorsClosed ∨ trainStopped

First-order predicate logic

This logic significantly extends the limited expressive power of propositional logic by introducing variables, constants, terms and quantification of variables. Terms are used to designate specific objects in the domain of interest. Atomic predicates on terms designate domain-specific relations over them. They can be prefixed by universal or existential quantifications and recursively composed through the propositional connectives to form statements. With those extensions we can now specify properties that involve specific trains among multiple ones, for example, and that refer to commanded acceleration as a function of train speed and location.

The *syntax* of first-order predicate logic simply reflects those extensions through the following rules. (The '*' meta-symbol means '0, 1 or more occurrences of'.)

```
<term> ::= <constant> | <variable> | <functionSymbol> (<term>*)
<atomicPredicate> ::= true | false | <predicateSymbol> (<term>*)
<statement> ::= <atomicPredicate> | (¬ <statement>)
          |(<statement> ∧ <statement>) | (<statement> ∨ <statement>)
          |(<statement> → <statement>) | (<statement> ↔ <statement>)
          | (∀ <variable>) (<statement>) | (∃ <variable>) (<statement>)
```

The *semantics* of first-order predicate logic is again provided by a set of rules for evaluating the truth value of a statement under a given way of interpreting its atomic elements.

To define an *interpretation* for a set of statements, we first need to define the *domain* of interest as a set of objects that the terms in those statements may represent – for example, are we talking about trains, meetings or books? Then we need to define what specific object in that domain a constant or unquantified variable in those statements designates, what specific function over the domain a function symbol designates, and what n-ary relation over the domain a predicate symbol on n arguments designates.

To illustrate this, suppose that we would like to specify in first-order logic that the distance between two successive trains should be kept sufficient to avoid collisions if the first train stops suddenly:

```
∀ tr1, tr2
Following (tr2, tr1) → Dist (tr2, tr1) > WCS-Dist (tr2)
```

To evaluate this statement semantically, we first need to fix an interpretation for its building blocks by saying that:

- The domain of interpretation for the statement is the set of trains in our system.

- The atomic predicate *Following (tr2, tr1)* is true if and only if the pair (tr2, tr1) is a member of the binary relation *Following* over trains, defined as the set of pairs of trains in which the first train in the pair directly follows the second.

- The function symbol *Dist* designates the real-valued function that, for two given trains, returns their exact distance from each other.

- The function symbol *WCS-Dist* designates the real-valued function that, for a given train, returns the worst-case distance needed for the train to stop in an emergency.

- The predicate symbol '>', used in infix form, designates the '>' binary relation over real numbers.

In the context of specifying requirements, domain properties or assumptions, two important points should be emphasized at this stage:

- It makes no sense to say that a formal statement is true or false in an absolute sense; truth is always relative to a given interpretation of interest.

- Whatever the specification formalism might be, making this interpretation fully precise in the documentation through such designations is essential to avoid ambiguity, inadequacy or misunderstanding of the specification. (This point, often neglected in practice, will be re-emphasized throughout the book.)

In first-order logic, the interpretation function val_I on the atomic elements of a set of statements under interpretation I captures the following:

- For a constant a, $val_I(a)$ designates a corresponding domain element.

- For an unquantified occurrence of a variable x, $val_I(x)$ designates a domain element as well.

- For a function symbol f, $val_I(f)$ designates a corresponding function over the domain.

- For a n-ary predicate symbol P, $val_I(P)$ designates a corresponding n-ary relation over the domain.

The *semantic rules* for first-order predicate logic are then recursively defined under an interpretation I as follows. (S, $S1$ and $S2$ denote arbitrary predicate statements, and $\{x \leftarrow d\}oI$ denotes the interpretation that extends the interpretation I by forcing variable x to represent the domain element d.)

$VAL_I(a) = val_I(a)$ for a constant a.
$VAL_I(x) = val_I(x)$ for an unquantified variable occurrence x.
$VAL_I(f(t_1,\ldots,t_n)) = (val_I(f))(VAL_I(t_1),\ldots,VAL_I(t_n))$ for a function symbol f on terms t_i.
$VAL_I(\textbf{true}) = T$, $VAL_I(\textbf{false}) = F$.
$VAL_I(P(t_1,\ldots,t_n)) = (val_I(P))(VAL_I(t_1),\ldots,VAL_I(t_n))$ for a predicate symbol P on terms t_i.
$VAL_I(\neg S)$, $VAL_I(S1 \wedge S2)$, $VAL_I(S1 \vee S2)$, $VAL_I(S1 \rightarrow S2)$, $VAL_I(S1 \leftrightarrow S2)$:
    the rules are similar to propositional logic.
$VAL_I((\forall x)S) = T$ if $VAL_{\{x\leftarrow d\}oI}(S) = T$ for each domain element d,
                F if $VAL_{\{x\leftarrow d\}oI}(S) = F$ for some domain element d.
$VAL_I((\exists x)S) = T$ if $VAL_{\{x\leftarrow d\}oI}(S) = T$ for some domain element d,
                F if $VAL_{\{x\leftarrow d\}oI}(S) = F$ for each domain element d.

The *proof theory* of first-order predicate logic enables much more expressive statements to be derived systematically from given ones. It includes the inference rules of propositional logic plus specific ones such as:

$$\frac{(\forall x)\, S}{S\,[x/t]}\ \text{instantiation} \qquad \frac{u_1 = v_1,\dots,\, u_n = v_n}{f\,(u_1,\dots,\,u_n)\ =\ f(v_1,\dots,\,v_n)}\ \substack{\text{functional}\\ \text{substitutivity}} \qquad \frac{u_1 = v_1,\dots,\, u_n = v_n}{P(u_1,\dots,u_n)\ \leftrightarrow P(v_1,\dots,\,v_n)}\ \substack{\text{predicate}\\ \text{substitutivity}}$$

The instantiation rule allows a universally quantified statement S to be instantiated to any term t; the quantification is eliminated and every occurrence of x is replaced by t. The two substitutivity rules refer to an equality predicate symbol (used in infix form), designating a reflexive, symmetrical and transitive relation in the domain of interpretation. These two rules amount to term/predicate rewrite rules under the condition that the corresponding arguments are equal.

First-order specification languages

Many specification languages are based on a first-order logic where the variables designate objects involved in the specification of requirements, assumptions or domain properties. Such variables have *values* that may be changing over time. Typically, the variables correspond to arbitrary entity instances from an entity–relationship diagram, whereas the function symbols and atomic predicates correspond to attributes and relationships in this diagram, respectively (see Section 4.3.2). A value for a variable designating an object then corresponds to a tuple of values for its attributes and relationships.

A *state* of a variable x is then defined as a functional pair (x, v) where v denotes a value for that variable. If the system is specified by a tuple X of such variables, a *system state* is a functional pair X, V where V denotes a tuple of corresponding values for the variables in X.

In many first-order languages, specifications are interpreted over system states; a specification is satisfied by specific system states and falsified by all other states.

The logic underlying many first-order specification languages is in general a *sorted* one; that is, the variables are 'typed'. A typed variable designates an instance in a specific set (called *sort*). A sort can typically be an entity from an entity–relationship diagram or a set of data values.

For example, the preceding statement would be written instead as:

∀ tr1, tr2 : *Train*
Following (tr2, tr1) → Dist (tr2, tr1) > WCS-Dist (tr2),

where the variables *tr1* and *tr2* designate arbitrary instances of the *Train* entity, the atomic predicate *Following* corresponds to a binary reflexive relationship on *Train*, and the function symbols *Dist* and *WCS-Dist* correspond to attributes of *Following* and *Train*, respectively. A state of variable *tr2* might be characterized by the fact that the designated train is following another train, designated by *tr1*, at a distance of 100 metres, say, and with a worst-case stopping distance of 50 metres in that state.

A formal specification consists of a structured set of such statements. It defines a *logical theory*; that is, a set of axioms from which new statements can be derived automatically as theorems using the inference rules from the proof theory. Such derivations may be used for adequacy checking, for example. Stakeholders may be shown the derived theorems, after translation into natural language, and asked whether they really want the consequences of what was specified. The inference rules can also be used for consistency checking; a sequence of derivations yielding the predicate **false** means that the theory formalizing the requirements, assumptions and domain properties is logically inconsistent. (We come back to this in Section 5.4.)

In this setting, the semantics of first-order logic allows for a more precise characterization of some of the specification flaws introduced in Section 1.1.7. A specification is *contradictory* if there is no interpretation of interest that can make all its statements true together. It is *ambiguous* if there are different interpretations of interest that make all its statements true together. It is *redundant* if some of the statements can be inferred as theorems from others.

4.4.2 History-based specification

A first specification paradigm consists of writing assertions that capture all the admissible histories of system objects, where a history is a temporal sequence of object states.

Instead of explicitly representing all admissible histories, we can use a logic-based formalism. An obvious candidate would be a first-order logic in which each variable would be 'stamped' by an additional time variable. For example, a predicate $P(x_1, t_1, x_2, t_2)$ would relate the state at time t_1 of an object designated by x_1 to the state at time t_2 of an object designated by x_2. Such explicit handling of time parameters would result in complex, awkward assertions.

Temporal logics allow us to specify all admissible system histories in a declarative and implicit way. The assertions written in such logics require no time parameters. We need to use additional logical connectives instead for reference to past, current and future states along histories, for example ◆P (meaning 'P did hold in some past state') or □P (meaning 'P will hold in every future state'). Assertions in temporal logics are interpreted over system histories; an assertion is satisfied by specific histories and falsified by all others.

There are many temporal logics available. The variants differ by the underlying time structure (discrete, dense or continuous ordered sets of time points or time intervals) and by the structure of the histories they allow us to capture (linear sequences of states, or trees with branching to alternative successor states).

Linear temporal logic (LTL)

This logic is defined over discrete time points and linear histories. It proves convenient for abstract specification of a large class of requirements, assumptions and domain properties. In addition to the usual propositional connectives and first-order constructs, LTL provides the following temporal connectives:

◇	(some time in the future)	◆	(some time in the past)
□	(always in the future)	■	(always in the past)
W	(always in the future *unless*)	*B*	(always in the past *back to*)
U	(always in the future *until*)	*S*	(always in the past *since*)
○	(in the next state)	●	(in the previous state)

A system history in LTL is an infinite temporal sequence of system states. Time is isomorphic to the set *Nat* of natural numbers, and a history H is more precisely defined as a function:

H: Nat → State (X)

This function assigns to every time point i in H the system state at that time point. X is the set of system variables and *State (X)* is the set of all possible states for the corresponding variables in X; see Section 4.4.1.

As mentioned before, LTL assertions are interpreted over linear system histories. To define the LTL semantics more precisely, we use the notation

(H, i) |= P

to express that the LTL assertion P is *satisfied* by history H at time position i ($i \in Nat$). The assertion P is satisfied by the entire history H if it is satisfied at the initial time position: (H, 0) |= P.

The semantic rules for LTL temporal connectives are then recursively defined as follows:

(H, i) |= ◇ P   iff for some j ⩾ i: (H, j) |= P

(H, i) |= □ P   iff for all j ⩾ i: (H, j) |= P

(H, i) |= P *U* Q   iff there exists a j ⩾ i such that (H, j) |= Q and for every k, i ⩽ k< j, (H, k) |= P

(H, i) |= P *W* Q   iff (H, i) |= P *U* Q or (H, i) |= □ P

(H, i) |= ○ P   iff (H, i+1) |= P

The semantic rules for the connectives over the past are similar. Two other frequently used temporal connectives are ⇒ (entails) and ⇔ (congruent), defined by

P ⇒ Q iff □ (P → Q),   P ⇔ Q iff □ (P ↔ Q)

In the context of specifying requirements and assumptions, it is often necessary to specify properties over time bounds. *Real-time temporal logics* are therefore necessary. Bounded versions for the above temporal operators are introduced, such as:

$\diamondsuit_{\leq d}$ (some time in the future within deadline d)

$o_{\leq d}$ (always in the future up to deadline d)

To define such operators, a temporal distance function has to be introduced:

dist: Nat $\times$ *Nat* $\to$ *D*,

D = {d | there exists a natural n such that d = n $\times$ u}, where u denotes a chosen time unit,

dist (i, j) = | j − i | $\times$ u

Multiple units can be used (e.g. second, day, week); they are implicitly converted into the smallest time unit. The o-operator then yields the nearest subsequent time position according to this smallest unit.

The semantics of the real-time operators is defined accordingly, for example:

(H, i) |= $\diamondsuit_{\leq d}$ P   iff for some j $\geq$ i with dist (i, j) $\leq$ d: (H, j) |= P

(H, i) |= $\square_{\leq d}$ P   iff for all j $\geq$ i such that dist (i, j) $\leq$ d: (H, j) |= P

As with any other logic, LTL has a *proof theory* enabling assertions to be derived systematically from others. For example, the following LTL-specific rules of inference can be used:

$$\frac{\square P}{P}\ \text{state particularization} \qquad \frac{P_1 \wedge P_2 \Rightarrow Q,\ \square P_1,\ \square P_2}{\square Q}\ \text{entailment modus ponens} \qquad \frac{P \Rightarrow Q}{\square P \Rightarrow \square Q}\ \text{montonicity}$$

In the first rule above, the conclusion P means 'P holds in some arbitrary current state'.

Let us give a sample of typical LTL specifications. The first-order predicate statement introduced in Section 4.4.1 can now be made stronger, and closer to what we want, by requiring a safe distance *always* to be maintained between successive trains:

∀ tr1, tr2 : Train

Following (tr2, tr1) $\Rightarrow$ Dist (tr2, tr1) > WCS-Dist (tr2)

Note that the '$\to$' propositional connective was replaced by the '$\Rightarrow$' temporal connective to prescribe that the implication should hold in *every future* state from any current one (in particular, from the initial state of the system). Other statements for our train control system might be specified in LTL as follows:

(Requirement:) *Train doors shall always remain closed between platforms unless the train is stopped in an emergency.*

∀ tr: Train, pl: Platform

• At (tr, pl) $\wedge\neg$ At (tr, pl) $\Rightarrow$ tr.Doors = 'closed' **W** [At (tr, next (pl)) $\vee$ Alarm (tr) $\wedge\neg$ Moving (tr)]

(Requirement:) *Trains shall reach their next platform within at most 5 minutes.*

∀ tr: Train, pl: Platform
At (tr, pl) ⇒ ◇$_{\leq 5m}$ At (tr, next(pl))

For our meeting scheduling system, we might write LTL assertions such as the following:

(Requirement:) *Intended participants shall be notified of the meeting date and location at least 3 weeks before the meeting starts.*

∀ p: Person, m : Meeting
Holds (m) ∧ Intended (p, m) ⇒ ♦$_{\geq 3\,w}$ Notified (p, m)

(Assumption:) *An intended participant will participate in a meeting if the meeting date and location are convenient and notified to him or her.*

∀ p: Person, m : Meeting
Intended (p, m) ∧ Notified (p, m) ∧ Convenient (m, p) ⇒ ◇ Participates (p, m)

(Assumption:) *A meeting convenient for a person remains so afterwards.*

∀ p: Person, m : Meeting
Convenient (m, p) ⇒ □ Convenient (m, p)

(Assumption:) *A meeting notified to a person remains so afterwards.*

∀ p: Person, m : Meeting
Notified (p, m) ⇒ □ Notified (p, m)

Branching temporal logics

These logics allow us to write assertions that are interpreted over branching system histories. Such histories have a tree structure with branching to alternative successor states. *Computation Tree Logic* (CTL) is a representative example of this type of logic. In CTL we can quantify a property over paths *and* over states along a path:

AG *P* means 'for **a**ll paths, *P* holds **g**lobally for all states along that path'
AF *P* means 'for **a**ll paths, *P* holds **f**inally in some state along that path'
EG *P* means 'there **e**xists a path where *P* holds **g**lobally for all states along that path'
EF *P* means 'there **e**xists a path where *P* holds **f**inally in some state along that path'

The logic is somewhat more expressive than LTL, in that reachability properties can also be formalized through *EF* quantifiers.

History-based specification: Strengths and limitations

Temporal logics allow us to formalize requirements, assumptions and domain properties in an abstract, declarative way. There is no need to care for system operations that should establish the assertions. Built-in historical referencing eliminates the need for extra variables to encode past or future states. The assertions, especially in LTL, are often close to their natural language counterpart. Such non-operational style of specification is convenient in the early stages of the RE process where the various operations to be implemented by the software-to-be might not have been identified yet.

On the downside, formal assertions in temporal logics may be hard to build in some cases – typically, in cases where what we want to assert requires overnesting of temporal connectives. It may then be very hard to assess whether the specification is adequate; that is, whether what we write is really what we want to express. For example, a frequent situation arises where we want to say that '*a state predicate* Q *should hold after a state predicate* P *held and before a state predicate* R *holds*'. This is adequately formalized in LTL by the formal assertion

$$\Box \neg P \lor \Diamond (P \land \neg R \, \boldsymbol{U} \, (Q \lor \Box \neg R)))$$

The mapping between the natural language formulation and its formalization is not straightforward in this case. *Specification patterns* address this problem by providing templates for frequent assertions requiring such overnesting of temporal connectives (Dwyer *et al.*, 1999). For example, the preceding assertion in their pattern catalogue is specified instead by the pattern

Q precedes *R* after *P*

Another problem with temporal logics as specification formalisms taken in isolation is their lack of structuring mechanisms. We cannot structure the variables to which the assertions refer or group assertions into cohesive chunks. This problem can be addressed by combining multiple formalisms, as we will see in Chapter 17.

4.4.3 State-based specification

Instead of characterizing the admissible histories of the system-to-be, we may characterize the admissible system states at some arbitrary snapshot. The requirements, assumptions and domain properties are specified in a sorted logic through system invariants and pre- and post-conditions on the system's operations:

- An *invariant* is a condition constraining the system's states at this snapshot. It must thus always hold in any state along the system's admissible histories.

- Pre- and post-conditions are conditions constraining the application of system operations at this snapshot. A *pre-condition* is a necessary condition on input variables for the operation to be applied; it captures the operation's applicability and must always hold in the state in which the operation is applied. A *post-condition* is a condition on output variables if the operation is applied; it captures the operation's effect and must always hold in the state right after the operation has been applied. For specification completeness we are interested in the least restrictive applicability condition – that is, the weakest pre-condition – and the most complete effect condition – that is, the strongest post-condition. A post-condition may be *constructive* or not depending on whether or not the effect condition defines the output variables explicitly through equations.

Languages such as Z, VDM, B, Alloy or OCL rely on the state-based paradigm. The main differences between them lie in the constructs available for structuring the system states, the mechanisms for organizing the specification into manageable units and the implementation bias of some of them. These languages were designed with different objectives in mind: systematic specification refinement towards an implementation (Jones, 1990; Abrial, 1996), efficient verification of bounded models (Jackson, 2006) or integration in UML design models (Warmer & Kleppe, 2003).

Let us have a closer look at Z as a good representative of state-based specification languages (Spivey, 1992). This will allow typical issues in formal specification to be covered in greater detail. Z is probably the easiest language to learn because of its conceptual simplicity and its standard notations. The language is conceptually simple as it based just on sets and tuples as primitives for structuring the state space. Most notations come from elementary mathematics for manipulating sets, tuples, relations, functions and sequences. These notations are pre-defined in terms of sets and tuples in an extendable specification toolkit. The language also provides simple yet powerful mechanisms for importing specification units and combining them piecewise to form the specification of the entire system. Moreover, Z's implementation bias is lower than other state-based languages such as B or VDM.

A Z specification is a collection of schemas together with some textual definitions. Each *schema* has a *declaration part* where the variables used in the schema are declared or imported from other schemas, and an *assertion part* where the assertions constraining the state space are specified. There are basically two kinds of schema:

- A *data schema* specifies a portion of the system's state space by declaring an aggregate of tightly coupled state variables and by stating invariants on them.

- An *operation schema* specifies a system operation by declaring the operation's input and output variables and by stating pre-conditions and post-conditions on these input and output variables, respectively.

The initial state of the system is defined through *initialization schemas* that particularize each data schema in this state. The specifier must also declare, in textual definitions, what the *given types* are in the specification. These are 'primitive' sets of conceptual instances or values on which Z declarations rely. It is therefore important to make precise what given types designate in the system.

Let us review the main features of Z through specification excerpts for our library system. We might specify our given types by the following declaration:

[Book, BookCopy, Author, Topic, Person]
Book: *set of all possible books that could ever be considered;*
BookCopy: *set of all possible book copies that could ever be considered;* etc.

Data schemas

The concept of Directory in our library system might be specified by the following data schema:

```
Directory _____
  WhichBook: BookCopy +-> Book
  WrittenBy: Book +-> PAuthor
  Covers: Book +-> PTopic
_____
  dom WrittenBy ⊆ ran WhichBook
  dom Covers ⊆ ran WhichBook
_____
```

This data schema specifies the Directory as an aggregation of three state variables: WhichBook, WrittenBy and Covers. Each one is declared in the upper part of the schema. The semantics of such a declaration is that the possible values for the variable on the left belong to the set represented on the right. For example, the possible values for the state variable Covers belongs to the set Book+->PTopic; that is, a value for Covers is a partial function from the set Book of all possible books to the set PTopic of all possible subsets of topics. The notations '+->' and 'P' are the standard ones in elementary mathematics to denote partial mappings and powersets, respectively. They are not primitives in Z. For example, a function is a specific kind of binary relation, which is a subset of a Cartesian product, which is a set of (binary) tuples. The function Covers is *partial* here because it is not defined everywhere on its input set Book; in any current state of our library system, Covers is defined only on a strict subset of all possible books (to which corresponds a specific subset of topics among all possible subsets of topics).

The two invariants in the assertion part of the *Directory* data schema constrain the three tightly coupled state variables further by interrelating the domains where they are everywhere defined and the ranges of values they return. The notations '⊆', 'dom' and 'ran' are the standard ones in mathematics to denote set inclusion and the domain and range of a function, respectively. For example, the second invariant states that every book for which Covers returns a subset of topics is a book corresponding to a book copy currently found in the library's directory.

In the preliminary description of the library system, access to certain facilities is restricted to specific user categories (see Section 1.1.2). We therefore introduce another data schema to structure our state space:

```
LibraryAgents _____
  OrdinaryPatron: PPerson
  Staff: PPerson
_____
  OrdinaryPatron ∩ Staff = ∅
_____
```

The invariant in this schema states that the two introduced sets have an empty intersection; that is, the same person cannot be both an ordinary patron and a staff member. We should specify and structure the system state space further by introducing a data schema for library shelves:

LibraryShelves _____

    LibraryAgents

    Available, OnLoan: $\textbf{P}$BookCopy

    BorrowedBy: BookCopy $\rightarrow\!\!\!+$ Person

    Available $\cap$ OnLoan $= \varnothing$

    OnLoan $=$ **dom** BorrowedBy

    ran BorrowedBy $\subseteq$ OrdinaryPatron $\cup$ Staff

    $\forall$p: OrdinaryPatron $\bullet$ #BorrowedBy^{-1}(| {p} |) $\leq$ LoanLimit

---

There is a *schema inclusion* in the declaration part of this schema. It amounts to importing all declarations and assertions from the included schema LibraryAgents to the including schema LibraryShelves. As a result, the declaration and invariant on OrdinaryPatron and Staff are implicit in the LibraryShelves schema.

The assertion part of LibraryShelves contains four invariants. (Assertions on multiple lines are implicitly conjoined.) The first invariant states a domain property; namely, that a book copy may not be both checked out and available for check-out at the same time. The second invariant is a definition; the variable OnLoan is defined as the set of book copies currently borrowed by people. The third invariant is a requirement; it restricts the set of borrowers to persons currently registered as ordinary patrons or staff members. The fourth invariant is a requirement as well; it restricts the number of book copies an ordinary patron may borrow at the same time. The notations '#S', 'R^{-1}' and 'R(|S|)' are the standard ones in mathematics to denote the number of elements in a set S, the inverse of a relation R, and the relational image of a set S by a relation R, respectively. The '$\bullet$' symbol, not to be confused with the LTL 'previous' operator, delimits quantifiers.

We may now complete our structuring of the system's state space through a new data schema that includes two previously defined ones plus a specific invariant:

LibrarySystem _____

    Directory

    LibraryShelves

---

    dom WhichBook $=$ Available $\cup$ OnLoan

This invariant states that any copy of a book currently listed in the library's directory is either checked out or available for check-out. (Note that this property is a global one; it could not be specified in the schema LibraryShelves as the variable WhichBook is not defined there.) In conjunction with the first invariant in LibraryShelves, we are saying that the set of book copies listed in the library's directory is partitioned, at any system snapshot, into the subset of copies checked out and the subset of copies available for check-out.

As mentioned earlier, every data schema has an associated *initialization schema* to define the initial state of the corresponding state variables. This is used in particular for inductive reasoning about properties of the specification (see Section 5.4). For example, the initial state of library shelves is specified by associating the following schema with the LibraryShelves schema, to add the property that the corresponding sets are initially empty:

InitLibraryShelves _____

    LibraryShelves
  _____

    Available = ∅ ∧ OnLoan = ∅ ∧ BorrowedBy = ∅

Operation schemas

In a Z specification building process, the elaboration of data schemas is highly intertwined with the elaboration of operation schemas. The introduction of state variables in the latter, for easier specification of pre- or post-conditions, has to be propagated to the former.

As in many specification languages, Z makes a distinction between two kinds of operation: *modifiers* change the state of some system variables whereas *observers* don't.

For our library system, the operation of checking out a copy of a book is a modifier. We specify it by the following operation schema:

CheckOut _____

    Δ LibrarySystem
    Ξ Directory; Ξ LibraryAgents
    p?: Person
    bc?: BookCopy
  _____

    p? ∈ OrdinaryPatron ∪ Staff
    bc? ∈ Available
    # BorrowedBy^{-1}(| {p?} |) < LoanLimit
    Available' = Available \ {bc?}
    OnLoan' = OnLoan ∪ {bc?}
    BorrowedBy' = BorrowedBy ∪ {bc? ↦p?}

The declaration part of this schema states that the CheckOut operation modifies the state of the variables imported from the included schema LibrarySystem (as expressed by the 'Δ' prefix). Among those, the variables imported from the included schemas Directory and LibraryAgents are, however, left unchanged (as expressed by their 'Ξ' prefix). The operation has two instance variables as input arguments: p and bc, whose sets of possible values are the given types Person and BookCopy, respectively. The '?' suffix to their name declares them as input arguments for the operation.

The notations '∈', '\' and '∪' appearing in the assertion part of the CheckOut operation schema are the standard ones for set membership, difference and union, respectively. The first three conditions refer to input arguments only; they are thus implicitly *pre-conditions* for the CheckOut operation. The first pre-condition states that the input borrower must be currently registered as an ordinary patron or a staff member. The second pre-condition states that the input book copy must be among the available ones. The third pre-condition states that the input borrower may not have reached his or her loan limit in the initial state before the operation is applied. The three next conditions are implicitly *post-conditions*; they are equations defining the effect, on the modified state variables, of checking out the book copy declared as an input argument. The first two post-conditions state that this book copy has migrated from the set of available copies to the set of borrowed copies. The third post-condition states that the function BorrowedBy includes a new functional pair bc? $\mapsto$ p? in the operation's final state.

As in most state-based formalisms, the prime suffix decorating a modified state variable, is necessary to distinguish the state of this variable before and after application of the operation (the corresponding equality would not be satisfiable here without such a distinction). Also note that, without the 'Ξ' prefix on Directory and LibraryAgents in the declaration part of the CheckOut operation, we should have included additional equations stating that the initial and final states of all variables declared in Directory and LibraryAgents are the same. The 'Ξ' prefix is a partial Z answer to the so-called *frame problem* of specifying in a state-based language that the operations make no other changes than the ones explicitly specified (Borgida *et al.*, 1993).

The inverse operation of returning a borrowed book may be specified by the following schema:

$$
\begin{array}{|l}
Return \underline{\hspace{5cm}} \\
\quad \Delta\ LibrarySystem \\
\quad \Xi\ Directory;\ \Xi\ LibraryAgents \\
\quad bc?: BookCopy \\
\hline
\quad bc? \in OnLoan \\
\quad Available = Available \cup \{bc?\} \\
\quad OnLoan = OnLoan \setminus \{bc?\} \\
\quad BorrowedBy = \{bc?\} \lhd BorrowedBy \\
\end{array}
$$

The last post-condition in this schema says that the function BorrowedBy in the operation's final state is the same as the one in the initial state except that it is no longer defined on its argument bc?; that is, the function no longer includes a functional pair whose first element is bc?. (The notation '$S \lhd R$' is the standard one in mathematics for restricting the domain of a relation R to the complement of set S.)

The *CheckOut* and *Return* operations are modifiers. Observers in our system include query operations. Among them, bibliographical search is a basic service to be provided by our system:

$$
\begin{array}{|l}
BiblioSearch \underline{\hspace{5cm}} \\
\quad \Xi\ Directory \\
\quad tp?: Topic \\
\quad booklist!: \mathbb{P}Book \\
\hline
\quad booklist! = \{x: Book \mid tp? \in Covers\ (x)\} \\
\end{array}
$$

As seen from the '!' suffix, this schema declares the variable *booklist* as an *external output* variable; the output of the *BiblioSearch* operation is not among the variables in the tuple of state variables defining the system's state space. (The '!' suffix on external output variables should not be confused with the prime suffix on state variables in an operation's output state.)

Note how simple the specification of *BiblioSearch* is thanks to the built-in relational style of expression supported by Z. Also note that the inclusion of the function *Covers* among the state variables declared in the Directory schema was motivated by this specification of the *BiblioSearch* functionality.

Combining schemas

Z has an elegant structuring mechanism for defining new schemas from finer-grained ones. The new schema is defined as a *logical combination* of the finer-grained ones using the propositional connectives introduced in Section 4.4.1. Such a definition amounts to introducing a new schema explicitly whose declaration part would include all declarations from the finer-grained schemas and the assertion part would include all assertions from these schemas, interconnected through the corresponding logical connective. For example, the specification:

NewSchema = Schema1 $\land$ Schema2 $\lor$ Schema3

amounts to the specification:

$$
\begin{array}{|l}
\hline
\textit{NewSchema} \underline{\hspace{6cm}} \\
\quad \text{All declarations from Schema1, Schema2, Schema3} \\
\quad \rule{3cm}{0.4pt} \\
\quad \text{(AssertionSchema1} \land \text{AssertionSchema2)} \lor \text{AssertionSchema3} \\
\hline
\end{array}
$$

where *AssertionSchema* denotes the conjunction of all assertions from *Schema*.

This structuring mechanism is most helpful for incremental elaboration of a specification piecewise and for reusing the same specification piece at multiple places in the specification.

Let us illustrate this point on a more robust version of the preceding specification of the Checkout operation. This specification did not cover any exception, in particular situations where one of the implicit pre-conditions is not satisfied. We therefore introduce fine-grained schemas for exceptions, for example:

$$
\begin{array}{|l}
\hline
\textit{NotRegisteredAgent} \underline{\hspace{4cm}} \\
\quad \Xi \text{ LibraryAgents} \\
\quad \text{p?: Person} \\
\quad \text{mes!: Message} \\
\quad \rule{3cm}{0.4pt} \\
\quad \text{p?} \notin \text{OrdinaryPatron} \cup \text{Staff} \\
\quad \text{mes! = 'this person is currently not registered'} \\
\hline
\end{array}
$$

Doing so for every identifiable exception, we obtain a robust version of the Checkout operation built from the previous one and from similarly specified exceptions:

$$\text{RobustCheckout} = \text{Checkout} \wedge \text{AuthorizedAgent} \vee \text{UnauthorizedAgent} \vee \text{UnregisteredUser}$$
$$\vee \text{ UnknownCopy} \vee \text{UnavailableBook} \vee \text{LoanLimitReached}$$

The schema operations for the exceptions UnauthorizedAgent and UnknownCopy might then be reused in a robust version of the operation *Return*.

This section has provided a sufficiently detailed account of a simple state-based specification language to provide deeper insights on typical notations and mechanisms used for elaborating a formal specification. Other features were left aside; notably, mechanisms for parameterizing and instantiating a specification.

State-based specification: Strengths and limitations

State-based languages are generally grounded on simple, standard mathematics to capture the system's state space and operations, at some arbitrary snapshot, through invariants and pre- and post-conditions. They offer simple yet powerful mechanisms for specification-in-the-large such as, in the case of Z, aggregation of related variables, schema inclusion and logical composition of specification units for piecewise specification building. As they are formal, the specifications written in state-based languages are amenable to various forms of automated analysis, such as type checking, deductive inference of consequences of the specification, consistency checking, proofs of invariance or verification of claims about the specification, with counterexample generation in case the claim is not satisfied (see Section 5.4). As they are operational, the specifications can be executed under certain conditions, for example when they define the outputs of operations equationally, to provide animations for adequacy checking.

On the downside, the expressive power of state-based languages has limitations. The specification is essentially functional; many of the non-functional properties discussed in Section 1.1.5 cannot be captured. We can specify permissions through pre-conditions, but not obligations; we cannot specify that something *must* happen when such or such a condition becomes true.

Compared with history-based specifications, there is a price to pay for the absence of historical referencing. As in programming, we need to introduce auxiliary variables to encode histories. This can make the specification unnecessarily complicated and unnatural at the requirements engineering stage. For example, suppose that we would like to know in our library system who was the last borrower of some copy of a book (e.g. to sue him or her in case the copy is found damaged on the shelves). In linear temporal logic, we would quite naturally formalize the statement that for any book copy bc and person p, that person was the last borrower iff there has been no person p' who has borrowed bc since p borrowed it:

$\forall$ bc: BookCopy, p: Person
LastBorrower (bc, p) $\Leftrightarrow$ ($\neg \exists$ p': Person) [BorrowedBy (bc, p') **S** BorrowedBy (bc, p)]

where '*S*' is the 'since' operator over past states introduced in Section 4.4.2. In a state-based language, we would need to introduce an auxiliary variable, *PrecedingLoan* say, to enable the specification of that query:

LastBorrower _____

   Ξ LibrarySystem
   bc?: BookCopy
   p!: Person
   _____
   bc? ∈ Available ∪ OnLoan
   p! = PrecedingLoan (bc?)

This is not the end of the story, though. We then need to declare the *PrecedingLoan* variable in the *LibraryShelves* schema, specify invariants there to define the domain and range of this function, and write adequate post-conditions to define the final state of this function in *every* Δ–operation schema on *LibraryShelves*, in particular in the *CheckOut* and *Return* operation schemas.

To sum up, state-based languages such as Z turn out to be especially appropriate in domains involving complex objects that need to be structured and inter-related. They produce more operational specifications than those obtained with history-based formalisms. They appear more appropriate for the later stages of the specification process where specific software services have been elicited from more abstract objectives. Parts II and III of the book will come back to this important point.

4.4.4 Event-based specification

Instead of characterizing the admissible system histories or the admissible system states at some arbitrary snapshot, we may characterize the required transitions between classes of states along admissible histories. Such transitions are caused by the occurrence of events. The requirements, assumptions and domain properties are then specified through formalizations of transition functions. Such functions may be represented by state machine diagrams (see Section 4.3.7). A formal specification makes transition functions more precise by formally characterizing the input and output states of transitions, their triggering events and their guard conditions. We can now specify obligations through trigger conditions and permissions through guards.

It is important not to confuse the notion of *state* used here with the one used in the history-based and state-based specification paradigms. A state in the former sense is an equivalence class of states in the latter sense; such a class is defined by the set of all system states in which a state variable has the same value (see the definition and examples of SM states in Section 4.3.7).

Languages such as SCR, RSML, STATEMATE, LTS or Petri nets rely on the event-based paradigm. The differences between them lie notably in the structuring of states, the association of side effects with transitions, the handling of concurrency and synchronization, assumptions on what may or may not happen when the specified component is in some state, and assumptions on the rate at which the component interacts with its environment.

Let us have a closer look at SCR as a good representative of event-based formalisms (Parnas & Madey, 1995; Heitmeyer *et al.*, 1996). This language is among those that are suitable for formal specification at requirements engineering time. It makes an explicit distinction between requirements and domain properties (see Section 1.1.4). The specification has a tabular format close to decision tables for better structuring, readability and checkability of complex combinations of conditions and events (see Section 4.2.1). It is output driven, allowing the specifier to concentrate on one single input–output function at a time and to investigate all the conditions under which the corresponding output must be produced. Last but not least, SCR is supported by a rich toolset automating a variety of analyses (see Chapter 5).

SCR is built on the four-variable model that defines requirements as a relation between monitored and controlled variables (see Section 1.1.4). The system globally consists of two components: the *machine*, consisting of the software-to-be together with its associated input–output devices, and the *environment*. The machine defines values for the controlled variables, whereas the environment defines values for the monitored variables.

An SCR specification defines the machine through a set of tables together with associated information such as variable declarations, type definitions, initial state definitions and assumptions. Each table defines a mathematical input–output function. The specification thus prescribes deterministic machine behaviours. The behaviour of the environment is non-deterministic.

An SCR table may be a mode transition table, an event table or a condition table.

Mode transition tables

A mode transition table specifies a mode class by defining its various modes as a function of the previous corresponding mode and events. A *mode class* is an auxiliary variable whose behaviour is defined by a state machine on *monitored* variables. The states are called *modes*. Modes amount to logical expressions on monitored variables; they are often used as abstractions to discretize continuous monitored variables. Mode transitions are triggered by events. An *event* occurs when a variable changes its value. In particular, an *input event* occurs when a monitored variable changes its value. A *conditioned event* occurs if an event occurs when a specified condition is true. Events are thus implicit in SCR; they are manipulated through notations such as:

@T(v) WHEN C,

which means, in terms of the prime notation introduced in the previous section,

$C \wedge \neg v \wedge v'$,

where C and v are evaluated in the current state whereas v' is v evaluated in the next state. For example, @T(Reset = On) WHEN Alarm = On amounts to $Alarm = On \wedge \neg Reset = On \wedge Reset' = On$. This event occurs when *Alarm* is 'On' and *Reset* is not 'On' in the current state, and *Reset* is 'On' in the next state.

Table 4.1 illustrates a mode transition table for our train control system. The mode class is *MovementState*; the variable *measuredSpeed* is monitored by the train controller. The first row in the table states that if *MovementState* is 'MovingOK' and the event @T(measuredSpeed = 0) occurs, then the *MovementState* is switched to 'Stopped'. Rows must be disjoint. If none of the rows applies to the current state, *MovementState* does not change.

Complex machines may be defined in terms of several mode classes operating in parallel.

Old Mode	Event	New Mode
MovingOK	@T (measuredSpeed = 0)	Stopped
Stopped	@T (measuredSpeed > 0)	MovingOK
MovingOK	@T (measuredSpeed ≥ blockLimit)	TooFast
TooFast	@T (measuredSpeed < blockLimit)	MovingOK

Table 4.1 *Mode transition table for mode class MovementState*

Mode	Events	
Stopped, MovingOK, TooFast	@T (Alarm = On)	@T(Reset= On) WHEN Alarm = On
Emergency	True	False

Table 4.2 *Event table for term Emergency*

Event tables

An event table defines the various values of a *controlled* variable or a term as a function of a mode and events. The mode belongs to an associated mode class (AMC). A *term* is an auxiliary variable defined by a function on monitored variables, mode classes or other terms. Using term names instead of repeating their definition helps make the specification more concise.

Table 4.2 illustrates an event table defining the auxiliary term *Emergency* to capture emergency situations in which appropriate actions must be taken. This term is defined as a function of the AMC *MovementState* and the monitored variables *Alarm* and *Reset*. The last column in Table 4.2 states that 'if the reset button is pushed in a state where the alarm is "*On*" then *Emergency* must become *false* whatever the current mode is'.

Condition tables

A condition table defines the various values of a *controlled* variable or a term as a total function of an AMC mode and conditions. A *condition* is a predicate defined on one or more monitored, controlled or internal variables. Conditions in a row are expected to be disjoint (for the table to be a function) and covering the entire state space (for the function to be total).

Table 4.3 illustrates the use of a condition table to specify the controlled variable *DoorsState* as a function of the AMC *MovementState* and the term *Emergency*. The first row and column state that if *MovementState* is 'Stopped' with *AtPlatform* or *Emergency* being true, then *DoorsState* must be 'Open'. An entry *False* in an event (or condition) table means that no event (or condition) may cause the variable defined by the table to take the value in the same column as the entry. Note that there is always one output value whose corresponding condition is true.

Mode	Conditions	
Stopped	AtPlatform OR Emergency	NOT AtPlatform AND NOT Emergency
MovingOK, TooFast	False	True
DoorsState	Open	Closed

Table 4.3   *Condition table for controlled variable DoorsState*

SCR is built on the *synchrony hypothesis*; that is, the machine is assumed to react infinitely fast to changes in its environment. It handles one input event completely before the next one is processed. This hypothesis explains why (a) a mode transition table may specifiy the next value of the mode class in terms of the current and next values of monitored variables (and the current value of the mode class); (b) an event table may specify the next value of the target variable in terms of the current and next values of other variables (and the current value of this variable); and (c) a condition table may define the next value of the target variable in terms of the next value of other variables.

It may be worth pointing out that event-based languages such as SCR have a different kind of semantics than specification languages based on temporal logic or state-based languages such as Z. The former have a *generative semantics*; that is, every state transition in the system is forbidden except the ones explicitly required by the specification. The latter have a *pruning semantics*; that is, every state transition in the system is allowed except the ones explicitly forbidden by the specification. Unlike Z, for example, event-based languages make it unnecessary to specify explicitly that 'nothing else changes' – in other words, there is a built-in solution to the frame problem.

Event-based specification: strengths and limitations

SCR provides useful features when used in the specification phase of the RE process. Localizing the definition of each target variable in a distinct table, rather than spreading it throughout the specification, makes it easier to identify the various cases to be considered in the definition and check their completeness. For condition tables, such cases must be disjoint and cover the entire state space. This can be checked automatically (Heitmeyer *et al.*, 1996). Being fully formal, the tables can also be checked against declarative properties. Simulations, test cases and portions of code can be generated. Even without tool support, the tabular format of the specification may make it easier to understand and review.

On the downside, event-based formalisms such as SCR are 'flat'. Unlike state-based languages, there is no mechanism for structuring system variables, for refining tables or for composing tables in an incremental specification process. This may be felt to be a serious limitation in large projects (Wiels & Easterbrook, 1999). Other event-based formalisms such as statecharts or RSML have tried to address this limitation, at the price of increased complexity in the definition of their semantics. Unlike history-based specification languages, historical referencing is limited. Like in other specification paradigms, the specifier can mainly capture the functional aspects of the system. It is also impossible to specify the rationale for speci-fication items, for example by linking them formally to other specification items that explain them.

Event-based languages such as SCR turn out to be especially appropriate in domains where the focus is on the software's required reactions to its environment, such as software controllers, and where there is a strong concern for automated analysis, such as safety-critical applications.

4.4.5 Algebraic specification

The general idea here is to group the system's operations by the concept to which they refer, and to define the effect of their combined application. The operations are declared as mathematical functions applied to or returning instances of the concept. Their combinations are specified as equations that capture their laws of composition. This way of defining a structure by the operations applicable to it corresponds to universal algebras in mathematics (hence the name of this paradigm), and to abstract data types in programming.

Let us first introduce a very simple example in the context of tracking trains in our train control system. We might associate operations such as EnterBlock and WhichTrain? with the concept of track, and declare their signature by specifying their input and output sets:

WhichTrain?: Block $\rightarrow$ Train
EnterBlock: Train $\times$ Block $\rightarrow$ Block

One assertion to specify these operations further might be the following law of composition:

$\forall$ tr: Train, bl: Block
WhichTrain? (EnterBlock (tr, bl)) = tr

The paradigm differs significantly from the previous ones in that there is no explicit or implicit notion of state. A system history here corresponds to a trace of successive applications of operations.

Specification languages such as OBJ, ASL, PLUSS or LARCH rely on the algebraic paradigm. They differ notably in the mechanisms available for structuring the specification into manageable units.

In addition to the signature of each operation associated with the target concept, the declaration part of a specification unit may *import* concepts and operations specified in other units. In some languages it is also possible to specify the structure of the target concept by the use of *type constructors* such as *SetOf[T]*, to construct sets of elements of type *T*; *SequenceOf(T)*, to construct sequences of elements of type *T*; *Tuple(T1,...,Tn)*, to construct tuples of elements of corresponding type; and so on. Such constructors are parameterized types that are algebraically pre-defined, together with their standard operations, in a specification toolkit. For example, we might add the following declaration to the preceding signatures:

Type Track is *SequenceOf* [Block]

In the assertion part of a specification unit, the equations defining combinations of operations are often *conditional*; they hold under some condition written in terms of operations defined in that unit or imported from other units. For example:

LeaveBlock (tr, EnterBlock (tr', bl)) = bl   **if** tr == tr'

where the '==' symbol denotes an equality predicate imported from Train.

Some of the operations can be partial functions. The assertion part may then include pre-conditions on their application to specify the domain where they are everywhere defined, for example:

Pre_ LeaveBlock (tr, bl) :   *On (tr, bl)*

where *On* is a Boolean operation specified as follows:

On: Train × Block → Boolean
On (tr, EnterBlock (tr', bl)) = **true if** tr == tr', **false** otherwise

A specification alternative to pre-conditions on partial functions is to extend the output set so as to make the function total (that is, everywhere defined):

LeaveBlock: Train × Block → Block ∪ UndefinedLeave
LeaveBlock (tr, EnterBlock (tr', bl)) = bl **if** tr == tr'
                                       = undef_leave **if not** tr == tr'

The effect *undef_leave* of the operation combination in the latter case corresponds to an exception (to be subsequently implemented by, for example, an error message).

Writing a consistent, complete and minimal set of composition laws in the assertion part of an algebraic specification unit is not necessarily obvious. Which pairwise operation combinations should be considered; which ones should not? The following heuristic answers this question and provides a systematic way of building the specification. It is based on a stateless counterpart of the classification of operations introduced in Section 4.4.3:

- *Modifiers* allow any instance of the target concept to be obtained by composition with other modifiers. A necessary condition for an operation to be a modifier is to have the target concept among the components of its output set. For example, the operations of creating an empty sequence, appending an element to a sequence, removing an element or concatenating two sequences are modifiers for the concept of sequence.

- *Generators* form a minimal subset of modifiers that allow any instance of the target concept to be generated through a minimal number of compositions of them. For example, the operations of creating an empty sequence and appending an element to a sequence form a generator set, as any sequence can be generated from these in a minimal number of compositions. Adding to this set the operation of element removal would result in redundant compositions to generate the target sequence. In our train example, the operation *EnterBlock* is a modifier in the generator set.

- *Observers* allow us to get information about any instance of the target concept. A necessary condition for an operation to be an observer is to have the target concept among the components of its input set. For example, the operations of getting the length of a sequence or checking whether some element occurs in it are observers. In our train example, the operation *On* is an observer.

A minimal set of composition laws can then be built systematically as follows.

Identify generator set *GS*;
For each generator *Gen* in *GS*:
    For each observer *Obs* [and condition <case>]: write an equation taking the form
        Obs (..., Gen (..., ...,...),...) = <term> [if <case>]
    For each modifier *Mod* not in *GS* [and condition <case>]: write an equation taking the form
        Mod (..., Gen (..., ...,...),...) = <term> [if <case>]

In this procedure, <term> specifies the effect of the corresponding composition, by means of operations defined in the same unit or imported from other units; <case> specifies the condition for the equation to hold (if any), in terms of arguments appearing in the left-hand side. The term <term> must denote an instance of the output set declared in the operation's signature. The conditions <case> often cover a *base case*, where the defined operation is applied to the generator of an empty concept instance, and a *recursive case*, where the defined operation occurs in the right-hand side as well, where it is applied to a strictly 'smaller' concept instance.

The correctness argument underlying this specification-building procedure is that the terms *Gen* (...) capture the various ways of generating any instance of the target concept, and all other operations are defined on each of these.

To get further insight into the difference between the algebraic and state-based paradigms, let us algebraically specify some of the library system operations that were specified in Z in Section 4.4.3. The specification unit for the Library concept might include the following declarations:

EmptyLib: ∅ → Library
AddCopy: Library × BookCopy → Library
RemoveCopy: Library × BookCopy → Library
CheckOut: Library × BookCopy → Library
Return: Library × BookCopy → Library
CopyExists: Library × BookCopy → Boolean
CopyBorrowed: Library × BookCopy → Boolean

As it is impossible to check out copies being borrowed, to return unborrowed copies or to remove non-existent copies, we need to assert pre-conditions on these operations:

Pre_CheckOut (lib, bc): ¬ CopyBorrowed (lib, bc)
Pre_Return (lib, bc): CopyBorrowed (lib, bc)
Pre_ RemoveCopy (lib, bc): CopyExists (lib, bc)

We then need to find out what the generators are. For the portion of the specification we are considering, we need to be able to generate an arbitrary set of book copies managed by our library system and an arbitrary set of copies on loan. The operations EmptyLib and AddCopy are the generators for the former set, whereas the operation CheckOut is the generator for the latter set. The other operations to be composed with them are RemoveCopy, Return, CopyExists and CopyBorrowed. Hence the following equations for a minimally complete set of composition laws regarding our declared operations:

∀ lib: Library, bc, bc': BookCopy
CopyExists (EmptyLib (), bc) = **false**
CopyExists (AddCopy (lib, bc'), bc) = **true if** bc = bc'
                                    = CopyExists (lib, bc) **if** bc ≠ bc'
CopyExists (CheckOut (lib, bc'), bc) = CopyExists (lib, bc)
CopyBorrowed (EmptyLib (), bc) = **false**
CopyBorrowed (AddCopy (lib, bc'), bc) = CopyBorrowed (lib, bc)
CopyBorrowed (CheckOut (lib, bc'), bc) = **true if** bc = bc'
                                      = CopyBorrowed (lib, bc) **if** bc ≠ bc'
RemoveCopy (AddCopy (lib, bc'), bc) = lib **if** bc = bc'
                                    = AddCopy (RemoveCopy (lib, bc), bc') **if** bc ≠ bc'
RemoveCopy (CheckOut (lib, bc'), bc) = RemoveCopy (lib, bc) **if** bc = bc'
                                     = CheckOut (RemoveCopy (lib, bc), bc') **if** bc ≠ bc'
Return (CheckOut (lib, bc'), bc) = lib **if** bc = bc'
                                 = CheckOut (Return (lib, bc), bc') **if** bc ≠ bc'
Return (AddCopy (lib, bc'), bc) = AddCopy (Return (lib, bc), bc') **if** bc ≠ bc'

As we can see, the right-hand side of many operation compositions consists of a *base case* and a *recursive one* on a smaller structure, for example a library with one copy less. In particular, the composition *RemoveCopy;Add Copy* has no effect if these operations apply to the same book copy *bc*; otherwise it amounts to the composition *AddCopy;RemoveCopy* where the *RemoveCopy* operation is applied to the remainder of the library's set of copies of books. Similarly, the composition *Return;CheckOut* has no effect if these operations apply to the same book copy *bc*; otherwise it amounts to the composition *CheckOut;Return* where the *Return* operation is applied to a smaller set of borrowed copies of books.

Also note that we dropped the compositions *Return(EmptyLib(),bc)* and *Remove-Copy(EmptyLib(),bc)* as they are ruled out by the stated pre-conditions. Similarly, the composition

Return(AddCopy (lib,bc'),bc) is ruled out in case *bc* = *bc'* because of the stated pre-condition *CopyBorrowed (lib,bc)* on the *Return* operation (and a domain property stating that an added copy is not borrowed). Some exception handling should have been specified without such pre-conditions, for example:

Return: Library × BookCopy → Library ∪ UndefReturn,   Return (EmptyLib(), bc) = undef_return,

in case no pre-condition is specified on the *Return* operation.

It is worth noticing that the equations specifying the effect of composing an operation *Op* with a generator *Gen* often fit one of the two following patterns:

Op (..., Gen (..., ... ,...),...) = Gen (..., Op (..., ...,...),...) *commutativity axiom pattern*
Op (..., Gen (..., ...,...),...) = Op (..., ...,...)   *independence axiom pattern*

The *commutativity axiom pattern* often applies to modifiers *Op* that are not in the generator set – see the modifiers *Return* and *RemoveCopy*. The *independence axiom pattern* often applies to observers *Op* – see the observers *CopyExists* and *CopyBorrowed*. Such patterns may be used to guide the specifier in writing a first specification sketch or to check it.

The algebraic specification of the *BiblioSearch* operation, specified in Z in Section 4.4.3, illustrates the importation of other specification units:

Type Directory is *SetOf* [*Tuple* [Book, BookCopy, Topic]]
Imports List [T]
SIGNATURES
    EmptyDir: ∅ → Directory
    AddEntry: Directory × Book × BookCopy × Topic → Directory
    BiblioSearch: Directory × Topic → List [Book]
EQUATIONS
    ∀ dir: Directory, b : Book, bc : BookCopy, tp, tp': Topic
    BiblioSearch (EmptyDir(), tp) = nil
    BiblioSearch (AddEntry (dir, b, bc, tp'), tp) = AddList (b, BiblioSearch (dir, tp)) **if** tp = tp'
                                    = BiblioSearch (dir, tp) **if** tp ≠ tp'

In this specification, the imported operations *nil* and *AddList* are the standard operations on lists for creating an empty list and appending an element to a list, respectively. They are defined in the parameterized specification unit *List [T]* imported by Directory.

Algebraic specification: Strengths and limitations

The main strength of algebraic specification languages is their effectiveness for automated analysis of the specification. Efficient term rewriting engines are available for equational languages, which makes deductions more efficient. By unfolding recursive definitions, the specification can be executed for quick prototyping of operations. It is sometimes argued that algebraic specifications are more abstract; hiding states removes the need for notational devices, such as the prime notation in state-based languages to distinguish the input and output states of an operation, or frame axioms to specify that the operations make no other changes. Algebraic languages also provide rich mechanisms for structuring and reusing specifications such as parameterization, inheritance or enrichment of specification units.

On the other hand, there are serious limitations for requirements engineering. Equational languages restrict what we can express. Like state-based languages, there is no built-in historical referencing. Casting a specification as a set of recursive equations defining operation compositions may be felt to be unnatural and turns out to be difficult in practice. We must identify the right set of generators and perform inductive reasoning on well-founded sets to build correct recursive equations – like when we are programming in a functional language. Algebraic specifications thus appear to be not that abstract on second thoughts.

4.4.6 Other specification paradigms

Higher-order functions

This specification paradigm is also logic based, but the logic used is more expressive. In higher-order logics we may quantify statements over variables, but also over functions and predicates. The price to pay for increased expressiveness is decreased efficiency in automated manipulations, and interaction with expert users during such manipulations.

As in algebraic specifications, the target system is specified as a structured collection of mathematical functions. The functions here are grouped into logical theories. Such theories contain type definitions, variable declarations and axioms defining the various functions in the theory. As the logic is higher order, functions may have other functions as arguments. Languages such as HOL or PVS rely on this paradigm.

In the context of our train control example, we might want to specify a function *AddTrain* to add a new train to the system. Since this train has to be located and tracked, the train-tracking function has to be updated accordingly. The latter function should thus appear as an argument of the *AddTrain* function. In a PVS specification this would look like the following:

```
TRACKING: TYPE = [Blocks → Trains]
trk: VAR TRACKING
AddTrain: [TRACKING, Blocks, Trains → TRACKING]
AddTrain (trk, bl, tr) = trk WITH [(bl) := tr]
```

Process algebras

This paradigm characterizes systems as collections of concurrent and communicating processes that can be executed by more or less abstract machines under specific laws of interaction (Hoare, 1985; Milner, 1989). This paradigm is used for specifying and analysing design solutions – in particular, required interactions among components of a software architecture, communication protocols or security protocols. It is therefore not relevant for specification at requirements engineering time.

4.4.7 Formal specification: strengths and limitations

The formal specification paradigms reviewed in this chapter aim to express both the declaration and assertion part of a specification in formal language. This language is logic based and provides a formal syntax, a precise semantics for interpreting statements, and rules for inferring new statements from given ones. The specification paradigms differ by their focus (histories, states, event-based transitions or operation compositions), their style (declarative or operational) and their structuring mechanisms for specification-in-the-large. Each paradigm has a built-in semantic bias making it more effective in specific situations. State-based and algebraic specifications focus on sequential behaviours while providing rich structures for defining complex objects. They are better targeted at transactional systems. Conversely, history-based and event-based specifications focus on concurrent behaviours while providing only fairly simple structures for defining the objects being manipulated. They are better targeted at reactive systems.

Formal specification approaches have common strengths. Unlike statements in natural language, formal assertions are less inclined to some of the specification defects discussed in Section 1.1.7, notably ambiguities, noises, forward references, remorse and unmeasurable statements. The reason is that the language in which they are written offers precise rules for interpreting statements and built-in mechanisms for structuring the specification into pieces.

Formal specification languages support much more sophisticated forms of analysis of the specification, such as specification animation for adequacy checking, algorithmic or deductive verification of desired properties and formal completeness checks. (We come back to these in the next chapter.) Such analyses can be automated by tools. Moreover, formal specifications allow other useful artefacts to be generated automatically, such as counterexamples to claims, failure scenarios, test cases, proof obligations, specification refinements and source code.

The by-products of formal specification and analysis are often recognized as important as the formal product itself. A better informal documentation is obtained by feedback from formal expression, structuring and analysis. The architecture, source code and test data are more likely to satisfy the specification.

On the downside, formal specification languages have limited expressiveness. They mostly address the functional aspects of the target system. The main exceptions are the timing properties we can capture with history-based or some event-based languages.

Formal specifications are hard to write and hard to read. Getting adequate, consistent and complete specifications requires expertise and training. The input–output formats of many analysis tools require encoding or decoding by experts. Formal specification approaches are thus not easily accessible to practitioners. We could hardly imagine showing them to stakeholders.

Process models that integrate formal specification approaches with conventional development practices, including inspections, reviews and testing, are also lacking (Craigen *et al.*, 1995).

Despite such limitations, there are many success stories using formal specifications for real systems (see the bibliographical notes at the end of this chapter). They range from the reengineering of existing systems to the development of new systems. Evidence has been reported that the projects where they were used, while resulting in products of much higher quality, did not incur higher costs; on the contrary. Although many of the stories concern safety-critical systems, notably in the transportation domain, there are other target areas such as information systems, telecommunication systems, power plant control, protocols and security. A fairly impressive example is the Paris metro system. The traffic on Line 14 (Tolbiac–Madeleine) is entirely controlled by software. The safety-critical components of the software were formally developed using the *B* state-based specification and refinement method (Abrial, 1996). The refinement-based development was entirely validated by formal, fully automated proofs. Many errors were found and fixed during development.

Formal specifications are mostly used in the *design* phase of a software project to elaborate, specify and analyse a functional model of the software-to-be. Chapters 17–18 will further describe how they can be used earlier for RE-specific tasks such as conflict management, risk analysis, the refinement of system objectives into software requirements and environment assumptions, and requirements animation. This requires a more lightweight and flexible framework where multiple specification paradigms are integrated, statements can be formalized only when and where needed, and RE-specific abstractions are supported.

4.5 Conclusion

The requirements emerging from the elicitation and evaluation phases of the RE process must be organized in a coherent structure and specified precisely to form the requirements document. The latter should meet the various qualities discussed in Section 1.1.7. This chapter has reviewed the main techniques available for requirements specification and documentation, from free to structured text, and from tabular formats to semi-formal diagrams to formal specifications.

Each technique was seen to be more suited to specific aspects of the target system, and to have its own merits and limitations in terms of expressive power, structuring mechanisms, analysability, usability and communicability. As those merits and limitations are complementary to each other, an optimal trade-off should be reached by combined use of multiple techniques.

Which combination works best may depend on the domain, the prominence of non-functional concerns such as safety-critical or security-critical ones and the project specifics, including the level of expertise and training of project participants.

Beyond such mutual reinforcement, the semi-formal and formal approaches in this chapter have common limitations with respect to the nature of the RE process discussed in Chapter 1.

Confusion between descriptions and prescriptions

The approaches reviewed make no distinction between domain properties, requirements, assumptions and definitions (SCR being an exception). For example, the left multiplicity in the ER diagram in Figure 4.15 states the requirement that a block may contain one train at most, whereas the right multiplicity states the domain property that a train cannot span more than two consecutive blocks.

Similarly, the second conjunct of the pre-condition in the following Z schema is a requirement stating that trains must be stopped for their doors to open; the first conjunct and the post-condition together form a domain property stating what door opening means in any domain.

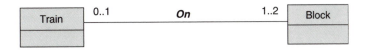

Figure 4.15 *– Confusing requirements and domain properties in ER diagrams*

As noted in Section 1.1.4, this distinction is essential in the context of engineering requirements. We can negotiate, weaken, change or find alternatives to requirements or assumptions; we cannot do so for domain properties.

Limited scope and absence of an intentional dimension

The approaches reviewed in this chapter address WHAT issues only. They do not cover the WHY and WHO dimensions of the RE process (see Section 1.1.3, Figure 1.2). Using them as such, we cannot specify the rationale for specification items. For example, the rationale explaining the requirements in the ER diagram and the Z schema above is not specified. To cope with an intentional dimension, we need higher-level abstractions that will be introduced in Part II, such as goals, goal refinements, agents and responsibility assignments.

As we noted before, the approaches reviewed in general do not address non-functional requirements. The latter form an important part of any requirements documentation and play a prominent role in the development process.

Lack of representation of alternative options

The semi-formal and formal approaches in this chapter do not allow alternatives to be captured and compared with each other for the selection of 'best' options. RE-specific approaches should provide support for reasoning about alternative refinements of objectives, alternative resolutions of conflicts or alternative assignments of responsibilities, based on criteria provided by non-functional requirements.

Lack of guidance

The approaches reviewed essentially provide sets of notations together with tools for a posteriori analysis. As a result, they induce a process of elaborating specifications by iterative debugging. In view of the inherent complexity of the RE process, we should consider a more constructive approach where the quality of the requirements documentation is ensured by the method followed.

The above limitations provide the main motivation for the goal-oriented, multiparadigm modelling and specification method presented in Parts II and III of the book.

Summary

- The requirements, assumptions and domain properties emerging from the elicitation and evaluation phases of the RE process must be organized into a coherent structure and specified precisely in the requirements document (RD). The specifications must be complete, consistent, adequate, unambiguous, measurable, pertinent, realistic and comprehensible.

- Free documentation in unrestricted natural language has no limitation in terms of expressiveness and communicability. However, it is much more likely to result in ambiguities, noises, forward references, remorse, unmeasurable statements and opacity.

- Disciplined documentation in structured natural language addresses some of these problems. The specifier may be guided by local rules on how statements should be formulated and structured, and by global rules on how the requirements document should be organized. Locally, we should follow technical writing principles, introduce decision tables for structuring and checking complex combinations of conditions, and use statement templates to further document statements with useful information such as their identifier, type, fit criterion, rationale, elicitation source and priority level. Globally, we may follow specific rules for grouping RD items within sections. Global templates allow us to organize the RD into specific sections according to organization-specific, domain-specific or international standards.

- Diagrammatic notations provide a means for summarizing portions of the requirements document in graphical language. This language is semi-formal in that the items relevant to a system view are declared formally, whereas the statements describing or prescribing their properties are informally stated in natural language. As they are formal, the declarations are amenable to surface-level analysis by automated tools to check their consistency and completeness. As they are graphical, they are easier to communicate. Diagrammatic notations differ by the specific aspect of the target system that they are intended to capture. They should be integrated, as those aspects are complementary. Integration can be achieved by enforcement of inter-diagram consistency rules.

- Context diagrams allow us to define the system scope in terms of relevant components and phenomena shared among them. A problem diagram further highlights the machine together with the controlled phenomena and the requirements constraining them. Some problem diagrams can be obtained by instantiation of frame diagrams that capture generic components and connections for common problem classes.

- Entity–relationship diagrams are a popular notation for capturing the structural aspects of the target system. Conceptual items are characterized by attributes and linked to others through domain-specific relationships. They can be aggregated or specialized into other conceptual items. Multiplicities formalize simple requirements and domain properties.

- SADT, DFD and use case diagrams allow us to capture the functional aspects of the system. SADT actigrams declare system operations by their input/output data, controlling data or events, and processing agents. Datagrams declare data in a dual way by their producing or consuming activities, controlling activities and the resources required to process them. DFD diagrams capture similar information in a simpler but less expressive way through bubbles interconnected by dataflows, with data repositories or system components as start and end points. Use case diagrams outline the system operations, grouping them by component and suggesting their interaction with external components. Those three types of diagram support functional decomposition.

- Event trace diagrams provide an easy-to-use notation for specifying examples of actual or desired interactions among system component instances. The concrete, narrative style of this notation makes it especially appropriate for scenario capture during requirements elicitation and for counterexample visualization during requirements verification.

- State machine diagrams focus on the behavioural aspects of the target system. The admissible behaviours of a system component are captured by sequences of possible state transitions for items that the component controls. Such sequences are paths in a directed graph where nodes represent states and arrows represent transitions triggered by events. Transitions may be guarded by conditions. Concurrent behaviours are represented by the parallel composition of state machine diagrams; a behavioural trace in the composite diagram is then a finite sequence of aggregated states from the composing SM diagrams.

- R-net diagrams visualize answers to *WHAT IF?* questions about external stimuli. An R-net specifies all the operations that a system component is required to perform, possibly under a particular condition, in response to a single input stimulus.

- Formal specification languages go one step further by formalizing the statements about RD items as well, not just their declaration. The benefits expected from this formalization are a higher degree of precision in the formulation of statements, precise rules for their interpretation and much more sophisticated forms of validation and verification that can be automated by software tools. In addition, the languages provide structuring mechanisms for organizing the specification into manageable units.

- Formal specification languages are grounded on some logic – often a sorted first-order logic to represent typed variables that can be quantified universally or existentially. The languages are defined by syntax rules, semantic rules for assigning a precise meaning to formal statements under some interpretation, and inference rules for generating new statements as consequences. When formal constructs are used for RE, it is essential to document explicitly and precisely what they designate in the target domain. Formal assertions generally refer to state variables designating objects involved in the requirements, assumptions or domain properties. Depending on the specification paradigm, the assertions are interpreted over system states or histories, being satisfied by some of them and falsified by the others.

- In the history-based paradigm, assertions capture admissible histories of system objects, where a history is a temporal sequence of states. Temporal logics support a declarative style of specification where such sequences are kept implicit thanks to temporal connectives for historical referencing to past and future states. LTL formulations tend to be close to their natural language counterpart. Specification patterns can be used when this is not the case.

- In the state-based paradigm, assertions capture admissible system states at some arbitrary snapshot. They are formulated as system invariants and pre- and post-conditions on system operations. State-based languages provide a variety of constructs for structuring the state space and for decomposing the specification into manageable units. Among them, Z is a fairly simple relational language that relies on sets and tuples as sole primitives for structuring the state space. A Z specification is essentially a collection of data and operation schemas that can be logically composed stepwise to form the entire specification.

- In the event-based paradigm, assertions capture event-driven transitions between classes of states along admissible system histories. A specification makes the transition function underlying the corresponding SM diagram more precise by formally characterizing the input and output states of transitions, their triggering events and their guard conditions. SCR is an event-based language, based on the four-variable model, especially suitable for formal specification of requirements for control systems. SCR specifications have a tabular format close to decision tables. Various kinds of tables are used to define controlled variables as functions of states of monitored variables, events and conditions. Each table represents a single input–output function. The specifier may concentrate on one table at a time and investigate all the conditions under which the corresponding output must be produced. Such output-driven specification provides a better guarantee of the completeness of requirements.

- In the algebraic specification paradigm, assertions are conditional equations capturing the admissible laws for composing system operations. They are grouped by the concept to which they refer. There is no notion of state; histories correspond to traces of successive applications of operations. A set of equations can be built systematically by identifying the set of generators for the associated concept and then by defining the effect of pairwise combinations of all other operations with each generator. The equations are most often decomposed into base cases and recursive cases; this requires some inductive reasoning. This more elaborate reasoning is the price to pay for the executability of the specification through term rewriting.

- Semi-formal and formal approaches may improve the structuring of the specification, augment its precision and increase its analysability. Their limitations with respect to

RE-specific needs call for a model-based, multiparadigm and goal-oriented method for RE.

Notes and Further Reading

Good advice for writing technical prose will be found in Day (1989) and Dupré (1998). The use of technical writing principles for documenting requirements is further discussed in Kovitz (1999). The building and use of decision tables are detailed in Pollack and Hicks (1971) and Chvalovsky (1983). Templates for structuring informal statements are also discussed in Sommerville and Sawyer (1997). The term 'fit criterion' is coined from Robertson and Robertson (1999), who make a strong case for requirements measurability.

Templates for organizing the entire requirements document are described in greater detail in Davis (1993). The VOLERE template is detailed in Robertson and Robertson (1999).

Context diagrams are introduced in DeMarco (1978). Their relevance to RE is convincingly argued in Jackson (1995a). The use of context, problem and frame diagrams for bounding the problem world is detailed in Jackson (2001). This book proposes a more extensive collection of problem frames and discusses satisfaction arguments for such diagrams. The use of problem frames for security requirements engineering is discussed in Haley *et al.* (2008). Another use for exploring the relationship between requirements and software architecture is reported in Rapanotti *et al.* (2004).

Entity–relationship diagrams were first introduced in databases for modelling concepts from which database schemas are derived (Chen, 1976; Pirotte, 1977). They are grounded on knowledge-representation languages such as conceptual graphs and semantic networks, which introduced structuring mechanisms such as aggregation and specialization with inheritance (Quillian, 1968; Smith & Smith, 1977; Brodie *et al.*, 1984; Sowa, 1984; Brachman & Levesque, 1985). The OMT modelling notation extends ER diagrams with operation signatures on classes (Rumbaugh *et al.*, 1991). The resulting notation is standardized in UML class diagrams (Rumbaugh *et al.*, 1999). The UML convention for multiplicity sides is taken here rather than the opposite one used earlier in the conceptual modelling literature.

Semi-formal notations that focus on data flows and functional decomposition are sometimes referred to as 'structured analysis'. SADT was a pioneering effort by Doug Ross and colleagues towards defining a first requirements specification language (Ross & Schoman, 1977b). A more detailed account is provided in Marca and Gowan (1988). DFDs are further detailed in DeMarco (1978). In spite of being found in OMT (Rumbaugh *et al.*, 1991), dataflow diagrams were banished from UML (Rumbaugh *et al.*, 1999). As far as RE is concerned, this decision was a mistake; data-flow diagrams are frequently used by system engineers to model information flows in organizations. The reason for such rejection was probably the major focus of UML on modelling notations for designers and programmers; data flows among architectural components contradict the principle of information hiding (Parnas, 1972) used in object-oriented programming.

Event trace diagrams were proposed in multiple forms, variants and extensions. Message Sequence Charts (MSC), the original ITU standard, is described in ITU (1996). A simple form of MSC was integrated into OMT (Rumbaugh *et al.*, 1991). Sequence diagrams, the UML variant, are described in Booch *et al.* (1999). The main extensions of event trace (ET) diagrams concern the representation of time and durations, co-regions to capture commutative interactions, ET prefixes as guards for ET suffixes to take place, and high-level MSCs to 'flowchart' MSCs (Harel & Thiagarajan, 2003). The language of Live Sequence Charts (LSCs) is a formal extension that makes an explicit distinction between possible, necessary and forbidden interactions (Harel & Marelly, 2003).

Variants of state machine diagrams have been known in automata theory since the early days as Mealy or Moore machines (Kain, 1972). They were used for modelling behaviours of a wide range of systems, including telephone systems (Kawashima, 1971) and user interfaces (Wasserman, 1979). Harel introduced statecharts as a significant extension to support concurrency and hierarchical structuring of states (Harel, 1987, 1996). An informal variant of statecharts was tentatively integrated into OMT (Rumbaugh *et al.*, 1991) and incorporated in the UML standards (Rumbaugh *et al.*, 1999). RSML (Leveson *et al.*, 1994) is a formal variant of statecharts further discussed below. Labelled transition systems are formal SM diagrams that support concurrency through a simple parallel composition operator; traces there are sequences of events rather than sequences of states (Magee & Kramer, 2006). The use of SM diagrams for specifying reactive systems is further discussed in Wieringa (2003).

There are many textbooks on logic. Manna and Waldinger (1993) and Gries (1981) are highly recommended for their orientation towards applications in computing science. The importance of explicitly documenting what formal predicates and terms designate in the domain is argued further in Zave and Jackson (1997). The ERAE specification language established an important bridge between ER diagrams and first-order logic (Dubois *et al.*, 1991).

There are also numerous textbooks on formal specification. A comprehensive presentation of the state-based and algebraic paradigms can be found in Turner and McCluskey (1994) or Alagar and Periyasamy (1998). A widely accessible introduction is Wing (1990). A road map on specification techniques and their strengths and limitations is given in van Lamsweerde (2000a).

The formal systems underlying history-based specification in linear and branching-time temporal logics are best introduced in Manna and Pnueli (1992) and Clarke *et al.* (1999), respectively. Time can be linear (Pnueli, 1977) or branching (Emerson & Halpern, 1986). Time structures can be discrete (Manna & Pnueli, 1992; Lamport, 1994), dense (Greenspan *et al.*, 1986) or continuous (Hansen *et al.*, 1991). The specified properties may refer to time points (Manna & Pnueli, 1992; Lamport, 1994), time intervals (Moser *et al.*, 1997) or both (Greenspan *et al.*, 1986; Jahanian & Mok, 1986; Allen & Hayes, 1989; Ghezzi & Kemmerer, 1991). Most often it is necessary to specify properties over time bounds; real-time temporal logics are therefore necessary (Koymans, 1992; Morzenti *et al.*, 1992; Moser *et al.*, 1997).

Invariants and pre-/post-conditions as abstractions of program executions were first proposed in Turing (1949). Different axiomatic systems were introduced almost simultaneously and independently to formalize this principle (Floyd, 1967; Hoare, 1969; Naur, 1969). The term 'snapshot' in the context of state-based specification is coined from the latter paper. A calculus for weakest preconditions appeared in Dijkstra (1976).

State-based specifications are sometimes called model-based specifications. The latter terminology is somewhat confusing, as virtually every type of specification for a complex system is based on a model whatever the underlying specification paradigm. The initial design of the Z language was reported in Abrial (1980). It was rooted in early work on the semantics of the binary relational model (Abrial, 1974). The Z user manual was developed from extensive experience at Oxford (Spivey, 1992). An interesting collection of specification case studies in Z is presented in Hayes (1987). Good textbooks on specification and refinement in Z include Potter *et al.* (1996) and Woodcock and Davies (1996). These books also provide further background on the underlying discrete mathematics. Object-oriented variants such as Object-Z and Z++ are described in Lano (1995). There have been many books on other state-based languages, their use, dedicated analysis techniques and refinement calculi. For *VDM*, the original book remains the main reference (Jones, 1990); it comes with a series of case studies (Jones & Shaw, 1990). A more recent book puts emphasis on the process of modelling in VDM-SL, the standardized version of the language (Fitzgerald & Larsen, 1998). For *B*, 'the' book is Abrial (1996); shorter introductions include Lano (1996) and Schneider (2001). A variety of B specification case studies is provided in Sekerinski and Sere (1999). For *Alloy*, the language and specification analyser are described in Jackson (2006). For *OCL*, the best reference probably remains Warmer and Kleppe (2003); as the language is being standardized by the Object Management Group (OMG), the latest version should be checked on the OMG website (www.omg.org/docs). The frame problem in state-based languages is discussed in great detail in Borgida *et al.* (1993).

There have been quite a few event-based specification languages, with fairly different semantics. The SCR notation was first introduced in Heninger (1980) based on experience in specifying the flight software for the A-7 aircraft (Heninger *et al.*, 1978). The language was updated and further detailed in Parnas and Madey (1995). The formal semantics used in the SCR toolset is described in Heitmeyer *et al.* (1996). RSML is an event-based language that extends statecharts with interface descriptions and direct communication among parallel state machines; state transitions are more precisely defined there (Leveson *et al.*, 1994). Like statecharts, RSML is a graphical formalism supporting hierarchical state machines. It integrates decision tables for the definition of outputs under complex combinations of conditions. Like SCR, the technique has been validated by experience in complex projects, notably, the documentation of the specifications of TCAS II, a Traffic Collision Avoidance System (Leveson *et al.*, 1994). The STATEMATE tool supporting statecharts was used as a basis for defining a formal semantics for statecharts (Harel *et al.*, 1990; Harel, 1996). A semantically simpler route is taken in the LTSA toolset by composing labelled transition systems in parallel (Magee & Kramer, 2006). The latter SM diagrams do not support hierarchical decomposition, however. Other event-based languages include SPL (Manna & Pnueli, 1992), the language used in the STeP verification environment, and PROMELA, the language used by the SPIN model checker (Holzmann, 1991). Petri nets are another event-based language for describing control flows and synchronization among concurrent processes (Peterson, 1977). Like other languages they support a wide range of analysis techniques, including reachability analysis and deadlock detection, but lack structuring mechanisms for complex system descriptions, which makes specifications hard to build. A meta-framework for defining and comparing the many semantic options taken by event-based languages is proposed in Niu *et al.* (2003).

The initial ideas and principles on algebraic specification can be found in two seminal papers, Liskov and Zilles (1975) and Guttag (1977). Algebraic specification languages designed with those principles, and incorporating increasingly rich structuring mechanisms, include CLEAR (Burstall & Goguen, 1981), OBJ (Futatsugi *et al.*, 1985), LARCH (Guttag *et al.*, 1993), ASL (Astesiano & Wirsing, 1986) and PLUSS (Gaudel, 1992).

Specification languages using higher-order functions include PVS (Owre *et al.*, 1995) and HOL (Gordon & Melham, 1993).

The need for multiparadigm specification frameworks is convincingly argued in Niskier *et al.* (1989). OMT's combination of entity–relationship, data flow and state machine diagrams was among the first attempts to achieve this at a semi-formal level (Rumbaugh *et al.*, 1991). The viewpoint construct in Nuseibeh *et al.* (1994) provides a generic mechanism for achieving such combinations in a coherent way through inter-view consistency rules. Integrations of semi-formal and formal languages include Faulk *et al.* (1992), which combines SCR specifications, entity–relationship diagrams and DFDs; Zave and Jackson (1996), which combines state-based specifications and state machine diagrams; and Dardenne *et al.* (1993), which combines semantic nets for navigation through multiple models at a semi-formal level, a real-time linear temporal logic for specifying goal and object models, and state-based specifications for the corresponding operation model. Another combination is UML/OCL, which combines a blend of semi-formal notations with a state-based specification language (Warmer & Kleppe, 2003). Integrations of different formal specification paradigms include LARCH (Guttag *et al.*, 1993) and RAISE (George *et al.*, 1995), which combine algebraic and state-based specification languages. The SDL specification language standardized by the International Telecommunication Union combines DFDs for data flows among processes, a state machine language for event-based specification of single processes, message sequence charts for scenarios of interaction among processes and algebraic specifications for the specification of user-defined data types (ITU, 2002).

A good account of the use of formal methods in industrial projects is provided in Hinchey and Bowen (1995). Success stories range from the reengineering of existing systems (Heninger, 1980; Craigen *et al.*, 1995) to the development of new systems (Hall, 1996). The Paris metro story is reported in Behm *et al.* (1999). Another interesting application is the Z security verification of the Mondex electronic purse system (Stepney *et al.*, 1998). Other good accounts can be found in Clarke and Wing (1996) and Science of Computer Programming (2000).

Exercises

- Define fit criteria for the following specification fragments from our running case studies.

  'Trains should run at high frequency during rush hours.'
  'In order to ensure comfortable transportation, trains should accelerate/decelerate smoothly.'
  'Meetings should be scheduled as quickly as possible once they are initiated.'

- Build a decision table for a checkout transaction in the library system with input conditions such as 'registered user', 'book copy available', 'loan quota reached' and output conditions such as 'loan granted', 'loan denied' and 'book copy reserved'.

- Show how the VOLERE documentation template in Robertson and Robertson (1999) can be mapped to the IEEE Std-830 standard.

- Elaborate a problem diagram for the following simplified version of a patient monitoring system. Then explore the possibility of obtaining some parts of it by instantiation of the problem frames represented in Figure 4.4.

  Each patient in an emergency service is monitored by an analogue device that measures factors such as pulse, temperature, blood pressure and skin resistance. The software monitors these factors on a periodic basis, customized to each patient, and keeps them in a database for patient history tracking. For each patient, safe ranges are specified for each factor. If a factor falls outside of a patient's safe range, the nurse's station is notified.

- Consider cash withdrawal transactions from your favourite cash machine (ATM):

  a. Delimit the ATM problem world by a problem diagram. The diagram should show system components that are relevant to the problem of getting cash.

  b. Build an entity–relationship diagram to declare and structure the data involved in cash withdrawal.

    c. Build SADT diagrams to document the activities and data involved in such transactions.

    d. Represent the information flow in such transactions through a dataflow diagram.

    e. Show some possible scenarios of interaction between you and the ATM through a few message sequence charts.

    f. Build a state machine diagram for the ATM that covers the scenarios you have identified (and more).

    g. Build an R-net for the stimulus 'cardInserted'.

- In the context of modelling the admissible behaviours of a simplistic telephone switching system, use the state machine notation introduced in this chapter to capture the sequences of possible state transitions for a telephone calling another telephone or being called by it. States for a calling telephone might include, among others, 'dial tone', 'connected' and 'ring tone', whereas a called telephone might have states such as 'ringing' or 'connected'.

- Specify a traffic light controller as a parallel composition of two sub-controllers: one controlling the car traffic lights and the other controlling the pedestrian traffic lights.

- Consider the two following assertions in first-order predicate logic:

$$(\forall x) \, [P \, (x) \wedge Q \, (x) \rightarrow (\exists y) \, R(x,y)]$$
$$(\forall x) \, [S \, (f(x)) \rightarrow Q \, (x)]$$

    a. Apply the syntax rules of predicate logic to check whether these assertions are grammatically well formed.

    b. In the context of the library system, define two possible interpretations for these assertions: one that makes the first assertion *true*, by application of the semantic rules of predicate logic, and one that makes the first assertion *false*.

    c. Define a possible interpretation making those two assertions true in the context of the meeting scheduling system.

- Formalize the following statements in first-order predicate logic:

    'E-auctions sell cellos that are fake copies of antique ones and have low value.'
    'Jim's antique cello is sold in an Egulf auction.'

Then apply inference rules of predicate logic to derive, from the above theory, the statement:

    'Jim's antique cello is a fake, low-value copy.'

- Write temporal logic assertions in LTL that adequately formalize the following statements:

  'Items bought in an e-auction must be paid for *within* three months.'
  'Items sent by an e-auction's seller must *have been* paid for by the buyer.'
  'Sellers may *never* sell an item under e-auction *before* the end of the auction.'
  'The winning bidder shall be notified *as soon as* the auction has ended.'

- Complete the Z specification of portions of the library system in Section 4.4.3 by providing robust versions of specifications for the *Return* operation and for the query operation returning the list of book copies currently borrowed by a patron. The latter operation may be applied by *Staff* agents without restrictions; *OrdinaryBorrower* agents may only get the list of their own loans.

- Build a Z specification for a simple diary management system allowing users to make appointments, cancel them, move them to another date and obtain the dates of appointments with a given person.

- Consider a simple patient monitoring system in which the software controller generates alarm signals when the patient's temperature or blood pressure falls outside safe ranges. The alarm signals and safe ranges are different for temperature and blood pressure. Identify the controller's monitored and controlled variables and, from there, what might be helpful mode classes and terms. Then specify SCR tables for this system.

- Complete the algebraic specification of portions of the library system in Section 4.4.5 by specifying the concept of registered patrons, Patrons say, and useful operations such as Register, to add a patron to the set Patrons of registered patrons, Unregister, to remove a patron from this set, Registered?, to check whether a patron is in this set, and PatronInfo?, to obtain relevant information about a patron. Don't forget the EmptyPatrons generator.

5

Requirements Quality Assurance

I n the spiral model of the RE process introduced in Chapter 1, requirements quality assurance comes next after requirements documentation (see Figure 1.6). Quality assurance is aimed at checking that the items specified in the requirements document (RD) meet the various qualities defined in Section 1.1.7.

The checks may reveal multiple defects of different types (see Table 1.1 in Chapter 1). Errors are especially harmful. Missing, contradictory, inadequate, ambiguous or unmeasurable RD items may have serious consequences for the subsequent development phase of the project and for the quality of the resulting product. The later such errors are found, the more costly their repair is.

Requirements quality assurance consists of detecting defects, reporting them, analysing their cause, and undertaking appropriate actions to fix them. The final result of this activity is a consolidated requirements document.

This chapter presents the main techniques available for requirements quality assurance:

- *Inspections and reviews* involve several independent inspectors that individually analyse the RD to search for defects, and then meet to discuss their findings and recommend appropriate actions for fixing agreed defects. This technique is discussed in Section 5.1. It is the widest in applicability and scope. Inspections and reviews can be applied to any kind of specification format, from free text to structured templates to diagrammatic notations to formal specifications, to search for any kind of defect.

- *Queries on a requirements database* require parts of the RD to be specified in terms of the diagrammatic notations reviewed in Section 4.3. The specification is maintained in a requirements database structured according to the constructs of the semi-formal language. Queries on this database allow for certain forms of checks for the structural consistency and completeness of the specification. This technique is discussed in Section 5.2.

- *Animation-based validation* requires parts of the RD to be specified in terms of the formal constructs reviewed in Section 4.4. The specification must be executable or transformable into some equivalent executable form. By submitting events simulating the environment to an animation tool, we can check the appropriateness of specified behaviours in response to such events. The primary quality being checked here is requirements adequacy. This technique is discussed in Section 5.3.

- *Formal verification* covers a wide range of more sophisticated checks that tools can perform on a formal specification. These include type consistency checks, completeness checks on decision tables, and algorithmic or deductive checking that a behaviour model satisfies a desired property. This family of techniques is discussed in Section 5.4.

As mentioned before, requirements quality assurance is intertwined with the activity of requirements documentation. It may start as soon as portions of the specification are available. As a consequence, parts of the material presented in this chapter are intertwined with corresponding parts of the previous chapter.

Some of the requirements evaluation techniques in Chapter 3 were also concerned with quality assurance. Inconsistency management and risk analysis are obviously aimed at producing more complete, consistent and adequate requirements. The difference between the techniques in that chapter and this one lies in the stages of the RE process at which they are applied. Requirements evaluation consists of earlier analysis of raw elicited material, with multiple options still being left open, whereas requirements quality assurance as we will discuss it now consists of later analysis of specifications along selected options.

5.1 Requirements inspections and reviews

The first, widely applicable technique for requirements quality assurance consists of asking selected people to inspect the RD individually for defects and then meet for reviews to agree on a list of problems to be fixed. Inspections and reviews are known to be quite effective for source code (Fagan, 1986). Empirical studies suggest that this technique can outperform code testing. More recent studies reveal its effectiveness when applied to requirements documents as well, in terms of high defect detection rates, quality benefits and cost savings (Doolan, 1992; Kelly *et al.*, 1992).

Section 5.1.1 explains the various phases of the requirements inspection process. Section 5.1.2 provides some guidelines for organizing it. Section 5.1.3 discusses various types of inspection checklists.

5.1.1 The requirements inspection process

Requirements inspection may be more or less structured. At one extreme, *walkthroughs* are internal inspections involving members of the project team.

In general, the process is made more formal through having external reviewers, meetings with specific agendas, preparation material sent in advance so that people can come prepared to the meetings, and inspection reports. Figure 5.1 shows the phases of a more structured inspection process.

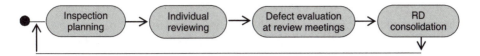

Figure 5.1   *Requirements inspection, review, and consolidation*

Inspection planning

This preliminary phase determines the size of and the members of the inspection team; the timing of the inspection process; the schedule and scope of each review meeting; and the format of inspection reports. Guidelines may be used for this; see Section 5.1.2.

Individual reviewing

Each inspector reads the RD or part of it individually to look for defects. This phase can be operated in several modes:

- *Free mode.* The inspector receives no directive on what part of the RD to consider specifically or what type of defect to look for. The review entirely relies on his or her initiative and expertise.

- *Checklist based.* The inspector is given a list of questions and issues to guide the defect search process. He or she may be directed to a specific part of the RD. (Checklists are discussed at the end of this section.)

- *Process based.* Each inspector is given a specific process to follow for defect search. The RD is distributed among inspectors playing different roles, according to different perspectives. Each of them is assigned specific targets, checklists and procedures or techniques for checking a specific class of defect. For example, one inspector for our train control system might be assigned the role of domain expert to check all safety-related requirements and assumptions using fault tree analysis (see Section 3.2.2). Another inspector might play the developer role and check all performance-related requirements and assumptions on the train–station communication infrastructure. In our meeting scheduling system, one inspector might be assigned the meeting initiator role to focus on functional requirements and check them for adequacy, consistency and completeness; another might play the meeting participant role to check convenience-related requirements; another might play the developer role to focus on interoperability requirements and so on.

Defect evaluation at review meetings

This phase takes place at the meetings scheduled in the planning phase. The defects found by each inspector are collected and discussed by the meeting participants in order to keep only those on which all agree. The causes of agreed defects are analysed, including causes in the RE process. The team recommends appropriate actions and documents the conclusions in an inspection report.

The aim of this phase is thus to discard false positives; these are concerns pointed out by one inspector which on second thoughts are perceived by the meeting participants not to be a real problem. The authors of the RD may sometimes participate in order to provide clarifications and counterarguments.

RD consolidation

The requirements document is revised to address all concerns expressed in the inspection report.

There have been quite different opinions on the importance of review meetings. People have argued that the primary source of defect detection is the individual reviewing phase (Parnas & Weiss, 1985). Empirical studies suggest that individual reviewing in *process-based* mode generally results in higher defect-detection rates and more effective reviews than reviewing in free or checklist-based mode – even to the point that inspection meetings bring no improvement in view of their cost (Porter *et al.*, 1995; Regnell *et al.*, 2000). On the other hand, review meetings appear effective in reducing false positives (Porter & Johnson, 1997).

5.1.2 Inspection guidelines

As for testing, there are general *WHAT–WHO–WHEN–WHERE* guidelines that may be used in the inspection process to make it more effective in finding actual defects:

- *WHAT?* The inspection report should be accurate and informative on specific points. It should contain substantiated facts, not opinions. It should be constructive and not offensive to the authors of the RD. It must be approved by all inspectors. A report structure may be suggested to provide inspector guidance in individual reading and defect collection. To reduce writing overheads, the report structure and format should be lightweight. To encourage active inspection, it should leave room for free comments.

- *WHO?* The primary objective of inspection and reviews is to find as many actual defects as possible. The inspectors should therefore be independent from the authors of the RD. They should not have a conflict of interest with them, or be in charge of evaluating them personally. To increase the coverage of the defect space, the inspection team should be representative of all stakeholder viewpoints. It should include people with different backgrounds, for example a domain expert, an end-user and a developer. A quality assurance specialist may be appropriate as well. The minimum team size usually advocated is three.

- *WHEN?* Requirements inspection should not be applied too soon, to avoid detecting defects that would have subsequently been caught by the authors anyway, nor too late, to avoid their downward propagation to subsequent project phases. Shorter, repeated meetings are more productive than longer, fewer ones. Two-hour meetings are generally recommended.

- *WHERE?* Empirical evidence from software testing suggests that the more defects are found at a particular place, the more scrutiny is required at that place and the places impacting on it or impacted by it. In any case, the inspection should carefully consider places where critical aspects of the system are presented, such as safety-related or security-related ones.

5.1.3 Requirements inspection checklists

The checklist-based and process-based modes of individual reviewing rely on lists of specific issues to address while searching for defects. The checklists may be defect based, quality specific, domain specific, language based or a blend of all those.

Defect-based checklists

These are lists of questions structured according to the various types of defects that we can find in a requirements document (see Section 1.1.7). Table 5.1 provides such a checklist for the

Omission	Is this concept precisely defined somewhere? Is this acronym defined? Are these definitions summarized in the glossary of terms? Is this objective operationalized through specific requirements? Are those requirements sufficient to ensure this objective? Is there any additional hidden assumption required for this? Is the rationale for this requirement (or assumption) made explicit somewhere? If this requirement or assumption relates to another, is the latter specified somewhere?
Contradiction	Is this statement consistent with the system objectives and constraints? Is this statement consistent with other related statements?
Inadequacy	Does this RD item formulate what stakeholders really expect?
Ambiguity	Can this statement be interpreted differently in different relevant contexts or by readers from different backgrounds? What are the possible interpretations? Are there other statements using this term with a different meaning?
Unmeasurability	Is there a fit criterion associated with this quality requirement? Is this fit criterion stated in terms of measurable quantities and measurement protocol? Can test data be derived from this statement to test that the implementation meets it? Is this statement stated in a way that discriminates it from alternative options?
Noise	Is this statement relevant to system objectives and constraints? Does the negation of this statement make any sense? (Otherwise the statement is a tautology.) Has this already been said without any reason for redundancy? Are there any other statements using this concept under different terms?
Overspecification	Does this statement entail a premature design choice? Would there be alternative sensible choices?
Unfeasibility	Is this RD item implementable in view of infrastructure, budget or timing constraints?

Table 5.1 *Defect-based checklist*

Unintelligibility	Will this statement be comprehensible by anyone who should use it? If not, why?
Poor structuring	Is the structuring rule for organizing these RD sections apparent? Is there any other structuring rule that would make them easier to understand? Is there any RD item related to this and described in an unrelated part of the RD? Does this RD item cover unrelated requirements? Does this RD item mix requirements and assumptions together? Does this RD item mix requirements and domain properties? Is there any unnecessary intermixing of functional and non-functional requirements?
Forward reference	Is this concept, so far undefined, defined somewhere later?
Remorse	Has this concept been used already before this definition?
Poor modifiability	Would any change to this RD item need to be propagated throughout major portions of the RD?
Opacity	Are there any inderdependent RD items whose dependencies are not made visible?

Table 5.1 Continued

defect table given in Chapter 1 (see Table 1.1). The table is split between errors and flaws. The granularity of an RD item may vary from a single statement to a group of statements following each other in the RD document.

Defect-based checklists cover the entire defect search space in terms of an extensible set of concrete questions for each defect type. Inspectors are thereby instructed on what to look for. The checklists remain fairly generic, though.

Quality-specific checklists

Such checklists specialize defect-based ones to specific categories of non-functional requirements, for example safety, security, performance, usability and so forth (see Section 1.1.5). For example, Lutz has defined a checklist for safety-related errors based on her studies of prominent error patterns in NASA safety-critical software. Her checklist specializes Jaffe's guidewords and correctness criteria to the context of interface and robustness requirements. (Guidewords were introduced in Section 3.2.2.) Omissions are the primary target defects here as their consequences are in general the most serious. Here is a sample (Lutz, 1996).

- Is there any unspecified response in this operation to out-of-range values of an input variable?

- Is there any unspecified response in this operation to not receiving an expected input value, or receiving it too early or too late?

- Does the logical OR of the input conditions on this operation form a tautology?

- Is there any recovery operation in case of input saturation?

- Can any output of this operation be produced faster than it can be handled by the consuming operation?

- Are all inputs from sensors used by the software controller?

- Does every state sequence from this hazardous state lead to a low-risk state?

- In case of error recovery by performance degradation, is the degradation predictable?

- Is there a check for data consistency performed before this decision is made based on those data?

Domain-specific checklists

These may specialize generic and quality-specific checklists to the specific concepts and standard operations found in the domain. The aim is to provide increasingly specific guidance in defect search. For example, we might define defect checklists specific to the meeting scheduling domain for the operations of initiating a meeting or determining a meeting schedule from participants' constraints. We might do the same in the train control domain for the operations of controlling train accelerations or doors opening.

Language-based checklists

Such checklists specialize the defect-based ones to the specific constructs of the structured, semi-formal or formal specification language used in the requirements document. The richer the language is, the more specific and dedicated the checklist will be. Moreover, most checks can be automated when those constructs are formalized (see Sections 5.2 and 5.4 hereafter).

For the *statement templates* discussed in Section 4.2.1, a checklist might be structured according to the specific template used, for example:

- Is there a value for every field in this template instantiation?

- Is this statement identifier used consistently throughout the RD?

- Does the statement type correctly indicate a requirement, assumption, domain property or definition?

- Is this fit criterion defined in terms of measurable quantities and measurement protocols?

- Is this rationale consistent with the system objectives?

- Is this priority consistent with the priority of other requirements to which this requirement contributes?

Train receives outdated acceleration command	T	T	T	T	F	F	F
Train enters station block at speed $\geq X$ m.p.h.	T	T	F	F	T	F	F
Preceding train is closer than Y metres	T	F	T	F	F	T	F
Full braking activated	X		X				
Alarm generated to station computer	X	X	X	X			

Table 5.2   *An incomplete decision table*

For the *decision tables* discussed in Section 4.2.1, completeness and redundancy checks can be performed almost for free – just by counting the number of columns and entry conditions. For example, consider the decision table in Table 5.2, inspired from our train braking example in Section 4.2.1.

This table has seven columns. For three input conditions, there should be eight columns to enumerate all possible combinations of conditions. One combination is thus missing. It turns out to be the critical case where the train does not receive an outdated command but is entering the station block too fast with a preceding train too close. In this missing case, full braking should be activated.

For a binary decision table with N entry conditions, there must be 2^N columns for the table to list all possible combinations of conditions exhaustively. If the number of columns is strictly less than 2^N, the table is incomplete; if this number is strictly greater than 2^N, the table is redundant. The missing combinations must be identified. Some might be impossible in view of domain properties, but this has to be documented in the RD. For those that are missing and actually possible, a corresponding effect condition must be specified to complete the specification.

For the *global templates* discussed in Section 4.2.2, a checklist might contain questions regarding the conformance of the RD organization to the structure prescribed by the template, and the matching of each section's actual content to the prescribed section heading.

For the *diagrammatic languages* discussed in Section 4.3, the checklists may include surface-level consistency and completeness checks within diagrams and between diagrams, for example:

- Does each input data flowing in this DFD operation appear as input data flowing in some upstream sub-operation in the DFD refining this operation? Does each output data flowing out of this DFD operation appear as output data flowing out of some downstream sub-operation in the DFD refining this operation?

- Are the input and output data of this DFD operation declared in an ER diagram?

- Does this relationship in this ER diagram have an adequate multiplicity?

- For the normal scenario described by this ET diagram, is there any possible exception scenario associated with it and not specified in the set of corresponding abnormal scenarios?

- Does the event labelling this interaction in this ET diagram trigger a transition in the SM diagram generalizing it? Is the event trace in the former diagram covered by a path in the latter diagram?

- Is there any state other than the final one in this SM diagram with no outgoing transition?

- Are the dynamic attributes or relationships defining this state in this SM diagram declared in an ER diagram?

Note that some of these questions correspond to the inter-view consistency rules discussed in Section 4.3.9, and to the kind of static semantics check performed by compilers – like 'Is this used variable declared?' or 'Is this declared variable used?'. These checks need not be manually performed by inspectors as tools can automate them (see Section 5.2).

For the *formal specification languages* discussed in Section 4.4, the checklists may include semantically richer consistency and completeness checks within specification units and between units. In Z, for example, a checklist may include questions such as the following:

- Is the type of the right-hand-side expression defining the output variable in this equational post-condition compatible with the declared type of that variable?

- If this variable is declared as a partial function in this data schema, is there an invariant in the schema to specify the input domain where this function is everywhere defined?

- If the output variable in this operation schema is a partial function, is there a corresponding pre-condition in the schema to specify where this variable is fully defined?

- Is this pre-condition consistent with invariants stated in the imported data schemas?

- Is there a corresponding exception schema for the case where this pre-condition does not hold?

- Does this OR-combination of schemas cover all possible cases?

- Does every imported variable in this Δ-operation schema have a post-condition to define its final state after the operation is applied?

- Is there an initialization schema for every data schema?

As the specification is fully formalized, many of these checks can be automated by tools (see Section 5.4 hereafter).

5.1.4 Conclusion

Inspections and reviews are an effective technique for requirements quality assurance. This technique appears to be even more effective than code inspection, in terms of type of defects found and their potential impact (Laitenberger & DeBaud, 2000). It is the widest in scope and applicability, and can be used to search for any kind of defect in any kind of specification format. For individual reviewing, a process-based mode relying on a blend of defect-based, quality-specific, domain-specific and language-based checklists is expected to be the most effective.

On the downside, there can be a large amount of inspection material to search through. The technique may require significant resources in time and manpower to be highly effective – especially if inspection meetings are required. Some efforts have been undertaken recently to alleviate the burden and costs through groupware tools that support document navigation, reduce paperwork and decrease the communication overhead (MacDonald & Miller, 1999; Grünbacher *et al.*, 2003). The danger still remains that important problems might be missed if they are not covered by specific checklists and if inspectors are overwhelmed with overly long, unmanageable checklists.

5.2 Queries on a requirements database

This tool-supported technique for requirements quality assurance is both simple and effective for large specifications. It may work on parts of the RD that are specified in terms of the diagrammatic notations reviewed in Section 4.3.

The idea is to maintain the specification in a *requirements database*. The schema of this database closely reflects the structure of the diagram language used for specification (Teichroew & Hershey, 1977). Queries on the requirements database allow for structural consistency and completeness checks. These correspond to some of the questions in the diagram-specific checklists in the previous section, and to the intra- and inter-view consistency rules discussed in Section 4.3.9.

The schema of the requirements database can be derived automatically, together with the language-specific database engine, by a meta-tool taking a meta-specification of the diagram language as input. The generated database engine includes a diagram-specific query language and processor for specification querying (Teichroew *et al.*, 1980; van Lamsweerde *et al.*, 1988; Jarke *et al.*, 1995).

Let us have a closer look at this on a concrete example. Suppose that we have specified some operational parts of our RD using a series of data-flow diagrams, where complex operations were recursively refined into finer-grained DFDs (see Section 4.3.4). Everywhere in the specification where an operation is refined, we would like to make sure that each data flowing out of this operation appears as data flowing out of one sub-operation (at least) in the DFD refining the operation.

A corresponding check negates this property. It might be formulated in natural language as follows:

> Is there any output data flowing out of this operation that is not flowing out of any of the refining sub-operations?

This check is a consistency check between adjacent levels of operation refinement, and a completeness check on the refining DFD. (It corresponds to the first question in the diagram-specific checklist in the previous section, simplified here for sake of clarity.)

In a DFD-specific query language, the check might look like the following:

```
Query DFD-refinementConsistency
  set out-data = Data
    which FlowsOut Operation with Operation.Name = 'myOperation'
    and which not FlowsOut ref-ops
      where set ref-ops = Operation which Refines Operation with Operation.Name = 'myOperation'
```

The diagram-specific query language is often an entity–relationship language having a set-theoretic flavour. The effect of a **set**-statement is to define a *group* of one or more elements from types or other groups (**where**-clause), by means of standard set operators and predicate expressions on relationships (**which**-clause) and attributes (**with**-clause) that are defined at the meta level.

If the set *out-data* returned by this query is non-empty, an inconsistency is detected; the returned set elements indicate the output flows missing in the DFD refining the operation.

Note that the words **Data**, **Operation**, **Name**, **FlowsOut** and **Refines** in the preceding query are keywords from the DFD language. The grammar of this language and the corresponding query engine are generated from a specification of the DFD language in an entity–relationship *meta*-language. Figure 5.2 shows the corresponding meta-specification, using the ER diagrammatic language described in Section 4.3.2 as the meta-language.

In practice, the analyst does not necessarily need to encode such structural checks in the query language. Many CASE tools offer an extensive, pre-cooked list of queries to check standard rules of intra- and inter-view consistency and completeness for the diagrams they support – see the diagram-specific checklist in the previous section for other examples of such rules. The diagrams can then be checked in 'press-button' mode to report violations of the rules encoded in this list.

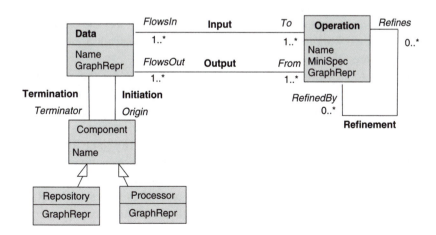

Figure 5.2   *An ER meta-specification of DFD diagrams for specification querying*

5.3 Requirements validation by specification animation

The main purpose of requirements *validation* is to check the adequacy of requirements and assumptions (see Section 1.1.7). We want to see whether the system-to-be as specified meets the actual expectations of stakeholders.

A first way of doing this consists of defining a representative sample of *validation scenarios*; we may then go through these with stakeholders to check whether the interactions among system components and their sequencing correspond to what stakeholders do really expect. When such scenarios are formalized as event trace diagrams, we can use scenario enactment tools that execute the scenarios and show the results of interactions along timelines in a visual form. (Scenarios were defined in Section 2.2.5 and their representation by ET diagrams was discussed in Section 4.3.6.). The problems we saw with elicitation scenarios remain the same. The identification of a representative scenario sample from the specified requirements and assumptions, for comprehensive system coverage, may not be easy.

Another approach, integrating the previous one, consists of animating parts of the specified system. To do this, we extract or generate an executable model of the software-to-be from the specifications. Then we simulate the system's behaviour using this model, and check with stakeholders whether a visualization of this simulation is adequate with respect to what they expect.

To simulate the system's behaviour, we submit events to the model that mimic possible behaviours of the environment, in order to execute the software model in response to these events. To visualize the simulation, we show how a suggestive representation of the system evolves dynamically as the model is being executed.

A *simulation* is thus an execution of the software model, whereas an *animation* is a visualization, in a suggestive form, of the simulated model in its environment.

Section 2.2.6 introduced prototyping as an aid to requirements elicitation. Prototyping and animation are related techniques, but they are not quite the same. A prototype is a quick implementation, in a very high-level programming language. It is not necessarily based on a model, and pays less attention to system visualization.

Requirements animation relies on an executable model. We therefore need a formal specification of what we want to check for adequacy. This specification must be executable or transformable into an equivalent executable form.

There are many tools working on this animation principle for the various specification paradigms reviewed in Section 4.4. For the state-based specification paradigm, the animators are interpreters of an executable subset of the corresponding language. Examples include the Jaza animator (for Z), the B-core and B-Toolkit animators (for B), the VDM-Tools animator (for VDM) and the Octopus and Together Designer animators (for OCL). For the transition-based specification paradigm, the animators execute state machine transitions that are triggered by input events from the environment. Examples include the SCR animator (for SCR), the STATEMATE and Rhapsody animators (for statecharts), the Nimbus animator (for RSML) and the LTSA animator (for labelled transition systems). For the history-based paradigm, the FAUST animator executes transitions in a state machine specification generated from pre-, post- and trigger conditions; these conditions are derived from temporal logic specifications of requirements and assumptions (we will come back to this in Chapter 18).

Let us have a closer look at how requirements animation typically works on a state machine specification.

5.3.1 Extracting an executable model from the specification

We first need to determine what part of the specification we want to animate for adequacy checking. If the selected part is written in an executable subset of the specification language, we can execute it directly. Otherwise we need to transform it into an executable version that must be semantically equivalent. For a state machine specification, the result is typically a set of parallel state machines – one per component class that we want to animate. In our train control system, for example, there might be one state machine for the dynamics of train doors, one for the dynamics of train moves and so forth.

5.3.2 Simulating the model

The extracted model must be instantiated for execution. We need to select component instances as 'test cases' – for example, do we want an animation with a single train and three stations, or two trains running in parallel on a track with four stations?

The instantiated state machines for the selected instances are then executed in parallel under control of a *NextState* function. This function controls the concurrent activation of multiple transitions fired by the occurrence of multiple triggering events. It also handles clock ticking for the animator's stepwise execution.

To see what the *NextState* function may look like, we need the following quantities. Let T denote a set of transitions, *CS* a global configuration of states and E a set of events:

Triggered (E):	set of transitions triggered by an event e in E.
Enabled (T, CS):	set of transitions in T whose source state is in *CS*.
Permitted (T, CS):	set of transitions whose guard is satisfied in configuration *CS* (guards were introduced in Section 4.3.7).
Consistent (T):	maximal set of transitions in T whose target states are not conflicting with each other (that is, the instantiated target state predicates are not inconsistent with each other).
EvGenerated (T):	set of output events generated when all transitions in T are executed.
newConfig (T, CS):	new global configuration produced by executing all transitions in T from configuration CS.

The *NextState* function is then recursively defined as follows;

```
NextState (E, CS):
      T = Triggered (E);
      T' = Enabled (T, CS) ∩ Permitted (T, CS) ∩ Consistent (T);
      if T' ≠ ∅ then
             E' = EvGenerated (T');
             CS' = newConfig (T', CS);
             NextState (E', CS');
      endif return
```

According to this definition of *NextState*, two transitions found to be conflicting with each other are both discarded; we do not consider alternative subsets of transitions with non-conflicting target states. We could be less strict and keep one of the conflicting transitions while discarding the others (Heimdahl & Leveson, 1996). The problem then is the arbitrary choice of which transition to keep. The user interacting with the animator might control this selection by moving the animation one step back and dropping one of the conflicting transitions of his or her choice.

5.3.3 Visualizing the simulation

The model simulation should be visualized in a suggestive way. For interaction with stakeholders, the animator should make it convenient to input events and watch the model's reactions. Animators typically support one or more of the following visualization formats:

- *Textual.* The input events are entered as textual commands; the model reactions are displayed as execution traces.

- *Diagrammatic.* The input events are entered by event selection among those applicable in the current state; the model reactions are displayed as tokens progressing along the model diagrams together with corresponding state visualization.

- *Domain-specific visualization.* The input events are entered through domain-specific control devices displayed on the screen; the model reactions are displayed as new values on domain-specific control panels. The entire animation may even be visualized as an animated scene in the software environment.

The third format for visualizing the simulation is obviously most appealing to stakeholders and, in particular, to domain experts. The SCR and RSML animators support control devices and panels. The LTSA and FAUST animators support domain scenes as well. Figure 5.3 shows a screenshot from the FAUST animator. As we can see there, the visualization is a mix of textual, diagrammatic and domain-specific formats. The textual window displays the trace of an animation scenario being replayed. The lower right window shows parallel state machines for train doors and train moves where the current state is highlighted. The two upper windows show snapshots, in this state, of two domain scenes taking place in parallel. One scene shows doors of train no. 1 opening and closing, whereas the other shows trains no. 1 and no. 2 moving along a single track with two stations and two railroad crossings. The window in the left middle of the screen shows an input–output control panel containing a speedometer and two joysticks for starting and stopping the train and opening and closing doors, respectively. Also note that this animation snapshot reveals a pretty bad problem in the simulated model, as seen visually but also pointed out by a property monitor on the lower left window – namely, the train is moving (see the speedometer) with the doors open.

5.3.4 Conclusion

Requirements animation is a concrete technique for checking a specification. It may reveal subtle inadequacies and other defects as well, in particular missing items – in Figure 5.3, a guard 'doors closed' missing on the 'start' transition from 'train stopped' to 'train moving'.

Due to its principle of 'What You See Is What You Check', animation is among the best ways of getting stakeholders and practitioners into the quality assurance loop. Moreover, 'interesting' animation scenarios may be recorded by the animator for later replay. In particular, these scenarios may provide *acceptance test data* for free. Animators can also be coupled with other analysis tools, such as monitors that detect property violations on the fly during animation (see the lower left window in Figure 5.3) or model checkers (discussed in the next section).

On the downside, there is a price to pay – we need a formal specification. Moreover, there is no guarantee that rewarding animation sequences will be played; these are interaction sequences revealing defects in the specification. To provide such a guarantee, the users of the animator should be carefully selected to be representative of experienced people who know about tricky things that can happen in the environment. Like test data, the animation scenarios should be carefully elaborated beforehand to ensure comprehensive model coverage. It should ideally be possible to simulate multiple events occurring independently and in parallel in the environment.

The gap between the animated model and the original specification may also be a problem. Is the model adequately capturing what was intended in the original, non-formal specification? If the animation reveals a bad symptom, where can the causes be found in the original specification?

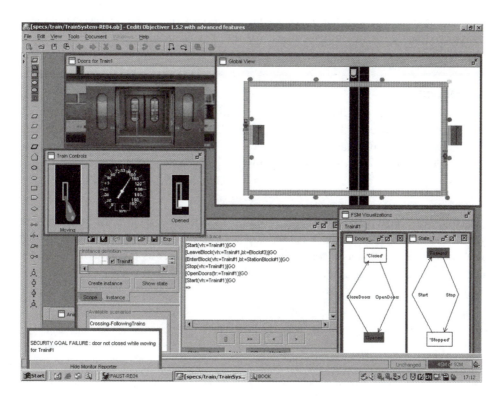

Figure 5.3 *Visualizing a model simulation during animation*

5.4 Requirements verification through formal checks *

The techniques in this section cover a wide range of more or less sophisticated checks on a specification that can be automated by tools. The specification must therefore be formal. The checks depend on the specific constructs of the specification language:

- Language checks are similar to those usually performed by compilers. They include syntax checks, type checks, static semantics checks, circularity checks and the like.

- The formal constructs provided by some languages allow for certain forms of consistency and completeness checking. We can use them to check that a specified input–output relationship is a function, in order to preclude non-deterministic behaviours, and is total, to cover all possible cases on its input set.

- A more sophisticated class of checks allows us to verify that the model we have specified formally satisfies some domain-specific property. Such verification can be done algorithmically by searching through the model for property violations; this is referred to as *model checking*. Alternatively, the verification can be done deductively by application of language-specific rules of inference to prove the property taken as candidate theorem.

5.4.1 Language checks

These checks correspond to what a syntax-directed editor or a compiler would typically do for us. Let us have a closer look at these for the Z specification of the library system in Section 4.4.3.

Syntax checking

Every expression in the specification must be grammatically well formed according to the syntax rules of the language. For example, a mistakenly written precondition 'bc?: Available' in the *CheckOut* operation schema in Section 4.4.3 would be detected by a Z syntax checker; declaration symbols may not appear in unquantified predicates.

Type checking

Each variable must have a specified type and all uses of this variable must be consistent with the type declaration. For example, a declaration 'Available: BookCopy' and pre-condition 'bc? $\in$ Available' would be detected as inconsistent by a Z type checker as the variable *Available* is not declared as representing a set, whereas it is used as a set. Similarly, in the *CheckOut* operation schema in Section 4.4.3, post-conditions such as

$$OnLoan' = OnLoan \cup bc?, \quad BorrowedBy' = BorrowedBy \cup \{bc? \rightarrow p?\},$$

---

* This section is provided here for comprehensive coverage of the topic of this chapter. It is based on Section 4.4 and may be skipped by fast-track readers only interested in a general overview of RE fundamentals or with no background in rudimentary discrete mathematics. Its material is, however, a prerequisite for Chapters 17–18.

where '$\rightarrow$' is the function declaration symbol, would be detected by a Z type checker as being inconsistent with the declaration 'bc?: BookCopy' and the imported declarations 'OnLoan: $\mathbb{P}$BookCopy', 'BorrowedBy: BookCopy $\twoheadrightarrow$ Person'.

Such structure clashes are found fairly often in informal requirements documents. For example, the constraints of a meeting participant could be defined at one place as a pair of sets of excluded and preferred dates, respectively, whereas at another place they are referred to as a set of excluded day slots. Finding such inconsistency through type checking may be quite helpful.

Static semantics checking

Each variable must be declared and have a specified initial value; variables must be used within their scope and so forth. For example, the misplacement of the invariant

dom WhichBook = Available $\cup$ OnLoan

in the *LibraryShelves* data schema in Section 4.4.3 would be easily detected as being outside the scope of the variable *WhichBook*. The Z schema import and initialization mechanisms make it easy to automate this type of check.

Circularity checking

No variable is being defined in terms of itself. Such checks are usually automated by detecting cycles in dependency graphs. A trivial example of circularity would be the following wrong post-condition in the *CheckOut* operation schema:

Available = Available \ {bc?}

Circular definitions are fairly frequent in technical reports such as requirements documents.

5.4.2 Dedicated consistency and completeness checks

A formal specification often relies on input–output relations to prescribe expected services and behaviours.

- Requiring such relations to be *functions* rules out undesirable non-deterministic behaviours; for every input situation there may be at most one corresponding output.

- Requiring such functions to be *total* ensures that there is an output for every possible input situation.

These properties can be easily checked when the relations are explicitly defined at single places in the specification.

Let us consider the SCR tables introduced in Section 4.4.4 to illustrate this kind of checking. We saw there that a condition table must specify the various values of a controlled variable or term as a total function of an associated mode class and conditions.

Checking disjointness of input cases for consistency

To check that the relation captured by a condition table is a function, we need to check, for each input row of the table, that the condition entries in that row are pairwise disjoint; there is then no input situation where two different outputs are defined. If $C1$, $C2$ denote a pair of condition entries, this amounts to checking that:

$$C1 \wedge C2 = \textit{false}$$

For example, consider the condition table in Table 5.3. (This table is a modified version of Table 4.3 in Section 4.4.4.)

Checking the entry conditions in the first input row for disjointness we obtain, by distributivity of AND over OR:

$$(\text{AtPlatform OR Emergency}) \text{ AND NOT AtPlatform} = (\text{AtPlatform AND NOT AtPlatform}) \text{ OR (Emergency AND NOT AtPlatform)}$$

$$= \textit{false} \text{ OR Emergency AND NOT AtPlatform}$$

$$= \text{Emergency AND NOT AtPlatform}$$

$$\neq \textit{false}$$

We thus have a problem here. Indeed, in situations where Emergency AND NOT AtPlatform holds, the table prescribes a non-deterministic behaviour where the doors may either be open or closed. This inconsistency must clearly be fixed by making the two conditions disjoint – here, by adding a conjunct NOT Emergency to the second condition.

Checking coverage of input cases for exhaustiveness

To check that the function captured by a condition table is total, we need to check that, for each input row of the table, the condition entries in that row cover all possible cases; an output is then defined in every possible input situation. If $C1$, $C2$, ..., Cn denote such condition entries, the following tautology must be checked:

$$C1 \vee C2 \vee \ldots \vee Cn = \textit{true}$$

For example, consider Table 5.4, the corrected version of Table 5.3. Checking the entry conditions in the first input row for coverage we obtain:

Mode	Conditions	
Stopped	AtPlatform OR Emergency	NOT AtPlatform
MovingOK, TooFast	False	True
DoorsState	Open	Closed

Table 5.3   *A condition table for controlled variable DoorsState*

Mode	Conditions	
Stopped	AtPlatform OR Emergency	NOT AtPlatform AND NOT Emergency
MovingOK, TooFast	False	True
DoorsState	Open	Closed

Table 5.4 *Corrected condition table for controlled variable DoorsState*

(AtPlatform OR Emergency) OR (NOT AtPlatform AND NOT Emergency) = AtPlatform OR Emergency
OR NOT AtPlatform
= **true** OR Emergency
= **true**

This formal derivation relies on rewritings based on propositional tautologies such as:

$(P \lor Q) \lor R \equiv P \lor Q \lor R$, $P \land Q \equiv Q \land P$, $P \lor \neg P \land Q \equiv P \lor Q$, $P \lor \textbf{true} \equiv \textbf{true}$.

Getting the same result for the second input row, we conclude that the table exhaustively covers all possible input cases.

In practice, tautology checkers are used by tools to automate such checks efficiently (Heitmeyer *et al.*, 1996). Similar techniques can be applied for other transition-based specification languages. In RSML, for example, the definition of the *NextState* relationship makes it possible to check such consistency and exhaustiveness compositionally for the entire system, structured as a set of hierarchical state machines (Heimdahl & Leveson, 1996).

5.4.3 Model checking

This technique is increasingly used to verify that a formally specified model satisfies some desired property. When checking a model at RE time, the property might be a requirement, an assumption or a domain property. Unlike theorem proving, the verification is algorithmic. The general idea is to explore the model in a systematic way to search for property violations. If a violation is found, the algorithm produces a counterexample that does not satisfy the property. This technique proves invaluable for debugging complex models involving safety-critical or security-critical aspects.

Figure 5.4 helps to visualize what model checking looks like. In the most frequent form of model checking, the inputs to the checker are a formal state machine model and a desired property formalized in temporal logic (see Section 4.4). There are two alternative outputs: '*Yes, the property is satisfied by the model*' or '*No, it is not satisfied, here is a counterexample*'.

The counterexample, if any, is a trace in the input state machine that does not satisfy the property. (A trace was defined in Section 4.3.7 as a sequence of successive states in the state machine up to a particular point. A temporal logic assertion was seen in Section 4.4.2 to be satisfied by historical sequences of states and falsified by others.)

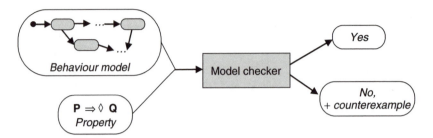

Figure 5.4 *Model checking*

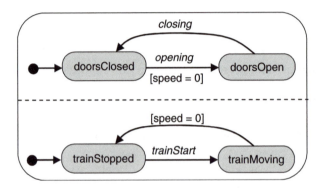

Figure 5.5 *A faulty SM model for the behaviour of a controller of train doors and movements*

Let us illustrate what a model checker can do on a concrete example inspired by Section 4.3.7. Figure 5.5 shows a faulty model for the behaviour of a component controlling train doors and movements in parallel.

As Section 4.3.7 explained, an SM state is an equivalence class of situations where an associated state variable has the same value. In particular, the states doorsClosed, doorsOpen, trainStopped and trainMoving stand for DoorsState = 'closed', DoorsState = 'open', MovementState = 'stopped' and MovementState = 'moving', respectively.

To check the model in Figure 5.5, we need to know which property to verify. (Part II of the book will show that a goal model can give us plenty of these.) Let us assume here that we want to model check that train doors always remain closed while the train is moving:

$\Box$ (MovementState = 'moving' $\rightarrow$ DoorsState = 'closed')

With this model and assertion as inputs, a model checker might produce the following counterexample trace, where each state is labelled by its incoming event:

init:	(doorsClosed, trainStopped);
start:	(doorsClosed, trainMoving);
[speed = 0]:	(doorsClosed, trainStopped);
opening:	(doorsOpen, trainStopped);
start:	(doorsOpen, trainMoving)

To find such a trace, a brute-force search algorithm builds the model's *reachability graph*. This graph contains the set of all possible states of the parallel state machine where those unreachable by allowed transitions have been removed.

- The reachability graph is explored exhaustively by recursively generating all next states from current ones, and testing whether those next states are 'bad' ones that result in property violation.

- The visited states are marked to avoid cycling.

- The algorithm terminates when a bad state is reached, in which case the violating path from the initial state to this bad state is produced, or when all states have been visited. In the latter case, the output is '*yes*' if no bad state was found, and '*no*' if a good state prescribed by the property was not found.

Model checkers can verify different types of properties on a parallel state machine:

- *Reachability* (or unreachability) properties are the easiest to verify. Such properties state that a particular situation can (or cannot) be reached. They are checked just by inspecting the reachability graph.

- *Safety* properties state that an undesirable condition may never hold (or a desirable condition must always hold). In a linear temporal logic, they take the form $\square\, P$. As soon as a trace is found to satisfy $\neg\ P$, the search algorithm terminates. (The word 'safety' used in this context is not necessarily related to safety-critical requirements.)

- *Liveness* properties state that a desirable condition must eventually hold. In a linear temporal logic, they take the form $\lozenge\ P$. When all states have been visited with no trace satisfying P the search algorithm terminates with a '*no*' output.

The combinatorial explosion of states to visit is an obvious problem with this kind of approach. As already noted in Section 4.3.7, a parallel state machine on N variables, each having M possible values, has M^N states. Fortunately enough, researchers in model checking have developed sophisticated techniques, based on theories of automata and data structures, in order to optimize the search and reduce the space for storing visited states by representing them implicitly. This makes it possible to explore a model with billions of states in reasonable time and space.

Another issue is the length and comprehensibility of counterexample traces generated by a model checker. For subtle bugs the trace can be long and provide little information on the causes of the symptom. Many model checkers take a *breadth-first* search strategy to produce the shortest violating traces. In the faulty model of Figure 5.5, the cause of the problem revealed by the counterexample is easy to spot; the guard DoorsState = 'closed' is missing on the *start* transition. For non-toy models and long traces, the mining of error causes is likely to be difficult, even if counterexample traces are the shortest ones.

There are multiple variants and refinements of the principles outlined here (Bérard *et al.*, 2001). The best-known variants and refinements are implemented in the SPIN and SMV model checkers.

In *SPIN*, the properties have to be formalized in Linear Temporal Logic (LTL). The state machine model must be expressed in PROMELA, a language close to guarded commands (Dijkstra, 1976). To address the state explosion problem, the visited states are maintained in a tunable hash table; the bigger the table, the smaller the likelihood of missing a bad state (Holzmann, 1997, 2003).

In *SMV*, the properties have to be formalized in Computation Tree Logic (CTL), a branching temporal logic where histories have a tree structure with branching to alternative successor states (see Section 4.4.2). This logic supports the formalization of reachability properties through *EF* quantifiers. To address the state explosion problem, sets of visited states are represented symbolically by binary decision diagrams (BDDs). Large sets of states can often be represented by small BDDs (Clarke *et al.*, 1999; Bryant, 1992).

The *Alloy* analyser fits the general scheme in Figure 5.4 but in a different specification paradigm. The input model is specified in Alloy, a state-based specification language. The property to verify is a 'claim' specified in Alloy as well. The model is first instantiated by restricting the range of the model variables to a few values, in order to avoid state explosion. The analyser then tries to satisfy the negation of the claim within that bounded model, using an efficient SAT solver. The counterexample produced, if any, is a set of values for the variables, within the restricted range, that satisfies the negated claim.

Model checking techniques have multiple strengths. Property verification is fully automated; unlike theorem proving, no human intervention is required during verification. As the analysis is exhaustive, flaws cannot be missed. For example, the bug shown as an example in this section *will* be detected. The same bug was revealed by animation in the previous section, but there we had to be lucky enough to decide to animate that trace. In fact, many model checking environments include an animator to visualize the generated counterexample traces. In practice, counterexamples prove to be the most helpful output of a model checker. They help debugging the specification and can be subsequently used as test data. These various strengths explain the increasing popularity of model checking technology in industry.

On the limitation side, the state explosion problem still makes model checkers unusable for the analysis of very large, complex models. *Bounded* model checkers address this limitation quite effectively; they check models instantiated to a few instances. But then we lose the original guarantee of not missing flaws. Much research work is also devoted to finding good abstractions to enable the analysis of infinite state models with finite state verification techniques. Other efforts focus on the explanation of complex counterexample traces to help find the causes of the problem in the model.

5.4.4 Theorem proving

Another approach to formal verification of a specification consists of verifying the desired property deductively rather than algorithmically. The formal system underpinning the specification language provides rules of inference to generate new assertions from given ones (see Section 4.4.1). The verification consists of showing that the target property, taken as the candidate theorem, can be derived from the formal specification, taken as a set of axioms, by a sequence of applications of inference rules. Such derivation can be automated by a theorem proving tool. Provers are generally interactive. An expert user may be required to confirm or reject generated lemmas that the tool cannot verify. The user may also need to provide proof strategies. These are combinations of rule applications that are more likely to produce shorter proofs.

A theorem prover can be used for other related purposes as well. By taking *false* as the candidate theorem, a set of specifications may be formally shown to be inconsistent. We can also derive new assertions from the specifications, show these to stakeholders after translation into natural language and ask them whether they want these consequences of what was specified.

In general, some of the inference rules come from the logic used whereas others are specific to the specification language. Suppose that we want to prove properties of a Z specification, for example. The inference rules might include, among others, the propositional *modus ponens* and *chaining* rules, the first-order *functional substitutivity* and *predicate substitutivity* rules (see Section 4.4.1) and the following Z-specific rule:

$$\frac{\textit{Prop [S}_0\textit{], \{Prop\} Op \{Prop\}} \text{ for every } \Delta\text{-operation } \textit{Op}}{\textit{Prop[s]} \text{ for every state s}} \quad \textit{invariance}$$

In this inference rule, *Prop [S]* means 'the property *Prop* is satisfied in state *S*', S_0 denotes the initial state and the expression {*P*} *Op* {*Q*} means 'if operation *Op* is applied in a state satisfying *P*, its application results in a state satisfying *Q*'. The rule encodes an induction principle over states. It says that a desired property can be inferred to hold in *any* state provided that it holds in the initial state and it is kept invariant along state transitions caused by any of the modifier operations.

To see what a proof may look like, let us get back to the Z specification of portions of our library system in Section 4.4.3. Suppose that we want to verify that the assertion

Prop: Available ∩ OnLoan = ∅,

from the *LibraryShelves* schema, does indeed hold in any state in view of the specification of the modifier operations on this schema. In other words, we want to prove that the modifiers as specified do preserve the invariance of this assertion. The above invariance rule allows us to derive the invariant from the specification of modifiers as follows:

- *Prop [S$_0$]* is trivially verified since the initialization schema *InitLibraryShelves* tells us that Available = ∅ and OnLoan = ∅ (see Section 4.4.3).

- We then need to show that {*Prop*} *RobustCheckOut* {*Prop*}.

    a. Since all exceptions UnauthorizedAgent, UnregisteredUser, UnknownCopy, UnavailableBook, LoanLimitReached in the specification of *RobustCheckOut* are Ξ-operations, we just need to focus on the *CheckOut* Δ-operation.

b. Assuming that *CheckOut* is applied in a state satisfying *Prop*, we use the post-conditions specified in *CheckOut* to compute the term Available ∩ OnLoan in the final state of *CheckOut* (see Section 4.4.3):

Available′ ∩ OnLoan′ = (Available \ {bc?}) ∩ (OnLoan ∪ {bc?})

(using the rule of functional substitutivity on function symbol '∩')

= Ø (because of the precondition bc?∈ *Available* and a known property in set theory, namely: **if** a ∈ A and A ∩ B = Ø **then** A \ {a} ∩ B ∪ {a} = Ø)

- The proof is similar for {*Prop*} *RobustReturn* {*Prop*}.

- Hence, by application of the invariance rule, we derive that *Available* ∩ *OnLoan* = Ø holds in any state.

Let us now illustrate how an inconsistency can be derived. Suppose that the following assertion is explicitly or implicitly specified in the *CheckOut* operation schema:

OnLoan′ = OnLoan

(Such an error is not uncommon when state variables are declared, through a Ξ–schema import, as being left unchanged.) From the invariant defining the OnLoan variable in the *LibraryShelves* data schema, we know that:

OnLoan = **dom** BorrowedBy   in *any* state

Using an instantiation rule, we conclude that in the states after application of the operation *CheckOut*, we have in particular:

OnLoan′ = **dom** BorrowedBy′

= **dom** (BorrowedBy ∪ {bc? ↦ p?})

(by the postcondition and functional substitutivity on function '**dom**')

= **dom** BorrowedBy ∪ **dom** {bc? ↦ p?}

(by a known property about domains in function theory)

= OnLoan ∪ {bc?}

(by folding the above definition of *OnLoan* and by functional substitutivity on '∪')

Getting back to the above wrong post-condition on OnLoan, we obtain by transitivity of equality:

OnLoan = OnLoan ∪ {bc?}

which is inconsistent in set theory as $A = A \cup B$ cannot be satisfied when B is not empty.

A similar kind of derivation can be applied to derive pre-conditions from invariants.

Note that the preceding two proofs rely on known properties from base theories. Tools automating such derivations include simplifier modules that access libraries of axioms and theorems about sets, relations, arithmetics and so on.

The main strength of theorem provers comes from the soundness and completeness of the underlying formal system used. Thanks to the deductive inference rules applied in the derivations, every derived conclusion is correct and every correct conclusion can theoretically be derived. In addition to property verification, these conclusions can be used for showing inconsistencies in the specification and inadequacies of logical consequences. Properties that cannot be verified by a model checker, for state explosion reasons, can be verified with a theorem prover. Infinite state spaces can be handled through induction-based inference rules. Failing proofs can also provide more insights into error causes.

The main problem is the difficulty of using theorem proving tools. A highly experienced user is needed to input, accept or reject lemmas that cannot be proved in practice, and to guide the application of inference rules. Unlike model checkers, no concrete counterexample is produced if the target property is not satisfied.

5.5 Conclusion

Requirements quality assurance is a major concern in view of the diversity of potential defects in the requirements document (RD), their consequences and the cost of late repair. The RD must be carefully analysed to detect defects and fix them – especially incomplete, inconsistent, inadequate, ambiguous or unmeasurable RD items.

The techniques reviewed in this chapter vary in scope, applicability and cost effectiveness:

- Inspections and reviews can in principle detect any kind of defect in any kind of specification format. Their cost can be controlled by a well-planned process and effective checklists. This technique is less likely to uncover subtle errors. Tool support is fairly limited.

- Queries on a requirements database can detect structural inconsistencies and omissions in semi-formal specifications. The technique is fairly cheap as it can be fully automated by easy-to-use tools. As queries address surface aspects of specifications only, they are not likely to find subtle errors.

- Requirements animation requires a formal, executable specification of what we want to animate. The main target defects are inadequacies, although missing items can also be detected. Suggestive visualizations of the simulation allow domain experts and end-users to be involved in the quality assurance process. Animators can point out subtle errors, but only along the animation scenarios followed. The main cost is that of building the specification to be animated.

- Formal verification can reveal ambiguous and unmeasureable RD items during specification formalization, and omissions, inconsistencies and inadequacies during specification analysis. They are supported by tools that can uncover subtle errors. However, they are less widely applicable as they all require a formal specification of what we want to analyse. The tools generally require experienced users to be available. Dedicated consistency and completeness checks may sometimes offer a good cost–benefit compromise; there is no need for building huge reachability graphs or using complex theorem proving technology. Empirical evidence, however, suggests that model checkers and theorem provers are champions at uncovering subtle, critical errors. In the former case, exhaustive exploration guarantees that no defects are missed; in the latter case, deductive derivations on declarative specifications are less exposed to state explosion problems.

Those complementary strengths and limitations lead to the conclusion that an ideal requirements quality assurance process should integrate inspections and reviews on the entire RD, queries on surface aspects of the conceptual, functional and behavioural facets of the system, and animation and formal checking for in-depth analysis of critical aspects, including safety- and security-related ones, if any.

This chapter did not cover all the approaches to requirements quality assurance. In particular, natural language paraphrasing of a formal specification has appeared promising in other areas (Swartout, 1983). Generating natural language sentences from a semi-formal or formal specification, for checking by stakeholders, might prove effective for adequacy or consistency checking (Dallianis, 1992; Gervasi & Zowghi, 2005).

There are other quality-related outcomes of requirements validation and verification that we did not cover but that are worth mentioning (see the bibliographical notes at the end of this chapter for some references):

- We can produce *test data* from interaction scenarios, R-net diagrams, decision tables or animations. We can generate them automatically with model checkers, constraint solvers applied to state-based or history-based specifications, or dedicated test data generators.

- We can also generate specification refinements towards implementations.

- Instead of verifying invariant properties, we can sometimes generate them algorithmically to check the adequacy of the specification, to complete it or to prune the state space.

- Formal reuse of specifications can be supported by specification matching tools.

The semi-formal and formal techniques in this chapter assume that an operational specification is fully available, such as a state machine specification or a structured system decomposition into data and operations. This strong assumption does not hold in the earlier stages of the RE process. The material available for early analysis is partial and made up of declarative statements such as objectives and constraints mixed with scenario examples. We therefore need complementary techniques for earlier, incremental checks on declarative specification fragments. Parts II and III of the book will present a sample of such techniques. A goal-oriented modelling framework will support a variety of semi-formal and formal techniques for earlier checking of partial models, in particular:

- To check that refinements of objectives into sub-objectives are correct and complete.

- To check that operationalizations of objectives into specifications of operations are correct and complete.

- To animate these operationalizations for adequacy checking.

- To point out incomplete specifications due to poor risk analysis and lack of anticipation of unexpected behaviours (as introduced in Section 3.2) and to resolve this incompleteness through appropriate countermeasures.

- To detect conflicts and divergences among objectives, requirements and assumptions (as introduced in Section 3.1) and to resolve them according to various strategies.

As we will see there, formal analysis can be restricted to specific parts of declarative models and applied only when and where needed.

Summary

- Requirements quality assurance consists of detecting defects in the requirements document (RD), reporting them, analysing their causes and undertaking appropriate actions to fix them. The final result of this activity is a consolidated RD. The main target of this process is the completeness, consistency, adequacy, unambiguity, measureability and comprehensibility of RD items. The later such defects are found with respect to these target qualities, the more costly their repair is. Other qualities to care for include pertinence, realism, good structuring, traceability and modifiability.

- Requirements inspection and reviews form an effective technique for quality assurance. It is the widest in scope and applicability. For individual inspection, a process-based mode relying on a blend of defect-based, quality-specific, domain-specific and language-based checklists is expected to be most effective. It may then even be the case that the review meetings normally following individual inspections are no longer cost effective.

- Queries are a simple but effective technique for checking diagrammatic specifications, maintained in a requirements database, against structural completeness and consistency. The query language is specific to the type of diagram used. The corresponding query engine is generated by meta-tools from a specification of the diagram languages, typically written in an entity–relationship meta-language. The specifications can be checked from pre-compiled queries that encode standard intra- and inter-diagram consistency rules.

- Requirements animation is a concrete technique for validating the adequacy of requirements and assumptions. It can uncover other subtle defects that may not be easily visible in the RD. Animation requires a formal specification of the part of the system that we want to check. This specification needs to be converted in an executable model. The latter reacts to input events that should simulate environmental behaviours. The model simulation can be visualized by domain-specific scenes for increased appeal to and feedback from stakeholders. Animation sequences must be carefully designed beforehand to increase the likelihood of discovering defects.

- When the specification to be analysed is fully formal, a wide range of more sophisticated checks can be performed. Beyond the standard language checks that compilers can do, tools can automatically check certain forms of specification consistency and completeness. Model checkers can algorithmically verify that the specification satisfies some desired property. Theorem provers can deductively verify this by taking the property as a candidate theorem.

- When the specification language allows expected functionalities and behaviours to be locally defined as input–output relations, we can formally verify input–output consistency by checking that the relation is a function, and input–output completeness by checking that this function is total. When the relationship is represented in a tabular format, these checks amount to simple checks along each table row for disjointness and coverage.

- Model checking is an increasingly popular technique for verifying that a formally specified model satisfies some desired property. If the property is not satisfied, a counterexample is generated. In the most frequent case, the input model is a parallel state machine, the property is formalized in a linear or tree temporal logic, and the output counterexample is a state machine trace showing how the property can be violated. The verification is performed by an exhaustive search for property violation through a reachability graph. Large models with complex concurrent behaviours entail a state explosion problem. A wide range of time/space optimization techniques is aimed at addressing this problem.

- Theorem proving is another approach to property verification. The verified property is formally derived from the specification by a sequence of applications of deductive inference rules associated with the specification language. This approach can also be used to show logical inconsistencies among specifications or to derive logical consequences for adequacy checking. Theorem provers may succeed in verifications where model checkers fail, but require the assistance of experienced users.

- An effective requirements quality assurance process for mission-critical systems should ideally combine inspections and reviews of the entire RD, queries on surface aspects of the conceptual, functional and behavioural facets of the system, animation-based validation and formal verification of critical aspects.

Notes and Further Reading

The principles and virtues of formal code inspection are discussed in Fagan's classic papers (Fagan, 1976, 1986). For requirements inspection, convincing cases are presented in Doolan (1992) and Kelly *et al.* (1992). Gilb and Graham provide comprehensive coverage of software inspection principles and guidelines (Gilb & Graham, 1993). The various phases of an inspection process are further discussed in Laitenberger and DeBaud (2000). Individual reviewing modes are surveyed in Basili *et al.* (1996). Process-based reviewing is often called 'scenario based' in the literature. We avoid this terminology in view of the possible confusion with the RE scenario concept. Porter and colleagues reported on an empirical study showing the effectiveness of requirements inspection and, in particular, individual reviewing in process-based mode (Porter *et al.*, 1995). Regnell and colleagues reported on another experimental study where the gain of the process-based mode was significant over the free and checklist-based modes in some of the experiments, whereas the difference was not significant in others (Regnell *et al.*, 2000). MacDonald and Miller provide a good survey of tool support for inspection (MacDonald & Miller, 1999). In particular, CSRS is a collaborative tool supporting customizable inspection processes (Johnson, 1994). More recently, the GRIP tool was developed to support all phases of the inspection process (Grünbacher *et al.*, 2003). General checklists for inspection are also discussed in Kotonya and Sommerville (1997). Safety checklists are detailed in Jaffe *et al.* (1991), Leveson (1995) and Lutz (1996). An inspection strategy for scenario specifications is proposed in Leite *et al.* (2005).

Queries for consistency checking on a specification database were first demonstrated in the pioneering *ISDOS* system (Teichroew & Hershey, 1977). This system was generalized into a meta-system for parameterization on diagram languages (Teichroew *et al.*, 1980). The *IDA* system was an example of instantiation of this meta-system to data-flow diagrams, entity–relationship diagrams and diagrams capturing the system dynamics in terms of events, processes, synchronization points and resources (Bodart *et al.*, 1985). In addition to queries, *IDA* supported system simulations. The *ALMA* system provided a specification management meta-system integrating formal specification languages as well (van Lamsweerde *et al.*, 1988). The *ConceptBase* meta-environment goes one step further by supporting some form of deductive inferencing on the specification database (Jarke *et al.*, 1995). Many CASE tools since then have been built around specification databases to support checks through queries. The OMG Meta Object Factory (MOF) is a recent effort to standardize entity–relationship specification meta-languages for generic tools (OMG, 2006).

The early systems for requirements animation produced simulations from diagrammatic specifications such as R-net diagrams (Alford, 1977) and simple state machine diagrams (Wasserman, 1979). The principle of executing a formal specification was first explored on an operational entity–relationship language in Balzer *et al.* (1982). An operational specification can also be formulated at several levels of abstraction, where the user may ask whether specific behaviours can happen (Benner *et al.*, 1993). State-based specifications may be restricted to equational subsets of languages such as Z, VDM or B, for direct interpretation or translation into a logic or functional programming language (Hekmatpour & Ince, 1988; O'Neill, 1992; Siddiqi *et al.*, 1997; Ledru, 1997; Hazel *et al.*, 1998). More information on the Jaza animator for Z can be found in Utting (2006).

As behaviour is the primary focus of animation, many efforts were devoted to animating event-based specifications (Harel *et al.*, 1990; Holzmann, 1997; Larsen *et al.*, 1997). A comprehensive comparison of tools emanating from this research can be found in Schmid *et al.* (2000). The SCR, RSML and LSC animators support input–output interactions through control panels (Heitmeyer *et al.*, 1997, 1998a; Thompson *et al.*, 1999; Harel and Marelly, 2003). The LTSA animator supports domain scenes as well (Magee *et al.*, 2000; Magee & Kramer, 2006). FAUST supports domain scenes visualizing simulations that are generated from operational versions of temporal logic specifications (Tran Van *et al.*, 2004). A more elaborate *NextState* function than the one described in this chapter is introduced in Heimdahl and Leveson (1996). Other types of model may be animated as well; for example, the tool described in Heymans and Dubois (1998) animates specifications of the obligations and permissions of concurrent system agents.

Formal consistency and completeness checks based on the constraint that input–output relations must be total functions are presented in greater detail in Heitmeyer *et al.* (1996) and Heimdahl and Leveson (1996). In the SCR toolset, the checks are local on the tables representing the relations. In the RSML toolset they are performed compositionally on the entire system specification. With the latter toolset, several sources of dangerous incompleteness and non-determinism were found in the specification of the *TCAS* air traffic collision avoidance system (Heimdahl & Leveson, 1996).

The original idea and principles of model checking were independently developed in Queille and Sifakis (1982) and Clarke *et al.* (1986). Model checkers were originally conceived for hardware verification. They are now widely used in the semiconductor industry, and are increasingly used for checking critical aspects of software systems. Some of the best-known uses are reviewed in Clarke and Wing (1996). There have been quite a few tutorials and books on model checking techniques, usually oriented towards the SPIN automata-based approach (Holzmann, 1997, 2003) or the SMV symbolic approach (McMillan, 1993; Clarke *et al.*, 1999). Those techniques were extended to support richer models such as timed models or hybrid models. A sample of model checkers along this track includes KRONOS (Daws *et al.*, 1994), UPPAAL (Larsen *et al.*, 1997) and LTSA (Magee & Kramer, 2006). A comprehensive presentation of techniques and tools with comparisons will be found in Bérard *et al.* (2001). Model checking techniques and tools were also developed for RE languages such as SCR (Atlee, 1993) or integrated into formal RE toolsets (Heitmeyer *et al.*, 1998b). Some efforts were made to apply model checking technology earlier in the RE lifecycle. For example, Fuxman and colleagues extended the *i** RE framework with a temporal logic assertion language in order to model check early requirements specifications using the NuSMV model checker (Fuxman *et al.*, 2001; Cimatti *et al.*, 2000).

Many tools for state-based specification languages provide a front end to a theorem prover. For example, the Z/Eves front end to the Eves theorem prover supports formal derivations of Z assertions. In particular, it derives pre-conditions and checks that partial functions cannot be applied outside their domains (Saaltink, 1997). For algebraic specification languages, flexible front ends to efficient term-rewriting systems are available as well (Clavel *et al.*, 1996). The higher-order *PVS* verification system is often used by front ends as it allows specific formalisms to be defined as embeddings; language-specific proofs can then be carried out interactively using the proof strategies and efficient decision procedures provided (Owre *et al.*, 1995). A SCR/PVS front end is described in Heitmeyer *et al.* (1998a). STeP is another verification system for LTL and event-based specifications that combines theorem proving and model checking facilities (Manna & The STeP Group, 1996).

Techniques for generating invariants from event-based specifications in languages such as SCR or RSML are described in Bensalem *et al.* (1996), Park *et al.* (1998) and Jeffords and Heitmeyer (1998). There have been numerous efforts to generate test cases and oracles automatically from logic-based specifications, including Bernot *et al.* (1991), Richardson *et al.* (1992), Roong-Ko and Frankl (1994), Weyuker *et al.* (1994) and Mandrioli *et al.* (1995). Classic references on the refinement of a state-based specification towards an implementation include Morgan (1990), Jones (1990) and Abrial (1996). Formal techniques for specification reuse are described in Katz *et al.* (1987), Reubenstein and Waters (1991), Zaremski and Wing (1997) and Massonet and van Lamsweerde (1997).

The benefits of combining multiple quality assurance techniques for finding different types of defects in requirements for safety-critical systems are convincingly illustrated in Modugno *et al.* (1997).

Exercises

- Prepare a process-based reviewing plan for the library system. From the preliminary problem description in Section 1.1.2, define a specific role for each reviewer and, for each role, inspection directives based on specific checklists.

- Based on the preliminary problem description in Section 1.1.2, elaborate an inspection checklist for the train control system.

- Show how the questions in the checklist from Lutz (1996) can be traced back to the guideword-based checklist in Jaffe *et al.* (1991).

- Elaborate an SCR-specific checklist based on the description of SCR in Section 4.4.4.

- Elaborate an entity–relationship meta-model for the language of event trace diagrams. While doing so consider the following structural consistency rules:

  a. Every agent instance in an ET diagram must be the source or target of an interaction.

  b. Every incoming interaction with a target agent instance must originate from a source agent instance in the diagram.

c. Every incoming stimulus interaction must be followed by an outgoing response interaction.

Formulate checks for these rules as queries in your favourite database query language.

- Formulate some of the questions in the diagram-specific checklist in Section 5.1 as entity–relationship queries on corresponding specifications.

- Elaborate interesting animation sequences for the meeting scheduling system.

- For the faulty model in Figure 5.5, find a shorter counterexample trace violating the property that train doors must remain closed while the train is moving.

- Consider the parallel state machine in Figure 4.13 that corrects the faulty model in Figure 5.5. Build a finer-grained version of this state machine with two '*open*' states for the *DoorsState* variable, *OpenNormally* and *OpenInEmergency*, say, and two '*moving*' states for the *MovementState* variable, *Accelerating* and *Decelerating*, say. Next, build the reachability graph for the finer-grained parallel state machine. Then, compare the worst-case number of explored states with the one in a finer-grained version of the latter state machine where two '*stopped*' states for the *MovementState* variable are now distinguished; namely, *StoppedNormally* and *StoppedInEmergency*.

- Complete the invariance proof about the library system in Section 5.4.4 by showing that

    {Available ∩ OnLoan = Ø} *RobustReturn* {Available ∩ OnLoan = Ø}.

- Specify a simplistic diary management system that allows you to make and cancel appointments with specific people on specific dates, and to know on which date you have an appointment with whom. A partial function *Appointment: Dates* $\rightarrow\!\!\!\!+$ *Persons* seems quite natural to introduce. You also need a state variable to denote the range of this function, *WithWhom* say. Using a derivation similar to those in Section 5.4.4, investigate the consequences of a post-condition *WithWhom′* = *WithWhom* in the *MakeAppointment* operation schema.

6

Requirements Evolution

The world keeps moving – our target system too. After the system-to-be come systems-to-be-next. The system objectives, conceptual structures, requirements and assumptions that have been elicited, evaluated, specified and analysed may need to be changed for a variety of reasons, including defects to be fixed; project fluctuations in terms of priorities and constraints; better customer understanding of the system's actual features, strengths and limitations; and a wide range of environmental changes, including new or alternative ways of doing things, new business opportunities, new or alternative technologies, organizational changes, new or alternative regulations and so on.

Such changes may be required at various stages of the project: during requirements engineering itself, as a result of requirements evaluation and analysis; during subsequent development of the software-to-be, as design or implementation may reveal problematic aspects implied by the requirements; or after system deployment, as experience with the new system is gained.

Requirements evolution raises a difficult information management problem. Large amounts of information need to be versioned and maintained in a consistent state. Changes to the requirements document (RD) must be propagated through other items that depend on the changed items in order to maintain their mutual consistency. These include other RD items and downward product items such as prototypes, design specifications, architectural descriptions, test data, source code, user manuals and project management information. Consistency maintenance requires the management of traceability links among items and propagating changes along such links.

Chapter 1 introduced evolution-related RD qualities. Good structuring and modifiability are aimed at making the required changes as local as possible, whereas traceability is aimed at localizing those required changes easily (see Section 1.1.7). Undocumented traceability links together with late, unanticipated and undocumented changes may have quite severe consequences in terms of maintenance cost and product quality. Requirements engineers therefore need to prepare for change, from the very beginning of the project, and manage the change process in a controlled way based on policies, techniques and tools.

Evolution is at the heart of the RE process as it triggers new cycles in the spiral process introduced in Chapter 1 (see Figure 1.6). The process of anticipating, evaluating, agreeing on and propagating changes to RD items is called requirements change management – or *requirements management* for short.

This chapter offers an overview of the various issues and techniques available for requirements change management. Section 6.1 introduces the two dimensions of evolution together with their causal factors; evolution over time yields system revisions whereas evolution across product families yields system variants. We will then follow the successive stages of a disciplined requirements management process. Section 6.2 introduces change anticipation as the first milestone for effective evolution support, and describes techniques for anticipating changes. Section 6.3 introduces traceability management as another milestone in this process, and reviews techniques for managing traceability for better evolution support. Section 6.4 then discusses the various aspects of change control, from the handling of change requests to the evaluation and consolidation of changes. Section 6.5 introduces a recent paradigm for dynamic evolution where changes in environmental assumptions are monitored at system runtime for dynamic adaptation to such changes.

As requirements evolution is highly intertwined with the earlier phases of the RE process, this chapter will partly rely on material from previous chapters.

6.1 The time–space dimensions of evolution: revisions and variants

When we talk about requirements evolution, we need to consider different types of RD items that are subject to change, including system objectives, domain concepts, functional and non-functional requirements and assumptions about the environment. The term *feature* is sometimes used to refer to a change unit. Functional and non-functional features refer to collections of functional and non-functional requirements, respectively. Environmental features refer to assumptions, constraints, structures and work procedures in the environment.

Every evolution cycle in Figure 1.6 produces a new *version* of the RD with some distinguishing features. Like for any software-related artefact, a new version may be a revision or a variant:

- A *revision* results from changes generally made to correct or improve the current version of a single product.

- *Variants* result from changes made to adapt, restrict or extend a master version to multiple classes of users or usage conditions. The variants share commonalities while having specific differences.

Revisions result from evolution over time, whereas variants result from evolution across product families (sometimes called *product lines*). Figure 6.1 helps visualize those two dimensions of evolution. At any single point in time along the system lifetime, multiple variants may co-exist

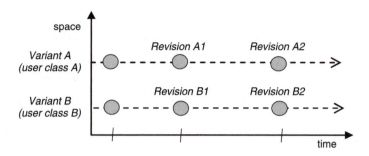

Figure 6.1 *Version types: the time-space dimensions of evolution*

at multiple places. Multiple revisions of the same item are expected to exist at different points in time, but not at the same time point.

Consider our meeting scheduling system, for example. The current version of the RD might evolve into a revised version or into multiple variants. A *revision* might fix a number of requirements omissions and inconsistencies that have been detected, and include improved features such as taking date preferences into account or notifying invited participants of the meeting date by an SMS message to their mobile phone. *Variants* might include a contracted version where meeting scheduling refers to meeting dates only; a version where both meeting dates and locations are handled; a variant of the latter where participants with different status are distinguished; and an extended version providing configurable rule-based conflict management facilities.

Revisions and variants define a two-dimensional space for defining product evolutions, rather than two separate tracks. Variants may evolve into revisions, and a revision may give rise to multiple variants. Requirements can also be *deferred* until subsequent product versions due to prioritization in view of project phasing, user skills and experience, technological risk and so on. (See Sections 3.4 and 6.4.2.)

Evolution types and causes

Changes in a requirements document may be of different types, caused by different factors, resulting in different types of versions and operated at different phases of the software lifecycle. Table 6.1 summarizes this quaternary relationship.

The linking of change causes, types, results and timing there is indicative of the complexity of the evolution process. The table suggests that RD changes may be required at any phase of the software lifecycle. The parentheses in the timing column designate software lifecycle phases where the corresponding change is less likely to take place. For example, better customer understanding is more likely to take place at RE time, if requirements prototyping or animation is used, and after software deployment, due to real experience with the running system.

Table 6.1 distinguishes among *corrective, ameliorative* and *adaptative* changes, and suggests the variety of environment changes calling for adaptations, extensions or contractions.

Causal factor	Change type	Version type	Change time
Errors and flaws in the RD (cf. Table 1.1)	Correction	Revision	RE, design, implementation, after deployment
Better customer understanding	Correction, extension	Revision	RE, (design), (implementation), after deployment
New functional feature	Extension	Revision, variant	(RE), (design), (implementation), after deployment
Improved quality feature	Amelioration	Revision	(RE), (design), (implementation), after deployment
Environmental change: new class of users or new usage condition	Adaptation, contraction, extension	Variant	RE, design, (implementation), after deployment
Environmental change: new way of doing things	Adaptation, extension	Revision	(RE), (design), (implementation), after deployment
Environmental change: alternative way of doing things	Adaptation	Variant	RE, (design), (implementation), after deployment
Environmental change: new regulation	Adaptation	Revision	(RE), (design), (implementation), after deployment
Environmental change: alternative regulation (e.g. in another country)	Adaptation	Variant	(RE), (design), (implementation), after deployment
Environmental change: organizational changes	Adaptation	Revision	(RE), (design), (implementation), after deployment
Environmental change: new technology	Adaptation, extension	Revision	(RE), (design), (implementation), after deployment
Environmental change: alternative technology	Adaptation	Variant	RE, design, implementation, after deployment
Environmental change: new opportunities	Extension	Revision, variant	(RE), (design), (implementation), after deployment
Process fluctuations: change in priorities, schedules or cost constraints	Contraction, Adaptation	Revision	RE, design, implementation

Table 6.1   *RD changes: Types, causes, results and timing*

6.2 Change anticipation

As a first step for the effective support of changes in system objectives, conceptual structures, requirements and environmental assumptions, we should anticipate such changes from the very beginning of the project. As we can never know whether the requirements we have are *actually* sufficient and adequate, we need to provide for adaptability very early on.

Change anticipation requires us to identify likely changes, assess their likelihood and document them in the RD. There are two main reasons for such documentation:

- *At RE time*, requirements and assumptions that are felt to be too volatile may call for alternative, more stable ones to reduce the evolution cost beforehand. When an assumption or requirement is kept in spite of its volatility, it deserves more attention during traceability management (see Section 6.3). We may also anticipate and record adequate responses to anticipated changes; this might be much cheaper than rediscovering them later on when the change occurs. Anticipated responses to likely changes further allow us to support runtime evolution, where volatile assumptions are monitored at system runtime and responses to changing assumptions are enacted on the fly (see Section 6.5).

- *At software development time*, the documentation of likely changes is essential for designing architectures that remain stable in spite of those changes, for example through their encapsulation or wrapping within dedicated, easily localizable components in the architecture. The contextual information about volatile requirements and assumptions is helpful for maintenance teams too.

For large, multiversion systems, change anticipation should ideally address the two dimensions of evolution. We can do this by classifying a requirement or assumption as *stable* or *volatile* from one system revision to the other, and as *common* or *distinct* from one system variant to the other.

More specifically, we may associate levels of *stability* or *commonality* with statements, as suggested in Section 4.2.1, or with sets of statements grouped into features. To enable comparative analysis, we may transpose some of the principles introduced in Section 3.4 for requirements prioritization:

- Each level should contain items of similar stability or commonality. The number of such levels should be kept small.

- The characterization of levels should be qualitative rather than quantitative, and relative rather than absolute, for example 'more stable than' rather than 'stable'.

Figure 6.2 suggests a feature ranking for the meeting scheduling system. Dedicated RD sections may then highlight those requirements and assumptions that are more volatile, or that are distinct from one variant to the other.

The elicitation techniques in Chapter 2 may help us determine adequate stability or commonality levels for the items that we are eliciting. Stakeholders should be involved in this

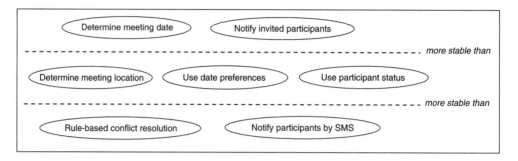

Figure 6.2 *Ordering features by levels of stability or commonality*

assessment to ensure its adequacy. In addition, we may base our analysis of likely changes on the following heuristic rules:

- *Regroup within features cohesive sets of statements that share the same stability or commonality level and address the same system objective.* It makes no sense to mix within the same change unit statements that are stable and statements that are highly volatile.

- *To help identify the most stable features, ask yourself what useful subset of features should be found in any contraction, extension or variant of the system.* Other features not in this subset should be classified as less stable. For example, any contraction, extension or variant of the meeting scheduling system should include a date determination feature and a participant notification feature whatever the type of meeting is – regular or episodic, physical or videoconferencing and so on.

- *Intentional and conceptual aspects are more stable than operational and factual ones.* High-level system objectives and domain-specific conceptual structures are more stable than operational ways of doing things, user characteristics, assumptions about ways of using the software or technology constraints. For example, the objective of informing invited participants of the meeting date is more stable than the operational requirement of sending them an SMS notification to achieve this.

- *Functional aspects related to the core objectives of the system are more stable than non-functional constraints for improvement or technology adaptation.* For example, the requirements for getting participant constraints are likely to be more stable than the requirements for a visual input–output calendar for increased usability of the constraint acquisition feature.

- *Decisions among multiple options deserve special scrutiny.* They may rely on incomplete knowledge or on assumptions that may no longer be valid later on in the system lifecycle. The requirements resulting from them are therefore likely to be more volatile:

  a. In the frequent case of incomplete knowledge at RE time, changes may be required later on as the missing knowledge becomes available. For example, we generally don't know all the potential security threats to the system, and new classes of attacks on similar systems may be revealed later on in the system lifecycle. We may also formulate architectural or inter-operability requirements without necessarily knowing all their implications for the development process; these implications might become apparent at software implementation time. Requirements set up with such incomplete knowledge are likely to be less stable.

b. Conflicts are another source of likely changes (see Section 3.1.3). When we explore alternative resolutions to a detected conflict, we might select a resolution based on conditions at RE time that are no longer valid later on. Requirements emerging from such conflict resolution are thus likely to be less stable.

c. Risks are another source of potential changes (see Section 3.2). The likelihood of a risk, assessed at RE time, may need to be revised later on based on new conditions or better knowledge of the real nature of the risk. When we explore alternative countermeasures to a particular risk, we might select a countermeasure that turns out to be no longer appropriate later on. Requirements emerging from this countermeasure are thus likely to be less stable.

d. There are often alternative ways of meeting a system objective through different combinations of sub-objectives. (Part II will come back to this at length.) We might choose one specific combination based on assumptions that might no longer be valid subsequently. Requirements emerging from such combination of sub-objectives are thus likely to be less stable.

e. There might be alternative ways of assigning responsibilities among system compo-nents. We generally choose specific responsibility assignments based on assumptions about system components that might no longer be valid later on in the system lifecycle. Responsibility assignments are another source of likely changes.

In all such cases it is worth documenting the reasons, conditions and assumptions under the selection of one specific option, as they are subject to change, and to document the alternative options that have been identified. These alternatives might give us appropriate responses to subsequent changes; we don't need to rediscover them when the corresponding change occurs.

6.3 Traceability management for evolution support

In view of the inevitability of evolution, we must prepare for change from the very beginning of the project and throughout its lifetime. Traceability management is another necessary ingredient for this. We may see it as the art of *documenting for evolution*. The overall objective of traceability management is to support consistency maintenance in the presence of changes, by ensuring that the impact of changes is easily localizable for change assessment and propagation. Traceability of RD items was therefore introduced in Section 1.1.7 as a target quality at which to aim.

Section 6.3.1 defines the notion of traceability more precisely and reviews the various types of links on which requirements traceability may rely. Section 6.3.2 discusses the traceability management process, its benefits and cost. Section 6.3.3 describes the techniques available for reducing this cost. To conclude, Section 6.3.4 discusses cost–benefit trade-offs for effective traceability management.

6.3.1 Traceability links

In a production chain, an item is *traceable* if we can fully figure out *where* the item comes *from, why* it comes from there, and *where* it goes *to* – that is, what it will be used for and how it will be used. Item traceability relies on the existence of *links* between items that we can follow *backwards*, towards source items, and *forwards*, towards target items.

Forward and backward traceability

Traceability links are thus aimed at localizing items, their origin, rationale and impact. To enable item tracing, such links must be made explicit and documented. By definition, they must be bi-directional to enable their traversal from source to target (*forward traceability*) and from target to source (*backward traceability*).

Vertical and horizontal traceability

In the context of engineering requirements for a software product, traceability concerns a diversity of items to be linked together: *RD items* such as objectives, concept definitions, functional and non-functional requirements and assumptions; and *downward software lifecycle items* such as design specifications, architectural decisions, test data, user manuals, source code, software documentation and project management reports.

- Within the RD, an item may rely on other RD items. We may wish to retrieve the definition of a concept involved in a requirement, for example, or the assumptions on which the requirement relies. Such traceability is called *horizontal traceability*.

- An RD item may originate from upward items found in the RD, such as business objectives or elicited items from interview transcripts or observation videotapes. It may give rise to lower-level RD items or downward software lifecycle items. Such traceability with upward and downward artefacts is called *vertical traceability*. Forward vertical traceability is sometimes called *downward traceability* whereas backward vertical traceability is sometimes called *upward traceability*.

Figure 6.3 helps visualize those basic notions. Note that some traceability links can be many to many; a source item can have multiple targets and a target item can have multiple sources. Let us consider some examples illustrating traceability paths in Figure 6.3.

- *Example 1.* Suppose that we have written our RD in a structured way according to the IEEE Std-830 standard (see Table 4.1 in Section 4.2.2). A requirement in RD Section 3.1 ('Functional requirements') might rely on a specific assumption about users reported in RD Section 2.3 ('User characteristics'). Likewise, a specific requirement in RD Section 3.3 ('Performance requirements') might rely on assumptions reported in RD Section 2.5 ('Assumptions and dependencies') and on interface requirements reported in RD Section 3.2 ('External interface requirements'). Many requirements involving a specific concept might rely on the definition of this concept and its structure, reported in RD

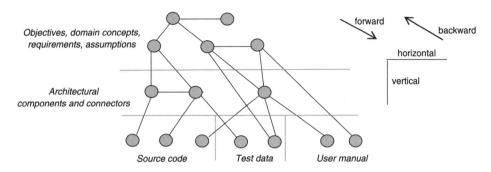

Figure 6.3 *Traceability links: forward, backward, horizontal, and vertical traceability*

Section 1.3 ('Definitions, acronyms and abbreviations'). These are all examples of where horizontal traceability is required for change management.

On the other hand, two security requirements in RD Section 3.6 might originate from an interview where attacks on the system-as-is were reported. These requirements might give rise to an *Access Control* module in the software architecture, to specific black-box test data on this module and to the description of a user authentication procedure in the user manual. Besides, distribution constraints reported in RD Section 3.4 ('Design constraints') might result in the selection of a *Publish–Subscribe* architectural style. These are all examples of where vertical traceability is required for change management.

- *Example 2.* Suppose now that we have specified the conceptual items involved in our meeting scheduler by the entity–relationship diagram in Figure 4.5 (see Section 4.3.2). The structuring of participant constraints in this diagram through excluded and preferred dates, and the distinction between important and normal participants, will give rise to specific requirements on how returned date preferences should be validated and handled (horizontal traceability). These requirements will give rise to the corresponding specifications of a *Constraints Handler* module in the architecture and the description of a constraints submission procedure in the on-line user manual (vertical traceability).

The implications of traceability in forward, backward, horizontal and vertical directions are important. Consider an RD item traceable along those directions:

- We can easily retrieve the context in which this item was created and changed, following traceability links backwards, and answer questions such as: '*Why is this here? Where is it coming from?*' For any target item we can thereby identify the source items that explain it. Likewise, we can retrieve the context in which the item is taken into account, following traceability links forwards, and answer questions such as: '*What are the implications of this? Where is this taken into account?*' We can thereby identify any item that exists because of the source item.

- As a consequence, we can easily localize the impact of creating, modifying or deleting traceable items in order to assess the impact along horizontal and vertical traceability chains.

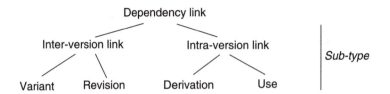

Figure 6.4   *A taxonomy of traceability link types*

Traceability link types

As traceability relies on links between items, we need to have a closer look at what such links convey more precisely. This is important for traceability management to determine whether two items should be linked or not. Figure 6.4 shows a typology of traceability links among RD items. Each link subtype inherits the parent definition while making it more specific.

Dependency   This is the most general traceability link type. There is a *Dependency* link between a target item B and a source item A if changing A may require changing B. We say that A *affects* B, in the forward direction for traceability, or B *depends on* A, in the backward direction (see Figure 6.5).

- *Example.* In our meeting scheduling system, B might be an RD section providing the functional requirements for determining the most convenient meeting date, whereas A might be an RD section defining what participant constraints are. B depends on A because, for example, if we decide in A to restrict the notion of participant constraints to excluded dates only, to define a simpler variant of our system, the functional requirements for determining the most convenient date in B must be simplified accordingly.

Dependency can be specialized in various ways. The more specialized the dependency, the more specific the reason for it, the more accurate the link, the easier its correct establishment and the more accurate its analysis for multiple uses in traceability management.

As Figure 6.4 shows, there are dependencies among different versions of the RD (left branch) and dependencies within a single version (right branch). Let us define the link types along the left branch first. (Remember that a feature was defined as a change unit.)

Variant   There is a *Variant* link between a target item B and a source item A if B has all the features of A while having its own distinguishing features. We say that B is a *variant* of the *master* version A (see Figure 6.6).

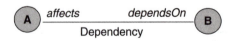

Figure 6.5   *Dependency link type*

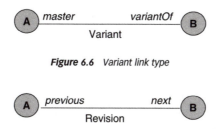

Figure 6.6 *Variant link type*

Figure 6.7 *Revision link type*

- *Example.* Consider an RD variant for our meeting scheduling system where participants have different status. This variant will share with other variants all features from the master RD version while having member status management and priority-based scheduling among its distinguishing features.

Revision There is a *Revision* link between a target item *B* and a source item *A* if *B* overrides certain features of *A*, adds new ones and/or removes others, while keeping all remaining features. We say that *B* is a *next* version of the *previous* version *A* (see Figure 6.7).

- *Example.* A revision of the current RD version for the meeting scheduler might override the current rule for optimal date determination by another rule taking date preferences into account, and add the new feature of notifying the scheduled date by an SMS message to participants, in addition to e-mail notification.

For better traceability among the linked items, *variant* and *revision* links are generally annotated with configuration management information such as the following:

- The *rationale* for their creation
- The *date* of creation
- Their *author*
- Their *contributors*; that is, the stakeholders who asked for or contributed to them
- Their *status*, e.g. 'proposed', 'under evaluation', 'approved', 'rejected' or 'deferred'.

Along the right branch in Figure 6.4, two kinds of dependency are distinguished within a single RD version.

Use There is a *Use* link between a target RD item *B* and a source RD item *A* if changing *A* makes *B* become incomplete, inadequate, inconsistent or ambiguous. We say that *A is used by B,* in the forward direction for traceability, or *B uses A*, in the backward direction (see Figure 6.8).

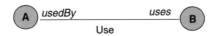

Figure 6.8 Use link type

- *Example 1.* In our library system, *B* might be an RD section providing the functional requirements for bibliographical search whereas *A* might be another section providing the functional requirements for directory management. *B* uses *A* because, at first sight, there might be requirements in *B* that rely on requirements in *A*. More precisely now, if we decide to extend the functional requirements on directory management to cover digital subscriptions as well, for example, the functional requirements for bibliographical search would become incomplete if they were not extended accordingly.

- *Example 2.* *B* might be a set of rules for loan management and *A* a definition of the concept of patron as someone who has registered with the library for the current academic year and paid a yearly deposit for potential fines. The rule set *B* may become inconsistent, ambiguous or incomplete if the definition *A* is changed in the RD's lexicon; therefore *B* uses *A*.

Derivation   There is a *Derivation* link between a target item *B* and a source item *A* if *B* is built from *A* under the constraint that *A* must be met. We say that *A is met by B*, in the forward direction for traceability, or *B is derived from A*, in the backward direction (see Figure 6.9).

Note that this definition does imply a dependency: changing *A* may require changing *B*, since *B* was built under the constraint of meeting the old *A*, not the new one. What it means for *A* to be met depends on the type of items being linked by *Derivation* links. In particular:

- *A* might be an objective stated somewhere in the RD and *B* a derived set of system requirements to achieve this objective.

- *A* might be a system requirement and *B* a derived set of software requirements and assumptions to ensure this system requirement (see Section 1.1.4).

- *A* might be a set of software requirements and *B* a derived set of architectural descriptions to ensure these software requirements.

- *A* might be a set of requirements and *B* a derived set of test data to test them.

   - *Example 1.* The objective of '*anywhere anytime notification*' for the meeting scheduler might have emerged from concerns expressed by frequent travellers during interviews (first *Derivation* link); this objective might be met by a SMS notification feature with corresponding requirements (second *Derivation* link); these requirements might in

Figure 6.9   Derivation link type

turn be met, in the software architecture, by specifications of specific methods of the *Notifier* class (third *Derivation* link) and, in the test plan, by test data covering these requirements (fourth *Derivation* link). See Figure 6.12 for a visualization of these links.

- *Example 2.* In the library system, the objective of *'regular availability of book copies'* might be met by a sub-objective of imposing a two-week limit on loan periods, from which requirements on sending reminders and charging fines are derived, from which specifications are derived for methods of the *Reminder* class in the software architecture.

The *Derivation* link type is a vertical dependency whereas *Use* is a horizontal one. The real difference between these two link types lies in *satisfaction arguments*. A *Derivation* link from a source item *A* to a target item *B* calls for an argument, to be documented, that *B* contributes to meeting *A*. No such argument is called for in the case of *Use* links.

Satisfaction arguments and derivational traceability links

When satisfaction arguments are documented in the RD, as highly recommended in Chapter 1, we get traceability links for free. The items involved in a satisfaction argument are connected through derivation links in a straightforward manner. For example, we introduced the following type of satisfaction argument in Section 1.1.4:

$$\{SOFREQ, \text{ ASM, DOM } \} \models SysReq,$$

meaning roughly 'the satisfaction of the software requirements in *SOFREQ*, under environment assumptions in *ASM* and domain properties in *DOM,* entails the satisfaction of the system requirement *SysReq*'. Considering the backward *'derived from'* direction, there is a one-to-many derivation link between the derived software requirements in *SOFREQ* on the one hand and the source system requirement *SysReq,* assumptions in *ASM* and properties in *DOM* on the other hand. The satisfaction of the software requirements in *SOFREQ* can no longer be argued to entail the satisfaction of *SysReq* if *SysReq* is changed *or if the environment assumptions in ASM or domain properties in DOM are changed.* As a consequence, if an environment assumption is no longer valid in *ASM*, the software requirements in *SOFREQ* need to be reconsidered for its satisfaction to entail the satisfaction of the system requirement *SysReq*. This applies a fortiori if *SysReq* is changed.

Part II of the book will introduce a richer typology of satisfaction arguments to support derivational traceability. *Goals* will be introduced to make the notion of system objectives more precise, and goal *operationalizations* into operations will be introduced to make the notion of system functionalities more precise. These new concepts will provide additional forms of satisfaction argument as extra sources for establishing traceability links, in particular:

$$\{REQ, \text{ ASM, DOM } \} \models G,$$

meaning roughly 'the system goal *G* is satisfied whenever the requirements in *REQ*, environment assumptions in *ASM* and domain properties in *DOM* are all satisfied'; and

$$OP \models G,$$

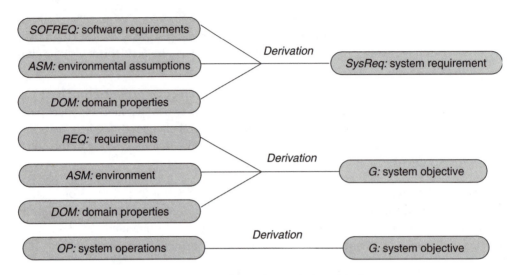

Figure 6.10   *Derivational traceability links implied by satisfaction arguments*

meaning roughly 'the system goal *G* is satisfied whenever the operation specifications in *OP* are satisfied'.

These additional types of satisfaction arguments will produce more derivational traceability links for free; see Figure 6.10.

Traceability link types: An entity–relationship model

The various subtypes of traceability links may be summarized in the ER model shown in Figure 6.11, using the graphical notations introduced in Section 4.3.2. Such a diagram can be used as a logical database schema for a traceability database management tool, as we will see in Section 6.3.3.

The left-hand part of the ER diagram in Figure 6.11 captures the inter-version dependencies. The right-hand part captures the intra-version dependencies. The edge labels denote the roles played in the relationship by the corresponding entities. Note that the *variant* and *revision* relationships are characterized by *CM* attributes corresponding to the configuration management information previously mentioned, such as their rationale, date of creation, contributors, status and so on.

RD items and software lifecycle items in Figure 6.11 are characterized by their attributes *RefName* and *Spec*. The *RefName* attribute designates a unique reference name. Each entity must obviously have a unique identifier for unambiguous reference throughout the documentation and, in particular, along traceability chains. The *Spec* attribute designates a precise specification of the corresponding item. It can be a natural language, diagrammatic or formal specification.

The branching down the *Derivation* link means that any instance of this link may have either an RD item or a software lifecycle item as target. The upper multiplicity of this relationship states that every RD item or software lifecycle item should meet one or more upward RD item (except root items, not represented to keep things simple). The lower multiplicity states that every RD item should be met by one or more downward RD or lifecycle item. Also note

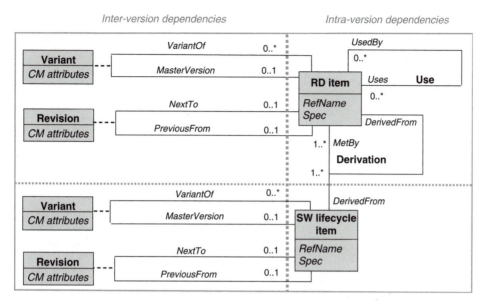

Figure 6.11　*Item traceability: an entity–relationship model*

the different multiplicities on the left-hand side of the *variant* and *revision* relationships; a master version may have multiple variants, whereas a single RD item version may have a single revision at most.

Figure 6.12 illustrates a possible instantiation of the traceability model in Figure 6.11 to RD items for our meeting scheduling system. It is based on examples previously introduced in this section. (The MS acronym there stands for 'meeting scheduler'.)

The various types of traceability links defined in this section remain fairly generic. In practice, they can be further specialized to the specifics of the organization, of the domain or of the type of project, when this is felt to be useful (Ramesh & Jarke, 2001).

6.3.2 The traceability management process, its benefits and cost

Traceability management refers to the process of establishing, exploiting and maintaining traceability links. This process provides multiple benefits for an extra cost to pay. A project-specific traceability policy should therefore be defined as an initial step of the process to regulate the next steps towards some optimal cost–benefit trade-off. Such a policy will be discussed in Section 6.3.4. Before that, we need to have a better understanding of the issues raised by the next steps, and the techniques we may use to reduce the cost of traceability management. This section follows those steps (see Figure 6.13).

Establishing traceability links

To enable forward and backward tracing of items, their origin, rationale and impact, we first need to identify *what RD items* need to be traceable and *what link types* should connect these items to enable their traceability.

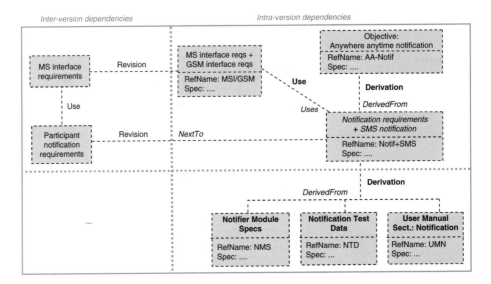

Figure 6.12   *Item traceability: model instantiation to meeting scheduling*

Answering these intertwined questions raises four issues to be settled: the granularity of a link, its semantic richness, its accuracy and the overhead required for its management.

- *Link granularity.* What does a source or target item of a link really cover? An entire section of the RD, a cohesive set of related requirements defining a feature or a single assumption? The granularity of a traceability link is determined by the granularity of the linked items.

- *Semantic richness.* Is the link intended to convey semantics, like the *Derivation* and *Use* links, or is it a purely lexical link, like keyword-based indexing or tagging?

- *Link accuracy.* Does the established link correctly stick to its semantics, as defined in the previous section? Is it focused enough for precise localization of dependencies? How accurate are the conclusions that can be drawn by retrieving the link?

- *Link overhead.* How important is the extra effort required for establishing and maintaining this link?

These four issues interact positively or negatively with each other. A finer-grained link contributes to higher accuracy, for example in localizing the impact of a change, but also to higher overhead; the finer the grain, the higher the number of links to be created and

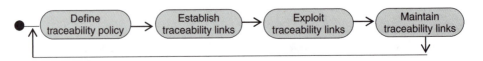

Figure 6.13   *Traceability management*

maintained. Likewise, a semantically richer link contributes to richer analysis and higher accuracy, for example in determining what needs to be rederived in the case of change, but also to higher overhead; we need then to check that the semantic definition really holds for the created or updated link.

These interactions call for an adequate cost–benefit trade-off that depends on project characteristics and expected gains. We come back to this after the multiple benefits of traceability have been discussed. As a general rule, however, we can a priori consider finer-grained traceability for two kinds of feature:

- Mission-critical features, in particular safety-critical and security-critical ones, as accuracy really matters for them.

- Features that are more likely to change, as discussed in the previous section, as the pay-off for them is more likely to outweigh the extra cost.

Deciding which RD items need to be linked and through which link types allows us to build a *traceability graph* where nodes are traceable items and edges are labelled by the corresponding link type (see Figure 6.12 for a possible visualization of such a graph). As previously mentioned, each node in the graph must be assigned a unique identifier for unambiguous reference. The traceability graph then needs to be recorded for later use.

For effective evolution support, a full traceability graph should cover inter-version, *Use* and *Derivation* links among selected items at a sufficiently fine-grained level. The resulting graph can be fairly large and complex to build. Section 6.3.3 will discuss techniques and tool support for alleviating that task.

Exploiting traceability links

Once identified and recorded, the linked items are retrieved by traversal of the traceability graph. This may be done for a variety of uses:

- *Evolution support.* The primary use is, of course, for consistency management during requirements evolution. When a change is requested on an item B, the context of the change is obtained by following dependency links backwards to get the source items A on which B depends. The impact of the change is assessed by following all dependency links forwards horizontally and vertically, to get the items C depending on B, and recursively. When the change is approved, it is propagated forwards along all those dependency links.

- *Rationale analysis.* The reasons for an RD item may be obtained by following derivation links upwards to obtain its sources and motivations. When a retrieved reason corresponds to an objective to be met by the system, we can check whether the RD item is sufficient for meeting it, and possibly discover other items that are missing for the objective to be fully met. When no reason is found, we may question the relevance of this item. Likewise, the reasons for an implementation feature may be obtained by following derivation links upwards from this feature. When a requirement is reached, we can check whether the feature is sufficient for meeting this requirement, and possibly discover missing or alternative implementation features for meeting the same requirement. When no requirement is found, the feature may either prove to be irrelevant 'gold plating' or reveal requirements that have been overlooked (and that perhaps might give rise to other implementation alternatives). Through rationale analysis we can thus find answers to questions about RD items and downward software items such as: 'Why is this here?' 'Is this enough?' 'Is this relevant?'

- *Coverage analysis.* We can also assess whether, how and where an RD item is met, by following derivation links downwards to other RD items and to architectural, implementation, test data, user manual and project management items. We can thereby find answers to questions raised at RE time or during the subsequent software development phases, such as: 'Is this concern, expressed during that interview, taken into account in the RD? Where?' 'Where and how is this assumption taken into account in the requirements?' 'Is this requirement taken into account somewhere in the design or implementation? Where?' 'Have all requirements been allocated?' 'Is this requirement exercised by an animation sequence?' 'Are there test data to exercise this requirement?'

- *Defect tracking.* In the case of a problem being detected during requirements animation or acceptance testing, we may follow derivation links upwards towards possible origins of the problem, such as the inadequacy of some upward requirement. Such cause–effect tracking is a pre-condition for effective, prompt repair.

- *Compliance checking.* When the traceable items include contractual clauses, regulations or standards prescriptions, we may follow derivation links upwards towards them in order to check or demonstrate that the RD meets them.

- *Project tracking.* When traceability chains include project management information about tasks, resources and costs, we may follow dependency links to monitor progress, allocate resources and control costs.

Maintaining traceability links

For the outcome of those various types of analysis to be correct and accurate, the traceability graph on which they are based must remain correct and accurate as the RD evolves. The graph must therefore be updated in accordance with changes once the latter have been made and propagated:

- When a new RD item is created, we should consider integrating it into the traceability graph with adequate new links.

- When a non-traceable RD item is modified, we should question whether the modified item should not be subsequently traceable and, if so, integrate it into the traceability graph.

- When a traceable RD item is deleted, we should delete it from the traceability graph together with its incoming and outgoing links – after all consequences of this change have been propagated.

- When a traceable RD item is modified, we should check all its incoming and outgoing links and, for each of them, determine according to its semantics whether it should be kept, deleted or modified.

- The presence of unconnected nodes, as a result of those manipulations, must be analysed to determine whether they should be 'garbage-collected' or whether new links should connect them.

6.3.3 Traceability management techniques

To take full advantage of the multiple benefits of traceability management, we need to reduce the complexity and cost of establishing and maintaining the traceability graph. This section reviews various techniques and tools to support the traceability management process.

Cross referencing

The first obvious possibility consists of configuring a standard text editor, spreadsheet or hypertext editor to support cross-referencing among the items we want to trace. This corresponds to the good old '*see Section X.y*' practice:

- The items to be traced are selected and assigned a unique name for cross-referencing.

- An indexing or tagging scheme is set up for the selected items to define which items are lexically linked to which others.

- The available search or browsing facilities are configured to this scheme.

- The items are then retrieved simply by following cross-reference chains.

This technique is lightweight and readily available. It can accommodate any level of granularity. It is, however, limited to a single link type that carries no semantics – namely, lexical reference. The information conveyed by the indexing scheme is implicit and may be inaccurate. As a result, the control and analysis of traceability information are very limited. The cost of maintaining the indexing scheme may turn out to be fairly high too.

Traceability matrices

Such matrices are often used in cross-referencing to represent the indexing scheme and to track cross-references. They can, however, be used to represent in matrix form any traceability graph built on a single relation – for example, the *Dependency* relation defined in Section 6.3.1.

Each row/column in the matrix is associated with the name of an item, for example an objective, a requirement, an assumption, a domain property, a document section, an architectural component, a set of test data and so on. The matrix element T_{ij} has a value '1' (say) if the item T_i is linked with item Tj, and '0' otherwise. Table 6.2 shows a very small example of a traceability matrix.

Looking at a specific row we easily retrieve, from the source item in the first column, all target items linked to it in the forward direction. Looking at a specific column we easily retrieve, from the target item in the first row, all source items linked to it in the backward direction.

Traceable item	T1	T2	T3	T4	T5
T1	0	1	0	1	0
T2	0	0	1	0	1
T3	1	0	0	0	1
T4	0	0	1	0	1
T5	0	0	0	0	0

Table 6.2   *A simple traceability matrix*

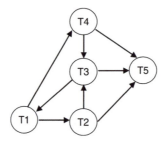

Figure 6.14   *Single-relation traceability graph represented by the matrix in Table 6.2*

For example, suppose that the traceability matrix in Table 6.2 captures a *Dependency* relation. The third row shows that item *T3* *affects* items *T1* and *T5*, whereas the third column shows that item *T3* *depends on* items *T2* and *T4*. The traceability graph represented by Table 6.2 is shown in Figure 6.14.

Traceability matrices provide a simple representation for traceability graphs. They allow for navigation in both forward and backward directions. They also support simple forms of analysis of the traceability graph, such as the detection of undesirable cycles. For example, the dependency cycle *T1* → *T4* → *T3* → *T1* in Figure 6.14 is easily detected through standard algorithms applied to the matrix in Table 6.2.

For large projects with many items to be traced, such matrices may become unmanageable. Filling in very large sparse matrices is error prone. A standard alternative against sparseness is the equivalent, unidirectional list representation; see Table 6.3. We can, however, then no longer navigate easily in the reverse direction.

A more serious limitation of traceability matrices and lists is their restriction to single relations. We cannot represent and navigate through traceability graphs with multiple link

Traceable item	forward-LinkTo
T1	*T2, T4*
T2	*T3, T5*
T3	*T1, T5*
T4	*T3, T5*
T5	–

Table 6.3   *Traceability list for the matrix in Table 6.2*

types, for example *Variant, Use* and *Derivation* links. Moreover, they are just a means for representing traceability links; we have no clue about which links should be established between which items.

Feature diagrams

Feature diagrams are another simple graphical representation dedicated to the *Variant* link type (Kang *et al.*, 1990). They allow us to capture multiple variants of a system family, with their commonalities and variations, within a single graph. The variants are retrieved by navigation through the graph with selection of corresponding features.

A node in a feature diagram represents a composite or atomic feature. The basic structuring mechanism is feature decomposition. A *composite feature* can be AND-composed of multiple sub-features that are mandatory or optional. It can also be OR-composed of alternative features that are exclusive ('one of') or non-exclusive ('more of'). An *atomic feature* is not decomposed any further.

A variant is retrieved from the feature diagram through a specific selection of atomic features in the diagram that meets the constraints prescribed by the diagram.

Figure 6.15 shows a small, simplified feature diagram for our meeting scheduling system. The diagram specifies the *MeetingScheduling* feature as an aggregation of four mandatory composite features (*MeetingInitiation, ConstraintsAcquisition, Planning* and *MeetingNotification*), as prescribed by the closed dot on top of each feature, plus an optional atomic feature (*RuleBasedConflictResolution*), as indicated by the open dot. The *ConstraintsAcquisition* feature is either a *byEmail* or a *byE-agenda* feature, as prescribed by the open triangle joining the parent feature to its child ones (exclusive OR). The *MeetingNotification* feature is a *byEmail* feature or a *bySMS* feature or both, as indicated by the closed triangle joining the parent feature to its children (non-exclusive OR). Note that there are three possible feature configurations for *MeetingNotification*.

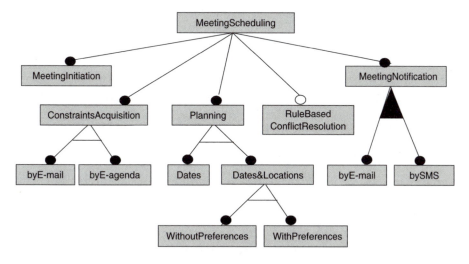

Figure 6.15 *Feature diagram for variants of the meeting scheduling system*

The diagram in Figure 6.15 captures a family of variants that share *MeetingInitiation* as a common feature. Note how compact this notation is; the number of variants captured in Figure 6.15 is equal to the number of possible feature combinations, that is:

$$1 \ (MeetingInitiation) \times 2 \ (ConstraintsAcquisition) \times 3 \ (Planning)$$

$$\times 2 \ (ConflictResolution) \times 3 \ (MeetingNotification) = 36.$$

Each of these 36 variants is retrieved by selection of a specific configuration of the leaf atomic features according to the graphical constraints prescribed by the graph. Also note that we do have control over the granularity of features here; we can build coarse-grained, simple, inaccurate diagrams or finer-grained, more complex, more accurate diagrams.

Traceability databases

For better scaleability and automated support of multiple link types, we can store all traceability information in a dedicated database and use database management facilities such as queries, views and versioning to manage that information.

A traceability database tool often manipulates a hierarchical structure of projects, documentation units within a project and data within a documentation unit. User-defined traceability attributes can be attached to the units and to the data. These may include, among others, the configuration management attributes mentioned before such as the date and the rationale for creation of the documentation unit/data, the author and contributors, the evaluation/approval status and so on. User-defined attributes can also encode dependencies among units and data such as *Use* and *Derivation* links.

The facilities provided by traceability database tools generally include the following:

- Creation and modification of documentation units and data together with their user-defined traceability attributes.

- Historical tracking of changes made to the units/data.

- Baselining of approved versions, for sharing among project members, until the next approved change.

- Forward and backward navigation through traceable units and data.

- Coverage checking.

- Database view extraction, visualization of traceability chains and report generation.

- Interoperability with other software engineering tools.

Several commercial tools provide this functionality, including DOORS (Telelogic), RTM (Chipware/Marconi) and RequisitePro (Rational/IBM). They are in a sense generic, allowing users to customize the tool to their own traceability attributes and granularity. They scale up to large projects and support forward, backward, horizontal and vertical tracing of requirements and assumptions. However, the manual intervention required for customizing the tool and for establishing the traceability graph may be difficult and error prone. One reason is the lack of structuring of traceability information, to be provided as 'flat', user-defined attributes, and the lack of guidance in feeding the tool with this unstructured information.

Traceability model databases

A *model-based* approach may be followed for better structuring of traceability information. The idea is to pre-define the traceability model for an organization or for a class of projects. Such a model defines which types of RD item and downward software item should be linked through which type of link. The model may also define process-level link types such as contributions of process actors under different roles to RD items, for example motivator, owner or documentor (Gotel & Finkelstein, 1995).

The traceability model may be specified using an entity–relationship notation, as already illustrated in Section 6.3.1 (see Figure 6.11). The logical schema of the traceability database for any project in the considered class is then derivable from the model specification. Model management meta-systems can generate instantiated, model-specific database management tools from this specification (Teichroew *et al.*, 1980; van Lamsweerde *et al.*, 1988; Jarke *et al.*, 1995).

For a particular project, the traceability model database is filled in with project-specific instances of the item/link types specified in the model, as illustrated in Figure 6.12. Each traceable item is an entity instance in the database, related to others through traceability links, and characterized by values for the attributes declared in the traceability model (which can be texts, diagram portions, formal expressions and so on).

Entity–relationship queries on the traceability model database allow us to navigate forwards or backwards through the database. The traceable entities are retrieved by following traceability relationship instances. This is quite similar to the principle of querying a requirements database for specification analysis (see Section 5.2).

For example, consider the following change scenario in our meeting scheduling system. Due to the latest GSM interface technologies, we need to make changes in the RD section containing the meeting scheduler interface requirements. The reference name of this item is *MSI/GSM* in Figure 6.12. To assess the impact of such changes, we would like to retrieve:

- Horizontally, all RD items that use *MSI/GSM*.

- Vertically, all downward software items that are derived from *MSI/GSM* or from the RD items that use *MSI/GSM* – architectural modules, test data, source code, project management information, user manual sections and so on.

In the entity-relationship query language introduced in Section 5.2, the following two simple queries do the job:

```
set ItemsUsingGsmInterfaceReqs = RD-Section
  which Uses (RD-Section with RD-Section.RefName = 'MSI/GSM')


set GsmDependentItems = ModuleSpecs ∪ TestData ∪ . . . ∪ UserManualSection
  which DerivedFrom (RD-Section (with RD-Section.RefName = 'MSI/GSM'
                    or in ItemsUsingGsmInterfaceReqs))
```

As for queries on a requirements database, we can define a pre-cooked list of traceability queries to retrieve dependency chains in 'press-button' mode.

A traceability model database can also include *executable traceability links* between requirements and executable models. A companion tool may then propagate speculative requirements changes to the executable model and re-execute the latter for change assessment, for example using database triggers. This principle has been explored with executable traceability links between performance requirements and simulations (Bodart *et al.*, 1985; Cleland-Huang *et al.*, 2003). It could also be used for traceability links between functional requirements and animations, or between usability requirements and user interface prototypes.

Specification-based traceability management

Instead of defining and maintaining an explicit traceability model, we can derive *implicit* traceability links from the structuring mechanisms provided by semi-formal and formal languages, when such languages are used for specifying portions of the RD.

Chapter 4 described a variety of structuring mechanisms supported by specification languages to organize a complex specification into manageable specification units – such as section templates in structured natural language specifications, stepwise decomposition in SADT, data flow or state machine diagrams, aggregation and specialization with inheritance in entity–relationship diagrams, inclusion and logical combination of Z schemas and so forth. Such structuring mechanisms provide built-in traceable RD items, granularities and language-specific specializations of the *Use* and *Derivation* link types. Let us illustrate this for a semi-formal and a formal specification language, respectively:

- Consider the structuring mechanism of decomposing SADT activities or data into finer-grained diagrams, or the structuring mechanism of decomposing DFD operations into finer-grained flows. This mechanism subsumes a *Use* dependency. To preserve specification consistency, changes to a parent activity, data or operation in the decomposition hierarchy need to be propagated down to the descendant, finer-grained activities, data or operations, respectively; for example a new output added to a decomposed DFD operation must appear in the diagram refining this operation.

- Consider the Z schema inclusion mechanism described in Section 4.4.3. This mechanism also subsumes a *Use* dependency link type. To make this clear, suppose that we change the definition of library shelves, previously specified as the set of book copies either checked out or available for check-out. We might revise this definition by introducing a third category of copies which can be used within the library room but may never be checked out (rare books, frequently used books and so on). When making such a change we need to change the data and operation schemas that include the *LibraryShelves* schema (see Section 4.4.3), otherwise the latter might become incomplete or inadequate.

In addition to the built-in traceability provided by specification-structuring mechanisms, inter-view consistency rules provide constraints to be maintained when changes are made to a multiview specification (see Section 4.3.9). Such constraints link traceable items to which they refer. For example, consider the following consistency rule:

> Every data in a flow or repository of a DFD diagram must be declared as an entity, attribute or relationship in an ER diagram.

This rule establishes *Use* links between data labels in DFD diagrams and corresponding entities, attributes or relationships in ER diagrams. When one of them is changed, the others linked to it by the consistency rule must be checked to see whether the consistency is maintained. Similarly, consider the consistency rule:

> Every interaction event in an event trace diagram must appear in a corresponding state machine diagram.

This rule establishes a *Use* link between event labels in ET diagrams and corresponding event labels in SM diagrams. When one of them is changed, the others linked to it by the rule must be checked to see whether the consistency rule is maintained. More semantically, the consistency rule of coverage of all ET traces by SM paths subsumes richer traceability links between the corresponding diagrams.

Traceability link generators

Another approach to the derivation of implicit traceability links consists of using information retrieval techniques for link mining in the RD (Huffmann Hayes *et al.*, 2003).

The idea is to formulate a query as a list of keywords characterizing a source RD item to be traced. A keyword-based information-retrieval algorithm may then compare the query with the terms used in other RD items in order to generate a list of candidate target items whose terms match the query sufficiently closely. Each item in the list yields a likely traceability link to the source item characterized by the query.

A similarity measure is used to compute how close the match is. The candidate target items in the returned list appear in descending order of similarity. For similarity assessment, the terms in an RD item may be weighted by their degree of importance in characterizing this item. Information retrieval algorithms may also use a thesaurus to handle keyword synonyms.

The performance of this technique is determined by its precision and its recall. *Precision* is the fraction of target items in the returned list that are really relevant to the source item specified by the query. *Recall* is the fraction of returned relevant items in the entire set of relevant items (returned or not returned).

The gain provided by this approach is somewhat compensated for by the loss. On the one hand, link generation may significantly reduce the manual effort of establishing and maintaining a traceability graph. On the other hand, the precision and recall might be far from satisfactory, resulting in a large number of false positives and missed links, respectively. To be sufficiently effective in precision and recall, the technique requires high lexical correlation between the source and target items. Even when this is the case, lexical correlation carries no semantics; we don't know much about the type of traceability link retrieved.

An alternative approach to keyword-based matching for link generation consists of defining explicit rules for matching related terms in source and target items. For example, the source items might be textual parts of the RD, whereas the target items might be semi-formal parts such as UML model portions. Interpreting these rules on actual RD items yields UML-specific types of dependency links among matching items (Spanoudakis *et al.*, 2004). This approach somewhat combines specification-based traceability management and automated link generation.

Consistency checkers

This last approach addresses the problem at its root. As one of the main objectives of traceability management is to maintain consistency in the presence of changes, we may merely need to detect and localize the sources of inconsistencies when such changes are made.

XlinkIt is a rule-based technique, supported by a tool, to achieve this (Nentwich *et al.*, 2003):

- The analyst identifies the items to keep consistent with each other, tags them and defines the various consistency constraints linking them. The constraints are specified in a rule language based on first-order logic (see Section 4.4.1). A link-generation semantics is associated with the first-order constructs. The latter do not simply return a truth value but also hyperlinks pinpointing the sources causing the truth value.

- For better manageability and scaleability, the traceable items and consistency rules are organized into cohesive document sets and rules sets, respectively, that can be composed hierarchically.

- When a change is made on some item in a document set, the rules in the corresponding rule set are evaluated.

- Any rule violation is highlighted by generating the hyperlinks to the violating items.

This approach is generic, as it makes no assumption about the nature of the documents to be linked nor the language in which the traceable items should be expressed. It can be used in distributed environments where the documents are distributed over the Web. XlinkIt is applicable in a variety of settings including natural language documents and semi-formal models. If we use multiple types of diagrams to specify portions of the RD semi-formally, we may use the intra- and inter-view consistency rules introduced in Section 4.3.9 as rules to be submitted to the XlinkIt rule engine.

6.3.4 Determining an adequate cost–benefit trade-off for traceability management

Traceability management should be cost effective. As a prerequisite, we need to determine an optimal balance between the expected gains from traceability analysis and the cost of creating and maintaining the traceability graph. A project-specific traceability policy should be defined as a result to regulate the subsequent steps towards an optimal cost–benefit trade-off (see Figure 6.13):

- On the one hand, the gains from evolution support, rationale analysis, coverage analysis, defect tracking, compliance checking and project tracking are generally decisive on the quality of the software engineering process and its resulting products.

- On the other hand, the cost of establishing and maintaining traceability links among a large amount and diversity of sources and targets, generally under different formats, may be significant. The task is hard, tedious and error prone.

Delayed gratification is an additional barrier. The price for traceability has to be paid at the beginning of the project, whereas the return on investment only comes later. Moreover, the ones who suffer from traceability management at the early stages of the project are generally not the ones who benefit from it at later stages.

On the other hand, poor traceability generally has quite expensive if not disastrous consequences. In the absence of any traceability documentation, it may be hard and time consuming, if at all possible, to recollect the context in which a requirement or an assumption was created, modified and used. Reverse engineering of untraceable rationale, impact and dependencies from downward artefacts, by other people, is likely to be expensive and unreliable. The *Ariane-5* disaster is one spectacular example of the cost of non-traceability of assumptions and their dependencies (Lions, 1996).

An effective cost–benefit analysis should determine output parameters from input ones. The *input parameters* include project characteristics that may affect the weight to put on traceability management, such as:

- The project's estimated size (in person-years) – the larger the project, the higher this weight.

- The size, distribution and estimated turnover of the development team – the larger, the more distributed and the more volatile the team, the higher the weight.

- The timing of the various development phases – the tighter the timing, the lower the weight.

- The estimated lifetime of the software-to-be – the longer the lifetime, the higher the weight on traceability management, as the system is more likely to undergo multiple, deep changes.

- The stipulation of explicit traceability requirements by customers and their priority level – the higher the priority level, the higher the weight.

- The estimated number of requirements and assumptions that should be involved in the traceability graph at some level of granularity or another – the higher this number, the higher the weight on traceability management.

- The estimated number and criticality of mission-critical requirements and assumptions – the higher these estimates, the higher the weight.

- The estimated number and volatility of requirements and assumptions that are subject to change – the higher these estimates, the higher the weight on traceability management.

The cost–benefit analysis should control *output parameters* from those input parameters, according to the weight assigned to traceability management. These output parameters include:

- The scope, granularity, accuracy, semantic richness and acceptable overhead of traceability management (as discussed before).

- The techniques and tools that will be used to reduce the cost of traceability management.

- The points along the project timeline where the traceability graph will be established, exploited for various analyses and updated – these typically correspond to points in time where approved versions are baselined.

- The people who will be responsible for traceability management.

A consistent set of values for these output parameters defines a *traceability policy* that guides the traceability management process. To remain consistent throughout the project, such a policy may need to be reevaluated and updated to take project fluctuations into account (as suggested in Figure 6.13).

As we saw before, the use of semi-formal or formal specification techniques may significantly contribute to reducing the cost of traceability management. The structuring mechanisms and consistency rules of the specification language yield built-in traceable items, granularities and traceability links. The richer the structuring mechanisms and consistency rules, the richer the support for traceability management. Part II will introduce further structuring mechanisms and consistency rules for goal refinement, goal operationalization, responsibility assignment and threat or hazard resolution by countermeasures. These will provide further fine-grained items to trace at low cost, and further link types for satisfaction arguments (see Figure 6.10).

6.4 Change control

The previous sections dealt with change anticipation and traceability management as two necessary conditions for effective requirements change management. Let us now have a closer look at the change process itself.

Change requests may arise at any time in the software lifecycle – during the early cycles of the spiral RE process, during software development or when the new system is running. The complexity of software-intensive systems and the potential impact of changes call for a systematic change control procedure.

Changes give rise to new cycles in the spiral RE process; see Figure 1.6 in Section 1.1.6. A new cycle is initiated by submission of a motivated change request; the request is evaluated by a review board; the approved changes are consolidated through new steps of specification, quality assurance and documentation. The change specifications are then implemented in a software revision or variant.

This section reviews the RE-specific steps of change initiation, evaluation and consolidation (see Figure 6.16). These steps can be made more or less formal depending on the importance of the proposed changes, the standards of the organization, the domain and the type of project. In particular, mission-critical projects generally undergo more formal change procedures.

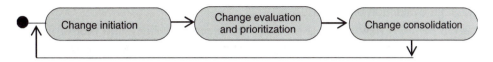

Figure 6.16 *Change control*

6.4.1 Change initiation

Section 6.1 introduced a variety of *causes* that may prompt different types of corrective, ameliorative or adaptative changes – errors and flaws in the RD, increased knowledge among customers or project members, wish for new or improved features, project fluctuations and a wide range of environmental changes including new or alternative ways of doing things, changes in organizational structures, new or alternative regulations, new or alternative technologies and so forth (see Table 6.1).

The team in charge of the project generally maintains a wishlist of possible changes identified by insiders or collected from outsiders. The wishlist may classify such changes by type (corrective, ameliorative or adaptative) and by perceived degree of emergency.

At certain time intervals, depending on causal factors, degree of emergency, type of project and organizational policy, the team consolidates the wishlist into a motivated *change request*. The latter typically provides the following information for each proposed change (or for each group of highly related changes):

- Its description, making it clear which RD items the change concerns – objectives, conceptual structures, functional or non-functional requirements or assumptions.

- The context in which such items were introduced and used in the previous version, including evaluation data when available.

- The rationale for this change, in terms of causal factors.

- The system stakeholders who asked for it.

- Its perceived degree of urgency, with some justification.

- A first estimation of the change impact on dependent software lifecycle items, on the resulting product and on the subsequent maintenance process.

- A first estimation of the cost and resources required for implementing it.

The change request may also suggest some priority ranking for the proposed changes, based on their type and on the criticality of the system aspects they concern. For example, a corrective change on mission-critical aspects has higher priority than an ameliorative change on non-functional aspects.

The change request is generally formulated on an ad hoc form for subsequent evaluation and tracking. It is submitted to a review board in charge of evaluation and approval.

6.4.2 Change evaluation and prioritization

The mission of the review board is to assess the merits, feasibility and cost of the changes proposed in the change request, according to change management policies that the board has pre-established. Based on this assessment, the board has to make an informed decision on which changes should be implemented, which ones should be deferred until later versions and which ones should be ignored.

The *review board* is generally an independent party that can make judgements objectively. It should be capable of cost–benefit assessments and entitled to make decisions. The board should ideally represent all stakeholder viewpoints, including people from marketing departments (where appropriate). In addition to project managers and decision makers, the review board should include, or be assisted by, domain experts and experienced developers.

To fulfil its mission, the review board needs to do the following:

- Understand the context of the requested changes based on the information provided in the change request and on documented traceability links, followed backwards.

- Check the well-foundedness of proposed changes, for example a proposed feature might already be supported by the current version in an insufficiently visible form; others might already be scheduled in a phased development where requirements were prioritized (see Section 3.4); a similar change might have been submitted and processed before and so on.

- Assess the benefits of proposed changes with respect to the system's objectives.

- Assess their impact on other items along traceability links followed forwards. Such items may need to be changed accordingly. Other requirements might overlap or even conflict with the proposed changes; assumptions about the environment might no longer be valid if the changes are made; past design decisions might be questioned; architectural specifications and test data may need to be modified accordingly and so forth.

- Detect potential conflicts among the proposed changes themselves.

- Assesss the risk of change against the risk of non-change.

- Estimate the cost and feasibility of the changes being considered in terms of required resources and timing.

- Prioritize the accepted changes, in case they cannot all be accommodated in the next version of the system.

The requirements prioritization techniques discussed in Section 3.4 apply to proposed changes as well; they are especially relevant here in the case of a large number of changes.

If preliminary estimations of costs, benefits and impact are available in the change request, the evaluators need to review them and refine them. They may need to consult and negotiate with stakeholders and developers of the previous version, if the latter are not sufficiently represented on the board.

The final outcome of the change evaluation step is a justified decision based on the recognized necessity, agreed benefits and estimated costs of the proposed changes. The change request can be approved, rejected or amended. In general, some proposed changes are approved, others are rejected and others are deferred until a subsequent version of the system. Deferred changes are then recorded in a list of requested changes together with the reasons for their postponement.

6.4.3 Change consolidation

The final step in Figure 6.16 consists of handling all approved changes to produce a new system version. This includes the following tasks:

- Forward propagation of all approved changes through the RD along horizontal links of the traceability graph, with a new cycle of specification, quality assurance and documentation in the spiral RE process (see Figure 1.6).

- Baselining of the new version of the RD for sharing among project members until the next version is baselined.

- Forward propagation of all RD changes downwards to software lifecycle items along vertical links of the traceability graph.

- Updating of the traceabiliy graph.

Tool support for change initiation, evaluation and consolidation

The overall change control process can be supported by various types of tools:

- A collaborative tool may support communications among the parties involved. Such a tool may be connected to a change request database, to keep track of change requests, and to a database where the specifications and traceability links are maintained.

- Dedicated tools can support some of the traceability management techniques in Section 6.3.3.

- Version control facilities provided by configuration management tools can store, baseline and retrieve variants and revisions of software lifecycle items.

- Prioritization tools may support the techniques explained in Section 3.4.

6.5 Runtime monitoring of requirements and assumptions for dynamic change

Requirements are frequently formulated under specific assumptions about the environment. As evolution is inevitable, some of these assumptions might no longer be valid when the system is deployed. In the longer term, it is even more likely that the system will sometimes run under conditions for which it was not designed. On the other hand, likely variations might already be foreseen at RE time but felt too costly to accommodate in the next software release.

Requirements monitoring is an evolution management paradigm aimed at addressing this problem (Fickas & Feather, 1995). The principle is as follows:

1. At RE time, we identify a number of assertions to be monitored. These might be requirements that are mission critical and likely to be violated from time to time, or assumptions that are felt unstable over time or from one class of users to another (see Section 6.2).

2. From the specification of each such assertion, we build a software monitor that will run concurrently with the software-to-be in order to detect specification violations.

3. At development time, we design and implement the software according to its original specifications. For each statement to be monitored, we may also design and implement an alternative course of action, if we want to automatically shift to it at system runtime in case of too frequent violations.

4. At system runtime, the monitor tracks events produced by the system and, in the case of a requirement/assumption violation, generates information for runtime reconfiguration. A warning may at least be produced together with the trace that led to the violation. More effectively, the information generated by the monitor is used by a 'compensator' module enabling the software to reconfigure itself automatically to the alternative course of action designed in Step 3. Such a reconfiguration may be governed by rules; for example it may take place at first violation or when the number of violations has exceeded a particular threshold.

Let us illustrate this dynamic evolution scheme for our meeting scheduling system. Consider the assumption that invited participants are responsive:

> If a participant receives an e-mail request for his/her constraints, he/she will provide these within X days.

This assumption is necessary for the satisfaction of requirements about prompt scheduling of a convenient date/location. It is thus critical for the mission of scheduling meetings effectively. It is also likely to be violated sometimes at system runtime, as it might require too much from highly busy people. This assumption, and the requirements dependent on it, are thus likely to change; we decide to monitor it (Step 1). We thus build a monitor to detect the absence of response events from participants within the prescribed deadline (Step 2). We design and implement alternative courses of action in the case of violations of this assumption, for example send a reminder to the participant, send an e-mail to his or her secretary or issue a warning to the meeting initiator (Step 3). At system runtime, the monitor detects violations and passes the information on to the compensator for rule-based decision on an alternative course of action.

Reconfiguration rules might look like these:

> If the number of times this participant has not returned his/her constraints within X days, over the past Y months, exceeds threshold Z
>> then send a reminder to alternative contact person P.

> If the number of times this participant has not returned his/her constraints within X days, over the past Y months, exceeds threshold Z
>> then get this participant's constraints from his/her e-agenda.

The first rule corresponds to a simple change of value for a controlled parameter (representing to whom to send reminders); the second rule captures an alternative design for getting participant constraints. The software will accordingly shift to these alternative solutions for the participant observed to be unreliable in that sense (Step 4).

Step 2 in this dynamic evolution scheme can be fully automated when the assertions to monitor are specified formally in temporal logic. As we saw in Section 4.4.2, such assertions are interpreted over system histories; that is, temporal sequences of events. The negation of a temporal logic assertion gives us the corresponding violation condition; a monitor for it will be watching for corresponding event traces. Such monitor can be automatically generated through two kinds of approaches:

- The negated temporal logic assertion is compiled into a temporal pattern of event combinations. When the system is running, a pre-defined generic monitoring system queries the historical database of system events for event sequences matching this pattern (Feather *et al.*, 1998; Robinson, 2006).

- The temporal logic assertion is compiled into a state machine representation. Every path to the error state in this state machine represents a sequence of events that violates the assertion. To detect assertion violations, the state machine runs synchronously with the system and issues warnings whenever the error state is reached (Giannakopoulou & Magee, 2003; Tran Van *et al.*, 2004).

The monitoring/compensation environment obviously relies on an ad hoc communication infrastructure for notifying, gathering, listening and reacting to events.

6.6 Conclusion

Evolution is inevitable. Requirements consistency, completeness and adequacy must be preserved under changing conditions. Maintaining the quality and timeliness of system revisions and variants remains a challenge.

An effective change management process should combine change anticipation, to ensure architectural stability and system flexibility; traceability management, to ensure accurate assessment and propagation of changes; and a rigorous procedure for initiating, evaluating and consolidating changes. The techniques in this chapter provide complementary ways of supporting this process.

Change management policies should determine which blend of techniques is most appropriate, and when and where to use them. Criteria for technique selection include their strengths and limitations, their potential synergies and project-specific characteristics such as project size and timing constraints, product lifetime, domain characteristics, mission-critical concerns and organizational standards.

The model-based RE method in Part II of the book will help us reduce the cost of change management. The goal-oriented models there will provide a structure for defining change units, natural granularities of traceable items, built-in derivation links and satisfaction arguments to be replayed in the case of change. Changes are made on the model along built-in traceability links, and the requirements document is regenerated from the model revision or variant.

Summary

- A three-word summary of this chapter might be: 'Prepare for change'. After the system-to-be come systems-to-be-next. Requirements evolution may concern system objectives, domain concepts, functional requirements, non-functional requirements and a wide variety of assumptions about the environment. These items may depend on each other. Downward software artefacts depend on them. Requirements evolution raises a difficult consistency management problem. The process of anticipating, evaluating, agreeing on and propagating changes to RD items is called requirements management.

- Changes to the RD may be of different types, caused by different factors, resulting in different types of versions and operated at different phases of the software lifecycle. A revision results from changes made to correct or improve the current version of the RD. Variants result from changes made to adapt, restrict or extend a master version to multiple classes of users or usage conditions. Many changes originate from changing conditions in the software environment and assumptions that are no longer adequate.

- Changes should be anticipated at RE time. We need to identify likely changes, assess their likelihood and document them in the RD. This information enables software developers to design architectures that will remain stable in spite of changing assumptions and requirements. To document likely changes, we may assign qualitative levels of stability to features or statements, or levels of commonality in the case of multiple variants. Such levels may be determined during requirements elicitation or by use of heuristic rules. In particular, decisions relying on incomplete knowledge or resolving conflicts, risks and other alternative options are likely to yield more volatile requirements and assumptions.

- The traceability of requirements and assumptions allows us to figure out where they come from, why they come from there and what they are used for. Traceability relies on the existence of documented links between items that we can follow backwards, towards source items, and forwards, towards target items. Horizontal traceability involves items from the same project phase that rely on each other. Vertical traceability involves items from different phases that give rise to each other. *Dependency* is the most general type of traceability link. It can be specialized into *Variant* and *Revision* links among versions, and into *Use* and *Derivation* links within a single version. The more specialized the dependency, the more specific the reason for it, the more accurate the link, the easier its correct establishment and the more accurate the change analysis. Derivation links call for satisfaction arguments. When such arguments are documented in the RD, we obtain rich traceability links for free.

- Traceability management refers to the process of establishing, recording, exploiting and maintaining traceability links in a traceability graph. It allows us to assess the impact of changes and to propagate actual changes for consistency maintenance within the RD and throughout the software lifecycle. This process also supports rationale analysis, coverage analysis, defect tracking, compliance checking and project tracking. There is, however, a cost to pay early for late gratification. Every project must settle an appropriate cost–benefit trade-off to define a traceability policy. Such a policy should determine the granularity, semantic richness and accuracy of traceability based on parameters such as project size, timing, development conditions and product characteristics. In particular, mission-critical and unstable features deserve finer-grained and more accurate traceability.

- Numerous techniques are available for alleviating the cost of traceability. Cross-referencing is a limited but readily available technique for lexical traceability. Traceability matrices are often used for representing and tracking single traceability link types. Feature diagrams capture commonalities and variations within a product family. Traceability database management systems provide facilities for storing, versioning, baselining and navigating through traceable items and their user-defined traceability attributes. Traceability model databases allow traceable items and links to be similarly managed under entity–relationship structures that instantiate a traceability meta-model. This model structures the database schema and may support multiple traceability link types. Specification-based traceability requires portions of the RD to be specified in a semi-formal or formal language; the language mechanisms for specification structuring provide built-in traceable units linked by specializations of *Use* and *Derivation* links. For multiparadigm specifications, inter-view consistency rules yield traceable items and links as well. Traceability link generators use keyword-based information-retrieval techniques to generate candidate lexical links from natural language text. Consistency checkers generate hyperlinks to items violating pre-defined consistency rules as they are changed.

- Change control is a more or less formal process depending on the domain, the organization and the prominence of mission-critical concerns in the project. A new cycle in the spiral RE process is initiated by submission of a motivated change request. The necessity, feasibility, benefits, impact and cost of the requested changes are evaluated by a review board. The approved changes are prioritized, if necessary, and the selected ones are consolidated through new steps of specification, quality assurance and documentation. The changes are then baselined and implemented in a new software revision or variant.

- Requirements monitoring is a recent paradigm for dynamic change at system runtime. Monitors are built for requirements or assumptions that are felt to be critical or too volatile. At system runtime, they run concurrently with the software to detect event sequences that violate the monitored assertions. They may report such violations to a rule-based compensator for system reconfiguration. Assertion monitors can be automatically generated if the requirements or assumptions to monitor are specified formally.

Notes and Further Reading

Surprisingly enough, the literature on requirements evolution is inversely proportional to the importance of the subject. Many RE textbooks hardly mention the problem. One notable exception is Kotonya and Sommerville (1997), which provides a comprehensive account of traceability policies and change control.

The dimensions of software evolution and the need for stable software architectures in spite of contracted, adapted and extended requirements were first discussed in Parnas (1979). Lehman pointed out that software applications keep evolving to accommodate changing requirements in the real world. His laws of software evolution suggest the inevitable decline of software functionality and quality unless rigorous adaptations are continuously made to catch up with the changing environment (Lehman, 1980; Lehman & Belady, 1985). Some of the software development methodologies in the 1980s made an explicit distinction between more stable items, such as conceptual data represented in the application's database, and more volatile items such as the processes manipulating such data. In JSD, for example, a distinction is made between the core 'entity' model, which should reflect the stable characteristics of the domain, and the functional processes, input–output formats and user interface, which are more subject to change (Jackson, 1978; Jackson & Zave, 1993).

A good survey of version control issues and models will be found in Conradi and Westfechtel (1998).

Palmer (1997) provides a general introduction to traceability. There were multiple definitions of this term before a commonly accepted one emerged (Gotel & Finkelstein, 1994). General overviews on forward, backward, horizontal and vertical traceability include Watkins and Neal (1994) and Ramesh (1998). The traceability of environmental assumptions is rarely considered, in spite of being among the most volatile items throughout the software lifecycle.

Process improvement standards such as ISO-9000 and CMMI emphasize the need for traceability management (Ahern *et al.*, 2003). Surveys reveal a wide range of traceability practices, from limited efforts by 'low-end' users to sophisticated procedures by 'high-end' users, depending on the target domain and the organization's maturity (Ramesh & Jarke, 2001). Usage-driven traceability has been proposed to master the cost of establishing and maintaining traceability links; the principle is first to define what traceability should be used for, in terms of project-specific needs, and then to derive what should be traced based on those definitions (Domges & Pohl, 1998).

Different types of links are proposed in the literature for defining traceability and recording traceability links. An early discussion can be found in Davis (1993). Pohl's thesis introduced principles for classifying such links and for defining them in a metamodel to support trace recording (Pohl, 1996). Ramesh and Jarke propose a reference typology of traceability links that include satisfaction, dependency, evolution and rationale links (Ramesh & Jarke, 2001). One difficulty with traceability link types found in the literature is that their precise semantics and orthogonality are not always clear. Horizontal and variant link types are generally neglected.

The principle of developing software families by parallel elaboration of variants, starting with commonalities, was formulated in Parnas (1976). This paper depicts the design process as a decision tree where branching corresponds to making differentiating design decisions among variants. Principles and processes for engineering product families can be found in Pohl *et al.* (2005).

The *Use* link type introduced in this chapter is inspired by Parnas (1979) with transposition to requirements engineering.

Models for representing design rationale in terms of goals, alternatives, issues and justifications are described in two classical papers (Potts & Bruns, 1988; Lee, 1991). These papers emphasize the importance of recording the design rationale. Techniques for capturing the design rationale to support requirements tracing are described in Bailin *et al.* (1990) and Shum and Hammond (1994).

Different types of satisfaction arguments are discussed in Yue (1987), Dardenne *et al.* (1993), Jackson (1995a), van Lamsweerde (2000b) and Hammond *et al.* (2001). These papers all point out the importance of satisfaction arguments for requirements traceability. This importance is now being recognized by practitioners too, for example under the term 'rich traceability' (Hull *et al.*, 2002).

Cleland-Huang advocates the combined use of multiple traceability techniques to fit the organization's maturity, the specifics of the domain and the pros and cons of each technique taken individually (Cleland-Huang *et al.*, 2004).

Traceability model database management systems are discussed in Teichroew *et al.* (1980), van Lamsweerde *et al.* (1988) and Jarke *et al.* (1995).

Feature diagrams were developed in the context of the FODA methodology for feature-oriented domain analysis (Kang *et al.*, 1990). Their role in software families, sometimes called product lines, is discussed in van Gurp *et al.* (2001). A formal definition of feature diagrams for analysis can be found in van Deursen and Klint (2002). Multiple variants of such diagrams were proposed in the literature; see Schobbens *et al.* (2006) for a review.

The idea of mining traceability links between source code and documentation using information retrieval (IR) techniques was explored in Antoniol *et al.* (2002). A good introduction to IR techniques may be found in Daeza Yates and Ribeiro-Neto (1999). Huffman Hayes and colleagues discuss the adaptation of IR algorithms for mining traceability links among RD items, and their evaluation against recall and precision (Huffman Hayes *et al.*, 2003).

Runtime requirements monitoring was introduced in Fickas and Feather (1995). It shares similarities with specification-based intrusion detection (Balepin *et al.*, 2003). The generation of assertion monitors from temporal logic specifications and their runtime exploitation for system self-adaptation is further discussed in Feather *et al.* (1998). The implementation of these ideas for requirement/assumption monitoring at model animation time is described in Tran Van *et al.* (2004). Robinson describes a requirements monitoring tool built on similar ideas for distributed event-based systems (Robinson, 2006). Efforts were recently made on monitor-based runtime self-adaptation for system customization to individual requirements and evolving skills (Hui *et al.*, 2003; Sutcliffe *et al.*, 2006).

The problem of managing changes so as to maintain related items in a consistent state has been thoroughly studied in artificial intelligence. Truth maintenance systems (TMS) keep track of assumption dependencies to highlight which assertions are no longer true in case of a changing assumption (Doyle, 1979; de Kleer, 1986). This work has received relatively little attention in the software engineering literature so far.

Exercises

- Based on the case study descriptions of the library management and meeting scheduling systems in Section 1.1.2, imagine change scenarios that illustrate the various rows in Table 6.1.

- Estimate stability levels, on a qualitative scale of {*low, medium, high*}, for a number of requirements and assumptions formulated in the case study description of the meeting scheduling system in Section 1.1.2. Explain the rationale for your estimates.

- List a number of features of your favourite e-auction system and, for each of them, estimate levels of stability and commonality from one country to another. Explain the rationale for your estimates.

- Find other examples of potential *variant* and *revision* links among RD items in the meeting scheduler case study described in Section 1.1.2, to complete those provided in Section 6.3.1.

- Let *B* be a set of rules for loan management in the library system and let *A* be a definition of the concept of patron as someone who has registered with the library for the academic year and paid a deposit for potential fines. To convince yourself that *B uses A*, explore specific changes in definition *A* and in rules in *B* that might make *B* become inconsistent, ambiguous or incomplete. (Remember that deposits are in particular utilized for fines on late returns.)

- Consider the meeting scheduling system where *B* is an RD section providing the functional requirements for determining the most convenient meeting date and *A* is an RD section defining what participant constraints are. What specific kind of dependency is this? Justify your answer.

- Based on the case study descriptions in Section 1.1.2, find further examples of horizontal and vertical traceability chains in addition to those provided in Section 6.3.1. From there, build portions of traceability graphs for those case studies.

- Extract a single-relation traceability graph from Figure 6.12, for the *Derivation* link type, and represent the same information by a traceability matrix. Imagine a few more links to augment those two representations.

- Consider the model of car you know best. Build a feature diagram that captures various optional features afforded by the manufacturer. Count the number of different variants represented by your diagram.

- Build a partial entity–relationship traceability model, in the style of Figure 6.12, for the library management case study. Formulate some relevant traceability queries on this model in the abstract entity–relationship query language introduced in Section 5.2.

- Explore implicit traceability links subsumed by the SCR tables described in Section 4.4.4.

- Based on the consistency rules listed in Section 4.3.9 and the description of *XlinkIt* in Nentwich *et al.* (2003), explain how this tool could be used to manage changes in semi-formal specifications.

- Section 6.3.4 lists a series of project characteristics that may affect the weight to be put on traceability management. Explain in greater detail why each of these characteristics may affect this weight in the way suggested there.

- Build a hierarchical dataflow diagram capturing the information flow in the change control process discussed in Section 6.4. Specify a few possible change control scenarios as event trace diagrams.

- Identify a number of volatile assumptions in the meeting scheduling system and explain how the monitor-based dynamic evolution scheme in Section 6.5 would work for them.

- Explore how the techniques reviewed in the previous chapters for requirements elicitation, evaluation and quality assurance may be replayed in the requirements change management process.

7

Goal Orientation in Requirements Engineering

I n our study of the various phases of the RE process, we have regularly found a common abstraction in the preceding chapters without really focusing on it. Chapter 1 introduced a variety of questions that the RE process must address, including *WHY*-questions about the objectives that the system-to-be should meet. As explained in Chapter 2, we need to understand the objectives of the system-as-is during domain analysis, and we need to discover the right reasons for a new system version during requirements elicitation. Chapter 3 discussed the early evaluation of elicited statements for potential conflicts, exposure to risks, selection of best alternatives and prioritization; the scope of this early evaluation included the objectives underlying requirements and environmental assumptions. The structured documentation templates in Chapter 4 allowed for specifying the rationale for specific requirements, unlike the semi-formal and formal specification languages reviewed there. Chapter 5 suggested the need for extending quality assurance techniques to enable earlier analysis, such as verification of the satisfaction of system objectives by operational requirements and assumptions. For evolution support, Chapter 6 confirmed the importance of satisfaction arguments and backward traceability to rationale.

This chapter focuses on system objectives as a core abstraction for requirements engineering. It introduces the concept of a goal to capture this abstraction and goal orientation as a basic paradigm for RE.

Section 7.1 defines this concept more precisely in relation to active system components called agents, and illustrates it through examples and counterexamples from our running case studies. Section 7.2 discusses the varying granularity of goals and clarifies their relationship to requirements and assumptions. Section 7.3 reviews the various types and categories of goals that we may need to elicit, evaluate, specify and consolidate while engineering requirements. Section 7.4 explains the key importance of goals by reviewing their multiple uses in the RE process. Section 7.5 discusses where and when goals can be found in this process. Section 7.6 finally relates goals to other requirements-related artefacts – such as scenarios of interaction between the software and the environment, operational specifications, use cases and properties used for finite state verification. This section also compares goal orientation with other paradigms such as agent orientation, object orientation and top-down system analysis. The bibliographical notes at the end of the chapter provide further information and credits on this increasingly important area of RE research and practice.

This brief chapter acts as a transition between the state-of-the-art part of the book and the model-building and analysis parts. While relying on various techniques introduced in Part I, we will use goals as a driving force for building and analysing system models in Parts II-III. Thanks to goal orientation, we will be able to reason about system models in terms of the *WHY* and *WHO* dimensions of RE.

7.1 What are goals?

Goal-oriented RE refers to the use of goals for requirements elicitation, evaluation, negotiation, elaboration, structuring, documentation, analysis and evolution.

A *goal* is a prescriptive statement of intent that the system should satisfy through the cooperation of its agents. An *agent* is an active system component playing a specific role in goal satisfaction. To fulfil such a role, the agent needs to restrict its behaviour by adequate control of system items.

In this definition, the word 'system' may refer to the system-as-is or the system-to-be. Goals are prescriptive statements like requirements and unlike domain properties, as the latter are descriptive (see Section 1.1.4). As implied by the wording 'prescriptive statement', goals are declarative, unlike operational procedures for achieving them. A key point in the definition is that *goal satisfaction requires the cooperation of system agents*. As a consequence, the goal must be formulated in terms of phenomena shared among agents; such phenomena are controlled by some agents and monitored by others (see Section 1.1.4). The system agents define the *scope* of the system. Goal satisfaction may involve a variety of system agents:

- Human agents playing specific roles, such as organizational units, operators or end-users.

- Devices such as sensors, actuators, measurement instruments or communication media.

- Existing software components such as legacy, off-the-shelf or foreign components in an open system.

- New software components forming the software-to-be.

Examples   Consider the following statement in our meeting scheduling system:

> Meetings shall be scheduled so as to maximize the attendance of invited participants.

This statement is clearly prescriptive – unlike the property 'a participant cannot attend multiple meetings at the same time'. It states an intent to be satisfied by agents of the system. No matter who these exactly are – although we expect them to include the meeting scheduler software, participants (who should attend) and initiators (who need to initiate meetings). The statement is thus a goal. Consider now the statement:

> Borrowed copies of books shall be returned within the prescribed deadline.

This statement is a goal that at first sight might involve borrowers (to return copies), the library software (to track loans and issue reminders) and perhaps library staff, depending on which option is taken to meet the goal (we don't really care at this point). Consider now the following statement about our train control system:

> The system shall guarantee safe transportation of all passengers.

We recognize a goal again that might involve various agents for its satisfaction, such as on-board train controllers (for control of safe acceleration), the station software (for issuing safe acceleration commands), the network communication infrastructure (for transmitting commands to train controllers rapidly), the tracking system (for keeping track of every train accurately), probably door actuators (for not opening doors if not commanded by the train controller), maybe passengers (for not forcing door opening during train moves) and so on. Again, no matter here who these agents exactly are; the point is that more or less complicated cooperation schemes are required to enforce this safety objective.

Counter-examples   Consider the following statement for the meeting scheduler:

> The system shall guarantee safe transportation of all participants to the meeting venue.

This statement looks like a prescriptive statement of intent. It cannot be considered as a goal of our meeting scheduling system, though; no cooperation among scheduler, participant and initiator agents can enforce it. Such an objective is out of the system's scope. Similarly, the prescriptive statement 'Make library users happy' is out of reach of the potential agents expected to form the library system-to-be. Consider now the following statement:

> To initiate a meeting, the initiator needs to prompt the meeting scheduler, authenticate him- or herself, fill in the ad hoc form to provide the date range and information about invited participants, and then confirm the request.

This statement is not a prescriptive statement of intent; it is not a declarative statement. It rather captures an operational procedure for achieving implicit goals such as 'Initiated meetings must be given a date range and contact information about invited participants' or 'Meeting initiation shall be restricted to authorized personnel'.

7.2 The granularity of goals and their relationship to requirements and assumptions

We obviously need to clarify the commonalities and differences between this notion of goal and the notions of requirement and assumption defined in Section 1.1.4 and used in the previous chapters.

The granularity of goals

Goals can be stated at different levels of abstraction:

- At higher levels, there are coarser-grained goals stating strategic objectives related to the business or the organization, for example:

    The system's transportation capacity shall be increased by 50%.
    The library system shall provide effective access to the state of the art.
    Meetings shall be scheduled so as to maximize the attendance of invited participants.

- At lower levels, there are finer-grained goals stating technical objectives related to system design options, for example:

    Acceleration commands shall be sent to every train every 3 seconds.
    Reminders for non-returned book copies shall be issued every week after expiration of the loan period.
    When no date can be found outside all excluded dates returned by participants, the constraints should be weakened by dropping the constraints of low-priority participants.

This difference in goal level and granularity suggests a specification-structuring mechanism based on *contribution links* among goals. A coarser-grained goal may be *refined* into finer-grained goals contributing to it or, conversely, finer-grained-goals may be *abstracted* towards coarser-grained goals to which they contribute. For example, the lower-level goal:

    Acceleration commands shall be sent to every train every 3 seconds

is expected to contribute to the higher-level goal:

    The system shall guarantee safe transportation of all passengers

through intermediate higher-level goals along a contribution chain. We will come back to this briefly in Section 7.4 and, in much greater detail, in Chapter 8.

Goals, requirements and expectations

This notion of goal and the varying granularity of goals bring us to a next important point. *The finer-grained a goal is, the fewer agents are required to satisfy it.* For example, the previous safe transportation goal was seen to require some cooperation among on-board train controllers, the station software, the network communication infrastructure, the tracking system, doors actuators, passengers and so on. Consider now the following finer-grained sub-goal contributing to it:

    All train doors shall always remain closed while a train is moving.

We expect this goal to involve much fewer agents; namely, the corresponding train controller, speed sensor and door actuators. Consider now the following finer-grained sub-goal contributing to the latter goal:

> *DoorsState* shall always have the value 'closed' when *measuredSpeed* has a non-null value.

This goal now only requires a single agent to enforce it; namely, the train controller software.

In this setting, the notions of requirement and assumption defined in Section 1.1.4 can be related to the notion of goal as follows.

A *requirement* is a goal under the responsibility of a single agent of the software-to-be. For example, the preceding statement is a requirement. Similarly, the following statements are requirements:

> Acceleration commands shall be sent to every train every 3 seconds.
>
> A loan coupon shall be issued if there is a copy of the requested book in the library database.
>
> The scheduled meeting date and location shall be sent to the e-mail address of every participant on the invitee list once they have been validated by the meeting initiator.

An *expectation* is a goal under the responsibility of a single agent in the environment of the software-to-be. For example, the following statements are expectations:

> Passengers get out of the train when the train doors are open at their destination platform.
>
> Acceleration commands sent to a train controller shall be received by it within X seconds at most.
>
> A borrower will return borrowed book copies within a week after the second threatening reminder.
>
> An invited participant will attend the meeting if the notified date and location fit the constraints he or she has returned.

The statement in the first example above is an assumption about the environment. It prescribes a specific behaviour for passenger agents. In the second example, it prescribes a behaviour for the communication infrastructure. (This assumption is required to achieve the higher-level goal of safe train acceleration based on real-time estimates of speed and position of the preceding train; otherwise the train might accelerate or decelerate based on outdated information about the preceding train.) By definition, expectations cannot be enforced by the software-to-be, unlike requirements.

Types of statement revisited in the presence of goals

Section 1.1.4 introduced various types of statement involved in the RE process, including system requirements, software requirements, domain properties and assumptions. The introduction of the goal concept results in a slight refinement of the terminology introduced there.

A *requirement* corresponds to what was called before a software requirement.

A *goal* might correspond to a system requirement or not, depending on which system agents are involved in its satisfaction; a system requirement as defined in Section 1.1.4 necessarily involved the software-to-be.

A *domain property* is still a descriptive statement about the environment, expected to hold invariably regardless of how the system behaves.

An assumption was defined in Section 1.1.4 as a statement to be satisfied by the environment. We observe now that some assumptions are prescriptive for environment agents. These are expectations as defined in this section. Other assumptions are descriptive, for example:

> Train tracks are in good conditions except the track segment X under maintenance.

This statement does not prescribe any agent behaviour. It is descriptive, but it is not a domain property. The assumption states some factual information that is subject to change, in this example once the segment maintenance has been done. This is not the case for a domain property such as:

> A train is moving if and only if its physical speed is non-null.

Environment assumptions will accordingly be specialized into expectations and hypotheses. An expectation as just defined is a prescriptive statement to be satisfied by a single environment agent; a *hypothesis* is a descriptive statement satisfied by the environment and subject to change. Here are a few more examples of hypotheses:

> The university library has about 20,000 patrons.
> Saturdays are excluded dates for meetings.

Figure 7.1 summarizes our refined typology of statements. In this typology, goals, requirements, expectations, domain properties and hypotheses are all formulated in terms of environment phenomena, in the vocabulary of stakeholders, with the restriction that requirements are now formulated only in terms of phenomena shared between the software and the environment. We will not talk about system requirements any further.

The importance of the distinction between descriptive and prescriptive statements should be recalled here. Goals may need to be refined into sub-goals, negotiated with stakeholders, assigned to agents responsible for them, weakened in the case of conflicts, or strengthened or abandoned in the case of unacceptable exposure to risks. Domain properties and hypotheses do not undergo such manipulation. Unlike prescriptive statements, they are not subject to decisions in the RE process. They are just there, for use in the RE process, and are pre-assigned to organizational components or Mother Nature.

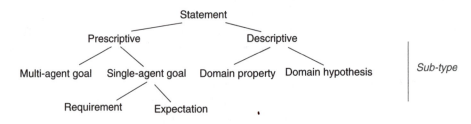

Figure 7.1 *Statement typology with goals*

7.3 Goal types and categories

Goals can be classified along two dimensions. On the one hand, a goal may be of one *type* or another depending on whether it prescribes intended system behaviours or preferences among alternative behaviours. On the other hand, goals allow us to capture functional and non-functional properties under a single abstraction; a goal may belong to one *category* or another depending on whether it prescribes a functionality or a quality constraint.

This section defines and illustrates the various types and categories of goals that we may find in the RE process. Chapter 8 will introduce diagrammatic notations for capturing them, together with techniques for building intentional system models through goal diagrams. Chapters 16 and 18 will detail further techniques for analysing such models.

7.3.1 Types of goal: behavioural goals vs soft goals

Figure 7.2 shows a taxonomy of goal types. The types there do not overlap; a goal is either a behavioural goal or a soft goal; a behavioural goal is either an *Achieve* goal or a *Maintain/Avoid* goal.

Behavioural goals

Such goals prescribe intended system behaviours declaratively. A *behavioural goal* implicitly defines a maximal set of admissible system behaviours.

A *system behaviour* is composed of parallel behaviours of the agents forming the system. An *agent behaviour* is captured by a sequence of state transitions for the items that the agent controls. These items are generally represented by *state variables*. A *state* of a variable x is a functional pair (x, v) where v denotes a particular value for x. A global system state is an aggregation of the state of all variables characterizing the system.

Figure 7.3 shows one admissible sequence of state transitions implicitly defined by the behavioural goal 'All train doors shall always remain closed while a train is moving'. There are implicitly two controlled state variables in this example: *trainMovement* and *trainDoors*, say. A possible state for the latter variable is the pair (trainDoors, 'closed'), denoted by *Closed* in Figure 7.3 for short. Each state there aggregates two sub-states: one for the controlled *trainMovement* and one for the controlled *trainDoors*.

A behavioural goal can be established in a clear-cut sense. We can always determine whether such a goal is established or not; that is, whether a specific behaviour is a member of the set of admissible behaviours implicitly defined by the goal. The phrase *goal satisfaction* thus makes sense for a behavioural goal, as we can observe that the goal is satisfied or that it is not.

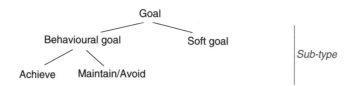

Figure 7.2 *A taxonomy of goal types*

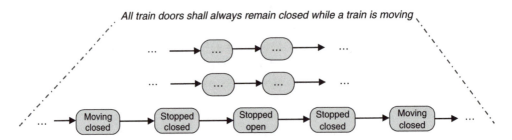

Figure 7.3 *Behavioural goals prescribe intended system behaviours*

As we will see in Part II of the book, behavioural goals may be used for building operational models of the target system such as UML use cases or state diagrams.

Behavioural goals can be further specialized into *Achieve* goals and *Maintain* goals (Dardenne *et al.*, 1993); see Figure 7.4.

Achieve goals
An *Achieve goal* prescribes intended behaviours where a target condition must *sooner or later* hold whenever some other condition holds in the current system state. When we want to highlight the goal type, we will prefix the goal name with the corresponding keyword. For an *Achieve* goal we will write: *Achieve [TargetCondition]*.

The corresponding specification has the following informal temporal pattern:

Achieve [TargetCondition]:   **[if** CurrentCondition **then] sooner-or-later** TargetCondition.

In this specification pattern, the *CurrentCondition* prefix is optional (in other words, it can be *true*).

An *Achieve* goal is sometimes denoted by *Cease [TargetCondition]* for the dual variant of this pattern:

Cease [TargetCondition]:   **[if** CurrentCondition **then] sooner-or-later *not*** TargetCondition.

- *Examples.* Here is a sample of *Achieve* goals, with the name of the goal followed by the pattern instantiation:

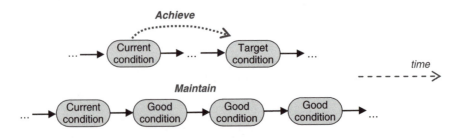

Figure 7.4 *Behavioural goals: Achieve and Maintain goals*

Achieve *[MeetingRequestSatisfied]*:
> **if** a meeting is requested **then sooner-or-later** the meeting takes place and is attended by all important invited participants.

Achieve *[BookRequestSatisfied]*:
> **if** a book is requested **then sooner-or-later** a copy of the book is borrowed by the requesting patron.

Achieve *[TrainProgress]*:
> **if** a train is at some platform **then sooner-or-later** the train is at the next platform.

In many instances of this pattern the target condition has to be established *sooner* rather than later, of course. This must be made further precise in the actual goal specification – typically, by prescribing a time interval within which the target condition must become true, for example:

Achieve *[BookRequestSatisfied]*:
> **if** a book is requested **then within a week** a copy of the book is borrowed by the requesting patron.

Achieve *[TrainProgress]*:
> **if** a train is at a platform **then within 5 minutes** the train is at the next platform.

Maintain goals

A *Maintain goal* prescribes intended behaviours where a 'good' condition must *always* hold (possibly under some other condition on the current state). Its specification takes the following informal temporal pattern:

Maintain *[GoodCondition]*:   **[if** CurrentCondition **then] always** GoodCondition,
in particular: **always** (**if** someCondition **then** GoodCondition).

A *Maintain* goal may also be denoted by *Avoid [BadCondition]* for the dual variant of this pattern:

Avoid *[BadCondition]*:   **[if** CurrentCondition **then] always *not*** BadCondition.

- *Examples.* Here is a sample of *Maintain* goals:

Avoid *[ParticipantConstraintsDisclosed]*:
> **always not** participant constraints disclosed to other invited participants.

Maintain *[AccurateBookClassification]*:
> **if** a book is registered in the library directory **then always** its keyword-based classification is accurate.

Maintain *[DoorsClosedWhileMoving]*:
> **always** (**if** a train is moving **then** its doors are closed).

Maintain *[WorstCaseStoppingDistance]*:
> **always** (**if** a train follows another **then** its distance is sufficient to allow the other to stop suddenly).

There are instances of the *Maintain/Avoid* pattern where the good/bad condition always has to be maintained/avoided up to some point, for example where another condition becomes true; this must of course be made further precise. We will come back to more specific *Achieve/Maintain* patterns in Part II while discussing goal-specification techniques.

Note that an *Achieve* goal refers to *some* future state, from an arbitrary current one, whereas a *Maintain/Avoid* goal refers to *every* future state (possibly up to some point).

Soft goals

Unlike behavioural goals, *soft goals* prescribe preferences among alternative system behaviours. They are more fulfilled along some alternatives and less along others.

Consider the following goal in our meeting scheduling system, for example:

> Interactions with invited participants should be limited as much as possible.

This goal prescribes that behaviours where there are fewer interactions (for example through e-agenda access) are to be preferred to behaviours where there are more interactions (for example through e-mail requests and reminders). Here is an additional sample of soft goals for our running case studies:

> The stress underpinning the working conditions of train drivers should be reduced.
> Passengers should be better informed of flight connections and airport facilities.
> The meeting scheduler software should be easy to use by administrative staff.
> The workload of library staff members should be reduced.

A soft goal cannot be established in a clear-cut sense. For example, we cannot say in a strict sense whether such or such a system behaviour in isolation satisfies the stress-reduction goal or not. We might, however, say that one system behaviour may reduce stress further than another. Put in more general terms, the phrase 'goal satisfaction' does not make too much sense for soft goals, as we cannot observe that they are satisfied by some behaviours and not satisfied by others. The phrase *goal satisficing* is sometimes used instead; a soft goal is more satisfied in one alternative than in another (Chung *et al.*, 2000).

Soft goals are therefore used as criteria for selecting one system option among multiple alternatives – in particular, one goal refinement among alternative ones, one risk countermeasure among alternative ones, one conflict resolution among alternative ones, or one goal responsibility assignment among alternative candidate agents. We will come back to this in Chapter 16.

In a way similar to *Achieve* and *Maintain* behavioural goals, we may prefix a soft goal name by a keyword indicating a corresponding pattern, such as:

> *Improve [TargetCondition],*
> *Increase [TargetQuantity],*   *Reduce [TargetQuantity],*
> *Maximize [ObjectiveFunction],*   *Minimize [ObjectiveFunction].*

As already introduced in Section 4.2.1, the specification of a soft goal should in addition clearly state a fit criterion to ensure its measurability.

Soft goals are not the same as goals whose satisfaction is required in X% of cases. The latter are behavioural goals sometimes called *probabilistic goals*. Unlike soft goals, we can observe whether a probabilistic goal is satisfied or not; satisfaction is only required 'on some average' due to limited resources, possibility of uncontrollable failure and so on. For example:

> The meeting scheduler should determine schedules that fit the diary constraints of all invited participants in at least 80% of cases.
>
> The distance between two consecutive trains should always be greater than the worst-case stopping distance of the train in front, with a mean time between hazards of the order of 10^9 hours.

Thus, the phrases 'satisficing' and 'partial degree of satisfaction' do not mean the same. The current state of the art in evaluating, validating and verifying probabilistic goals is still fairly limited, although such goals are frequently found in software projects (Letier & van Lamsweerde, 2004).

7.3.2 Goal categories: Functional vs non-functional goals

In a manner quite similar to the requirements categories introduced in Section 1.1.5, *goal categories* establish a distinction between functional and non-functional goals together with their respective specializations:

- A *functional goal* states the intent underpinning a system service, for example schedule convenient meetings, control acceleration of trains for rapid transportation.

- A *non-functional goal* states a quality or constraint on service provision or development, for example minimum interaction with participants during meeting scheduling, safe distance maintained between trains.

Figure 7.5 shows a goal taxonomy corresponding to the requirements taxonomy discussed in Section 1.1.5 (see Figure 1.5):

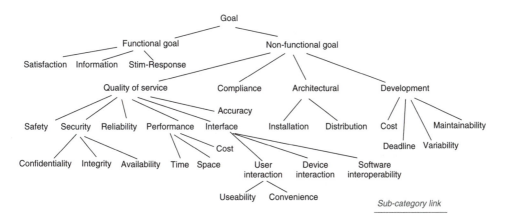

Figure 7.5 *Goal categories*

- *Satisfaction goals* are functional goals concerned with satisfying agent requests, for example 'Every relevant book request should be satisfied' or 'Every requested meeting should be scheduled if feasible'.

- *Information goals* are functional goals concerned with keeping agents informed about important system states, for example 'Passengers should be informed of what airlines are served at the next station' or 'Every invited participant should be notified as soon as possible of the scheduled meeting date and location'.

- *Stimulus–response* goals are functional goals concerned with providing appropriate responses to specific events, for example 'The on-board controller shall update the train's acceleration to the commanded one immediately on receipt of an acceleration command from the station computer'.

- *Accuracy goals* are non-functional goals requiring the state of variables controlled by the software to reflect the state of corresponding quantities controlled by environment agents accurately, for example 'The train's physical speed and commanded speed may never differ by more than X m.p.h.' or 'A copy of a book is stated as available if and only if it is physically on the shelves'.

- *Security goals* prescribe different types of protection of agent assets against unintended behaviours; such behaviours might be accidental or malicious, for example 'Date preferences of important participants may never be disclosed to anyone else than the meeting initiator' or 'Meeting initiation shall be restricted to authorized personnel'.

The definition of other goal categories in Figure 7.5 is obtained by transposing the corresponding definitions in Section 1.1.5.

For similar reasons to those discussed there, goal categories may overlap – unlike goal types. For example, consider the following goals:

Acceleration commands shall be sent to every train every 3 seconds
An ambulance shall be at the incident scene within 11 minutes

These goals are both functional and non-functional; they might be classified as satisfaction goals, safety goals and performance goals.

Using goal categories

In spite of their possible overlap, goal categories may prove useful in different RE contexts:

- *For eliciting or finding missing goals.* We may ask ourselves whether the RD covers all relevant goal categories for our system, for example:

  - Is there any accuracy goal for this critical system information?

  - Is there any confidentiality or privacy goal to protect this sensitive system information?

- *For detecting conflicts among goals.* We may reuse knowledge about negative interactions among the corresponding categories, for example:

  - Is there any conflict to be resolved between information and confidentiality goals about related information?

  - Is there any conflict to be resolved between accountability and confidentiality goals in the system?

  - Is there any conflict to be resolved between security and usability goals in the system?

- *For conflict resolution.* We may encode and reuse conflict-resolution heuristics, for example:

  - Safety goals have the highest priority in conflict resolution.

- *For specifying goals.* We may reuse heuristic rules guiding us in the specification process, for example:

  - Confidentiality goals are *Avoid* goals about knowledge that agents may have about each other.

Difference between goal types and goal categories

Types and categories provide independent ways of classifying the goals that we may consider in a system. The partition of goals into behavioural and soft goals is completely different from their classification into functional and non-functional goals. In the former case, the discriminating criterion is a semantic one; that is, whether a goal is satisfied by system behaviours in a clear-cut sense or not. In the latter case, the classification criterion is a pragmatic, more fuzzy one; that is, whether a goal prescribes intended system services or quality constraints on such services.

We should therefore not confuse soft goals with non-functional goals (as sometimes done in the RE literature). For example, goals such as:

Avoid constraints disclosure to other participants
Maintain doors closed while the train is moving
Participants should return their constraints within a week at most after request

would typically be classified as non-functional goals in the *Confidentiality*, *Safety* and *TimePerformance* category, respectively. All three are behavioural goals, though; for each of them, we can recognize whether a system behaviour satisfies it or violates it.

In practice, certain goals within a category are more frequently of a specific type. For example, many functional goals are expected to be *Achieve* goals. Many safety, security and accuracy goals are expected to be *Maintain* goals. User interaction, cost, development and some performance goals tend to be *soft goals*. In particular, '-ility' goals stating system-specific objectives related to usability, flexibility, maintainability or reusability are often soft goals.

7.4 The central role of goals in the requirements engineering process

There are multiple reasons for goals being so important in the RE process:

- *Goal refinement provides a natural mechanism for structuring complex specifications at different levels of concern*. A goal may be refined in a set of sub-goals that jointly contribute to it. For example, the high-level goal of *safe train transportation* can be partially refined into three sub-goals shown in Figure 7.6; namely, (1) Avoid train collisions, (2) Maintain train speed under the speed limit of the block the train is on, and (3) Maintain doors closed while the train is moving. These three sub-goals jointly contribute to the parent, higher-level goal. We may refine each of them in turn into finer-grained goals until we reach requirements on the software and expectations on the environment. (Chapter 8 will discuss goal refinement in much greater detail.)

- *Goals provide the rationale for requirements*. When the reason for a specific requirement is unclear, we can clarify it by checking what goals the requirement contributes to (if any). We can also explain the requirements to stakeholders by browsing goal refinement graphs such as the one in Figure 7.6 to visualize the contributions of requirements to higher-level goals

- *Goals drive the identification of requirements to support them*. Conversely, when a goal appears during the elicitation or evaluation phases of the RE process, we can explore various ways of achieving it to obtain new requirements contributing to it. (Chapter 15 will detail a method for goal-based requirements elaboration.)

- *Goals provide a richer structure for satisfaction arguments*. As suggested in Section 6.3.1, contribution links in a refinement graph provide the basis for chains of satisfaction arguments to show that higher-level concerns are met by lower-level ones (see Figure 6.10). Each argument in such chains takes the following form:

$$\{SUBGOALS, \text{ ASM, DOM }\} \models ParentGoal,$$

meaning: 'the goal *ParentGoal* is satisfied if its sub-goals in the set *SUBGOALS* are satisfied, assuming that the environment expectations in the set *ASM* and the domain properties and hypotheses in *DOM* are satisfied'. The bottom-end argument in such chains takes the form:

$$\{REQ, \text{ ASM, DOM }\} \models ParentGoal,$$

where *REQ* is a set of requirements. (We will come back to refinement-based satisfaction arguments in Chapters 8, 12 and 18.)

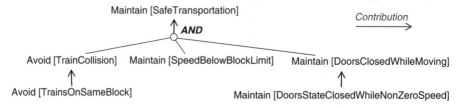

Figure 7.6 *Goal AND-refinement and contributions*

- *Goals provide a basis for showing the alignment of the system-to-be with the organization's strategic objectives.* Using such chains of satisfaction arguments, we can convince decision makers that the system-to-be will be in alignment with the organization's business goals at the top end of some chains – after all, this is what really matters to them.

- *Goals provide a precise criterion for requirements completeness.* A set of requirements is *complete* with respect to a set of goals if all the goals can be shown to be satisfied when the requirements are satisfied, assuming the environment assumptions and domain properties to hold. In other words, a set *REQ* is complete with respect to a set *GS* of goals, in view of known properties and hypotheses in *DOM* and expectations in *ASM*, if:

  for all *G* in *GS*, we can provide a satisfaction argument {*REQ*, ASM, DOM} $\models$ *G*

Achieving requirements completeness is a major concern of the RE process (see Section 1.1.7). Now we have a precise criterion we can check. A problem of course remains that the set of goals must be complete. Part III of the book will present techniques aimed at this, such as refinement checking, obstacle analysis, threat analysis and goal-oriented model animation.

- *Goals provide a precise criterion for requirements pertinence.* A requirement is *pertinent* with respect to a set of goals if it is used in the satisfaction argument of one goal at least. In other words, *r* in *REQ* is pertinent if:

  for some goal *G*, *r* is needed in a satisfaction argument {*REQ*, ASM, DOM} $\models$ *G*

Ensuring requirements pertinence is another important RE concern (see Section 1.1.7). Now we have a precise criterion we can check for this.

- *Goals provide a natural way of structuring the RD.* Goal AND-refinement structures may be used for organizing the RD, or portions of it, in a corresponding tree structure of sections and sub-sections. In fact, we can generate the RD semi-automatically from a goal-oriented model, as we will see in Chapter 16, Section 16.4.

- *Goals provide anchors for risk analysis.* A risk is usually defined as a loss of attainment of some corresponding objective (see Section 3.2). We can thus identify risks as goal negations, build risk trees as refinements of goal negations, and explore countermeasures as new goals to reduce, mitigate or reduce the identified risks. This can be done, in particular, for hazard analysis in safety-critical systems or for threat analysis in security-critical systems. (We will come back to goal-based risk analysis in Chapters 9, 16 and 18.)

- *Goals provide the roots for managing conflicts among requirements.* Conflicts among requirements are generally due to conflicts between the underlying goals to which the requirements contribute. The conflicting goals are owned by different stakeholders who have different viewpoints and concerns. For example, a goal of library staff members might be that:

  Borrowed book copies should be returned within two weeks

whereas a borrower's goal might be that:

> Borrowed book copies should be kept as long as they are needed.

To manage conflicts at goal level, we need to detect conflicts among goals; explore alternative conflict-resolution goals; select the best one based on soft goals; and propagate the selected resolution down to the requirements level. Conflict management at goal level proves much more effective. If we just handle apparent conflicts at the requirements level, we have no guarantee that a specific resolution among requirements would resolve the root conflict among the underlying goals; residual conflicts originating from the same root cause may be left unresolved elsewhere in the RD. (We will come back to goal-based conflict management in Chapters 16 and 18.)

- *Goals provide a criterion for delimiting the scope of the system.* The system is bounded by a set of goals to be satisfied through cooperation of 'good' agents. 'Bad' agents may obstruct some of these goals or threaten them. The set of 'good' and 'bad' agents defines the system's scope.

- *Goals support the analysis of dependencies among agents.* We can capture such dependencies in *i∗* diagrams that show agents depending on others for specific goals to be satisfied (Yu, 1993). Such diagrams can then be used for analysing strategic dependencies among organizational agents or for analysing dependency-based vulnerabilities in the system. (We come back to agent dependencies and *i** diagrams in Chapter 11.)

- *Goals provide a basis for reasoning about alternative options.* A system goal can be refined through alternative combinations of sub-goals. A fine-grained goal can be operationalized through alternative combinations of system services. The responsibility for a goal can be assigned to alternative agents. Incidental or malicious threats to a goal can be resolved through alternative countermeasure goals. A conflict among goals can be handled through alternative resolution goals. Those different types of alternatives are all captured at goal level, and generally result in fairly different system proposals. Goals thus provide the right RE abstraction for making alternative options explicit, exploring their respective implications and making effective decisions based on contributions to soft goals. For example, Figure 7.7 shows two alternative refinements of the goal *Avoid [TrainCollision]*. The first option consists of allowing one train at most on each block; the second option consists of allowing multiple trains to be on the same block provided that a worst-case stopping distance is maintained between successive trains. (Goal-based identification and

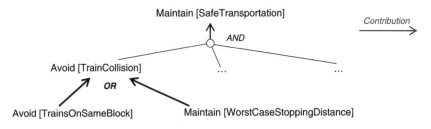

Figure 7.7   *Goal OR-refinement, alternative options, and system versions*

assessment of alternatives will be discussed in greater detail throughout Parts II and III of the book.)

- *Goals support traceability management.* As chains of satisfaction arguments are available from a goal-oriented RE process, there is no need to discover traceability links for evolution support – we get derivational traceability links for free, from low-level technical requirements to high-level strategic objectives (see Section 6.3.1).

- *Goals provide essential information for evolution support.* Section 6.2 discussed the identification of levels of stability and commonality as another important concern for managing requirements evolution. A requirement represents one particular way of achieving some underlying goal; the requirement is therefore more likely to evolve, towards another way of achieving that same goal, than is the parent goal itself. The higher level the goal, the higher its stability through successive revisions and the higher its commonality across variants of a system family. Multiple system revisions and variants generally share a common set of higher-level goals; they differ on the lower-level ones. In particular, the system-as-is and the system-to-be may correspond to alternative refinements of common parent goals. Their respective goals can be integrated into a single model, as we will see in Part II of the book. In Figure 7.7, the left-hand option contributing to the goal *Avoid [TrainCollision]* might correspond to the system-as-is, whereas the option on the right might correspond to the system-to-be, where more trains are allowed per block in order to increase train frequency and transportation capacity.

To sum up this discussion on the central role of goals in the RE process, we might say that requirements 'implement' goals much the same way as programs implement design specifications. Without a specification, we cannot develop the correct program that meets the specification. Without goals, we cannot engineer complete, consistent, pertinent and adequate requirements that meet them.

7.5 Where are goals coming from?

Goal identification is not necessarily an easy task. Sometimes goals are stated explicitly as system objectives during elicitation sessions. More often they are kept implicit and we need to 'mine' them from preliminary documents and from elicited material such as scenarios, workflow descriptions and other operational details provided by stakeholders.

The preliminary analysis of the system-as-is is an important source for goal identification. At higher levels, the business goals of the organization are generally apparent. Domain analysis also results in a list of complaints, deficiencies and other problems (see Chapter 2). *Avoiding* or *reducing* each of the listed problems yields an additional list of candidate goals to start from.

Another simple and quite effective means for goal identification consists of searching through preliminary documents and interview transcripts for intentional keywords, such as 'in order to' or 'so that' and keywords in the optative mood, such as 'has to' or 'shall'. Chapter 8 will detail these heuristics and others.

When goals are explicitly stated as system objectives, we may ask *HOW* questions during elicitation to find out contributing sub-goals. When they are kept implicit in the scenarios and operational descriptions being elicited, we may ask *WHY* questions to make them explicit.

In view of the central role played by goals in the RE process, the sooner a goal is identified and validated, the better. This does not entail any sort of waterfall-like requirements elaboration process, though. There is some inevitable intertwining of goal identification and requirements elaboration. Some goals may be identified in the elicitation phase; other goals may result from the requirements evaluation phase where problems are found such as conflicts and overexposure to risks; yet other goals may appear in the requirements quality assurance phase where problems are found such as omissions or inadequacies.

A variety of more sophisticated techniques for goal identification, refinement and abstraction will be detailed throughout Parts II and III of the book while discussing techniques for building and analysing goal models.

7.6 The relationship of goals to other requirements-related products and processes

This section relates goals to other RE artefacts such as scenarios, operational specifications, use cases and properties used in finite-state verification. The aim is to highlight the differences and complementarities among these notions. Goal orientation is then briefly compared with other candidate paradigms for RE such as agent orientation, object orientation and top-down analysis.

7.6.1 Goals and scenarios

Goals prescribe admissible or preferred behaviours of the agents forming the system. They are related to each other through refinement/contribution links. As we will see in Part II, such links can be gathered in a goal model to support various forms of early, declarative and incremental reasoning for goal refinement and operationalization, completeness checking, conflict management, hazard analysis, threat analysis, goal-oriented animation and generation of the requirements document. On the other hand, goals are sometimes felt to be too abstract by stakeholders. They cover classes of intended behaviours, but such behaviours are left implicit. Goals may sometimes be hard to elicit and make fully precise in the first place.

Scenarios capture typical examples or counterexamples of intended system behaviour through sequences of interactions among agents (see Sections 2.2.5 and 4.3.6). Their narrative and concrete style of description make them appropriate for requirements elicitation and validation, as they are easily accessible to stakeholders. On the other hand, scenarios are inherently partial and cover few behaviours of specific instances. They leave intended system properties implicit, and may entail premature decisions about event sequencing and distribution of responsibilities among agents.

Goals and scenarios thus have complementary strengths and weaknesses. As Parts II and III will show in greater detail, they can be combined synergistically for building and analysing system models.

The semantic relationship between goals and scenarios should become clear at this point. A behavioural goal implicitly defines a maximal set of admissible system behaviours (see Section 7.3.1). Such behaviours are composed of parallel agent behaviours, each captured by a sequence of state transitions of items that the corresponding agent controls. We can therefore make these state transitions explicit along agent timelines through corresponding agent inter-actions. A behavioural goal then *covers* the set of all positive scenario examples that illustrate

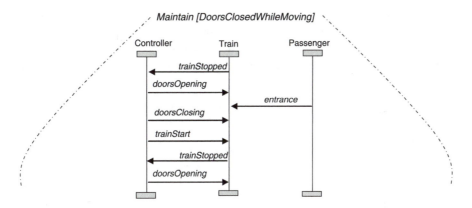

Figure 7.8 *Scenario coverage by behavioural goals*

it. Figure 7.8 depicts this coverage relationship between goals and scenarios by showing one member of the set of scenarios covered by the goal *Maintain[DoorsClosedWhileMoving]*.

7.6.2 Intentional and operational specifications

Goal specifications assert system intentions declaratively. Such intentional specifications allow us to reason early and incrementally on partial specifications, as we will see in Chapters 16–18.

On the other hand, most specification paradigms reviewed in Chapter 4 are operational; they refer to system operations, their data dependencies, their pre- and post-conditions, their laws of composition or the dynamics of their applications in terms of state transitions. Operational specifications support later forms of analysis on an entire specification, such as specification animation or model checking.

Intentional specifications leave the operations realizing them implicit, whereas operational specifications leave the intentions underlying them implicit. In terms of the various forms of analysis that they support, intentional and operational specifications complement each other. Chapter 12 will show how they can be integrated in a uniform framework, through a systematic mapping called goal *operationalization*, in order to support complementary types of analysis.

7.6.3 Goals and use cases

Use cases are a popular albeit fairly fuzzy form of operational specification (see Section 4.3.5). As their specification does not convey much, use cases are not really amenable to useful forms of analysis. However, they provide an outline view of the operations that an agent has to perform; such a view may prove useful for elicitation and communication with stakeholders. Like any operational specification, use cases leave their underlying functional and non-functional objectives implicit.

In Chapter 12 we will see how use cases can be easily generated from goal operationalizations.

7.6.4 Goals and model-checked properties

The properties that we can model check on state machine specifications can be descriptive or prescriptive (see Section 5.4.3). These properties are traditionally classified as safety or liveness properties; a *safety property* states that a 'bad' state may never be reached, whereas a *liveness property* states that a 'good' state is eventually reached.

A goal can of course be model-checked on an operational specification, like any prescriptive property. We deliberately avoid the standard safety/liveness terminology in this book for specific reasons:

- To avoid confusion between safety properties and safety requirements found in RE projects.

- To avoid confusion between safety/liveness properties and *Maintain/Achieve* goals. Unlike liveness properties, *Achieve* goals need to be bounded for realizability by system agents – the latter could otherwise unboundedly defer goal achievement; see Chapter 11. Strictly speaking, realizable *Achieve* goals are safety properties.

The important difference between goals and model-checked properties lies in the context and structure into which they fit. Goals pertain to AND/OR graphs that capture their refinement/contribution links together with their assignments to system agents. These graphs can be built systematically and are amenable to various types of earlier analysis, as we will see in the next chapters. Properties in the traditional model-checking sense do not come from structures built in a systematic way.

7.6.5 Goal orientation and agent orientation

Goal orientation is sometimes contrasted with agent orientation. On the one hand, the RE process may be more driven by the goals to be fulfilled by the system, from which the agents and their relationships are identified and analysed. On the other hand, the RE process may be more driven by the agents in the system and their dependencies, from which the goals are identified and analysed.

There is no fundamental difference between those two views, though. In goal-oriented approaches, the goals are identified and analysed based on the agents that can satisfy them. In agent-oriented approaches, the agents are identified and analysed based on the goals that they need to satisfy. Goal analysis and agent analysis are thus highly intertwined; a goal-oriented approach to RE is agent oriented as well, and vice versa. The difference is more a pragmatic matter of which driver, goal or agent is more effective at which stage of the RE process. The answer to this may depend on the domain and the type of project.

7.6.6 Goal orientation and object orientation

Chapter 10 will show how a conceptual object model can be derived systematically from a goal refinement graph and the specifications annotating this graph. The object model structures domain concepts in an extended entity–relationship form represented by a UML class diagram.

This is not to say that a goal-oriented approach to RE is object oriented. Object orientation, as usually defined, does not make any sense while engineering requirements. We certainly need specialization with inheritance as a concept-structuring mechanism, but we don't need the other basic ingredient of object orientation; that is, data encapsulation. The latter is a design concern; clustering operations and hiding implementation choices is not relevant at the RE stage as we are not concerned with design and implementation issues at all.

7.6.7 Goal orientation and top-down analysis

Some people sometimes mistakenly believe that goal-oriented approaches are top-down approaches, where we start from very high-level goals and proceed by stepwise goal decomposition until the requirements are obtained. This is by no means the case, of course; see Section 7.5. The material obtained from elicitation sessions most often covers a mix of strategic concerns, operational procedures, scenario examples, complaints, low-level details and so forth. No RE process can be made linear. We need to backtrack on issues as risks, conflicts and other problems become apparent.

In order to build a complete, consistent and adequate picture of the system-to-be from this hybrid and ill-assorted material, a goal-oriented approach must necessarily combine top-down and bottom-up processes driven by *HOW* and *WHY* questions, respectively.

Summary

- Goals provide a basic abstraction for addressing the *WHY* dimension of requirements engineering. A goal is a prescriptive statement of intent that the system should satisfy through cooperation of its agents. An agent is an active system component that can restrict its behaviour by adequate control of system items so as to satisfy the goals for which it is responsible. Goal-oriented requirements engineering refers to the use of goals for requirements elicitation, evaluation, elaboration, structuring, documentation, analysis and evolution.

- Goals can be defined at different level of abstraction. A goal at one level can be refined into sub-goals at the next level. Higher-level goals are coarser grained. The finer grained a goal is, the fewer agents are required to satisfy it. A requirement is a goal assigned to a single agent of the software-to-be. An expectation is a goal assigned to a single agent in the environment of the software-to-be. Unlike domain properties and hypotheses, goals may be refined, negotiated, assigned as responsibilities to agents and transformed in case of conflict or overexposure to risks.

- There are different types of goals. A goal is either a behavioural goal or a soft goal. A behavioural goal prescribes intended system behaviours declaratively. It can be established in a clear-cut sense; a system behaviour satisfies it or not. A behavioural goal is an *Achieve* goal or a *Maintain* goal according to the pattern of temporal behaviour that it prescribes. *Achieve* goals prescribe behaviours where some target condition must sooner or later become true. *Maintain* goals prescribe behaviours where some 'good' condition must be maintained or some 'bad' condition must be avoided. Behavioural goals are used for building operational specifications of the system. A soft goal prescribes preferences among alternative system behaviours. It is more fulfilled along some alternatives and less along others. Soft goals cannot be established in a clear-cut sense. They are used as criteria for selecting system options among multiple alternatives.

- There are different categories of goals that may overlap. A functional goal states the intent underpinning a system service. Satisfaction goals and information goals are common sub-categories of functional goals. A non-functional goal states a quality or constraint on service provision or on system development. Accuracy, safety and security goals deserve special attention in mission-critical systems.

- Goal types and categories provide different, independent ways of guiding requirements elicitation, specification and analysis. Non-functional goals should not be confused with soft goals. Many safety, security and accuracy goals are behavioural *Maintain* goals.

- Goal refinement provides a natural mechanism for structuring complex specifications at different levels of concern. A goal refinement graph shows the refinement and contribution links among goals. Requirements and expectations appear as leaf nodes in this graph.

- Goals play a crucial role in the RE process. They provide the rationale for requirements, drive the identification of requirements to support them and bound the scope of the system. They yield a precise criterion for requirements completeness and pertinence. Goal contribution links yield chains of satisfaction arguments that can be used for showing the alignment of the system-to-be with the organization's strategic objectives. Goals also provide anchors for risk analysis, conflict management and comparison of alternative options. Goal refinement structures provide useful information for evolution support and traceability management.

- Goals can be identified in all phases of the RE process, in particular during requirements elicitation, evaluation and consolidation. They are generally found by top-down refinement of higher-level concerns *and* by bottom-up abstraction from lower-level material such as scenario examples and operational descriptions.

- The complementary strengths and benefits of goals, scenarios and operational specifications call for their combined use for more effective requirements elicitation, evaluation and quality assurance.

Notes and Further Reading

Many old software development methodologies considered organizational objectives and user goals for early forms of analysis – called context analysis (Ross & Schoman, 1977b), definition study (Hice *et al.*, 1974) or participative analysis (Munford, 1981). This natural practice has led requirements documentation standards such as IEEE-Std-830 to require a specific document section for the objectives that the system should meet.

Means–ends analysis through AND-decomposition of problems into sub-problems has been standard practice in other disciplines for a long time. In artificial intelligence,

AND/OR problem reduction is a standard paradigm for problem solving (Nilsson, 1971). In human–computer interaction, AND-decomposition is a common mechanism for hierarchical modelling of user tasks (Rasmussen, 1986; Dix *et al.*, 2003). Goals are sometimes used in workflow models too (Ellis & Wainer, 1994). Business goals form an integral part of enterprise models (Loucopoulos & Kavakli, 1995; Boman *et al.*, 1997). In management science, Ishikawa diagrams (sometimes called fishbone diagrams) have a goal refinement structure for linking causes to problem symptoms in industrial processes (Kondo, 1994).

Goal orientation has proved also quite useful in other areas of software engineering. In software metrics, the Goal–Question–Metrics approach to measurement has proved quite effective for some time; it is goal driven and makes the distinction between intentional and operational levels (Basili *et al.*, 1988).

Surprisingly enough, goals have been, and still are, largely ignored in the literature on software modelling, specification and object-oriented development. Notable exceptions are the methodology described in Berzins and Luqi (1991), where goal hierarchies are used in the preliminary stages of software development, and the OBA approach, which uses goals as initial drivers of object-oriented analysis (Rubin & Goldberg, 1992). UML advocates sometimes confess the need for goals as higher-level abstractions not supported by the UML (Fowler 1997a, p. 45). Along these lines, practitioners have recommended the use of goal levels and goal decompositions as a means for building and structuring use cases to address them (Cockburn, 1997a, 1997b). The prominent tendency in software modelling research, however, has been to abstract programming constructs up to requirements level, rather than propagate requirements abstractions down to programming level (Mylopoulos *et al.*, 1999).

Yue was the first to argue that the integration of explicit goal representations provides criteria for requirements pertinence and completeness (Yue, 1987). The notion of operationalization of intentional specifications was introduced in Mostow (1985). The case for handling conflicts at goal level, rather than at the operational level, was convincingly made in Robinson (1989).

Feather developed a composite system design approach where local goals on individual agents are obtained from global system goals (called 'constraints' there). Agents have a choice of behaviour; an agent is responsible for a goal if restricting its individual behaviour is sufficient for ensuring goal satisfaction (Feather, 1987). In this framework, operational agent specifications and intentional system specifications can be analysed together to detect inconsistencies and resolve them by application of specification transformation operators (Fickas & Helm, 1992).

Two goal-oriented RE frameworks emerged independently in the early 1990s: *KAOS* (Dardenne *et al.*, 1991, 1993) and *NFR/i** (Mylopoulos *et al.*, 1992; Yu, 1993). While both frameworks addressed common targets such as goal refinement and conflicts, there were differences and complementarities in focus. In KAOS, the emphasis was more on semi-formal and formal reasoning about behavioural goals for derivation of goal refinements, goal operationalizations, goal-based risk analysis and conflict management (van Lamsweerde, 2000b). In NFR/i*, the emphasis was more on qualitative reasoning on soft goals for analysis of goal contributions, evaluation of alternative goal refinements and reasoning about goal dependencies among organizational agents (Chung *et al.*, 2000; Mylopoulos *et al.*, 2001). KAOS was more oriented towards goal satisfaction in the composite system design framework, whereas NFR/I* was more oriented towards goal satisficing.

Other goal-oriented RE frameworks emerged in the sequel (van Lamsweerde, 2001). In GBRAM, the focus was on guidelines and heuristics for identifying goals from raw material (Anton & Potts, 1998; Anton *et al.*, 2001). Most frameworks exploit the synergies between goals and scenarios for requirements elicitation and validation (Leite *et al.*, 1997; Anton & Potts, 1998; Haumer *et al.*, 1998; Rolland *et al.*, 1998; Sutcliffe, 1998; Kaindl, 2000). For embedded control software, the need for intentional specifications upwards of operational ones was recognized too (Leveson, 2000).

Some experience in using goal refinements as argumentation structures for safety-critical and security-critical systems is reported in McDermid (1994), Kelly and Weaver (2004) and Moore *et al.* (1999), respectively.

Goal types, and the distinction between *Achieve* and *Maintain* goals, were introduced in Dardenne *et al.* (1991, 1993). Their use is illustrated in, for example, Anton *et al.* (1994), van Lamsweerde *et al.* (1995). Goal categories were introduced in Mylopoulos *et al.* (1992) and Dardenne *et al.* (1993). A rich taxonomy of goal categories is proposed in Chung *et al.* (2000). Other goal classifications were proposed, in particular a classification according to desired system states, such as positive, negative, alternative, feedback or exception repair, and according to goal level, such as policy level, functional level or domain level (Sutcliffe & Maiden, 1993). Distinctions were also made between objective goals, which refer to objects in the system, and adverbial goals, which refer to ways of achieving objective goals (Anton *et al.*, 1994). Keywords were proposed to identify or represent goals in specific categories, for example qualitative verbs such as *Improve, Increase, Reduce, Make* and so on (Anton & Potts, 1998). Experience in using such categories for better requirements coverage is reported in Anton *et al.* (2001).

A great deal of work has been done on using goal specifications for a variety of early analyses, from informal to semi-formal to formal, in particular for:

- identifying goals from scenarios (Rolland *et al.*, 1998; van Lamsweerde & Willemet, 1998)

- checking goal refinements for completeness and realizability (Darimont & van Lamsweerde, 1996; Letier & van Lamsweerde, 2002a)

- deriving correct goal operationalizations (Letier & van Lamsweerde, 2002a)

- model checking early requirements (Fuxman *et al.*, 2001)

- identifying goal failure as source of new requirements (Potts, 1995; Cockburn, 1997b; van Lamsweerde & Letier, 1998; Anton & Potts, 1998; van Lamsweerde & Letier, 2000)

- managing conflicting goals (van Lamsweerde *et al.*, 1998; Robinson *et al.*, 2003)

- negotiating goal-based requirements (Boehm *et al.*, 1995; Robinson, 1990)

- reusing goal taxonomies and specifications (Massonet & van Lamsweerde, 1997; Anton & Potts, 1998; Sutcliffe & Maiden, 1998)

- elaborating or analysing security requirements (Anton *et al.*, 2002; Liu *et al.*, 2003; van Lamsweerde, 2004a)

- reasoning about partial goal satisfaction (Letier & van Lamsweerde, 2004)

- assessing or deriving software architectures from goal-based requirements (Gross & Yu, 2001; van Lamsweerde, 2003)

Goals are often defined in relation to the capabilities or skills of the agents responsible for their satisfaction (Dardenne *et al.*, 1993; Hui *et al.*, 2003). In their work on personal RE, Fickas and Sutcliffe have introduced the notion of *deferred goals* for dynamically customizable systems. Goals are ranked at RE time by levels of skills required for their satisfaction. The goals implemented in the first system versions are only those requiring elementary skills. As the system is running, higher-skill goals that were deferred are progressively incorporated into the system based on runtime monitoring of skill evolution (Sutcliffe *et al.*, 2006).

General overviews on goal-oriented RE can be found in van Lamsweerde (2000b, 2001). Case studies on goal-oriented analysis are presented in Anton *et al.* (1994), which illustrates the higher stability of goals with respect to operational descriptions; van Lamsweerde *et al.* (1995), and Dubois *et al.* (1998). Experience with goal-oriented RE in industrial projects is reported in van Lamsweerde (2004b).

Exercises

- Classify the following statements about a bank ATM system as *goal, requirement, expectation, domain property, hypothesis* or *definition*. Discuss the reasons for your classification. In particular, explain why some of these statements are not goals. For goal statements, identify the goal type and list system agents that might be involved in their satisfaction.

  a. ATM is an acronym for automatic teller machine.

  b. Ubiquitous cash services shall be provided.

  c. ATM passwords are 4-digit numbers.

  d. The likelihood of forgetting ATM cards at ATM counters shall be reduced as much as possible.

e. Users will take their ATM card back if the card is returned with a beep before cash delivery.

f. Any ATM card shall be kept after 3 wrong password entries.

g. Cash is delivered when the user password and the requested amount are valid.

h. Cash is delivered in multiples of banknote units.

i. ATM vaults contain single-currency banknotes.

j. Cash is taken by the cardholder when returned by the ATM.

k. To get cash the user must (i) enter his or her ATM card, (ii) type the correct password, (iii) select some amount below the acceptable limit, (iv) get his or her card back, (v) take the cash.

Explain why the distinction between *goal, requirement, expectation, domain property, hypothesis* and *definition* is important for engineering the requirements for such a system.

- Identify the type and the category of each of the following goals for an ambulance dispatching system. Discuss the reasons for your classification:

  a. The red button on the ambulance panel shall be pushed when the ambulance arrives at the incident scene.

  b. The stress inherent to working conditions of ambulance crews should be reduced.

  c. An ambulance is displayed by the software as being available if and only if it is actually ready for intervention at its ambulance station.

  d. The nearest available ambulance shall be mobilized for the incident.

  e. An ambulance may not be mobilized for an incident if it has not been allocated to that incident.

  f. Upon mobilization the selected ambulance shall receive a mobilization order on its mobile terminal.

- Formulate each behavioural goal in the two previous exercises as instantiations of *Achieve* or *Maintain/Avoid* patterns.

- Explain the rationale for the following statements about a traffic light system by making their underlying goals explicit:

  a. The light switch for pedestrians will be set to 'green' within x seconds after the pedestrian button has been pressed.

  b. The light switch for cars will be set to 'red' at least y seconds before the light switch for pedestrians is set to 'green'.

- Consider the following goal in a university library system:

  Book copies borrowed by students shall be returned within two weeks.

a. Identify a combination of sub-goals that would jointly contribute to this goal.

b. Find another combination of contributing sub-goals as an alternative system option.

- Build a preliminary refinement graph for your favourite bank ATM system, showing lower-level and higher-level goals together with their respective contribution links. Consider functional *and* non-functional goals by checking for pertinent instances of the various goal categories in Figure 7.5. Identify chains of satisfaction arguments from your graph.

Part II

Building System Models for Requirements Engineering

Part I of this book was dedicated to the fundamentals of Requirements Engineering. Once the motivations, conceptual background and terminology used in this discipline had been introduced, we studied a comprehensive sample of state-of-the-art techniques for requirements elicitation, evaluation, specification, consolidation and evolution.

As we noted, those techniques are faced with a recurring problem of *focus* and *structure*. The elicitation techniques in Chapter 2 raised the problem of focusing and structuring elicitation sessions (such as background studies, interviews, observations or group sessions) and elicitation artefacts (such as scenarios, prototypes or reusable knowledge fragments). The evaluation techniques in Chapter 3 raised the problem of identifying and comparing items at some common level of abstraction and granularity for risk analysis, conflict management, option selection or prioritization. The specification techniques in Chapter 4 offered mechanisms for structuring specifications, but did not tell us much about how we should structure a complex specification through those mechanisms. For quality assurance, the inspection techniques in Chapter 5 are more effective if inspections can be focused on structured specifications. The techniques for requirements validation and verification require the availability of structured specifications as well. Likewise, the evolution techniques in Chapter 6 are more effective when a rich structure is available for defining change units, granularities of traceable items, built-in derivation links and satisfaction arguments to be replayed in case of change.

A model-based approach to RE addresses this recurring problem of focus and structure. A *model* is an abstract representation of the target system, where key features are highlighted, specified and inter-related to each other.

The role of models in requirements engineering

A 'good' system model may act as a driving force for the RE process:

- It provides a comprehensive structure for what needs to be elicited, evaluated, specified, consolidated and modified.

- It allows us to abstract from multiple details to focus elicitation, evaluation, specification, quality assurance and evolution on key system aspects.

- It defines a common interface between those various RE activities, each acting as a producer or consumer of portions of it.

- It provides a basis for early detection and fixing of errors in requirements, assumptions and domain properties.

- It facilitates the understanding of complex systems and their explanation to stakeholders.

- It provides a basis for making decisions among multiple options and for documenting such decisions.

- It defines the core RE artefact from which the requirements document can be generated.

Requirements for RE models

To play such significant role in the RE process, a good model should meet the following requirements:

- *Adequate.* The model should adequately represent the essence of the target system while abstracting unnecessary details.

- *Complete and pertinent.* The model should capture all pertinent facets of this system along the WHY-, WHAT- and WHO-dimensions introduced in Section 1.1.3.

- *Precise and analysable.* The model should be accurate enough to support useful forms of analysis.

- *Multilevel.* The model should capture the system at different levels of abstraction and precision to enable stepwise elaboration and validation.

- *Open and evolvable.* The model should highlight important alternative options to be considered in the RE process together with the selected options.

- *Traceable.* The source, rationale and impact of modelling decisions should be easy to retrieve from the model.

- *Comprehensible.* The model should be easy to understand for stakeholders for further elicitation, evaluation, validation and modification.

A goal-oriented approach to model building

In the general setting established by Part I of the book, Part II presents a goal-oriented, model-based approach to RE aimed at producing models that meet those requirements. These models may capture both the system-as-is and the system-to-be.

To address the *completeness* requirement, a model will integrate multiple complementary views of the target system that cover the WHY-, WHAT- and WHO-dimensions:

- The *intentional* view captures the system objectives as functional and non-functional goals together with their mutual contribution links.

- The *structural* view captures the conceptual objects manipulated in the system, their structure and their inter-relationships.

- The *responsibility* view captures the agents forming the system, their responsibilities with respect to system goals and their interfaces with each other.

- The *functional* view captures the services that the system should provide in order to operationalize its functional goals.

- The *behavioural* view captures the required behaviours for the system to satisfy its behavioural goals; interaction scenarios illustrate expected behaviours of specific agent instances, whereas state machines prescribe classes of behaviour for any such instance.

To address the *traceability* requirement, those different views will be connected through traceability links showing how items in one view are explained by or derived from items in another view.

To address the *precision* requirement and support various forms of RE-specific analysis, the models will be expressed in terms of semi-formal notations augmented with structured annotations defining each model item precisely. The annotations can optionally be made formal, where and when needed, in order to support more sophisticated forms of analysis.

To address the *understandability* requirement, the models will be visualized through diagrammatic notations, in the style of those introduced in Section 4.3 but compliant with the UML standards wherever possible; that is, wherever the corresponding system view is supported by the UML under a simple, semantically well-defined and widely used form (Booch *et al.*, 1999; Dobing & Parsons, 2006).

The purpose of this part of the book is to introduce modelling techniques for capturing those various system views and for integrating them into a comprehensive system model. For each view, we will briefly introduce the modelling notations used, provide a precise yet simple semantics for them and illustrate their use in our running case studies. The main emphasis, however, will be on well-grounded heuristics for constructing 'good' models in the previously defined sense – this is where the difficulty lies in practice.

Chapter 8 is dedicated to the intentional view of the system. It presents techniques for modelling the system's functional and non-functional goals in terms of individual features, such as their specification, elicitation source or priority, and inter-relationships, such as their contributions to each other, their potential conflicts and their alternative refinements into software requirements and environmental assumptions. The resulting model is called *goal model*.

Chapter 9 complements the modelling techniques from the previous chapter with a goal-based form of risk analysis. The focus there is on what could go wrong with over-ideal versions of the goal model, typically obtained in the first stages of modelling. Obstacles are conditions for goal obstruction that are modelled as goal-anchored variants of the risk trees introduced in Section 3.2. The resulting model is called an *obstacle model*. New goals for a more robust system are then added to the goal model as countermeasures to the modelled obstacles.

Chapter 10 is dedicated to the structural view of the system. It presents techniques for building UML class diagrams to characterize, structure and inter-relate the conceptual objects manipulated in the system. The resulting model is called an *object model*. This chapter provides precise criteria for deciding whether a concept we want to capture in an object model is to be defined as an entity, attribute, relationship, event or agent. It discusses object-structuring mechanisms such as aggregation and specialization with inheritance. It also shows how a complete and pertinent object model can be derived from the goal model.

Chapter 11 is dedicated to the responsibility view of the system. The agents forming the system are modelled as active objects whose instances can restrict their behaviour so as to meet the goals for which they are responsible. Responsibility assignments rely on agent capabilities. The latter are defined in terms of ability to monitor or control the objects involved in goal formulations. An agent can also be decomposed into finer-grained ones with finer-grained responsibilities. It may be related to other agents through dependency links. The resulting model is called an *agent model*. We will also see how context diagrams can be derived from the goal model. (Context diagrams show the interfaces among agents; see Section 4.3.1.)

Chapter 12 is dedicated to the functional view of the system. The services to be provided are modelled as operations performed by system agents under specific conditions to operationalize the goals from the goal model. The techniques in this chapter will help us identify such conditions in a systematic way from goal specifications. The resulting model is called an *operation model*. We will also see how UML use cases can be derived in a straightforward manner from the operation model.

Chapter 13 is dedicated to the behavioural view of the system. A *behaviour model* is composed of scenarios and state machines. At the instance level, UML sequence diagrams are used for capturing interaction scenarios among specific agent instances. This chapter will provide heuristics for building a comprehensive set of sequence diagrams to illustrate the identified goals and obstacles, or to identify goals and obstacles from them. At the class level, simple forms of UML state diagrams are used for representing state machines that capture the admissible behaviours of any agent instance. The techniques discussed there will allow us to build UML state diagrams incrementally from interaction scenarios and from goal operationalizations.

Chapter 14 describes mechanisms for integrating the goal, object, agent, operation and behaviour models. These include the definition of a meta-model in terms of which the models can be defined and inter-related; the enforcement of inter-model consistency rules; and the grouping of related model fragments from different system views into cohesive model packages. The aggregation of the goal, object, agent, operation and behaviour models forms the entire *system model*.

Chapter 15 concludes this second part of the book by presenting a constructive method for elaborating a full, robust and consistent system model by incremental integration of the goal, object, agent, operation and behaviour sub-models. The requirements document is then produced in a systematic way by mapping the resulting model into a textual format annotated with figures. The document produced preserves the goal-oriented structure and content of the model, and fits prescribed documentation standards if required. The method will be shown in action there on a mine safety control system.

The figure below oulines the complementary system views studied in Part II. Their construction and use will be grounded on the general RE framework introduced in Part I. Part III will then present a variety of techniques for reasoning about the models built in Part II in order to analyse, evaluate and consolidate them.

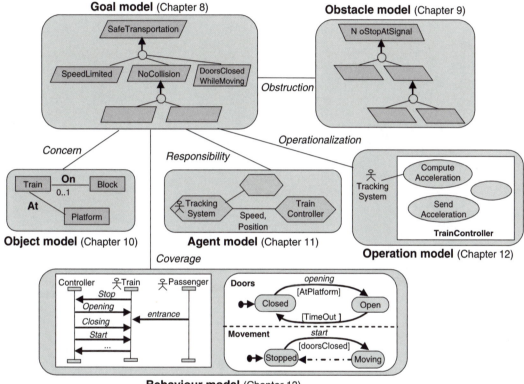

8

Modelling System Objectives with Goal Diagrams

T
his chapter is dedicated to the intentional view of the system that we want to model. This view covers the *WHY*-dimension of requirements engineering. It is provided by a goal model.

A *goal* was defined in Chapter 7 as a prescriptive statement of intent that the system should satisfy through the cooperation of its agents. Such a statement is formulated in terms of environment phenomena. The formulation is declarative – unlike operational procedures to 'implement' it. We may need to evaluate, negotiate, weaken or find alternatives to goals – unlike domain properties or hypotheses, which are descriptive statements holding regardless of how system agents behave. Goals may refer to high-level, strategic, coarse-grained objectives that the system should fulfil or to lower-level, technical, finer-grained prescriptions. The finer grained a goal is, the fewer agents are required to satisfy it. A *requirement* was defined in Chapter 7 as a goal under the responsibility of a single software agent; an *expectation* is a goal under the responsibility of a single environment agent. The instances of the responsible agent are then the only ones required to restrict their behaviour to satisfy the goal.

The *goal model* basically shows how the system's functional and non-functional goals contribute to each other through refinement links down to software requirements and environment assumptions. It may capture alternative ways of refining goals and potential conflicts among them. At its interface with other views of the system, the goal model captures inter-model relationships such as responsibility links between goals and system agents, obstruction links between goals and obstacles, reference links from goals to conceptual objects, or operationalization links between goals and system operations. The model also specifies individual features of each goal such as its name and precise specification, its type, category, priority, the elicitation source from which it comes and so forth. A formal specification of some goals may be optionally provided for further analysis.

Graphically, a goal model is represented by an AND/OR graph called a *goal diagram*. As we will see, goal nodes in such diagrams are annotated by their features and connected through various types of edges. *Refinement* links indicate how a goal is AND-decomposed into conjoined sub-goals. The same goal node can be the target of multiple such links; each of them indicates an alternative way of refining the goal into sub-goals. Leaf goals along refinement branches represent software requirements or environment assumptions needed to enforce parent goals. In a goal diagram, *conflict* links may interconnect goal nodes to capture potential conflicts among them. At the interface with other system views, a goal diagram may show alternative *responsibility assignments* connecting goal nodes to agents, *concern* links connecting goal nodes to the objects to which they refer, *operationalization* links connecting goal nodes to the system operations ensuring them and so forth.

Goal modelling makes it possible to capture the *system-as-is* and the *system-to-be* within the same model. In general, both system versions share high-level goals and differ along refinement branches of common parent goals.

The importance of the goal model derives from the central role played by goals in the RE process (see Section 7.4). In particular, we can derive other models in a systematic way from the goal model, such as the object and operation models. Moreover, the goal model enables early forms of RE-specific analysis such as risk analysis, conflict analysis, threat analysis or evaluation of alternative options (as Part III of the book will show).

Section 8.1 describes how goals are individually characterized within a goal model through various kinds of features annotating them. Section 8.2 discusses goal refinement as a basic mechanism for capturing goal contributions and for inter-relating goals, domain properties and hypotheses. Section 8.3 briefly introduces how conflicts among goals may be documented on the goal model for later resolution. Section 8.4 introduces other link types to connect goal model items to corresponding items in the object, agent, operation, behaviour and obstacle models. Section 8.5 explains how alternative options can be captured in a goal model through alternative goal refinements and assignments. Section 8.6 puts all the pieces together by showing how an entire goal model amounts to a special kind of AND/OR graph. Section 8.7 explains how a goal model can be further documented through features attached to goal refinements and assignments. Section 8.8 concludes this chapter by presenting a number of heuristics, tips and patterns for guiding modellers in the difficult task of building goal models.

8.1 Goal features as model annotations

In a goal model, each goal is annotated by a number of features to characterize the goal individually. Some of these correspond to slots of the statement templates discussed in Section 4.2.1. To help visualize these annotations, Figure 8.1 shows possible features of a variety of goals from our running case studies.

Each goal in a goal model is graphically represented by a parallelogram labelled by the goal's name, possibly prefixed by its type. The *Achieve* prefix on the first goal in Figure 8.1 indicates that this goal is a behavioural goal having the specification pattern: *[if CurrentCondition **then**] sooner-or-later TargetCondition* (see Section 7.3.1). Similarly, the *Maintain* prefix on the second goal in Figure 8.1 indicates that the goal is a behavioural one as well, but its specification pattern is: *[if CurrentCondition **then**] always GoodCondition*. The third goal is annotated as a soft goal, to be used for evaluating alternatives. The **Type** feature thus indicates which class of prescribed or preferred behaviour the goal refers to. Its range is {*Achieve, Maintain, SoftGoal*}.

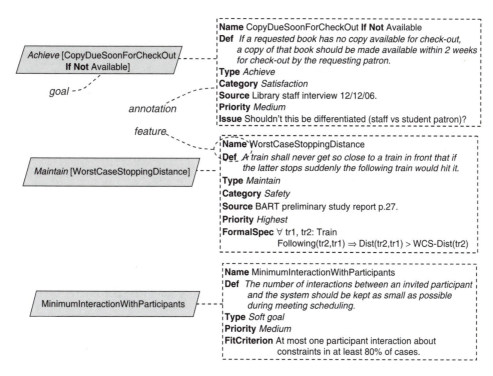

Figure 8.1   *Goal features as model annotations: examples*

Only two features are mandatory for any goal in a model: the goal's name and its specification. All others are optional.

- The **Name** feature must uniquely identify the goal throughout all views of the entire system model.

- The **Def** feature must precisely define, in natural language, what the goal prescribes in terms of phenomena that are monitorable and controllable in the system.

Goal names appearing in the goal model should be as suggestive as possible to enable their use as shortcuts for their complete definition. Names are just strings, however. For precise understanding, documentation and analysis of goals, they may never replace a complete, adequate and unambiguous goal specification in the **Def** feature. Moreover, goal specifications are used as input to the model-based generation of the requirements document (see Section 16.4).

In addition to the **Type** feature discussed above, the optional features of a goal include the following:

- **Category.** This feature indicates to which taxonomic categories the goal belongs. For example, the first goal in Figure 8.1 is concerned with satisfying agent requests, whereas the second goal is concerned with keeping the system in safe states. The use of such information for heuristic analysis was discussed in Section 7.3.2.

- **Source.** This feature indicates where the goal is coming from – a stakeholder who brought it up during elicitation, a specific section in a preliminary document used during background studies, a standard regulation in the domain and so forth. For example, the goal *Maintain[WorstCaseStoppingDistance]* in Figure 8.1 appeared at some place in a study report issued at a preliminary stage of the project. The use of such information for traceability management was discussed in Section 6.3.

- **Priority.** This feature indicates a qualitative level of goal priority for comparison with competing goals. The use of such information for conflict resolution and prioritization was discussed in Sections 3.1.3 and 3.4, respectively. For example, the goal *Maintain[WorstCaseStoppingDistance]* in Figure 8.1 is of the highest priority, like most safety goals. It should never be weakened in the case of conflict with performance goals regarding train speed or frequency, for example.

- **Stability.** This feature indicates a qualitative level of estimated stability with respect to other comparable goals. The use of such information for change anticipation was discussed in Section 6.2. Lower-level goals are expected to be less stable than the higher-level goals to which they contribute, as alternatives to the former might be considered to satisfy the latter.

- **FitCriterion.** This feature may annotate a *soft* goal to quantify the extent to which the goal should be met. It can be used for evaluating alternative options against it and for checking whether the goal is satisfactorily met by sub-goals. Fit criteria were discussed and illustrated in Section 4.2.1. The aim of this feature is to make soft goal specifications measurable (see also Section 1.1.7). For example, the fit criterion annotating the soft goal *MinimumInteractionWithParticipants* in Figure 8.1 provides a measurable threshold for what is meant by 'as small as possible' in the goal specification.

- **FormalSpec.** This feature may annotate a behavioural goal to formalize its informal **Def** specification and thereby enable a variety of formal analyses. The use of this feature will be deferred until Chapters 17 and 18. A real-time temporal logic, similar to the one introduced in Section 4.4.2, will be used there to formalize *Achieve* and *Maintain/Avoid* goals. The **FormalSpec** feature allows goal-based models to be analysed formally for adequacy, consistency and completeness – in alignment with the benefits of formal methods discussed in Section 4.4.7. Early formal analysis is especially relevant in the case of safety-critical or security-critical systems, as suggested by the train system's goal *Maintain[WorstCaseStoppingDistance]* in Figure 8.1.

- **Issue.** This process-level feature proves very useful in practice. It serves as a placeholder for recording questions raised about the goal during model elaboration. Such questions are to be addressed subsequently in the RE process. For example, the issue annotating the goal *Achieve[CopyDueSoonForCheckOutIfNotAvailable]* in Figure 8.1 records a modeller's question that should still be addressed, as different types of library user might deserve different service policies.

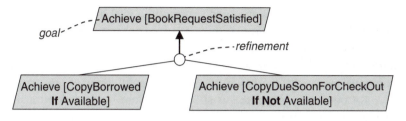

Figure 8.2 *AND-refinement*

8.2 Goal refinement

The core of the goal model consists of a refinement graph showing how higher-level goals are refined into lower-level ones and, conversely, how lower-level goals contribute to higher-level ones. Refinement graphs were briefly suggested in Section 7.4. We look at them in detail now.

In a refinement graph, an *AND-refinement* link relates a goal to a set of sub-goals. This set is called *refinement* of the parent goal. Each sub-goal in the refinement is said to *contribute* to the parent goal. The meaning of an *AND-refinement* is that *the parent goal can be satisfied by satisfying all subgoals in the refinement.*

For example, Figure 8.2 shows a possible AND-refinement of the goal *BookRequestSatisfied* in our library system. Graphically, a refinement is represented by a small circle connecting the contributing sub-goals to the refined goal; the latter is the target of the directed link. Semantically, this AND-refinement link expresses that the goal *BookRequestSatisfied* can be satisfied by satisfying the goal *CopyBorrowedIfAvailable* and the goal *CopyDueSoonForCheckOutIfNotAvailable*. (The latter sub-goal was characterized by an annotation in Figure 8.1.)

An AND-refinement of a goal G into sub-goals $G_1, G_2, \ldots, G_n$ should ideally be complete, consistent and minimal.

- *Complete refinement.* The satisfaction of all sub-goals $G_1, G_2, \ldots, G_n$ should be sufficient for the satisfaction of the parent goal G in view of all known domain properties and hypotheses in *Dom*. In short:

$$\{G_1, G_2, \ldots, G_n, Dom\} \models G$$

where $S \models A$ means: 'the statement A is always satisfied in any circumstance where all statements in S are satisfied'. In other words, no subgoal is missing for the parent goal to be satisfied. The refinement is then called a *complete refinement*.

A refinement that is arguably complete is graphically represented by a black circle. In Figure 8.2, the refinement circle should be blackened as it can be argued to be complete – either a copy is available and letting the requesting patron borrow it ensures that the book request is satisfied, or no copy is available and making sure that a copy becomes available within two weeks for loan by the requesting patron ensures that the book request is satisfied. All possible cases are thus covered.

To provide such completeness arguments, properties and hypotheses about the domain may be needed as contextual information. We come back to this below; see the example in Figure 8.4. Getting complete AND-refinements of behavioural goals is obviously essential for requirements completeness. A missing sub-goal will result in missing requirements or assumptions to satisfy it. This is the most harmful type of RE error, as we saw in Chapter 1. Completeness arguments should therefore be provided for mission-critical goals. Refinement patterns may be used informally to achieve this; see Section 8.8. Formal techniques for checking refinement completeness can be used as well; see Chapter 18.

- *Consistent refinement.* The sub-goals, domain properties and hypotheses may not contradict each other:

$$\{G_1, G_2, \ldots, G_n, Dom\} \not\models \textbf{false}$$

We clearly do not want the parent goal G to be trivially satisfied, as anything can be argued to hold in inconsistent situations.

- *Minimal refinement.* If one of the sub-goals in the refinement is missing, G_j say, the satisfaction of the parent goal is no longer always guaranteed:

$$\{G_1, \ldots, G_{j-1}, G_{j+1}, \ldots, G_n, Dom\} \not\models G$$

In a minimal refinement, the contribution of each sub-goal in the refinement is needed for the parent goal to be satisfied. We are not interested in imposing additional restrictions in the refinement that are not strictly required for the satisfaction of the parent goal. (Such additional restrictions might be needed for other reasons; they would then appear in refinements of parent goals capturing these other reasons.)

In an AND-refinement of a goal G, a sub-goal may itself be AND-refined, and recursively. The parent goal G may thus be the root of an AND-refinement tree. Figure 8.3 illustrates this for the AND-refinement in Figure 8.2.

The leaf nodes in refinement trees are nodes that need not be refined further. These include goals whose responsibility can be assigned to single software agents (as requirements) or to single environment agents (as expectations), or else descriptive statements used in the refinement. The latter might be domain properties or hypotheses. (Those different types of statements were defined in Section 7.2; see Figure 7.1.)

Figure 8.4 shows leaf nodes in a refinement tree. Graphically, they may be differentiated by a bold border. The 'home' shape is used for representing domain properties or hypotheses. Responsibility links are also shown, which are interface links with the agent model; see Section 8.4. Hexagons are used for representing system agents, with an inside 'fellow' icon if the agent is an environment one.

Note that a single sub-goal may sometimes be sufficient in a complete refinement (see the top refinement in Figure 8.4).

Also note that the portion of the goal model showing AND-refinement links will in general be a directed acyclic *graph* rather than a tree. There might be multiple root goals and a single goal node may contribute to multiple parent nodes. For example, the goal *HighFrequencyOfTrains*

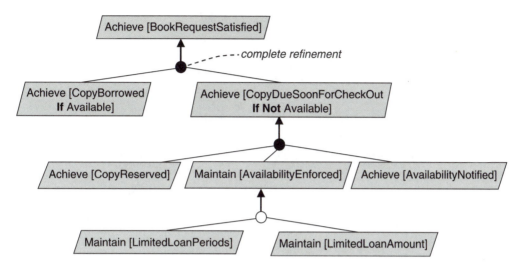

Figure 8.3   *AND-refinement tree*

contributes to the goal *RapidTransportationOfPassengers* but also to the goal *Transportation-CapacityIncreased* (see Figure 8.5). Similarly, the goal *AccurateBookClassificationByTopic* in the library system contributes to multiple parent goals such as *AccurateAnswerToBiblioQuery* and *EasyCopyLocalizationInShelves*.

It is important to emphasize that refinement links are two-way links – one way showing goal decomposition and the other way showing goal contribution. We may thus identify refinement links *top down*, asking ourselves how to satisfy a given goal by some AND-combination of subgoals; *bottom up*, asking ourselves which parent goals a given goal contributes to; or in a hybrid way, proceeding bottom up and then asking ourselves what other refinement links

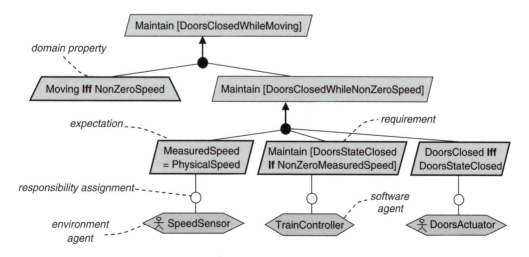

Figure 8.4   *Leaf nodes in an AND-refinement tree*

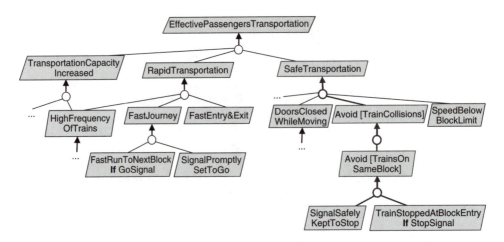

Figure 8.5   *Tree of satisfaction arguments on a goal model*

are required for the refinement of the identified parent goal to be a complete one. Goal modelling thus does not entail top-down decomposition, as sometimes mistakenly suggested in the literature on the subject. We come back to this important point in Section 8.8 while discussing heuristics for model building.

Goal refinement and satisfaction arguments

As suggested in Section 7.4, AND-refinement links in goal models support a rich structure of satisfaction arguments, each taking the form:

$$\{REFINEMENT,\ DOM\}\ \models\ ParentGoal$$

where *REFINEMENT* denotes a set of conjoined subgoals refining a goal *ParentGoal*, possibly in conjunction with domain properties and hypotheses in *DOM*. By chaining such arguments bottom up, we may show that a set of requirements and expectations ensures a parent goal, the latter ensuring its own parent goal together with others, and recursively, until a high-level goal of interest is thereby shown to be satisfied.

For example, consider the goal model fragment in Figure 8.5 for our train control system. We might argue that the goals *SignalSafelyKeptToStop* and *TrainStoppedAtBlockEntryIfStopSignal* together ensure the goal *Avoid[TrainsOnSameBlock]*; the latter ensures the goal *Avoid[TrainCollisions]*; the latter ensures the goal *SafeTransportation* together with others. At each step in this argumentation tree we should ask ourselves whether a sub-goal, domain property or hypothesis is missing for the refinement of the parent goal to be a complete one.

When domain properties or hypotheses are used in satisfaction arguments, it is very important also to check whether these are *adequate*. Fatal RE errors may originate from wrong properties or unrealistic hypotheses. For example, Figure 8.6 shows a correct goal refinement that involves an inadequate property about the domain (for better precision, we use simple propositions connected by implication/equivalence symbols instead of goal names). The wrong domain property there resulted in a major accident during a landing on a rainy day at Warsaw

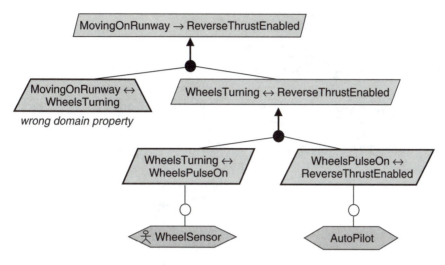

Figure 8.6 *Correct refinement based on wrong domain property for the Airbus A320 braking logic*

airport; see Section 1.2.1. Chapter 18 will show how this error could have been detected using formal obstacle analysis.

8.3 Representing conflicts among goals

In addition to positive contributions among goals, there might be negative ones. Section 3.1.1 introduced the notion of divergence among statements emerging from the RE process. A divergence captures a *potential* conflict, where some statements become logically inconsistent if a boundary condition becomes true. Goals in a refinement graph might be potentially conflicting in that sense.

Roughly, the goals $G_1, G_2, \ldots, G_n$ are *divergent* in a domain *Dom* if we can find a feasible boundary condition B under which the goals cannot be satisfied together:

$$\{G_1, G_2, \ldots, G_n, B, Dom\} \models \textbf{false}$$

(Section 16.2.1 will provide a more complete definition of divergence.)

Such potential conflicts among goals in a model often occur when the goals originate from multiple sources or viewpoints. For example, the goal *LimitedLoanPeriods* in Figure 8.3 might have been formulated by library staff stakeholders, whereas somewhere else in the model we might find the goal *CopiesBorrowedAsLongAsNeeded* that comes from interviews with patrons.

We must of course detect such situations and resolve them in an appropriate way. As discussed in Section 3.1.3, resolution should not take place too early in the RE process; conflicting statements might be a source for further elicitation of useful information. It may, however, be worth capturing potential conflicts in the goal model, when they are suspected, in order to return to them subsequently for deeper analysis (such analysis will be discussed in Chapters 16 and 18).

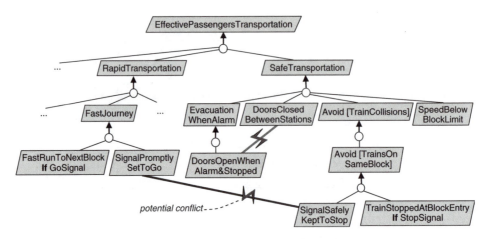

Figure 8.7 Capturing potential conflicts in a goal model

Graphically, a potential conflict among goals is represented by a 'flash' icon on a link connecting them. Figure 8.7 illustrates some possible conflicts in a goal model for the train control system. The goals *DoorsClosedBetweenStations* and *DoorsOpenWhenAlarm&Stopped* are potentially conflicting there; the former prescribes that train doors should always remain closed between two successive stations, whereas the latter prescribes that doors should be open when an alarm is raised and the train is stopped. A feasible boundary condition for conflict consists of a train being stopped between two stations with an alarm raised; under this condition the two goals cannot be satisfied together. (In Chapter 18 we will see how such a boundary condition can be derived formally from the goal specifications.) Similarly, the goals *SignalPromptlySetToGo* and *SignalSafelyKeptToStop* are potentially conflicting; a too prompt 'go' signal guarding the block that a train is waiting to enter might result in an unsafe situation where two trains are on that block (as the previous train did not have enough time to leave it); this would violate the goal *SignalSafelyKeptToStop*.

Soft goals often prescribe a target quantity to be increased or reduced. A frequent situation of potential conflict arises when one soft goal prescribes a quantity to be increased whereas another soft goal prescribes a related quantity to be reduced. Typically, the quantity to be increased may refer to some functionality or quality, whereas the related quantity to be reduced refers to cost, for example *JournalCoverageIncreased* vs *OperationalCostsReduced* in the library system, or *MoreControllersHired* vs *RunningCostsDecreased* in an air traffic control system. In such situations, it is important to annotate the soft goal with a FitCriterion feature so that feasible boundary conditions for conflict can be determined and acceptable thresholds found for conflict resolution.

8.4 Connecting the goal model with other system views

The core of a goal model consists of an annotated refinement graph where potential conflicts may be indicated. In addition to refinement and conflict links, the goal diagram representing the goal model generally shows interface links between the goal model and the other sub-models of the system model.

- The ***responsibility*** link type is defined at the interface between the goal model and the agent model. A responsibility assignment of a goal to an agent means that the instances of this agent are the only ones required to restrict their behaviour in the system so as to satisfy the goal. Responsibility links were illustrated in Figures 8.4 and 8.6. They will be further discussed when the agent model will be described; see Chapter 11.

- The ***obstruction*** link type is defined at the interface between the goal model and the obstacle model introduced for risk analysis. A goal is obstructed by an obstacle if the satisfaction of the obstacle prevents the goal from being satisfied. For example, the goal *TrainStoppedAtBlockSignalIfStopSignal* in Figure 8.5 is obstructed by the obstacle *SignalNotVisible* or the obstacle *TrainDriverUnresponsive*; the condition of an unresponsive driver failing to react to the 'stop' command issued by the train controller does indeed prevent that goal from being satisfied. Obstruction links will be detailed in Chapter 9 when the obstacle model is described.

- The ***concern*** link type is defined at the interface between the goal model and the object model. A goal concerns a conceptual object if its specification refers to this object. For example, the goal *Avoid[TrainsOnSameBlock]* concerns the conceptual entities *Train* and *Block*, and the conceptual association *On* between *Train* and *Block*. Concern links will be detailed in Chapter 10 when the object model is described.

- The ***operationalization*** link type is defined at the interface between the goal model and the operation model. A leaf goal is operationalized by a set of operations if the specification of these operations ensures that the goal is satisfied. For example, consider the leaf goal *DoorsStateClosedIfNonZeroMeasuredSpeed*, defined by

$$MeasuredSpeed \neq 0 \rightarrow DoorsState = \text{'closed'}.$$

  This goal is operationalized by operations such as *StartTrain* and *OpenDoors* through pre-conditions that restrict their applicability so as to satisfy the goal, for example '*MeasuredSpeed = 0*' is a pre-condition on the operation *OpenDoors* for the satisfaction of that goal. Operationalization links will be detailed in Chapter 12 when the operation model is described.

- The ***coverage*** link type is defined at the interface between the goal model and the behaviour model. A behavioural goal *covers* a scenario or a state machine if the sequences of state transitions expressed by the scenario or state machine capture some of the behaviours prescribed by the goal. Section 7.6.1 already introduced this link type and illustrated it for the goal *Maintain[DoorsClosedWhileMoving]*; see Figure 7.8. Coverage links will be further discussed in Chapter 13 when the behaviour model is described.

8.5 Modelling alternative options

As mentioned in the introduction to Part II, it is important for an RE model to capture multiple options that should be considered while engineering the requirements. When they are made explicit in the model, such options can be discussed with stakeholders to assess their pros and cons; they can be evaluated against soft goals; they can be negotiated with decision makers to reach agreement on the most satisfactory ones. Multiple alternatives in a model may also capture multiple versions of the modelled system (variants or revisions; see Chapter 6).

A goal model makes it possible to capture two kinds of alternative options:

- A goal might be refinable in different ways; each will result in a different system, satisfying a different set of sub-goals. Alternative goal refinements are discussed in Section 8.5.1.

- A leaf goal might be assignable to different agents in the system; each alternative assignment will result in a different system, with a different distribution of responsibilities. Alternative responsibility assignments are discussed in Section 8.5.2.

8.5.1 Alternative goal refinements

In a refinement graph, a goal node can be the target of multiple AND-refinements. Each refinement is then called an *alternative* for achieving the parent goal. An alternative refinement is thus one set of sub-goals, among others, that AND-refines the parent goal (see the definition of refinement in Section 8.2). The meaning of multiple alternative refinements is that *the parent goal can be satisfied by satisfying all sub-goals from any of the alternative refinements.*

For example, Figure 8.8 shows two alternative refinements of the goal *ConstraintsKnown-FromRequest* in the meeting scheduling system. This goal states that 'the time/location constraints of the invited participants listed in the meeting request shall be known to the meeting scheduler'. The two refinements connected to the goal *ConstraintsKnownFromRequest* in Figure 8.8 express that this goal can be satisfied by satisfying the sub-goals *ConstraintsRequested*, *ConstraintsTransmitted* and *CommunicationWorking*, or, alternatively, by satisfying the sub-goals *ConstraintsObtainedFromE-agenda*, *E-agendaUpToDate* and *E-agendaAccessible*. (In the second alternative, the goal *E-agendaUpToDate* is an expectation about participants, in the category of accuracy goals.)

Figure 8.9 illustrates alternative goal refinements in our other case studies. In the train control system, the goal *Avoid[TrainCollisions]* can be satisfied by making sure that a block will always contain one train at most (left-hand alternative in Figure 8.9) or, alternatively, by allowing multiple trains to be on the same block provided that a safe stopping distance is maintained between successive trains (right-hand alternative in Figure 8.9; see the characterization of this goal in Figure 8.1). In the library system, the goal *ComprehensiveLibraryCoverage* can be satisfied by satisfying the goal *EffectiveBookSupply* (left-hand alternative in Figure 8.9) or, alternatively, by satisfying the goal *AccessToForeignDigitalLibrary* (right-hand alternative in Figure 8.9).

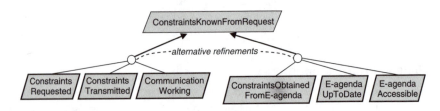

Figure 8.8 *Alternative goal refinements in the meeting scheduling system*

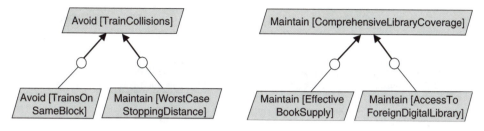

Figure 8.9 *Alternative refinements in the train control and library systems*

Alternative goal refinements generally result in different system designs that will produce different versions of the system. For example, the left-hand alternative in Figure 8.8 will result in a meeting scheduler with interaction through e-mail, whereas the right-hand, e-agenda alternative will result in a meeting scheduler with no interaction with participants for getting their constraints. Similarly, the left-hand alternative for the train system in Figure 8.9 corresponds to a system design incorporating signal management at every block, whereas the right-hand alternative corresponds to a system design without block signals but with dedicated management of acceleration commands to trains. Likewise, purchasing books or subscribing to digital libraries correspond to fairly different system designs for achieving comprehensive coverage.

A system might of course combine multiple alternatives to be considered under different conditions within the same version. In our meeting scheduling example, a hybrid of the two previous designs, with e-mail or e-agenda interaction depending on the type of participant, should certainly be worth considering. This would, however, correspond to a third alternative refinement in Figure 8.8, producing a third possible version of the system.

Each alternative goal refinement may have its pros and cons, to be evaluated and compared for the selection of a best option (see Section 3.3). The pros should correspond to soft goals in the model. If this is not the case, they should be added to the model as new soft goals, possibly to be refined. Similarly, the cons should be conflicting with soft goals; the latter should be added and refined if they are not found in the model. Alternative options are thus a source of further goal elicitation. We come back to this in Section 8.8. Section 16.3 will present techniques for evaluating alternative options based on their contribution to soft goals.

8.5.2 Alternative responsibility assignments

As introduced in Chapter 1, the WHO-dimension of requirements engineering concerns the distribution of responsibilities among system agents. We need to analyse carefully who is going to be responsible for what.

At the interface between the goal model and the agent model, *responsibility* links connect requirements and expectations to corresponding agents. The meaning of assigning a leaf goal to an agent is that the instances of this agent will be the ones (and the only ones) required to restrict their behaviour so as to satisfy the leaf goal.

In general, multiple agents might be envisaged for such behaviour restriction to ensure some leaf goal. The responsibility for that goal is then assignable to any of them. We capture

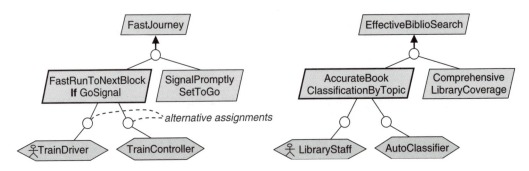

Figure 8.10   *Alternative responsibility assignments*

this in the model through multiple alternative responsibility links between the leaf goal and the candidate agents. Each alternative link is called an *assignment*.

Alternative goal assignments result in different system versions. These versions differ by the distribution of responsibilities among the agents forming the system. From one version to the other, more or less functionality might be automated.

For example, two alternative assignments might be considered for the goal *FastRun-ToNextBlockIfGoSignal* in our train system (see Figure 8.10). This goal might be under the responsibility of the *TrainDriver* agent or under the responsibility the *TrainController* agent in a driverless alternative with increased automation. In the library system, the goal *AccurateBookClassificationByTopic* is assignable to the *LibraryStaff* agent or, alternatively, to a software component that would retrieve relevant keywords from electronic abstracts supplied by publishers and classify books accordingly (this component is named *AutoClassifier* in Figure 8.10).

As for alternative goal refinements, alternative assignments have their respective pros and cons that should be made explicit as soft goals in the goal model. For example, the assignment of the goal *AccurateBookClassificationbyTopic* to the *AutoClassifier* agent might increase development costs and sometimes produce bizarre classifications; the alternative assignment of this goal to the *LibraryStaff* agent might result in an increased load on library staff and in delayed accessibility of books waiting for classification. In the train system, the goal *DoorsStateClosedWhileNonZeroMeasuredSpeed* was assigned to the *TrainController* agent in Figure 8.4. Alternative assignments might connect this goal to the *TrainDriver* agent or to the *Passenger* agent. The responsibility assignment to the *TrainDriver* agent results in transportation delays and in driver overload; those cons conflict with the soft goals of rapid transportation and reduced driver load, respectively. The responsibility assignment to the *Passenger* agent results in passengers getting control of door opening; this is conflicting with safe transportation goals.

The pros and cons of alternative assignments need to be evaluated and compared for selection of the best options. (Section 16.3 will present techniques for evaluating alternatives based on their contribution to soft goals.) As seen from the preceding examples, the goal assignments that will be selected among the considered alternatives determine what will be automated in the system-to-be and what will not – and, correspondingly, what are going to be the requirements on the sofware-to-be and the expectations on the environment. As a result, the *boundary* between the software-to-be and its environment will be established.

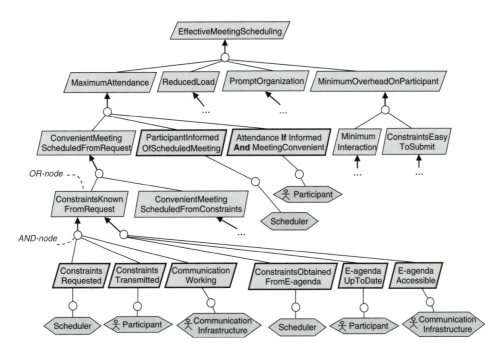

Figure 8.11 *Goal model fragment for the meeting scheduling system: AND-nodes and OR-nodes*

Note that alternative goal refinements generally entail different distributions of responsibilities, as illustrated at the bottom of Figure 8.11 for the meeting scheduling system.

8.6 Goal diagrams as AND/OR graphs

The previous sections showed piecewise what goal diagrams look like. Roughly, we have seen graphs where goal nodes are connected through refinement and conflict links, and connected to items from other models through interface links such as *responsibility* or *operationalization* links. Looking more closely at these graphs, we have seen other types of nodes; namely refinement nodes, 'home' nodes capturing domain properties or hypotheses, and nodes from other models that are connected to goals through these interface links. We have also seen that multiple refinements or assignments of the same goal node capture alternative options.

Figure 8.11 shows a larger fragment of a goal diagram for our meeting scheduling system. It contains high-level goals, requirements, expectations, refinement/contribution links and some possible responsibility assignments.

The core of a goal diagram shows alternative AND-refinements of the system's goals. It amounts to a special kind of graph known as an *AND/OR graph*. Non-leaf *goal* nodes are OR-nodes, whereas *refinement* nodes are AND-nodes (see Figure 8.11).

- An *OR-node* is satisfied provided that one of its successor nodes is satisfied.

- An *AND-node* is satisfied provided that all its successor nodes are satisfied.

(Note that some nodes might have one successor node only.) This semantics of *AND* and *OR* nodes is to be taken in a strict, clear-cut sense for behavioural goals. For soft goals, the wording 'satisfied' is to be understood as 'satisfied' or 'more or less satisfied' (see Section 7.3.1).

8.7 Documenting goal refinements and assignments with annotations

In the same way as we further characterize goals through annotations, we can attach useful features to refinements and assignments for better documentation of the goal model. These features are all optional.

- **Name.** This feature can be attached to a refinement or to an assignment for unambiguous reference when dealing with alternatives, for example 'the ConstraintsThroughE-agenda alternative' for the alternative goal refinement on the right in Figure 8.8 or 'the DriverlessStart alternative' for the alternative assignment to the TrainController agent in Figure 8.12.

- **SysRef.** The *system reference* feature can be attached to a refinement or to an assignment in order to indicate which alternative is taken in which version of the system. For example, the alternative assignment DriverlessStart and the alternative refinement AccelerationControl in Figure 8.12 are *both* taken in the system version named SystemToBe.

- **Status.** This graphical feature can be attached to a refinement to indicate whether the refinement is arguably complete for satisfying the parent goal. The value 'complete' is represented by blackening the refinement circle as introduced before (see Figure 8.4 or 8.12).

- **Tactic.** This feature can be attached to a refinement to document the tactic used for producing it. For example, 'Goal decomposition by cases' is a tactic that was used for refining the goal *BookRequestSatisfied* in Figure 8.2. The tactic 'Guard introduction' is attached to the refinement of the goal FastJourney in Figure 8.12 to explain how this refinement was found. A number of tactics are available as refinement patterns to help modellers refine goals. Section 8.8 will discuss them in detail. Documenting a model with the tactics used for building it makes it much easier to understand.

The annotation mechanism can be applied to other link types used for modelling the system. In particular, the *conflict* links introduced in Section 8.3 may be annotated with the boundary condition making the corresponding goals conflicting.

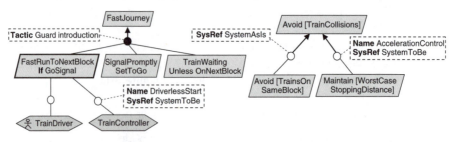

Figure 8.12 *Annotating refinements and assignments*

8.8 Building goal models: Heuristic rules and reusable patterns

Building a complete, consistent, minimal and adequate goal model for a complex system turns out to be surprisingly difficult in practice. This task is especially critical in view of the central role of goals in the RE process (see Section 7.4).

This section describes a variety of heuristic rules, tips, bad smells and common refinement patterns to support the model-building process. These may guide us in the elaboration of a first draft of the goal model. This draft will subsequently be enriched by building the obstacle, object, agent, operation and behaviour models, as the next few chapters will show. The resulting model needs to be consolidated through various forms of analysis, discussed in Chapters 16–18.

We first consider the elicitation of preliminary goals (Section 8.8.1). Rules for enriching the resulting sketches and for scoping them are provided next (Sections 8.8.2 and 8.8.3). Some common pitfalls are then reviewed (Section 8.8.4). Finally, Section 8.8.5 describes a number of reusable refinement patterns that encode common tactics for goal refinement.

8.8.1 Eliciting preliminary goals

The building of a preliminary draft of the goal model should proceed from the early stages of domain analysis and requirements elicitation. Several heuristics are available for eliciting individual goals to start with. We can analyse the current objectives and problems in the system-as-is, search for intentional keywords in elicitation material and browse goal taxonomies to explore relevant instantiations.

(H1) Analyse the current objectives and problems in the system-as-is

As we saw in Section 1.1.6, the early phases of the RE process are partly concerned with the identification of various types of objectives:

- There are strategic objectives of the organization, business goals and policies that are pervasive through any version of the system. When they appear during elicitation, they should be considered as candidate *high-level goals* for our goal model, to be connected later on to finer-grained contributing goals. In some cases policies might already be connected to underlying business goals through contribution links. For example, 'Effective access to state-of-the-art knowledge' is a strategic objective for a university that should be found in any version of a library system. Privacy policies regarding staff and students might be relevant as well. In our train system, we might elicit strategic objectives such as 'Serve more passengers' or 'Reduce operational costs'.

- There are domain-specific objectives that should be preserved from the system-as-is to the system-to-be. Each of these should be found in our goal model. For example, 'Satisfy book requests' or 'Accurate classification of books' are domain-specific concerns that might emerge from domain analysis and are likely to be found in any version of a library system.

- Requirements elicitation is partly concerned with the analysis of problems with the system-as-is in the light of opportunities to be exploited. Each such problem might raise the candidate goal of addressing it in the system-to-be. Multiple candidates might be considered as alternatives in the goal model; namely, to *avoid*, *reduce* or *mitigate* the problem or its causes by exploiting technology opportunities. For example, one of the problems with the library system-as-is is that 'bibliographical search is restricted to library opening hours' (see the list of stakeholder complaints in Section 1.1.2). The goal 'bibliographical search accessible from anywhere at any time' might be introduced in the goal model to counter this complaint. For the meeting scheduling system, one of the problems emerging from domain analysis is that 'people are unnecessarily inconvenienced by scheduling messages with which they are not concerned'. The soft goal 'avoid unnecessary interactions with invited participants' might be identified as a result – to be subsequently refined so as to make it precise what 'unnecessary interactions' means.

(H2) Search for goal-related keywords in elicitation material

Another simple, cheap and quite effective technique for identifying preliminary goals for the system-to-be consists of applying a standard text search engine to find prescriptive, intentional or amelioration keywords in interview transcripts and other preliminary documents involved in the elicitation process. The keywords are predefined in a table that drives the search. The phrases returned containing these keywords are considered for goal formulations. The underlying justification is that a goal by definition is a prescriptive statement of intent. Many goals moreover prescribe some amelioration with respect to the system-as-is. Table 8.1 shows a table of goal-related keywords that might drive goal search in elicitation material.

For example, a returned phrase such as 'passengers at a station should be informed in time about train arrivals' may call for the introduction of a corresponding goal in the goal model.

Although simple and useful, such blind search does of course have limitations. False positives may be obtained. The technique is applied to raw material that may contain many of the defects discussed in Section 1.1.7. It is also sensitive to specific formulations. Each phrase returned must therefore be analysed in its context for adequacy and precision.

The intentional keywords listed first in the second row of Table 8.1 are, however, fairly accurate in capturing intents. In particular, keywords such as 'in order to', 'so as to' or 'so that' are especially useful. When they are found, phrases like:

'In order to X, ... has to Y',   '... shall Y to X',   'Y so as to X',   'Y so that X'

Prescriptive	shall, should, must, has to, to be, may never, may not, should never, should not, ...
Intentional	in order to, so as to, so that, objective, aim, purpose, achieve, maintain, avoid, ensure, guarantee, want, wish, motivate, expected to, ...
Amelioration	improve, increase, decrease, reduce, enhance, enable, support, provide, make, ...

Table 8.1 *Keywords for goal search in elicitation material*

yield both a goal X and a refinement link from X to a contributing sub-goal Y. For example, consider the following phrase from the case study description in Section 1.1.2:

> The distance between two trains following each other shall always be sufficient to prevent the back train from hitting the front train in case the latter stops suddenly.

This phrase suggests a goal *Avoid [TrainCollision]* and a sub-goal *Maintain [WorstCaseStoppingDistance]* contributing to it.

(H3) Instantiate goal categories

Section 7.3.2 described a taxonomy of functional and non-functional goal categories. We can browse such a taxonomy and, for each leaf node in the classification tree, look for system-specific instantiations of it.

For example, we might ask questions about the train system such as: 'Is there any *information* goal concerning passengers?' As a result, we might elicit the goal 'passengers at a station should be informed about train arrivals' mentioned previously. For the meeting scheduling system, we might look for instantiations of *interoperability* goals in view of foreign services with which the meeting scheduler will have to interact. We might also look for *confidentiality* goals concerning participant information. In the library system, we might look for instantiation of *accuracy* goals relating physical book copies to their software 'image'.

8.8.2 Identifying goals along refinement branches

When a goal is found and its features are made precise, we should look for sub-goals contributing to it and for parent goals to which the goal contributes. Several heuristics are available to support this task.

(H4) Ask HOW and WHY questions

Let G be a goal already identified. We can systematically identify sub-goals and parent goals of G by asking two kinds of questions about this goal:

- *Goal refinement through HOW questions.* Sub-goals of G are found by asking questions such as:

  a. 'How can G be satisfied?'

  b. 'Is this sub-goal sufficient or is there any other sub-goal needed for satisfying G?'

- *Goal abstraction through WHY questions.* Parent goals of G are found by asking questions such as:

  a. 'Why should G be satisfied by the system?'

  b. 'Is there any other parent goal that G contributes to?'

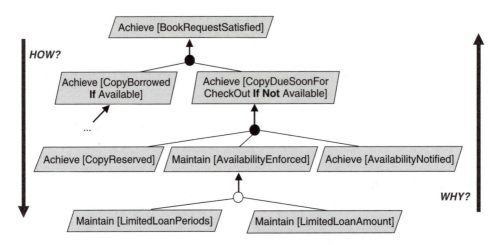

Figure 8.13   *Top-down and bottom-up identification of goals along refinement branches*

A frequent goal-acquisition pattern consists of asking a *WHY* question about goal *G*, directly followed by a *HOW* question about the parent goal just found, in order to find 'brothers' of *G* that might be missing for the parent goal to be satisfied.

For example, a *WHY* question about the goal *TrainStoppedAtBlockSignalIfStopSignal* in Figure 8.5 would result in identification of the goal *Avoid[TrainsOnSameBlock]*. A *HOW* question about the latter would then lead to the goal *SignalSafelyKeptToStop* that might have been overlooked.

Figure 8.13 illustrates such a HOW/WHY acquisition process on the library system. During interviews, library staff might have expressed the concern of limiting loan periods by time – hence the goal Maintain[LimitedLoanPeriods] at the bottom of Figure 8.13. By asking a *WHY* question about this goal we might identify the upper goal Maintain[AvailabilityEnforced]. A new *WHY* question about the latter goal might lead to identification of the upper goal Achieve[CopyDueSoonForCheckOut**IfNot**Available]. Back to the previous goal Maintain[AvailabilityEnforced], we might ask a *HOW* question about it to find the missing sub-goal Maintain[LimitedLoanAmount] that contributes to it as well.

Every time we ask a *HOW* question about a goal we can ask a *HOW ELSE* question next, in order to explore alternative options for refining that goal; see Figures 8.8 and 8.9 for examples.

WHY questions can also be asked about more operational material in order to identify the underlying goals. This applies particularly to *scenarios* that frequently arise in elicitation sessions (see Section 2.2.5).

Figure 8.14 illustrates this point for the meeting scheduling system. The goals ConstraintsKnownFromRequest and ParticipantsInformed, appearing in Figure 8.11 might have been elicited that way from episodes illustrating them in the scenario shown in Figure 8.14.

(H5) Split responsibilities

We may constrain *HOW* questions by requiring the resulting sub-goals to involve fewer potential agents in their satisfaction, when such agents are easily identifiable. The set of

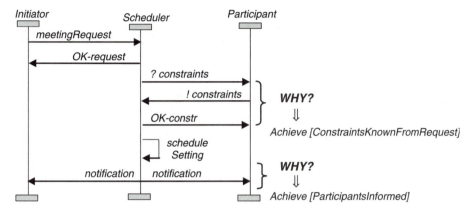

Figure 8.14   *Goal identification from WHY questions on scenario episodes*

potential agents that need to cooperate for the satisfaction of the parent goal is thereby decomposed into subsets associated with corresponding sub-goals. The use of this heuristic is important for ensuring that the refinement process makes progress towards a stage where all finer-grained goals are assignable as requirements on software agents or expectations on environment agents.

Figure 8.15 shows how this heuristic was applied in two refinement examples that appeared previously in this chapter. For example, the goal ConstraintsKnownFromRequest should involve the agents Scheduler, who must know the constraints of participants; Participant, who needs to provide such constraints; and CommunicationInfrastructure, which must communicate the constraints. The goal refinement was driven by a *HOW* question constrained by the splitting of responsibilities among those agents.

(H6) Identify soft goals by analysing the pros and cons of alternative refinements

As already noted in Section 8.5, a pro may suggest a soft goal that might not have been identified yet. If so, the corresponding refinement should be connected to this soft goal through a contribution link. In a dual way, a con may suggest a negated soft goal that might not have been identified yet. If so, the corresponding refinement should be connected to this soft goal via a conflict link.

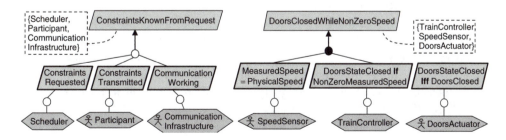

Figure 8.15   *Goal refinement by splitting responsibilities*

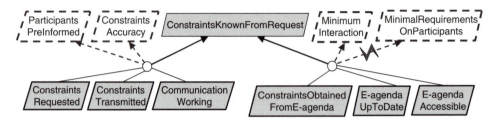

Figure 8.16   *Soft goals identifiable from pros and cons of alternative options*

For example, the two alternative refinements for the meeting scheduler to know the constraints of invited participants have their respective merits (see Figure 8.16). The ConstraintsThroughEmail alternative is likely to yield accurate constraints, as people know exactly what their actual constraints are. This alternative also results in invited people being pre-informed that the meeting will take place in the specified date range. On the other hand, the ConstraintsThroughE-agenda alternative contributes to ensuring minimum interaction with and inconvenience for invited participants. For each such merit, we may question whether it should be considered as a soft goal for the system. On the other hand, the downside of the ConstraintsThroughE-agenda alternative is that it puts extra requirements on the participant's side; namely, to be equipped with an e-agenda and to make it accessible from outside. Such simple analysis may bring the goal MinimalRequirementsOnParticipants to light, with which the ConstraintsThroughE-agenda alternative is conflicting.

(H7) Identify agent wishes

Another heuristics for further identification of goals consists of reviewing the list of human agents already identified at the current stage of the elicitation process. For each of them, we may ask stakeholders playing the corresponding role at the process level what goals this agent might wish the new system to satisfy.

In the meeting scheduling system, for example, goals such as MinimumInteraction or Minimal-RequirementsOnParticipants are desired by Participant and might be identified that way as well. The goal SchedulingLoadReduced might appear as a goal desired by the Initiator. In the library system, the goal BorrowedCopyReturnedOnTime might appear as being desired by LibraryStaff whereas the conflicting goal CopyBorrowedAsLongAsNeeded might appear as being desired by Patron.

(H8) Analyse obstacles, threats and conflicts

Various forms of analysis of the goal model provide another important source for identifying further goals in a consolidated model. In particular, the identification of obstacles to goal satisfaction raises the exploration of new goals to overcome them. The analysis of threats to security goals results in the introduction of countermeasures as new security goals in the goal model. The detection of conflicts among goals may result in new goals to resolve them. These analyses will be detailed in Chapters 9, 16 and 18.

(H9) Check the converse of Achieve goals

It is often the case that an *Achieve* goal of form:

if preCondition **then sooner-or-later** TargetCondition

has a converse *Maintain* goal associated with it taking the form:

always (**if** Target Condition **then** preCondition).

The latter goal is typically a safety or security goal that may have been overlooked if we have been primarily concerned with functional goals so far. If so, we need to integrate this new goal, possibly together with its parents and children, at some appropriate place in the goal model.

For example, let us suppose that we have found the functional *Achieve* goal for the A320 braking logic:

if WheelsPulseOn **then sooner-or-later** ReverseThrustEnabled

Once this goal has been identified, we should question whether the converse prescription makes sense; that is:

always (**if** ReverseThrustEnabled **then** WheelsPulseOn).

This converse is indeed an essential safety goal in this case, as enabling reverse thrust before the plane is on the ground would result in a disaster.

As another example, consider the following standard *Achieve* goal in an e-shopping system:

if ItemPaid **then sooner-or-later** ItemSent.

Using our heuristic, we should question whether the converse prescription makes sense; that is:

always (**if** ItemSent **then** ItemPaid),

which indeed is an essential security goal in any e-shopping system.

(H10) Check the complementary case of conditional Achieve goals

Suppose again that we have identified an *Achieve* goal of form:

if preCondition **then sooner-or-later** TargetCondition

We should ask a *WHAT IF* question about it to check whether a complementary goal should be prescribed, taking the form:

> **if not** preCondition **then** ??

For example, we might have identified the following *Achieve* goal for our train control system:

> **if** block signal set to 'go' **then sooner-or-later** the approaching train is on this block.

The *WHAT IF* question prompted by this heuristic would then lead us to elicit a companion goal of the form:

> **if** block signal set to 'stop' **then** ??

which in this case is an essential prescription to be made precise and integrated in the goal model (see Figure 8.5).

8.8.3 Delimiting the scope of the goal model

While expanding the goal model top down and bottom up along refinement branches, we need to know when the goal refinement/abstraction process should stop. The answer is quite simple; it derives from the definition of the concepts of goal, requirement and expectation (see Chapter 7).

(H11) Refine goals until they are assignable to single agents

The process of asking *HOW* questions along a refinement path in the goal model terminates when we reach a fine-grained goal that is assignable as a requirement to a software agent or as an expectation to an environment agent. The corresponding leaf goal will be operationalized into software operations or environment tasks depending on the type of agent responsible (see Chapter 12).

For example, the goal ConstraintsRequested in Figure 8.15 should not be refined further as it can be assigned to the Scheduler agent. Similarly, the goal DoorsStateClosed IfNonZeroMeasuredSpeed is a leaf goal in the goal model as it is assignable as a requirement to the TrainController agent.

As we will see in Chapter 11, agents may have varying granularities during model elaboration. An agent can be modelled as an aggregation of finer-grained agents. For example, an organizational department with specific goal responsibilities, for example LibraryDepartment, might be decomposed at some stage of the environment modelling process into several operational units with corresponding finer-grained roles and responsibilities, for example LibraryStaff, SubscriptionService, BookAcquisitionService etc. Likewise, a software agent with associated requirements, for example ConstraintsHandler in the meeting scheduling system, might be decomposed during architectural design into finer-grained components with corresponding requirements, for example constraintsRequestor and constraintsCollector. In such cases, the goals under the responsibility of the coarser-grained agent must be refined accordingly, with the finer-grained sub-goals being assigned to the finer-grained sub-agents (see Section 11.4).

(H12) Abstract goals until the system's boundary is reached

The process of asking *WHY* questions along a refinement path in the goal model terminates when we reach a high-level goal whose parent goals cannot be satisfied through the cooperation of the system's agents only. Such goals fall ouside the scope of the system.

For example, the goal 'eliminate greenhouse effect' is not within the scope of the train control system, as it requires the cooperation of additional parties that are not part of the system. The sub-goal of meeting transport regulations contributing to it might lie within the system's scope, though. Likewise, goals such as 'make library users cultivated' or 'make meeting participants happy' require the cooperation of additional parties and therefore fall outside the scope of the system. They are not specifically relevant to the problem world of managing a library or scheduling meetings.

8.8.4 Avoiding common pitfalls

There are a number of problems, confusions and bad smells frequently found in models produced by novice modellers that we should be aware of and avoid.

(H13) Do not confuse goals with operations

A goal is conceptually different from a particular action taken to satisfy that goal. For example, the goal of keeping doors closed while a train is moving is different from the action of opening doors under safe conditions to meet that goal.

A goal captures an objective that the system should satisfy; it is specified declaratively. An operation captures a functional service that the system should provide to satisfy such an objective and maybe others; it is specified by conditions characterizing its applicability and effect (see Chapter 12).

Semantically speaking, a behavioural goal constrains entire sequences of system state transitions; an operation constrains single state transitions within such sequences. For example, the goal Achieve[CopyBorrowedIfAvailable] in Figures 8.3 and 8.17 constrains sequences of system state transitions so that a copy of a requested book, if available, is eventually borrowed within an acceptable amount of time. On the other hand, the operation BorrowCopy constrains transitions from a state where the book copy is not borrowed to a state where it is borrowed; in the input state the book must be requested and the copy must be available.

As we will see in Chapter 12, operations from the operation model *operationalize* leaf goals from the goal model – in somewhat the same way as programs implement their specification. A goal is in general operationalized through multiple operations ensuring it. On the other hand, an operation may operationalize multiple goals underpinning it. For example, the goal *DoorsStateClosedIfNonZeroMeasuredSpeed* will be operationalized through operations such as

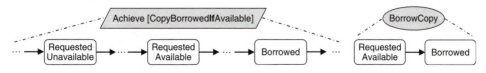

Figure 8.17 *Behavioural goals vs.operations: semantic difference*

OpenDoors, to be applied only when the train is stopped, and StartTrain, to be applied only when the train has its doors closed. On the other hand, the operation OpenDoors might itself operationalize other goals, such as Avoid[PassengersDelayed], through other restrictions – in this case, the additional restriction of being applied as soon as the train is stopped at a platform.

Furthermore, some goals may not have an operation counterpart. This is in particular the case for soft goals used for evaluating alternative options (see Section 16.3).

Terminology tip   To avoid possible confusion between a goal and an operation, use the past participle of a suggestive verb for the goal's name (e.g. 'CopyBorrowed') to refer to the target condition that the goal prescribes, and the infinitive tense for the name of a corresponding operation (e.g. 'BorrowCopy') to refer to single transitions to output states satisfying that target condition.

(H14) Do not confuse AND-refinements into multiple cases with OR-refinements into multiple alternatives

Through case analysis, we may refine a goal into multiple sub-goals where each sub-goal specializes the parent goal to some distinct case. This must be captured by an AND-refinement into such sub-goals; the refinement is complete if all possible cases that can occur in the system are covered. The left-hand diagram in Figure 8.18 illustrates such an AND-refinement into multiple cases – here, the case where a copy of the requested book is available and the case where such a copy is not available.

On the other hand, we may refine a goal in different, alternative ways. In such an OR-refinement, each alternative is aimed at ensuring the parent goal according to a distinct option. Different options result in different system proposals; a single option is taken in the target system. The right-hand diagram in Figure 8.18 illustrates such an OR-refinement into multiple alternatives.

Those two mechanisms for goal refinement are different and should not be confused with each other. An AND-refinement into cases introduces complementary sub-goals within the same system. An OR-refinement into alternatives introduces sub-goals for different systems. In Figure 18, it would be a modelling error to replace the AND-refinement in the left-hand diagram by alternative refinements as in the right-hand diagram – one for the case *Available*, another for the case NotAvailable. It would make no sense to consider one system proposal where requested books always have a copy available and another alternative system proposal where requested books never have a copy available.

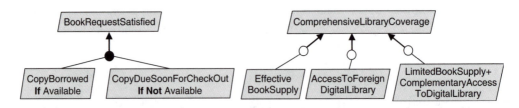

Figure 8.18   *AND-refinement into subgoals vs OR-refinement into alternatives*

Such error corresponds to the frequent confusion between the *and* and *or* connectives in case analysis. As pointed out in Section 4.1, the correct decomposition of the statement:

If (Case1 **OR** Case2) **then** <Statement>

is the statement:

If Case1 **then** <Statement> **AND if** Case2 **then** <Statement>.

(H15) Avoid ambiguities in goal specifications

The same goal might be understood in different ways by different people. To avoid this, the goal name should be chosen as a suggestive shortcut for what it prescribes. More importantly, what such a name exactly designates must be made fully precise in the goal specification provided in the goal's *Def* annotation (see Section 8.1). This specification must be adequate, complete, formulated precisely in terms of measurable system phenomena and agreed by all parties involved in the RE process.

Consider the goal named *DoorClosedWhileMoving*, for example. What is it really meant to prescribe? Do we mean that train doors should remain closed in any state where the train is moving? Or do we mean 'between stations' instead? What if a train is not moving, in particular between two successive stations? The answer to all such questions should be crystal clear and unambiguous from the *Def* annotation. For example, the specification 'train doors shall be closed in any state where the train is moving' imposes no restriction on states where the train is not moving; doors may be either open or closed then. Another goal should be introduced then to prescribe an appropriate behaviour in case of an emergency stop between stations – this goal can be derived from further analysis, as Part III of the book will show.

8.8.5 Reusing refinement patterns

The reuse of 'pre-canned' patterns provides quite effective guidance in the model-elaboration process. Such patterns suggest generic refinements/abstractions for instantiation to the specifics of the modelled system. The technique works as follows.

1. *Establishing a catalogue of refinement patterns.* Common patterns for refining a goal into sub-goals are predefined in a pattern catalogue. Each pattern encodes a specific tactic for goal decomposition.
   A pattern is characterized by a *name*, an *applicability condition*, a two-level *AND-refinement tree* showing how a generic behavioural goal can be refined into generic sub-goals, a number of possible *variants* and *examples* of use. The goal specifications refer to parameters representing conditions. For example, the refinement pattern shown as the left-hand diagram in Figure 8.19 has three parameters: TargetCondition, MilestoneCondition and CurrentCondition.
   The completeness of each generic AND-refinement in the catalogue is established once and for all through a formal proof, but the user of the pattern has no need to see any formal specification or proof.

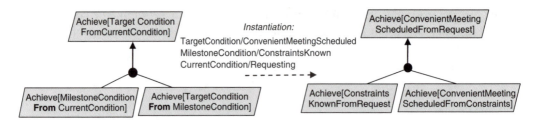

Figure 8.19   *The milestone-driven refinement pattern*

2. *Retrieving reusable refinement patterns.* At system modelling time, we may browse the catalogue to retrieve applicable patterns.

- A generic parent goal in a pattern might match the goal currently being considered. An AND-refinement is then obtained by instantiating the parameters in the generic sub-goals to corresponding system-specific conditions, including the parameter instantiations from the matching parent goal. For example, the AND-refinement shown as the right-hand diagram in Figure 8.19 is obtained by instantiating the pattern on the left; the parameters TargetCondition, MilestoneCondition and CurrentCondition are replaced by ConvenientMeetingScheduled, ConstraintsKnown and Request, respectively.

- Conversely, a set of generic sub-goals in a pattern might match the goals currently being considered. The root of a corresponding AND-refinement is then obtained by instantiating the parameters in the generic parent goal to the system-specific parameter instantiations in the matching sub-goals. The pattern is thereby used as an *abstraction pattern*. For example, the parent goal Achieve[ConvenientMeetingScheduledFromRequest] in the right-hand diagram in Figure 8.19 might have been obtained by such a reverse application of the pattern in the left-hand diagram.

- More frequently, a generic parent goal together with some sub-goals in a pattern might match the partial AND-refinement tree that we are currently building. The refinement is then *completed* by adding the pattern sub-goals that were missing in our current AND-refinement, and instantiating their parameters according to the match.

- Several candidate patterns might match a current modelling situation. This produces *alternative refinements* to be considered for inclusion in the goal model and for evaluation against soft goals from the model.

3. *Adapting the reused patterns.* The produced refinement, abstraction or completion may need to be adapted for adequacy with the specifics of the modelled system. To document the refinement and help users of the model understand it, the resulting refinement/abstraction may be annotated with the name of the pattern that was used (see the 'Tactic' annotation in Section 8.7).

A catalogue of common goal refinement patterns

The following patterns encode frequently used refinement tactics. As mentioned before, each pattern is described by a name, an applicability condition, a generic AND-refinement tree, variants and examples of use from our running case studies.

The milestone-driven refinement pattern

Applicability   This pattern is applicable to behavioural *Achieve* goals where an intermediate condition can be identified as a necessary milestone for reaching the target condition prescribed by the goal. More precisely, any behaviour prescribed by the goal must necessarily reach a state satisfying the milestone condition before reaching a state satisfying the target condition.

Refinement tree   The left-hand diagram in Figure 8.19 shows the generic AND-refinement tree for this pattern. Remember that the specification of *Achieve* goals has the following form (see Section 7.3.1):

> *Achieve [TargetCondition]:*   **[if** CurrentCondition **then] sooner-or-later** TargetCondition,

The first sub-goal in the left-hand diagram in Figure 8.19 is an *Achieve* goal with the milestone condition as a target condition; it states that sooner or later the milestone condition must hold if the condition *CurrentCondition* from the parent goal holds in the current state. The second sub-goal is an *Achieve* goal as well; it states that sooner or later the target condition of the parent goal must hold if the milestone condition holds in the current state. The completeness of the AND-refinement can be established from the definition of what a milestone condition is about.

Example of use   The right-hand diagram in Figure 8.19 shows an application of the milestone-driven refinement pattern for building the model fragment in Figure 8.11. The milestone condition expresses that the constraints of invited participants are known to the scheduler. This condition is indeed a prerequisite for determining a convenient date and location for the meeting. The first *Achieve* sub-goal in the instantiated refinement states that those constraints should be known to the scheduler within a reasonable time; the second sub-goal states that a convenient meeting date and location should be determined within a reasonable time once all participant constraints are known.

Variants   A first variant consists of considering several successive milestones to be reached on any path to a target state. For n milestones we obtain $n + 1$ sub-goals *Achieve [NextMilestoneConditionFromPreviousMilestoneCondition]*, where for the last sub-goal NextMilestoneCondition is TargetCondition, and for the first sub-goal PreviousMilestoneCondition is CurrentCondition ($n \geq 1$).

Another variant consists of taking a *Maintain* goal as parent goal in the pattern. The GoodCondition to be maintained acts as the TargetCondition. The *Achieve* sub-goals, if any, must guarantee that the milestone conditions are established sufficiently fast for the GoodCondition

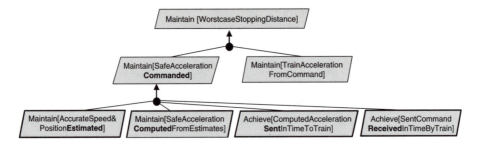

Figure 8.20 *Variants of the base pattern for milestone-driven refinement*

to be preserved. Figure 8.20 shows the use of both variants in our train control system. The past participles in sub-goal names are written there in bold to suggest corresponding milestone conditions.

Milestone-driven refinements and scenarios A milestone-driven goal refinement can often be mapped to a scenario that illustrates it. Conversely, an elicited scenario can often be mapped to a milestone-driven goal refinement that generalizes it. Each milestone condition then corresponds to a state assertion holding after an interaction along the scenario timeline. For example, the meeting scheduling scenario in Figure 8.14 corresponds to a milestone-driven refinement of the goal Achieve[MaximumAttendance] into sub-goals Achieve[ConstraintsKnownFromRequest], Achieve[ConvenientMeeting ScheduledFrom-Constraints] and Achieve[ParticipantsInformedOfScheduledmeeting] (see Figure 8.11).

Case-driven refinement patterns

These patterns introduce case conditions that guide the refinement of the parent goal. Two frequently used such patterns are the decomposition-by-cases pattern and the guard-introduction pattern.

The decomposition-by-case pattern

Applicability This pattern is applicable to behavioural *Achieve* goals where different cases can be identified for reaching the target condition. The cases must be disjoint and cover the entire state space.

Refinement tree Figure 8.21 shows the generic AND-refinement tree for this pattern. In each case a specific target condition must be reached. The refinement requires two domain properties, one stating the disjointness and coverage property of the case conditions, the other stating that the disjunction of the specific target conditions must imply the target condition of the parent goal. The completeness of the AND-refinement is derivable by use of those two domain properties.

Examples of use The decomposition-by-case pattern was applied in Figure 8.2 for refining the goal Achieve[BookRequestSatisfied] into sub-goals Achieve[CopyBorrowedIfAvailable] and Achieve[CopyCopyDueSoonForCheckOutIfNotAvailable]. The domain properties were left implicit there; the first states that if a copy of the requested book is borrowed or due soon for

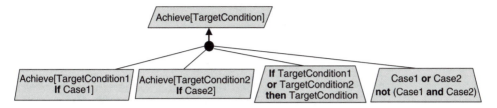

Figure 8.21 Decomposition-by-cases pattern

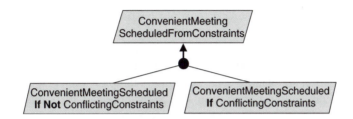

Figure 8.22 Instantiating the decomposition-by-cases pattern to meeting scheduling

check-out by the requesting patron, then the book request is satisfied. The second domain property tautologically states that a book either has an available copy or it has not. Note that the decomposition-by-case pattern could be used for refining the same goal according to different partitions into cases. For example, the goal Achieve[BookRequestSatisfied] could also be refined into sub-goals Achieve[BookRequest**ByStaff**Satisfied] and Achieve[BookRequest**ByOrdinaryPatron**Satisfied].

Variants The pattern in Figure 8.21 can be trivially generalized to *n* disjoint cases covering the entire state space, with specific target conditions associated with each of them ($n \geq 2$). It can also be particularized to the situation where the target conditions in the various cases all amount to the target condition of the parent goal. Figure 8.22 illustrates the use of the latter variant for refining the goal ConvenientMeetingScheduledFromConstraints that appeared in Figure 8.11.

Another variant concerns the decomposition of *Maintain/Avoid* goals by cases. The corresponding pattern is defined by replacing '*Achieve*' by '*Maintain* and '*TargetCondition*' by '*GoodCondition*' in Figure 8.21.

The guard-introduction pattern

Applicability This pattern is a case-driven refinement pattern applicable to behavioural *Achieve* goals where a guard condition must necessarily be set for reaching the target condition.

Refinement tree Figure 8.23 shows the generic AND-refinement tree for this pattern. The first sub-goal of the *Achieve* goal states that the target condition must be reached from a current condition where in addition the guard condition must hold. The second sub-goal states that the guard condition must be reached as a target from that current condition. The third

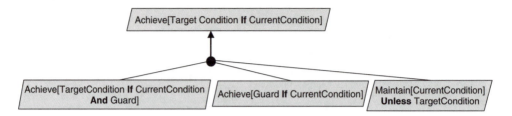

Figure 8.23   *Guard-introduction pattern*

sub-goal states that the current condition must always remain true unless the target condition of the parent goal is reached.

Example of use   The guard-introduction pattern was applied to refine the train system goal Achieve[FastJourney] in Figure 8.12. In this example, the guard for reaching the next block is the condition GoSignal. The sub-goals obtained by pattern instantiation are Achieve[FastRunToNextBlockIfGoSignal], Achieve[SignalPromptlySetToGo] and Maintain[TrainWaiting] **Unless** OnNextBlock.

Matching this pattern with the refinement of the same parent goal in Figure 8.7, we conclude that the refinement there is incomplete due to the missing sub-goal Maintain[TrainWaiting] **Unless** OnNextBlock. The completeness of the guard-introduction pattern can be established formally in temporal logic, and this completeness check can be automated, as we will see in Chapter 18.

The divide-and-conquer pattern

Applicability   This pattern is applicable to *Maintain* goals where the GoodCondition to be preserved is composed of two conjoined conditions.

Refinement tree   Figure 8.24 shows the generic AND-refinement tree for this pattern. The parent goal states that the conjoined good conditions must always be preserved unless some EndCondition becomes true. The refinement consists of splitting the parent goal according to the splitting of its good conditions.

Example of use   Figure 8.24 also shows an application of this pattern in the goal model for the library system. The goal of periodically sending reminders while increasing fines, unless the corresponding book is returned, is thereby split in two sub-goals.

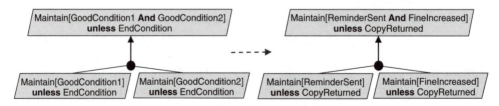

Figure 8.24   *Divide-and-conquer pattern*

A systematic use of the divide-and-conquer pattern improves the cohesion of goal models, as finer-grained goal specifications refer to single concerns only.

Variants The GoodCondition to be preserved may be composed of n conjoined conditions ($n \geq 2$). Another variant is the particular case where the EndCondition reduces to **true**, which results in dropping the 'unless' part in the goal/sub-goal specifications.

Unrealizability-driven refinement patterns

These patterns support the heuristic of splitting responsibilities among agents (see *(H5)* above). They are applicable to *Achieve* or *Maintain/Avoid* goals referring to conditions that cannot be monitored or controlled by the agents that are expected to take responsibility over them.

The general idea is to introduce monitorable or controllable counterparts of such conditions together with additional assertions mapping the original conditions to their monitorable/controllable counterpart. These assertions are accuracy goals or domain properties, depending on whether they are prescriptive or descriptive. (The notion of monitorable/controllable phenomena was introduced in Section 1.1.4. Accuracy goals were defined Section 7.3.2. The notion of goal realizability by an agent will be detailed in Chapter 11.)

The unmonitorability-driven refinement pattern

Applicability This pattern is applicable when a condition in a goal formulation, to be monitored by the agent expected to be in charge of the goal, cannot be monitored by the agent. The pattern is aimed at resolving such unmonitorability.

Refinement tree The left-hand diagram in Figure 8.25 shows the AND-refinement tree for this pattern.

Examples of use In the right-hand diagram in Figure 8.25, the agent expected to be responsible for the goal Maintain[DoorsClosedWhileNonZeroSpeed] is the software train controller. This agent cannot monitor the condition NonZeroSpeed though; there is no way the software controller could evaluate the train's physical speed. The pattern is therefore instantiated by the introduction of a condition NonZero*Measured*Speed, monitorable by the train controller, and a corresponding accuracy goal to be assigned as an expectation to a speed sensor agent. Figure 8.6 provides another example where the unmonitorability-driven refinement pattern was used twice. The first application to the top goal resulted in the introduction of a domain property rather than a goal (like the first application to the top goal in Figure 8.4).

Figure 8.25 *Unmonitorability-driven refinement pattern*

Figure 8.26 *Uncontrollability-driven refinement pattern*

The uncontrollability-driven refinement pattern

Applicability This pattern is applicable when a condition in a goal formulation, to be controlled by the agent expected to be in charge of the goal, cannot be controlled by the agent. The pattern is aimed at resolving such uncontrollability.

Refinement tree The left-hand diagram in Figure 8.26 shows the AND-refinement tree for this pattern.

Example of use In the right-hand diagram in Figure 8.26, the train controller cannot control the condition DoorsClosed as it cannot physically close train doors. The pattern is therefore instantiated by the introduction of a condition DoorsStateClosed, controllable by the train controller, and a corresponding accuracy goal to be assigned as an expectation to the doors actuator agent.

8.8.6 Reusing refinement trees associated with goal categories

The above refinement patterns encode general tactics commonly used for problem decomposition. They make no assumption about the goal category or the domain in which they will be reused. (Goal categories were discussed in Section 7.3.2.)

As a complement, we may encode typical ways of refining goals within a specific goal category. Such encoding yields larger refinement trees on category-specific concepts and conditions.

Model reuse may help us in the goal elicitation process, as discussed in Section 2.2.7. When a goal is introduced in the goal model, instead of starting a refinement from scratch we may check refinement trees in the corresponding category, instantiate reusable ones in system-specific terms, adapt them as necessary or simply reject them if they are felt inadequate. We may also compare them with the refinements we are elaborating to check for missing sub-goals or alternative refinements.

Figure 8.27 shows a reusable refinement tree in the category of *satisfaction* goals (see Figure 7.5). The goal RequestIssued is under the responsibility of the agent requesting the service. The service request is satisfied if there is a response to the request by an appointed server that meets the request. The server must remain appointed until the service is fully delivered.

The comparison between the reusable refinement tree in Figure 8.27 and the partial goal model for the meeting scheduling system in Figure 8.11 might raise questions for further

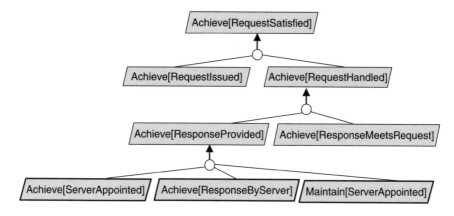

Figure 8.27 *A generic refinement tree for satisfaction goals*
Source: R. Darimont and A. van Lamsweerde, 1996.

goal elicitation, such as the absence of goals related to the issuing of requests by meeting initiators or the absence of goals related to scheduler appointment. For example, do we want multiple schedulers specialized to different types of meeting or distributed among multiple sites?

Figure 8.28 shows a reusable refinement tree in the category of *safety* or *security* goals. Forbidden states are avoided there by anticipating dangerous states that might lead to them. These dangerous states raise alarms or warnings to which responses must be provided by an appointed guard to clear the potentially dangerous situation. The goal ResponseByGuard is not necessarily a leaf goal, as it may require multiple agents to cooperate. For instance, a response can itself be a stimulus sent to other agents; stimuli can be chained, forwarded, broadcasted, acknowledged and so on.

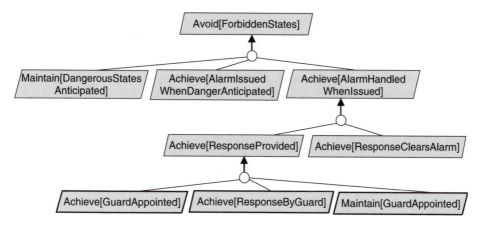

Figure 8.28 *A generic refinement tree for safety or security goals*

Summary

- A model-based approach to RE provides a focus on and a structure for what needs to be elicited, evaluated, specified, consolidated, explained and modified during the RE process. A model abstracts from multiple details to capture the essence of the *system-as-is* and the *system-to-be*. A good model should be adequate, complete, pertinent, traceable and comprehensible. It should support multiple levels of precision and highlight alternative options. To be complete, a model should cover the multiple facets of the system. These include the intentional facet (goals), the structural facet (objects), the responsibility facet (agents), the functional facet (operations) and the behavioural facet (scenarios and state machines).

- A goal model basically shows how the system's functional and non-functional goals contribute to each other through refinement links down to software requirements and environment assumptions. It may also capture potential conflicts among goals and alternative ways of refining goals. At its interface with other views of the system, the goal model captures responsibility links between goals and system agents, obstruction links between goals and obstacles, reference links from goals to conceptual objects, operationalization links between goals and system operations and coverage links between goals and scenarios or state machines.

- A goal model is graphically represented by a goal diagram. Its core is an AND/OR graph showing AND-refinements of goals into conjoined sub-goals and OR-refinements of goals into alternative AND-refinements. A goal AND-refinement means that the goal can be satisfied by satisfying all its sub-goals. A goal diagram can be built and browsed top down, bottom up or, most frequently, in both directions. Leaf goals correspond to requirements on the software-to-be or expectations on environment agents.

- Every goal in a goal diagram must be individually characterized through annotations. These include a precise goal specification and optional features such as the goal's type, category, priority, elicitation source or issue still to be addressed. Soft goals may be annotated with a fit criterion. Behavioural goals may optionally be annotated with a formal specification for more sophisticated forms of analysis.

- Goal refinements should be consistent with known domain properties and hypotheses. They should be complete, to avoid missing requirements, and minimal, to avoid unnecessary requirements. Those properties should be established, at least informally, through chains of satisfaction arguments along refinement paths in the goal model. Domain properties and hypotheses are often involved in such arguments. They must be checked for adequacy with respect to real-world phenomena.

- In addition to alternative goal refinements, a goal diagram may capture alternative responsibility assignments. Both kinds of alternative option result in different system proposals, distributions of responsibilities and boundaries between the software-to-be and its environment. These define system versions. Multiple options can be annotated by the system version to which they refer.

- To start building a goal model, we may obtain preliminary goals by analysing the strategic business objectives of the system-as-is, by identifying the domain-specific objectives to be preserved across system versions, and by addressing the reported problems and complaints about the system-as-is in the light of new opportunities. We may also search for prescriptive, intentional or amelioration keywords in interview transcripts and other preliminary documents involved in the elicitation process. In addition, we may browse the various goal categories to look for system-specific instantiations in each category.

- Once preliminary goals are obtained, we may build refinement and abstraction paths in a goal diagram by recursively asking HOW and WHY questions about available goals, respectively. HOW ELSE questions may help in identifying alternative refinements. A simple qualitative analysis of the pros and cons of alternatives may help identify corresponding soft goals that might be missing. *HOW* questions may be constrained by requiring the resulting sub-goals to involve fewer potential agents. Goals are to be refined until they are assignable to single agents. They should be abstracted until high-level goals are reached whose parent goals cannot be satisfied through cooperation of the system's agents only.

- Goals should not be confused with functional services that operationalize them. AND-refinements into multiple cases are different from OR-refinements into multiple alternatives. Annotating each goal in a model with an adequate, complete, precise and agreed definition of the goal in terms of measurable system phenomena is essential for avoiding ambiguities and misunderstandings.

- Refinement patterns provide effective guidance in the model elaboration process by encoding common tactics for goal decomposition. By instantiating a pattern in matching situations, we may produce a complete refinement, find some underlying parent goal or complete a partial refinement. Pattern instantiations must be checked for adequacy and adapted if necessary. Multiple matching patterns produce alternative refinements. The most commonly used patterns include the milestone-driven, decomposition-by-cases, guard-introduction, divide-and-conquer, unmonitorability-driven and uncontrollability-driven refinement patterns.

Notes and Further Reading

The integration of multiple views for model completeness is discussed in Nuseibeh *et al.* (1994). Earlier modelling frameworks were built on this principle. For requirements modeling, SADT and RML combine structural and functional views (Ross & Schoman, 1977a; Greenspan *et al.*, 1986); SA combines functional and contextual views (DeMarco, 1978); KAOS adds the intentional dimension to such views (Dardenne *et al.*, 1993). For modelling software designs, OMT and UML integrate structural, functional and behavioural views (Rumbaugh *et al.*, 1991, 1999; Jacobson *et al.*, 1999). A comparative evaluation of modelling frameworks can be found in Mylopoulos (1998).

Goal AND/OR graphs for RE were introduced in Dardenne *et al.* (1991) and Mylopoulos *et al.* (1992). These graphs are commonly used for problem reduction in artificial intelligence (Nilsson, 1971). The NFR modelling framework is more focused on capturing positive/negative contributions among soft goals (Mylopoulos *et al.*, 1992). The KAOS framework was originally more oriented towards behavioural goals and their refinement/conflict links (Dardenne *et al.*, 1991, 1993). It also covered alternative responsibility assignments and operationalization links. The latter were inspired by the concept of operationalization in Mostow (1983). The completeness, minimality and domain consistency of refinements are discussed in Darimont and van Lamsweerde (1996).

Many modeling frameworks integrate goals, scenarios and goal-scenario coverage links (Anton *et al.*, 1994; van Lamsweerde *et al.*, 1995; Leite *et al.*, 1997; Anton & Potts, 1998; Haumer *et al.*, 1998; Rolland *et al.*, 1998; Sutcliffe, 1998; Kaindl, 2000). Links between goals and failure scenarios were introduced in Fickas and Helm (1992).

The characterization of a goal by features such as its priority or feasibility was suggested first in Robinson (1989). Fit criteria as soft goal features are borrowed from Robertson and Robertson (1999). More sophisticated frameworks for capturing issues in models can be found in Potts and Bruns (1988) and Lee (1991). Formal specifications are introduced as goal features in Dardenne *et al.* (1993).

Heuristics for goal identification are discussed in Dardenne *et al.* (1993), including the elicitation of wishes of human agents and the splitting of responsibilities among agents. *HOW* and *WHY* questions for identifying goals along refinement links were introduced in van Lamsweerde *et al.* (1995). They are also used in Anton and Potts (1998). The effectiveness of keyword-based identification of goals in documents is discussed in Anton and Potts (1998), van Lamsweerde (2000b) and Anton *et al.* (2001).

The problem of scoping goals within the system's subject matter is addressed in Zave and Jackson (1997). This paper also emphasizes the need for precise definition of modelled concepts for unambiguous interpretation in terms of domain phenomena.

Refinement patterns can be seen as an RE counterpart of design patterns (Gamma *et al.*, 1995; Buschmann *et al.*, 1996). They were introduced in Darimont and van Lamsweerde (1996). A more comprehensive sample of patterns can be found in Darimont's thesis, together with larger refinement trees for certain goal categories and domains (Darimont, 1995). The milestone-driven pattern is inspired by a widely used heuristics in AI problem reduction (Nilsson, 1971). The reverse use of refinement patterns for abstraction from scenarios is discussed in van Lamsweerde and Willemet (1998). The unmonitorability-driven and uncontrollability-driven patterns were introduced in Letier and van Lamsweerde (2002a). They are discussed in greater detail in Letier's thesis (Letier, 2001).

Numerous efforts have been made to encode domain expertise in reusable models (Reubenstein & Waters, 1991; Sutcliffe & Maiden, 1998). These include structural models (Ryan & Mathews, 1993; Fowler, 1997b; Konrad *et al.*, 2004), behavioural models (Konrad *et al.*, 2004) and contextual models showing agent interfaces (Jackson, 2001). Patterns also emerged in workflow modelling (van der Aalst *et al.*, 2003).

Experience with goal models in industrial projects is reported in van Lamsweerde (2004b), Fairbanks *et al.* (2006) and Darimont and Lemoine (2007).

Exercises

- Consider the following integrity goal in the library system:

    Book copy return shall be encoded correctly and by library staff only.

    Elicit parent goals of this goal through WHY questions.

- In a simple patient-monitoring system, the goal NurseInterventionIfPulseThreshold Exceeded states that a nurse shall promptly assist a patient whose pulse rate is beyond a critical threshold.

    a. Consider the following sub-tree found somewhere in the refinement of this goal by a novice modeller (goal names there are sufficiently suggestive for what this modeller had in mind). In view of what the goals and goal refinement refer to, explain why this proposal makes no sense.

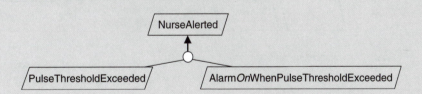

    b. A MonitoringSoftware agent is expected to help in the satisfaction of the goal NurseInterventionIfPulseThresholdExceeded. Since this agent cannot monitor the condition PulseThresholdExceeded nor control the condition NurseIntervention, apply the monitorability-driven and controllability-driven refinement patterns to split responsibilities and derive requirements on the software and expectations on environment agents. Your goal diagram should show individual responsibility assignments.

- Consider the following portion of a goal diagram for a light-control system proposed by a novice modeller:

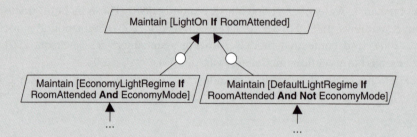

Explain what is wrong with this diagram and fix the error.

- Consider an ambulance-dispatching system with the following goal diagram and specifications:

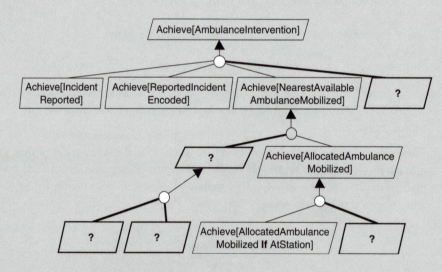

Goal   AmbulanceIntervention

Def: *For every urgent call reporting an incident, a first ambulance shall arrive at the incident scene within 11 minutes.*

Goal   NearestAvailableAmbulanceMobilized

Def: *For every encoded incident, the nearest available ambulance shall be mobilized within 3 minutes.*

a. Complete the goal diagram based on those specifications and using applicable refinement patterns. For each 'question mark' goal, provide a suggestive name and a precise specification.

b. In your completed diagram, list the goals that require further refinement and explain why.

c. Identify possible responsibility assignments in your diagram.

- Consider the leaf goals in the refinement tree in Figure 8.20. Can these be assigned to agents or do they need further refinement? If the former is the case, suggest possible responsibility assignments.

- Investigate alternative refinements and responsibility assignments for the goal Avoid[BookCopiesStolen] in the library system. Identify soft goals from the pros and cons of each alternative assignment.

- Consider the following goal model fragment for an air traffic control system. The parent goal roughly states that aircraft routes should be sufficiently separated. The refinement is intended to produce sub-goals for continually separating routes based on different kinds of conflict among routes.

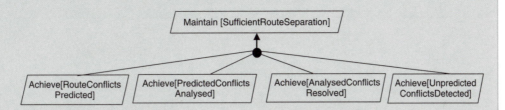

a. Identify the parent goal of the goal Maintain [SufficientRouteSeparation].

b. Restructure this model fragment by use of the decomposition-by-case and milestone-driven patterns so as to make the use of those two patterns explicit and separated.

c. By doing so, find an incompleteness in this model fragment and fix the anomaly.

- Extend the diagram in Figure 8.9 to capture a meeting scheduling system version where participant constraints are obtained, for important participants, from their e-agenda, and for ordinary participants through e-mail communication.

- Consider the case study description for the library management system in Section 1.1.2.

a. Based on the list of stakeholder complaints about the library *system-as-is*, reported in this case study description, apply the heuristics in Section 8.8.1 to identify some preliminary goals for a goal model of the library *system-to-be*.

b. Apply the keyword-based search heuristics to the case study description in order to complete this preliminary list.

c. From this list and the full case study description, use *WHY/HOW* questions, refinement patterns and other heuristics in Section 8.8 to build a goal model for the entire system-to-be. You may want to integrate some of the model fragments shown in this chapter.

- Consider the case study description for the meeting scheduling system in Section 1.1.2.

  a. Based on the reported list of the usual problems and difficulties in scheduling meetings, apply the heuristics in Section 8.8.1 to identify some preliminary goals for a goal model of the system-to-be.

  b. Apply the keyword-based search heuristics to the case study description to complete this preliminary list.

  c. From this list and the full case study description, use *WHY/HOW* questions, refinement patterns and other heuristics from Section 8.8 to build a goal model for the entire system-to-be. You may want to integrate some of the model fragments shown in this chapter. The model should explicitly capture the *system variants* suggested in Section 1.1.2.

9

Anticipating What Could Go Wrong: Risk Analysis on Goal Models

Chapter 3 made a strong case for analysing risks early in the requirements lifecycle. As illustrated in Section 1.2.1, many software failures originate from a natural inclination to conceive an over-ideal system where the environment and the software will always behave normally as expected. This is rarely the case in practice. The system is exposed to a variety of risks. If risks go unrecognized or underestimated, the requirements on the software and expectations on the environment will be inadequate and incomplete. Model-based RE should therefore integrate the identification, assessment and control of risks within the model-elaboration process.

A *risk* was defined in Chapter 3 as an uncertain factor whose occurrence may result in the loss of satisfaction of some corresponding objective. Product-related risks may result in the system's inability to satisfy some of its functional and non-functional objectives. The notion of risk is thus directly related to the notion of objective. As objectives are explicitly captured and structured in the goal model, we may anchor risk analysis on this model and perform this analysis while the goal model is being elaborated.

This chapter complements the goal-model-building techniques from the previous chapter. The general idea is to analyse what could go wrong in the first, over-ideal versions of the goal model – typically, because of unexpected agent behaviours. Obstacles are introduced as pre-conditions for goal obstruction. They can be refined in obstacle diagrams corresponding to goal-anchored variants of the risk trees introduced in Section 3.2. The main objective of obstacle analysis is *requirements completeness*. New or modified goals for a more robust system are added to the goal model as countermeasures to those leaf obstacles from the obstacle model that are likely to occur and have severe consequences. Such analysis is particularly important for mission-critical systems. The modelling techniques introduced in this chapter will provide a basis for more sophisticated forms of semi-formal and formal analysis of obstacles in Chapter 16 and Chapter 18, respectively.

Section 9.1 makes the notion of goal obstruction by obstacles more precise. Section 9.2 discusses obstacle AND/OR refinement as a basic mechanism for structuring obstacle diagrams. Section 9.3 then explains how a more robust goal model can be obtained systematically as a result of the identification, assessment and resolution of obstacles in such diagrams.

9.1 Goal obstruction by obstacles

Section 9.1.1 defines obstacles more precisely in relation to goals, domain properties and hypotheses. Section 9.1.2 explains what it means for a set of obstacles to be complete with respect to our knowledge of the domain. Section 9.1.3 briefly reviews important categories of obstacles.

9.1.1 What are obstacles?

Intuitively, an obstacle to an assertion is a pre-condition for the non-satisfaction of this assertion. The obstructed assertion is in general a goal. However, we are sometimes interested in exploring the consequence of non-satisfaction of descriptive assertions such as hypotheses; such non-satisfaction can propagate up to the non-satisfaction of other goals (as Section 9.2.3 will show). An obstacle must be compatible with known valid properties of the domain and satisfiable through system behaviours.

Let us make this more precise before looking at examples. In what follows, G denotes an assertion, O an obstacle to it and Dom a set of valid domain properties and hypotheses (see Figure 7.1).

An *obstacle* to an assertion is a statement meeting the following conditions:

1. $\{O, Dom\} \models$ not G *obstruction*
2. $\{O, Dom\} \not\models$ false   *domain consistency*
3. O can be satisfied by some system behaviour   *obstacle feasibility*

The obstruction condition (1) states that the satisfaction of obstacle O, constrained by the satisfaction of all properties in Dom, results in the non-satisfaction of assertion G.

For example, consider the goal *TrainStoppedAtBlockSignalIfStopSignal* in Figure 8.5. Let us call *DriverUnresponsive* the situation where a train driver fails to respond to a stop command such as a signal being set to 'stop'. We know the following descriptive property from the train control domain:

> **If** a train stops at a block signal set to 'stop' **then** the train driver has responded to the corresponding stop command,

or its equivalent contraposition:

> **If** a train driver has **not** responded to a signal's stop command **then** the train does **not** stop at that block signal.

Using this domain property, we conclude that the situation *DriverUnresponsive* results in the non-satisfaction of the goal *TrainStoppedAtBlockSignalIfStopSignal* when the signal is set to 'stop'.

In the above definition, the domain consistency condition (2) states that the obstacle O may not contradict properties about the domain. It makes no sense to pay attention to obstacles that are impossible in view of such properties. For example, imagine the situation where a signal is set to 'stop' while a train is arriving at extremely high speed, resulting in the train having no space enough to stop at the block signal. Such situation would result in the non-satisfaction of the goal *TrainStoppedAtBlockSignalIfStopSignal*; it cannot be considered as an obstacle, though, as trains in our domain could not physically reach such speed.

The feasibility condition (3) states that the obstacle O must be satisfiable through the behaviours of one or several agents in the system. For example, the obstacle *DriverUnresponsive* can be satisfied by driver behaviours, for example falling asleep or chatting on their mobile phone (as has sometimes happened in train accidents). If we now consider the goal *BookRequestSatisfied* in our library system, the obstacle of a patron never getting a copy of a requested book is satisfiable by a 'starvation' scenario involving a coalition of other patron instances; each time a copy of the requested book becomes available, this copy is borrowed by a patron different from the requesting one.

As we saw in Chapter 7, a behavioural goal prescribes a maximal set of admissible behaviours. An obstacle to such a goal defines a minimal set of inadmissible behaviours. (These correspond to negative scenarios as defined in Section 2.2.5.) A goal prescribes universal properties – to be satisfied for *any* train, stop signal, meeting or library patron. An obstacle to a goal characterizes existential situations – satisfiable at least by *some* train, stop signal, meeting or library patron. The definition of obstacles in terms of goal negations makes these notions dual to each other. In particular, goal obstruction yields sufficient obstacle conditions for the goal not to be satisfied; the negation of such obstacles yields necessary pre-conditions for the goal to be satisfied.

9.1.2 Completeness of a set of obstacles

For a critical goal or hypothesis, defensive RE would recommend as many likely obstacles as possible to be identified for subsequent resolution in a more robust system. Completeness is thus a desirable property for a set of obstacles – at least for obstacles to mission-critical assertions such as safety goals or security goals. Completeness is, however, bounded by what we know about the domain, as we will see now.

A set of obstacles $O_1, O_2, \ldots, O_n$ to an assertion G in a domain *Dom* is *domain complete* for G if the following condition holds:

$$\{\text{not } O_1, \text{ not } O_2, \ldots, \text{not } O_n, Dom\} \models G \qquad domain\ completeness$$

In other words, if none of the obstacles in the considered set is satisfied, then the assertion is necessarily satisfied.

To understand the implications of this definition, let us give an example. Suppose that we have identified two obstacles to the goal *TrainStoppedAtBlockSignalIfStopSignal*; namely, *DriverUnresponsive* and *BrakeSystemDown*. From the definition of domain completeness, claiming that those two obstacles form a complete set would amount to claiming that the following condition is known as a domain property:

> **If** StopSignal **and not** DriverUnresponsive **and not** BrakeSystemDown
>   **then** TrainStoppedAtBlockSignal

Such a strong domain property has to be questioned, of course. It is clearly inadequate in this example, as the train might not stop at the block signal in spite of the driver being responsive and the brake system working. For example, the signal might not be visible (this was the cause of a major train accident in the London area in the late 1990s). We can draw two conclusions from this:

- Obstacle completeness is relative to how much we know about the domain and how adequate our knowledge is.

- Obstacle analysis may help elicit and validate domain properties as well.

The assistance of domain experts is often needed to help us assess obstacle completeness and elicit relevant domain properties for goal-based risk analysis.

9.1.3 Obstacle categories

Section 7.3.2 introduced a taxonomy of goal categories (see Figure 7.5). In view of the duality between goals and obstacles to them, we can identify an obstacle category for each goal category:

- Hazard obstacles are obstacles that obstruct Safety goals.

- Threat obstacles are obstacles that obstruct Security goals. In particular, Disclosure, Corruption and Denial-of-Service obstacles obstruct Confidentiality, Integrity and Availability goals, respectively. As we will see in Section 16.2.3, such obstacles deserve special analysis in connection with the anti-goals of malicious agents in the environment.

- Dissatisfaction obstacles are obstacles that obstruct the satisfaction of agent requests (that is, Satisfaction goals). They can be further specialized into categories such as NonSatisfaction, PartialSatisfaction or TooLateSatisfaction obstacles.

- Misinformation obstacles are obstacles that obstruct goals of making agents informed about object states (that is, Information goals). They can be further specialized into categories such as NonInformation, WrongInformation or TooLateInformation obstacles.

- Inaccuracy obstacles are obstacles that obstruct the consistency between the state of variables controlled by software agents and the state of corresponding quantities controlled by environment agents.

- Unusablility obstacles are obstacles that obstruct Usability goals; and so on.

Knowing the category of a goal may prompt a search for obstructing obstacles in the corresponding obstacle category. More specific goal sub-categories result in a more focused search for corresponding obstacles. This provides a basis for heuristic identification of obstacles, as Section 16.2.2 will show.

9.2 Modelling obstacles

To support goal-based risk analysis, we need to capture obstacles in a causal model showing which goals or hypotheses they obstruct and how they can be AND/OR refined into finer-grained obstacles causing these obstructions.

An *obstacle model* is a set of obstacle diagrams associated with goals and hypotheses in a goal model. Each diagram is an obstacle refinement tree showing how the associated goal or hypothesis can be violated. We first describe what obstacle diagrams look like (Section 9.2.1). Obstacle refinements in these diagrams should meet certain conditions (Section 9.2.2). The obstructions identified there propagate up through AND-refinements in the goal model (Section 9.2.3). Like goal diagrams, obstacle diagrams should be annotated by features characterizing obstacles individually (Section 9.2.4).

9.2.1 Obstacle diagrams

An *obstacle diagram* is an AND/OR obstacle refinement tree anchored on an assertion G in a goal model:

- The root of the tree is the assertion *not* G; we will call it the *root obstacle*.

- An OR-refinement shows alternative ways of satisfying the parent obstacle in view of domain properties and hypotheses.

- An AND-refinement shows how a parent obstacle can be decomposed into sub-obstacles whose conjoined satisfaction is sufficient for the satisfaction of the parent obstacle in view of the domain properties and hypotheses.

- The leaves of a refinement tree are elementary obstacles whose satisfiability, likelihood and resolution can be determined more easily. Leaf obstacles are connected to countermeasure goals through *resolution* links.

The obstacle diagram in Figure 9.1 shows how the goal TrainStoppedAtBlockSignalIf StopSignal from Figure 8.5 can be obstructed. An obstacle is graphically represented by a 'reverse' parallelogram labelled by its name. The root of the diagram is the goal negation, connected to the goal by an obstruction link. This obstacle can be satisfied by satisfying any of the sub-obstacles SignalNotVisible, DriverUnresponsive or BrakeSystemDown. As their satisfiability, likelihood and resolution seem easy to determine, these sub-obstacles are not refined any further. For example, the obstacle SignalNotVisible can be satisfied with some likelihood for a signal surrounded by trees, through the combined action of Mother Nature and a negligent maintenance team. The diagram in Figure 9.1 also shows a new goal emerging as a countermeasure to the obstacle DriverUnresponsive. This goal prescribes periodic responsiveness checks on each train by regular sending of prompts to which the train driver has to react. This new goal needs to be refined or assigned in an updated version of the goal model.

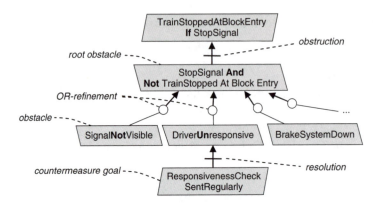

Figure 9.1 *Obstacle diagram*

The *obstruction* condition (1) in the definition of obstacles in Section 9.1.1 involves valid domain properties and hypotheses from *Dom*. The specific properties actually involved in goal obstruction are often left implicit in order not to clutter the diagram. It is, however, sometimes useful to make them explicit in the diagram as 'home' nodes involved in obstacle AND-refinements. For example, Figure 9.2 makes explicit the factual domain hypothesis under which the parent obstacle is satisfied; namely, the corresponding signal being set to 'stop'.

The obstacle diagram in Figure 9.1 does not show AND-combinations of sub-obstacles causing the satisfaction of a parent obstacle and the obstruction of the associated goal. In Figure 9.3, the obstacle AmbulanceLost is among the alternatives for obstructing the goal MobilizedAmbulanceAtIncidentInTime in an ambulance-dispatching system. This obstacle is itself AND-refined into sub-obstacles AmbulanceCrewInUnfamiliarArea and In-carGPSNotWorking. Both obstacles need to be satisfied for the parent obstacle to be satisfied. AND-refinements of obstacles are important for capturing *combinations* of circumstances that result in the parent obstacle being satisfied and the associated goal being obstructed. Major system disasters are often caused by such combinations.

Obstacle diagrams share similarities with the risk trees introduced in Section 3.2.2. Here, the nodes are conditions that are directly or indirectly connected to obstructed goals and to resolution goals.

The overall obstruction structure for a goal model is a directed acyclical graph in the most general case; a single obstacle may contribute to the obstruction of multiple assertions. Figure 9.4 illustrates this while showing multiple obstacle diagrams from an obstacle model for our train control case study. The goal tree on top appeared in Figure 8.20.

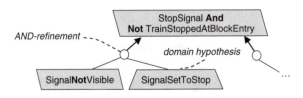

Figure 9.2 *Making domain properties or hypotheses explicit in obstacle refinements*

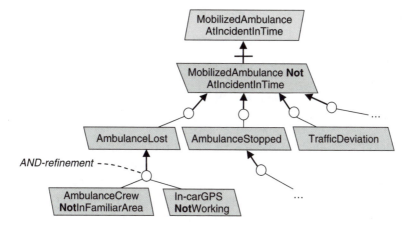

Figure 9.3 *AND-combination of subobstacles in an obstacle diagram*

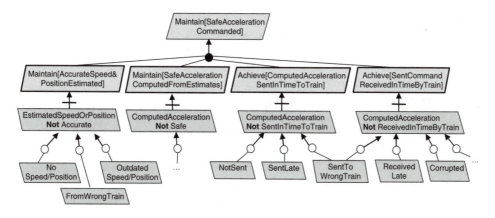

Figure 9.4 *Anchoring obstacle diagrams on a goal model*

9.2.2 Conditions on obstacle refinement

In an obstacle diagram, the AND/OR refinement of obstacles is subject to conditions similar to those discussed in Chapter 8 for the AND/OR refinement of goals.

An *AND-refinement* of obstacle O into subobstacles $O_1, O_2, \ldots, O_n$ should meet the following conditions:

$$\{O_1, O_2, \ldots, O_n, Dom\} \models O \qquad \text{\textit{complete AND-refinement}}$$
$$\{O_1, O_2, \ldots, O_n, Dom\} \not\models \text{false} \qquad \text{\textit{consistent AND-refinement}}$$
$$\{O_1, \ldots, O_{j-1}, O_{j+1}, \ldots, O_n, Dom\} \not\models O \quad \text{\textit{minimal AND-refinement}}$$

The first condition is needed for the satisfaction of the parent obstacle and the obstruction of the assertion on which the obstacle diagram is anchored. The second condition is needed for the sub-obstacle combination to be possible in the domain. The third condition is useful when looking for minimal ways of obstructing the associated assertion and, correspondingly, minimal resolutions.

An *OR-refinement* of obstacle O into alternative sub-obstacles O_i should meet the following conditions ($1 \leqslant i \leqslant n$):

$\{O_i, Dom\} \models O$	*entailment*
$\{O_i, Dom\} \not\models \text{false}$	*domain consistency*
$\{\text{not } O_1, \text{not } O_2, \ldots, \text{not } O_n, Dom\} \models \text{not } O$	*domain completeness*
$\{O_i, O_j, Dom\} \models \text{false } (i \neq j)$	*obstacle disjointness*

The first condition is needed for the satisfaction of the parent obstacle and the obstruction of the assertion on which the diagram is anchored. The second condition is just the domain-consistency condition for an assertion to be an obstacle (see Section 9.1.1). The third condition is useful when looking for a domain-complete OR-refinement; we then get all possible ways of obstructing the assertion associated with the diagram through satisfaction of the parent obstacle (see Section 9.1.2). The fourth condition is useful for looking at non-overlapping causes of the obstruction in order to explore specific resolutions for each distinct cause.

By chaining the preceding *entailment* condition and the *obstruction* condition defining obstacles in Section 9.1.1, we conclude that obstruction is a transitive relation along OR-refinement paths of an obstacle diagram:

> **if** *sO* is a sub-obstacle within an OR-refinement of an obstacle O obstructing G
> **then** *sO* obstructs G as well.

A goal may be thus be obstructed by multiple obstacles (and an obstacle may obstruct multiple goals, as illustrated in Figure 9.4).

9.2.3 Bottom-up propagation of obstructions in goal AND-refinements

There is a dual structure between goal AND-refinement and obstacle OR-refinement. Figure 9.5 illustrates this. If a goal G is *AND*-refined in two sub-goals $G1$ and $G2$, its root obstacle not G can be *OR*-refined in the root obstacles not $G1$ and not $G2$ of these sub-goals. This is a direct consequence of De Morgan's laws in propositional logic:

> **not** (G1 **and** G2)   is logically equivalent to   **not** G1 **or not** G2.

As an important consequence, obstruction propagates bottom up in AND-refinement trees of the goal model. This is helpful for assessing the *severity of the consequences* of an obstacle in terms of higher-level goals being obstructed.

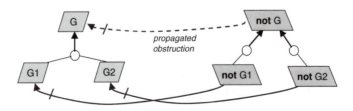

Figure 9.5 *Goal AND-refinement and obstacle OR-refinement*

Such bottom-up propagation explains why we are sometimes interested in exploring the obstruction of hypotheses, or even questionable domain properties, during obstacle analysis. When such a hypothesis or property is needed in a goal AND-refinement to ensure the parent goal, if we can obstruct it in a feasible, domain-consistent way, then we show that the parent goal can be obstructed as well.

9.2.4 Annotating obstacle diagrams

As for goals in a goal diagram, it is important to characterize individual obstacles precisely in obstacle diagrams through *annotations*. Figure 9.6 shows the obstacle DriverUnresponsive as an annotated diagram node.

Each obstacle in a diagram is annotated by various features:

- **Def.** This feature must provide a precise specification of the obstacle, in natural language, in terms of feasible system phenomena.

- **Category.** This optional feature indicates to which taxonomic categories the obstacle belongs. It may be used for heuristic identification of sub-obstacles (see Section 16.2.2).

- **Likelihood.** This feature estimates how likely the situation captured by the obstacle condition is. It may be expressed on a qualitative scale (e.g. very likely, likely, possible, unlikely) or on a quantitative scale (e.g. in a discrete range of probability values or intervals). This estimation is used for risk assessment (see Section 3.2.2). It should be elicited from domain experts.

- **Criticality.** This feature estimates how severe the consequences of the situation captured by the obstacle condition are. It may be expressed on a qualitative scale (e.g. catastrophic, severe, moderate, low) or on a quantitative scale (e.g. from *1* to *10*). This estimation is used for risk assessment as well (see Section 3.2.2).

- **Issue.** As for goals, this process-level feature may be used optionally as a placeholder for recording questions about this obstacle to be subsequently addressed.

- **FormalSpec.** This optional feature provides a temporal logic formalization of the informal **Def** specification to enable more sophisticated forms of obstacle analysis (see Chapter 18).

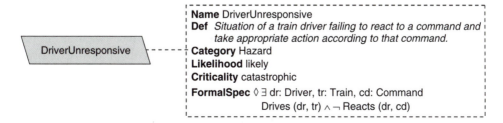

Figure 9.6   Obstacle attributes as model annotations

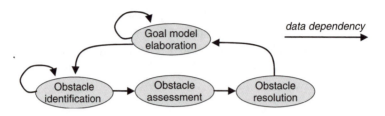

Figure 9.7   *Obstacle analysis and goal model elaboration*

9.3 Obstacle analysis for a more robust goal model

Like in any risk management process, obstacle analysis is an iteration of *Identify–Assess–Control* cycles (see Section 3.2.2). Each cycle consists of the following steps:

- IDENTIFY: select goals and hypotheses in the goal model and identify candidate obstacles to each of them.

- ASSESS: evaluate the likelihood and criticality of each identified obstacle.

- CONTROL: resolve each obstacle according to its likelihood and its criticality to produce new goals as countermeasures in the goal model.

These steps may be intertwined. The iterative obstacle analysis process is itself intertwined with the iterative elaboration of the goal model, as shown in Figure 9.7. During elaboration of the goal model by elicitation, refinement and abstraction, goals/hypotheses are selected and obstacles to them are identified. Such obstacles may be recursively refined (see the left-hand circular arrow at the bottom of Figure 9.7). The likelihood and criticality of the identified obstacles are assessed. Based on the result of this assessment, alternative resolutions are explored and the best resolutions are selected as new goals (or modified ones) in the goal model. These new goals may in turn trigger a new cycle of goal refinement and obstacle analysis. The goal–obstacle analysis loop in Figure 9.7 terminates as soon as the remaining obstacles are considered acceptable without further resolution. Acceptability thresholds are determined by cost–benefit analysis based on obstacle likelihoods and criticalities from the assessment step.

Let us have a closer look at each step of the *Identify–Assess–Control* cycle.

9.3.1 Identifying obstacles

Selecting goals and hypotheses for obstruction

As a prerequisite to obstacle identification, we need to determine which assertions in the goal model should be considered for obstacle analysis and, for each of them, how extensive such identification should be.

- The selected assertions should preferably be *leaf nodes* in the goal model. The finer-grained the target, the finer-grained the obstacles to it, the easier the identification and assessment of such obstacles. Higher-level goals yield higher-level obstacles that need to be refined significantly to identify precise circumstances whose feasibility, likelihood and criticality can be assessed easily and accurately. This refinement duplicates goal refinement in the goal model in view of the dual structure between goal AND-refinement and obstacle OR-refinement (see Figure 9.5). It is much easier and preferable to elicit and refine what is wanted than what is *not* wanted; we may then propagate the consequences of obstructing fine-grained goals bottom up along AND-refinement trees in the goal model to determine the consequences in terms of coarser-grained goals being obstructed.

- For a selected leaf goal, the extensiveness of obstacle identification will depend on the goal's priority and category. Higher-priority goals deserve more extensive obstacle identification than lower-priority ones. For critical goal categories such as Safety and Security, the search for obstacles should be quite extensive, and even exhaustive when possible (as the examples in Figures 9.1–9.4 might suggest). Even for less critical goal categories, though, a fairly systematic identification of obstacles is helpful for pointing out missing requirements or unrealistic assumptions that would result in the software failing to accomplish its mission satisfactorily. Figure 9.8 suggests this systematic identification of obstacles to leaf goals of our meeting scheduling system. In this example, the obstacle ParticipantNotCheckingEmail reveals an implicit expectation of participants regularly checking their e-mail. This might appear quite unrealistic in some cases, with the harmful consequence of meetings sometimes being scheduled without taking the constraints of important participants into account.

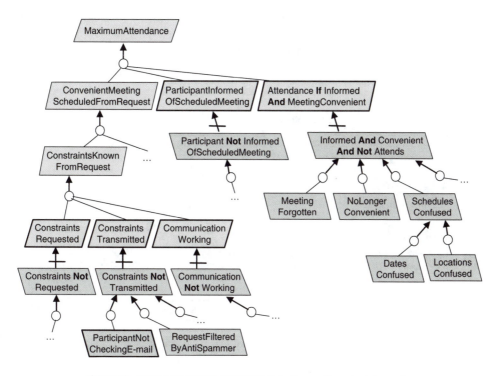

Figure 9.8 *Systematic obstacle identification for the meeting scheduling system*

Obstacle identification

Once leaf goals and hypotheses have been selected in the goal model, the overall procedure for identifying obstacles is as follows:

For each selected assertion G:

- Take the negation of G to obtain its root obstacle **not** G.

- Find AND/OR refinements of **not** G, according to the determined level of extensiveness, in view of valid domain properties and hypotheses,

- until obstruction pre-conditions are reached that are sufficiently fine-grained to enable an assessment of their feasibility, likelihood and resolvability.

The domain properties and hypotheses used in this procedure are either known or elicited during the refinement process (see Section 9.1.2). They must be valid for the analysis to be sound. When a domain property or hypothesis appears questionable, we should apply the same procedure to it in order to investigate how it could be broken.

In Figure 9.9, the obstacle-identification procedure is applied twice to a goal model fragment for the A320 braking logic (this example was introduced in Section 1.2.1 and used in Figure 8.6). The obstacle diagram on the left is produced by application of the procedure to the goal ReverseThrustEnabledIffWheelsTurning. The obstacle diagram on the right is produced by application of the same procedure to the questionable hypothesis WheelsTurningIffMovingOnRunway. The diagram shows how this invalid property can be broken.

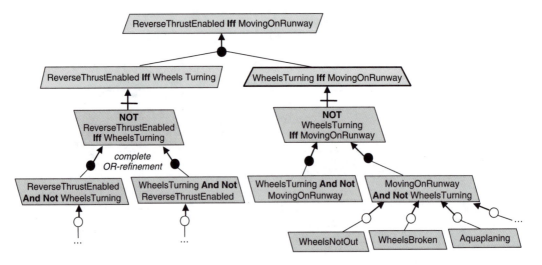

Figure 9.9 *Breaking goals and domain hypotheses in the Airbus A320 braking logic*

Obstacle-identification techniques

As noted before, the obstacle-identification procedure may require ingenuity and domain expertise. However, we can use semi-formal techniques to assist us.

Tautology-based refinement   In view of the negation prefixing the root obstacles, tautologies such as the following prove helpful in driving some of the refinements:

> not (A and B) *amounts to* not A or not B,   not (A or B) *amounts to* not A and not B,
> not (if A then B) *amounts to* A and not B,
> not (A iff B) *amounts to* (A and not B) or (not A and B)

Figure 9.9 illustrates the use of the latter tautology. One benefit of tautology-based decompositions is the *complete* OR-refinement we obtain when an or-connective is introduced in the rewriting of the parent obstacle. As for AND-refinements, we 'blacken' OR-refinement nodes when we can provide a completeness argument (as in Figure 9.9).

Identifying necessary conditions for the obstructed target   This technique is quite effective for finding obstacles to *Achieve* and *Maintain* goals. We have seen in Chapter 7 that the general form of an *Achieve* goal is:

> *Achieve [TargetCondition]:*   **[if** CurrentCondition **then] sooner-or-later** TargetCondition

By negating this goal, we obtain its root obstacle:

> [CurrentCondition **and] always not** TargetCondition   *(Obst)*

Suppose now that we can find or elicit a valid domain property giving us a necessary condition for the target condition to hold; that is:

> **if** TargetCondition **then** NecessaryCondition   *(Dom)*

which tautologically amounts to its contraposition:

> **if not** NecessaryCondition **then not** TargetCondition   *(Dom)*

Replacing *not TargetCondition* by *not NecessaryCondition* in *(Obst)*, we obtain the following assertion:

> [CurrentCondition **and] always not** NecessaryCondition   *(SubObst)*

We can see, by simple chaining, that *(SubObst)* does imply *(Obst)* when taken with *(Dom)*.

Figure 9.10 summarizes this simple reasoning as an *obstacle-refinement pattern*. The reasoning is similar for *Maintain* goals.

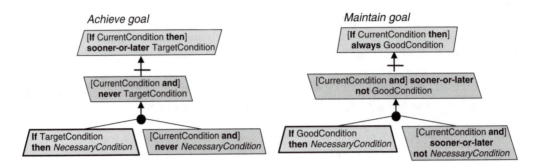

Figure 9.10   *Obstacle refinement driven by necessary conditions for the obstructed target*

For example, consider the *Maintain* goal *TrainStoppedAtBlockSignalIfStopSignal* in Figure 9.1. In the **Def** specification of this goal, the condition to be maintained is:

If a block signal is set to 'stop' **then** any arriving train is stopped at it.

The target GoodCondition to be preserved is thus: 'any arriving train is stopped at the stop signal'. The root obstacle for the goal is:

A block signal is set to 'stop' **and** some arriving train is **not** stopped at it.

We ask ourselves what are necessary conditions in the domain for the target condition that any arriving train stops at a stop signal. We might thereby find or elicit necessary conditions such as:

The train driver has responded to the signal's stop command.
The signal is visible.

We can then instantiate the obstacle refinement in the diagram on the right in Figure 9.10 to derive the obstacles of some train driver sooner or later failing to respond to a signal's stop command (*DriverUnresponsive*) or some block signal sooner or later being not visible (*SignalNotVisible*).

This simple technique can be made much more precise if we formalize the specifications of critical goals and domain properties in temporal logic. Chapter 18 will present a formal version where obstacles are generated through a formal calculus. The technique can then be applied at any level of an obstacle refinement tree for generating sub-obstacles from a parent obstacle. The idea remains the same: we look for necessary conditions for an obstructed target condition in the parent obstacle to hold, and negate these to produce sub-obstacles.

As another example of using this technique, consider the sub-obstacle MovingOnRunway **And Not** WheelsTurning in the right-hand diagram in Figure 9.9. The target condition being obstructed in this sub-obstacle is the condition WheelsTurning. Looking for necessary conditions in the domain for aircraft wheels to be turning, we may find conditions such as WheelsOut, WheelsNotBroken or **Not** Aquaplaning. The negation of each such necessary condition yields the corresponding sub-obstacles in Figure 9.9.

Using applicable refinement patterns

To find obstacle refinements, we may also apply refinement patterns from Section 8.8.5 that match the specification of the parent obstacle. The milestone-driven, case-driven and divide-and-conquer patterns are especially relevant.

In particular, the milestones may correspond to intrusion milestones in the case of an obstacle to some security goal. For the case-driven patterns, the cases correspond to obstruction cases.

9.3.2 Evaluating obstacles

For each leaf obstacle in an obstacle diagram, we must check whether it is compatible with what we know about the domain and find a possible system behaviour satisfying it – see the *domain-consistency* and *feasibility* conditions for a statement to be an obstacle in Section 9.1.1. We must then determine the *Likelihood* and *Criticality* features annotating this obstacle in the model.

To do this, we can use the risk assessment techniques discussed in Section 3.2.2. As noted before, the assistance of domain experts may be needed for estimating the likelihood of a leaf obstacle.

The following rules may also be applied for propagating *Likelihood* features bottom up in obstacle diagrams, from independent subobstacles sO_i to a parent obstacle O:

$$\text{Likelihood }(O) = \min_i (\text{Likelihood }(sO_i)) \quad \text{if } O \text{ is an AND-refinement into } sO_i;$$
$$\text{Likelihood }(O) = \max_i (\text{Likelihood }(sO_i)) \quad \text{if } O \text{ is an OR-refinement into } sO_i.$$

Such propagation rules produce rough estimates that may need to be refined through domain-specific weakenings (for AND-refinements) or strengthenings (for OR-refinements).

For the *Criticality* feature, the severity of the consequences of an obstacle can be estimated in terms of the higher-level goals to which the obstructed goal/hypothesis contributes. As we saw in Section 9.2.3, the obstruction propagates up recursively to the parent goals along goal AND-refinement trees (see Figure 9.5). If the obstructed goal/hypothesis contributes to several parent goals, the obstruction propagates up along each AND-refinement tree in which the goal/hypothesis is involved.

9.3.3 Resolving obstacles in a modified goal model

The identified obstacles, if likely and critical, must be resolved through adequate counter-measures. Obstacles are in general resolved at RE time by injecting countermeasures into the goal model. Such countermeasures may need to be refined like other goals in the model (see Figure 9.7).

Alternatively, the resolution of non-critical obstacles can be deferred until system runtime through obstacle monitoring (see Section 6.5). The resolution is then deployed dynamically as an anticipation or repair action when the monitor detects that the obstacle condition will or has become true, respectively.

In any case we need to determine adequate resolutions for each obstacle being considered. We can use goal-anchored versions of the risk control techniques in Section 3.2.2 for this. There are two steps:

1. We explore alternative countermeasures to the obstacle by the application of model transformation operators.

2. We select the best obstacle resolution from among the alternatives identified.

Exploring alternative countermeasures

The model transformation operators in Step 1 encode alternative tactics for transforming the goal model in order to eliminate the obstacle, reduce its likelihood or mitigate its consequences.

Here is a catalogue of resolution operators we may use. Let *O* denote the considered obstacle and *G* a goal obstructed by it.

Goal substitution *Find an alternative refinement of G's parent goal in which G and O no longer appear.* The corresponding model transformation is depicted in Figure 9.11a. The refinement involving sub-goal *G* there is replaced by another refinement of the parent goal *PG*, involving sub-goals *G'* different from *G*. If an alternative refinement of *PG* cannot easily be found, we may recursively look for alternative refinements of *PG*'s parents in the goal graph.

For example, consider the obstructed goal ReverseThrustEnabledIffWheelsTurning and the obstructed domain hypothesis WheelsTurningIffMovingOnRunway in Figure 9.9. To resolve both obstructions, we might get back to the parent goal ReverseThrustEnabledIffMovingOnRunway, and refine it alternatively into the sub-goal ReverseThrustEnabledIff*PlaneWeightSensed* together with the valid domain property PlaneWeightSensedIffMovingOnRunway.

For the meeting scheduling system, the obstacle E-agendaNotUpToDate might be resolved in this way by taking the alternative refinement of the parent goal ConstraintsKnownFromRequest in Figure 8.8, where participants' constraints are obtained by e-mail instead.

Agent substitution *Find an alternative responsibility assignment for the obstructed goal G so that there is no longer any possible agent behaviour making the obstructing obstacle O feasible.*

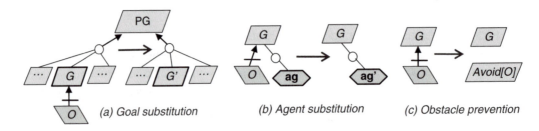

(a) Goal substitution   (b) Agent substitution   (c) Obstacle prevention

Figure 9.11 *Model transformation operators for eliminating obstacles*

The corresponding model transformation is depicted in Figure 9.11b. The assignment of goal G to agent ag there is replaced by an assignment to another agent ag' making O no longer feasible.

For example, the goal Maintain[SafeAccelerationComputed] in the train control system might have been assigned to the agent OnBoardTrainController. This allows for behaviours satisfying the obstacle ComputedAcceleration**Not**Safe due to this agent being not sufficiently reliable. To resolve the obstacle, we can assign the responsibility for that same goal to an ultra-reliable StationTrainController agent instead.

In the meeting scheduling system, the obstacle ParticipantNotCheckingEmail obstructing the goal ConstraintsTransmitted might be eliminated by assigning the responsibility for this goal alternatively to a Proxy agent (e.g. the participant's secretary).

Obstacle prevention *Introduce a new goal Avoid[O] in the model to prevent the obstacle from being satisfied* (see Figure 9.11c). If selected as a countermeasure, the goal needs to be refined until individual responsibility assignments are reached. This tactic is generally used for resolving obstacles to Safety and Security goals.

For example, the obstacle Corrupted appearing in Figure 9.4 should be resolved by the new goal Avoid[TrainAccelerationCommandCorrupted], if this obstacle is likely.

The obstacle MeetingForgotten appearing in Figure 9.8 might be resolved by introduction of the new goal Avoid[MeetingForgotten]. If selected as a countermeasure, this goal would be refined into a requirement Achieve[MeetingReminded] assigned to the meeting scheduling software.

Goal weakening *Weaken the specification of the obstructed goal to make it more liberal so that the obstruction disappears.* For a goal formulated as an **if-then** statement, such weakening is achieved syntactically by adding a conjunct in the **if**-part or a disjunct in the **then**-part.

For example, we saw in Figure 9.8 that the goal AttendanceIfInformedAndMeetingConvenient can be obstructed by the obstacle NoLongerConvenient. This goal states the following:

If the meeting was convenient to the participant at meeting scheduling time
   and the participant is informed of the schedule
then the participant will attend the meeting.

To make the obstruction disappear, we might weaken the goal formulation by strengthening the **if**-part:

If the meeting was convenient to the participant at meeting scheduling time
   and the participant is informed of the schedule
   and the participant has no last-minute impediment
then the participant will attend the meeting.

On another hand, the goal SectorControllerOnDutyIfBusySector in an air traffic control system can be obstructed by the obstacle NoSectorControllerOnDuty. We might weaken the goal formulation by weakening the **then**-part:

> **If** the sector is busy
> **then** (there shall always be a sector controller on duty
>   **or** a controller from an adjacent sector will be temporarily allocated to this sector too).

Obstacle reduction   Instead of eliminating the obstacle, we may *reduce its likelihood by introducing an ad hoc countermeasure.* For a goal assigned to a human agent, the countermeasure is typically intended to increase responsiveness, motivation or dissuasion.

For example, the likelihood of the obstacle DriverUnresponsive in Figure 9.1 can be reduced through the countermeasure goal ResponsivenessCheckSentRegularly intended to increase driver responsiveness.

In the library system, the likelihood of the obstacle BookCopyNotReturnedInTime is reduced through the countermeasure goal FineChargedIfNotReturnedInTime intended to dissuade negligent behaviour.

Goal restoration   The tactic here consists of tolerating the obstacle O while requiring the target condition of the obstructed goal G to be restored if the obstacle condition holds. A new goal is added to the goal model that takes the form:

> **if** O **then sooner-or-later** *TargetCondition*

This tactic is often used when the obstacle appears to be unavoidable. For example, sending reminders to negligent borrowers in the library system refines the resolution goal of enforcing the return of copies that are not returned in time.

In an ambulance dispatching system, the goal MobilizedAmbulanceAtIncidentInTime in Figure 9.3 might be restored by mobilization of another ambulance if the mobilized one has broken down.

Obstacle mitigation   The obstacle is also tolerated here, but the consequences of its satisfaction are mitigated. A new goal is added to the goal model to attenuate such consequences. Two forms of mitigation can be distinguished: weak or strong mitigation.

In a *weak mitigation*, the new goal ensures that a weaker version of the obstructed goal is satisfied whenever the obstacle is satisfied.

For example, let us again consider the obstacle NoLongerConvenient that obstructs the goal AttendanceIfInformedAndMeetingConvenient in Figure 9.8. The weak mitigation goal Achieve[ImpedimentNotified] ensures the following weaker version of the obstructed goal:

> **If** the meeting was convenient to the participant at meeting scheduling time
>   **and** the participant is informed of the schedule
> **then** the participant will attend the meeting **or** will be excused.

In a *strong mitigation*, the new goal ensures that the parent goal of the obstructed goal, or an ancestor of it, is satisfied whenever the obstacle is satisfied, in spite of the goal obstruction.

For example, a strong mitigation of the obstacle OutdatedSpeed/Position in Figure 9.4 results in the introduction into the goal model of the new goal Avoid[TrainCollisionWhen OutdatedSpeed/Position].

Do nothing The last tactic consists of applying no countermeasure at all. The goal model is left unchanged in spite of the obstacle. At system runtime, we may just tolerate the obstacle, or monitor it for dynamic anticipation or repair (see Section 6.5). This tactic is typically applied when the obstacle is unlikely or has non-severe consequences.

Selecting the best resolution Once alternative countermeasures have been identified, we need to compare them to select the best one. We may use comparison criteria such as the following:

- The number of obstacles resolved by an alternative.

- The likelihood and criticality of the resolved obstacles.

- The contribution of the alternative to non-functional goals in the goal model.

- Its cost.

The selection should be cost effective. It may be based on estimations of risk-reduction leverages (see Section 3.2.2) and on qualitative or quantitative reasoning about contributions to non-functional goals (see Section 16.3).

Multiple complementary countermeasures may be selected when the obstruction is not eliminated. For example, we might introduce into the library goal model both the countermeasure FineChargedIfNotReturnedInTime, to reduce the likelihood of the obstacle BookCopyNotReturnedInTime, *and* the goal restoration countermeasure Achieve [ReminderSentIfNotReturnedInTime].

When a new goal is introduced into the goal model as a selected resolution, it may be captured in the corresponding obstacle diagram through a resolution link (see Figure 9.1).

When the selected countermeasure consists of weakening the obstructed goal, the weakening must be propagated in the AND-trees where the weakened goal was involved in the goal model; the modified model must then be rechecked.

In any case, the new or modified goals need to be refined until assignable requirements and expectations are reached. The updated goal model will result in a more complete requirements document and a more robust system. As the new requirements and expectations can themselves be overexposed to new obstacles, a new *Identify–Assess–Resolve* cycle may be needed (see Figure 9.7).

Summary

- Anticipating what could go wrong with the system as designed is essential for the success of the project and for the quality of the resulting product. Such anticipation should take place at RE time by breaking over-ideal system specifications in order to produce more complete requirements for a more robust system. Obstacle analysis is a goal-based form of risk analysis aimed at identifying, assessing and resolving the possibilities of breaking assertions in the system's goal model. Such analysis is intertwined with the model elaboration process.

- An obstacle is a pre-condition for non-satisfaction of some goal, hypothesis or questionable domain property used in the goal model. It must be consistent with valid domain properties and hypotheses, and feasible through possible behaviours of system agents. Goals and obstacles are dual notions. We can therefore derive obstacle categories from goal categories. Goal obstruction propagates bottom up along goal AND-refinement trees.

- An obstacle diagram is a goal-anchored risk tree showing how a root obstacle to an assertion can be AND/OR refined into sub-obstacles whose feasibility, likelihood and resolution are easier to establish. OR-refinements show different ways of obstructing the assertion. They should ideally be domain complete. AND-refinements capture specific combinations of circumstances for obstruction. They should be complete, domain consistent and minimal. Leaf obstacles are connected to countermeasure goals through resolution links. The nodes in obstacle diagrams are individually characterized through annotations.

- The identification of a complete set of obstacles is highly desirable when a goal is mission-critical; the goal is guaranteed to be satisfied when none of the obstacles in this set can be satisfied. Completeness, however, depends on how much we know about the domain and how adequate our knowledge is. Obstacle analysis may help elicit and validate domain properties as well.

- Obstacle identification may require some assistance from domain experts. We can build obstacle diagrams systematically using techniques such as tautology-based refinement, finding necessary conditions in the domain for obstructed targets, and obstacle refinement patterns.

- Determination of the likelihood of an obstacle and the severity of its consequences relies on risk-assessment techniques. The latter may take advantage of the AND/OR refinement structure of the goal model. Obstacles estimated to be sufficiently likely and critical should be resolved.

- Obstacle resolution consists of exploring alternative countermeasures to select the best ones based on estimations of risk-reduction leverages and contributions to non-functional goals. The exploration of alternative countermeasures can be made systematic by the use of operators that transform the goal model so as to eliminate the obstacle, reduce its likelihood or attenuate its consequences. Such operators include goal substitution, agent substitution, obstacle prevention, goal weakening, obstacle reduction, goal restoration and obstacle mitigation.

Notes and Further Reading

A more technical treatment of obstacle analysis can be found in van Lamsweerde and Letier (2000). This paper also provides a comprehensive obstacle analysis case study covering the causes of major failures of an older version of the London Ambulance System (LAS, 1993; Finkelstein, 1996).

The seminal idea of associating obstacles with goals appeared in Potts (1995). Obstacles are considered there as negative scenarios associated with goals. They are used in Anton and Potts (1998) to identify scenarios and goals for goal-based analysis of evolving systems. Heuristics for identifying possible exceptions and errors in such scenarios are proposed in Sutcliffe *et al.* (1998), for example scenarios in which events happen in the wrong order or in which incorrect information is transmitted. Influencing factors such as agent motivation and workload are also used to help anticipate exception occurrences and assign probabilities to abnormal events. Generic requirements are attached to exceptions as possible ways of dealing with the problems identified.

Obstacles as obstruction pre-conditions were introduced first in van Lamsweerde and Letier (1998), where various techniques for identifying obstacles are presented including the generation of obstacles from goal negations and domain descriptions, the use of obstruction patterns and the use of obstacle categories. Lutz and colleagues discuss a convincing application of obstacle analysis to identify anomaly-handling requirements for a NASA unpiloted aerial vehicle (Lutz *et al.*, 2007).

The integration of hazard analysis in the early stages of the RE process is also advocated in Leveson (2002). Iterative approaches for defect-driven modification of requirements specifications in the context of system faults and human errors are proposed in Anderson *et al.* (1995) and de Lemos *et al.* (1995). Fault trees and threat trees are discussed as special types of risk trees in Leveson (1995) and Schneier (2000), respectively.

The separation between resolution exploration and resolution selection is discussed in Easterbrook (1994) in the context of conflict management. Some of the obstacle-resolution tactics in this chapter have been studied in relation to handling problematic situations in other contexts, for example exceptions and faults in fault-tolerant systems (Cristian, 1995; Gartner, 1999); feature interaction in telecommunication systems (Keck & Kuehn, 1998); inconsistencies in software development (Nuseibeh, 1996); or conflicts between requirements (Robinson &. Volkov, 1997; van Lamsweerde *et al.*, 1998). The distinction between strong and weak mitigation for obstacle resolution is an RE counterpart of the distinction between two notions of fault tolerance: one where the program meets its specification in spite of faults, and the other where the program meets a weaker version of the specification (Cristian, 1991).

Exercises

- Consider a simplistic engine-control system whose specification includes the following:

  (Goal)   **If** PressureTooLow **then** AlarmRaised
  (Domain property)   **If** StartMode **then not** PressureTooLow

  Explain why the condition:

  StartMode **and not** AlarmRaised

  cannot be considered as an obstacle to that goal.

- Consider the root obstacle ConstraintsNotTransmitted in the obstacle diagram anchored on the goal ConstraintsTransmitted in Figure 9.8. Explain why the *OR*-refinement of this root obstacle into the sub-obstacles shown there – namely, ParticipantNotCheckingEmail and RequestFilteredByAntiSpammer – is certainly *not* domain complete.

- Use your best domain knowledge about ambulance systems to complete the obstacle diagram sketched in Figure 9.3 for obstruction of the goal MobilizedAmbulanceAtIncidentInTime. Then, explore alternative countermeasures to the leaf sub-obstacles in your diagram using model transformation operators from Section 9.3.3.

- Consider the accuracy goal IncidentFormAccuratelyEncoded in an ambulance-dispatching system. This goal states that 'the incident details shall be accurately encoded from the information provided by emergency calls'. Incident details include the precise location of the incident, the type of incident, the estimated number of people requiring intervention, and the estimated ambulance resources needed for first aid on the incident scene. (Incident encoding is needed for mobilizing the right number and the right types of ambulance.) Elaborate an obstacle diagram anchored on the goal IncidentFormAccuratelyEncoded.

- Consider the goal AllocatedAmbulanceMobilized in an ambulance-dispatching system. Following the milestone-driven pattern, this goal was refined in the goal model into two sub-goals:

  MobilizationOrder SentTo AmbulanceMDT,   AmbulanceMobilized From OrderOnMDT,

  where *MDT* stands for the **m**obile **d**ata **t**erminal inside ambulances. Obstacle analysis revealed that the obstacle MDT-BrokenDown is likely and critical. Explore alternative countermeasures to this obstacle using model transformation operators from Section 9.3.3. Identify those among them that seem most appropriate, and explain why you believe this to be so.

- One goal in a nuclear power plant is to maintain an effective cooling system. The goal SafetyInjectionIffLossOfCoolant appears somewhere in the refinement of this goal. A software component for safety injection control is involved in the satisfaction of this goal. The following goal is a leaf sub-goal in the refinement of SafetyInjectionIffLossOfCoolant:

  SafetyInjection **Iff** (LowWaterPressure **and not** Overridden)

  Build a complete obstacle diagram anchored on this goal using tautology-based AND/OR refinements only. (The precise meaning of SafetyInjection, LowWaterPressure and Overridden in the domain of nuclear power plants is not necessary for this exercise.)

- Re-derive the various obstacles for the meeting scheduling system in Figure 9.8 using the technique of identifying necessary conditions for the obstructed targets.

- Consider the goal AuthenticatedAccess obstructed by the obstacle PasswordForgotten in a Web service. Explore goal restoration countermeasures to this obstacle.

- Identify goals, obstacles and alternative obstacle resolutions for the library management system based on the case study description given in Section 1.1.2.

- Consider the following simplified version of a patient-monitoring system. Elaborate a goal model for it and perform obstacle analysis to complete your goal model towards a more robust system.

  Each patient in an emergency service is monitored by an analog device that measures factors such as pulse, temperature, blood pressure and skin resistance. The software monitors these factors on a periodic basis, customized to each patient, and keeps them in a database for patient history tracking. For each patient, safe ranges are specified for each factor. If a factor falls outside of a patient's safe range, the nurse's station is notified.

10

Modelling Conceptual Objects with Class Diagrams

I n our multi-view modelling framework for RE, this chapter is dedicated to the structural view of the system. In this view, the conceptual objects manipulated in the system-as-is or system-to-be are defined precisely, characterized further through individual features and inter-related with each other through semantic links. The structural model resulting from this organization will be called the *object model*. Conceptual objects capture domain-specific concepts referred to by prescriptive or descriptive statements about the system. Depending on their nature, they are defined in the object model as entities, associations, agents or events. The model is represented by entity–relationship diagrams using the UML class diagram notation. These diagrams were introduced in Section 4.3.2. This chapter focuses on how we can build them in a systematic way.

An object model plays a significant role in model-based software development. At RE time, it provides the concept definitions and domain properties used by the goal, agent, operation and behaviour models. It yields the system state variables in terms of which goals, agents, operations and behaviours are specified. An object model thus introduces a common vocabulary to which to refer. We can generate a glossary of terms from this model on which all parties involved in the development can agree and which they can use for unambiguous reference. At software design time, the object model provides a basis for generating a database schema (if any) and for elaborating a software architecture.

Section 10.1 takes a closer look at conceptual objects, what they capture and how we can characterize them. Sections 10.2–10.4 make the notions of entity, association and attribute more precise in this setting, and illustrate their use for structural modelling. Section 10.5 discusses specialization and aggregation as model-structuring mechanisms. Section 10.6 presents a few more UML features that sometimes prove useful in practical modelling situations, such as OR-associations and associations of associations. Section 10.7 concludes this chapter by providing a variety of heuristics and tips to help us build 'good' object models. In particular, we will see there how a complete and pertinent object model can be built systematically from a goal model.

10.1 Representing domain concepts by conceptual objects

We first need to understand what precisely conceptual objects and their instances capture in terms of system phenomena. The types of object we can find in an object model are introduced next. We will then see how model annotations can be used for characterizing the individual features of a conceptual object and for collecting relevant domain properties as object invariants.

10.1.1 What are conceptual objects?

A *conceptual object* is a discrete set of instances of a domain-specific concept that are manipulated by the modelled system. These instances:

- are distinctly identifiable

- can be enumerated in any system state

- share similar features

- may differ from each other in their individual states and state transitions.

Every object instance has a built-in, immutable *identity* allowing it to be distinguished from other object instances – even when their common features have identical values. For example, we can identify and distinguish two instances of the Patron object having exactly the same last name, first name and birthdate, whereas we cannot distinguish two instances of the string 'Mary Smith', say.

In any system state, it must be possible to *enumerate* all the object instances involved in the system in that state. For example, we should be able to enumerate all instances of the BookCopy object that are currently involved in our library system.

The *features* shared by any object instance include individual features that characterize the object in isolation, such as the object's name, definition, type, domain properties and attributes; and the associations in which the object participates with other objects in the model. (Individual features are detailed in Section 10.1.5; associations are discussed in Section 10.3.) For example, any instance of the Train object in our train control system has common attributes such as *Speed*, *Location* and *DoorsState*, and common associations such as *On* and *At* linking that instance to corresponding instances of the Block and Platform objects, respectively. Any Train instance also satisfies the domain property stating that it is moving if and only if its speed is non-null (see Figure 10.2 below).

In a given system state, different instances of the same object generally have different values for their common attributes and associations. For example, different trains may in the same system state have different values for their Speed attribute and On association. Object instances may thus evolve differently from state to state according to specific values for their attributes and associations.

In accordance with the notion of state introduced in Section 7.3.1, a *state* of an object instance is a tuple of functional pairs $x_i \mapsto v_i$ where for every object attribute or association x_i

a value v_i is defined for that instance. For example, a state for an instance tr of the Train object might be:

(tr.Speed $\mapsto$ 0, tr.Location $\mapsto$ 9.25, tr.DoorsState $\mapsto$ 'open', On $\mapsto$ (tr, block13), At $\mapsto$ (tr, platform2))

10.1.2 Object instantiation: classes and current instances

Every conceptual object in an object model has a built-in semantic relation associated with it to determine which specific instances are members of the object in the current state; by *current state* we mean some arbitrarily chosen system state. This relation is defined as follows:

InstanceOf (*o*, *Ob*)   **iff**   *o* is an instance of object *Ob* in the current system state.

For example, *InstanceOf (bci, BookCopy)* expresses that the particular book copy identified as *bci* is currently a member of the set of book copies manipulated by our system. This instance might not have been a member one year before (as it was not purchased yet); it might no longer be a member one year after (as it might be permanently damaged or stolen).

The set of instances that are members of an object will thus generally change over time. An instance may also migrate from one object to another over time. For example, the same person might currently be a StudentPatron instance and later on a StaffPatron instance. The same instance might also be simultaneously a member of multiple objects. For example, the same person in our meeting scheduling system might simultaneously be an Initiator instance and a Participant instance.

When an individual becomes an instance of an object, the object's attributes and associations are instantiated as *state variables* in terms of which it can be characterized. For example, a new train *tr* getting into the system gets state variables such as tr.Speed, tr.Location, tr.DoorsState, On(tr,) and At(tr,). The current set of *system state variables* is defined by the set of all such state variables taken over all object instances currently in the system.

When we elaborate a structural view of the system, we model conceptual objects as abstractions of all their possible instances. We thus manipulate classes of instances and rarely refer to particular instances; the semantic *InstanceOf* relation is kept implicit in the model. The contexts in which we may want to refer to particular instances explicitly include the following:

- *For scenario specification.* The interaction sequences illustrating a desired system behaviour involve particular agent instances. The notation :*Ob* will then be used to denote a particular agent instance *o*, associated with a scenario timeline, such that *InstanceOf(o,Ob)*; see Section 13.1.

- *For specification of operations and for formal assertions.* When we specify the signature of an operation, we need *instance variables* to indicate object instances taken as input arguments or produced as output results (see Chapter 12). When we specify goals, domain properties or pre- and post-conditions of operations in a formal specification language, we also need instance variables to indicate object instances to which the assertions refer – see the instance variable *'tr'* in the domain properties attached to the Train entity in Figure 10.2, and the examples involving quantification of instance variables in Section 4.4.2. (The formalization of assertions attached to model components will be discussed in Chapter 17.) In all such cases we use notations like

o: Ob   as a shortcut for   **for** *o* **such that** InstanceOf *(o, Ob)*

- *For specification of acceptance test data.* Test data are particular instances of corresponding classes from the object model.

It is important not to confuse class-level conceptual abstractions and their instances. As we will refer to the former much more often than to the latter, we use the shorter term 'object' for the class-level abstraction and the longer term 'object instance' for their instances – rather than the alternative 'object class' vs 'object' terminology sometimes used in the literature.

10.1.3 Types of conceptual object

There are different kinds of object whose structure may be captured in an object model (see Figure 10.1).

An *entity* is an autonomous and passive object. Its instances may exist in the system independently of instances of other objects (unlike associations); they cannot control the behaviours of instances of other objects (unlike agents). For example, we can model the Train, Block and Platform objects in our train control system as entities. In the library system, the Book and BookCopy objects are entities as well. Entities were briefly introduced in Section 4.3.2 when we reviewed entity–relationship diagrams as a specification notation; we come back to them in Section 10.2.

An *association* is a conceptual object dependent on other objects that it links. Each linked object plays a specific *role* in the association. The instances of the association are conceptual links among corresponding object instances. For example, *On* is an association linking the Train and Block entities; *Copy* is an association linking the Book and BookCopy entities; *Loan* is an association linking the Patron agent and the BookCopy entity. In the latter association, Patron plays the role *Borrows* whereas BookCopy plays the role *BorrowedBy*. Associations were also briefly introduced in Section 4.3.2 under the synonymous term 'relationship' (originally used in the literature); we come back to them in Section 10.3.

An *agent* is an autonomous and active object. Its instances have individual behaviours captured by sequences of state transitions for the state variables that they control. These variables refer to attributes/associations of object instances. For example, a TrainController agent

Figure 10.1   *Object typology*

instance can control the acceleration attribute of Train instances; a Staff instance can control instances of the Loan association. Agents were briefly introduced in Chapters 7 and 8 when we discussed goal responsibility assignments; they will be further detailed in Chapter 11. Here, we are specifically concerned with modelling the structural features of an agent such as its attributes and the associations in which it takes part.

An *event* is an instantaneous object. Any event instance exists in a single state of the system only. For example, an instance of the *StartTrain* event in our train control system exists only in the state where a corresponding train instance is moving whereas it was stopped in the preceding state; an instance of the BookRequest event exists only in a state where a particular patron has made a loan request for a particular book. When in a specification we need to refer to an instance of an event *Ev* in the current state, we use the standard notation:

Occurs (Ev)   as a shortcut for   InstanceOf (ev, Ev).

Events were briefly introduced in Sections 4.3.6 and 4.3.7 when we reviewed event trace diagrams and state machine diagrams as specification notations; we come back to them in Chapter 13. Here, we are specifically concerned with modelling the structural features of an event such as its attributes and the associations in which it might take part. For example, the *StartTrain* event may need to be structurally linked to the Train entity to enable us to capture the occurrence of two different *StartTrain* events within the same system state, corresponding to two different Train instances starting simultaneously.

The sub-type edges in Figure 10.1 define a partition of object instances; any object instance is either an entity, association, agent or event instance. In an object model, we will therefore model conceptual abstractions directly as entities, associations, agents or events (rather than as objects).

10.1.4 Object models as UML class diagrams

We will represent object models by UML class diagrams. The notation was introduced in Section 4.3.2 and has been used occasionally (see Figures 5.2 and 6.11). A much more detailed account will be provided in the next few sections from a model-building perspective.

- Entities and the structural features of agents and events will be represented as operation-free UML classes (depicted by rectangles; see Figure 10.2).

- Associations will be represented as UML associations (depicted by labelled edges in the case of binary associations; see Figure 10.2).

Note that the RE notion of an 'object' is quite different from the notion of an 'object' used in object-oriented design:

- At RE time, we are not concerned with software objects. Only those objects shared by the software and its environment or owned by the environment are relevant (see Section 1.1.4, Figure 1.3).

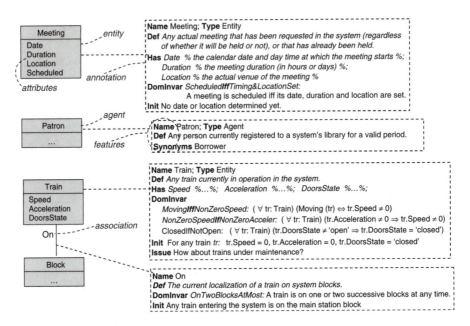

Figure 10.2   *Object features as model annotations: examples*

- Deciding which operations to cluster with which object is a design decision; there might be multiple alternative clusterings having their pros and cons from a design perspective. Encapsulation makes little sense at RE time. There is no information-hiding concern, as there should be no implementation aspect at this stage. The system operations are modelled in a separate view provided by the operation model; they may be clustered later at design time to form design classes.

10.1.5 Object features as model annotations

Like goals in a goal model, we may annotate the conceptual objects in an object model with textual features to characterize them individually. Figure 10.2 shows possible annotations of objects from our running case studies. An annotation may collect the following features of the object to which it is attached:

- The **Name** feature must uniquely identify the object for unambiguous reference throughout all views of the entire system model. We thereby know, for example, that the concept named Patron, structurally represented by a rectangle in the object model, is the same as the one represented by a hexagon in the goal and agent models (see the graphical representation of agents in Chapter 8, for example Figure 8.11). In a class diagram, object names appear as labels of nodes or edges.

- The **Type** feature allows us to declare textually whether an object represented as a UML class is an entity, an agent or an event.

- The **Def** feature must define the conceptual object precisely in natural language. This definition should provide a system-specific interpretation of the semantic *InstanceOf* relation introduced in Section 10.1.2, by stating the necessary and sufficient condition for an individual to be currently an instance of the object – or, equivalently, by stating the exact conditions for an individual to appear in and disappear from the system as an instance of this object. For example, Patron is defined in Figure 10.2 as any person currently registered with the library for a valid period; this allows us to determine whether a particular person is currently an instance of this object or not. Object definitions are essential for model accuracy; they must be sufficiently precise to preclude different interpretations by different people. Moreover, object definitions are used as inputs to the model-based generation of the requirements document and, in particular, the glossary of terms (see Section 16.4).

- The optional **Synonyms** feature lists a number of terms that may be used as synonyms when referring to this conceptual object, for example 'borrower' for 'patron' in Figure 10.2.

- The **Has** feature textually defines the meaning, in terms of system phenomena, of the various object attributes graphically declared in the lower part of the rectangle representing the object (attributes are further discussed in Section 10.4). Such a definition must be as precise as possible to preclude different interpretations. For example, the top annotation in Figure 10.2 makes precise to what a meeting *Date* refers. Such clarification is obviously essential for our meeting scheduling system.

- The **DomInvar** feature lists known domain properties about the object as invariants holding in any object state. Such properties are needed for building or checking models involving the object. In particular, the refinement of goals and obstacles often relies on domain properties (see Chapters 8–9); these are specified as domain invariants on the corresponding object in the object model. For example, the first domain invariant attached to the Train entity in Figure 10.2 appeared in the refinement of the goal Maintain[DoorsClosedWhileMoving] in Figure 8.4. The domain properties stating necessary conditions for target/good conditions, appearing in the pattern shown in Figure 9.10, are similarly attached to corresponding objects in the object model. As for goals, the specification of an invariant may be prefixed by a suggestive *name* for shortcut reference in graphical models.

- The **Init** feature states the initial value of the attributes and associations of any instance when it appears in the system as an instance of this object; that is, in the state in which the semantic condition *InstanceOf(o,Ob)* becomes true. This feature is often used for inductive reasoning about the object, for example in inductive arguments in the style introduced in Section 5.4.4.

- As in the goal and obstacle models, the **Issue** feature serves as a placeholder for recording questions about the object to be subsequently addressed in the model-elaboration process. For example, the issue attached to the Train entity in Figure 10.2 raises the question of whether the model should take trains under maintenance into account.

Domain properties in an object annotation generally refer to the object's attributes – see the domain invariants attached to the Meeting and Train entities in Figure 10.2. When they involve instances of multiple objects, they need to be attached to a corresponding association between these objects. For example, the domain property stating that trains span two blocks at most is attached to the On association in Figure 10.2 – and not to the Train entity as it involves the Block entity as well (see heuristic (*H4*) in Section 10.7.1 below).

The **DomInvar** and **Init** features may be specified in natural language, as shown in Figure 10.2 for the Meeting entity and the On association, or in a formal language for more sophisticated forms of model analysis, as suggested in Figure 10.2 for the Train entity. The benefits of formal analysis were discussed in Section 4.4.7. We come back to formal models and formal analysis in Chapters 17–18.

10.2 Entities

As introduced in Section 10.1.3, an *entity* is an autonomous and passive object. Like any conceptual object, the instances of an entity can be distinctly identified, enumerated and characterized by common features and specific behaviours. Such instances cannot control behaviours, though. They may currently exist in the system independently of instances of other objects.

The *Entity* concept is defined at the meta level as a specialization of the *Object* concept (see Section 14.1, Figure 14.4). As a consequence, it inherits all features of the *Object* concept. Entities are therefore individually characterized by a name, a definition, attributes, domain invariants and initializations.

When we define an entity in its **Def** feature, the system-specific conditions for an individual to appear/disappear as an instance of it must not necessarily refer to other objects in the model, because entities are autonomous (unlike associations). For example, we modelled the Meeting concept as an entity in Figure 10.2. Its **Def** feature does not refer to other concepts such as participant, initiator, constraints or schedule. In contrast, any definition of the Constraints concept will necessarily refer to the participant who is subject to the constraints and to the meeting to which the constraints apply.

Like any object instance, entity instances evolve individually from state to state depending on changes in the values of their state variables. These variables are instantiated from the entity's attributes and associations as the corresponding instances get into the system.

10.3 Associations

As introduced in Section 10.1.3, an *association* is a conceptual object linking other objects. Each linked object plays a specific *role* in the association. For example, the Train entity plays the role isOn in the On association, whereas the Block entity plays the role holdsTrain (see Figure 10.3).

An *instance* of an association is a conceptual link among instances of objects playing the corresponding role. If the association links objects $O_1, \ldots, O_n$ under respective roles $R_1, \ldots, R_n$, an instance of it structurally amounts to a tuple:

$$[o_1, \ldots, o_n],$$

where each linked instance o_i satisfies *InstanceOf*(o_i, O_i) and plays the role R_i in the link – see Figure 10.3. The *position* of each instance in the link is obviously important. A different ordering

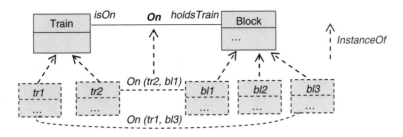

Figure 10.3 *An association with instances and roles*

of instances would define a different link, as instances in a different position would then play a different role.

When we need to refer to the semantic *InstanceOf* relation for an association *A*, we use the predicate notation:

$A(o_1, \ldots, o_n)$ as a shortcut for *InstanceOf* $([o_1, \ldots, o_n], A)$.

For example, we write *On (tr, bl)* instead of *InstanceOf ([tr, bl], On)* to specify that a specific *On*-link exists in the current state between train *tr* and block *bl*. This allows us to write goals that restrict the behaviours of associations, for example:

if On (tr, bl) **then not** On (tr′, bl)   for tr′ ≠ tr

Like any object, association instances can be distinctly identified, enumerated and characterized by common features and specific behaviours:

- The built-in immutable identity of an association is the tuple of built-in identities of the linked objects.

- As the *Association* concept is a specialization of the *Object* concept at the meta level, it inherits all the features of this concept. An association is therefore individually characterized by a name, a definition, attributes we can attach to it, domain invariants and initializations (see Figure 10.2).

- The instances of an association evolve individually from state to state. An instance appears in the system as the corresponding link is created; that is, as the corresponding predicate $A(o_1, \ldots, o_n)$ becomes true. It disappears from the system as the link is deleted; that is, as the corresponding predicate $A(o_1, \ldots, o_n)$ becomes false. For example, the link *On (tr, bl)* is created when train *tr* enters block *bl*; it is deleted when *tr* leaves *bl*. The state changes between link creation and deletion are caused by changes in values of the link's state variables. These variables are instantiated from the association's attributes and associations. For example, the state of a *Loan* instance in the library system might change between link creation and deletion by a change of value of the *TimeLimit* attribute attached to this link (see Figure 10.6).

An association is intrinsically dependent on the objects it links; its instances may currently exist in the system only if the participating instances are linked and are all currently instances of the corresponding objects.

Also note that an association may link objects of different types – entities, associations, agents or events. For example, the Loan association in the library system links the Patron agent and the BookCopy entity. (We come back to associations linking associations in Section 10.6.4.)

Arity of an association

The *arity* of an association is the number of objects linked by it. We speak of *binary associations* when this number is 2, and of *n-ary associations* when it is greater than 2.

Binary associations are frequently found in object models. They are graphically represented by edges labelled by the association name and connecting the participating objects. For example, the *On* association in Figure 10.3 and the *Constraints* association in Figure 4.6 are binary associations.

N-ary associations are used when more than two participating objects are required for defining links that need be distinguished. For example, consider the *Registration* association in our library system. Suppose that we want to model that patrons can be registered at different libraries for different registration periods and at a single library for one or two successive periods. If we do not consider the concept of Period as a separate, 'first-class' entity participating in the association, we cannot distinguish links involving those two periods separately. A Period attribute attached to a binary *Registration* association could not distinguish between two registration links that need be distinguished – one link for the first registration period, the other for the next. We could then not model punishment policies for late returns, prescribed in the goal model, such as suspension for the first registration period but not for the next one. We therefore end up with a ternary association linking the Patron agent, the Library entity and the Period entity under corresponding roles; see Figure 10.4. N-ary associations are graphically represented by diamonds labelled by the association name and connecting the participating objects.

Reflexive associations

An association can be reflexive; the same object then appears in the association at multiple positions under different roles. (Such an association is called a 'self-association' in UML.) For example, we need to model that trains follow each other in our train control system. This requires the introduction of an association *Following* that links Train, in the role *Follows*, and Train, in the role *FollowedBy*. In a completely different setting, suppose that we want to model a software architecture where data are exported among components. A reflexive ternary association would do the job here, *Export* say, linking the Component agent, in the role *Exports*, the Data entity, in the role *ExportedBy*, and the Component agent again, in the role *Imports*.

Multiplicities of an association

Multiplicities were already briefly mentioned in Section 4.3.2 when we introduced entity–relationship diagrams. An association has a multiplicity on each side of it; that is, for each role. The *multiplicity* on one side specifies the minimum and maximum number of

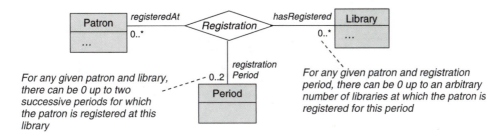

Figure 10.4 *A ternary association and its multiplicities*

object instances on this side that may be associated, in the same state, with a single sub-tuple of instances on the other sides. These numbers define a range, graphically represented by an interval *min..max*.

Figure 10.4 shows the multiplicities of the ternary *Registration* association mentioned before. For a binary association, the constraint expressed by a multiplicity *min..max* on one side of the association can be rephrased more simply as follows:

- *min* represents the minimum number of object instances on this side that, in any given state, *must* be the target of a given instance on the source side.

- max represents the maximum number of object instances on this side that, in any given state, *may* be the target of a given instance on the source side.

Figure 10.5 shows the multiplicities of the binary association represented in Figure 10.3. It also illustrates frequent values for *min* and *max* that capture the following *constraint patterns*:

- min = 0: *optional link* – there might be no target instance associated with a given source instance in some states. For example, a given block does not necessarily hold a train.

- min = 1: *mandatory link* – in any state, there must be at least one target instance associated with a given source instance. For example, a given train as defined in Figure 10.2 is necessarily on one block at least.

- max = 1: *uniqueness* – in any state, there may be no more than one target instance associated with a given source instance. For example, a given block as specified in Figure 10.5 may only hold one train at most.

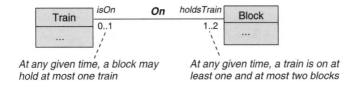

Figure 10.5 *A binary association and its multiplicities*

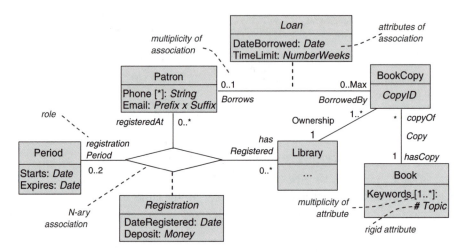

Figure 10.6 *Object model fragment for the library system*

- max = *: in any state, there may be an arbitrary number of target instances associated with a given source instance, *n* say, with *n* > 0. For example, a given Book instance may have an arbitrary number of BookCopy instances linked to it by the Copy association (see Figure 10.6).

We may use shortcut notations for multiplicities in the following situations:

- When min = max, we may just write the single value as a multiplicity, e.g. '1' for '1..1'.

- In the case of unconstrained multiplicities, we may just write '*' for '0..*'.

Multiplicities, domain properties and goals

Multiplicities formalize a restricted class of statements about linked objects. We can specify certain domain properties of associations, such as:

A train may be at one platform at most at a time

and certain goals constraining associations, such as:

A patron may not borrow more than *Max* book copies at a time.

As already noted in Section 4.5, there is no way to distinguish among multiplicities which ones are descriptive and which ones are prescriptive. While decorating associations systematically with adequate multiplicities in an object model, it is therefore important to spot those that are prescriptive in order to include the corresponding assertion in the goal model. As a result of object model decoration by multiplicities new goals might be elicited that have been overlooked so far.

For example, a WHY question about the prescriptive multiplicity *0..Max* on the BorrowedBy side of the Loan association in Figure 10.6 might result in discovering the goal *LimitedLoanAmount*, the parent goal AvailabilityEnforced, other missing sub-goals to satisfy the latter goal and sub-goals to satisfy the *0..Max* multiplicity assertion (see Fig. 8.3).

Needless to say, most descriptive and prescriptive statements about associations cannot be formalized through multiplicities, for example a domain property such as:

A book copy may not be both borrowed and available at the same time

or goals such as:

Any borrowed book must be returned within two weeks
Patrons may only access information about their own loans

Such statements need to be formulated in natural language as domain invariants or goals in the object or goal models, respectively, or expressed in a formal specification language for more sophisticated analysis; see Chapters 17–18. .

10.4 Attributes

Entities, associations, agents and events are structured in an object model through their attributes and associations with other objects.

An *attribute* is an intrinsic feature of an object regardless of other objects in the model. It has a name and a range of values. More precisely, an attribute *Att* of an object *Ob* is a partial function:

$$Att : Ob \rightarrow SORT,$$

where *SORT* denotes the range of possible values that the attribute may take.

We speak of *elementary* attributes when the attribute range is a set of atomic values, and *structured* attributes when this range is defined in terms of standard sort constructors such as *Tuple, SetOf, SequenceOf* or *Union*; each value in the range is then a tuple, set, sequence or alternative set of values, respectively.

Graphically, an attribute is declared in the lower part of the rectangle representing the object that it characterizes; this rectangle is hanging on the corresponding edge or diamond when the object is an association. Figure 10.6 shows a model fragment for our library system that includes a few attribute declarations. For example, Keywords is is an attribute characterizing the Book entity; Email is an attribute characterizing the Patron agent; and Deposit and TimeLimit are attributes characterizing the Registration and Loan associations, respectively.

For each declared attribute, a precise semantics must be stated in a **Has** annotation, as discussed in Section 10.1.5 (see Figure 10.2). For example, we should explicitly state in a corresponding annotation that TimeLimit captures the maximum loan period, in number of weeks, for a given patron and book copy.

As we can see in Figure 10.6, an attribute declaration provides the signature of the corresponding function; the function domain – that is, the set of object instances characterized by the attribute – is left implicit. The range can be declared through predefined sorts (such as

String or Boolean), domain-specific names or explicit enumeration. Here are some examples of attribute declarations:

CopyAvailable: **Boolean**	(elementary attribute of **BookCopy** entity, predefined sort)
CopyID: *Year* x **Integer**	(structured attribute of **BookCopy**, *Tuple* sort constructor)
Name: **String**	(elementary attribute of **Patron** agent, predefined sort)
Email: *Prefix* x *Suffix*	(structured attribute of **Patron**, *Tuple* sort constructor)
Keywords: **SetOf**[*Topic*]	(structured attribute of **Book**, *SetOf* sort constructor on domain-specific sort)
dateRange: **SeqOf**[*Date*]	(structured attribute of **Requesting** association, *SequenceOf* sort constructor)
SpeedLimit: *Speed*	(elementary attribute of **Block** entity, domain-specific sort)
DoorsState: {open, closed}	(elementary attribute of **Train** entity, enumeration sort)

Attribute multiplicity

We may declare the minimum and maximum number of values that an attribute can take. The multiplicity of an attribute appears as a suffix to the attribute's name. It provides a shortcut way of stating that the attribute is optional or mandatory, and elementary or structured:

- The multiplicity [0..y] declares an attribute possibly with no value; that is, an optional attribute (whatever y is).

- The multiplicity [y..*] declares an attribute whose value may be a *set of* values.

The default multiplicity [1..1] declares an elementary and mandatory attribute; it is generally left implicit in the model. Frequent multiplicities include [0..1], [1..*], [1..*fixedNumber*], and [*].

For example, the attribute declaration Keywords [1..*]: *Topic* within the Book entity in Figure 10.6 states that any book in the library system must, in any state, have at least one value for its Keyword attribute, whose sort is *Topic*, and may have an arbitrary number of such values within a single state.

Rigid attributes

It is sometimes useful to indicate that the value of an attribute is normally not expected to change over time. A *rigid* attribute keeps the same value throughout entire system behaviours. Such an attribute does not contribute to the definition of an object state and to the characterization of object behaviours. If we know that an attribute is rigid we do not need to represent it in a state transition diagram; we do not need to animate it or show it in counterexample traces produced by a model checker and so forth. A rigid attribute may be indicated by prefixing the sort name in its declaration by '#', for example:

CopyID: # *Year* x **Integer**   SpeedLimit: # *Speed*   Capacity: # *NumberOfPassengers*

Associations vs relations

At this point we may note the difference between an *association* (or relationship in the entity-relationship sense) and a *relation* (in the mathematical sense; see Section 4.4.3). An association instance is a *single* tuple that can be individually characterized by attribute–value pairs; a relation instance is *a set of* tuples to which attribute–value pairs cannot be individually attached.

10.5 Built-in associations for structuring object models

This section introduces two predefined, domain-independent associations that we may use as model-structuring mechanisms. We discuss object specialization/generalization first and object decomposition/aggregation next.

10.5.1 Object specialization

The set of current instances defining an object can often be divided into subsets sharing common features while having their own distinguishing features. For example, the set of patrons currently registered in our library system could be divided into student patrons and staff patrons. Patron instances in both subsets have an e-mail address and may borrow copies of books; student patrons might, however, be subject to stricter loan rules. Such subsets of instances can be disjoint and together cover all object instances, or not. In the former case they define a partition over the object instances.

A *specialization* link may be introduced in a model between an object *SubOb* and an object *SuperOb* if every current instance of *SubOb* is a current instance of *SuperOb* as well; that is:

for any individual *o*:   **if** InstanceOf (*o, SubOb*) **then** InstanceOf (*o, SuperOb*)

In this binary association, the object *SubOb* plays the role *Specializes* whereas the object *SuperOb* plays the inverse role *Generalizes*. Object specialization thus amounts to set inclusion. (The synonyms '*IsA*' or '*SubClassOf*' are sometimes used in the literature for '*Specializes*'.)

As a built-in consequence, the object *SubOb* by default inherits all features of the object *SuperOb*, in particular the attributes of *SuperOb*, the associations in which *SuperOb* participates and its domain properties. The object *SubOb* may in addition have its own attributes, associations and domain properties. These specific features are the only ones that need to be explicitly attached to *SubOb* in the model.

Figure 10.7 shows a better structuring of a portion of the library model fragment shown in Figure 10.6. On the one hand, the Patron agent is specialized into sub-classes StudentPatron and StaffPatron; it is indeed the case that any current instance of StudentPatron is a current instance of Patron in view of the respective definitions of these concepts (see Figure 10.2 for the definition of the Patron object.). On the other hand, the concepts of BookCopy, JournalCopy and ProceedingsCopy may have emerged from elicitation sessions; they are generalized in Figure 10.7 into the concept of BorrowableItem. It is indeed the case that any current instance of ProceedingsCopy is, in our system, a current instance of BorrowableItem as well. Note that such a bottom-up introduction of specialization links may result in generalized concepts that might not be physically apparent in the system; they might not have been mentioned during elicitation sessions either.

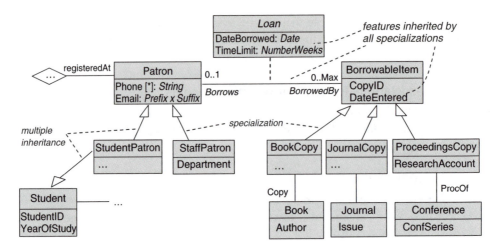

Figure 10.7   *Object specialization/generalization with inheritance of attributes and associations*

As a consequence of the specialization-based model structuring in Figure 10.7:

- The specialized agents StudentPatron and StaffPatron inherit, from the Patron agent, the attributes Phone and Email, plus the associations Loan and Registration and their attributes (such as TimeLimit of loans and Deposit on registrations).

- The specialized entities BookCopy, JournalCopy and ProceedingsCopy inherit, from the BorrowableItem entity, the attributes CopyID and DateEntered, plus the Loan association and its attributes.

Note that the specialized objects may have distinct features. For example, the StaffPatron entity has a Department attribute unlike StudentPatron; the ProceedingsCopy entity has a *ProcOf* association with Conference unlike the other specializations of BorrowableItem.

As specialization is a built-in association defined on conceptual objects, we can specialize entities, associations, agents and events. Feature inheritance includes the **Type** feature; the sub-class and super-class objects are both either entities or associations or agents or events.

We can also chain specialization links into paths with inheritance hierarchies as a result. For example, we might further specialize the StudentPatron agent in Figure 10.7 into a PhDstudentPatron agent, or further generalize the BorrowableItem entity in Figure 10.7 into a ReturnableResource entity. Such a richer structure should be introduced only if it is worth doing so; that is, if there are inheritable features to be captured in the model.

The benefits of specialization-based structuring of the object model should become clear at this point:

- Specialization links allow us to factor out features that are common to multiple objects into a single super-class object. Without feature duplication the resulting model is made lighter and simpler to understand.

- The introduction of super-class objects favours their reuse by specialization to other contexts. For example, the generalization of the entity BorrowableItem into ReturnableResource may lead to other specializations such as DVDcopy or VideoCopy and the reuse of the structural model in Figure 10.7, with slight adaptations, in a different system for DVD/Video rental (see Section 2.2.7 and the exercise at the end of this chapter).

- Specialization links may substantially increase the modifiability of large object models. The modifications of common, more general features are localized into the more general objects and propagated down by inheritance to all specializations.

Inhibiting inheritance

We may sometimes not want a feature to be inherited by default from the super-class object to the sub-class one. For example, the attribute declaration *Phone [*]: String* in the Patron agent in Figure 10.7 states that this attribute is optional; for staff patrons we may want this attribute to be mandatory, for example for quick pre-emptive access to copies under long-term loan. Inheritance is inhibited simply by redefining within the sub-class object, under the same name, those features that we don't want to inherit. As a general rule, *a more specific feature always overrides a more general one*. In this example, we would override the attribute declaration in the Patron agent simply by writing the declaration Phone [1..*]: String within the StaffPatron agent. The mechanism is similar for associations; an association redefined under the same name on the sub-class object overrides the association defined on the super-class object.

Multiple inheritance

An object may have multiple generalizations; any current instance of it must then be a current instance of each super-class object. For example, the StudentPatron agent in Figure 10.7 specializes both the Patron and Student agents; it is indeed the case that any individual who is currently a student patron must be registered both as a patron and as a student at the university. As a consequence, the sub-class object by default inherits all the features of all the objects it specializes. In Figure 10.7, the StudentPatron agent by default inherits, from the Patron agent, the attributes Phone and Email, the associations Loan and Registration together with their attributes and, from the Student agent, the attributes StudentID and YearOfStudy plus all associations in which the Student agent participates.

The previously noted benefits of specialization are thus boosted with multiple inheritance. We must, however, check that there is no *inheritance conflict*. This happens when the same feature is inherited from multiple sources under incompatible syntax or semantics. For example, let us assume that an Email attribute is attached to the Patron and the Student agents. Suppose that the **Has** annotation attached to the Patron agent states that this attribute captures the patron's private e-mail, whereas the **Has** annotation attached to the Student agent states that this attribute captures the student's university e-mail. There would be a semantic clash here in case of multiple inheritance of this feature in the StudentPatron agent. Once they are detected, inheritance conflicts are simply resolved by appropriate renaming of the conflicting attribute/association to remove the conflict. In our example, the conflict is resolved simply by renaming the Email attribute of Student into, say, UniversityEmail; the StudentPatron agent then inherits the Email and UniversityEmail attributes from the corresponding sources.

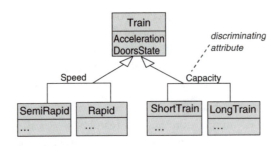

Figure 10.8 *Multiple specializations and discriminators*

Multiple specializations

In addition to multiple generalizations, an object may also have multiple specializations. This typically happens in modelling situations where we want to distinguish different subsets of object instances according to different criteria. The same object instance is then generally a member of multiple subsets – one per criterion. We speak of *discriminator* when the specialization criterion corresponds to different values of a single attribute in the super-class object; different discriminator values define different sub-class objects. The inherited attribute is then singled out as a discriminator labelling the corresponding specialization links. Figure 10.8 illustrates this for our train system. The Speed and Capacity attributes of the Train entity are taken out of this entity to label corresponding specializations as discriminators.

10.5.2 Object aggregation

We may sometimes need to model composite objects; these are structurally made of parts that are objects as well. For example, a library may structurally be seen as composed of parts such as a directory, shelves, an anti-theft device and so on.

An *aggregation* link may be introduced between an object $AggOb$ and objects $PartOb_1, \ldots,$ $PartOb_n$ if every current instance of $AggOb$ is a tuple of current instances of $PartOb_1, \ldots,$ $PartOb_n$:

for any individual o: **if** InstanceOf $(o, AggOb)$ **then** $o = [o_1, \ldots, o_n]$ **with** InstanceOf $(o_i, PartOb_i)$

In this built-in association, the object $AggOb$ plays the role *Aggregates* whereas the objects $PartOb_1, \ldots, PartOb_n$ play the role *PartOf*.

Composition is a particular case of aggregation where the composite object $AggOb$ and its parts $PartOb_i$ appear and disappear together in the system. The component object may be part of a single composite object only and, in addition to the preceding aggregation condition, we must have:

for any individual o: **if** $o = [o_1, \ldots, o_n]$ **and not** InstanceOf $(o, AggOb)$ **then not** InstanceOf $(o_i, PartOb_i)$

Figure 10.9 illustrates the use of aggregation and composition in structural modelling. An anti-theft device is introduced there as a structural component of a library. This component is

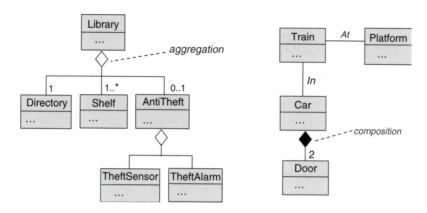

Figure 10.9   *Object aggregation and composition*

itself an aggregation of sensor and alarm devices. On the right-hand side of Figure 10.9, a train car is structurally defined as a composition of two doors. The latter exist in the system if and only if the former exists in the system as well; if a train instance disappears from the system so do its doors.

Like any association, aggregations may be decorated with multiplicities. We may in particular express whether the parts of an aggregation are mandatory or optional. In Figure 10.9, the anti-theft device is stated as optional.

Aggregation links are obviously antisymmetrical and transitive. In Figure 10.9, AntiTheft is not part of TheftAlarm, and TheftAlarm is among the parts of the Library entity. We may thus define *PartOf* hierarchies.

As aggregation is a built-in association defined on conceptual objects, we can aggregate entities, associations, agents and events. The parts may be of different types. For example, the objects Library and Shelve in Figure 10.9 are entities whereas AntiTheft is an agent.

Note that we cannot define attributes as aggregates of sub-attributes, as they are not objects. Attributes are structured by structuring the range in their declaration, for example the components of a Date attribute can be captured by a declaration Date: *Day×Month×Year*. Any Date value is thereby structured as a tuple of corresponding values for *Day*, *Month* and *Year*.

10.6 More on class diagrams

This section reviews a few more UML features that sometimes prove useful in practical modelling situations. These include derived attributes/associations, OR-associations, ordered associations and associations of associations.

10.6.1 Derived attributes and associations

It is sometimes convenient to introduce a controlled form of redundancy into a model by making explicit a structural feature that would otherwise be left implicit. Making such a feature explicit allows us to make shortcut references to it.

A *derived attribute* attached to an object is an attribute defined in terms of other attributes of this object. Likewise, a *derived association* on an object is an association defined in terms of other associations in which the object participates. To point out that a derived attribute/association is structurally redundant in the model, its name in the graphical declaration has to be prefixed by '/'. The attribute definition in a Has annotation must make it clear how the attribute/association can be derived from other object features.

For example, there might be multiple statements about reminders and fines in the library system that refer to the due return date of borrowed items. The attributes attached to the Loan association in Figure 10.7 include *DateBorrowed*, the date at which the loan is initiated, and *TimeLimit*, the maximum loan period. We may therefore add the following derived attribute to the Loan association:

> / ReturnDate: *Date*
> ... % ReturnDate: date at a time distance of *TimeLimit* weeks from *DateBorrowed* %...

For similar reasons, we might introduce a derived association / *DoorsOf* linking the Door and Train entities in Figure 10.9. This association is derived by relational composition of the *PartOf* and *In* associations. In Figure 10.2, it might be useful to attach *Moving* as a derived Boolean attribute to *Train*; the derivation rule is already provided there, see the first domain invariant in Figure 10.2.

10.6.2 OR-associations

There are associations where the same role can be played by multiple alternative objects. The set of instances playing this role is the *union* of the sets of instances defining those alternative objects. Such associations are called *OR-associations*. They are represented by a dotted line connecting the links to the alternative objects playing the same role.

Figure 10.10 illustrates a binary OR-association linking the BorrowableItem entity on one side and the Book and Journal entities playing the *MasterOf* role on the other side. This model fragment states that a borrowable item is a copy of either a book or a journal.

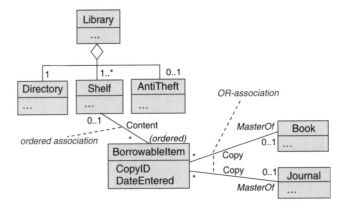

Figure 10.10 *OR-associations and ordered associations*

In Figure 6.3 in Chapter 6, the *Derivation* association is an OR-association as well (not represented there in the UML syntax for such associations). Two alternative objects play the *DerivedFrom* role in this association; namely, RD item and SW lifecycle item. The model in Figure 6.3 states that an RD item can be met by one or several other items, each being either a RD item or a downward software lifecycle item.

10.6.3 Ordered associations

When an association maps a single source instance onto multiple target instances, we can specify that these target instances are ordered according to some ordering to be defined in an annotation. (The single source instance is an object instance in the case of a binary association, or a (n-1)-tuple of object instances in the case of an n-ary association.) The target side of the association is decorated with the keyword *(ordered)* to indicate such ordering.

For example, the model portion in Figure 10.10 states that a library shelf contains a certain number of borrowable items that are ordered according to, say, year of purchase followed by serial number.

10.6.4 Associations of associations

As previously mentioned in Section 10.3, an association like any object may be involved in another association under a specific role. Associations of associations are sometimes needed in complex structural models.

For example, consider an online reservation system that allows us to reserve seats for performances, where a performance refers to a concert at a concert hall during a season. We might have good reason to consider the concepts of Concert, Hall and Season as first-class citizens to which we can attach attributes and associations. The Performance concept therefore must be structurally modelled as a ternary association on Concert, Hall and Season. As reservations refer to specific seats for specific performances, it is natural to model the concept of Reservation structurally as a binary association linking the Seat entity and Performance association; see Figure 10.11.

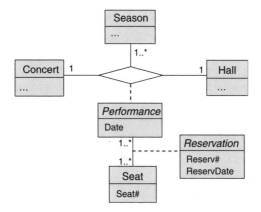

Figure 10.11 *Association of associations*

10.7 Heuristic rules for building object models

A good object model should be adequate, complete, consistent and pertinent. Building such a model for a complex system is commonly recognized in the literature on UML and conceptual modelling as a difficult task requiring skilled and highly experienced modellers. This section shows that, on the contrary, this task can be made surprisingly easy. The object model is built in a systematic fashion from the goal model through derivation rules and associated heuristics. By construction, the resulting model is complete, pertinent and traceable with respect to the goal model. (The notions of goal-oriented completeness and pertinence were defined in Section 7.4. Derivational traceability links were discussed in Section 6.3.1.)

Section 10.7.1 describes the overall process of deriving object models incrementally from goals and domain properties found in the goal model. A number of specific questions arise while following this process. They are addressed by heuristics presented in the next few sections. These include rules for determining whether a concept referenced in the specification of a goal or a domain property should be modelled as an object or as an attribute (Section 10.7.2) and, in the case of an object, whether it should be modelled as an entity, a binary or n-ary association, an agent or an event (Section 10.7.3). Other guiding rules can be used for deciding whether an attribute should be attached to an object or to an association linking it (Section 10.7.4), and for deciding whether an association should be a domain-specific one or an aggregation (Section 10.7.5). Heuristics for introducing object specializations/generalizations are presented in Section 10.7.6. Some common pitfalls and bad smells are finally reviewed in Section 10.7.7.

10.7.1 Deriving pertinent and complete class diagrams from goal diagrams

Concern links were briefly introduced in Section 8.4 as the interface between the goal model and the object model. A goal *concerns* a conceptual object if its specification refers to this object.

For example, the goal Maintain[SpeedBelowBlockLimit] is specified by a **Def** annotation stating that:

> The *speed* of a <u>train</u> <u>on</u> a <u>block</u> may never exceed the *limit* associated with that block.

This specification clearly refers to the Train and Block concepts. The instances of these concepts are distinctly identifiable, can be enumerated in any system state, share similar features and differ on states and specific behaviours. The goal therefore concerns the Train and Block objects. According to the first rule below, these objects should be found in the object model. The goal specification also refers to a train being *On* a block. According to the next rule below, *On* should be an association linking Train and Block; the goal concerns this association as well. According to rules introduced in the next sections, the Train and Block objects will be classified as entities. The concepts of Speed and SpeedLimit will emerge as attributes of Train and Block, respectively, as they are also referred to in the goal specification.

(H1) Deriving objects from the goal model

Introduce in the object model all conceptual objects which the goals and domain properties from the goal model refer to, and only those.

This heuristic rule ensures that (a) the object model will be *complete* with respect to the system goals, and (b) all objects in the model are *pertinent* with respect to those goals (see Section 7.4).

To apply this rule, we need to review all the concepts referred to in every goal/property specification from the goal model, and retain those satisfying the criteria for being an object (see Section 10.1.1). The above example illustrates this.

(H2) Deriving associations from the goal model

Identify associations and participating objects from linking expressions in the specification of goals and domain properties.

In every goal/property specification, we look for conceptual links from linking phrase patterns such as:

    <source> <linkingVerb> <target>   or   <linkingNoun> of <target> by <source>

The linking verb/noun yields an association, whereas the link source and target yield participating objects under corresponding roles. In such patterns, a source or target may refer to multiple objects in the case of an n-ary association.

In addition to the preceding example yielding the *On* association linking the Train and Block objects, consider the goal Maintain[WorstCaseStoppingDistance]. This goal states that:

    The distance between two trains <u>following</u> each other shall always be sufficient to prevent the *back*
    train from hitting the *front* train in case the latter stops suddenly.

The underlined linking expression indicates a binary reflexive association on the Train object with roles *back* and *front*, respectively.

Note that the heuristic rules in (*H1*) and (*H2*) provide yet another reason for goal/property specifications to be precise (in addition to those discussed in Section 8.1). The heuristic rule in (*H2*) may sometimes require specification rephrasing to highlight linking expressions.

The derivation of associations, participating objects and attributes becomes straightforward when the goal/property specifications are formalized (see Section 4.4.2 and Chapters 17–18). For example, the previous specification of the goal Maintain[SpeedBelowBlockLimit] is easily formalized by:

    $\forall$ tr: Train, bl: Block
    On (tr, bl) $\Rightarrow$ tr.Speed $\leqslant$ bl.SpeedLimit

In view of the predicate notation for the built-in *InstanceOf* relation on associations introduced in Section 10.3, the association *On* and participating objects Train and Block are derived directly, together with the attributes Speed and SpeedLimit of Train and Block, respectively. Similarly, the formalization of the preceding specification for the goal Maintain[WorstCaseStoppingDistance] is:

    $\forall$ tr1, tr2: Train
    Following (tr2, tr1) $\Rightarrow$ tr2.Position – tr1.Position > tr2.WCS-Dist,

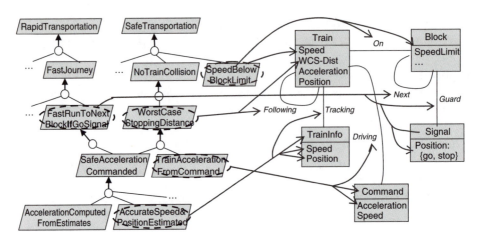

Figure 10.12 *Incremental derivation of an object model from a goal model*

which directly yields the *Following* reflexive association on the Train object, and the Position and WCS-Dist attributes of Train.

Figure 10.12 shows the incremental derivation of an object model from portions of a goal model. In addition to the previous derivations from the goals SpeedBelowBlockLimit and WorstCaseStoppingDistance, Figure 10.12 depicts the derivation of the *Next* and *Guard* associations from the goal FastRunToNextBlockIfGoSignal, together with participating objects and attributes; the derivation of the *Driving* association from the goal TrainAccelerationFromCommand, together with participating objects and attributes; and the derivation of the *Tracking* association from the goal AccurateSpeed&PositionEstimated, together with participating objects and attributes.

(H3) Introducing software-environment tracking associations

Identify tracking associations between environment objects and software counterparts for goal realizability by a software agent.

The unrealizability-driven refinement patterns in Chapter 8 capture a frequent situation where we would like a software agent to be responsible for a goal concerning an environment object that the agent cannot monitor or control (see Figures 8.25 and 8.26). A monitorable/controllable 'image' of the object should then be introduced at the interface between the software and the environment, together with an accuracy goal requiring this image to reflect the environment object accurately. This frequent situation results in the association pattern shown in Figure 10.13. The environment object named *Object* and its software image *Obj-Info* are linked by a generic one-to-one *Tracking* association constrained by the accuracy goal. The latter typically prescribes that every attribute *Att* of the shared image *Obj-Info* has the same value in the current state as the corresponding attribute *Att* of the environment object, possibly up to some acceptable difference – for example, the value in the environment at most x time units before, or some value within an acceptable error threshold y.

An instantiation of this pattern does in fact appear in Figure 10.12; the accuracy goal there concerns the estimated *Speed* and *Position* of the *TrainInfo* image of *Train*.

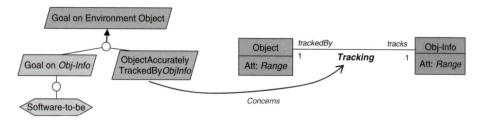

Figure 10.13 *Introducing a software counterpart of an environment object: the Tracking association*

The *Tracking* association pattern is applicable in any situation where a monitorable/controllable counterpart of unshared phenomena must be introduced for goal assignment to the software-to-be. In the library system, for example, this pattern leads to the introduction of new objects BookCopyInfo, LoanInfo and PatronInfo, which track their environment counterpart in Figure 10.6 and are controllable by the software-to-be.

(H4) Identifying associations from domain invariants on multiple objects

The domain properties used while modelling the system need to be attached as invariants on single objects (see Section 10.1.5). Such properties might seem to involve multiple objects. For example, consider the following physical constraint on meeting scheduling:

> Two meetings cannot take place in the same room at the same time.

What object should this invariant be attached to? The property might be seen to constrain the Meeting object or the Room object (a room cannot accommodate more than one meeting at a time). Such cases where it seems hard or arbitrary to attach the invariant to a single candidate reveal a possibly missing association between the candidate objects constrained by the property. This association should be made explicit in the model, and the property should be attached to it as domain invariant. In this example, the *Allocation* association should be introduced between the Meeting and Room objects as a result of this heuristic rule.

The heuristic rules in *(H1)–(H4)* are grounded on the objective of obtaining an object model that is complete, pertinent and traceable with respect to the goals and domain properties of the goal model. It should, however, be noted that the derivation links between those two models can be *bidirectional*:

- There might be objects or attributes that are felt necessary in the object model without being referred to by any goal from the goal model. In such cases, the questioning of *WHY* the object/attribute should appear in the object model may result in the discovery of a goal or domain property that was missing from the goal model.

- While systematically decorating associations with multiplicities on every side, we might specify prescriptive multiplicity constraints that are not found in the goal model. These should be added to it together with their WHYs and HOWs, as already discussed in Section 10.3.

10.7.2 Object or attribute?

While deriving the object model from the goal model, the question frequently arises of whether a conceptual item referenced in a goal/property specification should be modelled as an object or as an attribute of some object. For example, should the concept of Author of a book be structurally modelled as an object or as an attribute of Book? The following rule provides a definite criterion for deciding.

(H5) Identifying attributes

Model a conceptual item as an attribute when it is a function we don't want to structure conceptually; that is, (a) its instances need not be distinguished, (b) we don't need to attach attributes/associations to it, specialize it or aggregate/decompose it, and (c) its range is not a conceptual object we want to specialize or attach attributes/associations.

To be considered as an attribute, the item must be a function (by definition of what an attribute is). When applied to an object instance it may return at most one value, possibly structured. For example, Author might be candidate for being an attribute, declared by Author: SeqOf[Name], as it cannot return more than one value for the same book; that is, more than one sequence of book co-authors. Whether Author should be an object, linked to Book by a Writing association, or an attribute of Book depends on whether we need to consider book authors as first-class citizens or not. If we want to specialize this concept (for example to ScientificEditor) or attach attributes/associations to it (for example author's birth date or research interests), then we need to make it an object rather than an attribute of Book.

According to this heuristic rule the Speed and SpeedLimit items in the preceding specification of the goal Maintain[SpeedBelowBlockLimit] should be modelled as attributes; they meet criteria (a)–(c). On the other hand, the Department attribute of StaffPatron in Figure 10.7 might be questioned on those grounds. If the goal model requires university departments to be structured in terms of specializations (for example Science or Humanities departments) or of attributes/associations (for example departments *Managing* their own library), then we need to make Department an object rather than an attribute.

10.7.3 Entity, association, agent or event?

If a conceptual item referenced in a goal/property specification has been determined to be an object, the next question is whether this object should be an entity, an association, an agent or an event. The next rule is based on the definition of these types of object to provide a decision criterion.

(H6) Determining the type of an object

Model a conceptual object as an event if its instances may exist in a single state only; as an agent if its instances can control behaviours of instances of other objects; as an entity if its instances are passive and autonomous; and as an association if its instances are passive and dependent on other object instances they are linking.

According to this rule, a train *start* is an event instance; a train *actuator* is an agent instance; a *train* is an entity instance; and a train *being at* some platform is an association instance.

If a conceptual object referenced in a goal/property specification has been determined to be an association, the next question is whether this association should be a binary or n-ary one. The next rule provides a criterion for deciding.

(H7) Identifying n-ary associations

Model an association as an n-ary one (n > 2) if, for any of the n participating items, (a) the item needs to be considered as an object, and (b) association tuples that differ only on its instances need to be distinguished.

For example, consider the *allocation* of a meeting to a room with some equipment. A ternary association linking Meeting, Room and Equipment should be introduced if each of these concepts should be considered as an object (rather than an attribute), in view of goal/property specifications, and allocations of the same meeting to the same room with different equipment need to be distinguished as different allocations. This rule was also used to make *Registration* a ternary association in Figure 10.4; see the explanation for it in Section 10.3.

10.7.4 Attribute of a linked object or of the linking association?

If a conceptual item referenced in a goal/property specification has been determined to be an attribute, there might be hesitation about what object this attribute should be attached to. This arises particularly when the attribute explicitly qualifies an object while implicitly referring to an association linking this object. For example, a goal/property specification might refer to the borrowing date of a copy of a book; should we attach the DateBorrowed attribute to the BookCopy entity or to the Loan association? The following rule provides a criterion for deciding.

(H8) Attaching attributes to associations

Attach an attribute to an association when it directly or indirectly characterizes all participating objects, especially if there might be no instance currently participating in a particular role.

In other words, a 0..x multiplicity on one side of an association (whatever x is) calls for attachment to the association of attributes implicitly referring to all participating objects. The reason is that we lose information otherwise. For example, if DateBorrowed is attached to BookCopy instead of Loan, we cannot know which Patron instance was borrowing some BookCopy instance at some DateBorrowed earlier to the current state in which there is no Loan link among such instances (see Figure 10.14).

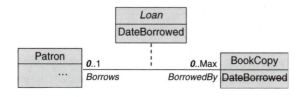

Figure 10.14   *Attaching attributes to associations with possibly unlinked parties*

10.7.5 Aggregation or association?

As an association instance and an aggregation instance are both tuples of objects (by definition), the question may arise whether a structural link type between a composite object and component objects should be modelled as an association or as an aggregation. The following rule provides a criterion for deciding.

(H9) Preferring associations to aggregations

Model a structural link type between a composite object and component objects as an association if any of the following conditions holds: (a) its semantic definition, in terms of the InstanceOf *relation, is domain specific; (b) the composite and component objects appear to be independent from each other; or (c) it might be worth attaching attributes/associations to the link type.*

In all other cases an aggregation or composition may be envisaged, by definition of these built-in associations. As conditions (a)–(c) cannot necessarily be evaluated in a clear-cut sense, we should go for a domain-specific association in the case of doubt.

For example, the structural link type named *In* in Figure 10.9 was chosen to be an association as Car and Train instances are relatively independent from each other (a train car might belong to one train in one state and to another train in subsequent states). Moreover we may want to attach attributes to *In*, for example the position of a car in a train. It may also be worth making it explicit, in a **Def** annotation, under what conditions a car may or may not be part of a train.

10.7.6 Specializing and generalizing concepts

Section 10.5.1 discussed the benefits of specialization-based structuring of object models – lighter and simpler models thanks to the factorization of common features in super-class objects; reuseability of model fragments in other systems; and increased modifiability of models by propagation of changed features down inheritance hierarchies. We should therefore introduce specialization/generalization links in our models wherever such benefits are expected. The following heuristics make this further explicit.

(H10) Identifying specializations

Identify specializations from classification expressions and discriminant factors in the specification of goals and domain properties.

In every goal/property specification from the goal model, we look for classification expressions from keywords such as 'type', 'category', 'class' and so on. We check whether the corresponding items meet the criteria for being objects (see Section 10.1.1). Then we look for commonalities and differences among them to check whether factorization in super-class objects and specialization into sub-class objects brings the expected benefits of feature inheritance. If so, we restructure the model accordingly through specialization links and attachment of common, inheritable attributes, associations and domain invariants to the super-class object.

Multiple classification schemes might appear when we apply this heuristic. To maximize the structural cohesion within each sub-class, it is preferable then to introduce different specialization schemes according to different discriminating factors (see Figure 10.8). Each sub-class object then meets a single classification criterion.

In the meeting scheduling system, for example, this heuristic rule might lead us to identify specializations of the Participant agent according to the Status of their instances. Such specialization might be derived from a goal prescribing discriminating rules for handling preference constraints. It should be kept separate from another specialization based on different access rights to the system.

(H11) Identifying generalizations

Identify generalizations from objects characterized by similar attributes, associations or invariants.

This heuristic complements the previous one in that here we proceed bottom up from already identified objects to find common abstractions that are not necessarily referred to in goal/property specifications. Such abstractions might not be physically observable in the system – see for example the BorrowableItem abstraction in Figure 10.7. While doing so, multiple generalization schemes might appear. They should be introduced in the model provided that the aforementioned benefits can be expected from multiple inheritance of features attached to the different abstractions.

For example, the generalization of the Meeting object into a Gathering abstraction that gathers attendants in specific rooms at specific dates might result in the handling of multiple meeting variants suggested in the case study description (see Section 1.1.2), and in the reuse of portions of the generalized object model for a course organization system where no constraints handling is required apart from some restricted rules for teachers.

10.7.7 Avoiding common pitfalls

Finally, there are a number of problems, bad smells and confusions frequently found in models produced by novice modellers that we should be aware of and avoid. They generally arise from implementation biases, due to the modeller's programming background, or from confusion among different system views.

(H12) Avoiding pointers as attributes

Avoid object attributes that amount to pointers to other objects: Use binary associations instead.

An attribute may not have a conceptual object as a range. Pointers are a programming construct, not a modelling one; they implement premature choices that can discard others. Such choices must be deferred to the implementation stage of the software part of the system. Figure 10.15 illustrates the problem.

(H13) Avoiding non-structural links

Do not pollute the object model with non-structural links between objects that pertain to other system views.

Figure 10.15 *Using pointers instead of associations*

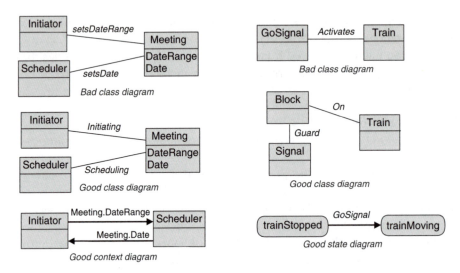

Figure 10.16   *Confusing system views*

The object model should capture static and structural links only. Monitoring/control links defining the interfaces among agents must be captured in the agent model, for example through context diagrams (see Chapter 11). Dynamic links among objects must be captured, in a more precise way, in the behaviour model of the system through scenarios and state machines (see Chapter 13).

Figure 10.16 illustrates such confusion among different system models and the representation of non-structural links in an object model. In the left-hand part, the upper diagram conveys interface information that should be found in the agent model. In the right-hand part, the upper diagram conveys dynamic information that should be found in the behaviour model of the system.

(H14) Avoiding obscure concept names

Names for objects, attributes and ranges should be chosen as a suggestive shortcut for what they actually designate. This is important for a quick understanding of the model while browsing through it. The selected names will also be used as entries in the glossary of terms. They define a common vocabulary among stakeholders to be used throughout the RE lifecycle (possibly with synonyms if the latter were agreed in an annotation; see Section 10.1.5).

We should therefore prefer specific names over unspecific ones (e.g. 'Patron' or 'Borrower' rather than 'Person'), avoid confusing names (e.g. 'Book' for 'BookCopy'), favour terms commonly used in the domain (e.g. 'Proceedings' rather than 'ConferenceBook') and avoid any implementation terminology or unnecessary jargon (e.g. use 'Directory' rather than 'BookFile').

More importantly, exactly what such names designate must be made fully precise in the definition of the conceptual item provided in **Def** and **Has** annotations (see Section 10.1.5). This definition must be adequate, complete, formulated precisely in terms of measurable system phenomena and agreed by all parties involved in the RE process.

Summary

- An object model provides a structural view of the system-as-is or system-to-be. It shows how the concepts involved in relevant environment phenomena are structured in terms of individual features and relationships with other concepts. The model gathers all concept definitions and domain properties used in the goal, agent, operation and behaviour models of the system. It introduces a common vocabulary to refer to. A glossary of terms can be generated from it on which all parties involved in the project should agree and which they should use for unambiguous reference.

- A conceptual object is a set of instances of a domain-specific concept; such instances are distinctly identifiable, can be enumerated in any system state, share similar features and differ on states and specific behaviours. The features shared by object instances include the object's definition, type, individual attributes, associations with other objects, domain invariants and initial state. The object's attributes and associations are instantiated as *state variables* in terms of which object instances can be characterized. Specific values for these variables define specific states of object instances. The built-in *InstanceOf* semantic relation, interpreted over system states, allows us to determine which individuals are instances of the object in the current state.

- There are different types of conceptual objects that we can model in the structural view of a system. An entity is an autonomous and passive object. An association is a passive object dependent on other objects it links conceptually. An agent is an autonomous and active object. An event is a single-state object.

- An attribute is a function from an object to a range that we do not want to model conceptually through other attributes and associations. Such a range may be structured through standard type constructors.

- An object model is graphically represented by an annotated UML class diagram showing conceptual objects, their attributes and the associations among them. Every object must be precisely defined in a **Def** annotation. Such a definition should provide a system-specific interpretation of the *InstanceOf* relation by stating the necessary and sufficient conditions for an individual to be currently an instance of the object. The **Has** annotation must precisely define the system-specific meaning of every attribute.

- An association structurally amounts to a tuple of objects each playing a specific role in the association. Every association can be characterized by a predicate on instance variables; this predicate holds in the current state if the corresponding object instances are currently linked. Even though binary associations are more common, n-ary associations are needed when we must distinguish links among n objects that differ just on one participating instance ($n > 2$). Multiplicities formalize a restricted class of statements about linked objects. Some of these may capture domain properties, others may capture goals that should be refined/abstracted in the goal model. We may also specify the multiplicity of an attribute in its declaration, in particular when we want to state that an attribute is optional or has multiple values.

- Object specialization is a built-in association corresponding to set inclusion. The sub-class object by default inherits all attributes, associations and domain invariants of the super-class object while having its own distinguishing features. Feature inheritance can be inhibited by feature override in the sub-class. An object may have different specializations according to different discriminators; and it may inherit features from multiple super-classes. Specialization-based structuring makes models simpler by factorization of common features in super-class objects; feature changes are propagated down along inheritance hierarchies; generalized objects can be reused in other systems.

- Aggregation is a built-in structural association between a composite object and component objects that are parts of it. Composition is a particular case of aggregation where the composite object and its components appear and disappear together in the system. If we need a system-specific definition of what is meant for an object to be part of another, we should use a domain-specific association instead.

- An object model can be built systematically from a goal model by application of derivation rules and associated heuristics. By analysing the specification of goals and domain properties, we can identify all the objects that they refer to. Associations are derivable from predicative expressions linking objects in those specifications. For goal realizability by a software agent, we often need to introduce monitorable/controllable counterparts of environment objects together with tracking associations. Object specializations can be identified from classification expressions and discriminant factors in goal/property specifications. Domain invariants on multiple objects may reveal an implicit, missing association between them. During such incremental derivation of an object model from a goal model, we may use a variety of heuristics for deciding whether a particular concept should be an object or an attribute; in the case of an object, whether it should be an entity, a binary or n-ary association, an agent or an event; and in case of an attribute, what object it should be attached to. By construction, the resulting object model is complete, pertinent and traceable with respect to the goal model. Conversely, *WHY* questions about concepts felt necessary in the object model and association multiplicities may reveal goals missing from the goal model.

- A conceptual object model may not include non-structural aspects that pertain to other system views, such as interface or behavioural aspects, and implementation aspects such as object attributes pointing to other objects.

Notes and Further Reading

Various forms of entity-association diagrams, with or without specialization and aggregation, have emerged from work in database conceptual modelling (Chen, 1976; Pirotte, 1977; Smith & Smith, 1977), semantic networks for knowledge representation (Quillian, 1968; Brachman & Levesque, 1985) and conceptual graphs (Sowa, 1984). Those efforts from different disciplines were integrated in Brodie *et al.* (1984). Many extensions have been published over the years in the *Proceedings of the Entity-Relationship Conference* series. Precise semantics for concept specialization and inheritance were studied in Touretzky (1986).

The OMT multi-view modelling technique adopted ER diagrams for modelling structural aspects of software designs (Rumbaugh *et al.*, 1991). The subsequent UML standardization efforts are reported in Rumbaugh *et al.* (1999).

In the RE literature, the RML modelling language used generalization, aggregation and classification to structure models made of entities, operations and constraints (Greenspan *et al.*, 1982). The latter were expressed in a formal assertion language providing temporal referencing constructs. RML was probably the first requirements modelling language to have a precise semantics, defined in terms of mappings to first-order predicate logic (Greenspan *et al.*, 1986).

The integration of entities, events and temporal constraints was also studied in Bubenko (1980). Such entities and events take part in the real world surrounding the software-to-be (Jackson, 1978).

The ERAE specification language integrated entities, associations, attributes, events and formal assertions within a unified framework with well-defined semantics (Dubois *et al.*, 1991). The further integration of agents as conceptual structures for object models appeared in Dardenne *et al.* (1993). This paper also introduced the predicate notation for associations and the *Tracking* association between environment objects and their software counterpart (called '*Mapping*' there). The use of the *Tracking* association in refinement patterns is discussed in Letier and van Lamsweerde (2002a).

The *InstanceOf* built-in semantic relation was introduced in Letier's thesis (Letier, 2001) as a simpler, more elegant variant of the *Exists* built-in feature attached to objects in Dardenne *et al.* (1993).

The systematic derivation of object models from goal models was first discussed in van Lamsweerde (2000b). Complementary guidelines for entity–relationship modelling can be found in Wieringa (2003).

The use of specialization/generalization mechanisms as a basis for reusing structural models in RE is discussed in Reubenstein and Waters (1991), Maiden and Suttcliffe (1993), Ryan and Mathews (1993), Fowler (1997b), Massonet and van Lamsweerde (1997), Suttcliffe and Maiden (1998) and Konrad *et al.* (2004).

Exercises

- Classify the following concepts in an ambulance-dispatching system as an entity, an association, an agent, an event or an attribute, and explain the reasons for your classification:

    ambulance, incident, reception of an incident call, call assistant, incident form, incident location, ambulance crew, mobilization (of an ambulance to an incident), ambulance location, GPS system, ambulance breakdown.

- Based on your limited expertise in ambulance systems, give a precise definition of the conceptual objects Incident and Mobilization (of an ambulance to an incident) by adequate instantiation of the *InstanceOf* relation to the ambulance-dispatching domain.

- Based on the case study description in Section 1.1.2, give a precise definition of the conceptual objects Participant and Constraints by adequate instantiation of the *InstanceOf* relation to the meeting-scheduling domain. Define other individual features that should annotate these objects in a structural model of the meeting scheduling system.

- Where should the following domain properties be attached in an object model of the corresponding systems: (a) 'a train may be at one platform at most at a time', (b) 'a book copy may not be both borrowed and available at the same time'.

- Consider the Loan association between patrons and book copies. When does an instance of it appear in and disappear from the library system? What corresponding predicate becomes true and false, respectively?

- Consider the Requesting association between initiators and meetings in Chapter 4, Figure 4.5. Explain why the *min* multiplicity on the Meeting side is *1* in view of some adequate definition of the Initiator agent.

- Make structural changes to the model fragment for the library system in Figure 10.6 in order to capture a system where the time limit for a loan is different for academic and holiday periods.

- Build a structural model for the enrolment of students on courses that are given by alternative professors and can be taken during alternative semesters. Specify the multiplicities on all sides. How should the notions of credits and marks be represented?

- Consider the organization of a university into schools, departments and independent research institutes. Provide a structural model for such organization that shows where different types of personnel such as students, administrative staff, research associates and faculty members fit in. Make sure that you specify multiplicities and annotate their meaning in natural language.

- Suppose that we model the relative importance of participants in a meeting by the attribute declaration *Importance: {high, low}*. Should this declaration be attached to the Meeting entity, the Participant agent or the association Invitation between Meeting and Participant? Explain the domain-specific reasons for your answer.

- Restructure the model in Figure 10.7 to model a system where only non-privileged patrons need to register at the library; among these, student patrons and university outsiders should be distinguished.

- Generalize and then respecialize the object model in Figure 10.7 so that it can be reused for rental of CDs, DVDs and videos. You may want to reread Section 2.2.7 to get some context and inspiration for this exercise (see Figure 2.4).

- Suppose that the attribute declaration CopyID: *#Year* x Integer is found within the BorrowableItem entity in Figure 10.7. While structuring the value of a copy identifier as a pair (edition year, serial number) might be adequate for book copies or proceedings, such structuring is inadequate for journal issues. How would you solve this modelling problem?

- Consider the following **Def** annotation of the goal Achieve[FirstAmbulanceIntervention] in an ambulance-dispatching system:

  > For every urgent call reporting an incident, the first ambulance should arrive at the incident scene within 8 minutes for category A incidents (immediately life threatening) and within 14 minutes for category B incidents (all others).

  Use the heuristics in Section 10.7 to derive from this goal specification (a) a domain-specific association, (b) attributes of the association and/or on the linked objects, and (c) specialization links.

- Apply the *Tracking* association pattern in Figure 10.13 to extend the library object model fragment in Figure 10.6 with new objects such as BookCopyInfo, LoanInfo and PatronInfo that track their physical counterpart in Figure 10.6. Which goals should be added to the goal model?

- From your answer to the goal modelling exercise on the ambulance-dispatching system at the end of Chapter 8, derive a corresponding object model fragment for this system.

- Consider the simplified version of a patient-monitoring system given as the last exercise in Chapter 9 and the goal model you have built for it. Derive a full object model for this system from your goal model.

- Consider the meeting scheduling case study description in Section 1.1.2 and the entity–relationship model fragment in Chapter 4, Figure 4.5.

  a. The Meeting entity there has a Location attribute capturing the meeting venue. Suppose now that we want to further model the rooms where meetings may take place together with the resources they provide (number of seats, audio-video equipment etc.). Should the Room concept be modelled as an object or as an attribute? Explain your answer.

b. Explain why the DateRange concept should be modelled as an attribute, rather than an object, and why it should be attached to the Requesting association between Initiator and Meeting, rather than to the Meeting entity.

c. Extend the model in Figure 4.5 from the goal model fragment in Chapter 8, Figure 8.11. The latter might concurrently be extended for wider coverage of the case study description in Section 1.1.2.

- Find a few common abstractions to a system for allocating berths to tankers and a system for allocating airport gates to landing aircrafts. The core concepts from these two systems should be generalized so that they can be defined as specializations of those common abstractions and inherit interesting features from them.

- Based on the case study description in Section 1.1.2 and the goal model fragments in Chapter 8, complete the object model fragments given in this chapter for the train control and library management systems. The goal model fragments in Chapter 8 might concurrently be extended for broader coverage of the case study description in Section 1.1.2.

- Section 3.2 defines the concept of project risk in terms of other concepts such as *objective* being not achieved, *likelihood* of occurrence, *consequences* and their *severity* and so on. Build an object meta-model linking such concepts structurally.

- Object models are structured in terms of concepts such as *object, entity, association, agent, event, attribute, range, arity, multiplicity, identification, specialization* and so on. Build an object *meta-model* linking such concepts structurally together. This meta-model should be structured in terms of meta-objects, meta-links and meta-attributes. It should provide an outline view of the material in this chapter.

11

Modelling System Agents and Responsibilities

In our multi-view modelling framework for RE, this chapter is dedicated to the responsibility view of the system we want to model – who is doing what, and why. This view covers the *WHO*-dimension of requirements engineering introduced in Chapter 1.

Agents were introduced in Chapters 7–8 as active system components that are responsible for the leaf goals in a goal model. The preceding chapter showed how their structural features can be modelled in an object model. This chapter complements that introductory material by focusing on how we can further model agents and their responsibilities. Responsibility assignments rely on agent capabilities. The latter are defined in terms of ability to monitor or control object attributes and associations defined in the object model. A goal assigned to an agent must be realizable by this agent in view of its capabilities. An agent can also be decomposed into finer-grained ones with finer-grained responsibilities. It may be related to other agents through dependency links. An *agent model* captures agent capabilities, responsibilities, interfaces and, possibly, refinements, wishes (for human agents), beliefs and dependencies. We can represent such a model by an agent diagram or, under a more restricted form, by a context diagram or a dependency diagram. (Context diagrams were introduced in Section 4.3.1.).

An agent model serves multiple purposes. It shows the distribution of responsibilities within the system and provides a basis for load analysis (we come back to this kind of analysis in Section 16.1). It defines the system scope and configuration, in terms of agents and their interfaces, and in particular the boundary between the software-to-be and its environment. We may formulate heuristics for responsibility assignment and capture dependency chains among agents for vulnerability analysis. An agent model may also serve as an input to software architecture design.

Section 11.1 summarizes what we know about agents from the previous chapters while making this notion more precise. Section 11.2 discusses the various features that we can capture about an agent in a model. Section 11.3 introduces agent diagrams, context diagrams and dependency diagrams as possible means for representing agent models or parts of them.

Section 11.4 describes agent refinement as a structuring mechanism for decomposing agents and responsibility assignments into finer-grained ones. Section 11.5 provides a number of heuristics and tips to help modellers build agent models. In particular, we will see how a context diagram can be derived systematically from a goal model.

11.1 What are agents?

As introduced in Section 7.1, an *agent* is an active system component playing a role in goal satisfaction. To play such a role, the agent instances need to restrict their behaviour by adequate control of system items. What matters here is not the agent's properties as an individual but the *role* that the agent plays in the system for goal satisfaction. In the meeting scheduling system, for example, we are not interested in the specific properties of Initiator or Participant instances as individuals but in their role in satisfying goals such as the prompt availability of meeting constraints.

From an operational standpoint, we might see an agent as a processor that performs operations under restricted conditions to satisfy the goals for which it is responsible. Such conditions correspond to permissions and obligations that are defined for every operation in the operation model (as the next chapter will show).

For reasoning about responsibilities and derivation of such permissions and obligations, we need to split multi-agent responsibilities on coarse-grained goals into single-agent responsibilities on fine-grained goals. The latter are leaf goals to be assigned to software agents as requirements or to environment agents as expectations.

For an agent to be assigned to a goal, the goal must be realizable by the agent in view of its capabilities. Agent capabilities are defined in terms of object attributes and associations that the agent can monitor or control. The notions of capabilities and goal realizability will be made precise in Section 11.2.

Complex systems are inherently concurrent. Global system behaviours are composed of multiple concurrent behaviours. Agent instances may therefore run concurrently with others. True concurrency turns to be necessary, as two different agent instances may need to fulfil their obligations in the same state by triggering their respective operations. (Concurrency based on interleaving of agent instances would therefore not work.)

When it has no obligation in the current state, an agent instance may decide to apply an operation, provided that the corresponding permissions are fulfilled, or to apply it later. The system is therefore non-deterministic. We come back to non-determinism and concurrency issues in Section 12.4 when the notion of operation will be more precisely defined.

Agent categories

There are different categories of agents that we can find in a system:

- *New software agents* to be developed such as software controllers, information managers or Web services.

- *Existing software agents* such as legacy, off-the-shelf or foreign components with which the software-to-be will have to interoperate.

- *Devices* such as sensors, actuators, measurement instruments, radars, communication media, network infrastructures and so on.

- *Human agents* playing specific roles such as organizational units, operators or end-users.

The system scope may be extended to include human agents that are malevolent. These agents are concerned with breaking system goals to satisfy their own malicious goals. They need to be modelled as well in order to elaborate countermeasures to threats and obtain a more complete set of security requirements. We come back to this in Section 16.2.3.

11.2 Characterizing system agents

In an agent model, an agent is characterized by a number of features such as its monitoring/control capabilities, its responsibilities and the operations it needs to perform to meet these responsibilities. For specific kinds of agents and analyses we may want to capture the agent's wishes with respect to goals, its beliefs and dependencies on other agents. Let us have a closer look at those various features.

11.2.1 Basic features

Like any object, an agent must have a *name* and a precise *definition* making it clear under what conditions an individual is currently an instance of the agent (see Section 10.1.5).

We may also annotate the agent with its *category* and, in particular, indicate whether the agent is a software-to-be agent or an environmental one – software, device or human agent; see the 'fellow' icon in Chapter 8, Figure 8.4.

The agent can also be characterized by attributes, associations with other objects and domain invariants; these are captured in the object model.

11.2.2 Agent capabilities

The capabilities of an agent are defined statically in terms of *monitoring* links and *control* links to objects in the object model (see Figure 11.1). Such links capture the agent's ability to monitor or control object attributes or associations. These attributes/associations act as monitored or controlled variables for the agent. When an individual becomes an instance of the agent, these variables are instantiated as *state variables* that this agent instance can monitor or control (see Section 10.1.2).

- An agent *monitors an attribute* of an object if its instances can get the values of this attribute from object instances. The agent *monitors an association* if its instances can evaluate whether this association holds between object instances.

Figure 11.1 *Agent capabilities*

- An agent *controls an attribute* of an object if its instances can set values for this attribute on object instances. The agent *controls an association* if its instances can create or delete association instances.

When modelling agent capabilities, we need to specify which agent instance monitors/controls the attribute or association of which object instance. This information is provided in a so-called *capability instance declaration* attached as annotation to the corresponding monitoring/control link in the agent model; see Section 11.3.1.

An agent is said to *monitor* (or *control*) an *object* when it monitors (or controls) all the object's attributes and associations.

Examples Consider the TrainController agent in our train case study. Its capabilities might include the following:

- To monitor the attributes Speed and Position of the TrainInfo entity declared in the object model (see Figure 10.12).

- To control the attributes Speed and Acceleration of the Command entity (see Figure 10.12) and the attribute DoorsState of the TrainInfo entity.

We will say that the TrainController agent has TrainInfo.Speed and TrainInfo.Position among its *monitored variables*, whereas it has Command.Speed and Command.Acceleration among its *controlled variables*.

Note that TrainController has no capability of controlling the physical acceleration of trains (that is, the Acceleration attribute of Train in Figure 10.12), whereas a TrainActuator agent does. Similarly, TrainController has no capability of monitoring the physical speed of trains (that is, the Speed attribute of Train) whereas a Speedometer agent does.

In the meeting scheduling system, the Scheduler agent includes among its capabilities the monitoring of the Requesting association between Initiator and Meeting, and the control of the Date and Location attributes of Meeting (see Chapter 4, Figure 4.6). It obviously has no capability of controlling the Attendance association between Participant and Meeting. The Participant agent includes among its capabilities the control of the Constraints association between Participant and Meeting and the Attendance association between Participant and Meeting, and the monitoring of the Notification association between Participant and Meeting. It obviously has no capability of monitoring nor controlling the Date and Location attributes of Meeting.

Agent interfaces Capabilities define the agent's interface with respect to other agents in the system; an agent monitors some object attribute or association controlled by some other agent.

Monitored/controlled conditions An extended, higher-level notion of capability is helpful when reasoning about agent capabilities for goal responsibility assignment. An agent *monitors a condition* if its instances can evaluate whether the condition holds. An agent *controls a condition* if its instances can make this condition true or false.

For example, consider the goal Maintain[DoorsStateClosedWhileNonZeroSpeed], defined as:

for any instance *tr* of TrainInfo: **always (if** tr.Speed $\neq$ 0 **then** tr.DoorsState = 'closed')

With regard to this goal, the TrainController agent has the capability, for an arbitrary instance *tr* of the TrainInfo object, to monitor the condition tr.Speed $\neq$ 0 and to control the condition tr.DoorsState = 'closed'.

11.2.3 Agent responsibilities and goal realizability

An agent is said to be *responsible* for a goal if its instances are the only ones required to restrict their behaviour, through adequate setting of their controlled variables, so as to satisfy this goal.

In the preceding example, the TrainController agent can be made responsible for the goal Maintain[DoorsStateClosedWhileNonZeroMeasuredSpeed] (see Figure 11.2). As this agent controls the variable TrainInfo.DoorsState its instances can, for corresponding instances *tr* of TrainInfo, keep tr.DoorsState to the value 'closed' when the monitorable condition tr.Speed $\neq$ 0 holds, without intervention of any other agent instance.

When modelling agent responsibilities we need to specify which agent instance is responsible for which goal instantiation to specific object instances. For example, the TrainController agent instance on board a train might only be responsible for the goal in Figure 11.2 instantiated to *this* train. Such information is provided in a so-called *responsibility instance declaration* attached as an annotation to the corresponding responsibility link in the agent model; see Section 11.3.1.

Goal realizability Responsibility assignments must take agent capabilities into account. If the responsibility for a goal is assigned to an agent, this goal must be realizable by the agent in view of its capabilities. Intuitively, this means that given the agent's monitoring and control capabilities, it is *possible* for the agent alone to get the goal satisfied without more restrictions than those required by the goal.

A more precise definition of realizability of behavioural goals can be formulated as follows. Remember that a behavioural goal implicitly defines a maximal set of admissible system behaviours; see Section 7.3.1. On the other hand, a set of possible behaviours of an agent instance can be captured by a transition system defined by a pair (*Init, Next*) where:

- *Init* is a set of initial states of the agent's controlled variables.

- *Next* is a transition relation mapping sequences of predecessor states of the agent's monitored and controlled variables to successor states of its controlled variables.

Figure 11.2 *Agent responsibility*

A goal G is then said to be *realizable* by an agent ag if and only if there exists a transition system TS_{ag} for ag such that:

$$\text{RUN } (TS_{ag}) = \text{BEHAVIOURS } (G),$$

that is, the set of possible runs of TS_{ag} is exactly the set of possible behaviours prescribed by G on those variables. (Set equality is taken in this definition rather than set inclusion to avoid restrictions on agent behaviours that are not strictly required by the goal.)

Figure 11.3 suggests the intuition behind this semantic definition of goal realizability by an agent. The set of behaviours prescribed by the goal coincides with a set of runs of a *possible* transition system for the TrainController agent. In the specific run provided as illustration, the agent's controlled variable is DoorsState (shown in italics).

In practice, determining the existence of a possible transition system might be quite difficult. We can use an equivalent, more tractable set of criteria when we need to assess goal realizability for responsibility assignment. A goal turns to be *unrealizable* by an agent if and only if one of the following criteria holds:

- The agent is unable to monitor a variable in the goal specification that needs to be evaluated for goal satisfaction.

- The agent is unable to control a variable in the goal specification that needs to be constrained for goal satisfaction.

- There is a variable in the goal specification that needs to be evaluated in a future state.

- The goal is an unbounded *Achieve* goal; that is, its target condition can indefinitely be postponed to future states.

- An external circumstance can make the goal unsatisfiable (e.g. a boundary condition; see Sections 3.1.1 and 8.3).

Example   According to this equivalent characterization of realizability, the goal

for any instance *tr* of TrainInfo: **always (if** tr.Speed $\neq 0$ **then** tr.DoorsState = 'closed')

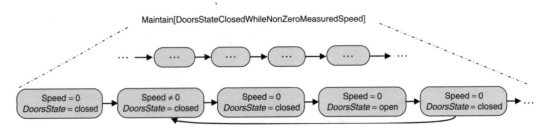

Figure 11.3 *Goal realizability and agent runs*

is realizable by a TrainController agent having the capability of monitoring the variable Train-Info.Speed and of controlling the variable TrainInfo.DoorsState. On the other hand, the goal

for any instance *tr* of Train: **always** (**if** train *tr* is moving **then** doors of train *tr* are closed)

is unrealizable by this agent. Its capabilities do not enable it to monitor whether the train *tr* is physically moving nor to control the physical opening and closing of doors.

Goal unrealizability provides the root motivation for applying the unrealizability-driven refinement patterns discussed in Section 8.8.5. Those patterns produce both finer-grained goals and finer-grained responsibilities.

Alternative responsibilities and assignment selection   A goal might be realizable by different agents. The responsibility for it is therefore assignable to alternative agents, as we have already seen in Section 8.5.2. Alternative responsibility assignments are captured in the goal model. The agent model captures the *selected* assignment only. Such a selection may be based on analysis of the contributions of each alternative to the soft goals from the goal model; see Section 16.3.

Unique Controller constraint   For the sake of simplicity of the underlying semantic framework, capability-based responsibility assignments are subject to the following constraint: once assignments have been selected, any attribute/association may be controlled by one agent at most. The *Unique Controller* constraint precludes interferences between concurrent agent behaviours.

11.2.4 Agents as operation performers

Another feature characterizing every agent in a model is the set of operations that the agent performs. An agent *performs* an operation if the applications of this operation are activated by instances of the agent (see Figure 11.4).

When modelling agents as operation performers, we need to specify which operation application is activated by which agent instance. This information is provided in a so-called *performance instance declaration* attached as an annotation to the corresponding performance link in the agent model; see Section 11.3.1.

The operations performed by an agent provide the means for its instances to set the agent's controlled variables so as to satisfy the assigned goals. Such a setting must be made

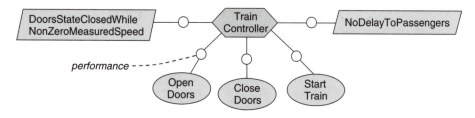

Figure 11.4   *Agent as operation performer*

under restricted conditions, specified as agent permissions or obligations on the corresponding operation in the operation model. (This will be detailed in the next chapter on the operation model.)

Example   The first arrow along the agent run illustrated in Figure 11.3 captures a state transition where the *StartTrain* operation is applied by a TrainController agent on a train instance, *tr* say. The permission condition for this operation to ensure the underlying goal is tr.DoorsState = 'closed'. This condition is fulfilled in the initial state where the operation was applied (see the first bubble in Figure 11.3). The third arrow along the agent run captures a state transition where the *OpenDoors* operation is applied by the agent. The permission condition for this operation to ensure the same goal is the condition tr.Speed = 0. This condition is fulfilled in the initial state where this operation was applied (see the third bubble in Figure 11.3). The *OpenDoors* operation additionally has an obligation condition, namely, '*train tr has just stopped at a platform*'; the TrainController agent *must* apply the operation as soon as this condition becomes true, in order to ensure the goal NoDelayToPassengers.

11.2.5 Agent wishes and beliefs

This section briefly introduces two optional agent features that we can introduce in agent models for specific kinds of analysis.

Wish links

A *Wish* link between a human agent and a goal in a model captures the fact that this agent would like the goal to be satisfied. For example, we might introduce a Wish link between the Staff library agent and the goal LimitedLoanPeriods, or a Wish link between the Patron agent and a goal LongLoanPeriods. In the meeting scheduling system, the goal MinimumInteraction in Figure 8.11 is wished by the Participant agent.

Wish links can be used for various purposes:

- *Goal elicitation.* We may browse the set of human agents already identified in the model and, for each of them, identify the goals they might wish (see heuristic (*H7*) in Section 8.8.2).

- *Responsibility assignment.* We may also use wish-based heuristics for discarding or favouring responsibility assignments to human agents, for example:

  a. Avoid assigning a goal to a human agent if the goal, or a parent of it, can be conflicting with the goals wished by the agent.

  b. Among alternative assignments of a security goal to different human agents, favour assignments to those wishing the goal; these agents will be more trustworthy in enforcing goal satisfaction.

According to the first assignment heuristic, we should avoid assigning the goal ReturnEncoded in Figure 11.11 to the Patron agent as the latter wishes the goal LongLoanPeriods that conflicts with a parent goal of ReturnEncoded; namely, LimitedLoanPeriods.

Agent belief and knowledge

An agent can be equipped with a local memory in which facts about its own environment are maintained. The agent's capabilities may then be extended to allow for reasoning on its local memory. The conditions under which facts get in and out of the agent's memory need to be stated through adequate domain properties.

In this setting, an agent *ag Believes* some fact F if F is found in its local memory. This is denoted by $Belief_{ag}$ (F). The agent *Knows* fact F if:

- It believes F.

- It is indeed the case that F holds.

Agent beliefs can be used for modelling an important class of obstacles known as *confusion obstacles*, where an agent can confuse instances of an object, or values of a state variable. Such obstacles are characterized by the following *wrong belief* pattern:

$Belief_{ag}$ (F) **and not** F

In the meeting scheduler, for example, Figure 9.8 showed the condition *DatesConfused* among the possible causal sub-obstacles of the no-show obstacle InformedAndConvenientAndNot Attends to the goal AttendanceIfInformedAndConvenient. This obstacle can be made more precise by writing:

$Belief_{Participant}$ (m.Date = d) **and** $m.Date \neq d$ for some meeting m and date d

Confusion obstacles can be particularly harmful when they obstruct safety or security goals – for example patient instance confusion or dose confusion in healthcare processes, or mode confusion in flight management systems. We come back to these in Section 16.2.2.

For system security, confidentiality goals prescribe what unauthorized agents may *not* know about sensitive information. Their specification pattern is $Avoid[Knows_{ag}$ (F)] where ag is an unauthorized agent, F is a property about some sensitive information and $Knows$ denotes the previously defined relation. We come back to confidentiality goals and threats in Section 16.2.3.

11.2.6 Agent dependencies

Obstacle analysis may reveal leaf goals in a goal model that might be obstructed under certain circumstances. In such circumstances the responsible agent fails to get the goal satisfied. One possible cause of failure might be another agent failing to get one of its assigned goals satisfied. Failure may then propagate along such dependency chains. For vulnerability analysis it may be worth making agent dependencies explicit in an agent model in order to anticipate appropriate responses through new goals in the goal model. When modelling an organization during domain analysis, it may also be worth modelling strategic dependencies among organizational agents.

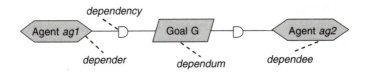

Figure 11.5 Agent dependency

An agent *ag1* is said to *depend on* another agent *ag2 for* a goal *G*, under the responsibility of *ag2,* if *ag2*'s failure to get *G* satisfied can result in *ag1*'s failure to get one of its assigned goals satisfied.

We may capture this in an agent model through a ternary *Dependency* link between *ag1*, playing the *Depender* role, *ag2*, playing the *Dependee* role, and *G*, playing the *Dependum* role (see Figure 11.5). Dependency links are generally represented in a dedicated diagram called *i** diagram (Yu, 1993); we come back to this in Section 11.3.3.

Examples   The Scheduler agent in the meeting scheduling system depends on the Participant agent for the goal ConstraintsTransmitted; if the latter fails to get this goal satisfied, the Scheduler agent may fail to get its assigned goal ConvenientMeetingScheduled satisfied (see Figure 8.11).

In our train control case study, the TrainController agent depends on the TrackingSystem agent for the goal AccurateSpeed&PositionEstimated; if the latter fails to get this goal satisfied, the TrainController agent may fail to get its assigned goal SafeAccelerationComputedFromEstimates satisfied (see Figure 8.20) – the computed accelerations might not be safe if the positions and speeds of trains running in the system are inaccurate.

Note that dependencies among agents, as defined here, do not infringe on the principle of individual responsibility. In the definition of dependency, the dependee *ag2* is by no means responsible for those goals assigned to the depender *ag1*, which could fail if the dependee fails to get the dependum *G* satisfied. The dependee might actually ignore these goals. Also note that, in case of the dependee *ag2* failing to get the dependum *G* satisfied, the failure propagates up to *G*'s parent goals in AND-refinement trees as well, for which *ag2* is jointly responsible with other agents.

Dependency is asymmetrical; the dependee *ag2* is obviously not dependent on the depender *ag1* for the dependum *G*.

Dependency chains

Dependency is transitive under certain conditions. If *ag1* depends on *ag2* for *G2* and *ag2* depends on *ag3* for *G3*, then *ag1* depends on *ag3* for *G3* whenever *G2* is among *ag2*'s goals that can fail if *ag3* does not manage to get *G3* satisfied. Such transitivity yields *dependency chains*.

An example of a dependency chain in our train system might be the following:

TrainController *depends on* AlarmTransmitter *for* AlarmNotified;
AlarmTransmitter *depends on* Passenger *for* AlarmRaised.

Dependency chains provide a basis for *vulnerability analysis*. Goal failure propagates back-wards along dependency chains, which might result in disastrous consequences in some cases. Such situations should be detected and resolved at RE time by 'cutting' critical dependency chains through alternative goal refinements and assignments so as to produce fewer and less critical dependencies.

Milestone-based dependencies

A common dependency situation arises when the milestone-driven pattern is used for refining a goal G into the following leaf sub-goals:

> G1: **if** C **then** M,   assigned to *ag1*,
> G2: **if** M **then** T,   assigned to *ag2*,

in the particular case where the reaching of the target condition T by *ag2* can fail if the milestone condition M is not properly reached by *ag1* (see Figure 8.19). In this case *ag2* depends on *ag1* for *G1*.

This is what happens in the preceding examples of dependency, for example between the TrainController depender, the TrackingSystem dependee and the milestone dependum Accurate-Speed&PositionEstimated.

11.3 Representing agent models

An agent model can be represented by different kinds of diagrams that capture different views on it. These include agent diagrams, context diagrams and dependency diagrams.

11.3.1 Agent diagrams and instance declarations

An *agent diagram* is an annotated graph showing the system agents, their respective capabilities, the responsibilities assigned to each of them (after selection from alternative assignments captured in the goal model) and the operations performed by each of them.

Figure 11.6 shows a portion of an agent diagram for our train control case study. The links between agents and goals are *Responsibility* links. The instance responsibility annotation there makes precise which TrainController instance is responsible for the computation of safe accelerations of which Train instances. The link between the TrainController agent and the SendCommand operation is a *Performance* link. An incoming arrow to an agent from an object indicates that the agent *Monitors* the object's attributes labelling the arrow. An outgoing arrow from an agent to an object indicates that the agent *Controls* the object's attributes labelling the arrow. If there is no label the agent monitors or controls the entire object. (Note that the Speed attribute of Train, monitored by TrackingSystem in Figure 11.6, captures the physical speed of trains; the Speed attribute of TrainInfo, controlled by TrackingSystem and monitored by TrainController, captures the measured speed of trains; and the Speed attribute of Command, controlled by TrainController, captures the commanded speed of trains.)

The annotations in an agent diagram are important, as they provide the agent definitions and their *instance declarations*:

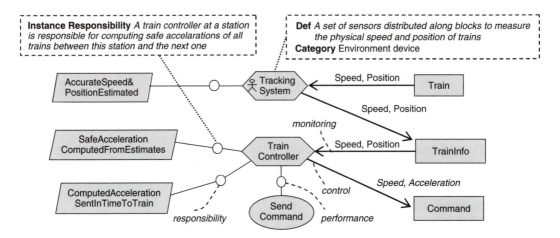

Figure 11.6 *Agent diagram*

- A *responsibility instance declaration* annotating a responsibility link in an agent diagram makes it precise which agent instance is responsible for which goal instantiation to specific object instances; see Figure 11.6. As another example, an instance declaration annotating the *Responsibility* link between the Participant agent and the goal ConstraintsTransmitted should state that 'if p is the Participant instance invited to the Meeting instance m who got a request for his/her Constraints instance c with respect to m, **then** p is the one responsible for the goal ConstraintsTransmitted specifically prescribing that his/her constraints c with respect to meeting m be transmitted to the scheduler'.

- A *capability instance declaration* annotating a monitoring or control link makes precise which agent instance is monitoring or controlling the attribute/association of which object instance. For example, consider the Participant agent controlling the Constraints association between Participant and Meeting in the object model of the meeting scheduling system. An instance declaration annotating the *Control* link between Participant and Constraints in an agent diagram should state that 'if p is the Participant instance, invited to the Meeting instance m, who got a request for his/her Constraints instance c with respect to m, **then** p is the one specifically controlling c'.

- Similarly, a *performance instance declaration* annotating a performance link in an agent diagram makes precise which agent instance is performing the operation on which input/output object instance. For example, an instance declaration annotating the *Performance* link between the Participant agent and the SendConstraints operation should state that 'if p is the Participant instance invited to the Meeting instance m who got a request for his/her Constraints instance c with respect to m, **then** p is the one performing the SendConstraints operation with c as specific input state variable'.

11.3.2 Context diagrams

Context diagrams were introduced in Section 4.3.1 as a standard means of capturing system components and their static interactions through shared phenomena. The nodes in such

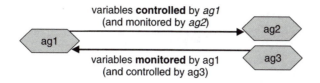

Figure 11.7 *Context diagram: agent interfaces*

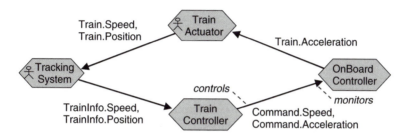

Figure 11.8 *Context diagram: an example*

diagrams represent active system components, whereas the edges represent communication between pairs of nodes through shared phenomena labelling them (see Figure 4.2).

We can use a variant of such a diagram to capture agents and their interfaces with each other. A node represents an agent; an edge here is directed from one agent to another and labelled by object attributes and associations declared in the object model. A variable labelling an arrow means that the source agent controls the variable, whereas the target agent monitors it (see Figure 11.7).

Figure 11.8 shows a context diagram for our train control system. The TrainController agent there controls the Acceleration attribute of the Command entity (declared in Figure 10.12), whereas the OnBoardController agent monitors this attribute. Both agents are software agents to be developed. Their respective environments are made of the agents with which they interface through the shared variables they monitor or control.

Note that the information conveyed by a context diagram is captured in an agent diagram as well. In fact, we can easily generate the former from the latter (see Section 11.5.2). In Figure 11.8, we just removed the goals and objects from the agent diagram in Figure 11.6, and for each removed object we merged the incoming and outgoing arrows labelled by the same variable so as to connect the corresponding source and target agents.

Context diagrams are simpler as they focus on capabilities only. By connecting the capabilities of one agent to those of other agents, they provide a useful, direct view of mutual interfaces among agents.

11.3.3 Dependency diagrams

Dependency diagrams allow us to capture dependencies among agents and, in particular, dependency chains (see Section 11.2.6). The *i** syntax may be used for dependencies. A ternary link between a depender agent, a dependee agent and a goal dependum is represented

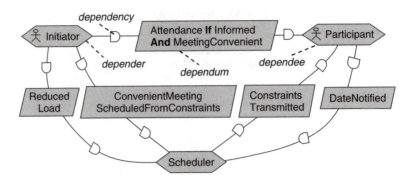

Figure 11.9 *Agent dependencies: i* diagram*

by a directed link from the depender to the dependee by way of the dependum; the 'D' link decoration shows the direction of the dependency.

Figure 11.9 shows a dependency diagram for our meeting scheduling system. The Initiator agent there depends on the Scheduler agent for the goal ConvenientMeetingScheduledFromConstraints. The latter itself depends on the Participant agent for the goal ConstraintsTransmitted.

Dependency diagrams focus on dependency links that agent diagrams do not capture. Dependency diagrams and agent diagrams are therefore complementary to each other.

11.4 Refinement of abstract agents

While building a system model, it may be convenient to consider a goal at some stage as being under the responsibility of a single, abstract, coarse-grained agent without caring too much what exactly the finer-grained agents composing the abstract agent are – some might not have been identified yet or the details of the finer-grained responsibility assignments might not matter at that stage. For example, the TrackingSystem agent in Figure 11.6 is structured from sensors distributed along system blocks. The specific details of such a structure might prove necessary only at a later stage of the model-building process. While modelling organizational structures and their responsibilities in the early stages of the RE process, it is similarly useful to model coarser-grained responsibilities of abstract organizational agents first, and to refine them later on in the process.

Like any object, an agent can be defined as an *aggregation* of components (see Section 10.5.2). These components are active in this case; they yield finer-grained agents composing the abstract agent.

We can then consider a goal *G* as being under the sole responsibility of the abstract agent *ag*, and then later on refine *G* into sub-goals *G1* and *G2* and, in parallel, agent *ag* into finer-grained agents *ag1* and *ag2*, with corresponding finer-grained responsibility assignments of *G1* and *G2* to *ag1* and *ag2*, respectively (see Figure 11.10).

Figure 11.11 shows an example of such goal–agent co-refinement. The library system goal LimitedLoanPeriods is put under the responsibility of an abstract agent named ReturnEngine. Later on in the model-building process, this goal is refined into the three sub-goals shown at the first level of refinement in Figure 11.11. The ReturnEngine agent is itself refined

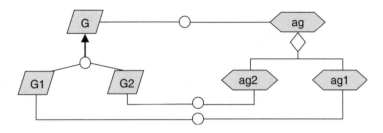

Figure 11.10   *Agent refinement and responsibility refinement*

into two agents: an abstract RemindEngine agent, responsible for the sub-goal Reminder-EmailedIf**Not**BackOnTime; and an abstract ReturnActors agent, responsible for the sub-goal Copies-BackOnTime. The RemindEngine agent is refined in turn into the LoanSoftware agent, which must meet the requirement ReminderIssuedIf**Not**BackOnTime, and an existing Mailer agent, responsible for the expectation ReminderTransmitted. On the other hand, the LoanActors agent is itself refined into the Staff agent, responsible for the expectations MaxLoanPeriodNotifiedUponCheckOut and ReturnEncoded; the Patron agent, responsible for the expectation CopiesReturnedOnTime; and the LoanSoftware agent again, responsible for the requirement ReturnedCopiesCheckedIn.

As another example, consider the meeting scheduling system and the assignment of responsibilities shown in Figure 8.11. We might not want to consider such fine-grained responsibility assignments in the first place. We could instead refine the goal ConstraintsKnownFromRequest in Figure 8.11 into two sub-goals, ConstraintsRequested and ConstraintsProvided, assigned to more abstract agents named SchedulerEngine and ParticipantEngine, respectively. Later on in the modelling process we could refine the agent ParticipantEngine into Participant and CommunicationInfrastructure, to obtain the fine-grained responsibilities shown in Figure 8.11. Note that those fine-grained responsibilities need eventually to be considered for the precise distribution of responsibilities and fine-grained analysis, such as the obstacle analysis discussed in Chapter 9.

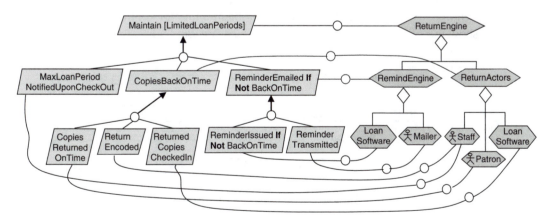

Figure 11.11   *Refining agents and their responsibilities: an example*

In the two preceding examples, the more abstract agents are hybrid ones in that they are composed of software agents and environment agents. We can similarly structure purely environmental agents or purely software ones:

- The case of environmental agent refinement is fairly common in the early RE stages where we assign global responsibilities to organizational structures that we later on decompose into, for example, departments, units or operators playing specific roles in the organization. The global responsibilities are then refined accordingly. For example, the goal AccurateBookClassificationByTopic in Figure 8.10 was assigned as an expectation of a LibraryStaff agent in one of the alternative options shown there. We might later on refine this agent into two finer-grained ones named ResearchStaff and AdministrativeStaff, with corresponding finer-grained responsibilities for the new sub-goals BookAccuratelyClassified and ClassificationCorrectlyEncoded, respectively.

- The case where we refine software-to-be agents arises in the early stages of architectural design, based on architectural criteria such as weak coupling and strong cohesion (see Section 16.5). For example, we might decompose our TrainController agent into finer-grained software agents such as AccelerationController, DoorsController and so on. Likewise, we might in the early phases of architectural design decompose our Scheduler agent into finer-grained software agents such as ConstraintsHandler, Date&LocationPlanner, MeetingNotifier and so on.

A goal–agent co-refinement pattern

Process control systems generally involve an abstract agent ProcessControlEngine in charge of an abstract goal ProcessControlledAdequately. This agent is refinable into three agents, DataSensor, SoftwareController and ProcessActuator, with corresponding finer-grained responsibilities for sub-goals ProcessInfoMonitoredAccuratelyFromData, ProcessInfoControlledAdequately and ControlledInfoActuatedAccuratelyOnProcess, respectively (see Figure 11.12).

This pattern corresponds to the four-variable model presented in Section 1.1.4 (see Figure 1.4) and to a particular case of the more general unrealizability-driven patterns discussed in Section 8.8.5 (see Figures 8.25–8.26). A problem frame for control systems could be defined to show the corresponding context diagram (see Section 4.3.1).

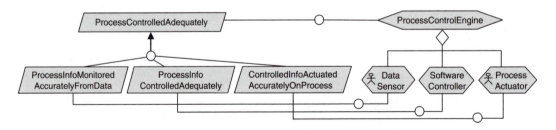

Figure 11.12 *Goal-agent co-refinement pattern in process control*

Note that agent refinement makes the terminologies introduced in Chapters 1 and 7 consistent with each other. A *system requirement* is under the responsibility of a coarse-grained system agent composed of software and environmental agents, whereas a *software requirement* is finer-grained and under the sole responsibility of a software agent.

11.5 Building agent models

This section complements the model-building issues initiated in the previous section by reviewing a number of heuristics and tips for building agent diagrams (Section 11.5.1) . It then shows how a context diagram can be directly derived from a goal model in a systematic fashion (Section 11.5.2).

11.5.1 Heuristics for building agent diagrams from goal models

Some rules may help us identify agents and their capabilities from information contained in the goal model. Other rules are more focused on responsibility assignments.

For *agent identification*, we may use the following rules:

- **Goal target.** *For a goal already identified in the goal model, review all the objects it refers to in order to single out the active ones; that is, those whose instances have the ability of restricting their behaviour. For each such object, determine what attribute and association in the object model the object can monitor or control.* (The *Concern* link type was discussed in Sections 8.4 and 10.7.1.) For example, the goal Achieve[BookRequestSatisfied] in the library system states that 'every book request by a patron should be satisfied within X weeks'. This goal concerns the Book, Requesting and Patron objects. While Book and Requesting object instances cannot restrict their behaviour, the Patron object instances can, for example through transitions from a state where a book copy is not borrowed to a state where it is borrowed. The Patron object is therefore identified as an agent having the capability of controlling the Loan association in Figure 10.6. This agent can also control the Requesting association and so forth. Note that any goal can be used for this heuristic, not necessarily those needing to be assigned.

- **Goal enforcer.** *For a goal already identified in the goal model, identify what agents could be made responsible for it. Then, for every object this goal refers to, determine the object's attributes and associations in the object model that could be monitored or controlled by those agents.* For example, the goal Maintain[AccurateLoanInfo] states that all the tracking information about loans in the library system should accurately reflect the actual state of these loans. (The *Tracking* association and corresponding accuracy goal were discussed in Section 10.7.1; see Figure 10.13.) We might identify Staff and Patron as alternative enforcers of this accuracy goal. The Staff agent can monitor and control all attributes attached to the LoanInfo andBookCopyInfo objects, whereas the Patron agent might have more restricted capabilities, for example he/she might not be able to control the TimeLimit attribute of LoanInfo. Likewise, the goal Avoid[StolenCopies] might yield the identification of an AntiTheft device agent to enforce it, to be later refined into finer-grained TheftSensor and TheftAlarm agents with corresponding finer-grained responsibilities (as suggested in Figure 10.9).

- **Goal wisher.** *For a goal already identified in the goal model, identify which human agents might wish this goal and which capabilities these agents might have.* This heuristic is symmetrical to heuristic (*H7*) in Chapter 8, Section 8.8.2. Here we look for unidentified agents from identified goals rather than unidentified goals from identified agents. For example, we might identify the agent ResearchStaff from the goal AccurateBookClassificationByTopic by use of this heuristic.

- **Variable monitor/controller.** *For an incoming (or outgoing) arrow in a partial context diagram, determine which agent might be the source (or target) of it and for what reason.* This heuristic may result in discovering new agents with corresponding new goals. For example, we might feel that there should be an outgoing arrow from the Scheduler agent, labelled by an attribute Meeting.RequiredEquipment – in other words, the scheduler software should determine the required equipment for the meeting. While questioning which agent this arrow should be connected to, we might elicit a LocalOrganizer agent monitoring this information to satisfy an underlying goal.

- **Do not confuse product-level agents and process-level stakeholders.** A product-level agent is defined by its role in the target system being modelled; a process-level stakeholder has a different role; namely, to provide input to the model-building process. For example, we should not confuse the LibraryStaff agent, with specific responsibilities and capabilities in the library system that we are modelling, and members of the library staff whom we are interviewing while building a model for this system. Even though a single instance can play both roles, these roles are different.

For *responsibility assignment*, we may use other heuristic rules complementing the preceding ones:

- **Assignment based on goal-capability matching.** *For a realizable leaf goal in the goal model, consider for alternative assignments any identified agent whose capabilities enable it to (a) monitor all variables that need to be evaluated in the goal specification, and (b) control all variables that are constrained by the goal specification.* As discussed in Section 11.2.3, the goal is realizable by any such agent.

- **Software counterpart of a human assignment.** *Consider the possibility of a software assignment as an alternative to a fine-grained assignment to a human agent, together with the pros and cons of both alternatives.* The assigned goal may need to be further refined for realizability by the software agent. The pros and cons of such an assignment may complement the soft goals already identified in the goal model, as discussed in Sections 8.5.2 and 8.8.2. For example, we might consider assigning the goal Accurate-BookClassificationByTopic to a software agent as an alternative to the assignment to the Staff agent. The pros would be to reduce the load of library staff and to speed up book availability; the cons would be to increase development costs and sometimes produce bizarre classifications.

- **Assignment refinement.** *Identify finer-grained assignments by goal–agent co-refinement.* This heuristic was discussed and illustrated in Section 11.4. It is supported by the realizability-driven refinement patterns in Figures 8.25–8.26 and the agent–goal co-refinement patterns in Figures 11.10 and 11.12.

- **Assignment selection based on soft goals.** *Use the soft goals identified in the goal model as criteria for selecting a best responsibility assignment.* The technique implementing this heuristic will be detailed in Section 16.3.

- **Assignment to wisher.** *Among alternative assignments of the same goal to different human agents, favour assignments to agents wishing the goal or a parent of it in the goal model.* For example, the assignment of the goal AccurateBookClassificationByTopic to the ResearchStaff agent wishing this goal should be favoured over the assignment to the AdministrativeStaff agent. This heuristic calls for the capturing of wish links in agent models; see Section 11.2.5. A negative variant of it is: *avoid assigning a goal to a human agent if the goal, or a parent of it, can be conflicting with the goals wished by the agent.* Such an assignment may introduce the risk of non-satisfaction of the assigned goal.

- **No critical dependency from assignment.** *Avoid goal assignments resulting in critical dependencies among agents.* Such assignments might result in critical failures and failure propagation. This heuristic calls for the capturing of dependency links in agent models; see Section 11.2.6. For example, the assignment of the goal AccurateBookClassificationByTopic to the AdministrativeStaff agent should be avoided according to this heuristic. Such an assignment results in a critical dependency for this goal between the BiblioSearchEngine depender and the AdministrativeStaff dependee; the depender will fail to satisfy its assigned goal AccurateResponseToBiblioQuery in the likely case of a non-expert AdministrativeStaff agent failing to satisfy the goal AccurateBookClassificationByTopic.

As a final note, remember that the links between the goal, object and agent models are bidirectional. We may therefore identify agents, capabilities and assignments from goals and object attributes already identified in a goal/object model, using the heuristics in this section, or, conversely, identify new goals or object attributes from agents and capabilities already identified in an agent model.

11.5.2 Generating context diagrams from goal models

Given a goal model where responsibilities for the leaf goals were assigned, we can easily produce a context diagram showing how the assigned agents are interfaced with each other.

The technique is based on a variant of the *goal–capability matching* heuristic for agent assignment and on the **if-then** structure of behavioural goal specifications (see Section 7.3.1). In this structure, the **if** part refers to conditions to be evaluated in the current state whereas the **then** part refers to conditions to be achieved or maintained. The goal specification takes the general form:

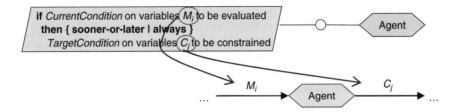

Figure 11.13   *Deriving agent interfaces from goal specifications*

if CurrentCondition on variables M_i (to be evaluated)
   then {**sooner-or-later** | **always** } TargetCondition on variables C_j (to be constrained).

If an agent is responsible for a leaf goal taking this form, it must necessarily be able to evaluate *CurrentCondition* and make or keep *TargetCondition* true. This requires the agent to monitor the variables M_i and to control the variables C_j.

In the system's context diagram, the agent should therefore have an incoming arrow labelled by the variables M_i and an outgoing arrow labelled by the variables C_j. Figure 11.13 depicts such an agent interface derivation. As a prerequisite, we need to determine which variables are *constrained* by the goal.

A context diagram is obtained piecewise by iterating such a derivation on leaf goals from the goal model; an agent with an outgoing arrow labelled by a variable is connected to all agents having an incoming arrow labelled with that variable. Figure 11.14 illustrates this piecewise derivation.

Figure 11.15 shows a more elaborate derivation of a context diagram fragment for the library system. This example also provides further details of the goal model for this system, and another illustration of the use of the *Tracking* association between environment objects

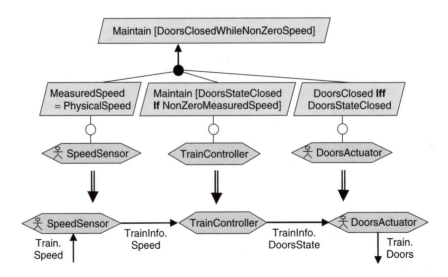

Figure 11.14   *Piecewise derivation of a context diagram: train example*

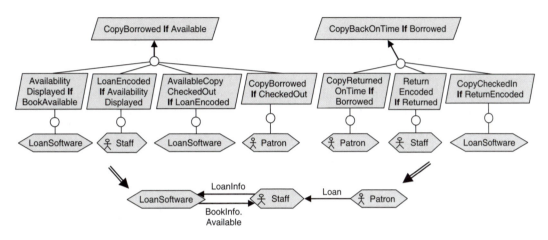

Figure 11.15   *Piecewise derivation of a context diagram: library example*

(Loan and Book) and their respective software counterpart (LoanInfo and BookInfo). The goal CopyBorrowedIfAvailable appeared in unrefined form in Figure 8.3. The *Tracking* association was discussed in Section 10.7.1; see Figure 10.13.

Similar to the derivation of associations and participating objects discussed in Section 10.7.1, the derivation of agent interfaces and context diagrams becomes straightforward and more accurate when the goal specifications are formalized in the specification language presented in Chapter 17. The **if-then** structure, variables to be evaluated and variables to be constrained then become fully apparent.

Summary

- An agent model captures the *WHO*-dimension of requirements engineering in terms of agents forming the target system, their capabilities, interfaces with each other and responsibilities for goals and operations. It may also show how agents and responsibility assignments are refined into finer-grained ones. An agent model defines the selected distribution of responsibilities, the system scope and configuration, and the boundary between the software-to-be and its environment. Such a model provides a basis for responsibility assignment heuristics, load analysis, vulnerability analysis and software architectural design. Some of these analyses may require additional features to be captured such as agent wishes, beliefs and dependencies.

- An agent is an active system object playing a specific role in goal satisfaction. It performs operations under restricted conditions so as to satisfy the goals for which it is responsible. Agent instances may run concurrently with each other. There are different agent categories such as software agents to be developed; legacy, off-the-shelf or foreign software components to be integrated; devices; and human agents.

- A goal under the responsibility of an agent must be realizable by the agent in view of its capabilities. Such capabilities are defined in terms of the system variables that the agent can monitor or control. These variables are object attributes and associations from the object model. Goal realizability requires in particular that the agent can monitor all variables to be evaluated in the goal formulation, and control all variables constrained by the goal formulation. An agent is responsible for a goal if its instances are the only ones required to restrict their behaviour, through adequate setting of their controlled variables, so as to satisfy this goal.

- Instance declarations must annotate responsibility, monitoring/control and performance links in an agent model to specify which agent instance is responsible for which goal instance, monitoring/controlling which object instance and performing which operation instance, respectively.

- A human agent wishes a goal if he/she would like this goal to be satisfied. An agent believes a fact if this fact is found in its local memory. It knows a fact if it believes this fact and the fact does actually hold. These notions are used in heuristics for goal elicitation, responsibility assignment, obstacle identification and threat analysis.

- A depender agent depends on a dependee agent for a goal if a dependee's failure to get this goal satisfied can result in a depender's failure to get one of its assigned goals satisfied. Agent dependency chains are subject to backward failure propagation. Critical dependency chains should therefore be resolved if possible through alternative goal refinements and assignments that eliminate or reduce dependency-based vulnerabilities.

- An agent model can be graphically represented in different ways showing different views on it. An agent diagram shows the responsibilities and capabilities of system agents together with the operations they perform. A context diagram shows agent interfaces in terms of variables that the agents monitor or control with respect to each other. A dependency diagram shows goal dependencies among agents.

- An agent can be structured as an aggregation of finer-grained agents. This mechanism supports abstract agents, responsible for coarse-grained goals, and an agent-goal co-refinement process where an agent and its assigned goals are refined in parallel into finer-grained agents, sub-goals and responsibility assignments.

- A variety of heuristics can be used for building agent diagrams from goal models. To identify agents, we may single out active objects among those referred to by goals, look for goal enforcers or goal wishers, or elicit agents that are the source/target of arrows in partial context diagrams. To identify assignments, we may match agent capabilities with goal formulations, consider software counterparts of fine-grained human assignments or refine assignments. To select an assignment among identified alternatives, we should take soft goals into account, favour wishers in the case of human assignments and avoid conflicting assignments or assignments introducing critical dependencies.

- A context diagram can be generated systematically from a goal model. For each goal assigned to an agent, the agent gets an incoming arrow labelled by the variables to be evaluated in the goal formulation and an outgoing arrow labelled by the variables constrained by the goal formulation. Agents with matching incoming/outgoing arrows are connected pairwise.

Notes and Further Reading

Feather's seminal paper on agent-based system design introduced agents as system components having choice of behaviour; an agent is responsible for a constraint if restricting its individual behaviour is sufficient for ensuring that constraint (Feather, 1987). The agent modelling framework in Dardenne *et al.* (1993) was grounded on this notion of agent and responsibility. The capabilities of an agent there were more operationally defined as a set of operations that the agent can perform, as in artificial intelligence planning. This modelling framework also included constructs for agent refinement and the capturing of agent wishes. Some of the responsibility assignment heuristics in this chapter originate from there.

The relationship between responsibility and capabilities, in terms of monitorability and controllability of system variables, is discussed more technically in Letier and van Lamsweerde (2002a). The characterization of requirements in Zave and Jackson (1997) is somewhat related to monitorability and controllability; a requirement may not be stated in terms of non-shared actions and may not constrain actions controlled by the environment. The system there consists of two agents, the machine and the environment, and the characterization is in terms of actions rather than object attributes/associations. The notion of realizability in this chapter is further studied in Letier (2001). It can be viewed as the RE counterpart, in terms of variables monitored and controlled by an agent, of the notion of realizability of a program specification; a specification is said to be realizable if there exists a program that implements it (Abadi *et al.*, 1989).

Systems for capturing and reasoning about agent knowledge are extensively discussed in Fagin *et al.* (1995). The use of agent beliefs for characterizing confusion obstacles and threats to confidentiality goals is discussed in van Lamsweerde and Letier (2000) and De Landtsheer and van Lamsweerde (2005), respectively. The mode confusion problem in flight management systems is described in Butler *et al.* (1998), together with formal methods for tackling it.

Instance declarations for higher model precision were introduced in Letier's thesis (Letier, 2001).

Agent dependencies were originally introduced in the *i** modelling framework (Yu 1993, 1997; Chung *et al.*, 2000; Castro *et al.*, 2002). Various types of agent dependency links are considered there to model situations where an agent depends on another for a goal to be achieved, a task to be carried out or a resource to become available. Operators associated with each dependency type may be combined to define plans that agents may use to achieve their goals. Various kinds of checks can then be supported, such as the viability of an agent's plan or the fulfilment of a commitment between agents. The notion of goal dependency there is not quite the same as the one defined in this chapter; it implicitly entails some form of responsibility delegation, unlike in this chapter. Although initially conceived for modelling the organizational environment of the software-to-be, recent efforts in the TROPOS project are aimed at using the agent–goal paradigm seamlessly through all phases of software development, from early requirements to software design to implementation on agent-oriented programming platforms (Castro *et al.*, 2002). The use of *i** models for vulnerability analysis is discussed in Liu *et al.* (2003) in the context of security RE.

Formal agent-oriented specification languages were developed for the later phases of the RE process. In the Albert language, agents and their assigned operations are specified in a real-time temporal logic extended with deontic constructs for capturing permissions and obligations (Dubois *et al.*, 1993). A case study integrating goal modelling for the earlier RE phases and agent specifications for the later ones can be found in Dubois *et al.* (1998). A good account of deontic constructs for such a specification style can be found in Meyer and Wieringa (1993).

Exercises

- Identify the basic capabilities of the Initiator agent in the meeting scheduling system.

- Explain why the goal CopyBackOnTimeIfBorrowed in Figure 11.15 is not realizable by the Patron agent.

- Annotate the responsibility links involving the Patron agent in Figure 11.15 with responsibility instance declarations.

- Consider the simplified version of a patient-monitoring system given as last exercise in Chapter 9, and the goal and object models you have built for it.

  a. Identify which capabilities the PatientMonitoringSoftware agent should have for realizability of the goals assigned to it.

  b. Write an annotated agent diagram for this system where instance declarations make clear what specific instances are involved in the *responsibility* and *performance* links.

- Consider the goal Avoid[StolenCopies] in the library system. Suppose that this goal has been assigned to a coarse-grained AntiTheft device. Apply the agent–goal co-refinement pattern in Figure 11.10 to produce finer-grained responsibilities, assuming that the AntiTheft agent is refined into the TheftSensor and TheftAlarm agents.

- Consider the following goals in an ambulance-dispatching system.

Achieve[AmbulanceAllocatedBasedOnIncidentInfo]

> **Def** *When an incident is encoded by the call operator and no ambulance has been already allocated to the incident, a first ambulance shall immediately be allocated by the dispatching software. This ambulance must be one available and nearest to the incident location, based on information recorded about ambulances.*

Achieve[AllocatedAmbulanceMobilized]

> **Def** *When an ambulance is allocated to an incident, the allocation and precise location of the incident shall be immediately notified on the mobile data terminal of this ambulance.*

a. Apply the various heuristics in Section 11.5.1 to identify agents and potential responsibility assignments for those goals.

b. Write instance declarations for those responsibilities.

c. Build a dependency diagram fragment involving those goals and the identified agents.

d. Derive interfaces among the identified agents based on those goal formulations.

- Show how the context diagram in Figure 11.8 can be derived piecewise from the goal model fragment shown in Figure 8.20.

- Derive a partial context diagram from the responsibility assignments in Figure 8.6 for the A320 braking logic. Complete this diagram using the *variable monitor/controller* heuristic in Section 11.5.1.

- Derive an agent diagram and a context diagram from the goal model fragment for the meeting scheduling system shown in Figure 8.11.

12

Modelling
System Operations

In our multi-view modelling framework for RE, this chapter is dedicated to the functional view of the system we want to model. This view covers the *WHAT*-dimension of requirements engineering introduced in Chapter 1. It focuses on the services the system should deliver in order to satisfy its goals. The goal, object and agent models were declarative; we now move to an operational model of the target system.

The system services are specified as operations performed under specific conditions to ensure that their underlying goals are satisfied. Operations were briefly introduced in the previous chapter from the perspective of the agents performing them. This chapter expands that introductory material by focusing on the process of operationalizing goals into operations ensuring them. An *operation model* captures the system operations in terms of their individual features and their links to the goal, object and agent models. The information conveyed by such a model includes, for each operation, its signature; the domain-specific pre- and post-conditions that intrinsically characterize the state transitions defined by the operation; goal-specific conditions that must further constrain any application of the operation for satisfaction of its underlying goals; and the agent controlling such applications in the software-to-be or the environment. An operation model can be represented by an operationalization diagram or, in a much more restricted form, by a UML use case diagram.

An operation model may be used for a variety of purposes. The model part covering software-to-be operations yields software specifications for input to the development process. We can use them in particular for deriving external specifications of functional components in the software architecture. The model part covering environment operations provides descriptions of tasks and procedures to be jointly performed in the environment for satisfaction of the system's goals. There are other products that we can derive from an operation model, such as black-box test data and executable specifications for system animation or software prototyping. The operation model can also be used for defining development work units, estimating development costs and schedules, and writing sections of the user manual. Last but not least, the explicit linking of operational specifications to the underlying system goals provides a rich basis for satisfaction arguments, traceability management and evolution support.

Section 12.1 makes the notion of an operation more precise and reviews different categories of operations that we can find in a system. Section 12.2 introduces various features that may characterize operations in a model, including their signature and their domain-specific pre- and post-conditions. The core of an operation model is a set of derivational links relating goals and operations. Section 12.3 discusses goal operationalization as an important RE milestone for rich satisfaction arguments and derivational traceability. An operation operationalizes its underlying goals through additional pre- and post-conditions that restrict its applications to ensure those goals. Section 12.4 provides a global semantic picture of what a system model conveys when we integrate its goal, object, agent and operation model components. Section 12.5 then introduces operationalization diagrams and UML use case diagrams as means for representing operation models. Section 12.6 concludes this chapter by proposing some heuristics and tips for building operation models from goal models. This section also shows how UML use cases can be generated as a simple by-product of goal operationalization diagrams.

12.1 What are operations?

An *operation* is a binary relation over system states. It has a tuple of input variables and a tuple of output variables defining its *signature*.

- An *input variable* designates an object instance to which the operation applies. The state of this instance affects the application of the operation.

- An *output variable* designates an object instance on which the operation acts. The state of this instance is changed by the application of the operation.

An input variable can be an output variable for the same operation. The variables in an operation signature are 'typed' by corresponding objects declared in the object model.

Remember that the *state* of an object instance was defined in Section 10.1.1 as a tuple of functional pairs $x_i \mapsto v_i$ yielding a value v_i for every attribute x_i of this object instance. If we denote the sets of states of the input and output variables of an operation Op by *InputState* and *OutputState*, respectively, Op is a set of input–output state pairs:

$$Op \subseteq InputState \times OutputState$$

A particular *application* of the operation yields a state transition from a state in *InputState* to a state in *OutputState*.

For example, the application of the OpenDoors operation to an instance *tr* of the TrainInfo object maps an input state comprising tr.DoorsState $\mapsto$ 'closed' to an output state comprising tr.DoorsState $\mapsto$ 'open'; see Figure 12.1. (The TrainInfo object was declared in the object model shown in Figure 10.12.)

The input and output variables associated with an operation will be called *instance variables*. As we saw in Section 10.1.2, the attributes characterizing an object are instantiated

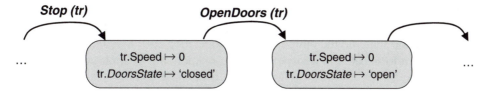

Figure 12.1 *Operation applications define state transitions*

as *state variables* characterizing its instances when the latter become instances of this object. Each instance variable thus has a set of state variables associated with it.

In Figure 12.1, *tr* is an instance variable for the TrainInfo object. This variable has tr.DoorsState among its state variables. It is both an input variable and an output variable for the Open-Doors operation.

Operation applications yield state changes on the operation's output variables; they form an important category of events captured in behaviour models, as we will see in Chapter 13. Instance variables that are not output variables for an operation are left unchanged by applications of this operation. When we define an operation in a model, we can further specify in its signature that the operation acts only on specific attributes of an output variable. This means that all other attributes of that variable are left unchanged by applications of the operation. We come back to this in Section 12.2.2.

Deterministic operations

We are generally interested by deterministic operations (especially in view of safety or security goals). Such operations may not produce multiple alternative output states from the same input state. Their relation is a function.

Operation atomicity

In our modelling framework, operations are *atomic*. They map input states to output states in the system's state coming immediately next; that is, one smallest time unit after. In other words, we cannot decompose operations into finer-grained ones. There are good reasons for this:

- From a semantic standpoint, the formal framework for defining the precise semantics of models is made conceptually simpler.

- From a methodological standpoint, we avoid the problems and pitfalls of functional decomposition. Decomposing an operation into sub-operations is often arbitrary; the traceability of sub-operations to their underlying goals is generally lost, and satisfaction arguments get more intricate. To preserve derivational traceability to goals and handle simpler and more precise forms of refinement, we will favour goal refinements in a purely declarative model, from which we derive fine-grained operations, over goal-free operation refinement in an operational model.

The conceptual simplification resulting from atomic operations might at first glance introduce limitations in model expressiveness. We may sometimes need to model operations lasting over multiple system state transitions. A common way of overcoming this problem consists of associating a pair of atomic operations with an operation having a particular duration – one making the operation start and the other making the operation end. Assertions about durational operations are then formulated in terms of events corresponding to applications of the atomic start/end operations.

Concurrency

As introduced in Section 11.1, agents may run concurrently with each other. In addition to such inter-agent concurrency, intra-agent concurrency is possible as well. An agent may need to apply multiple operations in parallel to fulfil its obligations with respect to the goals for which it is responsible. For example, a TrainController agent might simultaneously apply the OpenDoors operation in Figure 12.1 and the operation of displaying at which terminal platform the train is stopped. We will come back to concurrency issues in Section 12.4.

Operations and goals

The rationale for any operation to appear in a model should be made apparent. An operation must *operationalize* one or several goals underlying it. This is achieved by imposing restricted conditions on operation applications so as to enforce those goals. Such conditions are detailed in Section 12.2.4. Operationalization links between operations and goals form the core of an operation model.

Operation categories

There are different kinds of operations that we can find in a system:

- *Software operations* are performed by software-to-be agents. They sometimes automate corresponding operations performed manually in the system-as-is. A precise specification of software operations has to be passed on to software engineers for subsequent software development. Software operations are sometimes called services or functional features.

- *Environment operations* are performed by human agents, devices or existing software agents in the environment of the software-to-be. They are sometimes called *tasks* when they are performed by human agents. For some operations, a specification may be available, for example when they are performed by external devices or by legacy, off-the-shelf or foreign software with which the software-to-be needs to interoperate. For others, a specification needs to be elaborated, for example in the case of new tasks required for the operationalization of expectations on human agents.

In the meeting scheduling system, for example, PlanMeeting is a software operation performed by the Scheduler agent according to specifications to be made fully precise. SendConstraints is a task performed by the Participant agent. A specification of this task is needed for inclusion in the user manual or an online help facility.

12.2 Characterizing system operations

In an operation model, the individual features of an operation include the operation's name, definition and category; the operation's signature; the characterization of the operation's applicability and effect in terms of descriptive domain conditions; and the agent in charge of performing the operation. The prescriptive conditions for the operation to satisfy its underlying goals characterize operationalization links, discussed in the next section.

12.2.1 Basic features

Any system operation has a unique *name*. It must have a precise *definition* in terms of phenomena owned by the environment or shared with the software-to-be. We may also annotate the operation with its *category* to indicate whether the operation is a software-to-be one or an environment one.

12.2.2 Operation signature

The signature of an operation specifies the operation's input–output relation by declaring the input variables and output variables and, for each of them, the object to which the instance designated by the variable belongs. Such an object can be an entity, an association, an agent or an event. Operation signatures thus introduce explicit links between the operation model and the object model.

A signature may be specified graphically or textually (see the left- and right-hand parts of Figure 12.2). Textual declarations are written as model annotations taking a fairly standard form:

> **Operation** <operationName>
> **Input** <inputVariable>: <objectName>, ...
> **Output** <outputVariable>: <objectName>, ...

In such a declaration, the **Input** list identifies the object instances to which the operation applies, together with their corresponding object. Remember that the notation '*o: Ob*' means '*o such that InstanceOf (o, Ob)*'; see Section 10.1.2. Similarly, the **Output** list identifies the object instances on which the operation acts, together with their corresponding object. The variables introduced in an operation signature, such as *tr* in Figure 12.2, are *instance variables*.

Scope restriction

To delimit the scope of an operation, we may optionally restrict an object in the **Input** or **Output** declaration to specific attributes and/or associations of the object. This indicates that

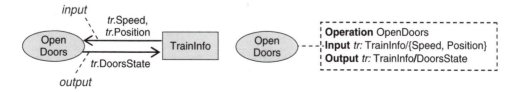

Figure 12.2 *Operation signature and scope restriction*

the operation *only* has access to these attributes and/or associations of the declared instance variable, in the case of an Input restriction, and *only* modifies these attributes and/or associations of the declared instance variable, in the case of an Output restriction.

Textually, we specify this by suffixing the object name in the operation's Input or Output list by the names of those attributes and/or associations. Graphically, we label the Input or Output arrow by those names (see Figure 12.2).

For example, the restricted textual declaration 'Output tr: TrainInfo/DoorsState' states that the OpenDoors operation *only* modifies the state variable tr.DoorsState; all other attributes or associations of the TrainInfo object instance *tr*, like its Speed or Position attributes, are left unchanged by this operation. Consider a completed version of the object model in Figure 10.12 where a Block-Info entity and OnInfo association have been introduced to account for the tracked counterpart of the physical Block entity and On association, monitorable by TrainController. The preceding declaration then states that the OnInfo association involving *tr* is left unchanged as well.

By default, when no scope restriction is declared on an input (or output) variable, the operation may access (or change) all its attributes and associations.

The instance variables introduced in the signature of an operation are used in the specification of the operation's pre- and post-conditions.

12.2.3 Domain pre- and post-conditions

Every operation is individually characterized by a pair of conditions called the domain precondition and the domain post-condition. These conditions together capture the class of state transitions defined by applications of the operation. They are descriptive as they capture what the operation intrinsically means in the domain:

- The *domain pre-condition* of an operation characterizes the class of input states when the operation is applied, regardless of any restriction required for goal satisfaction.

- The *domain post-condition* of an operation characterizes the class of output states when the operation has been applied, regardless of any restriction required for goal satisfaction.

Every operation in a model must be annotated with a specification of its domain pre- and post-condition. For example, the operation of opening train doors intrinsically means in the domain of train transportation that we get from a state where the doors are closed to a state where the doors are open; hence the domain pre- and post-condition annotating the OpenDoors operation in Figure 12.3. In these conditions, *tr* is the instance variable to which the operation applies, as declared in the operation's Input list in Figure 12.2.

Domain pre- and post-conditions are descriptive, not prescriptive. They do not prescribe when the operation must be applied nor when it may not be applied. Obligations and

Figure 12.3 *Domain pre- and post-conditions annotating an operation*

permissions appear in the model as *required* conditions for goal satisfaction. Such conditions annotate operationalization links between the operation and the corresponding goals; see Section 12.3. They strengthen the operation's domain pre- and post-conditions so as to ensure those goals. The need for separating the descriptive and prescriptive aspects in requirements specifications was discussed in Sections 1.1.4 and 4.5.

Pre- and post-conditions are assumed in this chapter to be specified in natural language. Their optional formalization in a logic-based language enables more sophisticated forms of derivation and analysis such as operationalization derivation, model animation and model checking (see Chapters 17–18).

12.2.4 Operation performer

Another feature characterizing every operation in a model is the agent performing it. As introduced in Section 11.2.4, an agent *performs* an operation if the applications of this operation are activated by instances of the agent. Operation performers are defined in the corresponding agent model (see Figure 11.4). The operation and agent models are therefore constrained by the following consistency rules:

- *Input/Output vs Monitoring/Control.* Every object attribute/association appearing in the Output (or Input) declaration of an operation performed by an agent must be controlled (or monitored) by this agent. If an object in the Output (or Input) declaration has no attribute/association suffix, then the agent must control (or monitor) all the object's attributes/
associations.

- *Unique Performer.* For consistency with the *Unique Controller* constraint in Section 11.2.3, every operation is performed by exactly one agent.

12.3 Goal operationalization

Operationalization refers to the process of mapping leaf goals, under the responsibility of single agents, to operations ensuring them. Each such operation is performed by the responsible agent under restricted conditions for satisfaction of its underlying goals. This section describes what such conditions consist of (Section 12.3.1), highlights the corresponding commitments required on the performing agents (Section 12.3.2) and discusses goal operationalization as a basis for derivational traceability and satisfaction arguments (Section 12.3.3).

12.3.1 Required pre-, post- and trigger conditions for goal satisfaction

Operationalization links were introduced briefly in Section 8.4, as they are defined at the interface between the goal model and the operation model. The sources of these links are leaf goals under the responsibility of single agents. A leaf goal is *operationalized by* a set of operations if the specification of these operations ensures that the goal is satisfied.

The specification of an operation therefore includes a set of prescriptive conditions on operation applications. These conditions, called *required conditions*, are aimed at ensuring that the goals underlying the operation are satisfied. The full specification of the operation is obtained by conjoining all its required conditions on the input states with its domain pre-condition, and all its required conditions on the output states with its domain post-condition.

A required condition may be a pre-condition, a trigger condition or a post-condition:

- A *required pre-condition* for a goal is a necessary condition on the operation's input states for satisfaction of this goal by any application of the operation. It captures a *permission*; under this condition the operation *may* be applied when the domain pre-condition holds. For example, a required pre-condition of the OpenDoors operation for the goal DoorsStateClosedIfNonZeroMeasuredSpeed is that '*tr.Speed = 0*' (see Figure 12.4); train doors *may* open *only if* the train is stopped.

- A *required trigger condition* for a goal is a sufficient condition on the operation's input states for satisfaction of this goal by any application of the operation. It captures an *obligation*; under this condition the operation *must* be applied when the domain pre-condition holds. For example, a required trigger condition of the OpenDoors operation for the goal FastEntry&Exit is that '*tr.Speed = 0 and tr.Position is a platform position*' (see Figure 12.4); train doors *must* open *as soon as* the train is stopped at a platform.

- A *required post-condition* for a goal is a condition on the operation's output states for satisfaction of this goal by any application of the operation. It captures an additional effect that the operation must have specifically to ensure the goal, in addition to the one captured by the operation's domain post-condition. For example, a post-condition of the operation SendAccelerationCommandToTrain, required for the goal Maintain[SafeAccelerationCommand], is that 'the commanded acceleration for tr is within a safe range'.

Notice the difference between a required pre-condition and a required trigger condition. A required pre-condition is a *necessary* condition for goal satisfaction; if the operation is applied then the condition must be true. A required trigger condition is a *sufficient* condition for goal satisfaction; if the condition becomes true in a state satisfying the domain pre-condition, then the operation must be applied.

Also note that the operation is not applied if a trigger condition becomes true in a state where the operation's domain pre-condition is not true. If the domain pre-condition becomes subsequently true and the trigger condition is still true, then the operation must be applied.

On the other hand, the operation is not applied if a required pre-condition becomes true in a state where the operation's domain pre-condition is not true. If the domain pre-condition becomes subsequently true and the required pre-condition is still true, then the operation may be applied – but not necessarily.

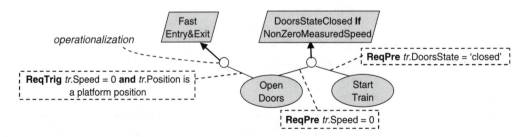

Figure 12.4 *Required conditions annotating operationalizations*

Consistency between required conditions

An operation does not necessarily have both a required pre-condition and a required trigger condition for the same goal. If it does, the possibility of the trigger condition becoming true in a state where the operation's domain pre-condition holds but not its required pre-condition would make the model inconsistent. The following consistency rule must therefore be enforced to prevent this:

> **if** ReqTrig **and** DomPre **then** ReqPre

This is easily achieved by letting the trigger condition cover the restriction captured by the ReqPre condition, if necessary; the actual trigger condition then amounts to ReqTrig and ReqPre.

Operation operationalizing multiple goals

A single operation may operationalize multiple goals, as depicted in Figure 12.4. Its specification must then include multiple sets of required conditions – one for each goal, consisting of a required pre-condition, trigger condition and/or post-condition for this goal. In our train example, a complete textual specification of the OpenDoors operation might look like this:

> **Operation** OpenDoors
>   **Def** Software operation controlling the opening of all doors of a train;
>   **Input** tr: TrainInfo; **Output** tr: TrainInfo/DoorsState;
>   **DomPre** tr.DoorsState = 'closed'; **DomPost** tr.DoorsState = 'open';
>   **ReqPre for** *DoorsStateClosedIfNonZeroMeasuredSpeed*: tr.Speed = 0;
>   **ReqPre for** *SafeEntry&Exit*: tr.Position is a platform position;
>   **ReqTrig for** *FastEntry&Exit*: tr.Position is a platform position **and** tr.Speed = 0.

Consider now the PlanMeeting operation in the meeting scheduling system. A partial specification showing the operationalization of the goal *ConvenientMeetingDate* might look like this:

> **Operation** PlanMeeting
>   **Def** Software operation setting a meeting date and location from the constraints of invited participants.
>   **Input** m: Meeting; **Output** m: Meeting/{Date, Location};
>   **DomPre** The meeting *m* has no date nor location; **DomPost** The meeting *m* has a date and a location;
>   **ReqPre for** *ConvenientMeetingDate*:
>   The constraints of every important participant invited to meeting *m* are available.
>   **ReqPost for** *ConvenientMeetingDate*:
>   The planned date *m*.Date is not among the excluded dates stated in the constraints of any important participant invited to meeting *m*.

Note that there is no scope restriction in the Input declaration of PlanMeeting. This operation therefore has access to all the attributes and associations defined for the Meeting entity in the object model (see Figure 4.5) and involving the instance variable *m* – including the *Invitation* and *Constraints* association instances involving *m* in the **ReqPre** and **ReqPost** conditions. Also note that the operation is declared to modify the attributes *m*.Date and *m*.Location only.

Consistency between multiple sets of required conditions

An operation operationalizing multiple goals may have multiple obligations and require multiple permissions. When its domain pre-condition holds, it must then be applied as soon as *one* of its trigger conditions is true, and may be applied provided that *all* its required pre-conditions are true. In other words, the operation's global trigger condition is the disjunction of its various trigger conditions, whereas its global required pre-condition is the conjunction of its various required pre-conditions. For M trigger conditions and N required pre-conditions, the *consistency rule* then takes the general form:

if DomPre **and** (ReqTrig$_1$ **or** ... **or** ReqTrig$_M$) **then** (ReqPre$_1$ **and** ... **and** ReqPre$_N$)

Goal operationalized by multiple operations

While a single operation may operationalize multiple goals, a single goal will in general be operationalized by multiple operations, as Figure 12.4 also shows. The goal is then ensured through multiple sets of required conditions – one for each such operation.

For example, the goal DoorsStateClosedIfNonZeroMeasuredSpeed in Figure 12.4 is operationalized through:

- the required pre-condition $tr.Speed = 0$ on the OpenDoors operation
- *and* the required pre-condition $tr.DoorsState = \text{'closed'}$ on the StartTrain operation.

Operationalization as an incremental process

A new goal might appear while building an operation model or after the model has been built. The operationalization of this new goal may require new associated operations or a new associated set of required pre-, trigger and/or post-conditions on operations previously identified and specified. As the goal model is declarative and because of the one-to-one correspondence between a goal and its required conditions, the modelling framework is compositional. While adding a goal and new required conditions for it, we just need to check that:

- The new goal introduces no conflict with other goals in the goal model.
- The consistency rule on ReqTrig/ReqPre conditions is preserved.

Operation signatures may also need to be extended as new input or output variables are referenced in the new required conditions.

12.3.2 Agent commitments

In the previous chapter we have seen that an agent is responsible for a goal if its instances are the only ones required to restrict their behaviour, through adequate setting of their controlled variables, so as to satisfy this goal. The operationalization of goals through required conditions on operations provides a more concrete view of what agents are committed to, namely:

for a goal *G* under responsibility of agent *ag*,
    for every operation *Op* operationalizing *G*,
        ag must guarantee that *Op* is applied *when* *Op*'s DomPre holds,
            as soon as one of *Op*'s ReqTrig holds *and only if* all *Op*'s ReqPre hold,
            so as to establish *Op*'s DomPost together with all *Op*'s ReqPost.

Such a commitment assumes that the following two rules are enforced by a model in addition to the *Unique Performer* rule in Section 12.2.4:

- An agent responsible for a goal performs all operations operationalizing that goal.

- If these operations operationalize other goals then the agent is responsible for those goals as well.

The capabilities required for an agent to fulfil its commitments can be now reformulated more explicitly as follows:

for a goal *G* under responsibility of agent *ag*,
    for every operation *Op* operationalizing *G*,
        ag must be able to monitor all *Op*'s pre- and trigger conditions
                and control all *Op*'s post-conditions

Agent non-determinism

Models exhibit a certain form of non-determinism in the way agents fulfil their commitments. While it is obliged to apply an operation when one of the operation's trigger condition becomes true, an agent instance has freedom to apply an operation or not when the operation's required pre-conditions are all true. For each operation performed by an agent, an agent instance may have eager or lazy behaviours:

- In an *eager* behaviour scheme, the agent instance applies the operation as soon as it can; that is, as soon as all required pre-conditions are true.

- In a *lazy* behaviour scheme the agent instance applies the operation when it is really obliged to do so; that is, when one of the operation's required trigger conditions becomes true.

Agent concurrency

Multiple trigger conditions might become true in the same system state. If these conditions refer to different operations of the same agent, an agent instance is obliged to apply them all in parallel. If they refer to operations of different agents, the corresponding agent instances are obliged to apply them in parallel. The model may thus exhibit intra- and inter-agent concurrency. Because of the obligations captured by trigger conditions, this is true concurrency, rather than operation interleaving.

Agent dependencies on operations

Agent dependencies on goals, as defined in Section 11.2.6, entail agent dependencies on operations operationalizing those goals. Modelling agent dependencies on operations/tasks is therefore not strictly needed, as it is redundant with dependency modelling at goal level.

12.3.3 Goal operationalization and satisfaction arguments

Chapters 1 and 6 already made the case for satisfaction arguments as a basis for establishing requirements 'correctness' with respect to higher-level objectives. Such arguments can be used for convincing stakeholders that their concerns are met by the requirements specification. They support derivational traceability among RE artefacts (see Sections 1.1.4 and 6.3.1).

Goal AND-refinement links in a goal model provided the first source of satisfaction arguments. As we saw it in Sections 7.4 and 8.2, this first type of argument is based on the notion of correctness of a goal refinement; it takes the form:

$$\{REFINEMENT,\ DOM\} \models ParentGoal,$$

where *REFINEMENT* denotes a set of conjoined sub-goals refining a goal *ParentGoal,* possibly in conjunction with domain properties and hypotheses in *DOM.* By chaining such arguments bottom up, we may show that a set of requirements and expectations ensure a parent goal, the latter ensuring its own parent goal together with others, and recursively, until a high-level goal of interest is thereby shown to be satisfied.

Operationalization links in an operation model provide a second, complementary source of satisfaction arguments in addition to refinement-based ones. To see what such arguments may look like, we first need to define what a correct operationalization is.

Correctness of a goal operationalization

A goal G is correctly operationalized into operations $Op_1, \ldots, Op_n$ if and only if the specifications $Spec(Op_1), \ldots, Spec(Op_n)$ of these operations in terms of domain and required conditions are necessary and sufficient for ensuring G; that is:

$$\{Spec(Op_1), \ldots, Spec(Op_n)\} \models G \qquad \textit{completeness}$$
$$Spec(Op_1), \ldots, Spec(Op_n)\} \not\models \textbf{false} \qquad \textit{consistency}$$
$$G \models \{Spec(Op_1), \ldots, Spec(Op_n)\} \qquad \textit{minimality}$$

(Remember that $S \models A$ means: 'the assertion A is always satisfied in any circumstance where all assertions in S are satisfied'.) The completeness criterion has similarities with the corresponding criterion for goal refinement in Section 8.2. A noticeable difference is in the definition of the minimality criterion. For operationalization, this criterion states that the required conditions should not be unnecessarily restrictive; they should not be stronger than what is strictly required by the goal. As we already noted in Section 11.2.3, an agent responsible for a goal must enforce it without being more restrictive than what the goal requires.

Goals provide thus a *completeness criterion* for an operation model. Such a model is complete with respect to a goal model if all satisfiable goals from the latter model are ensured by the specifications of the operations in the operation model.

Operationalization-based satisfaction arguments

Our second type of satisfaction argument is based on the above notion of operationalization correctness. It takes the form:

$$\{Spec(Op_1), \ldots, Spec(Op_n)\} \models OperationalizedGoal,$$

which means: 'the goal *OperationalizedGoal* is satisfied if the operations $Op_1, \ldots, Op_n$ are always applied in states satisfying their specifications $Spec(Op_1), \ldots, Spec(Op_n)$, respectively'.

By chaining operationalization-based arguments with refinement-based arguments, and chaining the latter bottom up, we may show that the specified operations ensure their underlying goals, the latter ensuring their own parent goals together with others, and recursively, until a high-level goal of interest is thereby shown to be satisfied.

Example Consider the goal *DoorsStateClosedIfNonZeroMeasuredSpeed* again. This goal states that:

for any tr: TrainInfo, **always (if** tr.Speed $\neq$ 0 **then** tr.DoorsState = 'closed')

To provide an informal satisfaction argument for this goal, based on its operationalization into operations OpenDoors and StartTrain, we need to argue that:

$$\{Spec(OpenDoors), Spec(StartTrain)\} \models DoorsStateClosedIfNonZeroMeasuredSpeed$$

Such an argument runs as follows. Because of the required pre-condition $tr.Speed = 0$ on the OpenDoors operation, we know that when this operation is applied to make its domain post-condition $tr.DoorsState = 'open'$ true, we necessarily have $tr.Speed = 0$ (by definition of a pre-condition). On the other hand, because of the required pre-condition $tr.DoorsState = 'closed'$ on the StartTrain operation, we know that when this operation is applied to make its domain post-condition tr.Speed $\neq$ 0, we necessarily have $tr.DoorsState = 'closed'$ from this pre-condition. Hence the goal maintained in both cases. Moreover, no other operation in the model can violate the goal; the OpenDoors and StartTrain operations are the only ones to have a *DomPost* affecting the goal's conditions DoorsStateClosed and NonZeroMeasuredSpeed, respectively.

Frame axioms A more rigorous argument relies on two so-called frame axioms that are built-in into operation models, namely:

- The operations have no other effects than the ones specified in their post-conditions.

- Any state transition corresponding to the domain pre- and post-condition of an operation necessarily implies that *this* operation has been applied.

Satisfaction arguments along the lines suggested here can be made formal if the goals and required conditions are expressed in a formal specification language. As Chapter 18 will show, we can then formally derive required conditions of operations, from goal specifications, by use of operationalization patterns.

Operationalization-based traceability

Operationalization links in an operation model give us other derivational traceability links for free, in addition to refinement links in the corresponding goal model. (These links were discussed in Section 6.3.1.) The separate specification of required pre, trigger and post-conditions of an operation, per goal, and their explicit connection to the goal requiring them yield derivational traceability links directly.

12.4 Goals, agents, objects and operations: The semantic picture

Figure 12.5 suggests an overall semantic picture of what a system model conveys when we integrate its goal, object, agent and operation model components.

As we saw in Chapter 7, the system's behavioural goals together prescribe a maximal set of admissible system behaviours. These behaviours are composed of parallel agent behaviours. A behaviour of an agent instance is captured by a sequence of state transitions for the object attributes and associations that the agent controls. These state transitions correspond to applications of operations performed by the agent; they take the smallest time unit (as discussed in Section 12.1). Agent instances evolve *synchronously* from state to state according to the obligations and permissions prescribed on their operations. As suggested in Figure 12.5, an agent instance might do nothing along system state transitions, while another might

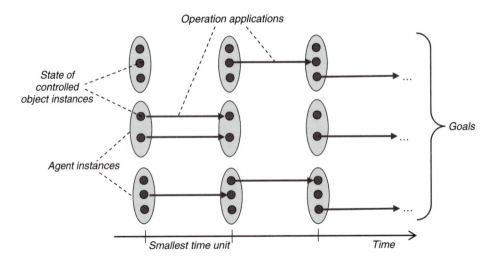

Figure 12.5 *Goals, objects, agents, and operations: the semantic picture*

be required to apply multiple operations in parallel because of multiple trigger conditions becoming true in the same state. Do-nothing behaviours may arise from lack of permission or from non-deterministic behaviour, as previously discussed.

12.5 Representing operation models

Operation models are represented by two kinds of diagram: operationalization diagrams and UML use case diagrams.

12.5.1 Operationalization diagrams

An operationalization diagram is an annotated graph showing the system operations, their operationalization links to goals in the goal model and input/output links to objects in the object model. Performance links may also be transferred from the agent model to indicate which agent performs which operation. An operation node is annotated with the specification of the operation's domain pre- and post-condition. An operationalization link is annotated with the specification of the required pre-, trigger and/or post-condition defining this operationalization.

Putting pieces from the previous sections together, Figure 12.6 shows an operationalization diagram fragment for the train control system. Operationalization links are represented by refinement arrows annotated with the conditions required for the target goal. In case of AND-operationalization of a goal by multiple operations, such links are AND-joined. The labelled arrows capture operation signatures through input and output links, labelled by the corresponding input and output variables, respectively. Such links are possibly qualified by the object attributes and associations to which the operation is restricted. As seen in Section 12.2.2, signatures can alternatively be specified textually as annotations on the corresponding operation.

Figure 12.7 shows a textual declaration for the library CheckOut operation. In this example, the predicate notation introduced in Section 10.3 for associations is used in the domain pre- and post-condition to specify the transition from a state where there is no Loan link between the input variables to a state where there is one such link.

12.5.2 UML use case diagrams

As introduced in Section 4.3.5, use case diagrams provide an outline view of restricted aspects of an operation model. For each agent, a rectangle includes all the operations that the agent

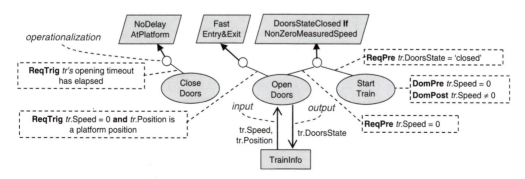

Figure 12.6 *Portion of operationalization diagram with annotations*

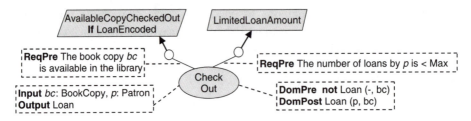

Figure 12.7 *Operationalization diagram excerpt for the library system*

performs. An inside operation bubble is connected to an outside agent icon if this operation 'interacts' with the agent in the environment of the operation performer. Figure 12.8 shows use case diagrams for the train control and library systems. The left-hand part shows operations performed by the TrainController and OnBoardController agents. Each agent appears in the environment of the other, where it interacts with some operations.

The right-hand part of Figure 12.8 illustrates the mechanisms for structuring use cases introduced in Section 4.3.5. The CheckReserved operation appears as a 'sub-operation' included in CheckOut. As we can see here, common sub-operations can thereby be factored out of multiple operations. The RefuseLoan operation appears as a variant extending the normal CheckOut operation; it has to be applied as an alternative course of action when the condition named *TooManyCopies* holds.

While providing a simple functional overview of system operations, use case diagrams are fairly vague. Operations and agents are captured only by their name; what is meant by an inter-action is unclear; the semantics of 'include' and 'extend' links appears obscure. The latter links should therefore be avoided. By favouring goal decomposition over operation decomposition, we can keep traceability to underlying goals and the prospect for satisfaction arguments.

To partially recover from the problems with use cases, we might annotate operation bubbles with pre- and post-conditions capturing the applicability and effect of each operation.

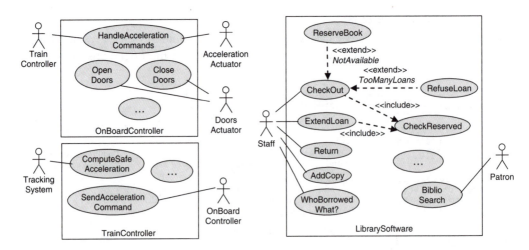

Figure 12.8 *Use case diagrams for train control and library management*

We might also detail what a bubble and its interaction links convey through a sequence diagram detailing inside interactions. (Sequence diagrams are the UML counterpart of the event trace diagrams introduced in Section 4.3.6; see Section 13.1.) With global pre- and post-conditions, however, we lose traceability to higher-level concerns and corresponding satisfaction arguments. With sequence diagrams, we get into the problems inherent to scenario specification – coverage problem, combinatorial explosion of cases, lack of structure and rationale, risk of overspecification (see Section 2.2.5). To overcome those problems, we can generate use cases automatically from richer, more precise representations in order to use them for what they are – an outline view of the system operations grouped by agent in an interacting environment. This generation is straightforward, as we will see in Section 12.6.2.

12.6 Building operation models

As for the other system views, the building of an operation model can be guided by heuristic techniques. The systematic building of operationalization diagrams from goal models and/or interaction scenarios is discussed first. Then we will see how use cases can be generated from operationalization diagrams.

12.6.1 Heuristics for building operationalization diagrams

To build an operationalization diagram, we essentially need to:

- Identify operations and their domain pre- and post-conditions, from which input and output variables are identified.

- Specify required pre-, trigger and/or post-conditions to annotate operationalization links between the identified operations and their underlying goals in the goal model.

Deriving operations from goal fluents

The idea here is to identify classes of state transitions that are 'meaningful' to behavioural leaf goals, as they are implicitly referred to in the goal specifications. To do this, we review *Achieve* and *Maintain* leaf goals in the goal model to analyse the inner structure of their specification (see Figure 12.9).

- For each goal specification G, we list the atomic state conditions P composing it through combinations of logical connectives. Any change in P's truth value can affect G's truth value.

- For each such condition P, we look for the operation whose applications make it **true** when it was **false**. This operation is called the *initiating operation* for P. By definition, P's initiating operation has *not* P and P as domain pre- and post-condition, respectively. Symmetrically, we look for the operation whose applications make P **false** when it was **true**. This operation is called the *terminating operation* for P. By definition, P's terminating operation has P and *not* P as domain pre- and post-condition, respectively.

Every atomic condition in a behavioural leaf goal yields a pair of initiating–terminating operations with corresponding domain pre- and post-conditions. These operations should be

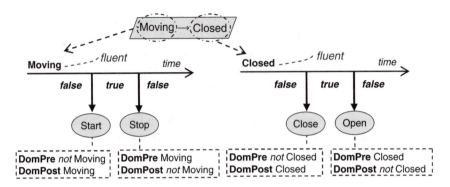

Figure 12.9 *Fluent-based derivation of operations*

considered as candidates for the operation model, since each of them can affect the goal's truth value. Such conditions defined by initiating and terminating operations are called *fluents* (Miller & Shanahan, 1999).

Example   Consider the leaf goal *Maintain [DoorsStateClosedIfNonZeroMeasuredSpeed]* shown in Figure 12.9. Its specification is:

always (if train's measuredSpeed $\neq$ 0 **then** train's doorsState = 'closed')

Let us write for short:

Moving: train's measuredSpeed $\neq$ 0,   *Closed:* train's doorsState = 'closed'

The **if** part of this specification contains just one fluent: *Moving*.

- The fluent's initiating operation has *not Moving* and *Moving* as *DomPre* and *DomPost*, respectively; we call this operation *StartTrain*.
- The fluent's terminating operation has *Moving* and *not Moving* as *DomPre* and *DomPost*, respectively; we call this operation *StopTrain*.

The **then** part of the goal specification contains another fluent: *Closed*.

- The fluent's initiating operation has *not Closed* and *Closed* as *DomPre* and *DomPost*, respectively; we call this operation *CloseDoors*.
- The fluent's terminating operation has *Closed* and *not Closed* as *DomPre* and *DomPost*, respectively; we call this operation *OpenDoors*.

Quite similarly, the goal AvailableCopyCheckedOutIfLoanEncoded in Figure 11.15 states that:

if the loan details for a copy of a book requested by a patron are encoded
then the loan is established between the patron and the book copy.

This specification yields the environment tasks *EncodeLoan* and *EncodeReturn* (from the **if** part) and the software operations *CheckOut* and *Return* on book copies (from the **then** part), together with corresponding domain pre- and post-conditions. For example, the fluent 'loan established between patron and book copy' has *CheckOut* and *Return* as initiating and terminating operations, respectively; the *CheckOut* operation has *not Loan(p,bc)* and *Loan(p,bc)* as domain pre- and post-condition, respectively (see Figure 12.7).

In such a systematic identification of operations relevant to goals, the input and output variables of each operation appear as they are referenced in their domain pre- and post-conditions. For example, *bc:BookCopy* and *p:Patron* are input declarations emerging from the domain pre-condition of the *CheckOut* operation (see Figure 12.7).

Identifying operations from interaction scenarios

In parallel with the fluent-based derivation of operations from declarative specifications, we may identify operations from more operational material when available. Scenarios were introduced as elicitation vehicles in Section 2.2.5; their representation by event trace diagrams was presented in Section 4.3.6 (the UML syntax for this representation will be introduced in the next chapter).

The heuristic technique for identifying operations from scenarios is again fairly simple. An interaction event in a scenario takes place between a source agent instance and a target agent instance. It might correspond to the application of an operation applied by the *source* agent; the output variables of this operation are monitored by the *target* agent. If the interaction carries attributes for information transmission, the attributes might be considered as candidate output variables. The source and target agent instances might be considered as candidate input variables of the operation.

For each interaction event we may thus ask ourselves to which operation application this event corresponds, which atomic condition intrinsically characterizes the state along the source agent's timeline right before the interaction (as candidate *DomPre*) and which atomic condition intrinsically characterizes the state along the source agent's timeline right after the interaction (as candidate *DomPost*).

Figure 12.10 illustrates the use of this heuristic on a meeting scheduling scenario introduced in previous chapters. The first interaction event is meetingRequest; it carries dateRange and withWhom as interaction attributes. Consistent with the object model in Figure 4.5 where Requesting appears as an association having those attributes, we identify an operation named RequestMeeting mapping a state satisfying the domain pre-condition *not Requesting(in,m)*, where there is no Requesting link instance between the variables *in* and *m*, to a state satisfying the domain post-condition *Requesting(in,m)*, where such a link instance now exists. The instance variable *m* appears as an output variable resulting from this link creation. The identification of other operations from the next interaction events proceeds similarly; see Figure 12.10.

Strengthening domain pre- and post-conditions with required conditions

Once operations are identified from goal specifications or scenarios, we need to find a correct set of required pre-, trigger and/or post-conditions on each of them so that their underlying goals are arguably satisfied.

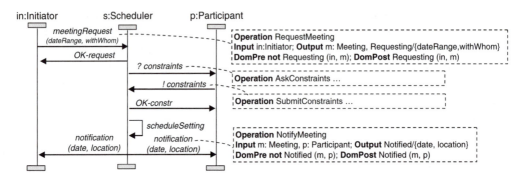

Figure 12.10   *Scenario-based identification of operations*

To do this, we review *Achieve* and *Maintain* leaf goals in the goal model and, for each of them, consider every operation whose *DomPost* effect may affect the goal specification. For each such operation we determine whether its applications need to be constrained by a permission, an obligation or an additional effect to enable a satisfaction argument in view of that *DomPost* effect.

Identifying required permissions

If the operation's *DomPost* effect can violate the goal specification under a condition *C*, we take ***not*** *C* as a required pre-condition of this operation to prevent applications in states resulting in goal violation.

For example, the *DomPost* effect of the library CheckOut operation in Figure 12.7 states that a Loan link is created between patron *p* and book copy *bc*. As a result, the number of loans by *p* is then increased by one unit. Such an effect may thus affect the goal Maintain[LimitedLoanAmount], which states that 'the number of loans by a patron may never exceed a threshold Max'; the goal is violated in the case *C* where the number of loans has already reached the upper bound *Max*. Hence the required pre-condition 'number of loans by p < Max' is obtained as a negation of the violation pre-condition.

Identifying required obligations

If the goal prescribes that the operation's *DomPost* effect must hold whenever a sufficient condition *C* becomes true, we take *C* as a required trigger condition of this operation to force its application in states where *C* becomes true.

For example, the goal ReminderIssuedIfNotBackOnTime in Figure 11.11 states that 'a reminder must be issued for a book copy borrowed by a patron if the return deadline is expired'. Using the fluent-based heuristic for operation identification, we find the IssueReminder operation whose *DomPost* is: 'a reminder is issued'. To enforce the goal, we therefore take the sufficient condition C: 'the return deadline has expired', in the goal's **if** part, as trigger condition on the operation.

When the operation has required pre-conditions, the trigger condition thereby obtained must be enriched to cover all of them, to meet the consistency rule discussed in Section 12.3.1.

Identifying required additional effects

The operation's *DomPost* effect might not be sufficient to ensure the target condition prescribed by the goal. If this is the case, we take the missing sub-condition C in the target condition as the required post-condition on this operation, to force its applications to reach the target.

For example, the *DomPost* effect of the PlanMeeting operation specified in Section 12.3.1 is: 'the meeting m has a date and a location'. This is not sufficient for operationalizing the goal ConvenientMeetingDate. The following missing target condition should therefore be taken as the required post-condition for this goal: 'the selected meeting date is convenient to important participants'.

The same heuristic in the train control system yields 'the sent acceleration is within a safe range' as a required post-condition on the operation SendAccelerationCommandToTrain for the goal Maintain[SafeAccelerationCommand]. The operation's *DomPost* effect is: 'the acceleration is sent to train *tr*', which obviously is not sufficient for the target.

While using the above heuristic technique for strengthening domain pre- and post-conditions with required conditions, we might find instance variables that are referred to in the goal specifications but not declared yet as input or output variables in the operation's signature. If this is the case, the signature must be extended accordingly.

The preceding technique for identifying operations and their required conditions is widely applicable but lacks precision – in particular, regarding the specific system states to which atomic conditions in goal specifications refer. A formalization of such specifications in temporal logic yields much higher precision. We can then elaborate formal satisfaction arguments and formally derive required conditions from goal specifications by the use of operationalization patterns. Such formal derivation is discussed in Chapter 18.

Refine goals, not operations

This point was made before in Section 12.1. It is sufficiently important to recall it here as a heuristic rule. Unlike operation refinement, goal refinement followed by operationalization has a precise semantics, supports simple satisfaction arguments, and provides derivational traceability to the functional and non-functional goals underpinning operations. In contrast, the refinement of operation pre- and post-conditions appears more complex and error prone, and requires more intricate satisfaction arguments. It is therefore preferable to refine goals and then derive operations from fine-grained goals assigned to single agents.

Bidirectional derivation: From operations to goals, scenarios, objects and agents

As we already noted for the model-building heuristics in the previous chapters, the links between an operation model and its corresponding goal, object and agent models are bidirectional. We may therefore identify and specify goals, objects, agents and scenarios from operations. An operation might sometimes be more apparent in elicitation material than its underlying goals or even than scenarios involving them. In such cases we need to start from the identified operations, investigate the conditions under which they may or must be applied, and then investigate the real reasons why such conditions should restrict operation applications, in order to elicit their underlying goals. Exploring examples of operation applications in interaction scenarios might help in the identification of domain and required conditions.

For example, it might be pretty clear from the beginning that checking out book copies is a loan management operation that should be automated in the system-to-be. While putting our finger on a pre-condition requiring the CheckOut operation to be applied only if 'the number of loans by p is < Max', we might ask ourselves why it should be so, in order to discover the underlying goal LimitedLoadAmount and its parent goal AvailabilityEnforced.

The goals thereby identified need to populate the corresponding goal model in order to support RE-specific types of analysis such as obstacle analysis, threat analysis, conflict analysis or reasoning about alternative options, as we will see in Chapters 16 and 18.

12.6.2 Generating use case diagrams from operationalization diagrams

An operationalization diagram shows system operations, their input–output objects and the goals they operationalize. A corresponding agent diagram shows the agents performing such operations and the object attributes/associations that those agents monitor or control. It is therefore fairly straightforward to generate UML use cases from them. The generation runs as follows:

> **for each** agent *ag* in an agent diagram
> > enclose all the operations *ag* performs in a rectangle bearing *ag*'s label;
> > **for each** such operation *op* in the corresponding operationalization diagram
> > > **for each** other agent *ag-env* in the agent diagram
> > > **if** *ag-env* controls one of *op*'s input object attribute/association
> > > > **or** monitors one of *op*'s output object attribute/association
> > > > **then** include *ag-env* around *ag*'s rectangle and draw an interaction link
> > > > > between *op* and *ag-env*

By transferring the annotations from the operationalization diagram to the use case diagrams, we obtain a more precise form of use case showing the domain pre- and post-condition of every operation together with its various required pre-, trigger and post-conditions for the associated goals. The generated use case diagram is then traceable to the goals underlying each operation.

Summary

- An operation model addresses the *WHAT*-dimension of requirements engineering by capturing the functional services that the target system should provide in order to meet its goals. The model part covering software operations yields software specifications as input to the development process. The model part covering environmental tasks yields descriptions of procedures to follow in the environment for satisfaction of the system's goals. We can obtain other products from an operation model, such as executable specifications for system animation or software prototyping, black-box test data and project management information.

- An operation is a binary relation mapping input variables to output variables. The input variables denote object instances to which the operation applies. The output variables denote object instances on which the operation acts. Operation applications yield atomic state transitions where the state of the output variables is changed.

- In an operation model, an operation is annotated by individual features such as its signature and its domain pre- and post-conditions. The signature declares the input and output variables. We can restrict declarations to specific object attributes and associations. The domain pre- and post-conditions capture what the operation intrinsically means in the domain, without any prescription for goal satisfaction, by describing the class of input states when the operation is applied and the class of output states when the operation has been applied.

- Operationalization refers to the process of mapping leaf goals, under the responsibility of single agents, to operations ensuring them. An operation may operationalize multiple goals. A goal may be operationalized by multiple operations. Each operation must be performed under restricted conditions for satisfaction of each underlying goal, including required pre-conditions, trigger conditions and post-conditions.

- Operationalization links support satisfaction arguments that complement the ones provided by AND-refinement links in the goal model. Here we need to argue that a set of operations satisfies an underlying goal thanks to the required pre-, trigger and post-conditions under which they are applied. By chaining operationalization-based arguments with refinement-based ones, we may show that the specified operations ensure a high-level goal of interest. Moreover, the separate specification of required pre, trigger and post-conditions of operations per goal yields derivational traceability links for free.

- Semantically, behavioural goals together prescribe a maximal set of admissible system behaviours. These behaviours are composed of parallel agent behaviours. The behaviour of an agent instance is captured by a sequence of state transitions for the object attributes/associations that the agent controls. These state transitions correspond to applications of operations performed by the agent. Agent instances evolve synchronously from state to state according to the obligations and permissions prescribed on their operations. An agent instance might do nothing along system state transitions, while another might be required to apply multiple operations in parallel because of multiple trigger conditions becoming true in the same state. Do-nothing behaviours arise from a lack of permission or from agent non-determinism.

- An operation model can be graphically represented by operationalization diagrams and UML use case diagrams. An operationalization diagram shows the system operations, their operationalization links to goals in the goal model, input/output links to objects in the object model, and possibly performance links to agents in the agent model. An operation node is annotated with domain pre- and post-conditions, whereas an operationalization link is annotated with required pre-, trigger and/or post-conditions. A use case diagram provides an outline view of an operation model by showing the operations that an agent performs together with interaction links with other agents. Use case diagrams are easily generated from operationalization diagrams.

- Various heuristics can be used for building operationalization diagrams. We may derive operations and their domain pre- and post-conditions by extracting fluents from goal specifications, together with their initiating and terminating operations. We may also identify operations from scenarios by considering interaction events as operation applications; domain pre- and post-conditions are obtained as state conditions right before and right after the interaction on the source agent's timeline. To specify required pre-, trigger and/or post-conditions, we may look for operations whose domain post-condition may affect behavioural goal specifications. Such operations may require a permission condition for avoiding goal violations, an obligation condition for enforcing the operation effect as stated by the goal or an additional effect condition to reach the goal target.

- The links between an operation model and its corresponding goal, object and agent models are bidirectional. When an operation is more apparent than its underlying goals, we may investigate the conditions under which it may or must be applied, and then elicit the operation's underlying goals by investigating the real reasons why such conditions should restrict operation applications.

- Goal refinement followed by operationalization is preferable to operation refinement, as it preserves goal traceability and supports simpler satisfaction arguments.

Notes and Further Reading

A more technical treatment of goal-oriented modelling and specification of operations can be found in Letier and van Lamsweerde (2002b).

Many requirements modelling languages offer a counterpart of operations, for example activities in RML (Greenspan et al., 1986) or tasks in i^* (Yu, 1993). Use cases were introduced in Jacobson et al. (1993). The UML notation for use cases is described in Booch et al. (1999). The CATALYSIS approach makes use cases more precise through pre- and post-conditions. Proposals for lifting use cases up for requirements engineering are discussed in Regnell et al. (1995). A tool generating use cases from operationalization diagrams can be found at www.objectiver.com.

The operations in this chapter are informally specified in a state-based style in the spirit of languages such as Z (Potter et al., 1996) or VDM (Jones, 1990). Here, we separate prescriptive conditions from descriptive ones, ensure traceability to underlying goals, and capture obligations that are generally not expressible in state-based languages.

The specification of agent permissions and obligations was already considered in the Forrest project (Finkelstein & Potts, 1987). Other formal frameworks for specifying permissions and obligations in requirements engineering can be found in Kent *et al.* (1993) and Dubois *et al.* (1993). A good account of this specification style from a logic standpoint can be found in Meyer and Wieringa (1993). Agent non-determinism and eager/lazy schemes for handling permissions are discussed in De Landtsheer *et al.* (2004) in the context of translating goal specifications into SCR specifications.

Goal operationalization has long been considered in AI problem solving (Mostow, 1983). A survey of its use in machine learning can be found in van Lamsweerde (1991). Operationalization processes for RE appeared in Dardenne *et al.* (1991), Mylopoulos *et al.* (1992) and Dardenne *et al.* (1993). Their application in business process reengineering is illustrated in Anton *et al.* (1994).

The principle of deriving operational specifications of a multi-agent system from more abstract ones is convincingly illustrated in Feather (1994).

Miller and Shanahan introduced fluents in their event calculus (Miller & Shanahan, 1999). For model analysis, fluents provide a nice connection between declarative and operational specifications (Giannakopoulou & Magee, 2003).

Exercises

- Explain what is wrong in the following specification of the software OpenDoors operation, and why:

  Operation OpenDoors
      Def Software operation controlling the opening of all doors of a train;
      Input tr: TrainInfo; **Output** tr: TrainInfo/DoorsState;
      DomPre *tr*.DoorsState = 'closed'; **DomPost** *tr*.DoorsState = 'open';
      ReqPre for DoorsStateClosedIfNonZeroMeasuredSpeed: *tr*.Speed = 0;
      ReqPre for *SafeEntry&Exit:* *tr*.Position is a platform position;
      ReqTrig for *FastEntry&Exit:* *tr*.Speed = 0.

- In the train control case study, the goal Maintain[AccelerationCommandSentInTime] requires the operation SendAccelerationCommandToTrain to be applied at least every 3 seconds (say). How would you capture this in terms of required conditions?

- Extend the operationalization diagram for the library system in Figure 12.7 with the operation of returning a copy of a book and its underlying goal Achieve[CopyReturnedOnTimeIfBorrowed]. Specify the signature and the domain pre- and post-conditions of this operation, and its required conditions for that goal. Insert your specifications as model annotations.

- Consider the following goal in an ambulance-dispatching system.

  Achieve[AmbulanceAllocatedBasedOnIncidentInfo]

  Def *When an incident is encoded by the call operator and no ambulance has already been allocated to the incident, the first ambulance shall immediately be allocated by the dispatching software. This ambulance must be one available and nearest to the incident location, based on information recorded about ambulances.*

  Specify the signature and domain pre- and post-conditions of the operation AllocateAmbulance operationalizing that goal. Then, specify the required trigger condition and the required post-condition for satisfaction of that goal. Build a satisfaction argument for the correctness of your operationalization.

- Consider the goal model fragment for the meeting scheduling system in Chapter 8 (Figure 8.11) and the specification of the PlanMeeting operation in Section 12.3.1. Build an operationalization diagram containing the operations that the meeting scheduler software should perform to ensure the leaf goals assigned to it in Figure 8.11. Then show the successive steps of generating a use case diagram for this agent from your operationalization diagram.

- Show in detail how the heuristics in Section 12.6.1 can be used to derive systematically the required pre- and trigger conditions on the train control operations in Figure 12.6.

- Apply the heuristics in Section 12.6.1 to determine adequate required conditions of the operation RemindMeeting in order to operationalize the meeting scheduling goal 'participants shall be reminded of the meeting date and location two weeks before the meeting'.

- Consider the following simplified specification of the braking logic in an aircraft-control system:

  The reverse thrust is set to 'enabled' **if and only if** the wheel pulses are set to 'on'.

  This requirement is assigned to the autopilot software, which controls the variable ReverseThrust and monitors the variable WheelPulses. Use the model-building heuristics in Section 12.6.1 to identify fluents, initiating and terminating operations together with their respective domain pre- and post-conditions, and the required conditions on these operations for the satisfaction of that requirement. Represent your answer by an annotated operationalization diagram and provide a requirement satisfaction argument for it.

- Consider the following simplified problem statement for a safety injection control system in a nuclear power plant (Courtois & Parnas, 1993):

  The purpose of safety injection is to prevent or mitigate damages to the core and coolant components on the occurrence of a fault such as loss of coolant. The ESFAS (Engineered Safety Feature Actuation System) is a software component that monitors steam pressure in the coolant system. If the pressure falls below some 'low' threshold, a safety injection signal is sent to a safety feature component to cope with the incident. A manual block button allows operators to override safety injection during a normal start-up or cool down of the reactor. The manual block must be automatically disabled when the pressure rises above a 'permit' threshold.

a. Build a goal model for this system showing how safety concerns are refined into leaf goals assigned to the ESFAS, SafetyFeature, CoolantSystem and Operator agents.

b. Derive a context diagram from your model that shows the interfaces among those agents, using the technique described in Section 11.5.2.

c. Build an annotated operationalization diagram for the requirement

   Maintain [SafetyInjection **If** LowPressure **And Not** Overridden]

under the responsibility of the ESFAS agent, using the heuristics in Section 12.6.1. As a hint, the annotating domain and required conditions should cover the StartSafetyInjection, StopSafetyInjection, OverrideSafetyInjection and DisableOverride operations performed by ESFAS.

13

Modelling
System Behaviours

I n our multi-view modelling framework for RE, this chapter is dedicated to the behavioural view of the system we want to model. A *behaviour model* captures the required behaviours of system agents in terms of temporal sequences of state transitions for the variables that they control. These transitions are caused by operation applications or by external events. The system's global behaviour is obtained as a parallel composition of agent behaviours.

As we saw in the previous chapters, a declarative goal model captures such behaviours implicitly; the corresponding operation model focuses on classes of input–output state transitions; the object model declares and structures the variables undergoing state transitions; the agent model indicates which variable is controlled by which agent. A behaviour model complements those various views by making the required behaviours fully *explicit*. In particular, it completes the static representation of system functionalities discussed in the previous chapter by capturing the required system dynamics.

While modelling the dynamics of an agent, we may consider specific behaviours of specific agent instances or all possible behaviours of any agent instance. Specific instance behaviours are captured through *scenarios*; general class behaviours are captured through *state machines*.

Scenarios and state machines were introduced in Chapter 4 when we reviewed diagrammatic notations for specifying statements in a requirements document (see Sections 4.3.6 and 4.3.7). This chapter expands on that introductory material in three ways:

- It highlights the complementarity and connections between a behaviour model and the corresponding goal, object, agent and operation models.

- It provides techniques for building behaviour models in a systematic way.

- It introduces the basics of UML syntax for representing scenarios and state machines by sequence diagrams and state diagrams, respectively.

A behaviour model may capture actual behaviours in the *system-as-is*. Such a model may be used during domain analysis to help understand how the system is running, what the problems might be with this and which dynamic aspects should be taken into account in the system-to-be.

A behaviour model of the *system-to-be* explicitly defines how this system should behave. As discussed in previous chapters, instance-level scenarios for the system-to-be provide partial, narrative representations that can be used for eliciting, validating or explaining behavioural requirements. We can also produce acceptance test data from them. Class-level state machines provide executable representations that can be used for model validation through animation, for model checking against formal specifications of domain properties and goals, or for code generation.

Section 13.1 summarizes what we know about scenarios from the previous chapters while providing further details on their structuring and their UML representation as sequence diagrams. Section 13.2 summarizes what we know about state machines while providing further details on their structuring and their UML representation as state diagrams. Section 13.3 presents a variety of techniques for identifying scenarios, for decorating them with explicit state information, for mining goals from scenarios and for building state machines systematically from scenarios and from goal operationalizations.

13.1 Modelling instance behaviours

As introduced in Sections 2.2.5 and 4.3.6, a *scenario* is a temporal sequence of interaction events among agent instances. The interacting instances may be instances of the same agent or of different ones. In the case of a *positive* scenario, the sequence of interactions illustrates a possible way of satisfying an implicit behavioural goal; the scenario captures one admissible behaviour of the interacting agent instances. In the case of a *negative* scenario, the sequence of interactions illustrates a possible way of satisfying an implicit obstacle to a goal; the scenario captures one inadmissible behaviour. A scenario may be sequentially composed of *episodes*; these are sub-scenarios associated with specific sub-goals of the goal underlying the scenario.

An *interaction event* is directed and synchronous. It typically corresponds to the source agent instance applying an operation whose effect is monitored by the target agent instance. The source agent is said to *control* the interaction, whereas the target agent *monitors* it. Like any event, an interaction is an instantaneous object; we can therefore declare attributes of it in the corresponding object model and label interaction instances with them to specify information transmission from source to target (see Figure 13.2 for examples of this).

Section 13.1.1 shows how the event trace diagram notation introduced in Section 4.3.6 is easily transposed for representing scenarios as UML sequence diagrams. Section 13.1.2 then presents mechanisms for refining scenarios by introduction of episodes or decomposition of agent instances.

13.1.1 Scenarios as UML sequence diagrams

Sequence diagrams are a UML variant of the event trace diagrams introduced in Section 4.3.6. Figure 13.1 shows a sequence diagram for our train control system. A minor variant of this scenario appeared in Section 7.6.1 to illustrate scenario coverage by behavioural goals (see

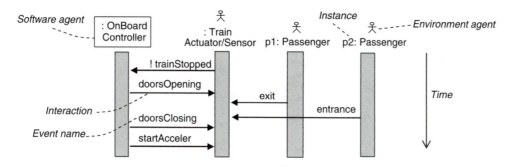

Figure 13.1 *Scenario represented by a sequence diagram*

Figure 7.8). The main difference in this example is the additional interaction event named *exit*, controlled by another instance of the Passenger agent.

The basic UML syntax for sequence diagrams is fairly similar to the one used in event trace diagrams. Timelines are represented by thin rectangles; software and environment agents are now graphically distinguished. The notation :*Ag* is used to denote a specific agent instance *ag* associated with a scenario timeline such that *InstanceOf(ag, Ag)*; see Section 10.1.2. Instance variables are introduced to distinguish instances of the same agent, for example the Passenger instances p1 and p2 in Figure 13.1.

Like in event trace diagrams, an interaction event is represented by an arrow labelled by the event name. The interaction is synchronously controlled by the source instance and monitored by the target instance. For example, the *startAcceler* event in Figure 13.1 is synchronously controlled by :OnBoardController and monitored by :TrainActuator/Sensor. It corresponds to an application of the startCommand operation by :OnBoardController. Note that state information, such as the commanded train speed becoming non-null right after this interaction, is kept implicit in that representation.

An agent timeline defines a *total* order on incoming/outgoing events; it is called a *lifeline* in UML. All events along a lifeline are comparable according to precedence. For example, we know from Figure 13.1 that the doorsOpening interaction event precedes the exit one on the :TrainActuator/Sensor lifeline. An entire sequence diagram defines a *partial* order for all events; events along non-interacting lifelines are not comparable according to precedence. For example, we cannot tell from a broader scenario involving multiple train instances, each having its own on-board software controller and actuator/sensors, the order in which two different passengers enter two different trains.

Figure 13.2 shows a loan scenario in our library system. The sequence diagram representing it illustrates other UML features.

A lifeline rectangle may be sized to capture the exact point in time where the corresponding agent instance *ag* appears in and disappears from the system – that is, the successive points in time where *InstanceOf(ag, Ag)* becomes true and then false; see Section 10.1.2. This typically applies to software agents. For example, the instance named :LoanManager in Figure 13.2 is shown to appear when a BookRequest interaction occurs and to disappear when a corresponding OK-Book interaction occurs.

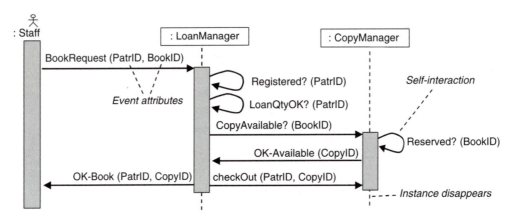

Figure 13.2 *Sequence diagram for a loan scenario*

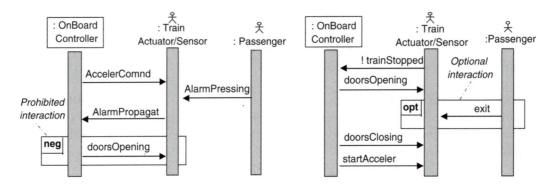

Figure 13.3 *Negative scenarios and optional interactions*

The scenario also shows information transmission through event attributes, for example the BookRequest event in Figure 13.2 carries identifiers of the corresponding patron and book instances as interaction attributes. Self-interactions are also shown there; these are 'internal' interaction events where the source and target instances are the same.

We can also enclose one or several successive interactions within a frame labelled by a keyword. In particular, the keyword **opt** means that the enclosed interactions are optional; the keyword **neg** means that the enclosed interactions may *not* happen. Negative scenarios can thereby be specified. Figure 13.3 illustrates the use of these constructs in two scenarios related to the one in Figure 13.1.

13.1.2 Scenario refinement: Episodes and agent decomposition

When elaborating complex scenarios stepwise, it may be convenient to express a coarse-grained scenario first and then incrementally refine it with further details. We can do this by introducing episodes or by decomposing an agent instance into finer-grained ones.

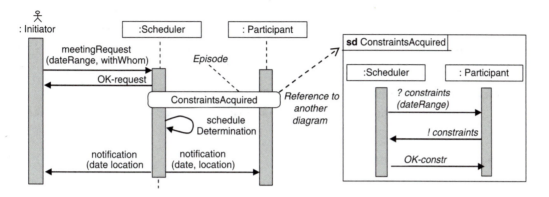

Figure 13.4 *Scenario refinement: introducing episodes*

Introducing episodes

We may sequentially decompose a scenario illustrating a goal into episodes illustrating sub-goals. The sequence of interactions defining an episode is shown in another sequence diagram labelled by the episode name. Figure 13.4 shows an example of such a scenario refinement for the meeting scheduling scenario appearing in Section 4.3.6 (see Figure 4.10). The scenario episode named *ConstraintsAcquired* is defined in another sequence diagram by a sequence of three interactions illustrating one possible constraints acquisition protocol.

Agent decomposition

It may sometimes be helpful first to consider interactions with a coarser-grained agent instance and later on refine this instance into finer-grained ones (in the way discussed in Section 11.4). New, finer-grained interactions may appear as a result. For example, the scenario in Figure 13.2 might result from a coarser-grained one shown on the left-hand part of Figure 13.5. The agent instance :LibraryManager has been decomposed into :LoanManager and :CopyManager. Similarly, the scenario in Figure 13.1 might be refined by decomposing the agent instance :TrainActuator/Sensor into :TrainSensor and :TrainActuator.

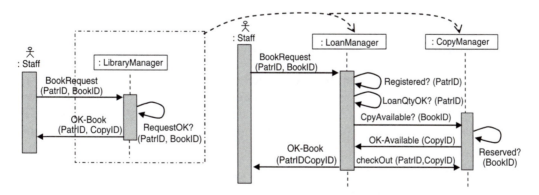

Figure 13.5 *Scenario refinement: agent decomposition*

It is worth noticing that a scenario being refined may involve coarse-grained interactions – see the RequestOK? interaction in Figure 13.5. These are strictly speaking not events as they are not instantaneous objects; they may last over multiple successive states. Such interactions are therefore sometimes called *macro-events*.

13.2 Modelling class behaviours

State machines complement the fragmentary information provided by scenarios in multiple ways:

- They make state information explicit.
- They capture the behaviour of any agent instance, not just a specific one.
- They are aimed at capturing all admissible sequences of state transitions, not just some specific ones.

As introduced in Section 4.3.7, a state machine (SM) captures admissible behaviours in terms of sequences of state transitions resulting from the occurrence of events.

In our multi-view modelling framework, we will model the required behaviour of an arbitrary instance of a system agent by the admissible sequences of state transitions for the time-varying variables that it controls. A global system behaviour is obtained by parallel composition of such behaviours.

A few notions introduced in previous chapters need to be recalled here. When an individual becomes an instance of an object, the object's attributes and associations are instantiated as *state variables* characterizing it; see Section 10.1.2. When an individual becomes an instance of the modelled agent, such variables are instantiated as state variables that this agent instance can monitor or control; see Section 11.2.2. A state variable may refer to an entire object instance when the agent controls all attributes and associations of the object; see Section 11.2.2. A *non-rigid* variable is a variable whose value is changing over time; see Section 10.4.

Two different notions of *state* are involved in behaviour modelling. It is important not to confuse them. Let us consider an object instance characterized by a number of state variables x_i.

- A *snapshot state* is a tuple of functional pairs $x_i \mapsto v_i$ where v_i denotes a possible value for x_i (see Section 10.1.1). For example, a snapshot state for an instance *tr* of the Train object might be:

   (tr.Speed $\mapsto$ 0, tr.doorsState $\mapsto$ closed, On $\mapsto$ (tr, block13), At $\mapsto$ (tr, platform2))

- A *SM state* is a class of snapshot states where some state variable always has the same value regardless of other state variables whose values may differ from one snapshot in this set to the other (see Section 4.3.7). For example, *doorsClosed* is an SM state for a train *tr* controlled by a TrainController agent instance. It includes multiple snapshot states such as:

   (tr.Speed $\mapsto$ 0, tr.doorsState $\mapsto$ *closed*, On $\mapsto$ (tr, block13), At $\mapsto$ (tr, platform2)),
   (tr.Speed $\mapsto$ 5, tr.doorsState $\mapsto$ *closed*, On $\mapsto$ (tr, block15), At $\mapsto$ (tr, nil)).

The state transitions captured by a state machine refer to SM states. The events causing these transitions are instantaneous objects to which attributes can be attached in the corresponding object model (see Section 10.1.3). Events can be of different types:

- *External events* are events that the agent associated with the state machine does not control. These include temporal events, such as an elapsed time period or a clock state change, and external stimuli occurring in state machines controlled by other agents, such as a state change there or some condition becoming true. For example, a time-out on doors opening or a passenger alarm are events that are external to the SM capturing the required dynamics of train doors.

- *Internal events* are events controlled by the agent associated with the state machine. They refer to applications of operations from the operation model by the corresponding agent instance, for example a *doorsClosing* event corresponds to an application of the CloseDoors operation. To highlight such a connection between a behaviour model and the corresponding operation model, it is advisable to take a lexical convention such as choosing a suggestive verb for an operation name and the corresponding noun for the internal event corresponding to applications of this operation.

Section 13.2.1 shows how the state machine notation introduced in Section 4.3.7 is easily transposed for representing state machines as UML state diagrams. Section 13.2.2 then presents mechanisms for refining state machines by sequential or parallel decomposition of states.

13.2.1 State machines as UML state diagrams

State diagrams are a UML variant of the state machine diagrams introduced in Section 4.3.7. They are sometime called *statechart diagrams* with reference to David Harel's original statechart notation. Figure 13.6 shows a state diagram for an arbitrary BookCopyInfo entity instance controlled by a LibraryManager agent. (Such an instance is defined at the software/environment interface to track a corresponding book copy in the physical library; see Figure 10.13.)

As we can see in Figure 13.6, the basic UML concrete syntax for state diagrams is fairly similar to the one used for SM diagrams in Section 4.3.7. The SM state onLoan in Figure 13.6 includes the set of all snapshot states of the BookCopyInfo instance having the form (..., Loan ↦ (thisCopy, PatrID), ...). The checkOut event carries *PatrID* as an attribute; it is an internal event corresponding to an application of the Borrow operation.

As in any SM diagram, a transition labelled by an event from a source state to a target state fires if an instance of the event occurs and the modelled instance is in the source state.

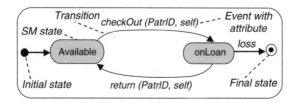

Figure 13.6 *A simple SM diagram for a BookCopyInfo entity controlled by LibraryManager*

The transition fires automatically if there is no event label (see the very first transition in Figure 13.6). In contrast to events that are instantaneous, a state has a duration; the modelled instance may remain in it for some time.

The initial and final states of the instance correspond to the states where it appears in and disappears from the system, respectively (that is, the states where the corresponding *InstanceOf* built-in predicate becomes true and false, respectively; see Section 10.1.2).

Guarded transitions

As in many state machine notations, we may in UML label a transition with a guard condition. A guard captures a necessary condition for transition firing; a transition labelled by an event and a guard fires *if* an event instance occurs and the modelled instance is in the source state, and *only if* the guard is true. The event instance thus has no effect if the guard is false.

Figure 13.7 shows a state diagram with guarded transitions for a BookInfo entity instance controlled by a LibraryManager agent. Guards are delimited by brackets. According to the lower-left transition in Figure 13.7, a book remains borrowable when a copy of it is being borrowed provided that this copy is not the last one to be available; otherwise the book gets into the UnBorrowable state, as expressed by the upper guarded transition. The guards in Figure 13.7 reference a condition name; we should in such a case specify in an annotation what this name designates. Guards may also be specified by Boolean expressions that reference state variables monitored or controlled by the modelled agent, or event attributes appearing in the diagram.

A guarded transition can have no event label. The guard then amounts to a *trigger condition*. Without it the transition would fire automatically, but with the guard the transition fires as soon as the guard condition becomes true. For example, the guard [Speed = 0] acts as a trigger condition on the event-free transition to the Stopped state in the upper left diagram of Figure 13.11 below; we get to the Stopped state as soon as the condition Speed = 0 becomes true.

Actions

An action is an auxiliary operation associated with a state transition. It is applied when the transition fires. Like any operation it is atomic. *Auxiliary* means that the action has no meaningful effect on the dynamics captured by the state diagram or by others. In other words, we do not want to capture in a state diagram the specific state resulting from the application of an action.

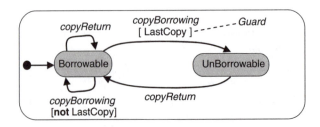

Figure 13.7   *A SM diagram for a BookInfo entity controlled by LibraryManager*

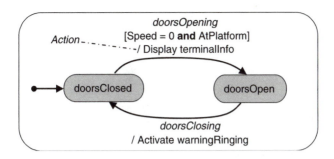

Figure 13.8 *Auxiliary actions in a state diagram*

Thanks to actions, we can prescribe certain operations to be applied in specific circumstances without cluttering the state diagram with uninteresting states that are not relevant to the dynamics of the considered state variable.

For example, Figure 13.8 shows the dynamics of the doorsState variable controlled by an OnBoardController agent. We want to prescribe that some information about the corresponding airport terminal be displayed in the train when the doors are opened at a platform. The action Display terminalInfo in Figure 13.8 does the job. Actions are prefixed by a '/' symbol. Without the actions in Figure 13.8 we would need to introduce auxiliary states such as TerminalInfoDisplayed and warningRinging; these states are not specifically relevant to the dynamics of train doors and would significantly clutter the diagram. (In passing, note the guard in the upper transition in Figure 13.8, aimed at ensuring the goals DoorsClosedWhileMoving and SafeEntry&Exit.)

It is of course essential not to use actions for operations whose applications produce states that are significant to the dynamics we want to capture; explicit events and state transitions must be introduced for these operations. Typical actions include the acquisition or display of necessary information from/to the environment of the agent being modelled, acknowledgements and the like.

Event notifications Event notifications form an important class of action where an event is notified by a 'producing' diagram to a 'consuming' diagram where this event causes transitions. This allows for synchronization among multiple diagrams. The UML format for such actions is:

/ **send** consumingDiagram. *producedEvent*

Figure 13.9 illustrates such an event notification from BookCopyInfo to BookInfo. The diagram in Figure 13.9 completes the one in Figure 13.6 for BookCopyInfo by notifying the event copyBorrowing to the diagram for BookInfo in Figure 13.7. This event is the one causing alternative state transitions in Figure 13.7; it is notified when the upper transition occurs in Figure 13.9.

Entry/exit actions There are modelling situations where we may want the same action to label all incoming transitions to a state or all outgoing ones. We can avoid this duplication by

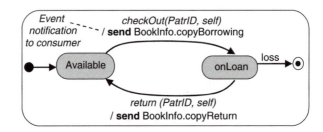

Figure 13.9 *Send actions for diagram synchronization: BookCopyInfo revisited*

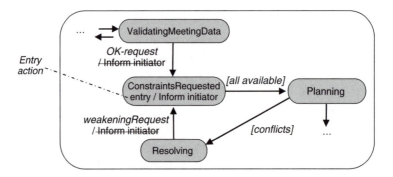

Figure 13.10 *Avoiding duplicated actions: entry and exit actions within a state*

inserting the action within the state, prefixed by the keyword **entry** to specify that the action has to be applied when entering the state (whatever the source states of the incoming transitions are), or by the keyword **exit** to specify that the action has to be applied when leaving the state (whatever the target states of the outgoing transitions are). Figure 13.10 illustrates this on a portion of the state diagram that appeared in Figure 4.11 for a meeting controlled by the meeting scheduler. Instead of duplicating the action *Inform initiator* on all incoming transitions

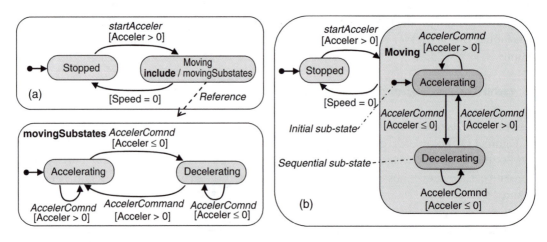

Figure 13.11 *Sequential state decomposition for the TrainInfo entity controlled by TrainController*

to the state ConstraintsRequested, we make it an entry action within that state. The action is applied at any incoming transition – in this case, at every transition labelled OK-request or weakeningRequest.

13.2.2 State machine refinement: Sequential and concurrent sub-states

As with scenarios it may be convenient, when we elaborate a complex state machine model stepwise, to specify first a coarse-grained state diagram that does not have too many states and then incrementally refine this diagram with more states that are finer-grained. We can do this by decomposing a state into sequential sub-states or into concurrent ones. In both cases the finer-grained sub-states are called *nested states*, whereas the super-state is called a *composite state*.

Sequential decomposition

An SM state may be decomposed into sub-states interconnected by new transitions. The composite state then itself becomes a state machine on the nested states. This simple structuring mechanism is recursive; a sub-state may in turn be sequentially decomposed.

Figure 13.11 illustrates two possible ways of representing a sequential state decomposition in a state diagram. On the left-hand side the state diagram refining the composite state is specified separately; the composite state has an **include** reference to it. On the right-hand side the refining diagram is graphically nested into the composite state. In both representations, the composite *Moving* state in the coarser-grained diagram is decomposed into sub-states *Accelerating* and *Decelerating* with adequate transitions inter-relating them.

The following semantic rules define sequential state decomposition more precisely:

- The instance modelled by the diagram is in the super-state if and only if it is in *one* (and only one) of the sequential sub-states. For example, the TrainInfo entity instance is in the Moving state if and only if it is either in the Accelerating state or in the Decelerating state.

- An incoming transition to the super-state is by default inherited by every sequential sub-state as an incoming transition to it. Likewise, an outgoing transition from the super-state is by default inherited by every sequential sub-state as an outgoing transition from it. For example, the transition guarded by [Speed = 0] in Figure 13.11b fires as soon as this guard becomes true *whichever sub-state the TrainInfo instance is in*. Such a default inheritance is useful for avoiding duplication of the same outgoing transition from every sequential sub-state; we merely need to make it an outgoing transition from the super-state. A generic example of such a situation arises when we want to model the dynamics of a transaction (such as an ATM or vending machine transaction) by a coarse-grained state TransactionState decomposed into sequential sub-states where a Cancel event in any of these causes the transaction to go back to its initial state. Instead of an outgoing Cancel transition from each sub-state, we merely need to specify a single outgoing Cancel transition from the super-state.

- There are, however, modelling situations where we may want to inhibit such a default inheritance of transitions. In particular, the inheritance of a super-state *incoming* transition should be avoided in view of the problem of non-deterministic choice of which alternative sequential sub-state to get into. The default inheritance of a super-state incoming or outgoing transition is inhibited by connecting this transition straight to the desired sub-states. As a more structured alternative, we may keep the transition connected to the super-state while inserting an initial sub-state (for a super-state incoming transition) or a final sub-state (for a super-state outgoing transition) within the nested diagram. An *initial sub-state* in a nested diagram defines the entry state from which the inner state transitions must start; a *final sub-state* defines the exit state where the inner state transitions must end. By connecting an initial sub-state to desired successor sub-states we are thus forcing the outer incoming transition to implicitly get into those desired states. For example, the initial sub-state inside the diagram refining the Moving state on the right-hand side of Figure 13.11 is connected to the Accelerating sub-state by an event-free transition; this forces any incoming transition to the Moving state to get straight to the Accelerating state (via the initial sub-state whose outgoing transition fires automatically). Similarly, by connecting a final sub-state to desired predecessor sub-states, we are forcing the outer outgoing transition implicitly to get out of those desired states.

Sequential sub-states may thus have specific transitions to/from other sub-states or other outer states connected to the super-state. Also note that *nested* initial or final states have a different meaning to non-nested initial or final states (as the latter represent states where the modelled instance appears in and disappears from the system; see Section 13.2.1).

Parallel decomposition

An SM state may also be decomposed into concurrent sub-states. As the latter may themselves be sequentially decomposed into sub-states, we can structure a composite state as a parallel composition of nested diagrams to model the dynamics of complex objects by hierarchical state machines. Such structuring has two main benefits:

- We can model the inherently concurrent behaviour of an agent controlling multiple state variables in parallel.

- We avoid the combinatorial explosion of the number of states in a diagram – for an agent controlling N variables each having K possible states, we need explicitly to represent $K \times N$ states instead of the K^N states required by a purely sequential state machine.

Figure 13.12 on the left shows the general state of a TrainInfo entity. This coarse-grained state, named TrainInfoState, is an aggregation of two concurrent sub-states, named MovementState and DoorsState, for the attributes of TrainInfo controlled by a TrainController agent – namely, Speed and doorsState. These concurrent sub-states are in turn decomposed into finer-grained sequential sub-states to produce the state diagram on the right of Figure 13.12. This diagram models the concurrent control of train moves and doors by the train controller. As in any parallel composition of behaviours, there can be interferences that need to be controlled through synchronization of shared events or guard conditions. In this example, the guard condition Speed = 0 in the lower sub-diagram acts as a synchronizing condition. In view of the guard semantics, this condition ensures that the lower sub-diagram gets into the state doorsOpen

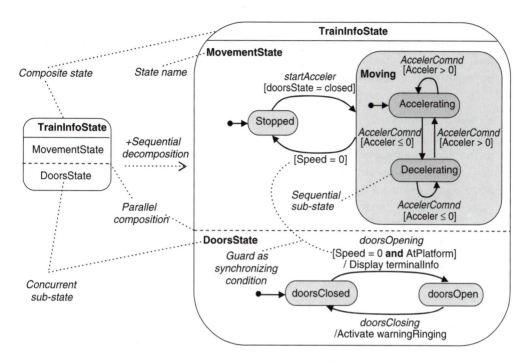

Figure 13.12   *Parallel state decomposition and hierarchical state machines*

only if the upper sub-diagram is in the state Stopped (the guard in the upper diagram tells us that the latter state is reached as soon as Speed = 0).

The following semantic rules define parallel state decomposition more precisely:

- The instance modelled by the state diagram is in the super-state if and only if it is in *each* of the concurrent sub-states. For example, the TrainInfo entity instance is in the coarse-grained state TrainInfoState if and only if it is simultaneously in the states MovementState and DoorsState. If the concurrent sub-states are themselves decomposed into sequential sub-states, then by the combined rules of parallel and sequential decomposition the instance is simultaneously in one (and only one) sequential sub-state of each concurrent state, for example Moving and doorsClosed in Figure 13.12. In Figure 13.13, the Loan

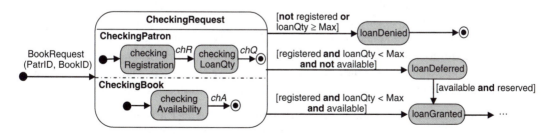

Figure 13.13   *Loan dynamics: a fragment with concurrent and sequential substates*

association instance is in super-state CheckingRequest if and only if it is simultaneously in sub-states CheckingPatron (that is, either checkingRegistration *or* checkingLoanQty *or* the final sub-state of CheckingPatron) *and* CheckingBook (that is, either checkingAvailability *or* the final sub-state of CheckingBook).

- An incoming transition to the super-state is inherited by every concurrent sub-state as an incoming transition to it. The firing rule corresponds to a *fork* mechanism. When the incoming transition to the super-state gets fired, all implicit incoming transitions to the concurrent sub-states get fired. In other words, when the super-state is entered each concurrent sub-state is entered simultaneously. For example, the occurrence of a BookRequest event in Figure 13.13 fires simultaneous incoming transitions to the concurrent sub-states CheckingPatron and CheckingBook (and, recursively, to their sequential sub-states checkingRegistration and checkingAvailability in view of the event-free transition from their respective initial sub-state).

- An outgoing transition from the super-state is inherited by every concurrent sub-state as an outgoing transition from it. The firing rule corresponds to a conditional *join* mechanism.

  a. If the outgoing transition from the super-state has no event or guard label, this transition is fired when all implicit outgoing transitions from the concurrent sub-states have been fired (in whatever order). In other words, the super-state is left when all concurrent sub-states have been left.

  b. If the outgoing transition from the super-state has an event or guard label, this transition is fired when the event occurs, provided that the guard is true (if any), forcing the exit from all concurrent sub-states. For example, the upper outgoing transition from super-state CheckingRequest in Figure 13.13 is labelled by the guard condition [not Registered or LoanQty ≥ Max]. As a result, the super-state is left whenever the requesting person is seen to be not registered, forcing the exit from sub-states checkingLoanQty and checkingAvailability while getting into the next state loanDenied.

The rules for parallel and sequential state decomposition sometimes make it difficult to understand what is really going on when we combine these mechanisms recursively. It is therefore highly advisable to use them in a disciplined manner according to the following *guidelines* for diagram well-formedness:

- To make it clear what state within a concurrent sub-diagram to get into when entering the sub-diagram, insert an *initial sub-state* in each sub-diagram with an outgoing transition to the desired state. Symmetrically, to make it clear what state in a non-cyclic concurrent sub-diagram to exit from when leaving the sub-diagram, insert a *final sub-state* in each sub-diagram with an incoming transition from the desired state. Figure 13.13 illustrates this. Also note that the two diagram patterns in Figure 13.14 are equivalent.

- Beware of 'spaghetti' diagrams in which transitions connect a sequential sub-state of a concurrent state to sequential sub-states of other concurrent states or to outer super-states

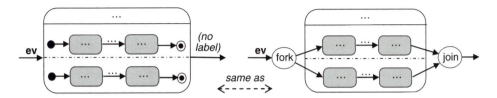

Figure 13.14   *Initial and final substates in concurrent subdiagrams*

in the state diagram. Unstructured diagrams tend to be unintelligible, unmanageable and flawed.

- When concurrent states are decomposed into sequential sub-states, check the resulting concurrent sub-diagrams carefully to see if they need to be synchronized:

    a. The same event may require transitions in multiple sub-diagrams (see Figure 13.13 for an example).

    b. An event causing a transition in a 'consuming' sub-diagram may need to be notified by a **send** action in a 'producing' sub-diagram (see Figures 13.7 and 13.9 for examples).

    c. Guards on the same attributes may be required in multiple sub-diagrams (e.g. the guard [Speed = 0] in Figure 13.12).

    d. A guard may be required in a sub-diagram to refer to an attribute modified by a transition in another sub-diagram (e.g. the guard [doorsState = closed] in Figure 13.12).

13.3 Building behaviour models

As noted in previous chapters, goals, scenarios and state machines have complementary strengths and limitations:

- Goals are declarative, capture functional and non-functional aspects, and support AND/OR structures that are particularly well suited to satisfaction arguments. As we will see in Chapters 16–18, goals support multiple forms of reasoning in the early stages of the RE process such as incremental refinement, completeness checking, conflict management, obstacle analysis, threat analysis, evaluation of alternatives, responsibility assignment, animation of goal operationalizations and requirements document genera-tion. On the downside, goals are sometimes felt to be too abstract by stakeholders. They cover entire classes of intended behaviours, but such behaviours are left implicit. As a consequence, goals may be hard to elicit and make fully precise in the first place.

- Scenarios support an informal, narrative and concrete style of expression. They are therefore easily accessible to stakeholders and prove to be an excellent vehicle for eliciting or explaining requirements (see Section 2.2.5). Positive scenarios allow us to detail what the fuzzy interactions in a use case diagram do capture. Their sequences of required interactions provide acceptance test data for free. On the downside, scenarios, like test cases, are inherently partial; they cover few behaviours of specific instances. For good coverage a large number of scenarios may be required. Scenarios leave intended system properties implicit. They may sometimes entail premature choices of event sequencing and distribution of responsibilities among agents.

- State machines provide visual abstractions of explicit behaviours of any agent instance in a class. They can be formally verified against goals or domain properties, yielding counterexample scenarios in case of violations (see Section 5.4.3). State machines are executable for model animation. They provide a good basis for code generation. On the downside, state machines are too operational in the early stages of the RE process. Building correct state machine models may be quite hard – especially in the case of a combined use of the parallel and sequential structuring mechanisms (as often needed for complex systems). As for scenarios, the requirements underlying them, including non-functional ones, are left implicit.

Table 13.1 summarizes the respective pros and cons of goals, scenarios and state machines. Also note that goals and state machines make state information explicit, whereas scenarios leave such information implicit. In view of their complementarities, we may expect goals, scenarios and state machines to form a win–win partnership for building complex models.

This section illustrates such a partnership through a few model-building techniques. Section 13.3.1 discusses how we can identify a set of scenarios with sufficiently good coverage. For scenario-based reasoning, it is often useful to make state information explicit; Section 13.3.2 shows how we can do this in a systematic way. We will then see how scenarios decorated with state information can help us build state machines (Section 13.3.3) and goal formulations (Section 13.3.4). Finally, we will see how goals and their operationalization can help us build state machines (Section 13.3.5). The model-building techniques in this section are kept

	Strengths	Limitations
Goals	Declarative, satisfaction arguments Expressive (functional, non-functional; alternative options) Entire classes of behaviours Variety of early analyses	Too abstract? Sometimes hard to elicit Implicit behaviours
Scenarios	Narrative, concrete examples Explicit behaviours Good for elicitation, explanation Acceptance test data	Few, partial behaviours Many required for good coverage Implicit requirements Premature choices?
State machines	Visual abstraction Entire classes of explicit behaviours Verifiable, executable, code generation	Hard to build and understand Implicit requirements

Table 13.1 *Complementarity of goals, scenarios, and state machines*

informal for wider accessibility. More precise, formal counterparts can be used as indicated in the bibliographical notes at the end of the chapter.

13.3.1 Elaborating relevant scenarios for good coverage

A sequence diagram illustrating typical interaction sequences among agent instances is in general more easily elaborated by focusing on pairwise interactions *one agent pair after the other*.

For pairwise interactions, we may consider coarse-grained agents and interactions first, and then refine these until we reach the level of granularity considered in the goal and agent models (see Section 13.1.2).

To ensure satisfactory scenario coverage, the following heuristics may be used while doing so.

Ensure goal coverage by positive scenarios

Make sure that all behavioural goals already identified in the goal model are properly illustrated by a representative sample of positive scenarios. For example, the identification of the goal BookRequestSatisfied may prompt the identification of a positive scenario such as the one appearing in Figure 13.2.

Ensure obstacle coverage by negative scenarios

Make sure that all obstacles already identified in the goal model are properly illustrated by negative scenarios. For example, the identification of the obstacle DriverUnresponsive in a train control system (see Figure 9.1) may prompt the identification of a negative scenario illustrating it.

Identify normal scenarios and their associated abnormal scenarios

Consider normal scenarios first and then abnormal scenarios for each of them. As introduced in Section 2.2.5, a *normal scenario* captures a course of interaction where everything proceeds as normally expected, for example the Loan scenario in Figure 13.2. An *abnormal scenario* is also positive, but captures an interaction sequence under a special or exceptional condition. For example, the scenario in Figure 13.15 captures an abnormal scenario associated with the normal one in Figure 13.2. *Associated* means that the two scenarios share a common prefix episode and then differ subsequently because of a possible exception case (captured by the event !notAvailable in Figure 13.15).

Exhaustive analysis of normal and abnormal cases is obviously important for scenario coverage. The abnormal scenarios associated with a scenario can be explored systematically as follows:

- We consider all prefix episodes of this scenario by increasing size.

- For each prefix episode, we question whether an exception can arise at its end.

- If so, a corresponding abnormal scenario should be specified.

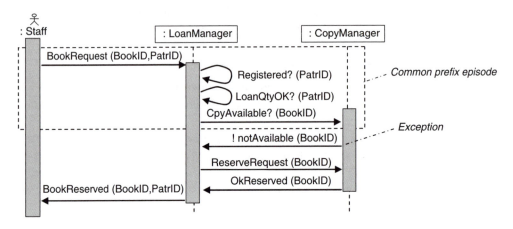

Figure 13.15   *Abnormal scenario associated with a normal Loan scenario*

To identify possible exceptions at the end of an episode, we may be guided by *exception patterns* such as invalid submitted data, unsatisfiable request, inadequate response, too slow response and timeout event, lack of response, cancellation event and so forth.

The systematic exploration of all prefix episodes of the Loan scenario in Figure 13.2 by increasing episode size leads us to three abnormal scenarios; namely, Unregistered, LoanQty-KO and !notAvailable. Each of these needs to be adequately specified in a dedicated sequence diagram.

Note that we may need to recursively explore new abnormal scenarios associated with the ones already identified. For example, we might need to consider an abnormal scenario *!notReservable(BookID)* associated with the abnormal scenario in Figure 13.15.

Identify auxiliary episodes

A sequence of interactions within a scenario may at some point require an auxiliary episode to get to the next interaction in the sequence, as the latter depends on this episode. For example, the scenario ConstraintsAcquired in Figure 13.4 is an auxiliary episode to get to the next interaction, scheduleSetting. Auxiliary episodes typically refer to requests for necessary information, agent authentication protocols, help requests and the like.

Identify responses to stimuli events

In event-driven systems, the events acting as system stimuli might be clearly identifiable from the very beginning. We may elaborate scenarios for such systems by listing those stimuli and for each of them explore which interaction sequence is needed to handle it. For example, which specific interaction sequence is needed to handle a meetingRequest event, a meetingCancellation event or a meetingReplanRequest event?

Check scenarios for clean-up

There are recurrent difficulties in elaborating sequence diagrams from scratch or transcribing them from stakeholder narratives. The same diagram might address unrelated concerns; it might contain irrelevant events; there might be impossible interactions; two related diagrams might show incompatible granularities of interaction. The identified scenarios should therefore be checked and cleaned up if necessary to facilitate the subsequent process of building state machines or goal formulations.

- *Unrelated concerns.* The same scenario might illustrate unrelated goals. Splitting such a scenario into multiple unrelated ones should be considered to reduce scenario complexity and increase scenario cohesion.

- *Irrelevant events.* A scenario might contain events that are not relevant to the implicit goal that it is intended to illustrate. Removing these events should be considered unless there are good reasons to keep them; that is, underlying related goals not identified so far. In particular, when there are successive interactions in the same direction along a timeline, without intermediate interaction in the other direction, we should check what such a unidirectional sequence is intended to convey. For example, the successive outgoing interactions doorsClosing and trainStart on the OnBoardController timeline in Figure 13.1 are relevant to the dynamics of doors under safe conditions; but how about the successive incoming interactions exit and entrance on the TrainActuator/Sensor timeline? Are the two of them needed? If so, what is the second intended to convey?

- *Impossible interactions: Lack of event monitorability or controllability.* An agent source of an interaction event might be unable to control it. Symmetrically, an agent target of an interaction event might be unable to monitor it. This should be checked and fixed if necessary, for example by splitting the interaction in two with an in-the-middle agent instance and timeline. For example, the BookRequest and OK-Book events in our library system are uncontrollable and unmonitorable by a Patron agent, respectively; this calls for the introduction of an in-the-middle Staff agent, as shown in Figure 13.2.

- *Incompatible or inadequate granularities.* Two episodes might refer to similar or related events that appear with different granularities in the corresponding diagrams. This makes it difficult to relate them or merge them when we build a state machine covering them (see Section 13.3.3). In such a case the diagrams should be restructured so that the related events appear at a common, adequate level of granularity for the goals that we want to illustrate. We should again particularly check successive interactions in the same direction with no intermediate interaction in the other direction. For example, four successive digitEntry events should be aggregated into a single PasswordEntry event when illustrating an authentication goal.

13.3.2 Decorating scenarios with state conditions

For scenario-based reasoning it is often useful to make state information explicit along a scenario. A *state condition* attached to a point on an agent's timeline captures the snapshot state of the non-rigid variables monitored or controlled by the agent instance at that time point. A *condition list* structures this condition in two sub-lists: a list of monitored conditions and a list of controlled conditions. A *monitored* (or *controlled*) *condition* is an atomic condition

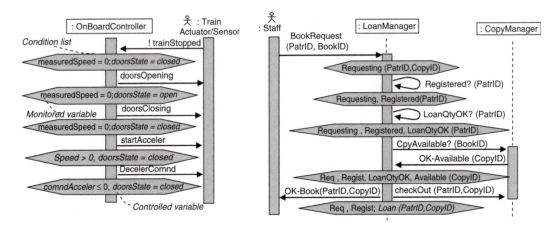

Figure 13.16   *Annotating scenarios with explicit state conditions*

characterizing the state of a monitored (or controlled) variable. All conditions in a condition list are implicitly connected by a conjunction.

For example, the condition list at the point right after the first interaction in the left-hand diagram in Figure 13.16 is <measuredSpeed = 0; *doorsState = closed>*. Controlled conditions are indicated in italics.

We can decorate each agent timeline of a sequence diagram in a systematic way as follows:

- We first determine the non-rigid state variables that the agent associated with the timeline monitors and controls. This information is available from the corresponding agent model, if already documented there; see Section 11.2.2. (Remember that non-rigid state variables are time-varying attributes or associations from the corresponding object model.)

- We then propagate the applicability and effect conditions of each interaction event down the timeline as follows:

  a. If the current event is an *outgoing* one, we add its *applicability* condition to the sub-list of *controlled* conditions right *before* it, and we add its *effect* condition to the sub-list of *controlled* conditions right *after* it, while removing from the latter sub-list any condition invalidated by the added condition. The event applicability and effect conditions are the *DomPre* and *DomPost* of the corresponding operation, respectively. They are obtained from the operation model; see Sections 12.2.3 and 12.6.1, Figure 12.10. If those conditions are not available yet in the operation model, we need to determine them and add them to this model as well.

  b. If the current event is an *incoming* one, we add its *effect* condition to the sub-list of *monitored* conditions right *after* it, while removing from this sub-list any condition invalidated by the added condition. This effect condition is the monitorable *DomPost* condition of the corresponding operation. If this condition is not available yet in the operation model, we need to determine it and add it to this model as well.

Note that any condition on a monitored or controlled variable is retracted from the corresponding sub-list if it is invalidated by a new effect condition being added. There is an underlying *frame principle*; namely, a condition at some point on a timeline remains subsequently true along this line until an interaction event is found whose effect is to make it false.

Figure 13.16 illustrates this down propagation of condition lists for the scenarios appearing in Figures 13.1 and 13.2. For example, the monitored condition measuredSpeed = 0 in the upper left condition list right after the !trainStopped event is the monitorable domain post-condition of the actuator's operation of physically stopping the train; the controlled condition *doorsState = closed* in that condition list is the domain pre-condition of the controller's operation whose application yields the doorsOpening event. In the next condition list down the timeline, the monitored condition measuredSpeed = 0 remains as it is not invalidated by the effect of the doorsOpening event. On the other hand, the controlled condition *doorsState = open* is added to that condition list as the domain post-condition of the operation corresponding to the doorsOpening event; the previous condition doorsState = closed is retracted from that list as it is invalidated by the new condition on the same variable.

13.3.3 From scenarios to state machines

State diagrams can be built incrementally from sequence diagrams by generalizing the latter into state machines that cover all behaviours captured by the positive scenarios and exclude all behaviours captured by the negative ones (if any).

Step 1: Decorate scenarios with state conditions

We first need to make state information explicit along the scenario timelines, following the procedure described in the previous section.

Step 2: Generalize scenarios into state machines

A state machine model is obtained from the decorated sequence diagrams as follows:

1. The system model is a parallel composition of state diagrams – *one per agent*, whose instances are illustrated by a scenario timeline at least.

2. For each such agent, the interaction sequences involving its specific instances in the positive scenarios are generalized to refer to *any* instance. The behaviour model of an arbitrary instance is a parallel composition of state diagrams – *one per state variable controlled by the agent.*

3. For each variable controlled by an agent, a candidate concurrent state diagram capturing its dynamics is built as follows:

   3.1. *Timeline selection.* All timelines of the agent that refer to the controlled variable are selected from the positive scenarios.

   3.2. *SM path derivation.* Each selected timeline is transformed into an SM path for the controlled variable as follows:

a. The sequence of states along the path is the sequence of conditions on the controlled variable along the timeline, from top to bottom, where each condition is converted into a corresponding SM state. For example, the condition *doorsState* = *closed* in Figure 13.16 becomes the SM state *doorsClosed*; the condition *Speed* > *0* becomes the SM state *Moving*; the condition *Loan(PatrID,CopyID)*, stating that a Loan association instance is created, becomes the SM state *loanGranted*.

b. An initial SM state is appended at the beginning of the path if the corresponding scenario can start in the initial state where the controlled object appears in the system.

c. The transition between two successive SM states on the path is labelled by the corresponding interaction event; that is, the event on the timeline between the controlled conditions yielding those states.

d. A transition resulting in a state change for the controlled variable is labelled by a candidate guard as well. This guard is formed by conjoining the 'fresh' conditions on other variables in the condition list on the timeline right before the transition; that is, the new conditions that appeared along the timeline since the last state change. The reason for this heuristic is that such new conditions set by the scenario might implicitly capture a pre-condition for the next outgoing interaction to take place.

e. The resulting SM path is simplified by pruning all transitions that do not result in a state change for the controlled variable. The path is then folded by introducing cycles to merge multiple occurrences of the same state into a single one.

Figure 13.17 illustrates such a transformation of a decorated agent timeline into an SM path for the variable doorsState controlled by the OnBoardController agent.

3.3. *SM path merge.* Finally, the derived SM paths are merged to form a candidate state diagram for the controlled variable. The merge proceeds as follows:

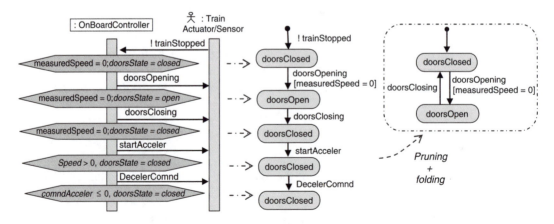

Figure 13.17 *Transforming an annotated agent timeline into a single SM path*

3.4.

    a. We select a first path starting with an initial state. (If there is no scenario that can start in the initial state, we need to elicit one.)

    b. Let *SD* denote the state diagram consisting of all paths merged so far. Until all paths are merged, we select a next path *P* to be merged. We traverse *P* from its start. Let *S* denote the next state in *P* to be considered for merge.

- If *S* is already in *SD*, we just add its incoming labelled transition in *P* to *SD* so as to connect *S* and the corresponding source state in *SD* (if this transition is not already in *SD*).

- If *S* is not already in *SD*, we add it to *SD* and connect its incoming labelled transition in *P* to the corresponding source state in *SD*.

Figure 13.18 shows the result of applying the merge procedure to the three SM paths on the left. In this illustration, S_i denotes a state whereas e_i denotes a transition labelled by an event name and/or a guard.

    Note that two transitions labelled by the same event and different guards are considered different by the merge procedure. We may optionally consider a further merge in such a case. The two transitions are merged into a single one, labelled by the common event only and leading to an intermediate state, CheckingGuards say, whose outgoing transitions are event free and labelled by the corresponding guard.

    Figure 13.19 illustrates such a merge for the two SM paths derived from the library loan scenarios in Figures 13.2 and 13.15. Note the application of step (d) of the SM path-derivation procedure, resulting in two different guards labelling the common BookRequest event. Also note that the resulting state diagram corresponds to the one in Figure 13.13.

    The state diagram obtained using the SM path merge procedure covers, by construction, all behaviours of the controlled variable that are captured by the input set of positive scenarios.

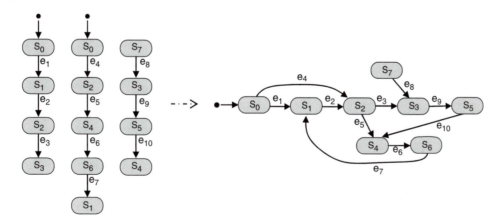

Figure 13.18 *Merging SM paths to form a state diagram*

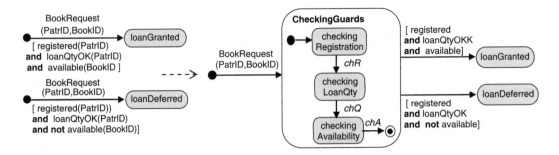

Figure 13.19   *Merging transitions labelled by the same event and different guards*

Step3: Check, extend and restructure the state machines as needed

Once the state diagrams for each variable controlled by the agent are composed in parallel, we need to check the resulting agent's state diagram for completeness and adequacy. This diagram might be incomplete, as the input scenarios it generalizes are inherently incomplete. It might be inadequate, as we might have overgeneralized the scenarios; the diagram might cover inadmissible behaviours. The checks can be organized by considering each concurrent sub-diagram in isolation first, and in combination next.

Intra-diagram checks   The following checklist may help in spotting and fixing problems within a single diagram associated with a controlled variable:

- *Unreachable states.* Some states in the diagram produced by the SM path merge procedure might not be reachable from the initial state through a sequence of state transitions covered by the diagram. This is generally due to scenario incompleteness. For example, the state S_7 in Figure 13.18 is unreachable. To fix the problem we need to elicit a new scenario for reaching such a state from the initial state; derive a new SM path from it; and apply the merge procedure to this path.

- *Missing states.* There might be other important values for the controlled variable that are not found in the timeline condition lists from which the SM states were derived. If so, new scenarios should be elicited to indicate how these values can be reached, and then integrated in the state diagram by replaying the path derivation/merge procedure. In case of non-cyclic behaviour, a *final state* should be included to indicate how the concurrent sub-diagram is left.

- *Missing or inadequate transitions.* The states in the diagram should be reviewed pairwise to check whether (a) additional transitions should connect them to cover admissible behaviours and, if so, with what event/guard label; (b) guards on captured transitions are missing; and (c) the guards inferred by the SM path-derivation procedure are adequate.

- *Missing actions.* Auxiliary actions such as information acquisition or display have not been considered so far. We may review each transition in the diagram to check whether any such side-effect action should be attached to the transition, to its input state or to its output state.

- *Coverage of negative scenarios.* If the input set includes negative scenarios, we need to check that the state diagram generalizing the positive scenarios does not cover any of them. To do this, we simply apply the SM path-derivation procedure to each negative scenario and search for the resulting paths in the state diagram. For any path found, we need to delete or restrict transitions on it so as to exclude the corresponding negative scenario.

- *Inappropriate structure:* We may sometimes want to restructure the diagram, for example by grouping multiple occurrences of the same transition into a single occurrence to/from a super-state aggregating the original target/source states.

Inter-diagram checks We also need to check that the parallel composition of sub-diagrams does not introduce inadmissible behaviours. The latter would result from undesired interleavings of transitions from different concurrent diagrams (such interleavings are sometimes called *implied scenarios*). Two levels of concurrency are involved here: the concurrent control of variables by a single agent, and the concurrent behaviour of multiple agents.

Checking concurrent diagrams for undesired implied scenarios may be quite hard in the case of complex models. Automated support is clearly suitable in view of the combinatorial explosion of possible interleavings introduced by concurrency; see the bibliographical notes at the end of this chapter. Without such support we need to check carefully whether the interfering diagrams are properly synchronized through shared events, synchronizing guards on shared variables, or event notification through **send** actions attached to transitions.

We also need to check the lexical consistency of event names – when the same event name occurs in different diagrams, do we really mean it to be the same event, causing synchronization among the diagrams? Lexical errors such as name confusions may have unintended effects on what the model really conveys.

13.3.4 From scenarios to goals

Positive and negative scenarios can also be used for producing declarative specifications of the goals underlying them. Such goals generalize the positive scenarios by covering more behaviours, left implicit, while excluding the inadmissible behaviours captured by the negative scenarios.

Asking WHY and WHY NOT questions about scenarios

As briefly introduced in Section 8.8.2, a simple but effective way of making the goals underlying a positive scenario explicit consists of asking *WHY* questions about sequences of interactions within it (see Figure 8.14).

When the goal underlying the scenario is an *Achieve* goal and the scenario is sequentially composed of cohesive episodes, we may consider the end of each episode as a milestone for reaching the goal target. By asking a *WHY* question about each episode, we can then obtain a milestone-driven refinement of the parent goal, associated with the scenario as a whole, into sub-goals associated with each episode (see Section 8.8.5 for the notion of milestone-driven refinement.)

For example, the meeting scheduling scenario in Figure 8.14 can be mapped to a milestone-driven refinement of the goal Achieve[MaximumAttendance] into sub-goals

Achieve[ConstraintsKnownFromRequest], Achieve[ConvenientMeetingScheduledFrom Constraints] and Achieve[ParticipantsInformedOfScheduledmeeting].

When a negative scenario is provided, a *WHY NOT* question about the specifically prohibited interaction is often quite effective too. The goal is obtained as the reason for not allowing this interaction after the preceding ones. For example, a *WHY NOT* question about the prohibited interaction doorsOpening after the interaction sequence *AccelerationCommand; AlarmPressing; AlarmPropagation* in Figure 13.3 would undoubtedly lead to the goal Maintain[DoorsClosedWhileMoving].

Mining behavioural goals from decorated scenarios

When positive scenario timelines have been decorated with condition lists (see Section 13.3.2), we can 'mine' *Achieve* and *Maintain* goal specifications by examining the conditions along a timeline.

Mining Achieve goals   A candidate *Achieve* goal is obtained by causally linking the conditions before and after an outgoing interaction event on a timeline. The goal specification takes a *stimulus–response* pattern:

> **If** ConditionBefore **then sooner-or-later** ConditionAfter

This goal is under the responsibility of the agent associated with the timeline.

Figure 13.20 illustrates such mining of *Achieve* goals. For example, the first curved arrow on the timeline of the agent instance *c2:OnBoardController* reveals the goal Achieve[TrainStoppedIfStopSignal] whose specification is:

The train's commanded speed shall be null if the block signal is set to 'stop'.

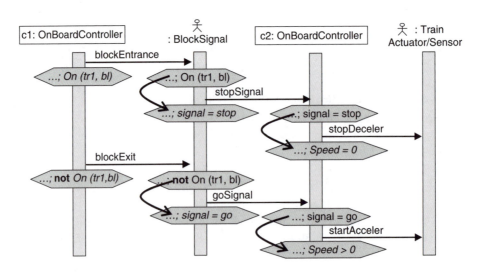

Figure 13.20 *Mining Achieve goals from stimulus-response interactions*

This goal is under the responsibility of the OnBoardController agent. Note that the condition 'signal = stop' in Figure 13.20 is synchronously monitored by the OnBoardController agent and controlled by the BlockSignal agent.

Mining Maintain goals   A candidate *Maintain* goal is obtained by finding a state transition *ST* along a timeline at which some condition *C* in the agent's condition list is true and remains subsequently true along the timeline up to some point where another condition *N* enters the list. The goal specification takes an *invariance* pattern:

> **If** *ST* **and** *C* **then always** *C* **unless** *N*

This goal is under the responsibility of the agent associated with the timeline.

For example, consider a variant of the train scenario in Figure 13.17, where the first two interactions !trainStopped and doorsOpening, with their resulting condition lists, appear at the end of the scenario instead. The interaction sequence in this scenario is thus:

> doorsClosing; startAcceleration; DecelerComnd; !trainStopped; doorsOpening.

The goal specification obtained from the decorated scenario is then:

> **If** Speed > 0 **and** doorsState = closed **then always** doorsState = closed **unless** measuredSpeed = 0

As scenarios are incomplete and informal, the goal specifications mined from them need to be checked for adequacy and completeness, and adapted if necessary.

13.3.5 From operationalized goals to state machines

The partnership among goals, scenarios and state machines can be exploited from another angle. We can derive state diagrams straight from goals and their operationalization in an operation model. The derivation procedure runs as follows:

1. The system model is a parallel composition of state diagrams – *one per agent* responsible for leaf goals in the goal model.

2. An agent's behaviour model is a parallel composition of state diagrams – *one per state variable controlled* by the agent.

3. For a variable controlled by an agent, a candidate concurrent state diagram capturing its dynamics is built as follows:

    3.1. *Operationalization selection.* We select all goals *G* assigned to the agent that constrain this controlled variable, together with all the operations operationalizing *G* whose **Output** list includes the controlled variable.

    3.2. *State machine derivation.* Each selected operation *Op* yields the following SM transition for the controlled variable:

a. The *source state* of the transition is the SM state defined by *Op*'s DomPre condition – by definition, the domain pre-condition of *Op* characterizes the class of input states when *Op* is applied, regardless of any restriction required for goal satisfaction (see Section 12.2.3).

b. The *target state* of the transition is the SM state defined by *Op*'s DomPost condition, conjoined with all *Op*'s ReqPost conditions (if any) – by definition, this condition characterizes the class of output states when the operation has been applied so as to satisfy all corresponding goals (see Sections 12.2.3 and 12.3.1).

c. The *event label* of the transition is chosen to clearly indicate that the event captures an application of *Op*.

d. The *guard* on the transition is defined by the conjunction of *Op*'s ReqPre conditions (if any) – by definition, each required pre-condition is a necessary condition for the transition to satisfy the corresponding goal (see Section 12.3.1).

e. If *Op* has trigger conditions in the operation model, the transition between the source and target states is an *event-free guarded transition* with the disjunction of ReqTrig conditions as guard – this corresponds to the event of one of the trigger conditions becoming true, which must force the transition to the output state for goal satisfaction. The event label capturing *Op* applications is kept implicit in this case. As briefly mentioned at the end of Section 12.3.3, a built-in frame principle tells us that any state transition from DomPre to DomPost necessarily implies that *Op* has been applied. Also remember that a consistent use of required pre- and trigger conditions must ensure that the formulation of the latter covers the former (see Section 12.3.1). In case such an implicit application of *Op* must trigger a transition in another diagram, the event-free guarded transition is also labelled by a **send** action for explicit notification of *Op*'s application to the consuming diagram.

In the state diagram thereby obtained, a label-free transition is added to connect the initial SM state to one of the derived states. The choice is based on the initialization of the controlled variable, available from the Init declaration for this attribute/association in the object model (see Section 10.1.5 and Figure 10.2).

Fig. 13.21 illustrates such a goal-driven derivation of a partial state diagram from a fragment of the corresponding operation model. A more detailed illustration will be provided in Section 15.2.7.

4. Check, extend, and restructure the state machines as needed. As for scenario-driven derivation, we need to check the resulting agent's state diagram for completeness and adequacy. The checks can be organized by considering each concurrent sub-diagram in isolation first and in combination next. We may use for this a checklist similar to the one provided in Section 13.3.3 for scenario-driven derivation.

Missing or inadequate guards result from missing or inadequate required pre- or trigger conditions, and perhaps missing or inadequate goals. For example, a missing AtPlatform

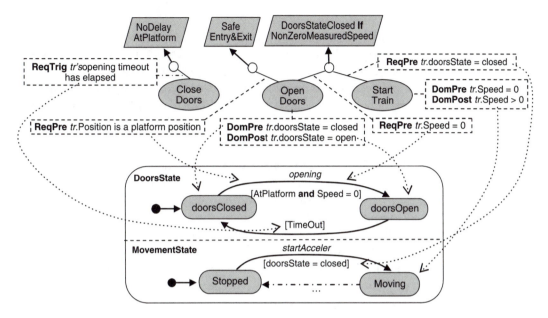

Figure 13.21 *Deriving state diagrams from operationalized goals*

condition in the upper guard in Figure 13.21 would reveal a missing ReqPre condition on the OpenDoors operation, and perhaps the missing goal SafeEntry&Exit. Likewise, missing or inadequate states or transitions result from missing or inadequate operations in the goal model, and perhaps missing or inadequate goals as well. The checks on the state machine model thus provide an extra source of checks on the goal and operation models.

Some of those checks can be supported by tools if the models are specified in a formal language. We can then in particular animate the models to check their adequacy, and verify that they satisfy leaf goals from the goal model and domain properties from the object model (see Section 5.3 and Figure 5.3).

Note that such goal-driven derivation of a behaviour model allows us to trace behavioural aspects back to their rationale. We thereby get derivational traceability links and satisfaction arguments for free.

Summary

- A behaviour model captures current behaviours in the system-as-is or required ones in the system-to-be. A global behaviour of the system is obtained by parallel composition of agent behaviours. Such behaviours are made explicit through scenarios showing sequences of interactions among specific agent instances or through state machines showing sequences of state transitions for the variables controlled by any agent instance within a class.

- A scenario is represented in UML by a variant of message sequence chart called a sequence diagram. With such diagrams we can capture synchronous interaction events along lifelines associated with agent instances; information transmission through event attributes; optional interactions; and prohibited interactions yielding negative scenarios. For stepwise scenario refinement we may also decompose a scenario into episodes or agent instances into finer-grained ones.

- A state machine is represented in UML by a variant of a statechart called a state diagram. A state in such a diagram captures a set of snapshot states where a controlled variable always has the same value. A state transition is caused by an event. External events are not controllable by the agent associated with the state machine, whereas internal events correspond to applications of operations by the agent. A transition in a state diagram may be labelled by the name of the causing event, by a necessary condition for transition firing and by auxiliary actions that are applied when the transition fires. These are operations yielding states that are not worth capturing in the diagram. To avoid duplication of the same action label on every incoming (or outgoing) transition, we may attach it to the target (or source) state as an entry (or exit) action.

- For stepwise refinement of a state diagram, we may decompose a state into sequential or concurrent sub-states. In the case of sequential decomposition, the super-state is itself a state machine on the sub-states; the instance modelled by the diagram is in the super-state if and only if it is in one of the sequential sub-states. A transition to/from the super-state is by default inherited by every sequential sub-state. To avoid this in the case of an incoming transition to the super-state, we should insert an initial sub-state connected to the sub-state to which we want the transition to get. In the case of a parallel decomposition, the instance modelled by the diagram is in the super-state if and only if it is in each of the concurrent sub-states. An incoming transition to the super-state is 'forked' to every concurrent sub-state. An outgoing transition from the super-state with an event or guard label is fired when the event occurs, provided that the guard is true, forcing the exit from all concurrent sub-states. A label-free outgoing transition from the super-state is 'joined' from every concurrent sub-state; it is fired when all sub-states are left.

- A hierarchical state machine is obtained by combining those two structuring mechanisms recursively. Concurrent diagrams allow us to model the inherently concurrent behaviour of an agent controlling multiple state variables in parallel while reducing the number of states to represent explicitly. There is a price to pay in increased model complexity. We need to take care of diagram synchronization through shared events, event notification or guards on shared variables. The sub-states at which to enter or to leave a concurrent diagram should be clearly indicated through initial or final sub-states, respectively.

- The complementary strengths and limitations of goals, scenarios and state machines call for their combined use for model building and analysis at the various stages of the RE process.

- To build a set of relevant scenarios with sufficiently good coverage, we may use a number of heuristics such as goal coverage by positive scenarios, obstacle coverage by negative ones, the systematic identification of abnormal scenarios associated with a normal one or the identification of auxiliary episodes. In any case the scenarios need be checked for coverage, cohesion, relevance, feasibility and compatibility.

- For scenario-based reasoning during model construction, it is often useful to decorate scenario timelines with conditions monitored or controlled by the corresponding agent. We can do this in a systematic way by propagating the domain pre- and post-conditions of the operations associated with each interaction down the timeline.

- A state machine model can be built from a set of scenarios by generalizing these to refer to any agent instance and to cover all behaviours captured by the scenarios. A state diagram for a variable controlled by an agent is obtained by merging SM paths, derived from the sequences of state conditions on this variable along the agent's timelines. The agent's behaviour model is obtained as a parallel composition of these diagrams. Due to the risks of scenario incompleteness and overgeneralization, the concurrent diagrams need to be checked individually and in combination.

- From scenarios we can also identify goals and elaborate their specification. We may merely ask WHY questions about episodes in a positive scenario or WHY NOT questions about prohibited interactions in a negative scenario. Candidate specifications for *Achieve* and *Maintain* goals can be more systematically mined from a scenario by finding stimulus–response patterns and invariance patterns, respectively, in state condition sequences along the scenario timelines.

- A state machine model can also be derived directly from goals and their operationalization. A state diagram for a controlled variable is obtained by retrieving all goal operationalizations where the variable appears as an operation output; the states, transitions and transition labels in the diagram are derived from the domain pre- and post-conditions of those operations together with their required pre- and trigger conditions. The agent's behaviour model is the parallel composition of such diagrams for the variables they control. We need to check this model for completeness and adequacy. The checks may reveal problems in the goal and operation models as well. Such a derivation provides satisfaction arguments and derivational traceability links for model evolution.

Notes and Further Reading

Some bibliographical notes on the origins, variants and extensions of sequence diagrams and state diagrams are provided at the end of Chapter 4. More details on those diagrams will be found in Rumbaugh *et al.* (1999). UML 2.0 has programming constructs for scenario composition such as loops, alternatives and parallel composition. There are also timing constructs for capturing time distance between interaction events.

Magee and Kramer provide an excellent introduction to concurrency issues in state machine models (Magee & Kramer, 2006). Instead of the state-oriented style of state diagrams, they use the event-oriented style of labelled transition systems (LTS), where SM paths are seen as sequences of events rather than sequences of states. The semantics of concurrency is simpler but the diagrams are harder for humans to read. A deep analysis of the complex semantic issues raised by state machine formalisms will be found in Niu *et al.* (2003).

Heuristics and taxonomies for scenario identification are also discussed in the OMT book (Rumbaugh *et al.*, 1991) and in an interesting compilation of papers on the use of scenarios in system development (Alexander & Maiden, 2004).

Condition lists were introduced in STRIPS-like planning systems to characterize state information along a robot's sequence of actions (Nilsson, 1971). They are used in van Lamsweerde and Willemet (1998) for goal inference from scenarios and in Whittle and Schumann (2000) for state machine inference from scenarios. For timeline annotation, this chapter keeps the simpler syntax of message sequence charts (MSC) instead of the rather clumsy syntax proposed in UML 2.0 for state invariants.

Formal counterparts of the model-building techniques in this chapter can be found in the literature. Most efforts were devoted to the inductive synthesis of state machine models from scenarios. This problem is known to be difficult (Bontemps *et al.*, 2005). Induction is unsound in general and introduces risks of overgeneralization. Concurrent behaviours introduce implied scenarios that might be undesirable (Uchitel *et al.*, 2001; Letier *et al.*, 2005). The main techniques available support the translation of MSC specifications into statecharts (Kruger *et al.*, 1998); the synthesis of UML state diagrams from sequence diagrams capturing positive scenarios (Whittle & Schumann, 2000; Mäkinen & Systä, 2001); and the synthesis of LTS models from MSC scenarios taken as positive examples of system behaviour (Uchitel *et al.*, 2003). These techniques all require additional input information beside scenarios: local MSC conditions (Kruger *et al.*, 1998); pre- and post-conditions of interactions (Whittle & Schumann, 2000); state machine traces local to agents (Mäkinen & Systä, 2001); or a high-level message sequence chart showing how MSC scenarios are to be flowcharted (Uchitel *et al.*, 2003). Such additional input may be hard to get from end-users, and may need to be refactored in non-trivial ways when the scenarios are provided incrementally (Letier *et al.*, 2005). To address this problem, the synthesis procedure can be made interactive through scenario questions; these are scenarios generated by the synthesizer that the end-user just needs to accept or reject (Damas *et al.*, 2005). The injection of constraints into the synthesis process may significantly reduce the number of scenario questions and improve the adequacy of the synthesized model. Such constraints include specifications of goals, domain properties, legacy components and architectural constraints (Damas *et al.*, 2006).

A formal counterpart of the technique suggested in this chapter for inferring goal specifications from scenarios will be found in van Lamsweerde and Willemet (1998). An alternative technique based on fluents is described in Damas *et al.* (2006).

An automated version of the technique described in Section 13.3.5 for building state machine models from goal operationalizations can be found in Tran Van *et al.* (2004). The compiler described there generates concurrent state machines for goal-oriented model animation.

Exercises

- Use the techniques in Section 13.3.1 to identify a comprehensive set of abnormal scenarios associated with the normal meeting scheduling scenario in Figure 4.10, and represent these by sequence diagrams.

- Modify the scenario in Figure 13.1 to capture a situation where, instead of automatic opening of train doors at platforms and closing after a timeout, the opening/closing of doors is regulated by the presence of more passengers wishing to enter/exit the train.

- Use the decoration technique in Section 13.3.2 to annotate the Scheduler timeline, in the meeting scheduling scenario in Figure 4.10, with condition lists after each interaction.

- Complete the state diagram in Figure 13.13, for the dynamics of the Loan association in the library system, by incorporating deadline extensions for loans, returns of borrowed books and fines for overdue returns.

- Consider the train information controlled by a software train controller and its dynamics captured in Figure 13.12.

   a. What is the global initial state of TrainInfoState?

   b. Explain the consequence of omitting the guard [doorsState = closed] in the MovementState transition from state *Stopped* to state *Moving*, by means of a sequence diagram showing a possible scenario covered by the state diagram without that guard.

- Consider the dynamics of a telephone controlled by a call switching agent with SM states such as Idle, offHookTone, Waiting, callingTone (for a caller telephone calling a non-busy telephone), busyTone (for a caller telephone calling a busy telephone), Ringing (for a non-busy callee telephone), errorNotified (in case of invalid callee number), and Connected (for the caller and callee telephones).

a. Elaborate a state diagram showing the required dynamics of a telephone in terms of those states.

b. For each SM state in your diagram, identify the attribute or association from the corresponding object model as the state variable to which the SM state refers, and give an example of a snapshot state pertaining to this SM state.

c. Find two different ways of prescribing in your state diagram that, when a telephone gets connected, the phone number of the telephone it is connected to is shown on its screen; then explain which way is preferable.

d. Provide a few illustrating scenarios as sequence diagrams where the lifeline of the switching agent is covered by a path in your state diagram.

- Build a state diagram modelling the required behaviour of a thermostat in a house temperature control system. The model should capture the dynamics of state variables controlled by the thermostat based on the following simplified problem statement.

> A thermostat shall regulate a house heating and air conditioning (AC) system. It must switch the heating sub-system *on* when the heating mode is *on* and the measured home temperature is below some user-specified temperature, and *off* when the heating mode is off or the measured home temperature is above that desired temperature. Symmetrically, the thermostat must switch the AC sub-system *on* when the cooling mode is on and the measured home temperature is above some user-specified temperature, and *off* when the cooling mode is off or the measured home temperature is below that desired temperature. The thermostat shall also control a user interface that will consistently display: (a) the current mode (heating or cooling), (b) whether the corresponding sub-system is running or not, and (c) the current measured temperature and the desired temperature entered by the user on a control panel.

Due to the inherent concurrency in this system, your state diagram should show nested parallel and sequential states.

- Consider a simple bank ATM system for delivering cash to bank customers at ATM cash machines.

a. Build a representative set of sequence diagrams showing typical scenarios of interaction between a person needing cash, an ATM counter, the ATM software controller and the bank account management software. Identify normal and abnormal scenarios. (You may want to consider a coarse-grained agent ATM-Machine first, and subsequently refine it into ATM-Counter and ATM-Controller.)

b. Using the decoration technique in Section 13.3.2, annotate the ATM-Controller timeline in each scenario with condition lists referring to the state variables monitored or controlled by this agent.

c. From there, use the SM path derivation and merge procedures in Section 13.3.3 to build a state diagram on the variables controlled by the ATM-Controller, covering all your scenarios.

d. If necessary, restructure your state diagram so that (a) dynamically irrelevant states are kept implicit through auxiliary actions properly located; (b) composite states such as Idle, Active or UnderMaintenance appear explicitly; (c) the Active state is decomposed into sequential sub-states, including among them a state ClosingState where the dynamics of cash delivery and card ejection is modelled by parallel sub-diagrams.

- Replay the previous exercise where, instead of starting from interaction scenarios, you start from a goal model together with its operationalization. Here, you need to start from goal formulations in order to identify controlled objects, dynamic attributes/associations of such objects, goal-relevant states, fluents, operation specifications and events.

- Replay the two previous exercises on your metro ticket-distribution machine (or your favourite vending machine if you do not use the metro).

14

Integrating Multiple System Views

Our multi-view modelling framework for RE includes an intentional view, captured by a goal model; a structural view, captured by an object model; a responsibility view, captured by an agent model; a functional view, captured by an operation model; and a behavioural view, captured by a state machine model together with illustrating scenarios.

The integration of these various models forms the entire *system model*. When putting them together we need to make sure that the models are consistently related and complement each other. This chapter describes mechanisms for this.

An initial integration mechanism consists of defining a common meta-model in terms of which all models can be defined and interrelated. Section 14.1 presents a simple meta-model integrating the various modelling abstractions introduced in Chapters 8–13. A second mechanism consists of making inter-model consistency rules explicit. Such rules structurally link elements of different models. They are defined on the meta-model and need to be enforced when we integrate the models. Section 14.2 reviews a sample of consistency rules for our models. A third mechanism consists of grouping related model fragments from different system views together into cohesive model packages. Section 14.3 introduces a standard packaging mechanism for doing this.

14.1 A meta-model for view integration

A *meta-model* is a model that defines and interrelates conceptual abstractions in terms of which other models are defined. When talking about meta-models it is important to recognize the three different levels of modelling involved (see Figure 14.1).

The meta level

This level refers to domain-independent abstractions. It is made up of *meta-concepts* (e.g. Agent, Goal, Operation, Association), *meta-relationships* linking meta-concepts (e.g. Responsibility, Performance, Input, Link), *meta-attributes* of meta-concepts or meta-relationships (e.g. *Load*

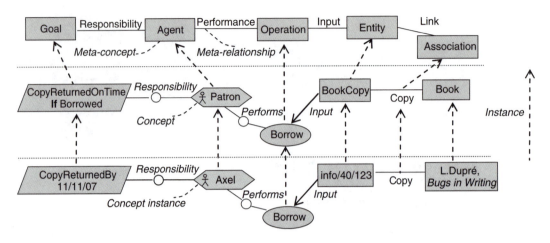

Figure 14.1   *The meta, domain, and instance levels*

of Agent, *DomPost* of Operation, *Multiplicity* of Link), and *meta-constraints* on meta-concepts and meta-relationships (e.g. 'an Agent *Performing* an Operation must *Control* the Output of this Operation').

The domain level

This level refers to concepts specific to the modelled system, for example library, loan, block signal, train acceleration command. It is made of *concepts* that are instances of meta-level abstractions. For example, the Patron concept in Figure 14.1 is an instance of the Agent meta-concept; the Borrow concept is an instance of the Operation meta-concept; the Copy concept is an instance of the Association meta-concept.

Domain-level concepts are linked through *instances* of the meta-relationships linking the corresponding meta-level concepts of which they are an instance, for example Patron *Performs* Borrow; Copy *Links* Book and BookCopy. Domain-level concepts must also satisfy instantiations of the meta-constraints on the corresponding meta-level concepts of which they are an instance, for example a Patron *Performing* a Borrow operation must *Control* the Loan association.

A system model is structured from domain-level concepts according to instances of the corresponding meta-relationships inherited from the meta level.

The instance level

This level refers to specific instances of domain-level concepts in the running system (see Figure 14.1).

The role of a meta-model

A meta-model is a conceptual model for the meta level, thus consisting of meta-level concepts, relationships, attributes and constraints. Such a model may play a significant role in the elaboration and management of multi-view system models:

- It defines the structure of the modelling language and provides a meta-language for describing it. Every modelling abstraction is defined within a single framework whatever view it pertains to.

- A meta-model provides a framework within which intra- and inter-view consistency rules can be defined (see Sections 4.3.9 and 14.2).

- It yields the logical schema of the model database in which models can be maintained and to which queries can be submitted for model analysis (as introduced in Section 5.2).

- It allows modelling methods to be defined as particular strategies for meta-model traversal.

- It summarizes the features of a modelling language or method and allows variants of a language or method to be compared.

- A meta-model provides a solid basis for tool support and integration. We can build generic tools that are parameterized on modelling languages. Such tools are instantiated by access to a meta-language specification of a particular modelling language.

Our meta-model for relating the goal, object, agent, operation and behaviour models of a system is a structural one. We will therefore use UML class diagrams to describe it. This section can therefore also be seen as a further illustration of the use of class diagrams, while providing a summary view of the modelling abstractions introduced in Chapters 8–13.

14.1.1 Overall structure of the meta-model

As a system model is made up of five views, Figure 14.2 shows the root meta-concept *SystemModel* as an aggregation of five meta-concepts corresponding to those views. Each of these is expanded below.

Every meta-concept in our meta-model is characterized by meta-attributes and meta-relationships whose instantiation results in a specific model at the domain level. Two meta-attributes are mandatory for any meta-concept whatever view it refers to: *Name* and *Def*.

- The values of *Name* allow for unambiguous reference to corresponding instances at the domain level, for example a goal model named 'TrainControl', a goal named 'DoorsClosed-WhileMoving', an association named 'AtPlatform'.

- The values of *Def* allow for unambiguous definition of corresponding instances at the domain level, for example 'Train doors should never be open while a train is moving on tracks' is the value for the *Def* attribute attached to the goal named 'DoorsClosedWhileMoving'.

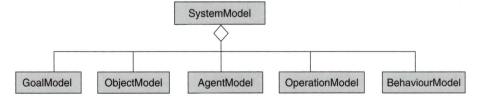

Figure 14.2 *Overall metamodel*

The *Issue* meta-attribute is optional for any meta-concept. As seen in previous chapters, its values record relevant process-related information when the corresponding instances are elaborated at the domain level.

14.1.2 The goal meta-model

Figure 14.3 summarizes how the modelling abstractions introduced in Chapters 7–9 are interrelated. The root meta-concept GoalModel appeared in Figure 14.2. The Goal meta-concept is obviously central to this part of the overall meta-model.

As a goal may be OR-refined into multiple alternative refinements, the meta-concept of Refinement is introduced together with the *Or-Ref* meta-relationship linking Goal and Refinement.

As a refinement may itself consist of multiple conjoined goals, the *And-Ref* meta-relationship is introduced between Refinement and Goal. This meta-relationship is represented by a UML OR-association because domain properties may be involved in the refinement as well.

Notice the multiplicities of those meta-relationships. A Goal may be OR-refined into *0* up to an arbitrary number of Refinements, whereas a Refinement refines one and only one Goal. On the other hand, a Refinement must be AND-refined into one Goal at least while possibly involving *0* up to an arbitrary number of DomDescript instances. (The latter meta-concept appears within dashed lines as it pertains to the Object meta-model.)

Figure 14.3 shows the various specializations of the Goal meta-concept detailed in Chapters 7–8. Each specialization by default inherits the meta-attributes and meta-relationships of its parent abstraction; LeafGoal does not inherit the *OR-ref* meta-relationship with Refinement.

A goal may be obstructed by obstacles (see Chapter 9) or by other goals conflicting with it (see Section 8.3). More general abstractions are introduced to capture both situations in a uniform way; namely, the ternary meta-relationship Divergence and the meta-concept

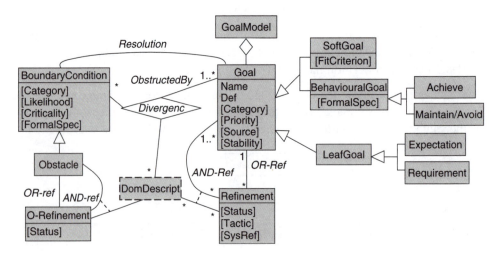

Figure 14.3 *The goal metamodel*

BoundaryCondition taking part in it. In the particular case of an obstacle, the multiplicity 1..* attached to the role ObstructedBy reduces to 1, as an obstacle obstruction involves a single goal. In case of conflicting goals, this multiplicity reduces to 2..*, as a boundary condition for conflict involves two divergent goals at least. Note that an obstacle can obstruct a domain description as well (see the multiplicity on the DomDescript side of Divergence). Obstacles may be AND/OR-refined to produce risk trees. Note that the O-Refinement meta-concept may not specialize the Refinement one (or a more general abstraction); obstacle refinements consist of sub-obstacles and domain descriptions only.

Figure 14.3 also shows some meta-attributes, for example the Goal meta-concept has Category, Source, Priority, Stability as optional meta-attributes (as introduced in Section 8.1). The SoftGoal and BehaviouralGoal meta-concepts have FitCriterion and FormalSpec as specific optional meta-attributes, respectively.

As introduced in Section 8.7, the Refinement meta-concept has optional meta-attributes such as Status, Tactic, SysRef (to indicate which alternative is taken in which version of the system) and so on.

As a specialization of BoundaryCondition, the Obstacle meta-concept inherits meta-attributes such as Likelihood and Criticality (see Section 9.2.4) together with the *Resolution* meta-relationship.

14.1.3 The object meta-model

Figure 14.4 shows how the abstractions introduced in Chapter 10 for structural modelling are inter-related. The root meta-concept ObjectModel appeared in Figure 14.2. The Object meta-concept is obviously central to this part of the overall meta-model. The meta-concepts pertaining to other views are indicated within dashed lines.

As we have seen before, domain-level objects are characterized by attributes and domain descriptions that are hypotheses or domain properties (called invariants) on their attributes. The initializations define attribute values when the Boolean *InstanceOf* meta-attribute becomes true

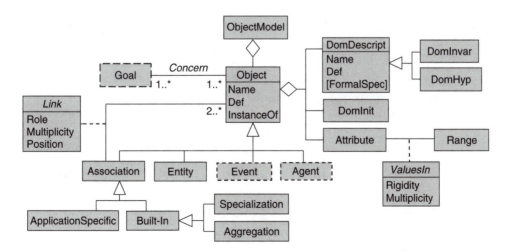

Figure 14.4 *The object metamodel*

for the corresponding instance (see Section 10.1.2). Attributes have values within a range; such values can be multiple and time varying or not, as indicated by the *ValuesIn* meta-relationship.

The various meta-specializations of the Object meta-concept inherit those characteristics. We can thus attach attributes and domain properties to associations, entities, events or agents. All meta-specializations inherit the *Link* meta-relationship between Object and Association. An association can thus in particular link other associations, as discussed in Section 10.6.4, or entities or agents.

Also note the Role, Multiplicity and Position meta-attributes of the *Link* meta-relationship; their values characterize links in domain-level associations.

Most of the multiplicities are not shown in Figure 14.4 to avoid cluttering the diagram. Note the multiplicity constraints on the *Concern* meta-relationship; an object must be referred to by one goal at least, to be relevant to the object model, and a goal must concern one object at least.

14.1.4 The agent meta-model

Figure 14.5 inter-relates the various abstractions defined in Chapter 11 for agent modelling. The root meta-concept AgentModel appeared in Figure 14.2.

The basic meta-relationships in which the Agent meta-concept participates are inter-view ones. In particular, the *Monitoring* and *Control* meta-relationships link Agent to the Attribute and/or Association meta-concepts in the object meta-model; Attribute and Association play the *stateVariable* role in these meta-relationships (see the agent capabilities in Section 11.2.2).

The *OR-Ass* meta-relationship between the LeafGoal and Assignment meta-concepts encodes the OR-assignment of leaf goals to agents (the same way as Refinement encodes goal OR-refinement in Figure 14.3). The 1..* multiplicity on the Assignment side of *OR-Ass* captures multiple alternative assignments of the same leaf goal. Like the Refinement meta-concept, Assignment has a SysRef meta-attribute to indicate which alternative is taken in which version of the system.

The *Responsibility* meta-relationship is defined pairwise among specializations of Agent and LeafGoal, with adequate multiplicities to account for individual responsibilities once an

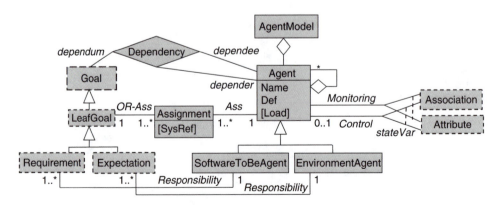

Figure 14.5 *The agent metamodel*

assignment is selected among alternative ones (see the 1..1 multiplicities on the agent sides of *Responsibility*).

To avoid cluttering the diagram, Figure 14.5 does not show the meta-attributes named *InstanceVariable* that are attached to the *Responsibility, Monitoring* and *Control* meta-relationships. These meta-attributes make precise what agent instance is linked to what goal instance or what object instance in the corresponding relationship at the instance level (see the instance declarations in Section 11.3.1).

Also note the possibility of refining agents through aggregation, as discussed in Section 11.4, and the *Dependency* meta-relationship defined in Section 11.2.6. The *Wish* meta-relationship defined in Section 11.2.5 is not shown in Figure 14.5. It links *Goal* and the HumanAgent meta-specialization of *EnvironmentAgent*.

14.1.5 The operation meta-model

Figure 14.6 summarizes the abstractions used for operation modelling. The root meta-concept OperationModel appeared in Figure 14.2.

The Operation meta-concept is linked to the goal model through the *Operationalization* meta-relationship that carries the required conditions for goal satisfaction as meta-attributes. The multiplicity constraints on this meta-relationship express that an operation must operationalize one leaf goal at least to be part of the model, and may operationalize multiple leaf goals as discussed in Section 12.3.1. On the other hand, a single leaf goal must be operationalized through one or more operations.

Any operation is individually characterized by its DomPre and DomPost conditions; see Section 12.2.3. The optional Category meta-attribute indicates the kind of operation (see Section 12.1).

Instantiations of the *Input* and *Output* meta-relationships yield operation signatures. The multiplicity of the *Performance* meta-relationship constrains the agent performing an operation to be unique.

To avoid cluttering the diagram, Figure 14.6 does not show the *InstanceVariable* meta-attributes attached to the *Performance* and *Input/Output* meta-relationships. These meta-attributes

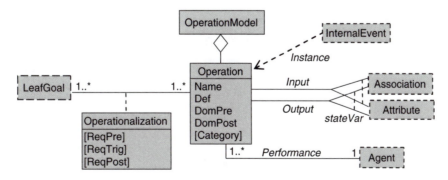

Figure 14.6 *The operation metamodel*

make precise which corresponding concept instances are linked together at the instance level (see the instance declarations in Sections 11.3.1 and instance variables in Section 12.2.2).

It is worth noticing that the context diagrams and use cases introduced in Chapters 11–12 require no specific abstractions in addition to those found in the agent and operation meta-models. The procedures explained in these chapters for generating those diagrams do in fact work on corresponding fragments of those meta-models (see the exercise at the end of this chapter).

Operation applications yield internal events (see Figure 12.1 and Section 13.2). The *Instance* meta-relationship therefore links the InternalEvent specialization of Event, defined in the behaviour meta-model below, and the Operation meta-concept.

14.1.6 The behaviour meta-model

Figure 14.7 inter-relates the various abstractions used for modelling system behaviours through scenarios and state machines. The root meta-concept BehaviorModel appeared in Figure 14.2.

The right part of the meta-model in Figure 14.7 is devoted to instance behaviours. The *History* meta-relationship structurally defines a scenario as a historical sequence of one up to an arbitrary number of timeline slices, each being a parallel composition of one or more interactions at the same point in time. Each interaction is defined by an interaction event instance, a source agent instance and a target agent instance. A scenario illustrates some goal(s) and may be decomposed through the *Episode* meta-relationship into sub-scenarios illustrating finer-grained sub-goals.

The left-hand part of Figure 14.7 is devoted to class behaviours. The AgentSM meta-concept structurally defines the behaviour of any agent instance within a class as an aggregation of

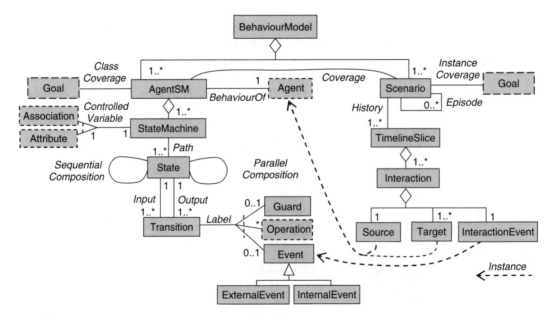

Figure 14.7 The behaviour metamodel

state machines – one per state variable that the agent controls. Each such state machine is defined by a path of one or more states that can be decomposed into sequential or concurrent sub-states. States are input or output states of transitions possibly labelled by an event, a guard and one or more operations. The set of SM paths must be included in the set of behaviours prescribed by the associated goal(s).

For the sake of clarity the diagram does not show the specializations of the State meta-concept that capture the concepts of initial state, final state, initial sub-state and final sub-state, respectively. These specializations do not inherit the SequentialDecomposition and ParallelDecomposition meta-relationships.

The overall meta-model presented in this section provides a common framework within which all views of a system model can be structurally defined and inter-related. The inter-view meta-relationships and meta-constraints are those connecting meta-concepts in Figures 14.3–14.7 to other meta-concepts represented within dashed lines. They play a prominent role in view integration, as the next section shows.

14.2 Inter-view consistency rules

Two views of a system model are said to be *structurally consistent* if they satisfy a set of rules constraining their respective elements for compatibility and complementarity.

Such rules correspond to the static semantics rules found in programming languages, such as 'every used variable must be declared', 'every declared variable must be used', 'every used variable must be initialized' and so on. Rule-based consistency checks across multi-view diagrams were introduced in Section 4.3.9.

Many structural consistency rules have the following *pattern*:

> **for every** item *it1* satisfying some property *P1(it1)* in view *V*1,
>> **there exists** a corresponding item *it2* in view *V*2 that satisfies some property *P2(it1,it2) linking it1 and it2*.

When a common meta-model is defined for view integration, the rules constrain meta-model components. (They are commonly called *meta-constraints*.) In particular, the preceding pattern amounts to a multiplicity constraint on inter-view meta-relationships:

> **for every** instance *ins1* of metaconcept *C*1 in metamodel *component MC1*,
>> **there exists** a corresponding instance *ins2* of metaconcept *C*2 in metamodel *component MC2*,
>>> linked to *ins1* by an instance of the inter-view metarelationship *IR*.

Rule violations drive model transformations towards structural consistency. As missing items are often revealed, the rules address structural completeness as well.

Such rules are to be determined at meta-model definition time, checked at model-building time when enough model elements are available in each view, and rechecked at model evolution time when the linked items are being changed.

Checking large models against a significant number of rules might be a daunting task. Fortunately, most checks can be fully automated through 'pre-cooked' queries on the model database. The principle was introduced in Section 5.2 and will be further detailed in Section 16.1. When there is no model database support, we can include the rules in model inspection checklists for manual review (see Section 5.1.3).

Here is a representative sample of inter-view rules linking the goal, object, agent, operation and behaviour views for structural consistency of the overall system model.

Structural consistency of the goal and object models

- Every conceptual item referred to in a goal specification in the goal model must appear as an attribute or object in the object model.
- Every goal in the goal model must concern at least one object in the object model.
- For every object in the object model, there must be at least one goal in the goal model concerning it.

Structural consistency of the goal and agent models

- One of the candidate agents in an OR-assignment to a leaf goal in the goal model must appear as the selected agent responsible for this goal in the agent model.
- Every goal under the responsibility of an agent in the agent model must appear as a leaf goal in the goal model.
- Every agent in the agent model must be responsible for at least one leaf goal in the goal model.
- Every requirement in the goal model must be under the responsibility of one and only one software agent.
- Every expectation in the goal model must be under the responsibility of one and only one environment agent.
- An agent responsible for a goal must have the capability of controlling the variables constrained by the goal specification and of monitoring the variables to be evaluated in it.
- If an agent responsible for a goal is refined in the agent model, each refining agent must be responsible for one or more sub-goals of this goal.
- If an agent depends on another for a goal in the agent model, this goal must appear in the goal model.

Structural consistency of the goal and operation models

- Every requirement in the goal model must be operationalized by at least one operation in the operation model.
- Every operation in the operation model must operationalize at least one leaf goal from the goal model.

Structural consistency of the goal and behaviour models

- Every scenario in the behaviour model must be covered by at least one goal in the goal model.

Structural consistency of the goal, object and agent models

- If an object is referred to by a goal under the responsibility of an agent, one or more attributes of it must be monitored or controlled by this agent.

Structural consistency of the goal, agent and operation models

- If an agent is responsible for a goal, it must perform all operations operationalizing that goal.
- If an agent performs an operation, it must be responsible for all the goals operationalized by this operation.

Structural consistency of the goal, agent and behaviour models

- Every parallel state machine capturing the behaviour of an agent in the behaviour model must show a set of paths prescribed by goals from the goal model that are assigned to this agent in the agent model.

Structural consistency of the object and agent models

- Every variable monitored or controlled by an agent in the agent model must appear as an attribute or object in the object model.
- An attribute or object in the object model may be controlled by at most one agent.
- Every agent in the agent model must control (or monitor) at least one attribute or object in the object model.

Structural consistency of the object and operation models

- Every input or output of an operation in the operation model must appear as an attribute or object in the object model.

Structural consistency of the object and behaviour models

- Every state of a state machine in the behaviour model must refer to a variable declared as an attribute or association in the object model.
- Every event attribute or event specialization in the behaviour model must appear as an attribute or a specialization of the corresponding object in the object model, respectively.

Structural consistency of the agent and operation models

- Every agent in the operation model must appear in the agent model.
- Every agent in the agent model must perform at least one operation in the operation model.

- Every operation in the operation model is performed by exactly one agent from the agent model.

- The inputs (or outputs) of an operation performed by an agent in the operation model must be monitored (or controlled) by the agent in the agent model.

- For every variable controlled by an agent in the agent model, there must be an operation performed by the agent whose output list includes this variable.

Structural consistency of the agent and behaviour models

- Every agent with a scenario timeline in the behaviour model must appear in the agent model.

- Every agent associated with a parallel state machine in the behaviour model must appear in the agent model.

- Every SM state in a parallel state machine associated with an agent in the behaviour model must refer to a variable controlled by this agent in the agent model.

Structural consistency of the operation and behaviour models

- The outputs of an operation are the only ones whose state can change by operation applications.

- Every scenario interaction in the behaviour model must correspond to the application of an operation performed by the source agent in the operation model.

- Every internal event labelling state machine transitions in the behaviour model must correspond to the application of an operation from the operation model.

14.3 Grouping related view fragments into packages

A third mechanism for integrating multiple views of the same system model consists of grouping related model fragments from different system views into cohesive model packages. The standard UML packaging mechanism supports this.

A *package* is a container in which model parts are defined and grouped together. Every model part is defined in one and only one 'home' package, which *owns* it. For organization and maintenance of large models, a package may *contain* other packages beside the model parts it owns – in the same way as a directory may contain files and other directories. We can thus define package inclusion trees.

In such a tree organization, all the names introduced in the model parts owned by a package are local to the package but visible to all the packages it contains and their descendants. Thanks to this visibility rule, the names of goals, objects, attributes, operations, scenarios and states are not necessarily global to the entire model. We are not obliged to choose names that are unique throughout the entire system model; the names must be unique within the home package and all its descendants.

A package may also *import* other packages. As a result, the names visible in the imported package become visible in the importing package as well. We can thereby reference external names within part of a model, while making sure that this importation does not introduce name clashes.

Import is one type of dependency among packages; the importing package depends on the imported package. A package *P depends* on another package *Q* if at least one element of *P* depends on one or more elements of *Q*; that is, a modification of those elements of *Q* may need to be propagated to the depending element(s) in *P*.

The packaging mechanism is obviously essential for organizing large models into coherent pieces, in particular for change control and model configuration management.

The *grouping rule* within a package has to be determined by the modeller. Several rules may be considered, which can be combined or not:

- A package might regroup model parts pertaining to the same view.

- It might contain model elements related to the same goal category, the same goal, the same functionality or the same agent.

- In any case, it should regroup elements that are likely to evolve together.

Figure 14.8 shows two overall organizations of a model according to two possible grouping rules. In the upper part, a library model is organized *by views* where each view is organized *by category* of the corresponding meta-concept. In the lower part, the same model is organized *by functionality*. Each package shown there regroups the goal, object, agent, operation and behaviour models associated with the corresponding functionality. Graphically, a package is represented by a 'folder' icon and a dependency by a dashed arrow.

As far as view integration is concerned, we can form cohesive multi-view packages – for example, to regroup the sub-goals, objects and operations related to a functional goal within a single package for presentation purposes. In this case a multi-view package will not define those elements but import the owner packages where the elements are defined.

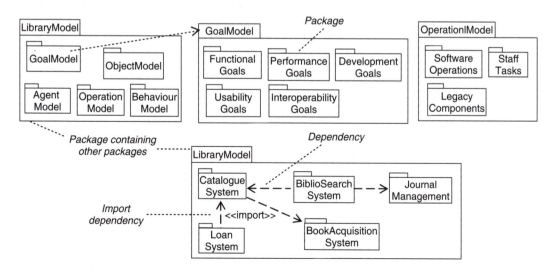

Figure 14.8 *Model packaging*

Summary

- A multi-view modelling framework must provide integration mechanisms to enforce the structural consistency, completeness and complementarity of different system views. For integration of the goal, object, agent, operation and behaviour models, we may inter-relate all views within a common meta-model, enforce inter-view consistency rules and organize multi-view model fragments into cohesive packages.

- A meta-model is a meta-level model providing abstractions in terms of which domain-level models can be defined and inter-related. Meta-models play multiple roles in model elaboration, model management and tool support. Structural meta-models can be organized in terms of entity–relationship structures. Meta-concepts are characterized by meta-attributes, linked to others by meta-relationships and further defined by meta-constraints. The goal-oriented meta-model in this chapter has one meta-level component per view. Each meta-model component summarizes how the abstractions used for modelling the corresponding domain-level view are inter-related.

- Meta-constraints on inter-view relationships play a prominent role in view integration. They yield rules to be enforced during model elaboration and evolution for the structural consistency and completeness of the model. Most rule-based checks can be fully automated through 'pre-cooked' queries on a model database structured according to the meta-model. Many rules follow a standard pattern. Among these are multiplicity constraints on inter-view meta-relationships.

- Model fragments can be grouped into packages. A package is the unique owner of the model elements it contains. It may contain other packages as well. The names of elements defined in a package are local to the package and its descendants. A package may import other packages to make visible the elements owned by the latter. We can thereby form multi-view packages where related model fragments are regrouped from single-view packages where they are defined. To facilitate model configuration and evolution, we should specify dependency links among packages. Elements that are likely to evolve together should be regrouped in the same package.

Notes and Further Reading

An earlier, restricted version of the meta-model in this chapter appeared in Dardenne *et al.* (1993). This paper describes the use of meta-models for requirements engineering, in particular for requirements acquisition through meta-model traversal. This use was inspired by learning-by-instruction systems such as Teiresias and the use of meta-rules for guiding knowledge acquisition (Davis, 1982). A similar distinction between meta- and object levels was used for requirements modelling in RML (Greenspan *et al.*, 1986).

The meta-model-based parameterization of tools on modelling languages, with instantiation through access to a meta-language specification of specific languages, is detailed in van Lamsweerde *et al.* (1988).

The use of consistency rules for integrating multi-view specifications was proposed in Niskier *et al.* (1989), where a PROLOG-based system is described for automating the checks. The principle was also used in OMT (Rumbaugh *et al.*, 1991) and the Viewpoint framework (Nuseibeh *et al.*, 1994). The automation of checks through queries on a model database is described in van Lamsweerde *et al.* (1988). A recent meta-model-based follow-up for formal multi-view consistency checking will be found in Paige *et al.* (2007).

A metamodel for UML is discussed in Evans *et al.* (2005). More details on the UML package mechanism may be found in Rumbaugh *et al.* (1999). Many modelling tools support the organization of large models in an *Explorer*-like fashion.

Exercises

- In the representation style of Figure 14.1, capture the main concepts involved in the various views of the meeting scheduling system as instances of elements of the meta-model depicted in Figures 14.3–14.7.

- Complete the diagrams in Figures 14.3–14.7 with adequate multiplicities on all meta-relationships.

- Highlight the agent meta-model part specifically used by the procedure for generating context diagrams in Section 11.4.2. Then rephrase this procedure in terms of meta-model elements.

- Highlight the part of the agent and operation meta-models specifically used by the procedure for generating use cases in Section 12.6.2. Then rephrase this procedure in terms of meta-model elements.

- Section 14.2 provides a sample of structural consistency rules constraining the goal, object, agent, operation and behaviour models of a system. Reformulate those rules as constraints on meta-concepts, meta-attributes and meta-relationships from the meta-model discussed in Section 14.1. Among those meta-constraints, point out the ones expressible as multiplicities on meta-relationships.

- Consider the *problem* and *frame* diagrams defined in Section 4.3.1. Build a structural meta-model for those diagrams. Explore suitable meta-constraints on your meta-model.

- Elaborate an overall organization of a multi-view model for the meeting scheduling system into cohesive packages. Explain the reasons for your grouping choices.

15

A Goal-Oriented Model-Building Method in Action

This chapter concludes the book's second part on multi-view modelling for RE by looking at the process of elaborating all views in a systematic, coherent and integrated way. Chapters 8–13 presented a variety of heuristics for building each view. Now we are concerned with the building of an entire system model out of those views. This chapter presents a constructive method for elaborating a robust and consistent model by incremental integration of the goal, obstacle, object, agent, operation and behaviour sub-models. The next chapter will then provide details on how we can further analyse that model and produce the requirements document systematically from it.

Figure 15.1 shows the various steps of the method we will follow. The first two steps concern the *system-as-is* whereas all other steps concern the *system-to-be*. The plain arrows in Figure 15.1 express data dependency, where a target step may require model items from the source step. These arrows are by no means to be interpreted as strict sequencing. Many steps are in fact intertwined, and backtracking to an upward step may be required from analysis at a downward step. The most frequent cases of step interleaving are suggested by dashed arrows. For example, the refinement of goals towards realizability may be influenced by agent capabilities modelled in the next step; goal identification may result from scenario illustrations and so on. Moreover, the various steps of model building are intertwined with further elicitation and validation with stakeholders.

The sections in this chapter follow those steps successively. Each section explains *what* the corresponding step consists of and *how* it may be run. The method is shown in action on a simple *mine safety control* system. As opposed to our three running case studies, this one is small enough to allow us to go into further details within a reasonable number of pages, and yet rich enough to illustrate most issues raised in a typical model-based RE process. The requirements document obtained from this model, using the generation technique explained in the next chapter, is shown on the book's Web site.

The following fragmentary notes summarize the outcome of the first elicitation sessions concerning the need for a new system for mine safety control.

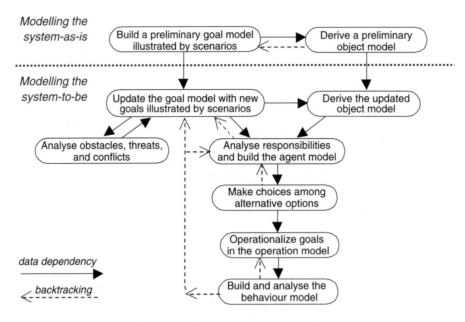

Figure 15.1 *Main steps of a model building method for RE*

Mine safety control

[*System-as-is.*] Miners are exposed to multiple hazards while working inside a mine. These include life-threatening levels of percolating water, carbon monoxide, methane and airflow.

Currently, dedicated supervisors have to alert miners inside the mine for prompt evacuation when any of those levels is estimated to be dangerous.

Sumps are placed at selected places in the mine for water collection. Each sump is equipped with a pump. The water level in each sump is regularly checked by dedicated operators to see if the water level is too high. When this level is too high, the corresponding pump must be turned on to pump the water out of the mine.

To avoid the risk of explosion, pumps may not be operated when the methane level exceeds a critical threshold.

The current situation results in unacceptable exposure to risks, due to: possible human lack of awareness or misjudgement of potentially dangerous situations; sudden flows of gas or water without operators at the right place to act on them; or pump-functioning problems. On the other hand, lack of accurate assessment sometimes results in unnecessary evacuations. The cost of manpower for safety control is another concern.

[*System-to-be*.] To address these problems, a distributed safety control system will be installed. Each sump will be equipped with water-level sensors to detect when the water is above a *high* or below a *low* level, respectively. A software-based controller shall turn a pump *on* whenever the water in the corresponding sump has reached the *high* water level, and *off* whenever the water has reached the *low* water level.

The mine will also be equipped with sensors at selected places to monitor the carbon monoxide, methane and airflow levels. An alarm shall be raised, and the operator informed within one second, whenever any of these levels has reached a critical threshold, so that the mine can be evacuated promptly.

Human operators can also control the operation of the pump, as previously, but within limits. An operator can turn the pump *on* or *off* if the water is between the *low* and *high* water levels. A special operator, the supervisor, can turn the pump *on* or *off* without this restriction.

The safety control system shall also maintain sensor readings and pump operation records for history tracking and analysis of anomalies.

15.1 Modelling the system-as-is

The first modelling phase takes place during domain analysis. Its purpose is to structure the goals and concepts constituting the core system business; that is, the stable goals and concepts that are expected to be common to any system version (*as-is, to-be* or *to-be-next*). For this, we analyse the system-as-is to extract preliminary goal model fragments and derive conceptual objects from them.

15.1.1 Step 1: Build a preliminary goal model illustrated by scenarios
WHAT

This step consists of analysing any available material to identify stable goals and inter-relate them through refinement links. Each goal is defined and classified in terms of its type and category (wherever possible). The goals are refined until we reach sub-goals that may differ from one system version to the other, or whose assignment in the system-as-is appears questionable. The goals are abstracted until the system's boundary is reached.

HOW

A preliminary goal model is built by application of the following heuristics to the *system-as-is*.

- Search for prescriptive or intentional keywords in statements about the system-as-is.

- Ask *HOW* and *WHY* questions about such statements.

- Check for explicit responsibility assignments in prescriptive statements.

- Elicit illustrative scenarios of current ways of doing things and ask *WHY* questions about them.

- Instantiate goal categories.

- Use goal refinement patterns to restructure the model.

These heuristics were detailed in Chapter 8.

Mine safety control example

A simple search for prescriptive or intentional keywords in the statements describing the system-as-is results in identification of the goals shown in Figure 15.2. Note that keywords such as *(in order) to* and *for* in those statements allow us to identify refinement links together with a goal–sub-goal pair.

The Def annotations in Figure 15.2 are obtained from corresponding statements in interview transcripts. They should be made more precise wherever necessary (e.g. 'prompt evacuation' or 'level too high'). More precision will be reached gradually as more knowledge is gained about the system.

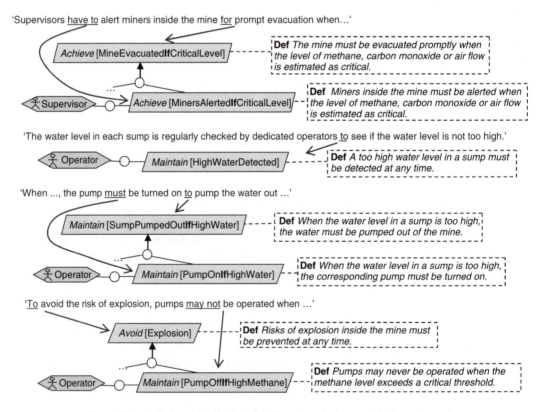

Figure 15.2 *Preliminary identification of stable goals and refinements in the system-as-is*

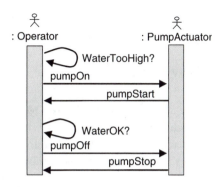

Figure 15.3 *Scenario illustrating the goal Maintain[PumpOnIfHighWater]*

We can also identify goal types in Figure 15.2 according to the patterns for behavioural goals discussed in Section 7.3.1. Note that some responsibility assignments arise from prescriptive statements in the system description.

The fragments in Figure 15.2 are refined/abstracted through HOW/WHY questions until the bottom/top boundaries of the system-as-is are reached, where the bottom nodes here call for alternative refinements or assignments in the system-to-be. Scenarios may be used as well to understand the system-as-is and prompt WHY questions. For example, the goal Maintain[PumpOnIfHighWater] might also have been elicited from the illustrative scenario in Figure 15.3.

Some model restructuring may take place while elaborating the goal graph for the system-as-is. For example, the different types of alerts (methane, carbon monoxide, airflow) call for an application of the decomposition-by-case pattern (see Figure 8.21). The use of the milestone-driven refinement pattern results in some restructuring too (see Figure 8.19). Figure 15.4 shows some fragments of the resulting goal model for the system-as-is.

Note the introduction of critical hypotheses that came out of satisfaction arguments. The hypotheses WaterPumpedOutIfPumpOn, SufficientPumpCapacity and LimitedWaterFlow in Figure 15.4

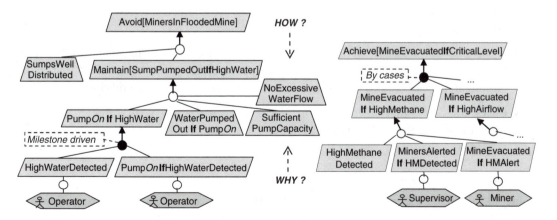

Figure 15.4 *Goal model fragment for the system-as-is*

were missing for the goal SumpPumpedOutIfHighWater to be satisfied from its sub-goal PumpOnIfHighWater. Such hypotheses will provide a source for obstacle analysis in Step 5 below.

15.1.2 Step 2: Derive a preliminary object model
WHAT
This step consists of identifying the *stable* concepts referred to in goal definitions or in elicited descriptions of the system-as-is. Each concept is defined and classified as an entity, association, attribute, agent or event. In particular, conceptual items that are inter-related in goal definitions or domain descriptions are linked through associations, attributes or specialization links. The *descriptive* statements about them are taken as corresponding domain invariants or hypotheses. A glossary of terms is obtained as a by-product of this step.

HOW
A preliminary object model is derived by application of the following heuristics to the *system-as-is*. (These heuristics were detailed in Chapter 10.)

- Take any conceptual object referred to by the goals identified in the previous step or by elicited domain descriptions, and only those.

- Identify associations and participating objects from linking expressions in those goals and descriptions.

- Identify associations from domain invariants/hypotheses on multiple objects.

- Use the heuristics in Section 10.7 to decide whether a concept should be an entity, association, attribute or event, and to which other concept this concept should be connected. Decorate all associations with multiplicities and determine whether each of these is descriptive or prescriptive (for inclusion in the goal model in the latter case).

- Identify specializations from classification expressions and discriminant factors in goals and domain descriptions.

- Identify generalizations from objects characterized by similar attributes, associations or domain descriptions.

- From goal formulations or domain descriptions about the system-as-is, sketch a preliminary state machine representation of domain objects whose dynamics is felt to be important, and identify to which attributes or associations such state machines refer.

- Check for conceptual objects that are not referred to by any goal identified so far, in order to elicit prescriptive statements about them if they really seem relevant. Drop them otherwise.

Mine safety control example
Figure 15.5 outlines the result of this step together with a few derivation examples. The concepts structured there from goal definitions and domain descriptions are expected to be stable throughout any system version.

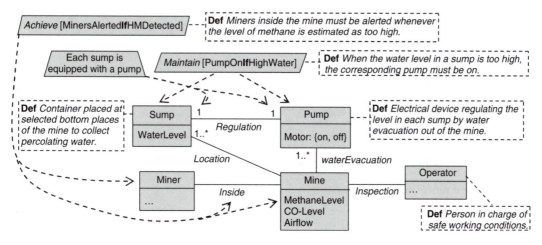

Figure 15.5 *Deriving a preliminary object model from goals and domain descriptions*

15.2 Modelling the system-to-be

The next modelling phase consists of expanding the preliminary structure of stable goals and domain concepts towards a model for the system-to-be. Based on reported problems with the system-as-is and elicited material about the system-to-be, we need to consider alternative goal refinements and assignments and, from there, operationalizations for the new system.

15.2.1 Step 3: Update the goal model with new goals illustrated by scenarios
WHAT

This step replays Step 1 on the system-to-be. The goal model obtained in Step 1 is expanded with *alternative* sub-goals and assignments specific to the system-to-be. The new sub-goals must meet the stable, higher-level goals identified in Step 1 as well as other goals that might emerge from new opportunities. Each new goal is defined and classified in terms of its type and category (wherever possible). The goals are refined until we reach alternative responsibility assignments; they are abstracted until the system's boundary is reached. Satisfaction arguments should be provided from the bottom of the goal model to show that the sub-goals ensure their parent goals.

HOW

The updated goal model is built by application of the following heuristics to the *system-to-be*:

- For each problem identified in the system-as-is, derive an improvement goal for the system-to-be in the light of opportunities to be exploited.

- Search for prescriptive, intentional or amelioration keywords in statements about the system-to-be.

- Ask *HOW* and *WHY* questions about goals already identified.

- Explore illustrative scenarios of alternative, better ways of doing things, and ask *WHY* questions about them.

- Identify wishes of human agents.

- Instantiate goal categories.

- Split responsibilities among agents.

- Identify soft goals by analysing the pros and cons of alternative refinements.

- Check the converse and complementary cases of *Achieve* goals.

- Use goal refinement patterns.

These heuristics were detailed in Chapter 8.

Mine safety control example

The list of reported problems with the system-as-is suggests soft goals such as:

Reduce [SafetyRiskExposure],
Reduce [SafetyControlCost],
Reduce [UnnecessaryEvacuations].

These soft goals will favour alternative goal refinements and assignments in view of recent progress in distributed multi-sensor technology.

New goals appear from prescriptive or intentional statements about the system-to-be, and from refinements or abstractions of these. Figure 15.6 shows a portion of the updated goal

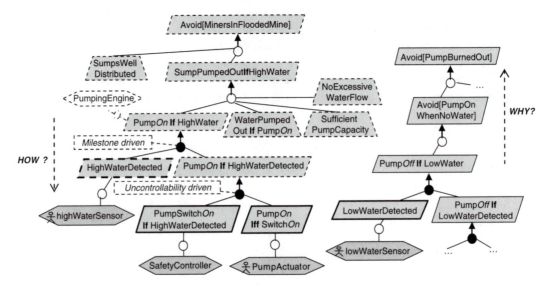

Figure 15.6   *Expanded goal model fragment for the system-to-be*

model obtained at this stage together with an indication of some of the heuristics and patterns used for deriving goal refinements or abstractions. The goals between dashed lines indicate stable goals that were already identified in Step 1 (see Figure 15.4).

Let us have a look at some derivation examples.

Maintain[HighWaterDetected] This goal was in the previous model but its assignment has changed after the statement 'each sump will be equipped with water-level sensors to detect when the water is above a high or below a low level'.

Maintain[PumpOnIfHighWaterDetected] This goal was in the previous model but its refinement has changed. The new refinement is obtained by use of the *uncontrollability-driven* refinement pattern (see Figure 8.26), leading to sub-goals PumpSwitchOnIfHighWaterDetected and PumpOnIfSwitchOn under the responsibility of the SafetyController and PumpActuator agents, respectively. Those assignments meet the statement 'a software-based controller shall turn a pump on whenever the water in the corresponding sump is reaching the high water level, and off whenever the water is reaching the low water level'.

As suggested in Figure 15.6, yet another way of building the refinement tree from the higher-level goal PumpOnIfHighWater would have been first to consider an abstract agent PumpingEngine, responsible for this goal, and then refine this agent and its responsibilities as discussed in Section 11.4 (see also Step 6).

Maintain[LowWaterDetected], Maintain[PumpOffIfLowWaterDetected] These new goals emerge from corresponding statements in the preliminary description of the system-to-be. Their refinement and resulting assignments are symmetrical to the left-hand part of Figure 15.6. Their rationale is obtained by abstracting them through *WHY* questions. For example, the reason for the goal PumpOffIfLowWater in Figure 15.6 is to prevent the pump from being burned out due to running without water in the sump.

Maintain[HighMethaneDetected] This goal was in the model of the system-as-is in Figure 15.4, but it is now assigned to a methane sensor integrated in the new computer-based system.

Achieve[MinersAlertedIfHMDetected] This goal was in the model of the system-as-is in Figure 15.4, but instead of being assigned to the Supervisor agent it is now further refined to account for the statement 'an alarm shall be raised, and the operator informed within one second, whenever any of these levels is reaching a critical threshold'. The refinement consists of two sub-goals, HMAlarmIfHMDetected and OperatorInformedIfHMDetected, and the hypothesis MinersAlertedIfHMAlarmAndOperatorInformed. This refinement is not detailed here for space reasons (see the exercise at the end of this chapter).

The handling of the airflow and CO alerts/evacuations is quite similar. Note that different types of sensors, alerts and evacuation procedures may be required for different types of alarms, which explains the decomposition by cases in Figure 15.4.

Annotating goals with their specification Every goal and domain description in the new model version must be given a **Def** annotation. Here is a sample of definitions. Note the significant number of accuracy goals.

PumpControllableManually, Readings**And**OperationsLogged   These goals are similarly identified, refined and abstracted.

Maintain[HighWaterDetected]. The high-water signal must be *on* whenever the water level in the sump is above some upper threshold.

Maintain[PumpOnIfHighWaterDetected]. The pump must be *on* whenever the high-water signal is *on*.

Maintain[PumpSwitchOnIfHighWaterDetected]. The pump switch must be set to *on* whenever the high-water signal is *on*.

Maintain[PumpOnIffSwitchOn]. The pump motor must be *on* if and only if the pump switch is set to *on*.

Maintain[LowWaterDetected]. The low-water signal must be *on* whenever the water level in the sump is below some lower threshold.

Maintain[PumpOffIfLowWaterDetected]. The pump must be *off* whenever the low-water signal is *on*.

Maintain[PumpSwitchOffIfLowWaterDetected]. The pump switch must be set to *off* whenever the low-water signal is *on*.

Maintain[PumpOffIffSwitchOff]. The pump motor must be *off* if and only if the pump switch is set to *off*.

NoExcessiveWaterFlow. The water flow in a sump is assumed to never exceed a worst-case figure of X litres per hour.

*Maintain[Readings**And**OperationsLogged]*. Readings from the high-water and low-water sensors in each sump must be logged together with the history of operations of all pumps to enable performance analysis and fault detection.

Using scenarios for elicitation or illustration   Some of the goals identified in this step might also have been discovered from new scenarios envisioned in the system-to-be. In any case, such scenarios help us to get a better grasp of some goals. Figure 15.7 shows the alternative scenario replacing the one in Figure 15.3. This scenario illustrates the goals Maintain[PumpSwitchOnIfHighWaterDetected] and Maintain[PumpSwitchOffIfLowWaterDetected].

15.2.2 Step 4: Derive the updated object model
WHAT

This step replays Step 2 on the system-to-be. The object model obtained in Step 2 is expanded by identifying the new conceptual objects specific to the system-to-be, as they are referred to in the goal definitions obtained in the previous step. Each new conceptual object is defined,

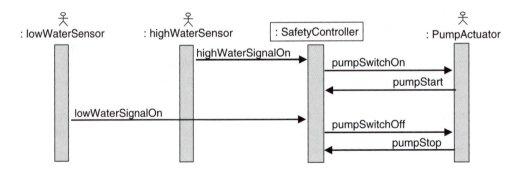

Figure 15.7   *New illustrative scenario in the system-to-be*

classified as an entity, association, attribute, agent or event, and linked to others based on the new goal definitions. Descriptive statements about the new objects are taken as domain invariants or hypotheses on them.

HOW

The updated object model is derived by application of the following heuristics to the *system-to-be*.

- Use all heuristics for object model derivation in Step 2, now applied to goals and descriptions of the *system-to-be*.

- Identify tracking associations between environment objects and software counterparts – see heuristic (*H3*) and Figure 10.13 in Section 10.7.1.

- Check the goal–object inter-view consistency rules in Section 14.2.

Mine safety control example

Figure 15.8 shows the updated object model resulting from this step. The objects between dashed lines indicate stable objects that were already identified in Step 2 (see Figure 15.5). Attributes in italics are new attributes arising from goals, domain properties or hypotheses obtained in the previous step. For example, the Switch attribute of the Pump entity comes from the goal PumpSwitchOnIfHighWaterDetected in Figure 15.6. The Capacity attribute of Pump comes from the hypothesis SufficientPumpCapacity appearing there. Note the introduction of specialization links from classification expressions and discriminant factors in goals and domain descriptions, for example 'a special operator, the supervisor, can turn the pump on or off without this restriction'.

The identification and integration of further goals and objects, and the making of goal/object definitions more precise, may continue in the subsequent steps of model elaboration as more knowledge is gained from complementary views of the system.

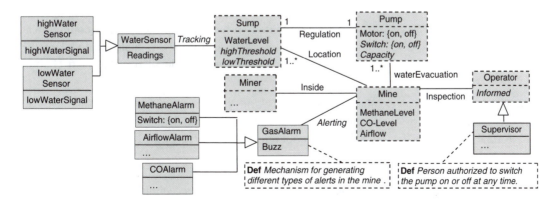

Figure 15.8 *Updated object model from goals and descriptions of the system-to-be*

15.2.3 Step 5: Analyse obstacles, threats and conflicts

WHAT

As the goals identified in the previous steps are likely to be over-ideal, we should adopt a pessimistic attitude and anticipate exceptional events or behaviours that might prevent important goals or hypotheses from being satisfied. A goal or hypothesis may become unsatisfiable because of obstacles obstructing it, including malicious ones set by malevolent agents to achieve their own anti-goals (such obstacles are called *threats*). A goal or hypothesis may also become unsatisfiable because of other goals conflicting with it under particular boundary conditions.

This step consists of:

- Identifying as many obstacles, threats and boundary conditions as possible.

- Assessing their likelihood and criticality.

- Exploring resolutions yielding new candidate goals as countermeasures in the goal model.

The selection of best resolutions is part of Step 7, where choices are made among alternative options.

HOW

Chapters 8–9 introduced some of the techniques that we can use in this step. The next chapters will provide more.

- To build an obstacle model and analyse it, we may use the heuristics and techniques described in Section 9.3. In particular, tautology-based refinement of obstacles is generally applicable as we start from goal/hypothesis negations; the identification of necessary domain conditions for the obstructed target, and its corresponding refinement pattern, is quite effective too (see Figure 9.10). Additional techniques for obstacle identification will be described in Sections 16.2.2 and 18.3. To explore alternative obstacle resolutions, we may apply the model transformation operators discussed in Section 9.3.3, including goal substitution, agent substitution, obstacle prevention, goal weakening, obstacle reduction, goal restoration and obstacle mitigation.

- To analyse threats against the model obtained so far and explore security countermeasures, we can apply an adapted version of obstacle analysis to build a model of the attacker's anti-goals and analyse it. This technique will be detailed in the next chapter (see Section 16.2.3).

- To detect potential conflicts among goals and explore conflict resolutions, we can generate boundary conditions for goal divergence and analyse these. Semi-formal and formal techniques for this will be described in Sections 16.2.1 and 18.5, respectively.

Mine safety control example

Figure 15.9 shows a systematic application of obstacle analysis techniques to a goal model fragment appearing in Figure 15.6. Each leaf goal or hypothesis is negated, and negations are

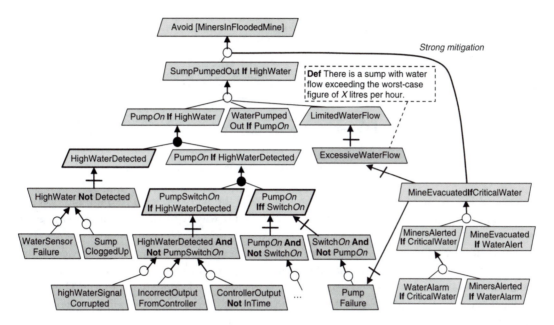

Figure 15.9 *Obstacle analysis: mine safety control examples*

OR-refined using standard tautologies and necessary domain conditions for the target of the obstructed assertion. For example, a necessary condition for the pump switch to be on is that the high-water signal from the water sensor should not be corrupted. When observable phenomena are reached in obstacle refinements, we analyse their likelihood and criticality. The sub-obstacles shown in Figure 15.9 are all fairly likely and critical as they obstruct goals in the *Safety* category. Each of them must therefore be resolved appropriately.

The resolution shown in Figure 15.9 is a strong mitigation (as defined in Section 9.3.3). The resolution goal MineEvacuatedIfCriticalWater ensures that the ancestor goal Avoid[MinersInFloodedMine] is satisfied in spite of descendant leaf goals being obstructed. This ancestor goal is our primary concern after all. The resolution goal has to be refined in turn; the milestone-driven refinement pattern was used in Figure 15.9 (see Figure 8.19).

Note that in this case the resolution goal resolves two critical obstacles – which provides a good reason for selecting it among alternative resolutions in Step 7. Also note that obstacle resolution sub-goals may be under the responsibility of the software-to-be, for example the requirement WaterAlarmSwitchOnIfPumpFaultDetected, refining the resolution sub-goal Water-AlarmIfCriticalWater in Figure 15.9. Other resolution (sub)goals might be under the responsibility of environment agents, for example the obstacle SumpCloggedUp will be resolved by an expectation SumpRegularlyCleanedUp, to be operationalized by a corresponding task for environment agents.

Figure 15.10 illustrates a typical potential conflict found in an RE process. On the one hand, the goal Maintain[PumpOnIfHighWater] is identified in Figure 15.6; on the other hand, the goal Maintain[PumpOffIfHighMethane] must be satisfied to ensure the goal Avoid[Explosion] in Figure 15.2. A boundary condition for conflict is that a system state is reached where the

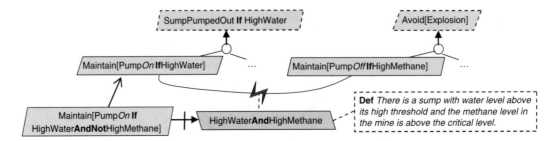

Figure 15.10   *Conflict analysis: mine safety control example*

water level in a sump is above the high threshold *and* the methane level in the mine exceeds its critical threshold; under such a condition there is no way we can satisfy those two goals together.

The conflict resolution shown in Figure 15.10 corresponds to a variant of the goal-weakening operator in Section 9.3.3, already introduced in Section 3.1.3 briefly. The lower-priority goal, PumpOnIfHighWater in this case, is weakened so as to cover the boundary condition. This yields the weakened goal PumpOnIfHighWaterAndNotHighMethane replacing the conflicting goal. The goal definition must be updated accordingly, for example:

> *Maintain[PumpOnIfHighWaterAndNotHighMethane]:* The sump pump must be *on* whenever the water level in the sump is above its high threshold and the methane level is not above its critical level.

Section 18.5 will describe formal techniques for detecting and resolving such divergences in a systematic way.

It is worth noticing that goal weakening for conflict resolution must in general be recursively *propagated* to related goals in the goal AND-tree in which the weakened goal appears. For example, the goal weakening in Figure 15.10 must be propagated to its parent goal, yielding the weakened version SumpPumpedOutIfHighWaterAndNotHighMethane, and to its sub-goal in Figure 15.6, yielding the weakened sub-goal PumpOnIfHighWaterDetectedAndNotHighMethane, and recursively.

While elaborating resolutions of obstacles or potential conflicts, we may use illustrative scenarios to make such resolutions more concrete. Figure 15.11 shows one such scenario for resolving the goal divergence in Figure 15.10.

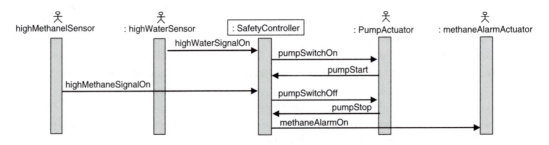

Figure 15.11   *Scenario illustrating a conflict resolution*

Finally, it is worth noticing that the analysis of risks and conflicts is performed early and at the goal level. Such analysis is made much simpler on declarative formulations. If we do it later, the analysis will be cluttered by operational details that may hide the underpinning problem causes and require backtracking on earlier decisions.

15.2.4 Step 6: Analyse responsibilities and build the agent model

WHAT

This step consists of exploring alternative responsibility assignments. For each leaf goal, the question we need to address is: *'Who is capable of controlling the state variables constrained by this goal and of monitoring the variables to be evaluated in it?'* The answer may lead to the identification of agents that were not already apparent from the earlier steps – including off-the-shelf components or foreign software services.

If not done earlier, all the agents forming the system need to be defined. The capabilities of each agent must be made precise in terms of state variables from the object model that the agent can monitor or control. The realizability of leaf goals by the agents tentatively assigned to them has to be checked; further goal refinement may be required to ensure realizability, and therefore we may need to backtrack to Step 3.

The agent model results from this step and from the selection among alternative assignments at the next step. In this model, we should annotate the capability links and responsibility links with *instance declarations* to specify what corresponding instances are involved in the links (see Section 11.3.1). A system context diagram can then be derived from the agent model.

HOW

Various heuristics were discussed in Chapter 11 to help in building an agent model. Let us summarize them:

- Identify any active object that a leaf goal concerns.

- Look for agents whose capabilities match the variables evaluated in and constrained by a leaf goal, respectively, and who may wish this goal (for a human assignment).

- Consider abstract agents and responsibilities first and then refine these until individual roles are reached.

- Wherever possible, avoid goal assignments resulting in critical dependencies among agents. If this is not possible, introduce defensive goals against such vulnerabilities in the goal model.

- Derive the system's context diagram using the technique in Section 11.5.2, and in the case of data-flow 'holes' in it, identify the missing data-flow controllers or monitors.

- Check for software counterparts of human assignments, including existing software components to be integrated (legacy components, off-the-shelf components or foreign services).

- To integrate an off-the-shelf software component once an assignment decision has been made in Step 7, plug into the goal model any goal for which this component can be made responsible; establish the system variables that this component can monitor or control in the object model; plug its operations into the operation model built in Step 8; plug its state machine model into the behaviour model built in Step 9.

- Check the inter-view consistency rules in Section 14.2 that link the goal, object and agent models.

Mine safety control example

Some potential responsibility assignments were already suggested in Figure 15.6. They were reached there by use of the unrealizability-driven refinement pattern in Figure 8.26 or, alternatively, by refinement of an abstract agent PumpingEngine (see Figure 11.8). The agent model in Figure 15.12 shows these assignments plus some others. The left-hand part shows responsibility assignments of leaf goals to agents emerging from the previous steps. The right part shows the monitoring and control capabilities of the agents on attributes of objects from the object model. Note that each goal is realizable by the assigned agent as its definition matches the agent's capabilities. Also note the consistency between those capabilities and the attributes appearing in the object model in Figure 15.8. The capabilities and responsibilities for handling the other critical gas levels are quite similar.

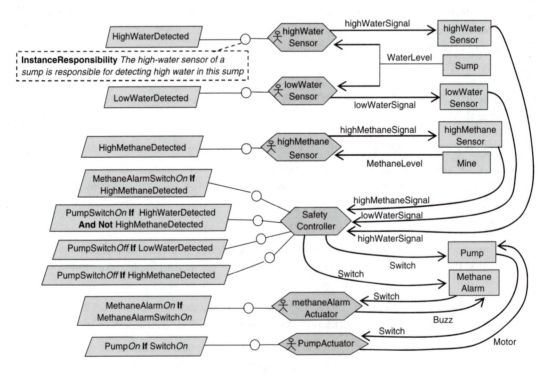

Figure 15.12   *Agent diagram for mine safety control*

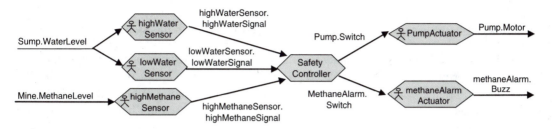

Figure 15.13   *Generated context diagram for mine safety control*

The agent diagram in Figure 15.12 does in fact show responsibility assignments that were selected after the evaluation of alternatives in Step 7 (taking place in parallel). Other alternatives include the following:

- We might consider a single water-level sensor per sump instead of two. This would result in alternative goal refinements and assignments. For example, the goal PumpOnIfHigh-Water**And**Not**HighMethane would instead be refined into sub-goals AccurateWaterMeasure and PumpOnWhenMeasureAboveHigh**And**Not**HighMethane; the former would be assigned to the unique WaterSensor agent, whereas the latter would be assigned to SafetyController. In this system variant, there would be corresponding alternatives for the goal PumpOffIfLowWaterOrHighMethane. The software agent SafetyController would now have the responsibility of comparing the measured water level to the High and Low thresholds.

- Instead of a single SafetyController agent in Figure 15.11, we might consider a distributed variant of the system with one software controller per sump and/or per gas sensor/alarm sub-system. This alternative might emerge from architectural requirements arising from the mine topology or from decisions taken at the architectural design phase of the project. (Architectural requirements were discussed in Section 1.1.5.)

Back now to the agent diagram in Figure 15.12, we may extract an agent interface view from it. Figure 15.13 shows the context diagram generated using the technique in Section 11.5.2.

15.2.5 Step 7: Make choices among alternative options
WHAT

Any model-based RE process is faced with alternative options resulting in multiple system variants (see Section 3.3). These include alternative goal refinements, risk resolutions, conflict resolutions and responsibility assignments. This step consists of evaluating the various options arising in the previous steps to select one 'best' set of options defining the final shape of the system-to-be. As we noted just above, this evaluation/selection may proceed in parallel with the preceding steps.

HOW

A number of heuristics and techniques are available to help us in this step:

- We may use qualitative reasoning techniques to select those options contributing the most to higher-priority soft goals related to quality and cost, without hurting lower-priority ones too much. Section 16.3.1 will present one such technique. While assessing the pros and cons of options we may elicit new soft goals as discussed in Chapter 8; see heuristic (*H6*) in Section 8.8.2.

- We may use more quantitative techniques, including multi-criteria analysis (Vincke, 1992). Section 16.3.2 will present a simple model-based quantitative technique that may help us.

- We may also use various kinds of heuristics, for example favour refinements or assignments introducing fewer or less severe risks, favour refinements or assignments introducing fewer or less severe conflicts, favour resolutions resolving more risks or conflicts or more severe ones, and so on.

Mine safety control example

When comparing the selected options shown in Figure 15.12 with the alternatives listed in Section 15.2.4, we might conclude that the ones in Figure 15.12 contribute the most to the highest-priority soft goal *Reduce[SafetyRiskExposure]* while contributing more to the soft goal *Reduce[SafetyControlCosts]* as well. For example, a single sensor per sump that continuously measures the water level is a more sophisticated device; it is more likely to break down (or to be clogged up) than two more rudimentary sensors, while costing more to purchase and/or to maintain. Similarly, a distributed safety control software might in a mine environment be more subject to external damage, synchronization errors or communication problems than a centralized, highly protected SafetyController agent; it might also be more costly to develop and maintain.

15.2.6 Step 8: Operationalize goals in the operation model
WHAT

This step consists of identifying and specifying the system services operationalizing the leaf goals in the goal model. For each behavioural leaf goal, the question we need to address is: *'What operations will ensure this goal?'* The answer results in a set of operations that each agent has to perform. Software operations must meet their requirements in the goal model, whereas environmental tasks must meet corresponding expectations. For this we need to specify, for all software operations at least, their signature, domain pre- and post-conditions, and the required pre-, trigger- and post-conditions ensuring their underlying goals. Satisfaction arguments should be provided to argue that the system leaf goals are ensured by the specifications of their corresponding operations.

The operationalization diagrams resulting from this step show, for each agent, the operations that it has to perform together with their specifications and their underlying goals. Performance instance declarations should specify which agent instance is performing an operation on which input/output object instances (see Section 11.3.1). A use case diagram can then be generated from this model to provide an outline view of it.

HOW

Various techniques and heuristics were discussed in Chapters 12–13 to help us build an operation model. Let us summarize them:

- Identify operations from interaction events in illustrative scenarios, and determine their domain pre- and post-conditions from state conditions characterizing the agent timeline right before and right after the corresponding interaction.

- *Derive operations from goal fluents.* For each atomic state condition P in a goal specification, determine its initiating operation, with domain pre-condition **not** P and domain post-condition P, and its terminating operation, with domain pre-condition P and domain post-condition **not** P.

- *Strengthen domain pre- and post-conditions with permissions, obligations and additional effects.* Consider any operation whose DomPost effect may affect some goal. If this effect can violate the goal under a condition C, take **not** C as a required pre-condition. If the goal prescribes that this effect must hold whenever a sufficient condition C became true, take C as a required trigger condition. If the effect is not sufficient to ensure the target condition prescribed by the goal, take the missing sub-condition C in the target as required post-condition. (A more systematic, formal version of this technique will be presented in Section 18.2.)

- Refine goals, not operations.

- Check the inter-view consistency rules in Section 14.2 that link the goal, object, agent and operation models.

- Generate use case diagrams using the algorithm presented in Section 12.6.2.

Mine safety control example

Figure 15.14 shows a portion of the operationalization diagram for the software agent Safety-Controller. The diagram outlines some of the operations that this agent performs together with their underlying goals and some signature information. These operations together with their

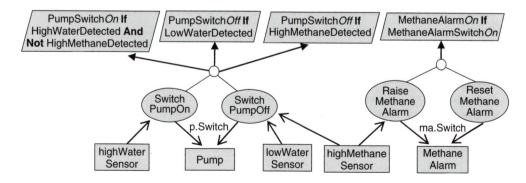

Figure 15.14 *Portion of operationalization diagram for the SafetyController agent*

DomPre and DomPost conditions were easily obtained from the fluents associated with those goals (see the corresponding goal definitions given in Steps 3 and 5).

The main information is to be found in the textual specifications annotating the corresponding operations in the diagram. These specifications were obtained by strengthening the domain pre- and post-conditions with permissions and obligations so as to meet the corresponding goal definitions. Here they are:

Operation SwitchPumpOn

  Def Software operation controlling pump activations in a sump.

  InstancePerformance The mine SafetyController software performs this operation for every sump regulated by a pump *p*, whose water level is tracked by high-water and low-water sensors *hWs* and *lWs*, respectively, under a mine high-methane sensor *hMs*.

  Input p: Pump, hWs: highWaterSensor, lWs: lowWaterSensor, hMs: highMethaneSensor;

  Output p: Pump/Switch;

  DomPre p.Switch = 'off'; **DomPost** p.Switch = 'on';

  ReqPre for *PumpSwitchOffIfHighMethaneDetected*: **not** hMs.highMethaneSignal = 'on'

  ReqPre for *PumpSwitchOffIfLowWaterDetected*: **not** lWs.lowWaterSignal = 'on'

  ReqTrig for *PumpSwitchOnIfHighWaterDetectedAndNotHighMethaneDetected*:

    hWs.highWaterSignal = 'on' **and not** hMs.highMethaneSignal = 'on'

Operation SwitchPumpOff

  Def Software operation controlling pump deactivations in a sump. **InstancePerformance** ...

  Input p: Pump, lWs: lowWaterSensor, hWs: highWaterSensor, hMs: highMethaneSensor;

  Output p: Pump/Switch;

  DomPre p.Switch = 'on'; **DomPost** p.Switch = 'off';

  ReqPre for *PumpSwitchOnIfHighWaterDetectedAndNotHighMethaneDetected*:

    not hWs.highWaterSignal = 'on' **or** hMs.highMethaneSignal = 'on'

  ReqTrig for *PumpSwitchOffIfLowWaterDetected*: lWs.lowWaterSignal = 'on'

  ReqTrig for *PumpSwitchOffIfHighMethaneDetected*: hMs.highMethaneSignal = 'on'

Operation RaiseMethaneAlarm

  Def Software operation controlling methane alarms in the mine. **InstancePerformance** ...

  Input p: Pump, ma: MethaneAlarm, hMs: highMethaneSensor; **Output** ma: MethaneAlarm/Switch;

  DomPre ma.Switch = 'off'; **DomPost** ma.Switch = 'on';

  ReqTrig for *AlarmSwitchOnIfHighMethaneDetected*: hMs.highMethaneSignal = 'on'

Operation ResetMethaneAlarm

  Def Software operation controlling methane alarm deactivation in the mine. **InstancePerformance** ...

  Input p: Pump, ma: MethaneAlarm, hMs: highMethaneSensor; **Output** ma:MethaneAlarm/Switch;

  DomPre ma.Switch = 'on'; **DomPost** ma.Switch = 'off';

  ReqPre for *AlarmSwitchOnIfHighMethaneDetected*: **not** hMs.highMethaneSignal = 'on'

The specifications of the controller's operations of raising and resetting the other alarms are similar. Note that the consistency rule linking required pre- and trigger conditions in

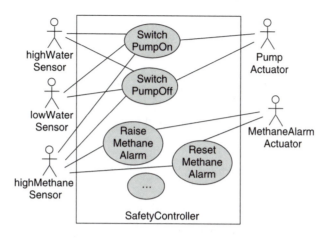

Figure 15.15 *Generated use case diagram for the SafetyController agent*

Section 12.3.1 is satisfied here. For the SwitchPumpOn operation, for example, there is a domain hypothesis telling us that *if* a high-water signal is on *then* the corresponding low-water signal is not on. (This hypothesis may need to be questioned by obstacle analysis to yield an adequate resolution for the case of one of the two water sensors failing to produce the right signal value.)

As we saw in Chapter 12, the overall pre-, trigger and post-condition of an operation is obtained by taking the conjunction of its domain pre-condition with all its required pre-conditions, the disjunction of all its trigger conditions, and the conjunction of its domain post-condition with all its required post-conditions. These overall conditions are those commonly passed on to software developers. Their split and explicit linking here to the underlying goals provide essential traceability back to their rationale for explanation and evolution support. It also allows us to generate state machine diagrams in the next step.

Figure 15.15 shows a use case diagram generated from Figure 15.14 using the algorithm in Section 12.6.2.

15.2.7 Step 9: Build and analyse the behaviour model
WHAT

This step consists of making the admissible system behaviours explicit from information supplied by the goal, object, agent and operation models. Such behaviours are captured by temporal sequences of state transitions resulting from external events and operation applications. They must meet the behavioural goals in the goal model and generalize the illustrative scenarios available. At the instance level, the scenario collection is extended for better coverage of admissible interactions among agent instances. At the class level, the required behaviours of an agent are specified by a parallel composition of state machines – one state machine per state variable that the agent controls. The system state machine is obtained by parallel composition of the agent state machines. If formalized, the resulting behaviour model can be analysed by animation for adequacy checking and by model checking against goals and domain properties. The result of such an analysis may prompt a new cycle of model revision through the preceding steps.

HOW

Various techniques and heuristics were discussed in Chapter 13 to help us build a behaviour model of the system. Let us summarize them:

- Ensure goal coverage by positive scenarios; ensure obstacle coverage by negative scenarios.

- Identify normal scenarios, their associated abnormal ones, auxiliary episodes and responses to stimuli events.

- Check scenarios against unrelated concerns, irrelevant events, impossible interactions and incompatible or inadequate granularities.

- Use the technique in Section 13.3.3 for generalizing scenarios into state machines.

- Use the technique in Section 13.3.5 for deriving state machines from operationalized goals.

- Use available decomposition mechanisms for refining or restructuring scenarios and state machines.

- Check the inter-view consistency rules in Section 14.2 that link the goal, object, agent, operation and behaviour models.

Mine safety control example

Figure 15.16 shows a portion of the behaviour model built with those techniques. There are four parallel state diagrams. The one on the left captures required behaviours of the SafetyController agent. The three diagrams on the right capture required behaviours of the PumpActuator, highWaterSensor and highMethaneSensor agents. (For the system dynamics to be fully modelled, the four diagrams should be further composed in parallel with diagrams for the other gas sensors and the alarm actuators.) The diagram on the left shows the parallel dynamics of some of the state variables controlled by SafetyController; namely, Pump.Switch, MethaneAlarm.Switch and WaterAlarm.Switch (the corresponding composite states are named accordingly). The diagrams on the right show the dynamics of state variables controlled by the corresponding agent; PumpActuator controls Pump.Motor, whereas highWaterSensor and highMethaneSensor control highWaterSignal and highMethaneSignal, respectively (see the agent model in Figures 15.12–15.13).

In view of a consistency rule linking the behaviour model and the object model, all those controlled variables should appear as attributes or associations in the object model; we can thereby see that an entity WaterAlarm with attribute Switch should be added to the object model fragment in Figure 15.8.

The state diagrams in Figure 15.16 were obtained from the goal-oriented operation model using the derivation technique in Section 13.3.5.

For example, the states pSwitchOff and pSwitchOn in the PumpSwitchState diagram are defined by the domain pre-condition p.Switch = 'off' and the domain post-condition p.Switch = 'on' of the SwitchPumpOn operation, respectively (see the specification of this operation

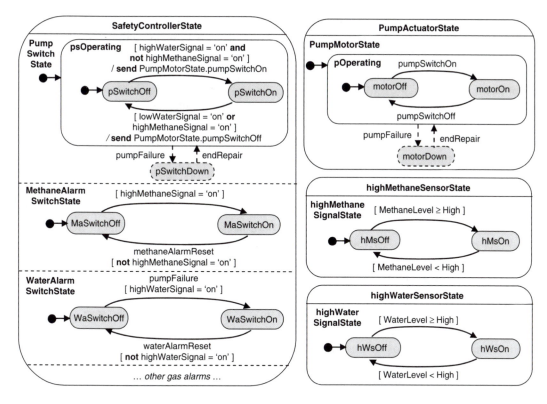

Figure 15.16 *Portion of a behaviour model for mine safety control*

in Section 15.2.6). As the latter operation has a trigger condition in the operation model, this trigger condition labels an event-free guarded transition from pSwitchOff to pSwitchOn (see the derivation rule for trigger conditions in Section 13.3.5). This guard implies the operation's required pre-conditions, as discussed in the previous section; the name of the pumpSwitchOn event, corresponding to an application of the SwitchPumpOn operation making the transition, is kept implicit. However, this event is notified by a **send** action to the PumpMotorState diagram as it must trigger a synchronized transition there from motorOff to motorOn.

When an operation has multiple trigger conditions, the derivation rule prescribes the corresponding event-free guarded transition to be labelled by their disjunction, see Section 13.3.5 and the transition from pSwitchOn to pSwitchOff in the PumpSwitchState diagram corresponding to an application of the SwitchPumpOff operation. When there is no trigger condition on an operation, the derivation rule prescribes the corresponding transition to be labelled by the name of the operation application together with its required pre-conditions as guards, see Section 13.3.5 and the transition from MaSwitchOn to MaSwitchOff in the MethaneAlarmSwitch-State diagram; this transition corresponds to an application of the ResetMethaneAlarm operation which only has a required pre-condition.

State diagrams equivalent to those in Fig. 15.16 could have been obtained as well by completing the scenario collection, initially comprising the scenarios in Figures 15.7 and. 15.11, and then by using the generalization technique in Section 13.3.3. Instead of the firing guard highWaterSignal = 'on' in Figure 15.16, we would instead have derived the equivalent firing event highWaterSignalOn appearing in Figures 15.7 and 15.11, for example. The goal-driven and scenario-driven derivations yield guard-oriented and event-oriented versions of the same state machine, respectively.

The PumpSwitchState and PumpMotorState diagrams in Figure 15.16 show that some state machine restructuring took place to introduce the composite sequential states psOperating and pmOperating, respectively. The reason for the introduction of these composite states is the pumpFailure event that may occur in any of their sequential sub-states. This event together with the 'dashed' states motorDown and pSwitchDown emerged from the obstacle analysis in Figure 15.9, where pump failure was found to be a likely obstructing condition. Accordingly, the object model in Figure 15.8 must be updated with a new 'down' value in the range of the attributes Motor and Switch of the Pump entity. New goals and corresponding operations must also be introduced in our model, if not done previously, to prescribe what should happen in the case of pump failure.

These small examples show how the multiple system views mutually strengthen each other. Checks and revisions towards a consistent and complete model are incremental and multi-directional. The steps of our method are thus not merely sequential, as said before. At the extreme end we might even have envisaged an elaboration process where a state machine model draft is sketched first, from which the underlying goals, objects, agents and operations are reverse engineered.

Whatever the actual elaboration process is, we can analyse a behaviour model such as the one in Figure 15.16, find errors in it, revise it and propagate the corrections back to the goal, object, agent and operation models thanks to the built-in traceability provided by the inter-model links. For large, complex models such analysis is tedious and error prone; model formalization allows us to automate the analysis through state machine animation and model checking (see Sections 5.3 and 5.4.3, and Chapter 18).

15.3 Handling model variants for product lines

Step 7 in our model-building method is devoted to making choices among the multiple alternative options arising in the modelling process. In case of a product family development project, we may instead want to keep such multiple options during this step so as to capture model commonalities and variations from one member of the family to another. What we then have to do is to define *model configurations*, where for each family member a specific set of options is taken to define its model. For this we need to (a) identify variations, (b) associate variations with a specific product family member, and (c) form a model configuration by taking, for a family member, its commonalities with other members together with its specific variations.

Defining commonalities and variations

In our modelling framework, a *commonality* refers to a parent goal being refined or assigned differently along alternatives, or to an obstacle or conflict being resolved differently along alternatives. *Variations* refer to alternative goal refinements, alternative agent assignments, alternative obstacle resolutions and alternative conflict resolutions. As different alternatives sometimes concern different objects, we may need to introduce corresponding variations in the object model as well.

Associating variations with product family members

To associate alternatives with specific family members, we attach the SysRef meta-attribute to every alternative node in the goal AND/OR graph – where an *alternative node* is an alternative refinement, assignment, or resolution node.

The value of SysRef at an alternative node identifies those members of the product family that are to be built along this specific alternative (see Sections 8.7 and 14.1). As multiple family members may share the same alternative, this attribute may reference multiple variants at the same node; its value has a list structure.

A predecessor node of an alternative node is called a *variation point*. This node and its ancestors yield commonalities of the family members referenced in the successor nodes of the variation point.

Such association of variations with family members must satisfy the following consistency rules:

- At any variation point, the SysRef values attached to different successor nodes must be disjoint from each other. As OR-refinements, OR-assignments and OR-resolutions define alternatives, the same family member may not be found in two different alternatives.

- The SysRef list of variant references at a successor node of a variation point must be included in the SysRef list of the predecessor alternative node of this variation point. The further we go down a path in the goal AND/OR graph, the further we discriminate among family members sharing the upper commonalities.

To cope with variations of an object, we need to introduce a generalized version of it that regroups all commonalities and specializations for each variation. SysRef attribute values are then attached to each specialization link.

Forming model configurations

A model configuration for a specific product family member M is obtained by traversing the entire goal model top down and breadth first. At each variation point we keep the upward commonalities and the successor alternative whose SysRef attribute includes M; all other successor alternatives are discarded. In the object model, we keep the generalized objects and their specialization referred to by the goals in the extracted single-alternative model. The agent, operation and behaviour models for M are those derived from this single-alternative model.

Figure 15.17 shows a simplified example of commonalities and variations in a damping sub-system for an automotive product line with two car series named *Y series* and *Z series*, respectively. Among their commonalities, the two car series share the three goals at the first level of refinement. This means that both car series will provide features for their common

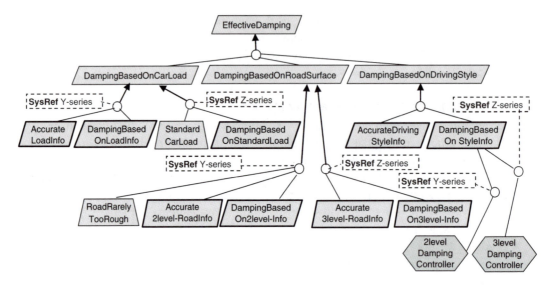

Figure 15.17   *Commonalities and variations in a product line model*

goal DampingBasedOnDrivingStyle, for example. As seen in Figure 15.17, the sub-goals of this commonality are common too. The variations between the two car series include the assignment of their common goal DampingBasedOnStyleInfo to distinct controllers having different levels of sophistication. Other variations include the sub-goal DampingBasedOnStandardLoad, specific to the Z series, and the sub-goal DampingBasedOnLoadInfo, specific to the Y series. Note that variations include *hypotheses* done in one system variant but not in another, for example Y series cars are assumed rarely to drive on very bad roads.

To get the model configuration for Z series cars, for example, we consider the goal model top down and breadth first and keep all commonalities, while taking alternative nodes whose **SysRef** attribute value includes 'Z series' at every variation point down the goal graph.

For comparison purpose, Figure 15.18 shows a portion of a product line model for the meeting scheduling system that corresponds to the feature diagram in Section 6.3.3 (see Figure 6.15). This example also shows **SysRef** values that are lists of references to variants. Note the consistent association of product versions to variations. For example, the goal DatePlanned is found in the model of the MS-light system variant, whereas the variants MS-Pro, MS-Pro+ and MS-Pro++ provide features for satisfaction of the goal Date&LocationPlanned (for space reasons the annotation for the latter product association is not shown in Figure 15.18). Going one step down, we can see that the sub-goal PlannedWithoutPreferences is found in the model for the MS-Pro product, whereas the alternative sub-goal PlannedWithPreferences is common to the models for the MS-Pro+ and MS-Pro++ products. The latter products differ by assignments of the same goal PlannedWithPreferences to the software agents DefaultConflictSolver and RuleBasedConflictSolver, respectively.

Figure 15.19 illustrates the use of the **SysRef** attribute for associating variations with object specializations in the object model that are referred to by corresponding goal variations in

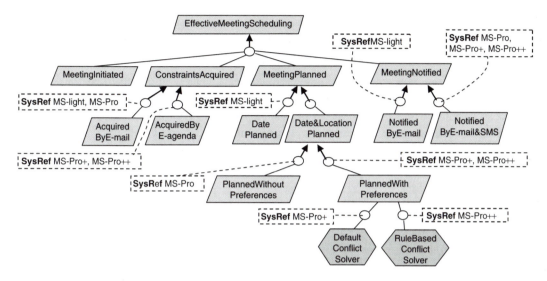

Figure 15.18   *Commonalities and variations in four meeting scheduling products*

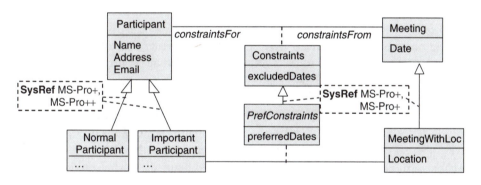

Figure 15.19   *Commonalities and variations in an object model*

the goal model. The objects common to all products there are specialized to specific ones as needed.

In comparison with the feature diagram representation for the same product line in Section 6.3.3, Figure 6.15, we may observe the following:

- The two representations basically have the same expressive power as they are both based on AND/OR graphs.

- The goal-oriented representation is more expressive, in that it is more explicit on the kind of distinguishing options; namely, different goals and operationalizations, different assumptions, different responsibility assignments, different obstacle resolutions, different conflict resolutions and different object specializations. Moreover, the association between options and product versions is made explicit.

- The goal-oriented representation carries more semantics as it captures satisfaction-based refinement rather than syntactic decomposition; lower-level options must arguably entail higher-level ones.

- The feature diagram representation is more compact as its built-in constructs for optional features and non-exclusive OR allow us to keep combinations implicit. For example, we need to introduce a third sub-goal of MeetingNotified in Figure 15.18 in case we want a product version where scheduled meetings are to be notified by SMS only.

Summary

- Building complex multi-view models requires a disciplined process for integrating all views of a system in a systematic, incremental and coherent way.

- In the process defined and illustrated in this chapter, a model for the stable goals and relevant objects in the *system-as-is* is built first using the heuristics and techniques presented in the previous chapters for goal modelling and object modelling, including the use of illustrative scenarios. The next steps are devoted to the *system-to-be*. The goal model is expanded with new goals illustrated by corresponding scenarios; the updated object model is derived from it; obstacles, threats and conflicts are detected on the goal model and resolutions are explored to yield alternative resolution goals in the goal model; alternative responsibility assignments are explored for the leaf goals together with the required agent capabilities on the object model; all alternative options raised are evaluated against soft goals in the goal model so that most preferred ones are selected; the selected leaf goals are operationalized into software operations and environmental tasks; a corresponding behaviour model of the system-to-be is derived and analysed. Each step is supported by dedicated heuristics and techniques discussed in the previous chapters, including the use of inter-view rules for enforcing model consistency and completeness.

- Those model-building steps are ordered by data dependencies; many of them are, however, intertwined and require backtracking to earlier steps as revisions are required from further analysis. The inter-view consistency rules are indeed multi-directional, not merely from one view to another.

- For software product line development projects, we need to keep alternative options rather than making selections. By associating product variants explicitly to alternative goal refinements, obstacle resolutions, conflict resolutions, agent assignments and object specializations, we can capture model commonalities and variations, and derive model configurations for each member of the product family.

Notes and Further Reading

A preliminary version of the model-building method in this chapter appeared in Dardenne *et al.* (1993) and was illustrated in van Lamsweerde *et al.* (1995) on a meeting scheduling system. The method has been refined from considerable industrial experience (van Lamsweerde, 2004b) and tool development (Darimont *et al.*, 1998; Ponsard *et al.*, 2007).

The mine safety control case study is inspired from partial descriptions of a mine pump control system in Kramer *et al.* (1983) and Joseph (1996). A formal development of an earlier model appeared in Letier's thesis (Letier, 2001).

Another illustration of the method in action can be found in van Lamsweerde and Letier (2004) for a simple safety injection system in a nuclear power plant (Courtois & Parnas, 1993).

Some experience on the use of an earlier version of the product line modelling technique in this chapter, for automotive systems, is reported in an MS thesis by de Schrynmakers and Accardo (2002).

Exercises

- Integrate and complete the goal model fragments in Figures 15.4, 15.6, 15.9 and 15.10 by further refining the goal PumpOffIfLowWaterDetected; and then by integrating, refining or abstracting the goals PumpOffIfHighMethane, PumpControllableManually, MineEvacuatedIfHighMethane, MineEvacuatedIfHighCO, MineEvacuatedIfHighAirflow, MineEvacuatedIfCriticalWater and ReadingsAndOperationsLogged, based on the preliminary description at the beginning of this chapter and the techniques available for the goal elaboration step. (Your model should integrate the stable goals relating to the system-as-is identified in Figure 15.4.)

- Follow the method presented in this chapter for an e-purse system whose preliminary description is as follows.

    An e-purse is a smartcard-based purse installed on a bank card. Money can be transferred at ATM counters from the owner's bank account to his or her e-purse. This requires PIN code authentication as for cash withdrawal. Buyers may use their e-purse at dedicated payment terminals installed in shops. To perform a payment from an e-purse, the buyer needs to insert his or her bank card into the seller's terminal (without authentication). The seller enters the amount due in the terminal. This amount is displayed to the buyer so that he or she can validate it by pressing an 'OK' button. The validated amount is transferred from the buyer's e-purse to the seller's terminal. This terminal is unloaded to the seller's bank account via a secured network. To avoid the risk of abuse, the e-purse balance may never become negative, and may not exceed a fixed, relatively small upper limit. The system should allow owners to know their e-purse balance; this information is however confidential and should not be disclosed to unauthorized third parties.

- Follow the method presented in this chapter on the following *airport gate allocation* case study. (The notes below are based on preliminary interviews.)

An airport consists of terminals, each containing a number of gates for flight departure or arrival. There are two types of gate: large capacity and small capacity. Both are generally arranged by different airlines and by different airport areas corresponding to different customs regulations.

The automated allocation of airport gates to aircrafts is envisioned for reducing flight delays due to aircraft waiting for a gate (waiting times are sometimes unacceptably long in the current system) and for better fit of multiple allocation constraints in addition to gate availability. In particular:

— The gate capacity must fit the flight capacity.

— The gate location should fit the airline location in the airport.

— In view of customs regulations, flights from specific countries need to be allocated to specific airport areas.

— In the case of an emergency or a significant flight delay, a flight should be allocated a gate that enables faster passenger exit and transfer.

In an aircraft-landing phase under the control of the new system, the pilot must ask the gate allocator for a gate. The allocator must then select a gate fitting all of the above flight constraints. The required information about gate availability, airline, where flights are coming from and degree of emergency of flight arrivals is to be maintained in a database for fast access and data integration. The only strong constraints are those about gate availability, flight capacity and flight origin. If no gate is available that fits those strong constraints, the allocator must inform the pilot and assign a position in the queue of waiting aircraft. This position is based on the degree of emergency and on the airline.

When an aircraft leaves a gate, the pilot must inform the allocator in order to make this gate available again for waiting or landing aircraft. The gate is then allocated to the longest-waiting aircraft in the queue that meets all strong constraints (if any).

To keep pilots informed on the state of airport gates, the allocator must also answer pilots' queries about gate capacity, which flights are waiting in the queue, which gates are currently allocated and to which flights, and which gates are currently available. Special requests may be issued by landing pilots; in such a case the allocator must notify a human controller who makes a decision based on the state of airport gates shown by the allocator.

Other constraints elicited so far include the following:

- A gate may be allocated to a flight only if it meets the strong constraints.

- A flight may be assigned a position in the queue only if all adequate gates are currently allocated.

- For confidentiality reasons a pilot may only know the allocation of gates to flights from the same airline.

Gate allocation must also take domain properties into account such as the following:

- At any time a gate may be allocated to one flight at most.

- A waiting aircraft may not be at two different positions in the queue.

- An aircraft may not be both in the queue and at a gate.

- An aircraft may not be at two different gates at the same time.

- Follow the method in this chapter on the following *e-shopping* case study. (The notes below are based on initial interviews.)

The RDS Records Company is a newly created online shop that sells records, books and DVDs. Its Web-based system shall enable potential customers to check available products, pick up desired ones, order them and receive them after payment. A Web interface shall describe the characteristics of each product such as its price, availability, expected delay when the product is not available, shipping costs for every likely location and approximate delivery time after payment.

RDS has made a deal with the BuddyCash Company (BCC) for billing. Every ordering customer must have a BuddyCash account. (RDS will have one BCC account as well.) A customer account must have associated personal information and a monthly credit limit. Every order made through the system must be paid for via a BuddyCash account. Clients shall get monthly bills from BuddyCash based on their account balance. RDS can at any time ask BuddyCash to transfer amounts of money from its account to a specified bank account.

BuddyCash shall notify customers by e-mail each time their account is accessed (typically when an order is made). Any order can be cancelled within 3 days following the transaction.

An order shall be processed as follows:

- The order is divided into two parts: available items, to be delivered immediately, and all other items requiring RDS orders to item providers.

- The amount to be paid is computed on the entire order, delivery cost included.

- A payment request is issued to BuddyCash for transmission to the client.

- The client is notified of the expected delivery time for available items and the expected order delay for the other items.

- The order part for available items is sent out to the shipping company, which returns a package ID for RDS to send back to the client for order tracking.

- A new notification is sent out to the client when the missing items become available to inform him or her about the expected delivery time.

RDS has also made a deal with the SPU company for shipping. SPU's main contractual obligations are the following:

- To conform to delivery times notified to the client for each order.

- To check the identity of the package receiver.

- To send back any package declined by the receiver or requested back by RDS.

- To offer a software package-tracking facility for use by RDS and its customers.

Two service levels will be available for delivery:

- Normal service: minimum 2 days and maximum 5 days between the time at which the package is received from RDS and the time at which it is delivered to the client.

- Express service: maximum 2 days between the time at which the package is received from RDS and the time at which it is delivered to the client. When a client decides to cancel a transaction on its BCC account, BuddyCash shall immediately inform RDS. If the package is still in the warehouse, the order is simply cancelled. If the package is in SPU's custody, it is requested by RDS and has to be sent back. If the package has already been delivered, SPU must get the package back from the client. The SPU officer must also check that the package is complete when he or she receives it from the client. When an order is cancelled, RDS shall reimburse, via the BCC accounts, any amount paid by the customer.

- Follow the method in this chapter on the following *power plant supervisory system*. The notes below are inspired by the PRECON system introduced in Ciapessoni *et al.* (1999).

The system is aimed at increasing both the efficiency and the reliability of power plant operations while reducing operation and maintenance costs. It should provide integrated support for acquiring performance data during operation from field sensors, detecting faults from those data, diagnosing them and raising appropriate alarms in the case of fault detection. In previous versions of the system, such functions were developed separately as stand-alone applications. Each application had its own facilities for data acquisition, processing and storage, and a dedicated human–machine interface. This resulted in significant costs for developing, installing and maintaining each application, in high training costs and in increased operational complexity. Users were often confused or distracted about what was really going on; this sometimes resulted in inadequate and possibly unsafe decisions. Reliability is a primary concern in power plants as hazardous substances such as fossil or nuclear fuel are manipulated for producing electricity.

To address those problems the new system must cover data acquisition, fault detection, diagnosis and alarm generation in a fully integrated way.

- Data acquisition: Relevant performance data must be periodically acquired from field sensors and pre-processed for fault handling. These data include measurements of analog and digital variables such as pressures and temperatures.

- Fault detection and diagnosis: The data must be analysed every 5 minutes to detect faults in the steam condenser or in the cooling circuit. Such analysis should also take place in parallel on request by operators, with a response time of 5 seconds at most. The variables computed during analysis and their input/output relation must be maintained in a repository (see below). Any fault must be notified to the alarm manager. For each type of fault detected, remedy actions should be suggested to the operator.

- Alarm management: Dedicated alarms must be raised for each type of fault within very short deadlines associated with the fault type. All alarms must be traced and their state recorded for later analysis.

- Dynamic reconfiguration: The system must be reconfigurable to particular features of specific plants – e.g. the amount of power produced or type of plant component.

– Data integration: A distributed repository sub-system will maintain all static and dynamic data from the acquisition, fault detection and diagnosis, alarm management and dynamic reconfiguration sub-systems.

– Integrated communication: All system components will communicate with each other through a common, fast, ultra-reliable communication infrastructure.

The system must also tolerate some faults. All field sensors and actuators must be continually monitored to detect possible device faults and malfunctions. The collected data should be validated, for example through device self-tests.

As the system is subject to both hardware faults and perturbations that may change the value of a state variable, the system should be able, when a hardware fault occurs and remains unrepaired for at least X seconds, to find the damaged part and put it off-line.

The system operates normally only if the value of state variables is not altered by perturbations. Data accuracy is of utmost importance for reliable operations.

Part III

Reasoning About System Models

The first part of the book introduced principles and state-of-the-art techniques for requirements elicitation, evaluation, specification, quality assurance and evolution. The second part presented a model-based method for requirements engineering in which complementary views of the target system are built incrementally and synergistically by systematic integration of goal, object, agent, operation and behaviour models. The chapters in this part presented a number of heuristics and techniques for guiding the model-building process.

The last part of the book complements this material with techniques for reasoning about the overall system model along the various steps of the method. Such techniques allow us to analyse model portions obtained so far, to derive new portions more systematically, or to derive downward products from the model such as the requirements document or a draft proposal for the software architecture. Some of the techniques are grounded on the principles introduced in Part I.

In the light of the distinction between semi-formal and formal approaches discussed in Chapters 4–5, the next chapters cover more or less sophisticated forms of reasoning and tool support.

Chapter 16 is dedicated to *semi-formal* reasoning. Queries on a model database allow us to check the structural consistency and completeness of a model, to retrieve model dependencies along traceability links, or to reuse model fragments from analogous systems. We may use heuristic rules based on the meta-model and on goal categories to help us detect conflicts, identify further obstacles and build anti-models of malicious environment behaviours against which countermeasures should be provided in the model. Qualitative and quantitative techniques may help us evaluate alternative options against soft goals. When a consolidated model is reached, a goal-structured requirements document can be generated semi-automatically from it. A preliminary software architecture can also be obtained in a systematic way from the model.

Chapters 17 and **18** are dedicated to *formal* model analysis. Such analysis requires that critical model items and the definitions annotating them be formalized in a machine-processable form. Once they are specified in the temporal logic language introduced in Chapter 17, we can use much more sophisticated techniques incrementally and locally, where and when needed. Chapter 18 presents formal techniques for goal refinement, goal operationalization, conflict management, obstacle analysis, threat analysis and synthesis of behaviour models for goal-oriented model animation.

16

Semi-Formal Reasoning for Model Analysis and Exploitation

The model-building method in the previous chapter includes several steps where the obtained model fragments need to be reviewed and analysed. This chapter discusses how we can perform such analysis in a semi-formal way and then derive downward products from the resulting model. As we saw in Chapters 4–5, 'semi-formal' means that the model elements and their links are declared in a formal language – in our case, the multi-view diagrammatic language introduced in Part II. The Def annotations of those elements must be as precise as possible but remain informally stated in natural language.

Queries on a requirements database were already introduced in Section 5.2 as a cheap but effective means for surface-level analysis of a large specification. Section 16.1 shows various ways in which this approach can usefully be applied during the various steps of our model-building method.

Step 5 in this method is fully devoted to analysing the model early enough against conflicts, obstacles and threats. Section 16.2 details further heuristics and techniques to help us in this step.

Step 7 in the method is devoted to the selection of best options among alternative goal refinements, risk resolutions, conflict resolutions and responsibility assignments. Section 16.3 provides qualitative and quantitative reasoning techniques to help us in this step.

Getting a high-quality requirements document is among the main objectives of system modelling at RE time. Section 16.4 outlines a semi-automated approach where the requirements document is generated by mapping the consolidated model into a textual format annotated with figures. The produced document preserves the goal-oriented structure and content of the model, and fits prescribed documentation standards if required.

As the requirements document is used in the later stages of software development, the underlying model should also be used for driving the architectural design process. Section 16.4 discusses one such process where a dataflow architecture is derived from the model and then refined using architectural styles and non-functional goals from the goal model.

16.1 Query-based analysis of the model database

The models we need to build for real systems are generally large. To enable concurrent development of a large model by multiple analysts involved in the project, we need a central repository in which consistent versions of the model can be created, updated and accessed by project members. Section 5.2 already introduced the principle of using a requirements database.

The logical schema of such a database is directly derived from the meta-model in terms of which models are defined – in our framework, the meta-model described in Chapter 14. All model elements are maintained in the database as *instances* of entity–relationship structures:

- There are instances of *meta-concepts* such as Goal, Refinement, Requirement, Expectation, Obstacle, Agent, Assignment, Entity, Association, DomProp, Operation, Scenario, Interaction, State or Transition.

- There are instances of *meta-relationships* linking meta-concepts such as Concern, Responsibility, Monitoring/Control, Performance, Input/Output or Coverage.

- There are instances of *meta-attributes* of meta-concepts or meta-relationships such as *Priority* of Goal, *FitCriterion* of SoftGoal, *SysRef* of Refinement or Assignment, *Likelihood* of Obstacle, *Multiplicity* of Link, *Load* of Agent, *DomPost* of Operation or *ReqPre* of Operationalization.

The resulting database is called a *model database*.

Model browsing

The first obvious exploitation of such structures consists of associating hyperlink types with meta-concepts, meta-relationships and meta-attributes. We can then generate HTML files from the model database, together with zoom-in and zoom-out facilities, for model browsing and circulation among stakeholders. Such files turn out to be quite helpful for preparing inspections and reviews (see Section 5.1). They may be included among the RE deliverables.

Beyond this, a model database supports multiple types of analysis through entity–relationship queries. We can use such queries for checking the structural consistency and completeness of the model (Section 16.1.1), for generating other views for dedicated analyses (Section 16.1.2), for traceability management (Section 16.1.3) and for analogical model reuse (Section 16.1.4).

16.1.1 Checking the structural consistency and completeness of the model

Structural rules state criteria for the model to be structurally consistent and complete. They include the inter-view consistency rules listed in Section 14.2. As we saw there, many such rules have a common pattern. The negation of that pattern yields the general form of an *inter-view check*:

> **Is there any** instance *ins1* of meta-concept *C1* in view *V1*
> **having no** corresponding instance *ins2* of meta-concept *C2* in view *V2*,
>   linked to *ins1* by an instance of the inter-view meta-relationship *IR* ?

For example, consider the following rule on the goal model:

Every unrefined goal in the goal model must be under the responsibility of an agent.

The corresponding check looks like this:

Is there any *unRefined* Goal instance **having no** *Responsibility* Assignment instance?

Such checks can be performed through queries on the model database. The query language might be a standard relational language provided by the database management system in use; or a dedicated entity–relationship query language generated from the meta-model, as discussed in Section 5.2; or a *XlinkIt*-like rule language with link-generation semantics for showing violating instances, as discussed in Section 6.3.3.

In the entity–relationship query language suggested in Section 5.2, now instantiated to the meta-model described in Chapter 14, a query for the above check looks like this:

Query leafGoalAssignmentCheck
    set unassignedGoals = **Goal**
        which not *OR-RefTo* **Refinement**
        and which not *OR-AssTo* **Assignment**

In this query, the keywords *OR-RefTo* and *OR-AssTo* correspond to roles in the *OR-Ref* and *OR-Ass* meta-relationships, respectively (see Figures 14.3 and 14.5). The query returns the set unassignedGoals of all unassigned leaf goals in the goal model for which assignments must be worked out (if not refined further).

Such structural rules are generally defined once and for all as meta-constraints on the meta-model. It therefore makes little sense to retype queries at every check; we may merely reuse a batch of *pre-cooked* queries for checks in 'press-button' mode.

In addition to the inter-view rules discussed in Section 14.2, the structural rules to be checked include intra-view ones. Here is a representative sample of *intra-view rules* for our modelling framework.

- Every leaf goal in the goal model must be specialized as a requirement or an expectation.
- The goal model may not contain refinement cycles.
- The object model may not contain inheritance cycles.
- Every object must appear in the object model as an entity, association, agent or event. Its specializations must be of the same sub-type.
- Every attribute must have an initialization (*DomInit*) in the object model.
- Every object referenced in a domain property (*DomInvar*) or hypothesis (*DomHyp*) must appear in the object model.

- Every interaction event in a scenario must appear as a transition label in the state machine generalizing the scenario.

- Every state in a state machine must have an incoming transition (except initial states). Every state in a state machine must have an outgoing transition (except final states).

- Every transition in a state machine must have an input state and an output state.

- Every loop in a state machine capturing non-cyclical behaviours must have an exit transition.

- Every event notified by a *send* action in a source state machine must label a transition in the target state machine.

The checks corresponding to those inter- and intra-view rules define *model checklists* that can be carried out by the database query engine on request. At any step of the model-building method we can thereby figure out what remains to be done.

16.1.2 Generation of other views for dedicated analyses

Besides structural consistency and completeness checks, we can use queries on the model database to extract other model views and visualize these for dedicated analyses.

Load analysis is one important example of analysis that we can perform from query-based view generation. By visualizing the result of the query:

> **GET all** *Responsibility* Assignments for *this* Agent,

we can spot problematic situations where a system agent appears overloaded. This may result in critical system vulnerabilities in the case of a human agent responsible for critical goals such as safety- or security-related ones. Alternative assignments or further refinements must then be sought, typically through increased automation; that is, alternative assignments to software agents.

Figure 16.1 suggests an example of such surface-level load analysis in an air traffic control system. The human agent SectorAssistant, in charge of an air traffic sector, appears overloaded by responsibilities that are all safety-critical. The PFS acronym there stands for 'Paper Flight Strip'. A paper flight strip records critical historical data about a specific flight in a fairly intricate format.

16.1.3 Traceability management

As discussed in Part II, some of the meta-concepts and meta-relationships in terms of which a model is built yield traceability link types for free. These include:

- *Derivation* link types such as *OR-Ref* and *AND-Ref* (between goals), *Resolution* (between goals and obstacles or boundary conditions), *Operationalization* (between goals and operations) and *Coverage* (between goals, scenarios and state machines).

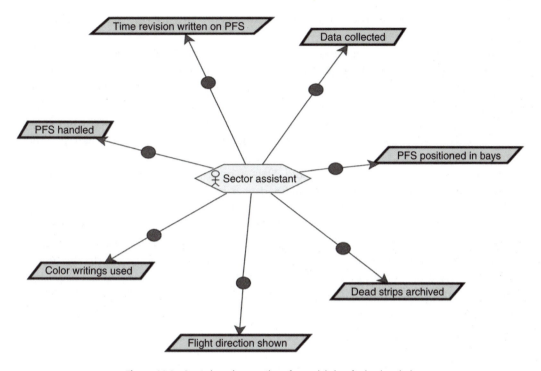

Figure 16.1   *Query-based generation of a model view for load analysis.*

- *Use* link types such as *Concern* (between goals and objects), Responsibility (between goals and agents), Dependency (among agents for goals), Monitoring/Control (between agents and objects) and Input/Output (between operations and objects).

(The *derivation* and *use* traceability link types were discussed in Section 6.3.1.)

We are thus freed from the pain of establishing and maintaining traceability links as they are built in to the model.

- We may use queries on derivation links to build satisfaction arguments – notably, queries on *AND-Ref* and *Operationalization* links.

- We may also follow *derivation* links and *use* links backwards or forwards to propagate model modifications along the required direction (see Section 6.3.2).

16.1.4 Analogical model reuse

A query-based engine can also automate a rudimentary form of analogical reasoning on models. The idea is to reuse portions of a known *source* model available in the model database to complete some parts of a *target* model that we are building.

Analogical reuse consists of mapping well-defined elements of the source model onto partially defined elements of the target model so that additional specifications of the target model can be obtained by source–target transposition. For example, the known source model might be a model for our train control system, whereas the target model we are building is a model for a lift control system.

Analogical reuse requires the model database to be hierarchically structured by layers of generalization/specialization. A layer contains multiple models defined as specializations of more abstract models found at the upper layer. This means that some of the goals, objects, agents, operations and behaviours of a model at a particular layer are defined as specializations of more abstract goals, objects, agents, operations and behaviours of models at the upper layer, respectively. Section 2.2.7 introduced such structuring for knowledge reuse during requirements elicitation; see Figure 2.4.

In our example, the *entities* Train and Station from our known source model might specialize entities Transporter and Place defined at a more abstract level, respectively. The *agents* TrainController and Passenger from our known source model might specialize the agents TransporterController and Transportee defined at that level, respectively. The *goals* Maintain[TrainDoorsClosedWhileMoving] and Achieve[PassengersInformedOfNextStation] in the source model might specialize the goals Maintain[TransporterDoorsClosedWhileMoving] and Achieve[TransporteeInformedOfNextPlace] defined at that more abstract level, respectively. *Operations* such as StartToNextStation and StopAtNextStation might specialize the operations

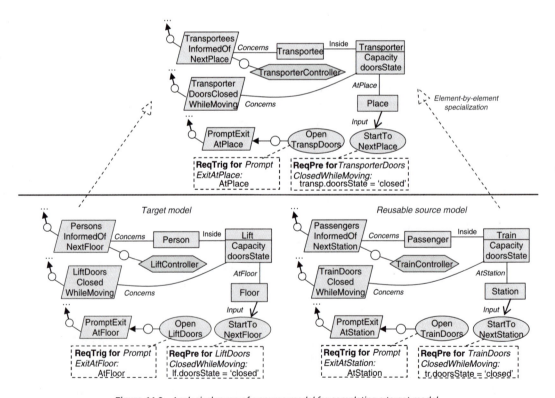

Figure 16.2 *Analogical reuse of a source model for completing a target model.*

StartToNextPlace and StopAtNextPlace defined at the more abstract level, respectively, and so on (see Figure 16.2). 'Defined' means that the definition of the goal, domain property or operation pre- or post-condition is formulated in the corresponding vocabulary of that level.

The notion of *IsA* specialization, defined only on the object model in Section 10.5.1, has to be extended accordingly. A model element such as a goal or an operation *specializes* another if its definition in the specialized vocabulary implies the definition of that other in the generalized vocabulary. For example, the prescriptive statement 'a passenger should be informed of airlines served at the next station' implies that 'this transportee should be informed about the next stopping place'.

As introduced in Section 2.2.7, a knowledge-reuse process is composed of *Retrieve–Transpose–Validate* cycles.

Retrieve–transpose step

This step is triggered by an *analogical query* that we need to submit to the *IsA*-structured model database. Such a query refers to elements from the target model that we want to check or complete. In our example, an analogical query about the target lift system might be:

set-similar liftGoals = **Goal which Concerns** Lift **or which Concerns** Person

Query satisfaction roughly consists of the following up-and-down traversal of the model database (see Figure 16.2):

1. *Query generalization.* The query is generalized by replacing the target elements in it by generalizations of them found at the upper layer. For example, the preceding query is generalized into:

   set-similar X = **Goal which Concerns** Transporter **or which Concerns** Transportee

2. *Search for source analogs satisfying the query.* The specialization trees in the model database are traversed down, from those generalized elements, to retrieve candidate source analogs that satisfy the query reformulated in their specialized vocabulary. The specialized elements in the latter query and the elements satisfying it must together meet the following *structural matching* constraints with respect to their target analog:

   - *Common abstraction.* The corresponding source and target elements must be specializations of the same generalized element. In particular, they must be instances of the same meta-concept; for example they must both be agents, events or soft goals. They must also be instances of the same category (where applicable); for example a Satisfaction goal may not match an Information goal, a Security requirement may not match a Performance requirement, a Modifier operation may not match an Observer operation.

   - *Same assertion pattern.* The corresponding source and target elements must have the same assertion pattern (where applicable). For example, an *Achieve* goal may not match a *Maintain* one.

- *Role preservation.* Source and target associations may match only if they have the same parity and if the respective objects that they link, taken in their order of occurrence, match pairwise. For example, the source association AtStation linking Train and Station and the target association AtFloor linking Lift and Floor may match only if Train and Station match Lift and Floor, respectively.

- *Same meta-relationship.* Linked elements within corresponding source and target pairs must be linked together by instances of the same meta-relationship. For example, the elements within the source pair (PromptExitAtStation, OpenTrainDoors) and within the target pair (PromptExitAtFloor, OpenLiftDoors) are linked together by instances of the Operationalization relationship.

3. *Solution transposition.* The matching elements satisfying the query in the source model are reformulated in the target vocabulary.

In our example, the source goals *PassengerInformedOfNextStation* and *TrainDoorsClosedWhileMoving* meet the structural matching constraints, while satisfying the preceding generalized query reformulated in the source vocabulary; that is, the query:

set-similar X = **Goal which Concerns** Train **or which Concerns** Passenger

These goals and their definitions are therefore transposed to the matching target vocabulary to yield the goals *PersonInformedOfNextFloor* and *LiftDoorsClosedWhileMoving*.

Validation step

The returned candidate elements must obviously be validated for adequacy. The analogical reuse of the three goals in Figure 16.2 appears adequate; the reuse of goals about acceleration or progress through blocks would, however, be inadequate for a lift system model.

We may then proceed to new *Retrieve–Transpose–Validate* cycles to reuse new elements linked to known ones, including goals, objects, agents or operations in the neighbourhood of reused ones. As suggested in Figure 16.2, we might thereby find required pre-conditions or trigger conditions on operations that were missing from the target model.

Such a way of completing a model by analogy with similar systems may especially be helpful for highlighting goals, obstacles or threats that have been overlooked so far.

16.2 Semi-formal analysis of goal-oriented models

The model-elaboration method in the previous chapter includes a step where the model is reviewed against conflicts, obstacles and threats. This section discusses techniques that may further help us in conflict analysis (Section 16.2.1), obstacle identification (Section 16.2.2) and threat analysis (Section 16.2.3).

16.2.1 Conflict analysis

As introduced in Section 3.1, conflicts inevitably arise in the RE process from different stakeholder viewpoints and from incompatible concerns expressed by the same stakeholder.

Conflicts should not be resolved too soon, to allow for further elicitation of potentially relevant information, nor too late as the subsequent software development process requires consistent input.

The general conflict management process discussed in Section 3.1 involves four steps:

- Identification of overlapping assertions.
- Detection of conflicts among them.
- Generation of resolutions for the detected conflicts.
- Selection of the best resolutions.

The main focus of this section is on conflict detection. Some tactics for generating conflict resolutions were reviewed in Section 3.1; Chapter 18 will come back to them in a more formal setting. Section 16.3 will discuss techniques for selecting the best alternatives.

In our modelling framework, conflicts among prescriptive assertions essentially arise in the goal model. There might be conflicts among required pre-, trigger or post-conditions in the operation model, but these are rooted in conflicts among their underlying goals. They should therefore be handled in the goal model.

Sections 3.1 and 8.3 briefly introduced the notion of divergence as a general form of conflict. This notion covers both strong conflicts and a weaker, more frequent form of potential conflict. Strong conflict amounts to logical inconsistency; we cannot satisfy a prescription P and its negation **not** P together. In a potential conflict, such strong conflict can arise under a boundary condition. Let us make this fully precise.

Goals $G_1, G_2, \ldots, G_n$ are *divergent*, given a set *Dom* of known domain properties, if there exists a boundary condition B such that the following conditions hold:

1. $\{B, G_1, G_2, \ldots, G_n, Dom\} \models \textbf{false}$ (*potential conflict*)

2. $\{B, G_1, \ldots, G_{j-1}, G_{j+1}, \ldots, G_n, Dom\} \not\models \textbf{false}$ for any j (*minimality*)

3. $B \neq \textbf{not}\,(G_1 \textbf{ and } G_2 \textbf{ and } \ldots \textbf{and } G_n)$ (*non-trivial boundary condition*)

Potential conflict The first condition in this definition states that the boundary condition B makes the goals $G_1, G_2, \ldots, G_n$ unsatisfiable together in view of known domain properties. (Remember that the notation '$\models$' means 'entails'.) Domain properties may need to be taken into account, as it makes no sense to consider conflicting situations that cannot happen in view of them.

Minimal conflict The second condition states that removing any of the potentially conflicting goals $G_1, G_2, \ldots, G_n$ no longer results in a potential conflict. For minimal resolution we want to highlight minimal conflict situations. For example, consider a first goal combination:

    Achieve [T When C1]: **if** C1 **then sooner-or-later** T,   Avoid [T When C2]: **if** C2 **then never** T, on the one hand, and a second goal combination

> Achieve [*T* When *C1*],   Achieve [*R* When (*C1 or C2*)],   Avoid [*T* When *C2*],

on the other hand. Both goal combinations are divergent. We can find a boundary condition making the goals in each combination unsatisfiable when they are taken together; if the condition *C1* and *C2* holds, we get into a strong conflict in both combinations. However, the first combination meets the above minimality condition, whereas the second does not – just remove the second goal from the latter and we still get into the same potential conflict. We are more interested in considering the first combination for simpler and minimal conflict resolution.

Feasible conflict The minimality condition precludes a trivial boundary condition *B* such that $\{B, Dom\} \models$ **false**; it would then no longer hold. Such a trivial boundary condition would make potentially conflicting any combination of non-conflicting goals. When the minimality condition seems hard to assess, we need at least to check that:

2a. $\{B, Dom\} \not\models$ **false**   (*feasibility*)

This can be assessed in more concrete terms by finding a *scenario* showing that the boundary condition *B* can be satisfied by the system in view of what we know about the domain.

Non-trivial conflict The third condition in the definition of divergence precludes the other trivial case where the boundary condition would be simply the negation of the goal AND-combination. Again, any goal combination would then be conflicting.

Divergence as defined is a fairly general notion covering two particular cases:

- A strong conflict corresponds to the case where $B =$ **true**.

- An obstacle, as defined in Section 9.1, amounts to a boundary condition in a situation involving a single goal in the 'conflict' (see the above definition with $n = 1$). This observation allowed us to capture the Obstacle meta-concept as a specialization of BoundaryCondition in our meta-model (see Chapter 14, Figure 14.3). Although risk analysis is traditionally distinguished from conflict analysis, some of the techniques are grounded on similar principles.

Regressing goal negations through overlapping goals

We may in particular adapt the technique introduced in Section 9.3.1 for obstacle identification and refinement (see Figure 9.10). Instead of determining under which condition a goal can be violated in view of known domain properties, we determine under which condition a goal can be violated in view of *other goals* overlapping it – where *overlapping* means that the goals *concern* one common object at least. For obstacle identification and refinement, we regressed

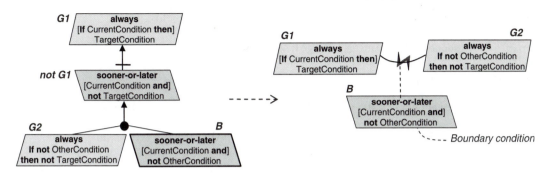

Figure 16.3 *Conflict detection: regressing a goal negation through overlapping goals*

the goal negation through domain properties (see Section 9.3.1). For conflict detection, we regress such negation through the overlapping goals.

Figure 16.3 illustrates this principle on a simple divergence pattern involving two *Maintain* goals. The root goal *G1* on the left is first negated. A pre-condition for this negation is then obtained by replacing the condition 'not TargetCondition' in the negation by the condition 'not OtherCondition', stated by another goal *G2* to imply the replaced condition 'not TargetCondition'. In this pattern, a one-step regression of *G1*'s negation through *G2* yields a boundary condition *B* for conflict. We can indeed argue that if the right-hand leaf condition *B* of the refinement tree in Figure 16.3 is satisfied and the left-hand leaf goal *G2* is satisfied, then the root goal *G1* is not satisfied.

In general, we need to iterate such a single regression step through other overlapping goals that might be involved in the divergence, and possibly through domain properties as well. The key point is that the divergent goals must be involved in the regression for a potential conflict involving them to be detected.

Let us illustrate this technique with two iterations, one involving a domain property. Consider the potential conflict appearing in the Mine Safety Control system in Chapter 15 (see Figure 15.10). Let us see how it can be systematically detected by derivation of a boundary condition for it.

The potentially conflicting goals were:

(G1) Maintain[PumOnIfHighWater]: **always (if** water above high threshold **then** pum on)

(G2) Maintain[PumOffIfHighMethane]: **always (if** methane above critical threshold **then** pum off)

We negate the first goal:

(**not** G1)   **sooner-or-later** water above high threshold **and not** pum on

A first regression step through the domain property:

(Dom)   **if** pump off **then not** pump on

allows us to replace 'not pum on' in (not G1) by 'pump off', which yields:

sooner-or-later water above high threshold **and** pum off

A second regression step through the overlapping goal (G2) yields:

sooner-or-later water above high threshold **and** methane above critical threshold

which is the boundary condition for making those two goals strongly conflicting.

A similar derivation allows us to detect that the library system goals Maintain[CopyKept-AsLongAsNeeded] and Achieve[CopyReturnedSoon] are divergent; see the exercise at the end of this chapter.

The divergence pattern in Figure 16.3 involves two *Maintain* goals. Similar patterns may be provided for *Achieve* goals or for a combination of *Maintain* and *Achieve* goals. Figure 16.4 shows one pattern involving an *Achieve* goal and an *Avoid* goal, in view of the domain property shown there. The divergence would involve three goals in case the latter property is prescriptive. More precise, formal patterns for such divergences will be provided in Chapter 18.

Heuristic identification of divergences

We may also use rules of thumb that are based on the meta-model and on goal categories to help us identify divergent goals. Such rules take the form:

If there are goals of this category in the goal model that overlap on this meta-relationship instance **then** check them for divergence.

Here is a sample of such rules.

- **(HRD1) If** *there is a* Performance *goal and a* Safety *goal concerning the same object,* **then** *check them for divergence.* For example, the divergence between the goals SignalPromptlySetToGo and SignalSafelySetToStop in Figure 8.7 might be identified through this rule. The former is a *Performance* goal, the latter a *Safety* goal, and both concern the Signal entity.

- **(HRD2) If** *there is a* Confidentiality *goal and an* Information *goal concerning the same object,* **then** *check them for divergence.* For example, the goals Achieve[ConstraintsKnown-ToInitiator] and Avoid[ConstraintsDisclosedToParticipants] are divergent in the meeting scheduling system because of the boundary condition of an initiator participating in the initiated meeting. The same rule may lead to the identification of a divergence

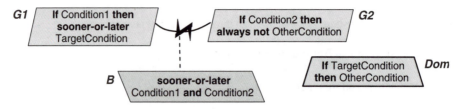

Figure 16.4 Divergence pattern with Achieve and Avoid goals

between the goals *Achieve[EditorsInformedOfFullReviews]* and *Maintain[ReviewAnonymity]* in an electronic journal management system, because of the boundary condition of an editor submitting papers to the journal.

- **(HRD3)** *If there is a Confidentiality goal having the form Maintain[AgentAnonymity] and an Accountability goal concerning the same agent,* **then** *check them for divergence.*

- **(HRD4)** *If there are two soft goals concerning the same object, one resulting in the increase of one of its attributes and the other resulting in the decrease of this attribute,* **then** *check them for divergence.* For example, a divergence between the library system goals Decrease[SubscriptionCosts] and Increase[JournalCoverage] might be detected that way. Both goals concern the Library entity. The former prescribes a decrease of the SubscriptionCosts attribute; the latter results in an increase of this attribute. In the train control system, we might thereby detect a divergence between the goals ShortStopAtStation and EnoughTimeForEntry&Exit – the resolution here will consist of an adequate compromise on the timeout value for doors opening.

- **(HRD5)** *If the same Satisfaction goal can be instantiated to multiple competing agent instances,* **then** *check these instantiations for divergence.* For example, two instantiations of the goal *Achieve* [RequestedMeetingScheduledWithinDateRange] are potentially conflicting in the meeting scheduler system in the case of multiple competing requests and short, overlapping date ranges. In an ambulance-dispatching system, this rule might lead to the identification of a divergence between multiple instantiations of the goal *Achieve* [NearestFreeAmbulanceDispatched] with a boundary condition of multiple accidents at equidistant places at the same time.

16.2.2 Heuristic identification of obstacles

Chapter 9 introduced obstacles, obstacle categories and various techniques for obstacle identification, evaluation and resolution. Heuristic rules may be used in addition for obstacle identification. As for conflict detection, such rules are based on the meta-model and on goal categories. Here they take the form:

If a model element has these characteristics **then** consider obstacles in this category.

Here is a sample of such rules.

(HRO1) *If an agent monitors or controls an object attribute or association for realizability of a goal under its responsibility,* **then** *consider obstacles in the following categories.*

- *InfoUnavailable.* The necessary state information on an object instance is not available to an agent instance.

- *InfoNotInTime.* The necessary state information on an object instance is available too late to an agent instance.

- *WrongBelief.* The necessary state information on an object instance, as recorded in the memory of an agent instance, is different from the actual state information on this object instance. (See the notion of agent belief introduced in Section 11.2.5.)

In the meeting scheduling system, this heuristic might help identify obstacles such as Meet-ingDatesConfusedByParticipant or ExcludedDatesConfusedByParticipant. For an electronic journal-reviewing process, an obstacle such as ReviewerBelievesWrongDeadline might be identified that way.

In the preceding identification rule, the *WrongBelief* obstacle category may be further refined into the following sub-categories:

- *WrongInfoProvided.* The necessary state information provided by *another* agent instance about an object instance is incorrect (e.g. too high or too low values for an object attribute).

- *InfoCorrupted.* The state information from the provider has been corrupted by a third party.

- *InfoOutdated.* The state information provided to the agent instance is no longer correct at the time of use.

- *InfoForgotten.* The state information provided to the agent instance is no longer available at the time of use.

- *WrongInference.* The agent instance has made a wrong inference from the available state information.

- *InfoConfusion.* The agent instance is confusing the necessary state information with some other information.

The sub-category of *InfoConfusion* obstacles may be further refined into the following sub-categories:

- *InstanceConfusion.* An agent instance is confusing the necessary state information about an object instance with state information about *another* instance of the same object.

- *ValueConfusion.* An agent instance is confusing different values for the same attribute of an object instance.

- *UnitConfusion.* An agent instance is confusing different units in terms of which values of an object attribute are expressed.

Figure 16.5 shows the taxonomy of *monitoring/control obstacles* on which the preceding identification rule is based.

In the meeting scheduling system, the preceding rule might help us identify several obstacles, for example participants confusing meetings or dates, meeting initiators confusing participants resulting in the wrong people being invited, confusions in constraints and so on.

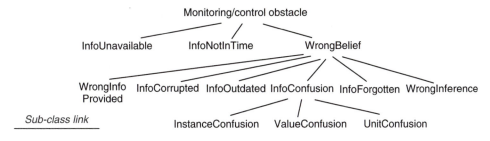

Figure 16.5 *A taxonomy of Monitoring/Control obstacles*

(See Figure 9.8.) In an ambulance-dispatching system, the obstacle of an ambulance going to the wrong place might similarly be identified. An important, domain-specific specialization of InfoConfusion obstacles in the aviation domain is *ModeConfusion*, where a pilot agent gets confused about the state of the cockpit software agent and what the latter is doing.

(HRO2) *If an agent needs a resource to realize a goal under its responsibility, **then** consider obstacles in categories such as* ResourceUnavailable, ResourceAvailableTooLate, ResourceOutOfOrder, WrongResourceUsed, or ResourceConfusion.

(HRO3) *If a goal* Achieve[TargetCondition**From**CurrentCondition] *requires some other condition to hold persistently before the TargetCondition is reached, **then** consider an obstacle where that persistent condition becomes false before the TargetCondition is reached.*

(HRO4) *If an* Information *goal is in the sub-category* MessageDelivered, ***then*** *consider obstacles in categories such as* MessageUndelivered, MessageDeliveredAtWrongPlace, MessageDeliveredAtWrongTime *or* MessageCorrupted.

(HRO5) *If a goal is in the* StimulusResponse *category, **then** consider the following obstacle categories*:

- Stimulusignored, TooLatePickUp, IncorrectValue or StimuliConfused *obstacles to the abstract goal* StimulusPickedUp.

- NoResponse, ResponseTooLate, Responseignored or WrongResponse *obstacles to the abstract companion goal* ResponseProvided.

Note that the more specific the goal/obstacle sub-categories, the more focused the search for corresponding obstacles.

16.2.3 Threat analysis: From goal models to anti-goal models

System security is an increasingly important concern. We frequently depend on distributed, heterogeneous, mission-critical software components in our systems. Such components are often highly vulnerable to sophisticated attack technology. The consequences of successful attacks can be quite severe – think of a man-in-the-middle attack resulting in disclosing sensitive information about credit cards, or a denial-of-service attack on medical records that prevents urgent surgery from being undertaken under the right conditions. In some cases, security and safety concerns can even interfere.

The earlier that security is addressed in the system lifecycle, the better. We must therefore carefully anticipate security-related problems at RE time by analysing threats and resolving them through adequate security countermeasures to be included in the requirements document.

As far as software is concerned, the security aspects we need to consider at RE time concern the *application layer* rather than the crypto, protocol or system/language layers. This layer is made of application-specific security requirements to be implemented later on in terms of primitives from those lower layers. Such requirements must, for example, prevent malicious users of an e-shopping system from getting an item without having paid for it.

Security threats

To address security concerns at RE time, we must anticipate both unintentional and intentional threats. A *threat* is the possibility of an agent asset in the system going unprotected against unintended behaviours. It corresponds to a security goal violation (see the definition of security goals in Section 7.3.2).

- An *unintentional* threat is a possibility of inadvert violation of a security goal – for example, some confidential information might be incidentally disclosed to unauthorized agents.

- An *intentional* threat is a possibility of proactive violation of a security goal by exploitation of unprotected data and system knowledge acquired through malicious behaviours, calculations, deductive inferences and so on. To cope with intentional threats, we clearly need to expand the system scope to cover malicious agents called *attackers*. These can be people that are insiders or outsiders of the original system, tools or fake devices.

From a semantic standpoint, an intentional threat is a class of possible behaviours of one or more attackers to break security goals through system state variables that they can monitor or control. An *attack* is one such behaviour. It amounts to a scenario showing how a corresponding security goal can be violated.

Note that the target of a threat can be other agents or objects in the system, not just software agents or objects, for example the defrauded seller in the e-shopping example.

Threats as obstacles

To support threat analysis, a model-based approach to RE should integrate threat models in system models. In our goal-oriented modelling framework, *threat models* are obstacle models augmented as follows:

- *Threats* are obstacles to security goals. Among such obstacles, intentional ones are to be satisfied by attackers to satisfy their own anti-goals. An *anti-goal* is an intentional obstacle or some other goal that an attacker may want to achieve. For example, an anti-goal for an e-shopping system might be Achieve[ItemReceivedAndNotPaid].

- A *threat tree* is an AND/OR obstacle tree anchored on a security goal; its root negates this security goal.

- A *threat model* is made of threat trees, expanded with attacker anti-goals in the case of intentional threats. Such model shows how the system's security goals can be obstructed unintentionally or intentionally. In each threat refinement tree, the leaf goals are specified in terms of conditions that can be monitored or controlled by an unauthorized agent or by an attacker.

For unintentional threats, threat analysis reduces to mere obstacle analysis on security goals. This section therefore concentrates on *intentional threats*.

The purpose of threat analysis then is to identify intentional threats that are likely and critical, based on the attacker's anti-goals and their capabilities, and elaborate countermeasures as new security goals in the goal model.

Let us see how we can do this in a systematic way. Section 18.4 will provide formal techniques to complement the semi-formal techniques in this section.

Attacker capabilities

We need to figure out what the capabilities of an attacker are. Capabilities will be captured by two sets of system conditions that the attacker can monitor and control, respectively. (Monitored/controlled conditions were defined at the end of Section 11.2.2.) These capabilities define the interface between the attacker and its own environment. The latter environment in particular includes the software-to-be.

For example, the attacker of a vulnerable e-shopping system might have the capability of controlling the conditions *ItemPaidByCustomer* and *PaymentNotificationReceivedBySeller*.

In the tradition of the *Most Powerful Attacker* view taken in cryptographic protocol analysis, we will assume a *Most Knowledgeable Attacker* (MKA) that knows everything about the model being attacked. In particular, the attacker is assumed to know the goal model, the domain properties and hypotheses used in the goal model, and the operation model.

The reason for this assumption is that *worst-case* threat analysis is desirable for complete exploration of security countermeasures. The MKA assumption is trivially satisfied here as the role of the attacker at RE time is played by the system modeller looking for missing countermeasures. The MKA assumption also implies that the attacker has no need to dynamically increase its knowledge through observation of system behaviours in response to the attacker's stimuli – as model builders we' have that knowledge already.

Analysing intentional threats

The overall procedure for threat analysis runs as follows.

1. Build threat graphs from anti-goals:

   a. Get initial anti-goals to be refined or abstracted.

   b. Identify classes of attackers wishing these, together with their capabilities.

   c. For each initial anti-goal and attacker class:

build an anti-goal refinement/abstraction graph as an argument showing how the anti-goals can be satisfied in view of the attacker's knowledge and capabilities; refinement terminates when leaf conditions are reached that meet the attacker's capabilities.

2. Derive new security goals as countermeasures to counter the leaf anti-goals from the threat graphs.

Let us now review and illustrate the various steps in this procedure.

Step 1: Identify initial anti-goals   We need to find preliminary anti-goals as malicious obstacles to be refined and abstracted in threat graphs. For this we may browse the goal model systematically in order to negate security goals, or determine whether some goal negation might be wished for malicious reasons.

Let us consider a web banking system, for example. One obvious security goal in such a system is the confidentiality goal:

Avoid [MoneyTransferMeansKnownByUnauthorizedPeople]

By simply negating it we get an anti-goal to start with:

Achieve [MoneyTransferMeansKnownByUnauthorized]

Step 2: Identify attackers and their capabilities   This step is obviously intertwined with the previous one; the negation of an application-specific goal raises the question of who might benefit from it. We may also use available attacker taxonomies to identify attackers.

For example, by asking who could benefit from the preceding anti-goal we could elicit agent classes such as Thief, Hacker, BankQualityAssuranceTeam and so on.

Step 3: Build threat graphs   For each initial anti-goal and attacker class identified, we need to build an anti-goal refinement/abstraction graph as a basis for exploring countermeasures. We may use for that all the goal-modelling heuristics provided in Chapter 8. In particular, we may ask *WHY* questions to identify parent anti-goals and *HOW* questions to identify offspring anti-goals. We may also use the refinement patterns discussed in Section 8.8.5.

Whatever technique is used, the anti-goal refinement along a branch stops as soon as we obtain an obstruction pre-condition that is monitorable or controllable according to the attacker's capabilities.

Let us consider a Thief agent in our web banking example. Starting from the initial anti-goal Achieve[MoneyTransferMeansKnownByUnauthorized], *WHY* questions lead us to a parent anti-goal Achieve[AccountsAttacked] and a grand-parent anti-goal Achieve[MoneyStolenFromBankAccounts]; see Figure 16.6. The milestone-driven refinement pattern in Figure 8.19 yields a missing sub-goal of the latter anti-goal; namely, Achieve[MoneyTakenFromAttackedAccounts]. Back to our initial anti-goal Achieve[MoneyTransferMeansKnownByUnauthorized], the milestone-driven refinement pattern again yields three sub-goals for it; namely, Achieve[BankSelected], Achieve[AccountStructureKnown] and Achieve[AccountNumber&Pin Known].

Let us refine the third sub-goal Achieve[AccountNumber&Pin Known]. We may use a *HOW* question about this anti-goal while noting the symmetry and multiplicities of the *Matching*

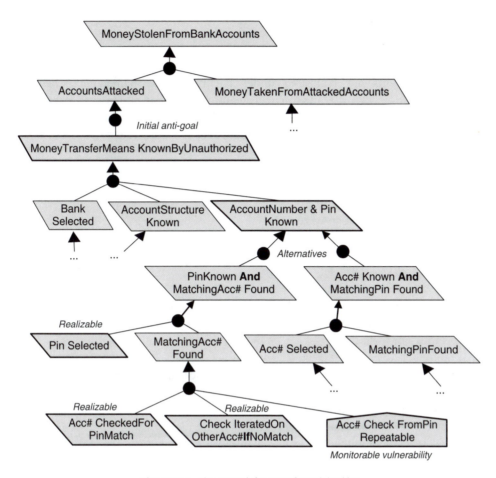

Figure 16.6   *Threat graph fragment for web banking.*

association between account numbers and PINs in the object model – an account number has exactly one matching PIN, whereas the same PIN may match multiple accounts. As a result we obtain two *alternative*, symmetrical sub-goals, namely:

Achieve [Account# Known **And** MatchingPin Found],

Achieve [Pin Known **And** MatchingAccount# Found].

(Section 18.4 will show how these goals and their precise specification can be derived formally.)

The refinement process goes on until we reach terminal conditions that are either realizable anti-requirements in view of the attacker's capabilities or observable vulnerabilities of the attacker's environment (including the target software). In the alternative refinement shown in Figure 16.6, the anti-requirements on the Thief agent are:

> *Achieve* [Account# CheckedFor PinMatch],
>
> *Achieve* [Check IteratedOn OtherAccount# **If** NoMatch].

These anti-requirements are realizable under the hypothesis named Acc#CheckFromPin-Repeatable, which states that the attacker can iterate on account numbers to check whether they match a selected 4-digit number. This property of the attacker's environment is a necessary sofware vulnerability for the attack modelled in Figure 16.6 to succeed. It does in fact correspond to a real, successful attack (dos Santos *et al.*, 2000).

Along the alternative refinement, not fully elaborated in Figure 16.6, we obtain symmetrical leaf goals:

> *Achieve* [Pin CheckedFor Account#Match],
>
> *Achieve* [CheckIteratedOn OtherPins **If** NoMatch],
>
> PinCheckFrom Acc# Repeatable.

The two first sub-goals are realizable anti-requirements, whereas the third condition is a vulnerability precluded by standard banking systems (beyond a very few PIN trials). This alternative is thus not realizable.

Step 4: Derive countermeasures
Based on the threat graphs built for each initial anti-goal, we may obtain new security goals by application of the model transformation operators discussed in Section 9.3.3 for obstacle resolution.

In security-critical systems the operator *Avoid [X]* is frequently used, where *X* is instantiated to an anti-goal or a vulnerability. For example, in our web banking system we would certainly take the following goals as new goals to be refined:

> Avoid [Acc#Check FromPin Repeatable],
>
> Avoid [PinCheck From Acc# Repeatable].

Resolution operators can be further specialized to malicious obstacles. In particular, the two following tactics should be considered for countermeasures:

- Make a vulnerability condition *unmonitorable* by any attacker.
- Make an anti-requirement *uncontrollable* by any attacker.

The alternative countermeasures obtained through such resolution operators must generally be further refined along alternative OR-branches in the updated goal model.

Such alternatives must be compared to select 'best' ones, based on contributions to other non-functional goals, as we will see below, and on conflicts that might arise with other goals in the goal model (see Section 16.2.1). A new cycle of threat analysis may then need to be undertaken for these new goals.

16.3 Reasoning about alternative options

Exploring alternative options is at the heart of the RE process. At different places in the book we have been faced with the problem of evaluating options for the selection of 'best' ones. Section 3.3 briefly introduced qualitative and quantitative techniques for decision support. We may expect such techniques to take advantage of the structure provided by a system model.

In our goal-oriented modelling framework, alternative options refer to goal refinements, conflict resolutions, obstacle resolutions, threat resolutions and responsibility assignments. As we saw in Chapter 15, Step 7 of the model-building method is devoted to the evaluation of such alternatives for making selections. Different alternatives contribute to different degrees of satisfaction of the soft goals identified in the goal model. This section expands on the material introduced in Chapter 3 to provide qualitative and quantitative techniques for selecting among alternatives in goal-oriented models.

16.3.1 Qualitative reasoning about alternatives

The general idea here is to use qualitative estimations for assessing the positive or negative contribution of alternative options to soft goals in the goal model (Mylopoulos *et al.*, 1992). The aim is to determine, for each alternative, a qualitative degree of satisficing of the top-level soft goals in the goal refinement graph; the option with the best degrees of satisficing is then selected. (The notion of soft goal satisficing was discussed in Section 7.3.1.)

To achieve this we need, for each alternative option, to:

- Assess its positive or negative influence on each leaf soft goal in the model.

- Propagate such influences bottom up in the goal graph until we reach the top-level soft goals.

Let us make these steps more precise while seeing them in action on our meeting scheduling system. Figure 16.7 shows a portion of the goal model with soft goal refinements and conflicts.

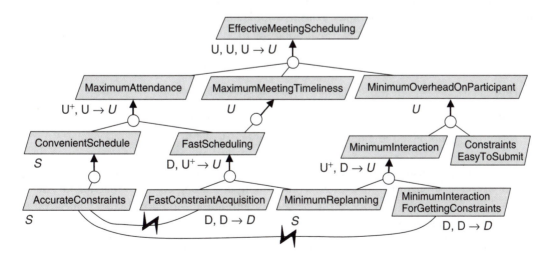

Figure 16.7 Upward propagation of satisficing labels in a soft goal refinement hierarchy

	Alternative options		
Leaf soft goals	ConstraintsAcquired By E-mail	ConstraintsAcquired From e-Agenda	Constraints Taken ByDefault
AccurateConstraints	+	−	−
FastConstraintAcquisition	−	+	+
Minimum Replanning	+	−	−
Minimum Interaction ForGettingConstraints	−	+	−

Table 16.1 *Qualitative contributions of options to leaf soft goals*

In particular, conflicts arise as the faster the constraint-acquisition process or the fewer the interactions with a participant, the less accurate the acquired constraints with respect to his or her actual constraints.

Assessing the qualitative contribution of alternative options to leaf soft goals

We first need to assess qualitatively the extent to which each alternative contributes to the various leaf goals in soft goal refinement hierarchies, for example '++' (very positively), '+' (positively), '−' (negatively), '− −' (very negatively), 'n' (neutral). This amounts to putting some *qualitative weight* on refinement and conflict links in the goal model. Table 16.1 suggests such initial assessment for three alternative options that we might consider for acquiring the constraints of participants invited to a meeting. (The names in option cells are names of corresponding refinements in the goal model; see Section 8.7.)

Bottom-up propagation of qualitative contributions

The next step consists of propagating such contributions upwards in the soft goal hierarchy through refinement and conflict links. For this we may use a procedure that assigns qualitative labels to each node in the hierarchy (Mylopoulos *et al.*, 1992). A node is labelled:

S (satisficed):   if it is satisficeable and not deniable,

D (denied):   if it is deniable but not satisficeable,

C (conflicting):   if it is both satisficeable and deniable,

U (undetermined):   if it is neither satisficeable nor deniable.

The procedure propagates such labels bottom up along refinement links, marked as '+' or '++' according to the strength of the positive contribution, and along conflict links, marked as '−' or '− −' according to the severity of the negative contribution. Additional label values can be assigned at intermediate stages of the procedure, for example:

U^+: unconclusive positive support, U^-: unconclusive negative support,

?: user intervention required for getting an adequate label value.

An upward propagation step from offspring nodes to their parent node goes as follows:

- The individual effect of a weighted link from an offspring to its parent is determined according to propagation rules such as the ones shown in Table 16.2 (we only consider a few weights to make things simpler). One additional rule states that *if* a node is a refinement node and all its offspring nodes have a *S* label, *then* this node gets an *S* label. A node will thus in general have multiple labels – one per incoming link.

- The various labels thereby collected at a parent node are merged into a single label. The user is first asked to combine U^+ and U^- labels into one or more S, D, C and U labels. The result is then combined into a single label by choosing the minimal label according to the following ordering:

$$S, D \geq U \geq C$$

This upward propagation step is applied recursively until the top-level soft goals get a single label.

Let us see how this technique works on the goal model portion shown in Figure 16.7. We consider the first option ConstraintsAcquiredByEmail in Table 16.1; it therefore gets an 'S' label to start with. According to Table 16.2, its '+' contribution links to AccurateConstraints and MinimumReplanning yield an 'S' label for these two leaf soft goals (as no other sub-goal is shown for the latter goals in the goal model; otherwise they would instead get a 'U$^+$', unless all other sub-goals have an 'S'). On the other hand, the '−' links from this first option to FastConstraintAcquisition and MinimumInteractionForGettingConstraints yield a 'D' label for these two leaf soft goals.

At the next step, the 'S' label of AccurateConstraints yields an 'S' label for ConvenientSchedule, through a '+' link and a 'D' label for FastConstraintAcquisition, through the '−' conflict link shown in Figure 16.6. Based on the above ordering, the labels 'D,D' on the latter goal get merged into a single 'D'.

At a next step, this 'D' label on FastConstraintAcquisition gets propagated through a '+' link to the parent goal FastScheduling as a 'D' label again, whereas the latter goal also gets a 'U$^+$' label through a '+' link from its offspring MinimumReplanning (see Table 16.2). After user intervention this 'U$^+$' might become 'U' and the resulting label merge yields, according to the pre-defined label ordering, a single 'U' label for FastScheduling. The process goes on upwards until we obtain 'U, U, U' labels for the top soft goal EffectiveMeetingScheduling, which get merged into a single 'U' label.

	Link weight		
	+	–	n
Offspring label	**Parent label**		
S	U$^+$	D	U
D	D	U$^+$	U
C	?	?	U
U	U	U	U

Table 16.2 *Qualitative label propagation rules*

A similar upward propagation for the second option in Table 16.1 – namely, ConstraintsAcquiredFrom-eAgenda – yields 'D, U, U' labels for the top soft goal. Globally the two options seem comparable, as they get the same top label after merge; namely, 'U' (undetermined). However, the second option has a 'D' label (denied) among the top labels, which might make it less preferred. The third option of merely taking default constraints (such as working days) gets one 'D' more at the top, which might be a good reason for discarding it.

This example shows the main limitation of such a qualitative approach; the propagation rules make the labels rapidly inconclusive as we move up in a too elaborate soft goal hierarchy. To overcome this, we might refine the qualitative labels, weights and propagation rules in Table 16.2 to make them less rough.

Still, the various types of labels and weights have no clear meaning. Qualitative reasoning schemes provide a quick and cheap means for rough evaluations in the early stages of the RE process. Their applicability for effective decision support based on accurate arguments appears limited.

16.3.2 Quantitative reasoning about alternatives

We can also decide which option to select by quantitative comparison of alternatives. Qualitative labels and weights are replaced by numerical scores. Such scores should be grounded on domain expertise and measurable system phenomena to make sense.

Model-based score matrices

Section 3.3 introduced weighted matrices as a simple technique for quantitative evaluation. In our model-based framework, the structure of such matrices is obtained directly from the goal model:

- The alternative refinements, assignments or resolutions are taken as options.

- The leaf soft goals are taken as evaluation criteria.

For a given set of alternative options, we need to score each option numerically against the leaf soft goals and collect these scores in a weighted matrix. A *score X* means that the option is estimated to satisfice the soft goal in X% of cases.

One advantage here with respect to qualitative contributions is the relative weighting that we can specify on different soft goals to distinguish their relative importance or priority. The last row in the matrix yields the total score of each option as a weighted summation of its scores with respect to each leaf soft goal (see Section 3.3).

Table 16.3 shows such a quantitative evaluation for the options and soft goals evaluated qualitatively in Table 16.1. In this evaluation, the soft goal AccurateConstraints is considered relatively much more important than the soft goals MinimumInteractionForGettingConstraints and MinimumReplanning (the latter having the same level of limited importance). The first option, ConstraintsAcquiredFromE-Agenda, is estimated to satisfice the soft goal AccurateConstraints in

Leaf soft goals	Significance weighting	Option scores		
		Constraints- Acquired By E-mail	ConstraintsAcquired From e-Agenda	Constraints Taken ByDefault
AccurateConstraints	0.50	0.90	0.30	0.10
FastConstraint Acquisition	0.30	0.50	0.90	1.00
MinimumReplanning	0.10	0.80	0.30	0.10
MinimumInteraction ForGettingConstraints	0.10	0.50	1.00	1.00
TOTAL	**1.00**	**0.73**	**0.55**	**0.46**

Table 16.3 *Weighted matrix for evaluating alternative options against leaf soft goals*

90% of cases, as invited participants are expected to directly express their own constraints; the 10% remaining stands for participants confusing dates, having taken other commitments in between and so on. Overall, this first option outperforms the others in view of the relative weights assigned to each soft goal.

The main problem with this approach is the determination, at RE time, of adequate option scores against soft goals. Note that the accuracy of each individual score taken in isolation is not what really matters. We can still draw meaningful comparative conclusions as long as *all scores are set consistently, from one alternative to the other, as a common basis for making comparisons*. Nevertheless, to avoid subjective estimations resulting in questionable decisions, the scores should be grounded on domain expertise, experience with similar systems and interpretations in terms of measurable system phenomena.

Determining option scores from measurable system phenomena

To complement the above technique, the goal model may help us determine option scores grounded on measurable phenomena. The idea is to identify gauge variables referred to in the definition of the soft goals and their fit criterion. (Fit criteria were introduced in Section 4.2.1. They are used in a goal model to characterize soft goals; see Section 8.1.)

A *gauge variable* is a variable associated with a specific leaf soft goal from the goal model. It captures a quantity such as:

- A quantity the soft goal prescribes to *Improve, Increase, Reduce, Maximize* or *Minimize*.

- The estimated cost of satisficing the soft goal.

- The estimated time taken for satisficing the soft goal.

Consider the leaf soft goal *MinimumInteractionForGettingConstraints* in the meeting scheduling system. The variable ExpectedNumberOfInteractions might be a gauge variable derivable from

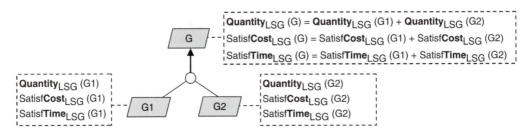

Figure 16.8 *Cumulative propagation of gauge variables*

this soft goal; it estimates the average number of interactions between a participant and the scheduler to get the participant's constraints.

A gauge variable should be cumulative and allow for comparisons:

- *Option comparability.* The variable should provide a measure related to soft goal satisficing for option comparison.

- *Cumulative quantity.* The variable should propagate additively along the AND-trees refining the options that we need to compare in the goal model.

Figure 16.8 explains what is meant by additive propagation. Let *LSG* denote a leaf soft goal used for option comparison. In view of the semantics of goal AND-refinement, the value of a gauge variable associated with *LSG* at a parent goal *G* in the refinement tree of an option is obtained by summing up the values of this variable at the sub-goals *G1* and *G2*. When a value for the variable at a particular sub-goal makes no sense, we merely ignore it in the summation.

The merits of an option with respect to a leaf soft goal *LSG* are obtained by upward propagation of the cumulative values of the gauge variables associated with *LSG* starting from the option's leaf sub-goals. The option score against *LSG* is the value of *LSG*'s gauge variables at the root of the option's refinement tree. By repeating this for the various leaf soft goals used as comparsion criteria, we obtain a set of scores for each option (one per soft goal).

Table 16.4 illustrates an evaluation of gauge variables that might result in the determination of the scores in Table 16.3. For example, the value '2' for the gauge variable ExpectedNumberOfInteractions in the option *ConstraintsAcquiredByE-mail* is obtained by summing the value '1' for the sub-goal ConstraintsRequested (one interaction per requested constraints) and the value '1' for the sub-goal ConstraintsTransmitted (another interaction per returned constraints). The value '3' in the same column results from '0 (time taken to request constraints) + 3 (estimated average time, in days, for a participant to return his or her constraints)'. Note that each gauge variable in Table 16.4 is derived from the corresponding leaf soft goal in Table 16.3.

16.4 Model-driven generation of the requirements document

Getting a high-quality requirements document (RD) is among the main objectives of system modelling at RE time. A goal-oriented model allows us to produce a corresponding RD semi-automatically. The generated RD preserves the goal-oriented structure and content of the model, and may fit prescribed documentation standards.

	Option values		
Soft goal gauge variable	ConstraintsAcquired By E-mail	ConstraintsAcquired From e-Agenda	ConstraintsTaken ByDefault
Expected Number of Correct Free Half-Days per Week	9	3	1
Expected Constraint Acquisition Time (in days)	3	1	0
Expected Number of Replannings	0.5	2	4
Expected Number of Interactions	2	0	0

Table 16.4   Values of gauge variables for soft goal satisficing by alternative options

The general idea is to generate a textual structure for the RD from the structure of the model and the structure of the required standards. The generated structure is filled in with the **Def** annotations of all model elements, inserted at an appropriate place in the corresponding document section.

The resulting text is expanded by additional items such as model diagram portions, tables, interview excerpts, illustrative scenarios, examples and so on. These additional items are inserted from the annotated model using a 'drag-and-drop' facility.

We may of course add text items, in particular introductory or concluding sentences, and adapt any generated RD item. Model-related modifications must, however, be performed on the model to maintain the consistency between the model and the generated RD.

Let us have a look at how the technique may work for the IEEE Std-830 standard template introduced in Section 4.2.2 (see Figure 4.1). For each template section the generation goes as follows.

1. Introduction

1.1 Document Purpose

A generic introduction is proposed here for adaptation.

1.2 System Purpose

The *top-level goals* from the goal model are inserted in a generic introductory text together with their definitions (**Def** annotations).

1.3 Definitions, acronyms and abbreviations

This section is produced from the *object model*. A glossary is generated by listing all object names in alphabetical order together with their definition (**Def** annotation), synonyms (if any), domain properties (**DomInvar** annotations) and initialization (**Init** annotation); see Figure 10.2. If an object has attributes and specializations, its presentation has a corresponding tree structure for listing attributes and specializations.

The textual presentation is expanded, if desired, by drag-and-drop of diagram portions from the object model.

1.4 References

(The documents referenced elsewhere in the RD need to be listed here with full reference information.)

1.5 Overview

A generic overview text is proposed here on the organization of the remainder of the document.

2. General description

2.1 System perspective

This section is produced from the *agent model*. The software-to-be is related to its environment by listing all system agents together with their interfaces in terms of the state variables that they monitor and control.

The textual presentation may then be expanded by drag-and-drop of portions of context diagrams generated from the agent model.

2.2 User requirements

This section is produced by a pre-order traversal of the *goal model* from top to bottom. The depth of subsection nesting is a user-definable parameter. By default, each goal diagram defines a sub-section where the diagram is displayed and the features of each goal, including its priority, are listed after its **Def** annotation (see Figure 8.1).

Cross-references are inserted to refer to other diagrams or texts. Each *requirement* is clearly distinguished in the generated text; beside its name, definition and features it gets a unique identifying number (see Section 4.2.1). The expectations of environment agents are not listed here as they appear in another section.

2.3 User characteristics

(A characterization of intended software users in terms of educational level, experience and technical expertise needs to be supplied here.)

2.4 General constraints

(A description of developmental constraints that may limit software design and implementation options needs to be supplied here.)

2.5 Assumptions and dependencies

The goal model is used here again to list all *expectations* assigned to environment agents. These include expectations on software agents whose **Category** has been stated in the agent model to be 'external' (legacy, off-the-shelf or foreign components; see Section 11.1).

All *obstacle*s left unresolved are listed in this section as well.

All items listed in this section are presented with their Def annotation and any other feature annotating them in the goal or obstacle model.

2.6 Apportioning of requirements

To indicate which requirements may be delayed until future system versions, a table is generated here that lists all the requirements presented in the preceding 'User requirements' section, sorted by priority level obtained from Priority annotations (see Figure 8.1).

3. Software requirements

3.1. Detailed requirements

3.1.1 General organization

The *agent model* is used here to list, for each software-to-be agent, the requirements from the goal model for which it is responsible.

Relevant portions of agent diagrams or context diagrams may then be dragged-and-dropped here.

3.1.2 Shared objects

The *object model* is used here to present class diagrams that contain objects Concerned by the requirements on the software agents. Each diagram is explained in terms of the objects composing it together with their attributes and associations, their definition (Def annotation), domain properties (DomInvar annotations) and initialization (Init annotation), as in the glossary.

3.1.3 Software operations

The *operation model* is used here to produce, for each software agent, the specification of all the operations it must perform. This includes, for each operation, its domain pre- and post-conditions, and its required pre-, trigger and post-conditions with respect to all the requirements for which the agent is responsible. At the end of the section, a table is produced showing the operations performed by each agent and, for each operation, the requirements operationalized by it.

The textual presentation may be expanded by drag-and-drop of the corresponding operationalization diagrams.

3.1.4 Software behaviours

The *behaviour model* is used here to produce, for each software agent, the interaction scenarios involving it and the statecharts on its controlled variables.

3.2. Summary

3.2.1 Functional requirements

This section lists all requirements whose Category has been stated in the goal model to be 'functional' (see Section 8.1).

3.2.2 External interface requirements

This section lists all requirements whose **Category** has been stated in the goal model to be 'interoperability', 'user interaction' or 'device interaction' (see Figure 7.5).

3.2.3 Performance requirements

This section lists all requirements whose **Category** has been stated in the goal model to be 'performance'.

3.2.4 Design constraints

This section lists all requirements whose **Category** has been stated in the goal model to be 'development' or 'architecture' (see Figure 7.5).

3.2.5 Software quality attributes

This section lists all remaining non-functional requirements whose **Category** has another value, e.g. 'safety' or 'accuracy'.

The requirements document generated from the model elaborated in Chaper 15, using the generation technique explained in this section and implemented by the *Objectiver* tool, can be found on the book's Web site.

16.5 Beyond RE: From goal-oriented requirements to software architecture

As the requirements document is used in the later stages of software development, we might expect its underlying model to be useable for driving the software architecture design process. *Architectural design* is concerned with the organization of the software-to-be into *components* and *connectors*. Connectors capture, at a sufficiently abstract level, the required interactions among components to be developed or to be supplied (Shaw & Garlan, 1996; Bosch, 2000). Architectural design is commonly recognized to have a deep impact on non-functional requirements related to security, fault tolerance, performance, interoperability and maintainability (Perry & Wolf, 1992).

It may be worth recalling that a number of *system* design decisions have already been taken at this point. These refer to the selection among alternative options in Step 7 of the method discussed in Chapter 15, according to the techniques presented in Section 16.3. Although such decisions have an impact on the scope and structure of the software-to-be, we should not confuse system design and *software* design, which is what we are concerned with in this section. Architectural design decisions result in specific ways of decomposing software-to-be agents into finer-grained components that interact through connectors so as to meet the non-functional requirements in the goal model.

On the other hand, architectural design and RE are often intertwined, as briefly discussed in Section 1.1.9. Architectural aspects may emerge fairly soon in the software engineering process. This may be due to the organization of environmental components with which the software-to-be has to interact, to constraints imposed by the integration of external or legacy software components, or to the early decision to reuse an existing architectural framework. Early architectural choices generally hide underlying domain properties and goals. The latter should be mined from them, and integrated in the object and goal models for increased completeness.

This section presents a model-driven approach for building a first draft proposal for the software architecture. The approach will be illustrated on our meeting scheduling system. The software data architecture is easily derived from the object model (Section 16.5.1). In parallel, an abstract dataflow architecture is derived from the agent and operation models (Section 16.5.2). Based on known architectural styles, this dataflow architecture is refined so as to meet the architectural requirements identified in the goal model (Section 16.5.3). The resulting architecture is then recursively refined to meet the various quality and development requirements found in the goal model (Section 16.5.4).

16.5.1 Deriving a software data architecture from the object model

In most cases the software-to-be relies on a so-called *logical database*, to be subsequently implemented in a distributed or centralized way using the file, database or object persistency management system supported by the implementation platform. An entity–relationship structure for the logical schema of such a database is obtained in a straightforward manner as follows.

- We browse the object model and check, for each conceptual object, whether it should have a software counterpart whose instances need be maintained in such a database, and why. (The answer to the latter question might reveal requirements that were overlooked.)

- Each selected object is mapped onto a software replica with a corresponding structure of attribute/association replicas. The association multiplicities are transposed as database integrity constraints.

- The standard operations of creating, accessing, updating and deleting corresponding 'records' are named in system-specific terms and added as fined-grained database operations on the corresponding class in the transposed class diagram.

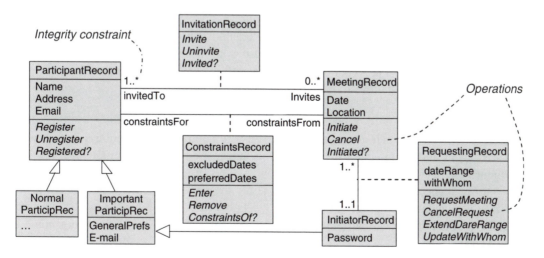

Figure 16.9 *Logical database schema with database access operations*

- Accuracy goals are added to require such mappings to be consistent; the state of each database element must accurately reflect the state of the corresponding environment element it represents.

Figure 16.9 shows a draft structure for the meeting scheduler's database derived from the object model fragment in Figure 4.5. In the transposed class diagram organizing the software object classes, operations such as RequestMeeting, Initiated?, ExtendDateRange and Uninvite correspond to *create, access, update* and *delete* operations on corresponding database elements, respectively. Some of these operations might already have emerged as software operations in the operation model. If they do, their specification is transferred from this model. If they don't, it would be the right time to elicit their underlying requirements and update the operation and goal models accordingly.

Here are some examples of new accuracy goals to be introduced in the goal model for linking environment elements and their software counterpart:

- *Maintain [ParticipantRecordedAsInvited Iff InvitedByInitiator].* A participant is recorded in the database as invited to this meeting if and only if he or she is actually invited by the initiator of this meeting.

- *Maintain [RecordedDatesExcluded Iff DatesExcludedByParticipant].* The dates recorded as excluded for this meeting by this participant in the database are those actually returned by the participant.

- *Maintain [MeetingCancellationRecorded Iff MeetingCancelledByInitiator].* A meeting is recorded as cancelled in the database if and only if the initiator has actually cancelled the meeting.

Such new accuracy goals need to be operationalized by adequate exception-handling operations, including data validation and recovery operations.

16.5.2 Deriving an abstract dataflow architecture from the agent and operation models

A first architectural draft is obtained by deriving the data dependencies among software agents assigned to functional requirements. Such dependencies yield abstract dataflow connectors linking the agents. In the derivation, the coarse-grained software-to-be agents in the agent model are decomposed into fine-grained software components C, each associated with a specific functional goal, so as to address the design soft goal *Maximize* [Cohesion (C)].

The derivation of a dataflow architecture proceeds as follows.

Step 1 For each software-to-be agent in the agent model, we consider the functional goals assigned to it. For each such goal, we define a software component clustering a finer-grained dedicated agent and all operations that this agent has to perform to operationalize the goal. The agent's interface is defined by the corresponding sets of variables that the agent monitors and controls, respectively. In other words, we apply the agent refinement mechanism to the software-to-be agents in the agent model (see Section 11.4), and derive the agent interfaces using the *goal-capability matching* heuristic (see Section 11.5.1 and the derivation scheme in Figure 11.13).

Step 2 For each pair of obtained components *C1* and *C2*, we derive a dataflow connector from *C1* to *C2*, labelled by the variable *d*, if and only if *d* is among *C1*'s controlled variables and *C2*'s monitored variables:

DataFlow (d, C1, C2) **iff** Controls (C1, d) **and** Monitors (C2, d)

Figure 16.10 shows a partial result of Step 1 for a portion of the goal model for the meeting scheduling system in Figure 8.11. The Scheduler software-to-be agent has been split up into the Requestor, Merger, Planner and Notifier agents so as to meet the design goal *Maximize*[Cohesion(C)]. Note that the Requestor's interface, for example, is derived from the definition of the goal ConstraintRequested assigned to it (see the derivation scheme in Figure 11.13).

Figure 16.11 shows the dataflow architecture resulting from Step 2. The arrows there denote dataflow connectors. They are labelled by the data flowing through them.

In this architecture, each software component is specified by the definition of the goal assigned to it, together with the pre-/trigger/post-conditions of the various operations operationalizing this goal.

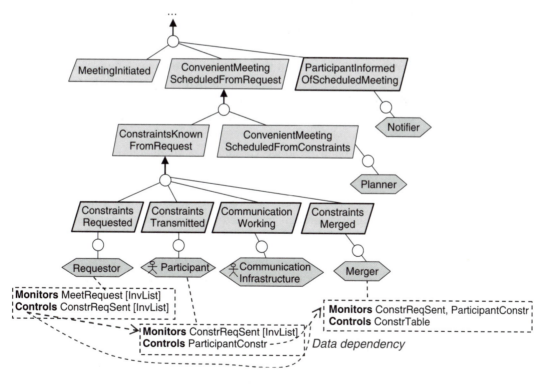

Figure 16.10 *Finer-grained software agents, their interfaces, and their data dependencies.*

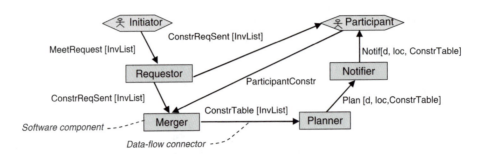

Figure 16.11 Derived dataflow architecture.
Source: Based on A. van Lamsweerde, 2003, with kind permission of Springer Science and Business Media.

16.5.3 Selecting an architectural style from architectural requirements

The abstract dataflow architecture defines our refinement space. Before exploring alternative ways of refining components and connectors locally, this space may need to be globally constrained by architectural requirements. The latter typically arise from the organization of environment components with which the software components will have to interact, for example the distribution of human agents, of organizational data or of physical devices that the software-to-be must control (see Section 1.1.5).

The dataflow architecture should therefore be refined by imposing an architectural style whose underlying soft goals match the architectural requirements.

A catalogue of architectural styles should be available for this, where each style is documented by applicability conditions and effect conditions on the matching architecture. The applicability conditions of a style may include domain properties together with the soft goals that the style is intended to achieve.

This process is semi-formal but can be made systematic by use of **if–then** *transformation rules*. Figure 16.12 shows a transformation rule for the introduction of the *event-based* style. The upper part of the left-hand rectangle captures the *applicability conditions* of this style:

- The first condition is a domain property stating that the environment agents interacting with software components through produced/consumed events are geographically distributed.

- The second condition is a target goal of the event-based style, stating that the software components in the style should know nothing about each other.

The lower part of the left-hand rectangle in Figure 16.12 and the right-hand rectangle show the matching architectural drafts before and after application of the transformation rule, respectively. A dashed arrow labelled ?d means that the source component *registers interest* to the target component for events corresponding to productions of *d*. An arrow labelled !d means that the source component *notifies* the interested target component of events corresponding to

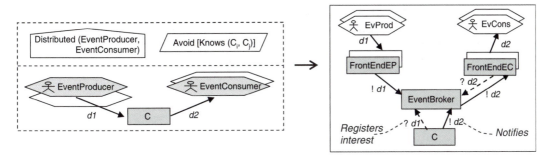

Figure 16.12 *Architectural refinement: imposing an event-based architectural style.*
Source: Based on A. van Lamsweerde, 2003, with kind permission of Springer Science and Business Media.

productions of d. The latter events carry corresponding values for d. The standard arrows still denote dataflow connectors.

Figure 16.13 outlines a portion of the result of applying the style-based transformation in Figure 16.12 to the abstract dataflow architecture in Figure 16.11. According to the event-based style, the dataflow connectors were replaced by pairs of '?register – !notify' interactions.

Note that there are still data flowing through the event notification arrows as the events carry the corresponding data among their attributes. *Any refinement must preserve the properties of more abstract connectors and components.* In this case, an abstract dataflow channel between two components must be preserved either directly or indirectly through intermediate components – such as the EventBroker component in Figure 16.13.

16.5.4 Architectural refinement from quality requirements

After style-based refinement of the abstract dataflow architecture to meet architectural constraints, we need to make further refinements to achieve the quality goals and the development

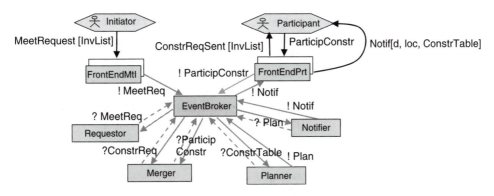

Figure 16.13 *Style-based architecture to meet architectural requirements.*
Source: Based on A. van Lamsweerde, 2003, with kind permission of Springer Science and Business Media.

goals from the goal model. For example, the event broker in Figure 16.13 should be split up into several brokers handling different kinds of events to meet the development goal *Maximize*[Cohesion(EventBroker)].

Many quality goals constrain component *interactions*. For example:

- Security goals constrain component interactions to restrict information flows along channels.

- Accuracy goals constrain interactions to maintain a consistent state between corresponding objects.

- Usability requirements constrain user–software interactions.

Development goals such as *Minimize*[Coupling(C1,C2)] or InformationHidden(C1,C2) also impose specific constraints on the way in which components $C1$ and $C2$ may interact. Other non-functional goals impose constraints on single components only, for example *Maximize*[Cohesion(C)].

The next architectural refinement phase proceeds on a more local basis. Its aim is to 'inject' quality goals and development goals within pairs of interacting components or within single components. In the former case we refine a connector, whereas in the latter case we refine a single component. The derivation proceeds as follows:

> For each quality or development requirement G in the goal model,
>
> Step 1: Identify all connectors and components constrained by G in the architecture.
>
> Step 2: Instantiate G to them.
>
> Step 3: Refine each of them so as to meet this instantiation.

The refinement of a constrained connector or component in Step 3 can be driven by *architectural refinement patterns*. Such patterns are expressed as architecture transformation rules. The left-hand side of a rule consists of a source component/connector template and a generic quality or development requirement; the right-hand side is a refinement of the source template that meets the target requirement or satisfices it (in case of a soft requirement).

Figure 16.14 shows an example of such a pattern. On the left-hand side of the rule, the source template consists of a dataflow connector between two generic components; the target requirement is a confidentiality requirement about the data flowing. On the right-hand side, the resulting connector refinement consists of splitting the dataflow connector into two dataflow connectors with a new SecurityFilter component in between.

A pattern may be selected if its left-hand side matches the constrained connectors, components and instantiated G obtained from Step 2 above.

Several patterns might be applicable, as a particular connector or component might be constrained by multiple instantiated Gs. In such cases, we might select one based on prioritization of the instantiated Gs (see Section 3.4) or on qualitative or quantitative reasoning about the alternative options (see Section 16.3 in this chapter). The matching pattern is then applied to produce the refinement on its right-hand side, instantiated accordingly.

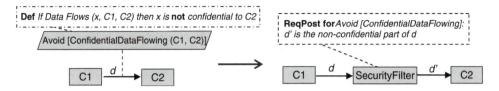

Figure 16.14 *Confidentiality-driven connector refinement pattern.*

Let us illustrate this pattern-based architectural refinement for the architectural draft obtained in Figure 16.13. After conflict resolution, the goal model contains the weakened confidentiality requirement:

Avoid [ParticipantConstraintsKnown To *NonInitiator* Participants]

(see Section 16.2.1). Step 1 above results in localization of the impact of this quality requirement on the dataflow connector between the Planner and the Notifier components via the EventBroker component (see Figures 16.11 and 16.13). In Step 2, the confidentiality-driven pattern in Figure 16.14 is seen to match by considering two disclosure levels: one for meeting initiators, the other for normal participants. The application of the instantiated pattern results in the

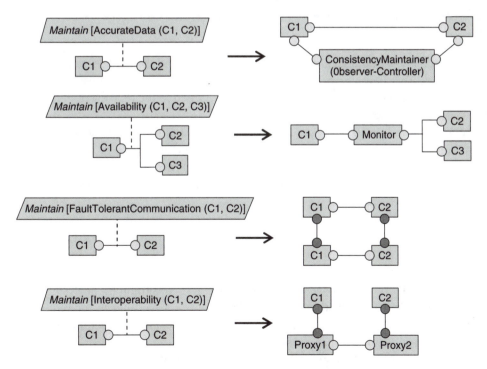

Figure 16.15 *Architectural refinement patterns for quality goals.*
Source: Based on A. van Lamsweerde, 2003, with kind permission of Springer Science and Business Media.

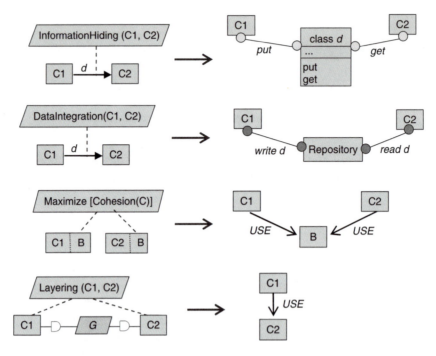

Figure 16.16   *Architectural refinement patterns for development goals.*
Source: Based on A. van Lamsweerde, 2003, with kind permission of Springer Science and Business Media.

introduction of a new component between the EventBroker and the Notifier; namely, Participant-ConstraintsFilter. This new component will ensure that the participant constraints are filtered out, for normal participants, from the PlanningDetails attached to the Notif event transmitted from the Planner to the Notifier via the EventBroker.

Figures 16.15 and 16.16 suggest a sample of architectural patterns for quality goals and development goals, respectively. The links between connectors represent constrained connectors obtained in the current design state. For our meeting scheduling software, the first pattern in Figure 16.15 might be used to introduce an abstract data type ConstraintsTable for use by the Merger and Planner components.

Summary

- A main strength of model-based approaches to RE is their support for analysing a model while building it, in order to check, evaluate, reuse and consolidate the requirements elaborated and structured in the model. We can moreover derive useful products from a model, including the requirements document itself and a preliminary architecture for the software part of the system. The depth of such analysis depends on the degree of model formalization. Simply by considering the semi-formal specification provided by the graphical representation of the model, we can already perform some useful forms of surface-level analysis.

- A multi-view model can be maintained in a database structured according to the underlying meta-model. A model database supports concurrent development, model browsing and multiple types of analysis through queries. We can use pre-cooked queries for checking the structural consistency and completeness of the model, for generating other views for dedicated analyses such as load analysis, and for managing traceability along the built-in *derivation* and *use* links provided by the model. Queries also allow us to check and complete a target model by analogical reuse of structurally matching model fragments in a database structured by specialization layers.

- A goal model can be analysed semi-formally against conflicts among overlapping goals, obstacles to goal satisfaction and threats to security goals. A divergence is a situation where a conflict arises if some boundary condition becomes true. We can detect divergences by regressing goal negations through overlapping goals or by heuristic identification rules based on the meta-model and on goal categories. Other heuristic rules may help us identify obstacles in specific categories.

- Threat analysis is aimed at breaking the model at RE time in order to anticipate security problems and complete the model with adequate security countermeasures. Threats amount to obstacles to security goals. They can be unintentional or intentional. The analysis of intentional threats calls for modelling malicious agents, their anti-goals and their capabilities. A threat model and its associated countermeasures can be elaborated systematically, like a goal refinement model, starting from negations of security goals and ending up when fine-grained anti-goals are reached that are realizable by attackers in view of their assumed capabilities.

- Any RE process is faced with alternative options among which to decide. In a goal-oriented modelling framework, alternative options refer to goal refinements, conflict resolutions, obstacle resolutions, threat resolutions and responsibility assignments. Different alternatives contribute to different degrees of satisfaction of the soft goals identified in the goal model. To select the best options, we can use qualitative or quantitative approaches. On the qualitative side, we can compare options against high-level soft goals in the model by assessing their contribution to each leaf soft goal through qualitative labels; such labels are propagated bottom up along refinement and conflict links in the goal graph until the top-level soft goals are reached.

- For quantitative reasoning, we may replace such labels by numerical scores. The technique of weighted matrices in Section 3.3 can be adapted to determine the total score of each option as a weighted summation of its scores with respect to each leaf soft goal in the model. For non-subjective conclusions, the option scores should be grounded on measurable system phenomena. Gauge variables can be identified from leaf soft goals to provide measures for comparing options; they propagate additively along the AND-trees refining alternative options in the model.

- A goal-oriented model allows us to produce the requirements document semi-automatically. The textual structure of this document is first generated from the structure of the goal model according to required documentation standards. This structure is then populated with the annotations of all model elements at an appropriate place. In particular, the glossary of terms is generated from the object model; the section on user requirements is produced by a pre-order traversal of the goal model from top to bottom; the section on assumptions and dependencies is generated from the expectations on environment agents and the unresolved obstacles. The resulting text is expandable by 'drag-and-drop' of model diagram portions and any other item with which the model is hyperlinked.

- The model underlying such a requirements document can be used in the later stages of software development. We can derive the software data architecture from the object model and an abstract dataflow architecture from the agent and operation models. This architecture can be refined through architectural styles that match the architectural requirements found in the goal model. The components and connectors in this architecture can then be refined by the use of architectural refinement patterns meeting the quality and development requirements in the model.

Notes and Further Reading

Some notes on requirements databases and the use of queries for structural checks are provided at the end of Chapter 5.

Analogies are generally seen as source–target mappings that preserve relations holding in the source analog (Gentner, 1988; Falkenhaimer *et al.*, 1989). The corresponding sources and targets do not necessarily have to be 'similar'; they are placed into correspondence according to the role they play in the relational structure. The intuition is that analogies are more about relations than about individual features. This principle was applied for analogical reuse of requirements in Maiden and Sutcliffe (1993), Massonet and van Lamsweerde (1997) and Sutcliffe and Maiden (1998). A heuristic search algorithm for the query satisfaction process outlined in this chapter is provided in Massonet and van Lamsweerde (1997). The principle of specializing assertions, not merely objects, was found in the RML requirements modelling language (Greenspan *et al.*, 1986).

Nuseibeh (1996) discusses useful principles on conflict management. Robinson *et al.* (2003) have done a broad literature survey on this important topic. A more technical treatment of the approach in this chapter will be found in van Lamsweerde *et al.* (1998).

The general principle of using heuristic rules for obstacle identification is somewhat similar in spirit to the use of HAZOP-like guidewords for eliciting hazards (Leveson, 1995) and, more generally, to the use of safety checklists (Jaffe *et al.*, 1991; Lutz, 1996; Sommerville & Sawyer, 1997). Mode confusion obstacles receive considerable attention in aviation systems as they were recognized to be responsible for a significant number of critical incidents (Butler *et al.*, 1998). Practical experience with the obstacle identification rules in this chapter is reported in Lutz *et al.* (2007).

Threat analysis with anti-goals was introduced in van Lamsweerde (2004a). It was applied in a large industrial project to model, analyse and explore countermeasures to on-board terrorist threats against civil aircraft. The goal model with derived countermeasures was used for elaborating the requirements for a threat detection/reaction system (Darimont & Lemoine, 2007).

Attack trees are a popular means for representing threats and interrelating them (Amoroso, 1994; Schneier, 2000). Such trees are built systematically here and anchored on a goal model; the countermeasures are integrated in the model too. The Most Powerful Attacker principle for cryptographic protocol analysis is discussed in Kemmerer *et al.* (1994).

Other modelling notations allow us to capture attacker features at RE time – notably, misuse cases that complement UML use cases (Alexander, 2003; Sindre & Opdahl, 2005). Anti-requirements as requirements for breaking existing requirements were introduced in Crook *et al.* (2002). A follow-up can be found in Haley *et al.* (2008), where a framework combining goals and problem frames is proposed for security requirements engineering. Goal-based approaches were also used for analysing internet privacy policies (Anton *et al.*, 2002). Liu and colleagues have extended the i^* agent-based RE framework in Yu (1993) to identify attackers inside the system, analyse vulnerabilities through agent dependency links and suggest counter-measures; vulnerabilities are propagated along agent dependency links (Liu *et al.*, 2003). As a follow-up to this work, the Secure Tropos methodology integrates other security-related notions such as ownership, delegation and trust among agents (Giorgini *et al.*, 2005; Mouratidis & Giorgini, 2007).

The importance of reasoning about alternatives at RE time is discussed in Mylopoulos *et al.* (2001). The qualitative technique in this chapter for evaluating alternatives is taken from Mylopoulos *et al.* (1992). The WinWin framework supports such qualitative reasoning as well (In *et al.*, 2001).

A more technical treatment of quantitative reasoning about alternative options will be found in Letier and van Lamsweerde (2004). Quality variables are used there instead of gauge variables. They are random variables with probability distribution functions. The analysis then is more accurate, but more heavyweight. Bayesian networks are another quantitative evaluation technique for making predictions about non-functional properties such as safety or reliability (Fenton & Neil, 2001).

Fairly little work has been reported since Parnas' seminal work on heuristics for identifying architectural components and dependencies among them (Parnas, 1979). In

Moriconi *et al.* (1995), a formal framework is proposed in which correctness-preserving transformations are applied to refine abstract architectures into concrete ones. Refinement patterns are also proposed there which are proved formally correct once for all and can be reused in matching situations. Bosch and Molin (1999) suggest an informal, iterative process for architecture elaboration based on successive evaluations and transformations of architectural drafts to meet non-functional concerns. In the other direction, Rapanotti *et al.* (2004) suggest how early architectural choices can facilitate problem analysis and decomposition in their problem frame approach. Gross and Yu (2001) discuss how the goal-oriented qualitative framework in Chung *et al.* (2000) can be used to document design patterns for selection during the architectural design process. A good compilation of architectural design patterns will be found in Buschmann *et al.* (1996). The USE relation in some of the refinement patterns in this chapter is discussed in Parnas (1979).

Exercises

- Outline a logical schema for a model database fitting the meta-model described in Chapter 14.

- Use your favourite database query language to formulate checks for the following structural consistency rules:

    a. (inter-view:) Every operation in the operation model must operationalize at least one leaf goal from the goal model.

    b. (inter-view:) If an agent performs an operation, it must be responsible for all the goals operationalized by this operation.

    c. (intra-view:) Every attribute must have an initialization (DomInit) in the object model.

    d. (intra-view:) Every state in a state machine must have an outgoing transition, except final states.

- Replay the analogical reuse process discussed in this chapter to acquire portions of a target model for a video rental management system by reuse of portions of a model for a library management system. The target system rents DVDs, video games and so on. While doing this, you should elaborate a counterpart of Figure 16.2. You may want to use model fragments for the library system shown in the previous chapters, and their generalization into model portions for a returnable resource management system (see Section 2.2.7 for some suggestions).

- Consider the library system. A stakeholder having the borrower's viewpoint might state that a borrower should keep a borrowed book as long as he or she needs it. A stakeholder having the staff's viewpoint might state that a borrower should return a borrowed book within two weeks, say. Use the regression technique in Section 16.2.1 to derive the boundary condition showing that the two following goals are divergent:

> *Maintain[CopyKeptAsLongAsNeeded]:* **if** copyOnLoan **then**
> **always** (**if** copyNeeded **then** copyOnLoan)
>
> *Achieve[CopyReturnedSoon]:* **if** copyOnLoan **then within-2-weeks** copyReturned
>
> (Dom) **if** copyOnLoan **then not** copyReturned
>
> (We know, of course, that **'not within-2-weeks** copyReturned' amounts to **'after-2-weeks not** copyReturned'.)

- Find the heuristic identification rule in Section 16.2.1 and corresponding boundary conditions that lead to the conclusion that the following goals are divergent:

  a. Achieve[PatientInformedOfOwnData] *vs* Avoid[CriticalPatientDataDisclosed] in a hospital management system.

  b. Increase[NumberOfAmbulancesAtStation] vs Decrease[OperationalCostsOf-Station] in an ambulance-dispatching system.

- Consider a system for delivering drugs to pharmacists. The drug provider's goal is to reduce delivery costs by reducing the number of deliveries. The pharmacist's goal is to improve drug availability to patients. Is there any heuristic rule in Section 16.2.1 that might help identify a divergence among these two goals? If so, what would a boundary condition look like, and what resolution strategies among those reviewed in Section 3.1.3 seem appropriate?

- Consider the safety-critical obstacles shown in Figure 9.4 for the train control system. Classify them in terms of the heuristic classifications in Section 16.2.2. Is there any other obstacle we might consider using those heuristic rules that is not shown in Figure 9.4?

- Use the heuristic rules in Section 16.2.2 to identify other meeting scheduling obstacles in addition to those shown in Figure 9.8.

- Build a goal model for your favourite e-shopping system. The milestone-driven refinement pattern in Chapter 8 should help you significantly in this task (see Figure 8.19). Your model should in particular include the functional goal *Achieve* [ItemSent If Item-Paid]. Using the heuristic of checking the converse of *Achieve* goals – see (H9) in Section 8.8.2 – you should also include in your model the security goal:

> *Avoid* [ItemSent **And Not** ItemPaid].

Elaborate a threat model showing possible attacks in a vulnerable system. The vulnerabilities should appear as leaf anti-goals or domain hypotheses in your model.

- Elaborate a threat model and security countermeasures for the e-purse system described in the second exercise at the end of Chapter 15.

- Elaborate a simple goal model, a threat model and security countermeasures for the following e-signature system.

   An electronic signature system enables people to sign documents electronically. Signers sign documents to show their agreement. Recipients need this agreement to act on the document. The signature system includes an ID smartcard (called an e-ID), an interface between the e-ID and the signer (called a sign box) and a PC to which the sign box is connected. The PC has an e-ID reader and a keypad where the signer can dial his or her pin code for signature.

- Table 16.2 shows the upward propagation of qualitative labels for the option *ConstraintsAcquiredByE-mail* in Table 16.1. Replay this propagation for the second option in Table 16.1; namely, *ConstraintsAcquiredFrom-eAgenda*.

- Consider an ambulance-dispatching system with the following soft goal refinements. Two options are being envisaged for this system. In *option A*, the functional goal of getting every ambulance call processed effectively is refined into sub-goals prescribing on-screen call taking and recording of incident details, with an e-map facility for locating incidents accurately. In *option B*, the same goal is refined into sub-goals prescribing paper-based call taking and recording of incident details, with manual incident localization on a map. The qualitative contribution of each option to the leaf soft goals is estimated in the table below.

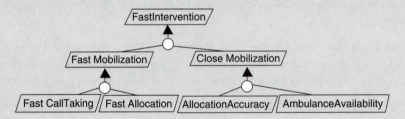

   a. Apply the qualitative technique in Section 16.3.1 to evaluate these two options against each other.

   b. Apply the quantitative technique in Section 16.3.2 to evaluate these two options against each other.

   c. Extend your analysis by introducing cost concerns in the soft goal graph.

   d. Explain which technique seems preferable in this case.

| | Alternative options | |
Leaf soft goals	Option A	Option B
Fast Call Taking	−	+
Fast Allocation	+	−
Allocation Accuracy	+	−
Ambulance Availability	+	−

- Apply the approach in Section 16.5 to derive a preliminary architecture for the library management system.

17

Formal Specification of System Models

In spite of their benefits and wide applicability, the model analysis and derivation techniques in the previous chapters are limited in depth. For example, the heuristic rules and patterns for goal refinement, obstacle identification or conflict detection refer to structured formulations in terms of keywords such as *'if-then'*, *'always'* or *'sooner-or-later'*. The goals, domain properties and pre-, trigger and post-conditions remain informally specified in natural language. We cannot automate any derivation or check on informal statements, or synthesize executable versions from them for model animation. Such statements tend to be imprecise. For example, when we say 'sooner or later', do we mean immediately next, or within some strict deadline or some time later on in the future? We often have seen structured formulations of form *'if* C *then* T'; are C and T meant to be evaluated exactly in the same state or in different states and, if so, which ones?

As discussed in Section 4.4.7, formal methods are harder to use and less widely applicable; but they provide much higher precision and richer forms of analysis and derivation supported by tools. The two last chapters are dedicated to formal methods for model-based RE.

Such methods require critical model items to be specified in a formal, machine-processable language. This chapter expands on the material introduced in Section 4.4 to present a formal specification language in which we can rigorously specify the goals, domain properties and operations in our models. This language will enable the use of the formal techniques presented in the next chapter for goal refinement, goal operationalization, conflict management, obstacle analysis, threat analysis and model synthesis for animation and model checking.

The overall approach to model analysis is a 'two-button' one though. The formal analysis button is pressed only when and where needed to formalize and analyse critical goals, domain properties, obstacles, threats or operations. The button pressed by default is the semi-formal one, where the model building and analysis techniques from the previous chapters are used.

Section 17.1 further details how the real-time temporal logic introduced in Section 4.4.2 fulfils our needs for formal RE. We will then see how this logic can be used for specifying goals and their patterns (Section 17.2), domain properties in the object model (Section 17.3) and the domain and required conditions on operations in the operation model (Section 17.4).

17.1 A real-time temporal logic for specifying model annotations

Linear Temporal Logic (LTL) was introduced in Section 4.4.2 as a formal language for specifying admissible system histories in a declarative way, without the need to make time explicit. This formalism is defined over discrete time points and linear histories (unlike the branching histories captured by the branching temporal logics briefly introduced there too).

LTL closely fits our *Achieve–Maintain* goal patterns. Moreover, what LTL assertions convey fits the semantic picture of our models discussed in Section 12.4 (see Figure 12.5).

An LTL-based language therefore seems adequate to our needs but for one thing. As goals often prescribe real-time constraints on system behaviour, we need a sufficiently expressive temporal logic. To see what such a logic looks like and how it fits our modelling framework, we first need to understand what state assertions refer to (Section 17.1.1). We will then review the temporal operators available for referring to future and past states (Section 17.1.2), before turning our attention to various types of real-time constructs (Section 17.1.3).

17.1.1 State assertions

A *state assertion* is a predicate intended to express that some descriptive or prescriptive property holds in some arbitrarily chosen *current* state. For example, we may assert that the goal of maintaining a worst-case stopping distance between two trains following each other is satisfied in the current state:

> Following (tr2, tr1) → Dist (tr2, tr1) > WCS-Dist (tr2)

This state assertion refers to variables *tr1* and *tr2*. In our context, the *variables* designate arbitrary instances of entities, agents or events declared in the goal model. They correspond to the *instance variables* discussed in Section 10.1.2. In this example, the variables *tr1* and *tr2* designate arbitrary instances of the *Train* entity. These formal variables should not be confused with the state variables used in Chapters 8–16; *a state variable* corresponds to an attribute or association of the corresponding formal variable.

The variables in a state assertion are generally typed; their *sort* is the corresponding entity, agent or event. The *value* of a variable is a tuple of values for the attributes and associations of the object instance that the variable designates. This value is changing over time. A *state* of a variable x is defined as a functional pair (x, v) where v denotes some value for that variable.

The language for expressing state assertions is a first-order sorted language. This means that we can write assertions on typed variables that are universally or existentially quantified, for example:

> ∀ tr1, tr2 : *Train*
> Following (tr2, tr1) → Dist (tr2, tr1) > WCS-Dist (tr2)

A state assertion is built recursively from atomic *predicate symbols* such as 'Following' and '>', applied to terms such as 'tr2', 'Dist (tr2, tr1)' or 'WCS-Dist (tr2)', linked by logical connectives and quantified over typed variables.

- The *atomic predicates* may capture relational operators, such as '>', or associations from the object model, such as 'Following' – see the predicate notation for associations in Section 10.3 and Figure 10.12 for an object model where this reflexive association is declared.

- The *terms* are built from constants, variables and function symbols applied to terms. The function symbols may capture mathematical functions (e.g. arithmetical operators), or attributes declared in the object model, such as the 'WCS-Dist' attribute of the entity 'Train' or the 'Dist' attribute of the association 'Following' (see Figure 10.12).

- The logical connectives are the propositional operators ∧ ('and'), ∨ ('or'), ¬ ('not'), → ('implies') and ↔ ('equivalent to').

- The quantifiers are ∀ ('for all') and ∃ ('there exists').

17.1.2 Temporal assertions

The descriptive or prescriptive properties that we may want to specify do not refer to the current state only. When we characterize admissible system histories in a declarative way, we need to refer to future and/or past states. State assertions therefore need to be prefixed by temporal operators indicating which states they refer to.

A *temporal assertion* is built recursively from state assertions, temporal operators, logical connectives and quantifiers. For example, we obviously want the preceding state assertion *always* to hold in any future state:

∀ tr1, tr2 : *Train*
☐ (Following (tr2, tr1) → Dist (tr2, tr1) > WCS-Dist (tr2))

As we saw in Section 4.4.2, temporal assertions are interpreted over system histories. In LTL logics, time is isomorphic to the set *Nat* of natural numbers; a history *H* is a function:

H: Nat → State(X)

where *X* is the set of system variables and *State(X)* is the set of all possible states for the corresponding variables in *X*. The notation

(H, i) ⊨ P

means that the temporal assertion *P* is *satisfied* by history *H* at time position *i*. The assertion *P* is satisfied by the entire history *H* if it is satisfied at the initial time position *0*:

(H, *0*) ⊨ P.

Section 4.4.2 introduced a few temporal operators for LTL. Here is a more complete list.

Future operators

$\diamond$ P ('sooner or later'), with semantics: (H, i) $\models \diamond$ P   **iff**   for some j $\geq$ i: (H, j) $\models$ P

$\square$ P ('always'), with semantics: (H, i) $\models \square$ P   **iff**   for every j $\geq$ i: (H, j) $\models$ P

P $\mathcal{U}$ Q ('always until'), with semantics: (H, i) $\models$ P $\mathcal{U}$ Q   **iff**   there exists a j $\geq$ i such that (H, j) $\models$ Q

and for every k, i $\leq$ k $<$ j: (H, k) $\models$ P

P $\mathcal{W}$ Q ('always unless'), with semantics: (H, i) $\models$ P $\mathcal{W}$ Q   **iff**   (H, i) $\models$ P $\mathcal{U}$ Q or (H, i) $\models \square$ P

o P ('next'), with semantics: (H, i) $\models$ o P   **iff**   (H, i+1) $\models$ P

P $\Rightarrow$ Q ('entails'), equivalent to: $\square$ (P $\rightarrow$ Q)

P $\Leftrightarrow$ Q ('congruent'), equivalent to: $\square$ (P $\leftrightarrow$ Q)

There is thus an implicit outer $\square$ operator in every entailment. Note that $\square$ P amounts to P$\mathcal{W}$ **false**. It may also be worth noticing that the '$\square$' and '$\diamond$' operators correspond to universal and existential quantification over time, respectively. Similar duality principles thus apply, for example,

$$\neg \square P \Leftrightarrow \diamond \neg P, \quad \neg \diamond P \Leftrightarrow \square \neg P$$

Past operators

$\blacklozenge$ P ('some time in the past'), with semantics: (H, i) $\models \blacklozenge$ P   **iff**   for some j $\leq$ i: (H, j) $\models$ P

$\blacksquare$ P ('has always been'), with semantics: (H, i) $\models \blacksquare$ P   **iff**   for every j $\leq$ i: (H, j) $\models$ P

P $\mathcal{S}$ Q ('always in the past *since*'), with semantics: (H, i) $\models$ P $\mathcal{S}$ Q   **iff**   there exists a j $\leq$ i such that (H, j) $\models$ Q

and for every k, j $<$ k $\leq$ i: (H, k) $\models$ P

P $\mathcal{B}$ Q ('always in the past *back to*'), with semantics: (H, i) $\models$ P $\mathcal{B}$ Q   **iff**   (H, i) $\models$ P $\mathcal{S}$ Q or (H, i) $\models \blacksquare$ P

$\bullet$ P ('previous'), with semantics: (H, i) $\models \bullet$ P   **iff**   (H, i $-$ 1) $\models$ P with i $>$ 0

@ P, equivalent to: ($\bullet \neg$ P) $\wedge$ P

It is sometimes convenient to evaluate terms in the previous state or in the next state – notably for specifying the post-conditions of an operation. The *previous* and *next* operators are therefore defined on terms as well. If F denotes a term and $\text{VAL}_{H,i}(F)$ denotes the value of term F at time position i along history H, we have:

$$\text{VAL}_{H, i} (\bullet F) = \text{VAL}_{H, i-1} (F) \quad \text{for } i > 0, \quad \text{VAL}_{H, i} (oF) = \text{VAL}_{H, i+1} (F)$$

17.1.3 Real-time temporal constructs

Goals often prescribe real-time constraints on system behaviour, for example:

Acceleration commands shall be sent to a train every two seconds.

Bounded versions for the preceding temporal operators are therefore necessary. The time bounds can be *relative* to the current state, *absolute* time bounds or *variable-dependent* time bounds.

Relative time bounds

Such time bounds refer to some time distance from the current state. The preceding statement is an example; in any current state where no acceleration command is sent to a train, one must be sent to this train within two seconds – from that state. We therefore need to introduce a *temporal distance* function between states:

$dist: Nat \times Nat \to D$ where $D = \{d \mid$ there exists a natural n such that $d = n \times u\}$
$dist(i, j) = \mid j - i \mid \times u$

In this definition, u denotes a chosen time unit. Multiple units can be used, for example microsecond, second, day, week; they are implicitly converted into the *smallest time unit*.

The 'o' and '•' operators then refer to the *nearest* subsequent and preceding time positions according to this smallest time unit, respectively. This time unit may be chosen to be arbitrarily small. Intuitively, these operators mean '*immediately after*' and '*immediately before*', respectively.

The preceding temporal operators are extended to capture relative time bounds. Here are the most frequently used *relative* real-time operators:

$\diamond_{\leq d} P$ ('some time in the future within deadline d'),
   with semantics: $(H, i) \models \diamond_{\leq d} P$ **iff**   for some $j \geq i$ with $dist(i, j) \leq d$: $(H, j) \models P$

$\square_{\leq d} P$ ('always in the future up to deadline d'),
   with semantics: $(H, i) \models \square_{\leq d} P$ **iff**   for every $j \geq i$ such that $dist(i, j) \leq d$: $(H, j) \models P$

$P \, \mathcal{U}_{\leq d} \, Q$ ('always until at least'),
   with semantics: $(H, i) \models P \, \mathcal{U}_{\leq d} \, Q$ **iff**   for some $j \geq i$ with $dist(i, j) \leq d$: $(H, j) \models Q$
                                                   and for every $k, i \leq k < j$: $(H, k) \models P$

$P \, \mathcal{W}_{\leq d} \, Q$ ('always unless at least'),
   with semantics: $(H, i) \models P \, \mathcal{W}_{\leq d} \, Q$ **iff** $(H, i) \models P \, \mathcal{U}_{\leq d} \, Q \, or \, (H, i) \models \square_{\leq d} P$

$\blacklozenge_{\leq d} P$ ('some time in the past up to'),
   with semantics: $(H, i) \models \blacklozenge_{\leq d} P$ **iff**   for some $j \leq i$ with $dist(i, j) \leq d$: $(H, j) \models P$

$\blacksquare_{\leq d} P$ ('has always been up to'),
   with semantics: $(H, i) \models \blacksquare_{\leq d} P$ **iff**   for every $j \leq i$ with $dist(i, j) \leq d$: $(H, j) \models P$

$P \, \mathcal{S}_{\leq d} \, Q$ ('always since at least'),
   with semantics: $(H, i) \models P \, \mathcal{S}_{\leq d} \, Q$ **iff**   there exists a $j \leq i$ such that $(H, j) \models Q$
                                                   and for every $k, j < k \leq i$: $(H, k) \models P$

$P \, \mathcal{B}_{\leq d} \, Q$ ('always *back to* at least'),
   with semantics: $(H, i) \models P \, \mathcal{B}_{\leq d} \, Q$ **iff** $(H, i) \models P \, \mathcal{S}_{\leq d} \, Q \, or \, (H, i) \models \blacksquare_{\leq d} P$

Absolute time bounds

Such time bounds refer to an absolute system time. For example, a library system goal might prescribe that 'every borrowed book copy shall be returned by the end of the year for inventory'.

We therefore need to introduce a clock function that assigns to every time point its actual time:

clock: Nat→Time
clock (i) = clock (0) + dist (0, i)

The absolute real-time operators are then defined accordingly, for example:

$\diamond_{\leq ct}$ P ('some time in the future before clock time *ct*'),
  with semantics: (H, i) $\models \diamond_{\leq ct}$ P **iff** for some j $\geq$ i with clock (j) $\leq ct$: (H, j) $\models$ P
$\square_{\leq ct}$ P ('always in the future before clock time *ct*'),
  with semantics: (H, i) $\models \square_{\leq ct}$ P **iff** for every j $\geq$ i such that clock (j) $\leq ct$: (H, j) $\models$ P

We may occasionally need to refer to the time of the current state in some assertions; in such cases the notation '*now*' is generally used instead of 'clock (i)'.

Variable-dependent time bounds

Such time bounds refer to one or more state variable declared in the object model; that is, an attribute or association whose value may be changing over time. For example, there might be a goal in the meeting scheduling system prescribing that 'the meeting date and location shall be notified to invited participants at least three weeks before the meeting takes place'. Here, the deadline for notification depends, for a meeting *m*, on the state variable *m.Date*. Such real-time constraints where time bounds are not constants are fairly frequent in practice.

To support them, we need to introduce time distances and clocks whose values may refer to state variables. The former are used for variable-dependent *relative* time bounds whereas the latter are used for variable-dependent *absolute* time bounds.

The variable-dependent real-time operators are then defined accordingly, for example:

$\diamond_{\leq d(sv)}$P with semantics: (H, i) $\models \diamond_{\leq d(sv)}$ P **iff** for some j $\geq$ i: (H, j) $\models$ P
  and for every k, i $\leq$ k $\leq$ j: clock (k) – clock (i) $\leq$ VAL$_{H, k}$ (d(sv)),
$\diamond_{\leq ct(sv)}$P with semantics: (H, i) $\models \diamond_{\leq ct(sv)}$ P **iff** for some j $\geq$ i: (H, j) $\models$ P
  and for every k, i $\leq$ k $\leq$ j: clock (k) $\leq$ VAL$_{H, k}$ (ct(sv)),

where *sv* denotes a state variable and VAL$_{H, k}$ (d(sv)) and VAL$_{H, k}$ (ct(sv)) denote the value of the variable-dependent deadline d(sv) and clock time ct(sv) at time position *k* along history *H*, respectively.

17.2 Specifying goals in the goal model

The real-time LTL in the previous section is used for formalizing the definition of behavioural goals. In addition to **Def** annotations stating such definitions informally, we may provide a formal counterpart as **FormalSpec** annotation of critical goals that call for formal analysis. Soft goals by definition cannot be formalized as they cannot be satisfied in a clear-cut sense.

For example, the formal specification of the goal *Maintain* [WorstCaseStoppingDistance] at the beginning of Section 17.1.2 annotates this goal in Figure 8.1. The preceding informal definition of the goal about acceleration commands to be sent on time to trains might be specified as follows, to annotate the goal formally in the goal model:

Goal *Achieve* [AccelerationCommandSentInTimeToTrain]
   FormalSpec ∀ tr: TrainInfo
      ¬ (∃ cm: CommandMessage) (cm.Sent ∧ cm.TrainID = tr.ID)
         ⇒ ◇$_{\leq 2s}$ (∃ cm: CommandMessage) (cm.Sent ∧ cm.TrainID = tr.ID)

In this specification, TrainID and ID are attributes of the CommandMessage and Train entities, respectively. The 's' symbol subscripting the '◇' temporal operator denotes the 'second' unit (as the required relative time bound here is two seconds). Remember that the ' ⇒' symbol hides a □ operator; 'P ⇒ Q' is the same as '□ (P → Q)'. In the preceding goal formalization, the implication indeed has to hold in every future state.

Goal specification patterns

Consider the *Achieve* and *Maintain* specification patterns for behavioural goals introduced in Section 7.3.1 and used throughout Part II of the book. These patterns can now be made fully precise together with their variants.

Achieve [TargetCondition]:

CurrentCondition ⇒ ◇ TargetCondition	(Unbounded *Achieve*)
CurrentCondition ⇒ ◇$_{\leq x}$ TargetCondition	(Bounded *Achieve*)
CurrentCondition ⇒ o TargetCondition	(Immediate *Achieve*)

Cease [TargetCondition]:

CurrentCondition ⇒ ◇ ¬ TargetCondition	(Unbounded *Cease*)
CurrentCondition ⇒ ◇$_{\leq x}$ ¬ TargetCondition	(Bounded *Cease*)
CurrentCondition ⇒ o ¬ TargetCondition	(Immediate *Cease*)

Maintain [GoodCondition]:

CurrentCondition ⇒ GoodCondition	(Permanent *Maintain*)
CurrentCondition ⇒ □ GoodCondition	('After' *Maintain*)
CurrentCondition ⇒ GoodCondition $\mathcal{W}$ NewCondition	('Between' *Maintain*)
GoodCondition ⇒ • PreCondition	('Transition' *Maintain*)
□$_{\leq x}$ (CurrentCondition → GoodCondition)	(Temporary *Maintain*)
CurrentCondition ⇒ □$_{\leq x}$ GoodCondition	(Temporary 'After' *Maintain*)
CurrentCondition ⇒ GoodCondition $\mathcal{W}_{\leq x}$ NewCondition	(Temporary 'Between' *Maintain*)

Avoid [BadCondition]

CurrentCondition ⇒ ¬ BadCondition	(Permanent *Avoid*)
CurrentCondition ⇒ □ ¬ BadCondition	('After' *Avoid*)
CurrentCondition ⇒ ¬ BadCondition $\mathcal{W}$ NewCondition	('Between' *Avoid*)
¬ BadCondition ⇒ • PreCondition	('Transition' *Avoid*)
□$_{\leq x}$ (CurrentCondition → ¬ BadCondition)	(Temporary *Avoid*)
CurrentCondition ⇒ □$_{\leq x}$ ¬ BadCondition	(Temporary 'After' *Avoid*)
CurrentCondition ⇒ ¬ BadCondition $\mathcal{W}_{\leq x}$ NewCondition	(Temporary 'Between' *Avoid*)

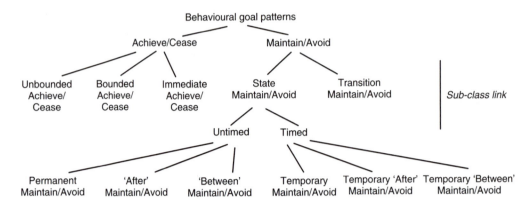

Figure 17.1 *A taxonomy of formal specification patterns for behavioural goals*

Figure 17.1 summarizes those various patterns in a pattern taxonomy for easier retrieval. Note the redundancy between *Achieve* and *Cease* patterns and between the *Maintain* and *Avoid* patterns; they are similar up to negation. Distinguishing among them proves convenient in practice, however, as each of them is matching frequent patterns of informal statements made by stakeholders. Patterns thereby enable non-expert specifiers to use elementary temporal logic without even knowing it.

Specifying requirements and expectations

The realizability of leaf goals in the goal model constrains the particular form that specifications of requirements and expectations may take. As discussed in Section 11.2.3, the agent responsible for a leaf goal must be able to monitor the variables to be evaluated in the goal specification, and to control the variables constrained for goal satisfaction. Moreover, there may be no variable in the goal specification to be evaluated in a future state, and the TargetCondition may not be indefinitely postponable to future states – in other words, the goal specification may not have the *Unbounded Achieve* pattern.

In particular, when we instantiate a pattern to specify a requirement or an expectation:

- No CurrentCondition on the left-hand side may contain a '$\Diamond$' operator.

- No Condition on the right-hand side may contain a '$\Diamond$' operator with no time-bound subscript.

Specification examples

Here is a representative sample of goal specifications for functional and non-functional goals that were informally specified in the previous chapters.

Goal *Maintain* [PumpOn**If**HighWater**AndNot**HighMethane]
   Def *Whenever the water level in a sump is too high and the methane level is below its critical threshold, the corresponding pump must be on.*

FormalSpec ∀ m: Mine, s: Sump, p: Pump

Located (s, m) ∧ Regulating (p, s) ∧ s.WaterLevel ≥ 'high' ∧ ¬ m.MethaneLevel ≥ 'critical'

⇒ p.Motor = 'on'

%% See the object model in Fig. 15.8 where the attributes and associations yielding terms and predicates are declared. %%

Goal *Maintain* [AccurateWaterMeasure]

Def *The water level measure monitored by a pump controller must accurately reflect the physical water level in the sump.*

FormalSpec ∀ s: Sump, p: Pump, pctrl: PumpController

CtrlPump (pctrl, p) ∧ Regulating (p, s) ⇒ pctrl.WaterLevelMeasure = s.WaterLevel

Goal *Achieve* [MineEvacuatedIfCriticalWater]

Def *If the water level in the sump remains above the high threshold for more than X minutes, the mine should be evacuated within one hour.*

FormalSpec ∀ m: Mine, s: Sump

Located (s, m) ∧ $\blacksquare_{\leq Xm}$ s.WaterLevel ≥ 'high' ⇒ $\diamondsuit_{\leq 1h}$ ¬ (∃ mr: Miner) Inside (mr, m)

Goal *Maintain* [DoorsClosedWhileNonZeroSpeed]

Def *The state of train doors shall always be 'closed' while the train's measured speed is non-null.*

FormalSpec ∀ tr: Train

tr.MeasuredSpeed ≠ 0 ⇒ tr. DoorsState = 'closed'

Goal *Achieve* [FastJourney]

Def *A train on some block shall be on the next block within X minutes.*

FormalSpec ∀ tr: Train, bl: Block

On (tr, bl) ⇒ $\diamondsuit_{\leq Xm}$ On (tr, next(bl))

Goal *Achieve* [ParticipantsInformedOfScheduledMeetingOnTime]

Def *Intended participants shall be notified of the meeting date at least three weeks before the meeting takes place.*

FormalSpec ∀ p: Participant, m: Meeting

Scheduled (m) ∧ Invitation (p, m) ∧ ¬ Notified (p, m) ⇒ $\diamondsuit_{\leq m.Date-3w}$ Notified (p, m)

Specifying obstacles and anti-goals

Formal analysis of obstacles and anti-goals requires their formalization as well. To specify them, we may use the same logic and similar specification patterns wherever applicable. While goal specifications are generally universally quantified and prefixed by an outer '□' operator, their negating obstacles and anti-goals are existentially quantified and prefixed by an outer '◇' operator. Here are some examples from previous chapters:

Obstacle DriverUnresponsive

FormalSpec ◇∃ dr: Driver, tr: Train, cd: Command

Drives (dr, tr) ∧ ¬ Reacts (dr, cd)

AntiGoal Achieve [ItemReceivedWithoutHavingBeenPaid]

FormalSpec ◇∃ b: Buyer, s: Seller, it: Item

Selling (s, it) ∧ ItemSent (it, b) ∧ ¬ ♦ ItemPaid (it, b)

17.3 Specifying descriptive properties in the object model

As we saw in Sections 7.2 and 10.1.5, descriptive properties of the system include *domain properties, hypotheses* and *initializations*. Descriptive properties may be given a name and are informally stated in the object model as annotations attached to the conceptual objects to which they refer. As shown in Figure 10.2, these annotations can be specified informally or formally. Our real-time temporal logic is used for their formal specification.

Initializations

The specification of an **Init** annotation reduces to a state assertion on the object's attributes. This assertion holds in a single state – the one where the corresponding object instance appears in the system (that is, the state where the built-in predicate *InstanceOf(o,Ob)* becomes true for this instance; see Section 10.1.2). Temporal operators therefore make no sense there. For our train system, for example, we may write descriptive properties that hold initially for any train instance entering the system, such as:

Init   ($\forall$ tr: Train) (tr.Speed = 0 $\wedge$ tr.Acceleration = 0 $\wedge$ tr.DoorsState = 'closed')

Domain properties and hypotheses

The specifications of **DomInvar** and **DomHyp** annotations have no such restrictions. We can in principle use any temporal construct we need, including real-time ones. However, the formal specification of domain properties or hypotheses should not constrain future states as such properties are not prescriptive.

In practice, there are a few recurring kinds of descriptive properties that are worth pointing out:

- Some domain properties refer to *laws* on environment phenomena, such as physical laws or organizational rules, that are generally stated as invariant properties holding in any current state. They typically take the general form:

    Condition1 $\Rightarrow$ Condition2,   Condition1 $\Leftrightarrow$ Condition2

    Examples:

MovingIffNonZeroSpeed:	($\forall$ tr: Train) (Moving (tr) $\Leftrightarrow$ tr.Speed $\neq$ 0)
NonZeroSpeedIfNonZeroAcceler:	($\forall$ tr: Train) (tr.Acceleration $\neq$ 0 $\Rightarrow$ tr.Speed $\neq$ 0)
ClosedIfNotOpen:	($\forall$ tr: Train) (tr.DoorsState $\neq$ 'open' $\Rightarrow$ tr.DoorsState = 'closed')
ScheduledIffTiming&LocationSet	$\forall$ m: Meeting
	Scheduled (m) $\Leftrightarrow$ ($\exists$ d: Dt, l: Loc) (m.Date = d $\wedge$ m.Location = l)
UnborrowableIfBorrowed	$\forall$ bc: BookCopy
	Borrowable (bc) $\Rightarrow$ $\neg$ ($\exists$ p: Patron) Loan (p, bc)

- Other domain properties refer to *causal links* among environment phenomena. They typically take the general form:

    Condition1 $\Rightarrow$ $\blacklozenge$ Condition2

Examples:

OnBlock**OnlyIf**FromPrevious	∀ tr: Train, bl: Block
	On (tr, bl) ⇒ ♦ On (tr, previous(bl))
Using**OnlyIf**Requested**And**Available	∀ r: Resource, u: User
	Using (u, r) ⇒ ♦ (Requesting (u, r) ∧ Available (r))
Scheduled**OnlyIf**Requested	∀ m: Meeting
	Scheduled (m) ⇒ ♦ (∃ in: Initiator) Requesting (in, m)

- Some hypotheses refer to the *stability of associations* declared in the object model. If an association links participating object instances, these instances remain linked for some time.

Examples:

KeepsRequesting**Unless**Using	∀ r: Resource, u: User
	Requesting (u, r) ⇒ Requesting (u, r) $\mathcal{W}$ Using (u, r)
DatesRemainConvenient	∀ m: Meeting, p: Participant
	Convenient (m, p) ⇒ □ Convenient (m, p)

As we will see in the next chapter, the formalization of domain properties and hypotheses may be required for formal goal refinement, obstacle analysis and threat analysis. In particular, we need to formally regress obstacle specifications through domain properties to generate sub-obstacles, and sometimes break hypotheses or questionable domain properties. Wrong hypotheses might have severe consequences; see the A320 braking logic example in Figure 9.9. As another example, the model for the Mine Safety Control system in Chapter 15 relies on the following hypothesis that should deserve careful attention:

DomHyp SumpHasPump
    Def A mine sump has always a pump regulating it and a pump controller controlling it.
    FormalSpec ∀ m: Mine, s: Sump
        Located (s, m) ⇒ □ (∃ p: Pump, pctrl: PumpController)
            Regulating (p, s) ∧ CtrlPump (pctrl, p)

Definitions

As introduced in Section 1.1.4, definitions are another type of assertion that may be introduced in formal specifications as well. Unlike other assertions, they have no truth value; they just introduce auxiliary concepts for reuse throughout the specification, for example:

    Definition BookAvailable (b, lib) $=_{\text{def}}$ (∃ bc: BookCopy) (Copy (bc, b) ∧ Borrowable (bc))

This definition allows us to reuse the predicate on its left-hand side in multiple places without need for writing the longer expression on its right-hand side. This mechanism can make specifications substantially shorter and more understandable. Definitions are attached as annotations to the concept in the object model of which they are an auxiliary – in this example, the Book entity.

17.4 Specifying operationalizations in the operation model

The domain and required conditions for critical operations in the operation model are specified in our temporal logic under a restricted form.

As a preliminary observation, we know that operations do operationalize *realizable* leaf goals only. Their domain and required conditions therefore make no reference to future states – in other words, their specification contains no $\diamond$ operator. An applicability condition depending on subsequent states or an effect condition characterized in terms of subsequent states would indeed make no sense.

Domain pre- and post-conditions

Domain conditions by definition refer to a single state. A domain pre-condition characterizes the *input state* when the corresponding operation is applied (regardless of any restriction required for goal satisfaction); the resulting domain post-condition characterizes the *output state* when the operation has been applied. The formal specification of domain conditions therefore takes the form of *state assertions* on the corresponding state:

- The DomPre condition of an operation holds in the operation's initial state and refers to the instance variables declared in its Input list.

- The DomPost condition of an operation holds in the operation's final state and refers to the instance variables declared in its Output list.

These variables are left unquantified as they are declared in the operation's signature.

Required pre- and trigger conditions

The required pre- and trigger conditions of an operation refer to its input state; they may also refer to preceding states:

- In case of a ReqPre condition, the necessary condition for goal satisfaction may prescribe some prerequisite to have been established previously.

- A ReqTrig condition often captures the obligation of applying the operation because of some accumulation of previous events (see examples below).

Required post-conditions

The required post-conditions of an operation refer to its output state; they may also refer to the operation's input state; that is, the state just before this output state. (Remember that operations are atomic; see Section 12.1.) In particular, such conditions often refer to a variable taken in the input state where the operation was applied, or relate the states of the same variable before and after application of the operation. In such situations, we use the terms $\bullet x$ and x to make a distinction between the variable in the input state and in the output state of the operation, respectively (see Section 17.1.2).

Specification examples

Here is a representative sample of specifications of operations that were informally specified in the previous chapters:

Operation OpenDoors

    Input tr: Train; **Output** tr: Train/DoorsState

    DomPre tr. DoorsState = 'closed'; **DomPost** tr. DoorsState = 'open'

    ReqPre for *DoorsClosedWhileNonZeroSpeed*: tr.MeasuredSpeed = 0

    ReqPre for *SafeEntry&Exit*: (∃ pl: Platform) At (tr, pl)　%% The train is at some platform. %%

    ReqTrig For *FastEntry&Exit*: @ (tr.MeasuredSpeed = 0) ∧ (∃ pl: Platform) At (tr, pl)

                               %% The train has just stopped at some platform. %%

Operation SendAccelerationCommand

    Input tr1, tr2: TrainInfo;

    Output cm: CommandMessage;

    DomPre ¬ cm.Sent; **DomPost** cm.Sent ∧ cm.TrainID = tr1.ID;

    ReqTrig for *AccelerationCommandSentInTimeToTrain*:

        ■$_{\leq 2s}$ ¬ (∃ cm': CommandMessage) (cm'.Sent ∧ cm'.TrainID = tr1.ID)

               %% No acceleration command has been sent to this train in the last two seconds. %%

    ReqPost for *SafeAccelerationCommanded*:

        • FollowingInfo (tr1, tr2) → cm.Acceleration ≤ F (tr1, tr2)

                        ∧ cm.Speed ≤ G (tr1, tr2) ∧ cm.Speed >tr1.Speed + 7

    %% The acceleration and speed commanded to this train are bounded by domain-specific functions on information about this train and about the train *tr2* known to precede it. %%

Operation SwitchPumpOn

    Input p: Pump, hWS: highWaterSensor, lWs: lowWaterSensor, hMs: highMethaneSensor;

    Output p: Pump/Switch;

    DomPre p.Switch = 'off'; **DomPost** p.Switch = 'on';

    ReqPre for *PumpSwitchOffIfHighMethaneDetected*: ¬ hMs.highMethaneSignal = 'on'

    ReqPre for *PumpSwitchOffIfLowWaterDetected*: ¬ lWs.lowWaterSignal = 'on'

    ReqTrig for *PumpSwitchOnIfHighWaterDetected**AndNot**HighMethaneDetected*:

        hWs.highWaterSignal = 'on' ∧ ¬ hMs.highMethaneSignal = 'on'

Operation SendReminder

    Input p: Patron, bc: BookCopy; **Output** Reminded

    DomPre ¬ Reminded (p, bc); **DomPost** Reminded (p, bc);

    ReqTrig for *ReminderSent*: ■$_{\leq 2w}$ Loan (p, bc) ∧ ¬ ♦$_{\leq 1w}$ Reminded (p, bc)

               %% This patron has borrowed this book copy for two weeks at least

                    and no reminder has been sent for one week. %%

Operation ScheduleMeeting

    Input m: Meeting, Invitation, Constraints; **Output** m: Meeting/{Scheduled, Date}

    DomPre ¬ Scheduled (m); **DomPost** Scheduled (m);

    ReqPre for *ConvenientMeetingDate*:

> (∀ p: ImportantParticipant) (Invitation (p, m) → Constraints (p, m))
> %%The constraints of every important participant invited to this meeting are available.%%
> **ReqPost for** *ConvenienMeetingDate:*
> (∀ p: ImportantParticipant) (• Invitation (p, m) → m.Date ∉ • Constraints[p, m].excludedDates)

Note the difference, in the specification of ScheduleMeeting, between the use of the Constraints association as a *predicate* 'Constraints(p,m)' in the **ReqPre**, to express that a Constraints link exists between participant *p* and meeting *m* (see Section 10.3), and the use of this association as an *object* 'Constraints[p, m]' in the **ReqPost** (see Figure 4.5).

We should of course ask ourselves whether those formal specifications correctly operationalize the underlying goal specifications. This question will be addressed in the next chapter (see Section 18.2).

17.5 Back to the system's semantic picture

Section 12.4 provided an overall picture of what a system model semantically conveys when we put the goal, object, agent and operation models together; see Figure 12.5. With a formal model we can make that picture a bit more precise.

The global state of the system at some time position is the aggregation of the local states of all its agents at that time position. The local state of an agent at some time position is the aggregation of the states, at that time position, of all the state variables that the agent controls. The state of a state variable at some time position is a mapping from its name to its value at that time position.

The system evolves synchronously from system state to system state, where the time distance between successive states is the *smallest* time unit defined in the real-time temporal logic.

The system's state transitions are caused by applications of applicable operations that the agents may or must perform on the state variables that they control. As it is atomic, an operation applied in the current state maps the corresponding agent's state to the next state one smallest time unit later.

When multiple trigger conditions become true in the same state, the corresponding operations must fire simultaneously. A system's state transition is thus composed of parallel transitions on local states (see Figure 12.5). This is thus true concurrency; the interleaving semantics often used in design models involving concurrency is not possible in view of the obligations expressed by trigger conditions.

The system's non-determinism arises from the non-deterministic behaviour of its agents. While an agent *must* perform an operation when one of the operation's trigger conditions becomes true, the agent has the freedom to perform an operation or not when its required pre-conditions are all true. Such non-determinism, while suitable at a more abstract level for declarative reasoning, must in general be removed when the specification is translated into a more operational language (in particular, for specification animation and for other checks on the operational version). A choice must then be made between an eager or lazy behaviour scheme for each operation performed by the agent:

- In the *eager* behaviour scheme, the agent performs the operation as soon as it can; that is, as soon as all required pre-conditions are true. This corresponds to a *maximal progress* property.

- In the *lazy* behaviour scheme, the agent performs the operation when it is really obliged to do so; that is, when one of its required trigger conditions becomes true.

In this framework, a system behaviour is defined by a temporal sequence of system state transitions. The system *satisfies a behavioural goal* if the set of all its possible behaviours is included in the set of behaviours prescribed by the temporal logic specification of the goal (as defined in Section 17.1.2).

Pruning semantics and frame axioms

Our declarative language for specifying goals, objects and operations has a pruning semantics, unlike operational specification languages which have a generative semantics:

- With a *pruning semantics*, every state transition is allowed except the ones explicitly forbidden by the specification.

- With a *generative semantics*, every state transition is forbidden except the ones explicitly required by the specification.

Generative semantics view operations as generating the set of admissible system behaviours; these cover the only possible transitions. There is thus a built-in assumption that nothing changes except when an operation specification explicitly requires it. As a consequence, generative semantics avoid the *frame problem*; the specifier is relieved from explicitly specifying what does *not* change.

Built-in frame assumptions, however, make it difficult to support incremental reasoning about partial model fragments – as nothing else may change.

With a pruning semantics, the specification prunes the set of admissible system behaviours. Incremental elaboration and reasoning through composition of partial models is then made possible. New specification fragments further prune the set of admissible behaviours.

The frame problem must, however, be addressed then. Two built-in axioms in our framework relieve the specifier from explicitly stating everything that does not change.

- *Frame axiom 1.* Any state variable *not* declared in the **Output** list of the specification of an operation is left unchanged by any application of *this* operation.

  This frame axiom is enforced by requiring the *DomPost* and *ReqPost* conditions of an operation to refer only to those state variables that are explicitly declared in the **Output** list of the operation.

- *Frame axiom 2.* Every state transition that satisfies the domain pre- and post-conditions of an operation corresponds to an application of this operation:

  for any operation *op*:
  DomPre (op) ∧ o DomPost (op) ⇒ Performed (op)

Summary

- Critical goals, domain properties, hypotheses and operations in a system model should be formally specified for higher precision, unambiguous interpretation and deeper analysis.

- A sorted, first-order, real-time linear temporal logic closely fits the semantic framework of our models together with common goal specification patterns. In this logic, the specifications are built recursively from state assertions on typed variables using logical connectives, quantifiers and temporal operators over future and past states. The sorts of variables designate objects declared in the object model. Such specifications are interpreted over system histories.

- To capture the timing constraints often prescribed in goal formulations, the temporal operators are extended with real-time constructs. The time bounds in these constructs can be relative to the current state, absolute time bounds or variable-dependent time bounds.

- The specification language based on this real-time temporal logic has a pruning semantics; every system state transition is allowed except the ones explicitly forbidden by the specification. Incremental model elaboration and reasoning through composition of partial fragments is thereby made possible. Some axioms must, however, be built in to the language to address the frame problem.

- Many behavioural goals match specification patterns in this real-time temporal logic. The patterns allow non-expert specifiers to use temporal logic without really knowing it. They can be arranged in an *Achieve/Maintain* taxonomy for easier retrieval. Patterns in this taxonomy differ on the timing for satisfaction of target conditions with regard to other conditions.

- Requirements and expectations in the goal model must be realizable by the agent responsible for them. Their specification therefore requires some restricted use of temporal operators. Obstacles and anti-goals are existentially quantified and prefixed by an outer '◇' operator.

- Many domain properties and hypotheses match specification patterns too. They often refer to laws on environment phenomena that hold in any current state, to causal links among environment phenomena, or to stable associations. The introduction of auxiliary definitions in the object model allows for shorter and more understandable formal specifications.

- For the sake of realizability, the specification of domain and required conditions in the object model makes no use of the ◇ operator. Domain pre- and post-conditions amount to state assertions on their input and output variables, respectively. Required pre-conditions and especially trigger conditions can refer to previous states. Required post-conditions often refer to the state of variables in the operation's initial state, in addition to the operation's final state.

Notes and Further Reading

An excellent introduction to linear time temporal logic will be found in Manna and Pnueli (1992). The real-time temporal logic in this chapter is inspired by Koymans (1992). It was introduced for annotating goal-oriented models in Dardenne *et al.* (1993). Similar logics were used earlier in other requirements modelling or specification languages, including ERAE (Dubois *et al.*, 1991) or TRIO (Morzenti *et al.*, 1992). The useful distinction between relative, absolute and variable-dependent time bounds was introduced in Letier's thesis (Letier, 2001). The variable-dependent time bounds are a declarative counterpart of the bounded obligations on operations in Kent *et al.* (1993).

The *Achieve* and *Maintain* goal patterns were introduced in Dardenne *et al.* (1993) and refined in Letier and van Lamsweerde (2002b). Some of them fit the specification patterns in Dwyer *et al.* (1999). The latter paper demonstrates the usefulness of specification patterns for hiding complex formalization details, thereby making analysis tools more accessible to non-expert users. The approach has been extended with patterns for behaviour model specifications (Smith *et al.*, 2002).

The issues raised by the frame problem in specification languages are discussed in depth in Borgida *et al.* (1993). Languages such as Z, LARCH and other temporal logic-based formalisms have a pruning semantics, whereas SCR, statecharts and VDM have a generative semantics (see the bibliographical notes at the end of Chapter 4). The first frame axiom in this chapter was similarly built in to LARCH.

Exercises

- Formalize the following goal definitions in real-time temporal logic. You may want to use goal specification patterns to help you in this task.

    Goal *Maintain* [PumpOff **If** LowWater]
    > **Def** *Whenever the water level in a sump is too low, the corresponding pump must be off (see object model in Fig. 15.8).*

    Goal *Avoid* [Explosion]
    > **Def** *No explosion may occur in the mine at any time.*

> **Goal** *Achieve* [MineEvacuated**If**CriticalGasLevel]
>> **Def** *If any of the carbon monoxide level, methane level, or aiflow level becomes critical, the mine must be evacuated within one hour (see object model in Fig. 15.8).*
>
> **Goal** Achieve[AmbulanceIntervention]
>> **Def** *For every urgent call reporting an incident, an ambulance must arrive at the incident scene within 14 minutes.*
>
> **Hypothesis** WillParticipate**If**Convenient**And**Informed
>> **Def** *An intended participant will participate in a meeting if the meeting date and location fit his/her constraints and are notified to him/her in time.*

- Interpret the assertions you have formalized in the previous exercise over system histories by showing, for each of them, examples of state sequences that are implicitly covered and examples of state sequences that are implicitly excluded from the specification.

- Using system history examples, show the difference between what the two following goal patterns are prescribing:

  CurrentCondition $\Rightarrow$ GoodCondition   (Permanent *Maintain*)
  CurrentCondition $\Rightarrow$ $\square$ GoodCondition   ('After' *Maintain*)

- Using system history examples, show the difference between what the two following goal patterns are prescribing:

  $\square_{\leq x}$ (CurrentCondition $\rightarrow$ $\neg$ BadCondition)   (Temporary *Avoid*)
  CurrentCondition $\Rightarrow$ $\neg$ BadCondition $\mathcal{W}_{\leq x}$ NewCondition   (Temporary 'Between' *Avoid*))

- Use the semantic rules for temporal operators, given in Section 17.1, to prove the following temporal congruences often used in practice:

  $\square (P \wedge Q)$ $\Leftrightarrow$ $\square P \wedge \square Q$
  $\diamond (P \vee Q)$ · $\Leftrightarrow$ $\diamond P \vee \diamond Q$

- Find history *counter*examples showing that the following temporal congruences do *not* hold in general. Since P $\Leftrightarrow$ Q amounts to P $\Rightarrow$ Q and Q $\Rightarrow$ P, split each congruence in two entailments to consider the two cases separately. A graphical representation by sequences of states annotated by truth values for P and Q might help you.

  $\square (P \vee Q)$ $\Leftrightarrow$ $\square P \vee \square Q$
  $\diamond (P \wedge Q)$ $\Leftrightarrow$ $\diamond P \wedge \diamond Q$
  $\diamond \square P$ $\Leftrightarrow$ $\square \diamond P$
  $\diamond \square P \wedge \diamond \square Q$ $\Leftrightarrow$ $\diamond (\square P \wedge \square Q)$

- Use the semantic rules for temporal operators in Section 17.1, and those of predicate logic in Section 4.4.1, to prove the following temporal congruences very often used for generating obstacles. (A graphical representation by sequences of states annotated by truth values for P and Q might help you.)

$$\neg \Box P \Leftrightarrow \Diamond \neg P, \quad \neg \Diamond P \Leftrightarrow \Box \neg P, \quad \neg \blacklozenge_{\leq d} P \Leftrightarrow \blacksquare_{\leq d} \neg P$$
$$\neg (P \; \mathcal{W} \; Q) \Leftrightarrow \neg Q \; \mathcal{U} \; (\neg P \wedge \neg Q)$$

- Complete the following operation specifications from our running case sudies and formalize their domain and required conditions.

> **Operation** CloseDoors
>   **Input** ...; **Output** ...
>   **DomPre** ...; **DomPost** ...
>   **ReqTrig For** *NoDelayAtPlatform*: ...   %% The doors opening timeout for <u>this</u> platform has elapsed.%%
>
> **Operation** StartTrain
>   **Input** ...; **Output** ...
>   **DomPre** ...   %% The train's speed is null. %%;   **DomPost** ...
>   **ReqPre for** *DoorsStateClosed* **If** *NonZeroMeasuredSpeed:* ...
>
> **Operation** CheckOutBookCopy
>   **Input** ...; **Output** ...
>   **DomPre** ...   %% This book copy is not borrowed by any patron %%;   **DomPost** ...
>   **ReqPre For** *AvailableCopyCheckedOutIfLoanEncoded*: ...   %% This book copy is available in the library.%%
>   **ReqPre For** *LimitedLoanAmount:* ...   %% The number of loans by this patron has not reached the *Max* quota.%%
>
> **Operation** NotifyMeeting
>   **Input** ...; **Output** ...
>   **DomPre** ...; **DomPost** ...;
>   **ReqPre for** *AccurateNotificationOfSchedule*: ...
>   **ReqTrig for** *ParticipantsInformedOfScheduledMeetingOnTime:* ...
>
> **Operation** StopSafetyInjection
>   **Input** WaterPressure, Overridden; **Output** SafetyInjectionSignal
>   **DomPre** SafetyInjectionSignal = 'On';   **DomPost** ...
>   **ReqPre/Trig For** SafetyInjection**Iff**LowWaterPressure**AndNot**Overridden: ...

- Reverse engineer the goals underlying the following operational specification in an ambulance dispatching system and formalize these goals accordingly.

Operation Mobilize
   Input inc: Incident;   **Output** amb: Ambulance, Mobilized
   DomPre ¬ (∃ a: Ambulance) Mobilized (a, inc);   **DomPost** Mobilized (amb, inc)
   RequiredPre for ??:   Available (amb) ∧ TimeDist (amb.Location, inc.Location) ≤ 11 min
   RequiredTrig for ??: $\blacksquare_{\leq 3m}$ (∃ cl: Call) (Responded (cl) ∧ About (cl, inc))

Formal Reasoning for Specification Construction and Analysis

18

As introduced in Chapters 4 and 5, formal methods for RE provide much higher precision and richer forms of analysis that can be supported by tools (see Sections 4.4 and 5.3–5.4). As they are harder to use and less widely applicable, we should concentrate their use on model portions appearing to be mission-critical. In a 'two-button' mode, the formal analysis button should be pressed only when and where needed to formalize and analyse critical goals, domain properties, obstacles, threats or operations. The button pressed by default is the semi-formal one where the model building and analysis techniques from Chapters 8–16 are used.

When goals, domain properties, hypotheses and operations are specified formally, we can prove that an AND-set of sub-goals entails a desired goal or show that there are missing sub-goals. We can verify that a set of requirements ensures that an underlying goal is satisfied. We can verify that a goal operationalization is correct. In other words, our satisfaction arguments become formal and more reliable. We can also show that a goal can be obstructed through a feasible scenario. More constructively, we can sometimes formally derive missing sub-goals, derive operation specifications from goal specifications, generate obstacles, threats or boundary conditions for conflict, and synthesize state machines from scenarios or goals.

This chapter presents formal techniques for doing that. Some of them formalize informal heuristics and techniques described in the previous chapters. The difference here is that they are made more precise, established on formal grounds and amenable to automation by tools. Other techniques in this chapter have no informal counterpart in the previous chapters.

Section 18.1 discusses formal goal refinement and the checking of the correctness and completeness of refinements. Section 18.2 is devoted to formal goal operationalization and the checking of operationalization correctness. Section 18.3 presents a formal version of the regression technique informally sketched in Chapter 16 for generating obstacles. It also presents formal goal obstruction patterns as an effective means for shortcutting formal derivations. The application of this technique for generation of security anti-goals in a threat model is shown in Section 18.4. Section 18.5 adapts the regression technique to the generation of boundary conditions for conflict detection. Conflict patterns and formal operators for conflict resolution are presented there as well. Finally, Section 18.6 discusses techniques for generating state machine models inductively from interaction scenarios and goal specifications.

18.1 Checking goal refinements

A first kind of RE-specific model verification consists of checking that the refinements of behavioural goals in the goal model are correct and complete. Such checking is important, as missing sub-goals result in incomplete requirements.

As introduced in Chapter 8, a set of goals $\{G_1, \ldots, G_n\}$ correctly refines a goal G in a domain theory *Dom* if and only if

$$\{G_1, \ldots, G_n, Dom\} \models G \qquad\qquad completeness$$
$$\{G_1, \ldots, G_n, Dom\} \not\models \textbf{false} \qquad\qquad consistency$$
$$\{\wedge_{j \neq i} G_j, Dom\} \not\models G \text{ for any } i \in [1..n] \quad minimality$$

We can follow several approaches to verify the correctness of a goal refinement, including theorem proving, the use of a catalogue of formal refinement patterns or SAT solver technology.

18.1.1 Using a theorem prover

A straightforward approach would consist of using a theorem prover dedicated to linear temporal logic, such as STeP (Manna *et al.*, 1996) or an interactive higher-order theorem prover such as PVS (Owre *et al.*, 1995) in which we could encode our real-time temporal logic. In view of the preceding definition of correctness, we would ask such a tool to prove the theorem G under the consistency and minimality constraints, taking $G_1, \ldots, G_n$ and the domain properties in *Dom* as axioms (see Section 5.4.4).

This approach appears a bit too heavyweight at RE time. It requires the assistance of an expert in theorem-proving technology. Feeding the theorem prover with intermediate assertions or confirming the lemmas or claims proposed by the tool may be far from trivial. Moreover, we generally get no real clue if the verification fails.

18.1.2 Formal refinement patterns

An alternative approach consists of using formal patterns to check, complete or explore refinements. This approach formalizes the semi-formal approach discussed in Section 8.8.5. The generic goals involved in a refinement pattern are now specified in our temporal logic. The conditions they refer to are meta-variables to be instantiated when we use the pattern.

A set of common refinement patterns is formalized and organized in a *pattern catalogue* for easy retrieval. The patterns encode known refinement tactics. Each of them is proved formally correct and complete once for all, for example using the STeP theorem prover. The patterns are then reused in matching situations through instantiation of their meta-variables.

Figure 18.1 shows formal versions of the *Milestone-Driven* and *Guard-Introduction* refinement patterns in Figures 8.19 and 8.23, respectively. The conditions C, T, M, D are meta-variables. Variants with time bounds on the ◇-operator are easily obtained.

Such patterns are reusable at will in any in matching situation. Figure 18.2 illustrates the use of the *Guard-Introduction* pattern. We want to check the refinement

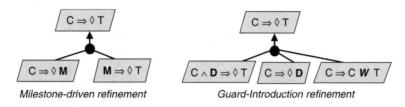

Figure 18.1   *Formal refinement patterns.*
Source: Reprinted from A. van Lamsweerde (2007), with permission from IOS Press.

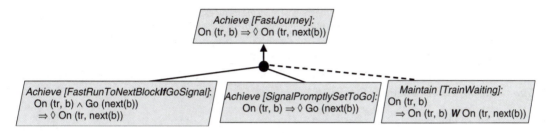

Figure 18.2   *Pointing out a missing subgoal through pattern instantiation.*

of the goal Achieve[FastJourney] into sub-goals Achieve[FastRunToNextBlockIfGoSignal] and Achieve[SignalPromptlySetToGo]. This refinement appeared in a goal model portion for our train control system; see Figure 8.5. (The variables in Figure 18.2 are implicitly quantified universally, and the time bounds on the ◇-operator are omitted for sake of simplicity.) An incomplete refinement is detected by pattern matching. The match reveals the missing third sub-goal in Figure 18.1, indicated by a dashed line in the instantiated refinement in Figure 18.2. The train must remain waiting on its current block until it moves to the next block; it may not go back to the previous block.

Exploring refinements

Formal refinement patterns support a constructive approach to refinement correctness. While a goal is being partially refined we can retrieve all matching patterns from the catalogue and explore alternative ways of completing the partial refinement. Figure 18.3 illustrates this. Three alternative sub-goals appear as possible responses to the refinement query on the left-hand side. Once instantiated, the three returned alternatives should be evaluated against the soft goals in the goal model to select the one that meets them best; see Section 16.3.

Hidden proofs

Another benefit of refinement patterns is the formal correctness proof of the instantiated refinements that we get for free. As mentioned earlier, each pattern in the catalogue is proved once for all. The proof of the instantiated refinement is just the corresponding instantiation

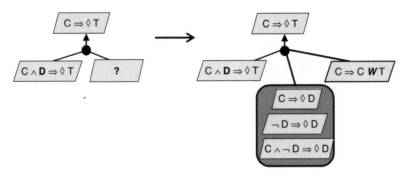

Figure 18.3 *Generating alternative goal refinements for exploration of alternatives.*
Source: Reprinted from A. van Lamsweerde (2007), with permission from IOS Press.

of the generic proof. To visualize such benefit, let us have a quick look at the proof of the *Guard-Introduction* pattern in Figure 18.1:

1.	$C \Rightarrow \Diamond D$	Hyp
2.	$C \wedge D \Rightarrow \Diamond T$	Hyp
3.	$C \Rightarrow C \, \mathcal{W} \, T$	Hyp
4.	$C \Rightarrow (C \, \mathcal{U} \, T) \vee \Box C$	3, def of *Unless*
5.	$C \Rightarrow \Diamond T \vee \Box C$	4, def of *Until*
6.	$C \Rightarrow \Diamond D \wedge (\Diamond T \vee \Box C)$	1, 5, strengthen consequent
7.	$C \Rightarrow (\Diamond D \wedge \Diamond T) \vee (\Diamond D \wedge \Box C)$	6, distribution
8.	$C \Rightarrow (\Diamond D \wedge \Diamond T) \vee \Diamond (D \wedge C)$	7, trivial lemma
9.	$C \Rightarrow (\Diamond D \wedge \Diamond T) \vee \Diamond \Diamond T$	8, 2, strengthen consequent
10.	$C \Rightarrow (\Diamond D \wedge \Diamond T) \vee \Diamond T$	9, $\Diamond$-idempotence
11.	$C \Rightarrow \Diamond T$	10, absorption

Instead of having to redo such a tedious and error-prone proof at every critical goal refinement while building the goal model, we get a proof merely by instantiating the meta-variables accordingly in the available generic proof of the applied pattern.

Realizability-driven patterns

Some refinement patterns might be seen as high-level inference rules in our real-time temporal logic. Others are specifically aimed at refining goals towards leaf goals that are realizable. Section 8.8.5 presented semi-formal patterns for introducing finer-grained sub-goals to resolve unrealizability problems. Figure 18.4 shows their formal counterpart. The root goal *G* involves a condition *p(m)* on a variable *m* unmonitorable (pattern on left) or uncontrollable (pattern on right) by the agent candidate for assignment. To resolve this, a monitorable (or controllable) 'image' variable *im* and condition *q(im)* on it are introduced under the constraint that they must accurately reflect their unmonitorable (or uncontrollable) counterpart; see the right sub-goals in Figure 18.4. The left-hand sub-goals are rewritings of the parent goal where all occurrences of the condition '*p(m)*' are replaced by the condition '*q(im)*'.

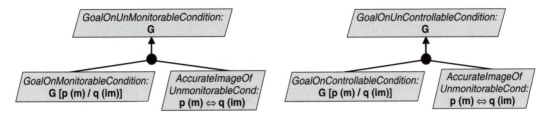

Figure 18.4 *Patterns for resolving goal unrealizability: Introduce Accuracy Subgoal.*

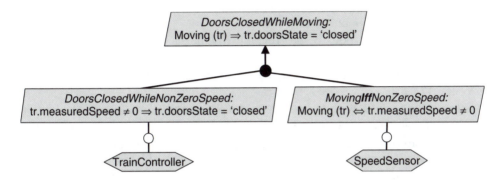

Figure 18.5 *Using the pattern "Introduce Accuracy Subgoal" for resolving unrealizability.*
Source: Reprinted from A. van Lamsweerde (2007), with permission from IOS Press.

Figure 18.5 illustrates the use of this pattern. The example suggests that such patterns are helpful for producing agent assignments as well.

First-order patterns

The preceding patterns are propositional; they involve logical connectives and temporal operators without quantifiers. We can also use first-order versions of them. Figure 18.6 shows a frequently used first-order refinement pattern corresponding to a mix of the preceding *Guard-Introduction* and *Milestone-Driven* refinement patterns.

Note that the offspring nodes in a refinement pattern are not necessarily all prescriptive once they are instantiated. Some might be descriptive (and should be represented with a 'home'

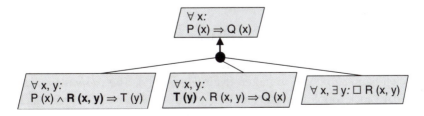

Figure 18.6 *First-order goal refinement pattern*

shape in the goal model). They can highlight important hypotheses or domain properties that have been overlooked. The offspring node on the right in Figure 18.6 typically captures a stability hypothesis about an association R in the environment (see Section 17.3).

The use of formal refinement patterns appears more constructive and lightweight than the application of a theorem prover to every critical refinement that we want to check. It is, however, more limited, as the parent goal in a refinement that we want to check has to match a root goal in the pattern catalogue.

18.1.3 Using bounded SAT solvers

In addition to using a theorem prover or a catalogue of formal refinement patterns, we can make a round-trip use of a bounded SAT solver.

SAT solvers are efficient tools for determining whether a given propositional assertion is satisfiable. If the assertion is satisfiable, they show a solution example that satisfies it. When the assertion is specified in temporal logic, the solution example is a system history satisfying it (see Section 17.1.2).

Bounded SAT solvers allow some user-defined upper bound to be imposed on the length of satisfying histories. The checks then become highly efficient in spite of the size of the state space to be explored. We lose completeness, though, as we cannot draw any conclusion if a bounded history is not found.

Let us consider the refinement of a goal G into sub-goals $G_1, \ldots, G_n$ in a domain theory *Dom*. In view of the definition of what a correct refinement is, we may apply the refutation principle in logic to reformulate our problem as one of determining whether the temporal logic formula:

$$G_1 \wedge \ldots \wedge G_n \wedge Dom \wedge \neg G$$

is satisfiable and, if so, finding a historical sequence of states satisfying it. If a solution satisfying this formula is found, we have found a history counterexample showing that the refinement is *not* complete. (The consistency and minimality conditions for refinement correctness are used as additional constraints in this process.)

In practice, we can use a front-end tool to a SAT solver. Such a tool does the following:

1. Ask the user to instantiate the above formula to selected object instances, in order to get a propositional formula.

2. Translate the result into the input format required by the selected SAT solver.

3. Ask the user to determine a maximal length to bound counterexample histories.

4. Run the SAT solver.

5. Translate the output back to the level of abstraction of the graphical input model.

Figure 18.7 shows the result produced by such a tool on the refinement in Figure 18.2 where only the two left-hand sub-goals are taken (as in Figure 8.5). The properties in *Dom* describe a simple circular block topology. After instantiation in Step 1, we get three blocks with their signal and two trains, say. The counterexample generated on the right-hand lower window is

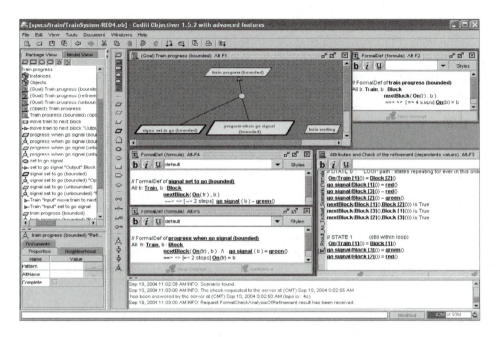

Figure 18.7 *Roundtrip use of a bounded SAT solver for checking goal refinements.*
Source: Reprinted from A. van Lamsweerde (2007), with permission from IOS Press.

a bounded sequence of states showing one train getting back to the previous block, which suggests the missing sub-goal of the train waiting on its current block until the signal is set to 'go'.

Such use of a bounded SAT solver allows partial goal models to be checked and debugged incrementally as the model is being built. The major pay-off resides in the counterexamples that may suggest missing sub-goals. A bounded universe, however, makes it possible to show the presence of bugs in a model, not their absence; there might be counterexample histories whose length exceeds the specified bound or which involve more object instances.

18.2 Deriving goal operationalizations

Another kind of RE-specific model verification consists of checking that the operationalizations of behavioural leaf goals in the goal model are correct. This is important for mission-critical operations; we must make sure that their specification in the operation model guarantees that their underlying goals are satisfied.

To perform such checks in a temporal logic framework, we first need a temporal logic semantics for operations. Let us denote by $[|C|]$ the LTL formula defining the meaning of a construct C.

An operation *op* defines a relation on input–output variables; see Section 12.1. In view of the definition of domain conditions in Section 12.2.3 and the semantic considerations in Section 17.5, we can define this relation as follows:

$$[|\ op\ |] =_{\text{def}} \text{DomPre}\,(op) \wedge o\,\text{DomPost}\,(op),$$

where *DomPre (op)* and *DomPost (op)* denote *op*'s domain pre- and post-condition, respectively, and '*o*' is the 'next' LTL operator introduced in Section 17.1.2.

Let *ReqPre(op), ReqTrig(op), ReqPost(op)* denote the sets of required pre-, trigger- and post-conditions for *op* to operationalize its underlying goals. In view of the definition of these conditions in Section 12.3.1, we have:

If $R \in$ ReqPre (op) **then** $[|R|] =_{\text{def}} (\forall *) [| \text{ op } |] \Rightarrow R,$

If $R \in$ ReqTrig (op) **then** $[|R|] =_{\text{def}} (\forall *) \text{DomPre } (op) \wedge R \Rightarrow [| \text{ op } |],$

If $R \in$ ReqPost (op) **then** $[|R|] =_{\text{def}} (\forall *) [| \text{ op } |] \Rightarrow \text{ o } R,$

where '$(\forall *)$' denotes the universal closure operator, meaning that any free variable in its scope gets universally quantified.

Section 12.3.3 defined what a correct operationalization is. We can now reformulate this definition in a more explicit form using the LTL semantics for operations.

A set of required conditions $R_1, \ldots, R_n$ on operations in the operation model correctly operationalizes a goal *G iff:*

$$[| R_1 |], \ldots, [| R_n |] \models G \qquad completeness$$
$$[| R_1 |], \ldots, [| R_n |] \not\models \textbf{false} \qquad consistency$$
$$G \models [| R_1 |], \ldots, [| R_n |] \qquad minimality$$

Every operationalization thus defines a proof obligation. Several approaches can be followed to verify the correctness of a goal operationalization.

18.2.1 Using bounded SAT solvers

As for checking goal refinements, we can make a round-trip use of a bounded SAT solver. Here we want to know whether the temporal logic formula

$$[| R_1 |] \wedge \ldots \wedge [| R_n |] \wedge \text{ Dom } \wedge \neg G$$

is satisfiable and, if so, find a historical sequence of states satisfying it.

The same front-end tool can be used to check bounded operationalizations and generate counterexample histories.

18.2.2 Formal operationalization patterns

The principle is similar to goal refinement patterns. A catalogue of operationalization patterns is built and formally proved correct, for example using the STeP or PVS theorem prover. The patterns cover common goal specification patterns. The generic operationalizations and their correctness proof are reused in matching situations by instantiation of their meta-variables.

Figure 18.8 shows a pattern for operationalizing goals having the '*Immediate Achieve*' pattern introduced in Section 17.2. Consider the following safety goal on train signals:

∀ b: Block
[(∃ tr: Train) On (tr, b)] ⇒ o ¬ GO (b),

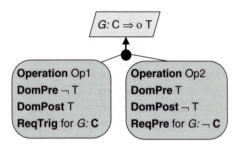

Figure 18.8 *Operationalization pattern for "Immediate Achieve" goals*
Source: E. Letier and A. van Lamsweerde, © 2002 ACM, Inc. Reprinted by permission.

where GO (b) means that block b's signal is set to 'go'. If we apply the pattern in Figure 18.8 to this goal, we obtain two operations; namely, SetSignalToStop(b) and SetSignalToGo(b), together with:

- A **ReqTrig** condition on the operation SetSignalToStop(b): ($\exists$ tr: Train) On (tr, b).

- A **ReqPre** condition on the operation SetSignalToGo(b): $\neg$ ($\exists$ tr: Train) On (tr, b).

A catalogue of operationalization patterns

We can systematically define operationalization patterns for the various goal specification patterns organized in the taxonomy discussed in Section 17.2 (see Figure 17.1). Figure 18.9 shows a frequently used pattern for operationalizing bounded *Achieve* goals.

The operation model fragment in this pattern states that, in order to operationalize a goal taking the form $C \Rightarrow \Diamond_{\leq d} T$, we need to introduce an operation with domain pre- and post-condition $[\neg T, T]$ and with a required trigger condition stating that the operation *must* be applied if T has remained false since C was true $d-1$ time units ago without T being true.

Let us illustrate this pattern on the Mine Safety Control case study. Consider the goal Achieve[AlarmWhenCriticalMethaneLevel] whose formal specification is:

$\forall$ c: PumpController
c.MethaneMeasure $\geq$ 'Critical' $\Rightarrow$ $\Diamond_{\leq d}$ c.Alarm = 'On'

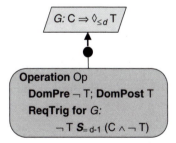

Figure 18.9 *Operationalization pattern for "Bounded Achieve" goals*
Source: E. Letier and A. van Lamsweerde, © 2002 ACM, Inc. Reprinted by permission.

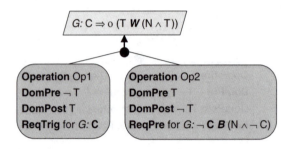

Figure 18.10 *Operationalization pattern for "Between Maintain" goals*
Source: E. Letier and A. van Lamsweerde, © 2002 ACM, Inc. Reprinted by permission.

This goal matches the root of the '*Bounded Achieve*' operationalization pattern. The operational specification derived after instantiation of the matching meta-variables is the following:

> **Operation** RaiseAlarm
> > **DomPre** c.Alarm ≠ 'On'; **DomPost** c.Alarm = 'On'
> > **ReqTrig for** *AlarmWhenCriticalMethaneLevel:*
> > > c.Alarm ≠ 'On' $S_{=d-1}$ (c.MethaneMeasure ≥ 'Critical' ∧ c.Alarm ≠ 'On')

The derived trigger condition captures an obligation to perform the operation if the methane measure has been above critical level $d-1$ time units ago with the alarm remaining off since then.

Figure 18.10 shows a pattern for operationalizing *Maintain/Avoid* goals. The root goal is a variant of the standard form $C \Rightarrow T\ W\ N$, where T must be maintained but is not instantly enforceable in a state where C holds. The operation model fragment in this pattern states that, in order to operationalize the root goal, two operations *Op1* and *Op2* need to be introduced; the former with domain pre- and post-condition $[\neg T, T]$ and a required trigger condition stating that it *must* be applied when C holds (provided the domain pre-condition $\neg T$ holds); the latter with domain pre- and post-condition $[T, \neg T]$ and a required pre-condition stating that it *may* be applied only if C has not been true *back to* (and including) *the last time* N was true.

To illustrate the pattern in Figure 18.10, consider the following goal for a simplified light control system:

> **Goal** Maintain [LightOnWhenRoomOccupied]
> > **Def** *A room light must remain 'On' between the time the first person enters the room and the time the last person leaves it.*
> > **FormalSpec** ∀ r: Room
> > > r.FirstEntry ⇒ o (r.Light = 'On' W (r.LastExit ∧ r.Light = 'On'))

The goal specification matches the root of the '*Between Maintain*' operationalization pattern. The operational specification derived after instantiation of the matching meta-variables is the following:

> **Operation** TurnLightOn
> > **Input** r: Room; **Output** r: Room/Light
> > **DomPre** r.Light ≠ 'On'; **DomPost** r.Ligth = 'On'
> > **ReqTrig for** *LightOnWhenRoomOccupied:* r.FirstEntry

Operation TurnLightOff
  Input r: Room; **Output** r: Room/Light
  DomPre r.Ligth ≠ 'Off'; **DomPost** r.Ligth = 'Off'
  ReqPre for *LightOnWhenRoomOccupied:* ¬ r.FirstEntry **B** (r.LastExit ∧ r.Light = 'On')

The required pre-condition states that the light may be turned off only if no first entry in the room has been detected back to the last time the last exit from the room was detected with the lights being on. Note that this derived pre-condition and the original goal as formulated do not require the light to be turned off as soon as the last exit occurs. Also note that the o-operator is introduced in the goal specification to ensure that the goal is realizable by the LightController agent; the latter cannot both detect the first entry and switch the light on within the same state.

Operationalization patterns may be used backwards for 'mining' the goals kept implicit behind a set of operation specifications. In this case, the offspring nodes must match the operation specifications in order to derive the parent goal instantiated accordingly (see the exercises at the end of the chapter).

18.3 Generating obstacles for risk analysis

Chapter 9 introduced obstacle models as a means for anticipating what could go wrong in an over-ideal system. Obstacle analysis iterates on *Identify–Assess–Control* cycles. Section 9.3.1 showed that the obstacle identification step in such cycles consists of building AND/OR risk trees anchored on goals, hypotheses or questionable domain properties involved in the goal model. (Risk trees were introduced in Section 3.2.2.) This section shows how such trees can be built systematically and formally.

According to the definition of obstacles in Section 9.1.1, we are looking for feasible conditions O such that:

$$\{O, Dom\} \models \neg\, G, \quad Dom \not\models \neg\, O,$$

where *Dom* is a set of valid properties that we know about the domain and G denotes a goal, hypothesis or questionable domain property that we want to analyse for potential obstruction of goals in the goal model.

While building risk trees anchored on G, we must make sure that obstacle refinements satisfy the following conditions introduced in Section 9.2.2:

$\{O_1, \ldots, O_n, Dom\} \models O$	*refinement completeness*
$\{O_1, \ldots, O_n, Dom\} \not\models \textbf{false}$	*domain consistency*
$\{\wedge_{j \neq i} O_j, Dom\} \not\models O$ for each $i \in [1..n]$	*minimal cause for obstruction*

We should also ideally care for the domain completeness of the set of obstacles $O_1, \ldots, O_n$ that we can find:

$$\{\neg\, O_1, \ldots, \neg\, O_n, Dom\} \models G$$

Obstacles can be generated abductively from $\neg\, G$ and *Dom*. While doing so, we may elicit new domain properties that are required in the formal derivation. There are two approaches.

We will first look at a calculus that formalizes the semi-formal technique in Section 9.3.1 (see Figure 9.10). Then we will see how goal obstruction patterns can help us shortcut formal derivations.

18.3.1 Regressing obstructions through domain properties

As we are looking for conditions O such that $\{O, Dom\} \models \neg G$, a pre-condition calculus might help us derive pre-conditions for $\neg G$ from properties in Dom that are known or elicited on the fly. Let us assume that domain properties have a standard form $A \Rightarrow C$.

The regression procedure for calculating pre-conditions for obstruction works as follows:

> *Initial step:*
>> take $O := \neg G$
>
> *Inductive step:*
>> let $A \Rightarrow C$ be the domain property selected,
>>> with C matching some L in O whose occurrences are all positive in O,
>>
>> then $\mu := \text{mgu}\,(L, C)$;
>>> $O := O\,[L/A.\mu]$.

This procedure relies on the following definitions and notations:

- For a formula $\varphi(u)$ with one or more occurrences of the sentence symbol u, an occurrence of u is said to be *positive* in φ if it does not occur in a sub-formula of the form $p \leftrightarrow q$ and it is embedded in an even (explicit or implicit) number of negations.

- The expression $mgu\,(F1, F2)$ denotes the most general unifier of $F1$ and $F2$.

- The expression $F.\mu$ denotes the result of applying the substitutions from unifier μ to F.

- The expression $F\,[F1/F2]$ denotes the result of replacing every occurrence of $F1$ in formula F by $F2$.

The soundness of the regression procedure follows from a monotonicity property of linear temporal logic (Manna & Pnueli, 1992):

> If all occurrences of u in $\varphi(u)$ are positive, then
>> $(p \Rightarrow q) \rightarrow (\varphi(p) \Rightarrow \varphi(q))$
>
> is valid.

Every iteration in the regression procedure produces potentially finer sub-obstacles to the assertion G on which the obstacle tree we are building is anchored. It is up to the specifier to decide when to stop, depending on whether the obstacles obtained are meaningful and precise enough to (a) easily identify satisfying scenarios for checking their feasibility, (b) easily assess their likelihood and severity, and (c) explore resolutions through the operators described in Section 9.3.3 (see Figure 9.11).

Examples Let us see this procedure in action for generating obstacles in the simplified A320 braking logic example in Section 9.3.1. We consider propositional specifications to make things simpler. One goal for landing control states that:

(G) MovingOnRunway ⇒ o ReverseThrustEnabled

As the autopilot software cannot monitor the variable MovingOnRunway, we apply the *'Introduce Accuracy Sub-goal'* refinement pattern in Figure 18.4 to produce the following sub-goals:

(G1) MovingOnRunway ⇔ WheelsState = 'turning'
(G2) WheelsState = 'turning' ⇒ o ReverseThrustEnabled

The sub-goal (G2) is a requirement on the autopilot software. The sub-goal (G1) is further refined into the following assertions:

(H) MovingOnRunway ⇔ WheelsTurning,
(E) WheelsTurning ⇔ WheelsState = 'turning'

The assertion (E) is an expectation on the wheel sensor. The assertion (H) states two hypotheses about the domain. The first says:

(H1) MovingOnRunway ⇒ WheelsTurning

Let us start our obstacle analysis on this hypothesis by obstructing it. We therefore negate (H1), which yields

$$\diamond \text{MovingOnRunway} \wedge \neg \textit{WheelsTurning}$$

We refine this negation by regressing it through the domain. We look for, or elicit, domain properties that are *necessary conditions* for the target condition *WheelsTurning* in the hypothesis that we want to obstruct. We might find, or elicit from domain experts:

$$\text{WheelsTurning} \Rightarrow \text{WheelsOut,}$$
$$\text{WheelsTurning} \Rightarrow \neg \text{WheelsBroken,}$$
$$\text{WheelsTurning} \Rightarrow \neg \text{Aquaplaning, etc.}$$

Let us select the third domain property, equivalent to its contraposition:

$$\text{Aquaplaning} \Rightarrow \neg \textit{WheelsTurning}$$

The consequent of this implication unifies with one of the conjuncts in the negated hypothesis above. We may therefore regress that negated hypothesis backwards through this domain property, which yields the following sub-obstacle obstructing the target assumption:

$$\diamond \text{MovingOnRunway} \wedge \text{Aquaplaning}$$

The generated obstacle is satisfiable by the environment (in this case, with the help of Mother Nature). It was indeed satisfied during the Warsaw plane crash (see Section 1.2.1). As the preceding derivation suggests, obstacle analysis may be used to elicit unknown domain properties as well.

Let us now consider an example involving first-order formalizations. In our meeting scheduling system, one goal states that the intended people should participate in meetings of which they are aware and that fit their constraints:

Goal *Achieve* [InformedParticipantsAttendance]
    FormalDef ∀ m: Meeting, p: Participant
        Invitation (p, m) ∧ Notified (p, m) ∧ Convenient (p, m) ⇒ ◇ Participates (p, m)

The initialization step of the regression procedure consists of taking the negation of this goal, which yields:

(NG)   ◇∃ m: Meeting, p: Participant
       Invitation (p, m) ∧ Notified (p, m) ∧ Convenient (p, m) ∧ □ ¬ Participates (p, m)

Suppose now that the domain theory contains the following property:

∀ m: Meeting, p: Participant
Participates (p, m) ⇒ Holds (m) ∧ Convenient (p, m)

This domain property states that a necessary condition for a person to participate in a meeting is that the meeting is being held and its date and location are convenient to him or her. A logically equivalent formulation is obtained again by contraposition:

(D)   ∀ m: Meeting, p: Participant
       ¬ [Holds (m) ∧ Convenient (p, m)] ⇒ ¬ Participates (p, m)

The consequent in (D) unifies with a litteral in (NG). Regressing (NG) through (D) then amounts to replacing in (NG) the matching consequent in (D) by the corresponding antecedent. We thereby derive the following potential obstacle:

(O1)   ◇∃ m: Meeting, p: Participant
    Invitation (p, m) ∧ Notified (p, m) ∧ Convenient (p, m)
    ∧□ [¬ Holds (m) ∨ ¬ Convenient (p, m)]

This obstacle covers the situation of an invited participant being notified of a meeting convenient to him or her but no longer convenient in any future state where the meeting is held. Further OR-refinement would result in two sub-obstacles that might be named MeetingPostponedIndefinitely and LastMinuteImpediment, respectively. Scenarios satisfying their respective assertions are straightforward in this case.

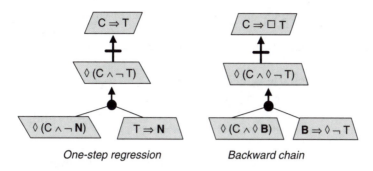

One-step regression   *Backward chain*

Figure 18.11   *Obstruction patterns for Maintain goals.*

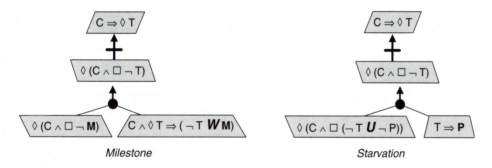

Milestone   *Starvation*

Figure 18.12   *Goal obstruction patterns for Achieve goals*

18.3.2 Using formal obstruction patterns

We can also use a pattern-based approach for generating obstacles. A catalogue of common obstruction patterns is built where each pattern is proved formally. The patterns are reused by instantiation in matching situations. Figures 18.11 and 18.12 show a few common obstruction patterns for *Maintain* and *Achieve* goals, respectively.

The left-hand pattern in Figure 18.11 is very common. It encodes a single step of the regression procedure. Some of the derivation examples in the previous section can therefore be seen as applications of this pattern as well.

As an example of using the *Starvation* pattern in Figure 18.12, consider a general resource management system and the goal:

∀ u: User, r: Resource
Requesting (u, r) ⇒ ◇ Allocated (r, u)

We know the following domain property:

Allocated (r, u) ⇒ ¬∃ u' ≠ u: Allocated (r, u')

This property suggests reusing the *Starvation* pattern with instantiations:

C: Requesting (u, r) T: Allocated (r, u) P: ¬∃ u' ≠ u: Allocated (r, u')

The following starvation obstacle is thereby derived:

◇∃ u: User, r: Resource
Requesting (u, r) ∧□ [¬ Allocated (r, u) 𝒰 ∃ u' ≠ u: Allocated (r, u')]

This obstacle captures a feasible coalition among other users that prevents the requesting user from ever getting the resource.

Once generated, the obstacles need to be assessed for feasibility, likelihood and severity. For feasibility, a SAT solver might be used to check that the obstacle assertion is satisfiable by the environment. For likelihood and severity, standard risk management techniques should be used; see Section 9.3.2.

18.4 Generating anti-goals for security analysis

Section 16.2.3 described a semi-formal approach for analyzing intentional threats against the goal model in order to explore security countermeasures and integrate these in the model. In this approach, attacker anti-goals need to be identified and refined until attacker capabilities are reached. This section describes formal techniques that may help us identify anti-goals and refine them.

We first need to see what formal specifications of security goals look like (Section 18.4.1). For identification of preliminary anti-goals, we identify security goals formally and negate them (Section 18.4.2). For anti-goal refinement, we can adapt the obstacle refinement techniques from the previous section (Section 18.4.3).

18.4.1 Specifying security goals

As introduced in Section 16.2.3, security goals prescribe different types of protection of system assets. Such protection sometimes restricts what agents may know about system objects. Section 11.2.5 introduced agent beliefs and knowledge based on properties that an agent can get from its local memory. Our real-time linear temporal logic needs to be augmented with constructs for specifying what agents know or may not know.

Specification constructs on agent knowledge

The epistemic operator $KnowsV_{ag}$ is defined on state variables as follows:

$KnowsV_{ag}$ (x) $=_{def}$ ∃ v: $Knows_{ag}$ (x = v)   ('knows value')
$Knows_{ag}$ (P) $=_{def}$ $Belief_{ag}$ (P) ∧ P   ('knows property')

The operational semantics of the epistemic operator $Belief_{ag}(P)$ is:

'P is among the properties stored in the local memory of agent ag.'

An agent thus *knows a property* if that property is found in its local memory and it is indeed the case that the property holds. Domain properties or hypotheses must make it precise under which conditions the property P appears in and disappears from the agent's memory.

Specification patterns for security goals

Security properties are generally classified in different categories (Kemmerer, 2003). We can formally specify those categories to obtain corresponding specification patterns. Instantiating the meta-variables in such patterns to system-specific 'sensitive' objects provides candidate security goals for our system, to be refined in the goal model and to be obstructed in an anti-goal model.

In particular, the following specification pattern defines confidentiality in a generic way:

> *Confidentiality:*   **Goal** *Avoid* [SensitiveInfoKnownByUnauthorizedAgent]
>   **FormalSpec** $\forall$ Ag: Agent, ob: Object
> $\neg$ Authorized (ag, ob.Info) $\Rightarrow$ $\neg$ KnowsV$_{ag}$ (ob.Info)

In this pattern for confidentiality goals, *Authorized* is a generic predicate to be instantiated through a domain-specific definition. For web banking services, for example, we would certainly consider the instantiation Object/Account while searching through the object model for sensitive information to be protected. We might then introduce the following instantiating definition:

> $\forall$ ag: Agent, acc: Account
> Authorized (ag, acc) $\Leftrightarrow$ [Owner (ag, acc) $\vee$ Proxy (ag, acc) $\vee$ Manager (ag, acc)]

Other specification patterns may be defined for privacy, integrity, availability, authentication, accountability or non-repudiation goals. In particular:

> *Privacy:*   **Goal** *Maintain* [PrivateInfoKnownOnlyIfAuthorizedByOwner]
>   **FormalSpec** $\forall$ ag, ag': Agent, ob: Object
>   KnowsV$_{ag}$ (ob.Info) $\wedge$ OwnedBy (ob.Info, ag') $\wedge$ ag $\neq$ ag'
> $\Rightarrow$ Authorization (ag, ob.Info, ag')

> *Integrity:*   **Goal** *Maintain* [ObjectInfoChangeOnlyIfCorrectAndAuthorized]
>   **FormalSpec** $\forall$ ag: Agent, ob: Object, v : Value
>   ob.Info = v $\wedge$ $\circ$ (ob.Info $\neq$ v) $\wedge$ UnderControl (ob.Info, ag)
> $\Rightarrow$ Authorized (ag, ob.Info) $\wedge$ $\circ$ Integrity (ob.Info)

> *Availability:*   **Goal** *Achieve* [ObjectInfoUsableWhenNeededAndAuthorized]
>   **FormalSpec** $\forall$ ag: Agent, ob: Object, v : Value
>   Needs (ag, ob.Info) $\wedge$ Authorized (ag, ob.Info)
> $\Rightarrow$ $\Diamond_{\leq d}$ Using (ag, ob.Info)

Such patterns can be diversified through variants capturing different security options. For confidentiality goals in particular, we may consider variants along two dimensions:

- The degree of approximate knowledge to be kept confidential – the exact value of a state variable, or the lower/upper bound, or the order of magnitude or any property about the value.

- The timing according to which that knowledge should be kept confidential – confidential in the current state, or confidential until some expiration date, or confidential unless/until some condition or confidential for ever.

18.4.2 Identifying security goals and initial anti-goals

In the threat analysis approach presented in Section 16.2.3, we need preliminary security goals and anti-goals to start building threat graphs. We may use two heuristics for this.

Instantiate security specification pattern and negate the instantiated specification

To obtain candidate specifications for security goals specific to our system, we may check the specification patterns for relevant instantiations:

- We instantiate the meta-model concepts in these patterns, such as Object and Agent, and the generic attributes, such as *Info*, to system-specific sensitive classes, attributes and associations in the object model.

- We specialize the abstract predicates, such as Authorized, UnderControl, Integrity or Using, through substitution by system-specific conditions.

Consider the *Confidentiality* specification pattern and our web banking example. Sensitive information about bank accounts includes the objects Acc# and PIN. The latter are defined in the object model as entities composing the aggregated entity Account and linked through a *Matching* association (see the example in Section 16.2.3). Instantiating the *Confidentiality* pattern to this sensitive information yields the following specification for inclusion in the goal model:

> **Goal** *Avoid* [AccountNumber&PinKnownByUnauthorized]
> **FormalSpec** $\forall$ p: Person, acc: Account
> $\quad \neg$ [Owner (p, acc) $\vee$ Proxy (p, acc) $\vee$ Manager (p, acc)]
> $\quad \Rightarrow \neg$ [KnowsV$_p$ (acc.Acc#) $\wedge$ KnowsV$_p$ (acc.PIN)]

If the instantiated specification is worth considering as a security goal in our model, we simply negate it to get a preliminary anti-goal to start our threat analysis. For the preceding goal, we obtain:

> **AntiGoal** *Achieve* [AccountNumber&PinKnownByUnauthorized]
> **FormalSpec** $\Diamond \exists$ p: Person, acc: Account
> $\quad \neg$ [Owner (p, acc) $\vee$ Proxy (p, acc) $\vee$ Manager (p, acc)]
> $\quad \wedge$ KnowsV$_p$ (acc.Acc#) $\wedge$ KnowsV$_p$ (acc.PIN)

Check the converse of asset-related Achieve goals

According to one of the heuristics in Section 8.8.2, an *Achieve* goal of form:

$$\text{preCondition} \Rightarrow \Diamond \text{ TargetCondition}$$

has a converse assertion

$$\text{Target Condition} \Rightarrow \text{preCondition}$$

that might be worth considering as a *Maintain* goal.

We should therefore check every asset-related *Achieve* goal in the goal model, form the converse *Maintain* assertion, check whether this assertion is worth considering as a candidate security goal in the goal model and negate it if so to get a preliminary anti-goal.

For example, while browsing the goal model of an online shopping system, we might stop on the goal stating that every paid item shall be sent within two days after payment:

$$\text{ItemPaidToSeller} \Rightarrow \Diamond_{\leq 2d} \text{ ItemSentToBuyer}$$

The converse *Maintain* assertion is:

$$\text{ItemSentToBuyer} \Rightarrow \text{ItemPaidToSeller}$$

which is indeed a security goal that we might have overlooked. Its goal negation is:

$$\Diamond (\text{ItemSentToBuyer} \wedge \neg \text{ItemPaidToSeller}).$$

This goal is obviously going to be desired by a number of malicious shoppers. We should therefore consider it among the preliminary anti-goals for threat graph building.

18.4.3 Refining anti-goals

When goals, domain properties and anti-goals are specified formally, we can use the regression procedure in Section 18.3.1. The main difference here is that the domain theory *Dom* through which anti-goals are regressed is augmented with goal specifications from the goal model – in particular, the software requirements and environmental expectations. For anti-goal satisfaction, the attacker may indeed use its knowledge of the goal model; see the *Most Knowledgeable Attacker* assumption in Section 16.2.3. We thereby obtain anti-goal pre-conditions to be satisfied by the attacked software and its environment as *vulnerabilities*.

Let us see how the threat graph for web banking services, elaborated semi-formally in Section 16.2.3, can be formally derived (see Figure 16.6). We focus on the formal derivation of refinements for the initial anti-goal Achieve[AccountNumber&PinKnownByUnauthorized], whose formal specification was obtained in the previous section.

We need properties of the attackers's environment to regress this goal through. Looking at the formal specification of this anti-goal, we might ask ourselves, 'What are sufficient conditions in the domain for an unauthorized agent to know both the number and PIN of an account simultaneously?' (see Section 9.3.1). We might also use the symmetry and multiplicities of the *Matching* association between account numbers and PINs in the object model. As a result we find, or elicit, two symmetrical domain properties:

∀ p: Person, acc: Account
¬ [Owner (p, acc) ∨ Proxy (p, acc) ∨ Manager (p, acc)]
    ∧ KnowsV$_p$ (acc.Acc#) ∧ (∃ x: PIN) (Found (p, x) ∧ Matching (x, acc.Acc#))
    ⇒ KnowsV$_p$ (acc.Acc#) ∧ KnowsV$_p$ (acc.PIN)

¬ [Owner (p, acc) ∨ Proxy (p, acc) ∨ Manager (p, acc)]
    ∧ KnowsV$_p$ (acc.PIN) ∧ (∃ y: Acc#) (Found (p, y) ∧ Matching (acc.PIN, y))
    ⇒ KnowsV$_p$ (acc.Acc#) ∧ KnowsV$_p$ (acc.PIN)

We may then regress the above anti-goal Achieve[AccountNumber&PinKnownByUnauthorized] through each of these properties to obtain two sub-goals as alternative pre-conditions for satisfying it. We thereby obtain an OR-refinement of the anti-goal in two alternative, symmetrical anti-sub-goals, namely,

AntiGoal *Achieve* [AccountKnown&MatchingPinFound]
    FormalSpec ◇∃ p: Person, acc: Account
        ¬ [Owner (p, acc) ∨ Proxy (p, acc) ∨ Manager (p, acc)] ∧ KnowsV$_p$ (acc.Acc#)
        ∧ (∃ x: PIN) [Found (p, x) ∧ Matching (x, acc.Acc#)]

AntiGoal *Achieve* [PinKnown&MatchingAccountFound]
    FormalSpec ◇∃ p: Person, acc: Account
        ¬ [Owner (p, acc) ∨ Proxy (p, acc) ∨ Manager (p, acc)] ∧ KnowsV$_p$ (acc.PIN)
        ∧ (∃ y: Acc#) [Found (p, y) ∧ Matching (acc.PIN, y)]

This regression-based refinement may go on until we reach terminal conditions that are either realizable anti-requirements, in view of the attacker's capabilities, or observable vulnerabilities of the attacker's environment (including the target software); see Figure 16.6.

There was no regression through goal specifications in the preceding derivation. One of the exercises at the end of this chapter requires such regression; see the goal model for an on-line shopping system in the exercises section.

18.5 Formal conflict analysis

Section 3.1 discussed a general conflict management process where overlapping assertions are identified; conflicts among them are detected; resolutions of the detected conflicts are generated; and best resolutions are selected. Section 16.2.1 described semi-formal techniques for detecting potential conflicts, called divergences, by semi-formal and heuristic identification of boundary conditions for conflict. This section describes the formal counterpart of these techniques to enable more precise and systematic detection of conflicts (Section 18.5.1). Resolution operators based on formal goal specifications are discussed next (Section 18.5.2).

18.5.1 Deriving boundary conditions for conflict

According to the definition of divergence in Section 16.2.1, a boundary condition B for conflict among overlapping goals $G_1, G_2, \ldots, G_n$ must meet the condition:

$$\{B, G_1, G_2, \ldots, G_n, Dom\} \models \textbf{false},$$

together with the minimality and non-trivialness conditions. We can derive such a B by regression or by the use of formal divergence patterns.

Regression-based derivation of boundary conditions

The technique is based on the observation that the preceding condition is equivalent to:

$$\{Dom, B, \wedge_{j \neq i} G_j\} \models \neg\, G_i$$

We may thus formally derive B as a pre-condition for one of the negated goals $\neg\, G_i$, by regression through an augmented theory:

$$\{Dom, \wedge_{j \neq i} G_j\},$$

where the goals G_j must be used in the regression to be involved in the divergence. The regression procedure is similar to the one given in Section 18.3.1.

Examples   Let us see this procedure in action for generating a boundary condition for conflict in our train control system. Consider the following two goals provided by stakeholders:

Maintain [DoorsClosedBetweenPlatforms]:   (AtPlatform ∧ o ¬ AtPlatform) ⇒ DoorsClosed $\mathcal{W}$ AtNext
Achieve [DoorsOpenIfAlarm**And**Stopped]   • (Stopped ∧ Alarm) ⇒ DoorsOpen

We start by negating one of the goals. Let us take the first one. Because of the tautology:

$$\neg\, (P\mathcal{W}Q) \Leftrightarrow \neg Q\, \mathcal{U}\, (\neg P \wedge \neg Q),$$

we get as negated goal:

$$\text{AtPlatform} \wedge \text{o} \neg \text{AtPlatform} \wedge \neg \text{AtNext}\, \mathcal{U}\, (\neg\, \text{DoorsClosed} \wedge \neg \text{AtNext})$$

A first regression through the domain property:

$$\text{DoorsOpen} \Rightarrow \neg\, \text{DoorsClosed}$$

yields:

$$\text{AtPlatform} \wedge \text{o} \neg \text{AtPlatform} \wedge \neg \text{AtNext}\, \mathcal{U}\, (\textit{DoorsOpen} \wedge \neg \text{AtNext})$$

Let us now regress this assertion through the goal Achieve [DoorsOpenIfAlarm**And**Stopped]. The atomic condition *DoorsOpen* after the above 'until' operator unifies the consequent of the implication in the specification of this other goal. The regression through the other goal therefore yields:

$$\text{AtPlatform} \wedge \text{o} \neg \text{AtPlatform} \wedge \neg \text{AtNext } \mathcal{U} \text{ (} \bullet \text{ (Stopped} \wedge \text{Alarm)} \wedge \neg \text{AtNext)}$$

This derived boundary condition precisely captures the situation of a train being between two platforms until an alarm was raised and the train stopped. This condition is obviously satisfiable and shows that the two goals cannot be satisfied together when it holds.

Let us now consider an example involving first-order formalizations. The following two security goals are found in an electronic reviewing process for a scientific journal:

> **Goal** *Maintain* [ReviewerAnonymity]
> > **FormalSpec** ∀ r: Reviewer, p: Paper, a: Author, rep: Report
> > > Reviews (r, p, rep) ∧ AuthorOf (a, p) ⇒ □ ¬ KnowsV$_a$ (Reviews[r,p,rep])
> **Goal** *Maintain* [ReviewIntegrity]
> > **FormalSpec** ∀ r: Reviewer, p: Paper, a: Author, rep, rep': Report
> > > AuthorOf (a, p) ∧ Gets (a, rep, p, r) ⇒ Reviews (r, p, rep') ∧ rep' = rep

In this specification, the object Reviews[r,p,rep] designates a ternary association capturing a reviewer *r* having produced a referee report *rep* for paper *p*. The predicate Reviews(r,p,rep) expresses that an instance of this association exists in the current state (see Section 10.3). The predicate Gets(a,rep,p,r) expresses that author *a* has the report *rep* by reviewer *r* for his paper *p*. The *KnowsV* predicate is the epistemic construct introduced in Section 18.4.1 for specifying security goals.

The two preceding goals are not logically inconsistent. However, let us see whether they are potentially conflicting. We take the goal *Maintain*[ReviewerAnonymity] for the initialization step of the regression procedure. Its negation is:

> ◇∃ r: Reviewer, p: Paper, a: Author, rep: Report
> Reviews (r,p,rep) ∧ AuthorOf (a,p) ∧ ◇ KnowsV$_a$ (Reviews[r,p,rep])   (NG)

Regressing (NG) through the ReviewIntegrity goal, whose consequent can be simplified to Reviews(r,p,rep) by term rewriting, yields:

> ◇∃ r: Reviewer, p: Paper, a: Author, rep: Report
> AuthorOf (a,p) ∧ Gets (a, rep, p, r) ∧ ◇ KnowsV$_a$ (Reviews[r,p,rep])   (NG1)

Let us assume that the domain theory contains the following sufficient conditions for identifiability of reviewers (the outer universal quantifiers are left implicit for simplicity):

> Gets (a, rep, p, r) ∧ Identifiable (r, rep) ⇒ ◇ KnowsV$_a$ (Reviews[r,p,rep])   (D1)
> Reviews (r, p, rep) ∧ SignedBy (rep, r) ⇒ Identifiable (r, rep)   (D2)
> Reviews (r, p, rep) ∧ French (r) ∧ ¬∃ r' ≠r: [Expert (r', p) ∧ French (r')]
> > ⇒ Identifiable (r, rep)   (D3)

In these property specifications, the predicate Identifiable(r,rep) means that the identity of reviewer r can be determined from the content of report rep. Properties (D2) and (D3) provide explicit sufficient conditions for this. The predicate SignedBy(rep,r) means that report *rep* contains the signature of reviewer *r*. The predicate Expert(r,p) means that reviewer *r* is a well-known expert in the domain of paper *p*. Property (D3) states that a French reviewer notably known as being the only French expert in the area of the paper is identifiable (as he/she makes typical French errors in English usage).

The third conjunct in (NG1) unifies with the consequent in (D1). The regression yields, after corresponding substitutions of variables:

◇∃ r: Reviewer, p: Paper, a: Author, rep: Report
AuthorOf (a, p) ∧ Gets (a, rep, p, r) ∧ Identifiable (r, rep)

The last conjunct in this formula unifies with the consequent in (D3); the regression yields:

◇∃ r: Reviewer, p: Paper, a: Author, rep: Report
AuthorOf (a, p) ∧ Gets (a, *rep*, p, r) ∧ Reviews (r, p, rep) ∧ French(r) ∧¬∃' ≠r: [Expert (r', p) ∧ French (r')]

This condition is satisfiable through a report produced by a French reviewer, who is the only well-known French expert in the domain of the paper, and sent unaltered to the author (as variable *rep* is the same in the Reviews and Gets predicates). We thus formally derived a boundary condition making the goals Maintain [ReviewerAnonymity] and Maintain [ReviewIntegrity] logically inconsistent when it holds.

The space of derivable boundary conditions can be explored by backtracking on each applied property to select another applicable one. After having selected (D3), we could select (D2) to derive another boundary condition:

◇∃ r: Reviewer, p: Paper, a: Author, rep: Report
AuthorOf (a, p) ∧ Gets (a, *rep*, p, r) ∧ Reviews (r, p, rep) ∧ SignedBy (rep, r)

which captures the situation of an author receiving the same report as the one produced by the reviewer with signature information found in it.

Formal divergence patterns

We may sometimes shortcut such formal derivations by instantiating common patterns of divergence among goals. The patterns highlight generic boundary conditions under which the goals become logically inconsistent. Their reuse in matching situations is similar to the obstruction patterns in Section 18.3.2.

Figure 18.13 shows a few common patterns. The one on the left is a formal version of the semi-formal pattern in Figure 16.4.

18.5.2 Formal resolution of divergences

As introduced in Section 3.1.3, we can explore alternative resolutions through operators that capture different resolution tactics. When the divergent goals are formally specified, such operators are defined more precisely; their use can be made more systematic. Here is a sample of formal resolution operators.

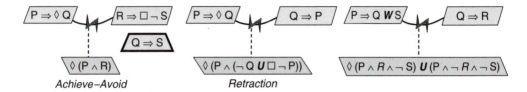

Achieve–Avoid   Retraction

Figure 18.13 *Formal divergence patterns.*

Avoid boundary condition

An *Avoid* goal is introduced taking the form:

$$\Box \neg B.$$

Restore divergent goals

A new goal is introduced taking the form:

$$B \Rightarrow \Diamond \bigwedge_{1 \leq i \leq n} G_i$$

Anticipate conflict

This tactic is applicable when a persistent condition P can be found such that, in a context C, we inevitably get into a conflict after some time if the condition P has persisted over too long a period:

$$C \wedge \Box_{\leq d} P \Leftrightarrow \Diamond_{\leq d} \neg \bigwedge_{1 \leq i \leq n} G_i$$

In such cases, we may introduce the following new goal to avoid the conflict by anticipation:

$$C \wedge P \Rightarrow \Diamond_{\leq d} \neg P$$

Goal weakening

We can weaken lower-priority goals involved in a divergence so as to make the divergence disappear. Such goals are made more liberal by making them cover the boundary condition. The goal weakenings must be propagated through the goal model; the weakened versions must replace the original ones in a way in which satisfaction arguments can still be made.

Here are a few wakening operators:

- *Syntactic weakening.* Add a disjunct in the consequent of a lower-priority divergent goal, or a conjunct in its antecedent.

- *Temporal relaxation:*

  Weaken $\Diamond_{\leq d} A$ to $\Diamond_{\leq c} A$ $(c > d)$.

  Weaken $\Box_{\leq d} A$ to $\Box_{\leq c} A$ $(c < d)$.

- Resolve the *Achieve–Avoid* divergence pattern in Figure 18.13 by:

  a. Weakening the first assertion into $P \land \neg R \Rightarrow \Diamond Q$.

  b. Keeping the second assertion $R \Rightarrow \Box \neg Q$.

  c. Strengthening the overall specification by adding the new goal: $P \Rightarrow \Diamond (P \land \neg R)$.

Examples In the journal reviewing system, we might resolve the detected divergence by avoiding the boundary condition (that is, not asking a French reviewer if he/she is the only French expert in the domain of the paper) or by weakening a divergent goal (for example weakening the lower-priority integrity requirement to allow for correction of typical French errors in English usage).

Conflicts should be carefully considered in safety-critical systems. An interesting example arises in our train control system. One goal might state that the commanded speed may not be 'too high', because otherwise it forces the distance between trains to be too high (for safety reasons). Another goal might state that the commanded speed may not be 'too low', because otherwise it may force acceleration that is uncomfortable for passengers. These goals are more precisely specified as follows:

Goal Maintain [CmdedSpeedCloseToPhysicalSpeed]
  FormalSpec ∀ tr: Train
    $r.Acc_{CM} \geq 0 \Rightarrow tr.Speed_{CM} \leq tr.Speed + f \text{ (distance-to-obstacle)}$
Goal Maintain [CmdedSpeedAbove7mphOfPhysicalSpeed]
  FormalSpec ∀ tr: Train
    $tr.Acc_{CM} \geq 0 \Rightarrow tr.Speed_{CM} > tr.Speed + 7$

The boundary condition for making these two goals logically inconsistent is easily derived:

$$\Diamond (\exists tr: Train) (tr.Acc_{CM} \geq 0 \land f \text{ (dist-to-obstacle)} \leq 7)$$

The selected resolution operator should be goal weakening in this case; we should keep the higher-priority safety goal as it is, and weaken the convenience goal in order to remove the divergence by covering the boundary condition:

Goal Maintain [CmdedSpeedAbove7mphOfPhysicalSpeed]
  FormalSpec ∀ tr: Train
    $tr.Acc_{CM} \geq 0 \Rightarrow tr.Speed_{CM} > tr.Speed + 7 \lor f \text{ (dist-to-obstacle)} \leq 7$

18.6 Synthesizing behaviour models for animation and model checking

As discussed in Section 13.3, goals, scenarios and state machines form a win–win partnership for system modelling and analysis (see Table 13.1). In particular, state machine models are amenable to animation or model checking against goals and domain properties (see Chapter 5).

As they are generally hard to build, we can use the techniques informally described in Section 13.3.3 and Section 13.3.5 to derive such models from goal operationalizations and scenarios. When formal specifications of goals, operations or scenarios are available, these techniques can be automated.

This section discusses formal counterparts of the techniques in Section 13.3.2–13.3.5. We briefly look at goal-driven approaches to state machine synthesis before turning our attention to scenario-driven synthesis.

18.6.1 Goal-driven model synthesis

A formal specification of mission-critical goals, domain properties and operations enables us to:

- Automatically compile parallel state machines from these specifications, using the algorithm given in Section 13.3.5.

- Use the animation engine outlined in Section 5.3 to animate the generated state machines from input events, entered by the user, or from pre-cooked scenarios of environment behaviour.

- Visualize such animations in terms of domain-specific scenes, as discussed in Section 5.3.3; see Figure 5.3.

18.6.2 Scenario-driven model synthesis

Suppose that we have an MSC-like specification of scenarios that includes formalized state conditions along the agent timelines (see Section 13.3.2). We can then generate state machines inductively from them using the algorithm given in Section 13.3.3.

Formal state conditions might, however, not be easy to obtain, as scenarios are intrinsically stateless. In such a case, we can use an alternative approach that does not necessarily require state conditions. Before looking at a stateless approach to model synthesis, we need some background.

Event-oriented state machines

The diagrams introduced in Sections 4.3.7 and 13.2 for specifying behaviour models are state oriented; their states explicitly capture classes of values for state variables declared in the object model. For stateless model synthesis, we will consider an event-oriented form of state machine known as a labelled transition system.

A *labelled transition system* (LTS) is an automaton defined by a structure (Q, Σ, δ, q_0), where Q is a finite set of implicit states, Σ is a set of event labels, δ is a transition function mapping $Q \times \Sigma$ to 2^Q and q_0 is an initial state. Figure 18.16 shows what an LTS looks like. Instead of focusing on state sequences, we focus on event sequences.

The target system is modelled as a parallel composition of LTS – one per system agent. Concurrent LTS behave asynchronously but synchronize on shared events.

Scenarios and LTS

As introduced in Section 13.1, a positive scenario illustrates a desired system behaviour. A negative scenario captures a behaviour that may not occur. It is captured by a pair (p, e) where

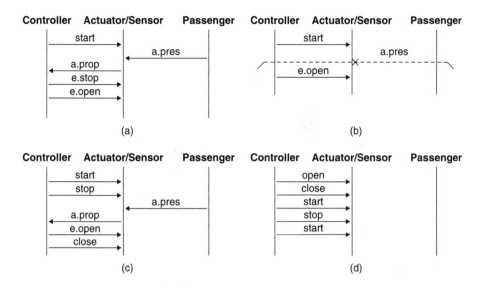

Figure 18.14   *Input scenarios for a train system*
Source: C. Damas, B. Lambeau and A. van Lamsweerde, © 2006 ACM, Inc. Reprinted by Permission.

p is a positive message sequence chart (MSC), called a *MSC pre-condition*, and *e* is a prohibited subsequent event. The meaning is that once the admissible MSC pre-condition has occurred, the prohibited event may not label the next interaction among the corresponding agents.

Figure 18.14 shows a collection of input scenarios for behaviour model synthesis. The upper right-hand scenario is a negative one. The intuitive, end-user semantics of two consecutive events along an MSC timeline is that the first is *directly* followed by the second.

We can define an LTS semantics for MSCs (Uchitel *et al.*, 2003). An MSC timeline defines a finite LTS execution capturing a behaviour of the corresponding agent instance. An MSC defines an execution of the parallel composition of each agent LTS.

LTS synthesis as grammar induction

The overall procedure for synthesizing an LTS behaviour model from a collection of positive and negative scenarios has two steps:

1. The input scenarios are generalized into an LTS for the entire system, called a *system LTS*.

2. This LTS is projected on each agent using standard automaton transformation algorithms (Hopcroft & Ullman, 1979).

The system LTS resulting from Step 1 covers all positive scenarios and excludes all negative ones. It is obtained by an interactive extension of a grammar induction algorithm known as RPNI (Oncinan & Garcia, 1992). Grammar induction aims at learning a language from a set of positive and negative strings defined on a specific alphabet. The alphabet here is the set of event labels; the strings are provided by positive and negative scenarios.

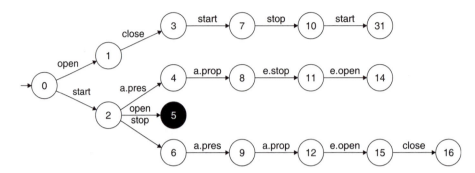

Figure 18.15 *PTA built from the scenarios in Fig. 18.14*

Representing the input scenario collection as a PTA RPNI first computes an initial LTS solution, called *Prefix Tree Acceptor* (PTA). The PTA is a deterministic LTS built from the input scenarios; each scenario is a branch in the tree that ends with a 'white' state, for a positive scenario, or a 'black' state, for a negative one. The scenarios are assumed to start in the same initial state.

Figure 18.15 shows the PTA computed from the scenarios in Figure 18.14. A black state is an error state for the system. A path leading to a black state is said to be *rejected* by the LTS; a path leading to a white state is said to be *accepted* by the LTS. By construction, the PTA accepts all positive input scenarios while rejecting all negative ones.

Generalizing scenario behaviours Behaviour generalization from the PTA is achieved by a generate-and-test algorithm that performs an exhaustive search for equivalent state pairs; equivalent states are *merged* into equivalence classes forming generalized states in the synthesized LTS.

Two states are considered *equivalent* if they have no incompatible continuation; that is, there is no subsequent event sequence leading to a white state from one and to a black state from the other.

At each generate-and-test cycle, RPNI considers merging a state q in the current solution with a state q' of lower rank. Merging two candidate states q and q' may require further merging of subsequent state pairs to obtain a deterministic solution; the same outgoing transition from a candidate generalized state to two different states results in merging the latter. Shared continuations of q and q' are folded up by such further merges. When this would end up merging black and white states, the candidate merging into a generalized state $(q, q'$ is discarded and RPNI continues with the next candidate pair.

Figure 18.16 shows the system LTS computed by the synthesizer for our train example. The resulting classes of equivalent states yielding implicit LTS states are:

$$\{0, 3, 6, 10, 16\}; \{2, 7, 13\}; \{4\}; \{5\}; \{9\}; \{8\}; \{11, 12\}; \{1, 14, 15\}.$$

The notion of state equivalence used by this generalization process shows the important role played by negative scenarios in avoiding merging *non*-equivalent system states, which would produce incorrect generalizations. RPNI is guaranteed to find the correct system LTS when the input scenario sample is rich enough; two distinct system states must be distinguished in

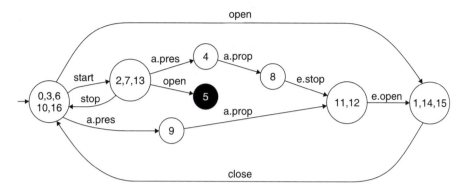

Figure 18.16 *Synthesized system LTS for the train example*
Source: C. Damas, B. Lambeau and A. van Lamsweerde, © 2006 ACM, Inc. Reprinted by Permission.

the PTA by at least one continuation accepted from one and rejected from the other. When the input sample does not have enough negative scenarios, RPNI tends to produce poor generalizations by merging non-equivalent states.

Scenario questions for better generalization

To overcome this problem, the LTS synthesizer extends RPNI in two directions:

- *Blue fringe search.* The search is made heuristic through an evaluation function that favours states sharing common continuations as first candidates for merging (Lang *et al.*, 1998).

- *Interactive search.* The synthesis process is made interactive through *scenario questions* asked by the synthesizer whenever a generalized state gets *new* outgoing transitions that one of the merged states did not have before.

To answer a scenario question, the user has merely to accept or reject the new MSC scenario generated by the synthesizer. The answer results in confirming or discarding the current candidate state merge. Scenario questions provide a natural way of eliciting further positive and negative scenarios to enrich the scenario sample. Figure 18.17 shows a scenario question that can be rephrased as follows:

> If the train starts and a passenger presses the alarm button, may the controller then open the doors in an emergency and close the doors afterwards?

This scenario should be rejected, as the train may not move with open doors.

While interaction takes place in terms of simple end-user scenarios, and scenarios only, the number of scenario questions may sometimes become large for interaction-intensive systems with complex composite states (as experienced when using the technique for non-trivial Web applications).

An *optimized version* of the LTS synthesis process can reduce the number of scenario questions drastically while producing an LTS model consistent with knowledge about the

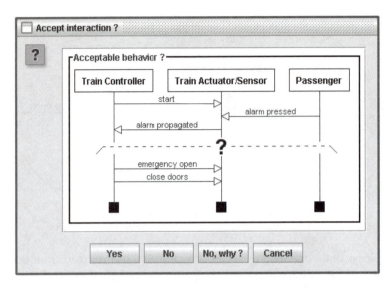

Figure 18.17   *Scenario question generated during synthesis*
Source: C. Damas, B. Lambeau and A. van Lamsweerde, © 2006 ACM, Inc. Reprinted by Permission.

domain and goals of the target system. The general idea is to constrain the induction process in order to prune the generalization search space and, accordingly, the set of scenario questions. The constraints include:

- State assertions generated along agent timelines from definitions of fluents.
- System goals and domain properties.

Let us look at how the induction process can be significantly improved through these constraints.

Constraining generalization by propagation of fluents through the PTA

Fluent definitions provide simple domain knowledge for constraining induction. As introduced semi-formally in Section 12.6.1, a fluent *Fl* is a proposition defined by a set $Init_{Fl}$ of initiating events, a set $Term_{Fl}$ of terminating events and an initial value $Initially_{Fl}$ that can be true or false. The sets of initiating and terminating events must be disjoint. A fluent definition takes the form:

fluent Fl = $< Init_{Fl}, Term_{Fl} >$ initially $Initially_{Fl}$

In our train example, the fluents *DoorsClosed* and *Moving* are defined as follows:

fluent DoorsClosed = $<$ {*close doors*}, {*open doors, emergency open*} $>$ initially **true**
fluent Moving = $<$ {*start*}, {*stop, emergency stop*} $>$ initially **false**

To constrain the induction process, we decorate the PTA with the value of every fluent at each node. The rule for pruning the generalization search space is to *avoid merging inconsistent states*; that is, states whose decoration has at least one fluent with different values. Two states are now considered *equivalent* if they have the same value for every fluent. The decoration of the merged state is simply inherited from the states being merged.

The algorithm for PTA decoration is based on the following observation. A fluent *Fl* holds at some point if either of the following conditions holds:

- *Fl* holds initially and no terminating event has yet occurred.

- Some initiating event has occurred and no terminating event has occurred since then.

The fluent definitions are thereby propagated forwards by symbolic execution along PTA paths (Damas *et al.*, 2005). The PTA nodes are then decorated with the conjunction of such values. Note that this propagation-based decoration is done only once, at the initial step after PTA construction.

Figure 18.18 shows the result of propagating the values of the fluent *DoorsClosed*, according to its above definition, along the PTA shown in Figure 18.15.

Constraining generalization by injecting goals and domain properties in the synthesis

For goals or domain properties formalizable as safety properties, we may generate a property *tester*; that is, an LTS extended with an error state such that every path leading to the error state violates the property (Giannakopoulou & Magee, 2003). Consider, for example, the goal:

$$\text{DoorsClosedWhileMoving} = \Box \, (\text{Moving} \rightarrow \text{DoorsClosed})$$

Figure 18.19 shows the tester LTS for this property (the error state is again the black one). Any event sequence leading to the error state from the initial state corresponds to an undesired system behaviour. In particular, the event sequence *<start, open>* corresponds to the initial negative scenario in Figure 18.14. The generated tester thus provides *many more negative scenarios*. Property testers can in fact provide potentially infinite classes of negative scenarios.

To constrain the induction process further, the PTA and the tester are traversed jointly in order to decorate each PTA state with the corresponding tester state. This is again performed

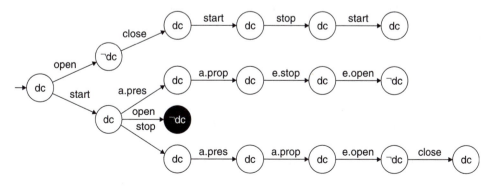

Figure 18.18 *Propagating fluent values along a PTA (dc is a shorthand for DoorsClosed)*
Source: C. Damas, B. Lambeau and A. van Lamsweerde, © 2006 ACM, Inc. Reprinted by Permission.

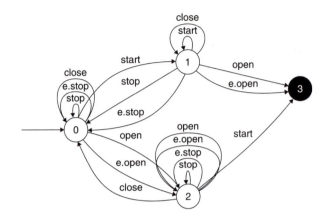

Figure 18.19   *Tester LTS for the goal **DoorsClosedWhileMoving***
Source: C. Damas, B. Lambeau and A. van Lamsweerde, © 2006 ACM, Inc. Reprinted by Permission.

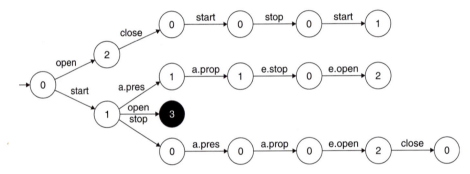

Figure 18.20   *PTA decorated using the tester LTS from Figure 18.19*
Source: C. Damas, B. Lambeau and A. van Lamsweerde, © 2006 ACM, Inc. Reprinted by Permission.

once, after PTA construction. Figure 18.20 shows the PTA decorated using the tester in Figure 18.19.

The pruning rule constraining induction is now to avoid merging states decorated with distinct states of the property tester. Two states are considered *equivalent* here if they have the same property tester state.

This pruning technique provides the additional benefit of ensuring that the synthesized system LTS satisfies the considered goal or domain property. A tester for a safety property is a canonical automaton; that is, minimal and deterministic (Giannakopoulou & Magee, 2003). A bijection thus exists between states and continuations. In other words, two states are distinct if and only if there is at least one continuation to distinguish them. In the particular case of the tester LTS, two states are distinct if and only if they do not have the same set of continuations leading to the error state.

The question remains as to where these goals and domain properties come from. There are complementary answers to this:

- We can pick them up in the goal model, when they are available.

- We can get them by asking the end-user the reason why a scenario is rejected as a counterexample when he or she answers a scenario question.

- We can infer some of them automatically by inductive inference from scenarios (Damas *et al.*, 2006). The inferred property then needs to be validated by the user. If it turns out to be inadequate, the user is asked to provide a counterexample scenario that will enrich the scenario collection.

Summary

- A temporal logic specification of critical goals in the goal model allows us to check that goal refinements are correct and complete. We can use a theorem prover, formal refinement patterns or a bounded SAT solver. Formal refinement patterns encode common goal refinements in temporal logic; we may reuse them in matching situations. All patterns informally presented in the book are easily formalized in LTL. Formal patterns may guide refinements while hiding the formal details. Such patterns are proved correct once for all. Once instantiated, they can point out missing sub-goals and drive the exploration of alternative formal refinements. *SAT solvers* are efficient tools for determining whether a given propositional specification is satisfiable by showing examples of satisfying solutions. We can build front ends to bounded SAT solvers for temporal logic to produce bounded system histories showing that a goal refinement is incomplete.

- A formal semantics for goal operationalization allows us to check the correctness of operationalizations by the use of SAT solvers or of formal operationalization patterns. Such patterns are organized for easy retrieval according to a taxonomy of goal specification patterns. They are proved correct once for all too. They can be used forwards, to formally derive operations with their domain conditions and required pre-, trigger and post-conditions; or backwards, for goal mining from operational specifications.

- Obstacles can be generated formally by regressing goal negations through formal specifications of domain properties. Regression is a declarative pre-condition calculus for abductive reasoning. It may be used to elicit domain properties as well. Formal obstruction patterns, when applicable, allow us to shortcut the formal derivations involved in regression.

- For threat analysis, we need to specify security properties in terms of epistemic constructs that capture what agents may or may not know. Such formalization together with formal anti-goal regressions through properties of the attacker's environment, including the system's goals, allows us to derive portions of a threat model formally. We can then explore security countermeasures on a more solid basis.

- We can also regress goal negations formally through overlapping goals to generate boundary conditions showing that the goals are potentially conflicting. Formal divergence patterns may be used here too as a cheap alternative. Formal resolution operators may help us resolve goal divergences in more solid and accurate ways.

- We need state machines for animating models and model-checking behaviour models against goals and domain properties. With formal models, we can synthesize state machines automatically or interactively from goal operationalizations or from scenarios. When formal state conditions along scenario timelines are not available, we can alternatively use grammar induction techniques and scenario questions for state machine synthesis. Such techniques can be significantly optimized by injection of fluents, goals and domain properties to prune the search space of possible generalizations.

Notes and Further Reading

Formal refinement patterns are detailed in Darimont and van Lamsweerde (1996) and extended with unrealizibility-driven patterns in Letier and van Lamsweerde (2002a). First-order patterns are described in much greater detail in the former paper. A tool automating goal refinement checking based on SAT solver technology is described in Ponsard *et al.* (2007).

The temporal logic semantics for operations is further discussed in Letier and van Lamsweerde (2002b). This paper describes the use of goal operationalization patterns and provides a richer sample of patterns.

Regression has been used in in AI planning for a long time (Waldinger, 1977). It can be seen as a declarative counterpart of Dijkstra's weakest precondition calculus (Dijkstra, 1976). The adaptation of regression techniques for formal analysis of obstacles and anti-goals is further detailed in van Lamsweerde and Letier (2000) and van Lamsweerde (2004a), respectively. The former paper provides a richer sample of goal obstruction patterns.

The agent knowledge and belief constructs for threat analysis are inspired from epistemic logics (Fagin *et al.*, 1995). Variants of specification patterns for confidentiality goals according to the degree of approximate knowledge and its timing are provided in De Landtsheer and van Lamsweerde (2005), where a model checker for such properties is described.

Formal analysis of conflicts and divergences is further detailed in van Lamsweerde *et al.* (1998).

Tran Van *et al.* (2004) describe a goal-oriented animation tool that synthesizes state machines from formal goal operationalizations according to the algorithm outlined in

Section 13.3.5. The generated state machines are animated within goal scopes in terms of domain scenes.

Quite a lot of effort was devoted to the synthesis of state machines from various forms of scenarios. For example, an LTS model can be synthesized from MSCs taken as positive examples of system behaviour (Uchitel *et al.*, 2003). MSC specifications can be translated into statecharts (Kruger *et al.*, 1998). UML state diagrams can be generated from sequence diagrams capturing positive scenarios (Whittle & Schumann, 2000; Mäkinen & Systä, 2001). Goal specifications in linear temporal logic can also be inferred inductively from MSC scenarios taken as positive or negative examples (van Lamsweerde & Willemet, 1998). These techniques all require additional input information besides scenarios; namely, a high-level message sequence chart showing how MSC scenarios are to be flowcharted (Uchitel *et al.*, 2003); pre- and post-conditions of interactions, expressed on global state variables (van Lamsweerde & Willemet, 1998; Whittle & Schumann, 2000); local MSC conditions (Kruger *et al.*, 1998); or state machine traces local to a specific agent (Mäkinen & Systä, 2001). This additional input information may be hard to get from stakeholders, and may need to be refactored in non-trivial ways if new positive or negative scenario examples are provided later in the requirements/design engineering process (Letier *et al.*, 2005). The inductive synthesis approach addressing this problem through scenario questions is detailed in Damas *et al.* (2005). The injection of formal specifications for constraining the induction space is detailed in Damas *et al.* (2006).

Exercises

- Elaborate variants of the *Milestone-Driven* and *Guard-Introduction* patterns in Figure 18.1 where time bounds are put on $\Diamond$ operators. Then adapt the instantiation in Figure 18.2 accordingly.

- Provide formal versions of the refinement patterns shown in Figures 8.21 and 8.24. Make sure that you are using the right temporal connectors, in particular for implications. Then explore formal instantiations on the examples illustrating those semi-formal patterns in Section 8.8.5.

- Consider the following meeting scheduling goal:

    Goal *Achieve* [ParticipantConstraintsKnown]
        FormalSpec ∀ p: Participant, m: Meeting
            Invitation (p, m) $\Rightarrow \Diamond$ ConstraintsKnown (p, m)

    Apply the formal milestone-driven refinement pattern in Figure 18.1 to derive sub-goals of this goal together with their formal specification.

- Consider the following goal in the context of the oversimplified A320 braking logic example used in previous chapters:

WheelsPulseOn ⇒ o ReverseThrustEnabled
  % *Reverse thrust shall be enabled when the wheels pulse is on* %

Use the operationalization patterns in Section 18.2 to derive the specification of the operations ensuring this goal.

- Consider the following statement about a simple autopilot system:

  If the pilot dials in an altitude that is more than 1,200 feet above the current altitude and then presses the alt_eng button, the altitude mode will not directly engage. Instead, the altitude engage mode will change to 'armed' and the flight-path angle select mode is engaged. (Butler, 1996)

The operation *EngageFPAmode* might be identified from this statement and specified as follows:

  Operation EngageFPAmode
  Input a: AutoPilot, alt_eng: ALTengageEvent; **Output** AutoPilot/FPAmode
  DomPre a.FPAmode = 'off'; **DomPost** a.FPAmode = 'on';
  ReqTrig for ??: Occurs (alt_eng) ∧ ALTtarget − ALTactual > 1200
                % *If the pilot presses the alt_eng button when the target altitude is more than 1,200 feet above the current altitude, the FPA mode is engaged* %

Use the operationalization patterns in Section 18.2 to infer the goal underlying this specification.

- Use the techniques in Section 18.3 to formally derive the obstacle tree shown in Section 9.2.1 (see Figure 9.1). Are there any further obstacles you could generate that way?

- Consider the meeting scheduling system goal:

  ∀ m: Meeting, p: Participant
  Invitation (p, m) ⇒ ◇ Participates(p, m)

Suppose that the following complete refinement has been derived formally for this goal:

  Invitation (p, m) ∧ Notified (p, m) ∧ Convenient (p, m) ⇒ ◇ Participates(p, m),
  Invitation (p, m) ⇒ ◇ (Notified (p, m) ∧ Convenient (p, m)),
  Invitation (p, m) ⇒ □ Invitation (p, m).

Complete the formal analysis in Section 18.3.1 to generate further obstacles to these goals.

- Formally rederive the obstacles to the meeting scheduling system in Figure 9.8 that you did not generate in the preceding exercise. Are there any further obstacles you could generate that way?

- Consider the car handbrake release problem described at the end of Section 1.2.1. In a way similar to the A320 braking logic example in Section 18.3.1, apply the regression procedure to generate corresponding obstacles.

- Complete the regression-based derivation of anti-goals in Section 18.4.3 to formally rederive the bottom of the threat graph for web banking in Figure 16.5.

- Consider the following formal goal model for an online shopping system. By formal regression through this goal model, derive a threat model anchored on the following security goal obtained as a converse *Maintain* assertion of one of the *Achieve* goals in this model:

ItemSent $\Rightarrow$ ItemPaid.

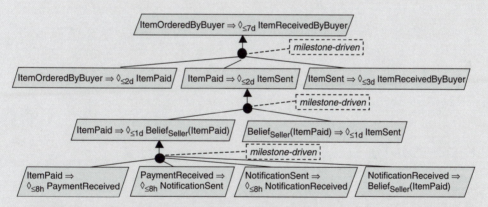

The attacker has the capability of *controlling* two conditions: ItemPaid and Notification-Received.

- Formally detect and resolve the divergence among the following two resource management goals:

$\forall$ u: User, r: Resource
Using (u, r) $\Rightarrow$ o [Needs (u, r) $\rightarrow$ Using (u, r)]   (*user's view*)

$\forall$ u: User, r: Resource
Using (u, r) $\Rightarrow$ $\Diamond_{\leq d} \neg$ Using (u, r)   (*staff's view*)

Bibliography

Abadi, M., Lamport, L. and Wolper P. (1989). 'Realizable and Unrealizable Specifications of Reactive Systems', *Proceedings of 16th ICALP*, LNCS 372, 1–17.

Abrial, J.R. (1974). 'Data Semantics', in Kimbie & Hoffman (eds), *Data Semantics in Data Management Systems*, North Holland.

Abrial, J.R. (1980). 'The Specification Language Z: Syntax and Semantics'. Programming Research Group, Oxford University.

Abrial, J.R. (1996). *The B-Book: Assigning Programs to Meanings*. Cambridge University Press.

Ahern, D., Clouse, A. and Turner, R. (2003). *CMMI Distilled: A Practical Introduction to Integrated Process Improvement*. Addison-Wesley.

Alagar, V.S. and Periyasamy, K. (1998). *Specification of Software Systems*. Springer-Verlag.

Alexander, I. (2003) 'Misuse Cases: Use Cases with Hostile Intent', *IEEE Software*, Jan/Feb, 58–66.

Alexander, I. and Maiden, N. (2004). *Scenarios, Stories, Use Cases Through the Systems Development Lifecycle*. John Wiley & Sons Ltd.

Alford, M. (1977). 'A Requirements Engineering Methodology for Real-Time Processing Requirements', *IEEE Transactions on Software Engineering*, Vol. 3, No. 1, January, 60–69.

Allen, J.F. and Hayes, P.J. (1989). 'Moments and Points in an Interval-Based Temporal Logic', *Computational Intelligence*, Vol. 5, 225–238.

Amoroso, E.J. (1994). *Fundamentals of Computer Security*. Prentice-Hall.

Anderson, R.J. (2001). *Security Engineering: A Guide to Building Dependable Distributed Systems*. John Wiley & Sons Ltd.

Anderson, T., de Lemos, R. and Saeed, A. (1995). 'Analysis of Safety Requirements for Process Control Systems', in *Predictably Dependable Computing Systems*, B. Randell, J.C. Laprie, B. Littlewood and H. Kopetz (eds), Springer-Verlag.

Anton, A.I. and Potts, C. (1998). 'The Use of Goals to Surface Requirements for Evolving Systems', *Proceedings of ICSE-98: 20th International Conference on Software Enginering*, Kyoto, April.

Anton, A.I., Carter, R., Dagnino, A., Dempster, J. and Siege, D.F. (2001). 'Deriving Goals from a Use-Case Based Requirements Specification', *Requirements Engineering Journal*, Vol. 6, 63–73.

Anton, A.I., Earp, I. and Reese, A. (2002). 'Analyzing Website Privacy Requirements Using a Privacy Goal Taxonomy', *Proceedings of RE'02 – International Requirements Engineering Conference*, Essen, September.

Anton, A.I., McCracken, W.M. and Potts, C. (1994). 'Goal Decomposition and Scenario Analysis in Business Process Reengineering', *Proceedings of CAISE'94*, LNCS 811, Springer-Verlag, 94–104.

Antoniol, G., Canfora, G., Casazza, G., De Lucia, A. and Merlo, E. (2002). 'Recovering Traceability Links between Code and Documentation', *IEEE Transactions on Software Engineering* Vol. 28 No. 10, October, 970–983.

Astesiano, E. and Wirsing, M. (1986). 'An introduction to ASL', *Proceedings of IFIP WG2.1 Conference on Program Specifications and Transformations*, North-Holland.

Atlee, J.M. (1993). 'State-Based Model Checking of Event-Driven System Requirements', *IEEE Transactions on Software Engineering* Vol. 19, No. 1, January, 24–40.

Bailin, S., Moore, J.M., Bentz, R. and Bewtra, M. (1990). 'KAPTUR: Knowledge Acquisition for Preservation of Tradeoffs and Underlying Rationale', *Proceedings of KBSA-5: Fifth Annual Knowledge-Based Software Assistant Conference*, September.

Balepin, I., Maltsev, S., Rowe, J., Levitt, K., Vigna, G., Jonsson, E. and Kruegel, C. (2003). 'Using Specification-Based Intrusion Detection for Automated Response', *Proceedings of RAID'2003: International Symposium on Recent Advances in Intrusion Detection*, Pittsburgh (PA), LNCS 2820, Springer-Verlag, 136–154.

Balzer, R.M. (1991). 'Tolerating Inconsistency', *Proceedings of ICSE-91: 13th Intrnational Conference on Software Engineering*, Austin (TX), May.

Balzer, R.M., Goldman, N.M. and Wile, D.S. (1982). 'Operational Specification as the Basis for Rapid Prototyping', *ACM SIGSOFT Software Engineering Notes* Vol. 7, No. 5, December, 3–16.

Basili, V. and Rombach, H.D. (1988). 'The TAME Project: Towards Improvement-Oriented Software Environments', *IEEE Transactions on Software Engineering*, Vol. 14, No. 6, June, 758–773.

Basili, V., Green, S., Laitenberger, O., Lanubile, F., Shull, F., Soerumgaard, S. and Zelkowitz, M. (1996). 'The Empirical Investigation of Perspective-Based Reading', *Empirical Software Engineering*, Vol. 1, No. 2, 133–164.

Behm, P., Benoit, P., Faivre A. and Meynadier, J.M. (1999). 'Météor: A Successful Application of B in a Large Project', *Proceedings of FM-99 – World Conference on Formal Methods in the Development of Computing Systems*, LNCS 1708, Springer-Verlag, 369–387.

Bell, T.E. and Thayer, T.A. (1976). 'Software Requirements: Are They Really a Problem?', *Proceedings of ICSE-2: 2nd International Conference on Software Enginering,* San Francisco, 61–68.

Benner, K.M., Feather, M.S., Johnson W.L. and Zorman, L.A. (1993). 'Utilizing Scenarios in the Software Development Process', *Information System Development Process*, Elsevier Science (North-Holland), 117–134.

Bensalem, S., Lakhnech, Y. and Saídi, H. (1996). 'Powerful Techniques for the Automatic Generation of Invariants', *Proceedings of CAV'96 – 8th International Conference on Computer-Aided Verification*, LNCS 1102, Springer-Verlag, 323–335.

Bentley, R., Hughes, J., Randall, D., Rodden, T., Sawyer, P., Shapiro, D. and Sommerville, I. (1992). 'Ethnographically-Informed System Design for Air Traffic Control', *Proceedings of ACM Conference on Computer-Supported Cooperative Work*, Toronto, 123–129.

Bérard, B., Bidoit, M., Finkel, A., Laroussinie, F., Petit, A., Petrucci, L. and Schnoebelen, P. (2001). *Systems and Software Verification: Model Checking Techniques and Tools*. Springer-Verlag.

Bernot, G., Gaudel, M.C. and Marre, B. (1991). 'Software Testing Based on Formal Specifications: A Theory and a Tool', *Software Engineering Journal*, Vol. 6, No. 6, 387–405.

Berzins V. and Luqi, L. (1991). *Software Engineering with Abstractions*. Addison-Wesley.

Beyer, H. and Holtzblatt, K. (1998). *Contextual Design: Defining Customer-Centered Systems*. Morgan Kaufmann.

Blum, B.I. (1992). *Software Engineering: A Holistic View*. Oxford University Press.

Bodart, F., Hennebert, A.M., Leheureux, J.M. and Pigneur, Y. (1985). 'Computer-Aided Specification, Evaluation, and Monitoring of Information Systems, *Proceedings of 6th International Conference on Information Systems*, Indianapolis.

Boehm, B.W. (1981). *Software Engineering Economics*. Prentice-Hall.

Boehm, B.W. (1988). 'A Spiral Model of Software Development and Enhancement', *IEEE Computer*, Vol. 21, No. 5, May, 61–72.

Boehm, B.W. (1989). *Software Risk Management*. IEEE Computer Society Press.

Boehm, B.W. (1991). 'Software Risk Management: Principles & Practice', *IEEE Software*, Vol. 8, No. 1, January, 32–41.

Boehm, B.W. and Papaccio, C. (1988). 'Understanding and Controlling Software Costs', *IEEE Transactions on Sofware Engineering*, Vol. 14, No. 10, October, 14–66.

Boehm, B.W., Abts, C., Brown, A.W., Chulani, S., Clark, B.K., Horwitz, E., Madachy, R., Reifer, D. and Steece, B. (2000). *Software Cost Estimation with COCOMO II*. Prentice Hall.

Boehm, B.W., Bose, P., Horowitz, E. and Ming June Lee (1995). 'Software Requirements Negotiation and Renegotiation Aids: A Theory-W Based Spiral Approach', *Proceedings of ICSE-17 – 17th International Conference on Software Engineering*, Seattle, 243–253.

Boman, M., Bubenko, J.A., Johannesson, P. and Wangler, B. (1997). *Conceptual Modeling*. Prentice Hall.

Bontemps, Y., Heymans, P. and Schobbens, P.Y. (2005). 'From Live Sequence Charts to State Machines and Back: A Guided Tour', *IEEE Transactions on Software Engineering*, Vol. 31, 12.

Booch, G., Rumbaugh J. and Jacobson, I. (1999). *The Unified Modeling Language User Guide*. Addison-Wesley.

Borgida, A., Mylopoulos J. and Reiter, R. (1993). 'And Nothing Else Changes: The Frame Problem in Procedure Specifications', *Proceedings of ICSE'93 – 15th International Conference on Software Engineering,* Baltimore, May.

Bosch, J. (2000). *Design and Use of Software Architectures: Adopting and Evolving a Product Line Approach*. Addison-Wesley.

Bosch, J. and Molin, P. (1999). 'Software Architecture Design: Evaluation and Transformation', *Proceedings of IEEE Symposium on Engineering of Computer-Based Systems*.

Brachman, R.J. and Levesque, H.J. (1985). *Readings in Knowledge Representation*. Morgan Kaufmann.

Bray, I.K. (2003). *An Introduction to Requirements Engineering*. Addison-Wesley.

Brodie, M., Mylopoulos, J. and Schmidt J. (eds). (1984). *On Conceptual Modeling: Perspectives from Artificial Intelligence, Databases, and Programming Languages*. Springer-Verlag.

Brooks, F.P. (1987). 'No Silver Bullet: Essence and Accidents of Software Engineering', *IEEE Computer*, Vol. 20, No. 4, April, 10–19.

Brown, A.W., Earl A.N. and Mc Dermid, J. (1992). *Software Engineering Environments: Automated Support for Software Engineering*. McGraw-Hill.

Bryant, R.E. (1992). 'Symbolic Boolean Manipulation with Ordered Binary Decision Diagrams', *ACM Computing Surveys*, Vol. 24, No. 3, 293–318.

Bubenko, J. (1980). 'Information Modeling in the Context of System Development', *Proceedings of IFIP Congress '80*, North Holland, 395–411.

Budde, R. (1984). *Approaches to Prototyping*. Springer-Verlag.

Buschmann, F., Meunier, R., Rohnert, H., Sommerlad, P. and Stal, M. (1996). *Pattern-Oriented Software Architecture: A System of Patterns*. John Wiley & Sons Ltd.

Butler, R.W. (1996). *An Introduction to RequirementsCapture Using PVS: Specification of a Simple Autopilot*. NASA Technical Memo 110255, NASA Langley Research Center, May.

Butler, R.W., Miller, S.P., Potts, J.N. and Carreno, V.A. (1998). 'A Formal Methods Approach to the Analysis of Mode Confusion', *Proceedings of DASC'98 – 17th Digital Avionics Systems Conference*, Seattle, November. See also http://shemesh.larc.nasa.gov/fm/fm-now-mode-confusion.html.

Byrd, T.A., Cossick, K.L. and Zmud, R.W. (1992). 'A Synthesis of Research on Requirements Analysis and Knowledge Acquisition Techniques', *MIS Quarterly*, Vol. 16, No. 1, 117–138.

Carlisle Scott, A., Clayton, J.E. and Gibson, E. L. (1991). *A Practical Guide to Knowledge Acquisition*. Addison-Wesley.

Carr, M.J., Konda, S.L., Monarch, I., Ulrich, F.C. and Walker, C.F. (1993). *Taxonomy-Based Risk Identification*. Report CMU/SEI-93-TR-006, Software Engineering Institute, Pittsburgh (PA), June.

Carroll, J.M. and Rosson, M.B. (1995). 'Narrowing the Specification Implementation Gap in Scenario-Based Design', in *Scenario-Based Design: Envisioning Work and Technology in System Development*, J.M. Carroll (ed.), John Wiley & Sons Ltd, 247–278.

Castro, J., Kolp, M. and Mylopoulos, J. (2002). 'Towards Requirements-Driven Information Systems Engineeering: The TROPOS Project', *Information Systems*, Vol. 27, 365–389.

Charette, R. (1989). *Software Engineering Risk Analysis and Management*. McGraw-Hill.

Chen, P. (1976). 'The Entity Relationship Model – Towards a Unified View of Data', *ACM Transactions on Database Systems*, Vol. 1, No. 1, March, 9–36.

Chung, L., Nixon, B., Yu E. and Mylopoulos, J. (2000). *Non-Functional Requirements in Software Engineering*. Kluwer Academic.

Chvalovsky, V. (1983). 'Decision Tables', *Software – Practice and Experience*, Vol. 13, 423–449.

Ciapessoni, E., Mirandola, P., Coen-Porsini, A., Mandrioli, D. and Morzenti, A. (1999). 'From Formal Models to Formally Based Methods: An Industrial Experience. *ACM Transactions on Software Engineering and Methodology (TOSEM)*, Vol. 8, No. 1, January, 79–113.

Cimatti, A., Clarke, E.M., Giunchiglia, F. and Roveri, M. (2000). 'NuSMV: A New Symbolic Model Checker', *International Journal on Software Tools and Technology Transfer*, Vol. 2, No. 4, 410–425.

Clarke, E.M. and Wing, J.M. (1996). 'Formal Methods: State of the Art and Future Directions', *ACM Computing Surveys*, Vol. 28, No. 4, December.

Clarke, E.M., Emerson, E.A. and Sistla, A.P. (1986). 'Automatic Verification of Finite-State Concurrent Systems Using Temporal Logic Specifications', *ACM Transactions in Programming Language Systems*, Vol. 8, No. 2, 244–263.

Clarke, E.M., Grumberg, O. and Peled, D.A. (1999). *Model Checking*. MIT Press.

Clavel, M., Eker, S., Lincoln, P. and Meseguer, J. (1996). 'Principles of MAUDE', *Proceedings of First International Workshop on Rewriting Logic and Applications, Electric Notes on Theoretical Computer Science*.

Cleland-Huang, J., Chang, C.K. and Wise, J. (2003). 'Automating Performance-Related Impact Analysis Through Event-Based Traceability', *Requirements Engineering Journal*, Vol. 8, No. 3, August, 171–182.

Cleland-Huang, J., Zemont, G. and Lukasic, W. (2004). 'A Heterogeneous Solution for Improving the Return on Investment of Requirements Traceability', *Proceedings of RE'04 – 12th IEEE Joint International Requirements Engineering Conference*, Kyoto, September.

Cockburn, A. (1997a). 'Goals and Use Cases', *Journal of Object-Oriented Programming*, Vol. 10, 35–40.

Cockburn, A. (1997b). 'Using Goal-Based Use Cases', *Journal of Object-Oriented Programming*, Vol. 10, 56–62.

Conradi, R. and Westfechtel, B. (1998). 'Version Models for Software Configuration Management', *ACM Computing Surveys* Vol. 30, 232–282.

Courtois, P.-J. and Parnas, D.L. (1993). 'Documentation for Safety Critical Software', *Proceedings of ICSE'93 – 15th International Conference on Software Engineering*, 315–323.

Craigen, D., Gerhart, S. and Ralston, T. (1995). 'Formal Methods Technology Transfer: Impediments and Innovation', in *Applications of Formal Methods*, M.G. Hinchey and J.P. Bowen (eds), Prentice Hall, 399–419.

Cristian, F. (1991). 'Understanding Fault-Tolerant Distributed Systems', *Communications of the ACM*, February.

Cristian, F. (1995). 'Exception Handling', in *Software Fault Tolerance*, M.R. Lyu (ed.), John Wiley & Sons Ltd.

Crook, R., Ince, D., Lin, L. and Nuseibeh, B. (2002). 'Security Requirements Engineering: When Anti-Requirements Hit the Fan', *Proceedings of RE'02 – IEEE International Requirements Engineering Conference*, Essen, September, 203–205.

Curtis, B., Krasner, H. and Iscoe, N. (1988). 'A Field Study of the Software Design Process for Large Systems', *Communications of the ACM*, Vol. 31, No. 11, 1268–1287.

Daeza Yates, R. and Ribeiro-Neto, B. (1999). *Modern Information Retrieval*, Addison-Wesley.

Dallianis, H. (1992). 'A Method for Validating a Conceptual Model by Natural Language Discourse Generation', *Advanced Information Systems Engineering*, LNCS 593, Springer-Verlag.

Damas, C., Lambeau, B., Dupont, P. and van Lamsweerde, A. (2005). 'Generating Annotated Behaviour Models from End-User Scenarios', *IEEE Transactions on Software Engineering*, Special Issue on Scenarios and State Machines, Vol. 31, No. 12, December, 1056–1073.

Damas, C., Lambeau, B. and van Lamsweerde, A. (2006). 'Scenarios, Goals, and State Machines: A Win–Win Partnership for Model Synthesis', *Proceedings of FSE'06, 14th ACM International Symposium on the Foundations of Software Engineering*, Portland (OR), November.

Dardenne, A., Fickas, S. and van Lamsweerde, A. (1991). 'Goal-Directed Concept Acquisition in Requirements Elicitation', *Proceedings of IWSSD-6 – 6th International Workshop on Software Specification and Design*, Como, 14–21.

Dardenne, A., van Lamsweerde, A. and Fickas, S. (1993). 'Goal-Directed Requirements Acquisition', *Science of Computer Programming*, Vol. 20, 3–50.

Darimont, R. (1995). 'Process Support for Requirements Elaboration'. PhD Thesis, Université Catholique de Louvain, Dépt. Ingénierie Informatique, Louvain-la-Neuve, Belgium.

Darimont, R. and van Lamsweerde, A. (1996). 'Formal Refinement Patterns for Goal-Driven Requirements Elaboration', *Proceedings of FSE'4 – Fourth ACM SIGSOFT Symposium on the Foundations of Software Engineering*, San Francisco, October, 179–190.

Darimont, R. and Lemoine, M. (2007). 'Security Requirements for Civil Aviation with UML and Goal Orientation', *Proceedings of REFSQ'07 – International Working Conference on Foundations for Software Quality*, Trondheim (Norway), LNCS 4542, Springer-Verlag.

Darimont, R., Delor, E., Massonet, P. and van Lamsweerde, A. (1998). 'GRAIL/KAOS: An Environment for Goal-Driven Requirements Engineering', *Proceedings of ICSE'98 – 20th International Conference on Software Engineering*, Kyoto, April, Vol. 2, 58–62. (Earlier and shorter version found in *Proceedings of ICSE'97 – 19th International Conference on Software Engineering*, Boston, May 1997, 612–613.

Davis, A.M. (1993). *Software Requirements: Objects, Functions, and States*. Prentice-Hall.

Davis, R. (1982). 'Teiresias: Applications of Meta-Level Knowledge', in *Knowledge-Based Systems in Artificial Intelligence*, R. Davis and D. Lenat (eds), McGraw-Hill, 227–490.

Daws, C., Olivero, A. and Yovine, S. (1994). 'Verifying ET-LOTOS Programs with KRONOS', *Proceedings of FORTE'94: Formal Description Techniques*, Bern, October, 227–242.

Day, R.A. (1989). *How to Write and Publish a Scientific Paper*. Cambridge University Press.

de Kleer, J. (1986). 'An Assumption-Based TMS', *Artificial Intelligence*, Vol. 28, 127–162.

de Landtsheer, R. and van Lamsweerde, A. (2005). 'Reasoning About Confidentiality at Requirements Engineering Time', *Proceedings of ESEC/FSE'05*, Lisbon, Portugal, September.

de Landtsheer, R., Letier, E. and van Lamsweerde, A. (2004). 'Deriving Tabular Event-Based Specifications from Goal-Oriented Requirements Models', *Requirements Engineering Journal*, Vol. 9, No. 2, 104–120.

de Lemos, R., Fields, B. and Saeed, A. (1995). 'Analysis of Safety Requirements in the Context of System Faults and Human Errors', *Proceedings of the IEEE International Symposium and Workshop on Systems Engineering of Computer Based Systems*. Tucson, Arizona, March, 374–381.

DeMarco, T. (1978). *Structured Analysis and System Specification*. Yourdon Press.

de Schrynmakers, A. and Accardo, N. (2002) 'Goal-Oriented Modeling of Requirements Families for Automotive Software'. M.S. Thesis, Department of Computing Science, Université Catholique de Louvain.

van Deursen, A. and Klint, P. (2002). 'Domain-Specific Language Design Requires Feature Descriptions', *Journal of Computing and Information Technology*, Vol. 10, No. 1, 1–17.

Dijkstra, E.W. (1976). *A Discipline of Programming*. Prentice-Hall.

Dix, A., Finlay, J., Abowd, G. and Beale, R. (2003). *Human–Computer Interaction*. Third edition, Prentice Hall.

Dobing, B. and Parsons, J. (2006). 'How UML Is Used', *Communications of the ACM*, Vol. 49, No. 5, May, 109–113.

Domges, R. and Pohl, K. (1998). 'Adapting Traceability Environments for Project-Specific Needs', *Communications of the ACM*, Vol. 41, 54–63.

Doolan, E.P. (1992). 'Experience with Fagan's Inspection Method', *Software – Practice and Experience*, Vol. 22, No. 2, 173–182.

dos Santos, A., Vigna, G. and Kemmerer, R. (2000). 'Security Testing of the Online Banking Service of a Large International Bank', *Proceedings of 1st Workshop on Security and Privacy in E-Commerce*, November.

Doyle, J. (1979). 'A Truth Maintenance System', *Artificial Intelligence*, Vol. 12, No. 3, 251–272.

D'Souza, D.F. and Wills, A.C. (1999). *Objects, Components, and Frameworks with UML: The CATALYSIS Approach*. Addison Wesley.

Dubois, E., Du Bois, P. and Petit, M. (1993). 'Object-Oriented Requirements Analysis: An Agent Perspective', *Proceedings of ECOOP'93 – 7th European Conference on Object-Oriented Programming*, Springer-Verlag, LNCS 707, 458–481.

Dubois, E., Hagelstein, J. and Rifaut, A. (1991). 'A Formal Language for the Requirements Engineering of Computer Systems', in *Introducing a Logic Based Approach to Artificial Intelligence*, A. Thayse (ed.), Vol. 3, John Wiley & Sons Ltd, 357–433.

Dubois, E., Yu, E. and Petit, M. (1998). 'From Early to Late Formal Requirements: A Process-Control Case Study', *Proceedings of IWSSD'98 – 9th International Workshop on Software Specification and Design*, Isobe, IEEE CS Press, April, 34–42.

Dupré, L. (1998). *Bugs in Writing: A Guide to Debugging your Prose*. Addison-Wesley.

Dwyer, M.B., Avrunin, G.S. and Corbett, J.C. (1999). 'Patterns in Property Specifications for Finite-State Verification', *Proceedings of ICSE-99 – 21st International Conference on Software Engineering*, Los Angeles, 411–420.

Easterbrook, S. (1994). 'Resolving Requirements Conflicts with Computer-Supported Negotiation', in *Requirements Engineering: Social and Technical Issues*, M. Jirotka and J. Goguen (eds), Academic Press, 41–65.

Ellis, C.A. and Wainer, J. (1994). 'Goal-Based Models of Collaboration', *Collaborative Computing*, Vol. 1, 61–86.

Emerson, E.A. and J.Y. Halpern, J.Y. (1986). '"Sometime" and "not Never" Revisited: On Branching versus Linear Time Temporal Logic', *Journal of the ACM*, Vol. 33, No. 1, 151–178.

Evans, A., Maskeri, G., Moore, A., Sammut, P. and Willans, J. (2005). A Unified Superstructure for UML. *Journal of Object Technology*, Vol. 4, No. 1, 165–181.

Fagan, M.E. (1976). 'Design and Code Inspections to Reduce Errors in Program Development', *IBM Systems Journal*, Vol. 15, No. 3, 182–211.

Fagan, M.E. (1986). 'Advances in Software Inspections', *IEEE Transactions on Software Engineering*, Vol. 12, No. 7, 744–751.

Fagin, R., Halpern, J.Y., Moses, Y. and Vardi, M.Y. (1995). *Reasoning About Knowledge*. MIT Press.

Fairbanks, G., Bierhoff, K. and D'Souza, D. (2006). 'Software Architecture at a Large Financial Firm', *Proceedings of OOPSLA'06*, Portland (OR).

Falkenhaimer, B., Forbus, K.D. and Gentner, D. (1989). 'The Structure-Mapping Engine: Algorithm and Examples', *Artificial Intelligence*, Vol. 41, 1–63.

Faulk, S., Brackett, J., Ward, P. and Kirby, J. (1992). 'The CORE Method for Real-Time Requirements', *IEEE Software*, September, 22–33.

Feather, M. (1987). 'Language Support for the Specification and Development of Composite Systems', *ACM Transactions on Programming Languages and Systems*, Vol. 9, No. 2, April, 198–234.

Feather, M. (1994). 'Towards a Derivational Style of Distributed System Design', *Automated Software Engineering*, Vol. 1, No. 1, 31–60.

Feather, M.S. and Cornford, S.L. (2003). 'Quantitative Risk-Based Requirements Reasoning', *Requirements Engineering Journal*, Vol. 8, No. 4, 248–265.

Feather, M.S., Cornford, S.L., Hicks, K.A. and Johnson, K.R. (2005). 'Application of Tool Support for Risk-Informed Requirements Reasoning', *International Journal of Computer Systems Science and Engineering*, Vol. 1, 5–17.

Feather, M., Fickas, S., Finkelstein, A. and van Lamsweerde, A. (1997). 'Requirements and Specification Exemplars', *Automated Software Engineering*, Vol. 4, 419–438.

Feather, M., Fickas, S., van Lamsweerde, A. and Ponsard, C. (1998). 'Reconciling System Requirements and Runtime Behaviour', *Proceedings of IWSSD'98 – 9th International Workshop on Software Specification and Design*, Isobe, IEEE CS Press, April.

Fenton, N., and Neil, M. (2001). 'Making Decisions: Using Bayesian Nets and MCDA', *Knowledge-Based Systems*, 14, 307–325.

Fickas, S. and Feather, M. (1995). 'Requirements Monitoring in Dynamic Environments', *Proceedings of RE'95 – 2nd International IEEE Symposium on Requirements Engineering*, March, 140–147.

Fickas, S. and Helm, R. (1992). 'Knowledge Representation and Reasoning in the Design of Composite Systems', *IEEE Transactions on Software Engineering*, June, 470–482.

Finkelstein, A. (1996). 'The London Ambulance System Case Study', Succeedings of IWSSD8 – 8th International Workshop on Software Specification and Design, *ACM Software Engineering Notes,* September.

Finkelstein, A. and Potts, C. (1987). 'Building Formal Specifications Using Structured Common Sense', *Proceedings of IWSSD-4 – 4th International Workshop on Software Specification and Design*, IEEE, April, 108–113.

Finkelstein, A., Gabbay, D., Hunter, A., Kramer, J. and Nuseibeh, B. (1994). 'Inconsistency Handling in Multi-Perspective Specifications', *IEEE Transactions on Software Engineering*, Vol. 20, No. 8, 569–578.

Fitzgerald, J. and Larsen, P.G. (1998). *Modelling Systems: Practical Tools and Techniques for Software Development*. Cambridge University Press.

Floyd, R.W. (1967). 'Assigning Meanings to Programs', *Proceedings of the Symposium in Applied Maths*, Vol. 19, American Mathematical Society, New York, 19–32.

Fowler, M. (1997a). *UML Distilled*. Addison-Wesley.

Fowler, M. (1997b). *Analysis Patterns: Reusable Object Models*. Addison-Wesley.

Futatsugi, K., Goguen, J., Jounnaud, J.-P. and Mesguer, J. (1985). 'Principles of OBJ', *Proceedings of POPL'85: ACM Symposium on Principles of Programming Languages*, 52–66.

Fuxman, A., Pistore, M., Mylopoulos, J. and Traverso, P. (2001). 'Model Checking Early Requirements Specifications in Tropos', *Proceedings of RE'01 – 5th International Symposium in Requirements Engineering*, Toronto, August.

Gamma, E., Helm, R., Johnson, R. and Vlissides, J. (1995). *Design Patterns: Elements of Reusable Object-Oriented Software*, Addison-Wesley.

Garlan, D., Monroe, R. and Wile, D. (1997). 'ACME: An Architecture Description Interchange Language', *Proceedings of CASCON'97*, Toronto, November, 169–183.

Gartner, F.C. (1999). 'Fundamentals of Fault-Tolerant Distributed Computing in Asynchronous Environment', *ACM Computing Surveys*, Vol. 31, No. 1, March, 1–26.

Gaudel, M.-C. (1992). 'Structuring and Modularizing Algebraic Specifications: The PLUSS Specification Language, Evolutions and Perspectives', *Proceedings of STAS'92*, LNCS 557, 3–18.

Gause, D. and Weinberg, G. (1989). *Exploring Requirements: Quality Before Design*. Dorset House.

Gentner, D. (1988). 'Analogical Inference and Analogical Access', in *Analogica*, A. Prieditis (ed.), Pitman, 63–88.

George, C., Haxthausen, A.E., Hughes, S., Milne, R., Prehn, S. and Pedersen, J.S. (1995). *The RAISE Development Method*. Prentice Hall.

Gervasi, V. and Zowghi, D. (2005). 'Reasoning about Inconsistencies in Natural Language Requirements', *ACM Transactions on Software Engineering and Methodology (TOSEM)*, Vol. 14, No. 3, 277–330.

Ghezzi, C. and Kemmerer, R.A. (1991). 'ASTRAL: An Assertion Language for Specifying Real-Time Systems', *Proceedings of ESEC'91 – 3rd European Software Engineering Conference*, LNCS 550, Springer-Verlag.

Giannakopoulou, D. and Magee, J. (2003). 'Fluent Model Checking for Event-Based Systems', *Proceedings of ESEC/FSE 2003*, 10th European Software Engineering Conference, Helsinki.

Gilb, T. and Graham, D. (1993). *Software Inspection*. Addison-Wesley.

Giorgini, P., Masacci, F., Mylopoulos, J. and Zannone, N. (2005). 'Modeling Security Requirements through Ownership, Permission, and Delegation', *Proceedings of RE'05, International Joint Conference on Requirements Engineering*, IEEE, Paris.

Glass, R.L. (ed.) (2003). Special Issue on the State of the Practice of Software Engineering, *IEEE Software*, Vol. 20, No. 6, November–December.

Goguen, J. and Jirotka, M. (eds) (1994). *Requirements Engineering: Social and Technical Issues*. Academic Press.

Goguen, J. and Linde, C. (1993). 'Techniques for Requirements Elicitation', *Proceedings of RE'93 – First IEEE Symposium on Requirements Engineering*, San Diego, 152–164.

Gomaa, H. and Scott, P. (1981). 'Prototyping as a Tool in the Specification of User Requirements', *Proceedings of ICSE-5: Fifth International Conference on Software Engineering*, Washington, IEEE Press, 333–342.

Gordon, M. and T.F. Melham, T.F. (1993). *Introduction to HOL*. Cambridge University Press.

Gotel, O. and Finkelstein, A. (1994). 'An Analysis of the Requirements Traceability Problem', *Proceedings of ICRE'94: First International Conference on Requirements Engineering*, IEEE, 94–101.

Gotel, O. and Finkelstein, A. (1995). 'Contribution Structures', *Proceedings of RE'95 – 2nd International IEEE Symposium on Requirements Engineering*, IEEE, 100–107.

Gottesdiener, E. (2002). *Requirements by Collaboration: Workshops for Defining Needs*. Addison-Wesley.

Greenspan, S.J., Borgida, A. and Mylopoulos, J. (1986). 'A Requirements Modeling Language and its Logic', *Information Systems*, Vol. 11, No. 1, 9–23.

Greenspan, S.J., Mylopoulos, J. and Borgida, A. (1982). 'Capturing More World Knowledge in the Requirements Specification', *Proceedings of ICSE-6 – 6th International Conference on Software Engineering*, Tokyo.

Gries, D. (1981). *The Science of Programming*. Springer-Verlag.

Gross, D. and Yu, E. (2001). 'From Non-Functional Requirements to Design through Patterns', *Requirements Engineering Journal*, Vol. 6, 18–36.

Grünbacher, P., Halling, M. and Biffl, S. (2003). 'An Empirical Study on Groupware Support for Software Inspection Meetings', *Proceedings of ASE'03: 18th International Conference on Automated Software Engineering*.

van Gurp, J., Bosch, J. and Svahnberg, M. (2001). 'On the Notion of Variability in Product Lines', *Proceedings of 2nd IFIP Working Conference on Software Architecture*, IEEE, 45–54.

Guttag, J.V. (1977). Abstract Data Types and the Development of Data Structures, *Communications of the ACM*, June.

Guttag, J.V., Horning, J.J., Jones, K.D., Sarland, S.J., Modet, A. and Wing, J.M. (1993). *Larch: Languages and Tools for Formal Specification*. Springer-Verlag.

Haley, C., Laney, R., Moffett, J., and Nuseibeh, B. (2008). Security Requirements Engineering: A Framework for Representation and Reasoning. *IEEE Transactions on Software Engineering*, forthcoming.

Hall, A. (1996). 'Using Formal Methods to Develop an ATC Information System', *IEEE Software*, Vol. 12, No. 6, March, 66–76.

Hall, R.P. (1989). 'Computational Approaches to Analogical Reasoning: A Comparative Analysis', *Artificial Intelligence*, Vol. 39, 39–120.

Hammond, J., Rawlings, R. and Hall, A. (2001). 'Will it Work?', *Proceedings of RE'01 – 5th International IEEE Symposium on Requirements Engineering*, Toronto, IEEE, 102–109.

Hansen, K.M., Ravn, A.P. and Rischel, H. (1991). 'Specifying and Verifying Requirements of Real-Time Systems', *Proceedings of ACM SIGSOFT'91 Conference on Software for Critical Systems*, New Orleans, December.

Harel, D. (1987). 'Statecharts: A Visual Formalism for Complex Systems', *Science of Computer Programming*, Vol. 8, 231–274.

Harel, D. (1996). 'The STATEMATE Semantics of Statecharts', *ACM Transactions on Software Engineering and Methodology,* Vol. 5, No. 4, 293–333.

Harel, D. and Marelly, R. (2003). *Come, Let's Play: Scenario-Based Programming Using LSCs and the Play-Engine*. Springer-Verlag.

Harel, D. and Thiagarajan, P.S. (2003). 'Message Sequence Charts', in *UML for Real Design of Embedded Real-Time Systems*, L. Lavagno, G. Martin, and B. Selic (eds), Kluwer.

Harel, D., Lachover, H., Naamad, A., Pnueli, A., Politi, M., Sherman, R., Shtull-Trauring, A. and Trakhtenbrot, M. (1990). 'STATEMATE: A Working Environment for the Development of Complex Reactive Systems', *IEEE Transactions on Software Engineering*, Vol. 16, No. 4, April, 403–414.

Hart, A. (1992). *Knowledge Acquisition for Expert Systems*, Second edition, McGraw-Hill.

Haumer, P., Pohl, K. and Weidenhaupt, K. (1998). 'Requirements Elicitation and Validation with Real World Scenes', *IEEE Transactions on Sofware Engineering*, Special Issue on Scenario Management, December, 1036–1054.

Hayes, I. (ed.) (1987). *Specification Case Studies*. Prentice Hall.

Hazel, D., Strooper, P. and Traynor, O. (1998). 'Requirements Engineering and Verification using Specification Animation', *Proceedings of Automated Software Engineering Conference*, 302–305.

Heimdahl, M.P. and Leveson, N.G. (1996). 'Completeness and Consistency in Hierarchical State-Based Requirements', *IEEE Transactions on Software Engineering*, Vol. 22, No. 6, June, 363–377.

Heitmeyer, C., Jeffords, R. and Labaw, B. (1996). 'Automated Consistency Checking of Requirements Specifications', *ACM Transactions on Software Engineering and Methodology*, Vol. 5, No. 3, July, 231–261.

Heitmeyer, C., Kirby, J. and Labaw, B. (1997). 'Tools for Formal Specification, Verification, and Validation of Requirements', *Proceedings of COMPASS '97*, June, Gaithersburg (MD).

Heitmeyer, C., Kirkby, J., Labaw, B. and Bharadwaj, R. (1998a). 'SCR*: A Toolset for Specifying and Analyzing Software Requirements', *Proceedings of CAV'98 – 10th Annual Conference on Comuter-Aided Verification*, Vancouver, 526–531.

Heitmeyer, C., Kirkby, J., Labaw, B., Archer, M. and Bharadwaj, R. (1998b). 'Using Abstraction and Model Checking to Detect Safety Violations in Requirements Specifications', *IEEE Transactions on Software Engineering*, Vol. 24, No. 11, November, 927–948.

Hekmatpour, S. and Ince, D. (1988). *Software Prototyping, Formal Methods, and VDM*. Addison-Wesley.

Heninger, K.L. (1980). 'Specifying Software Requirements for Complex Systems: New Techniques and their Application', *IEEE Transactions on Software Engineering*, Vol. 6, No. 1, January, 2–13.

Heymans, P. and Dubois, E. (1998). 'Scenario-Based Techniques for Supporting the Elaboration and the Validation of Formal Requirements', *Requirements Engineering Journal*, Vol. 3, No. 3–4, 202–218.

Hice, G.F., Turner, W.S. and Cashwell, L.F. (1974). *System Development Methodology*. North Holland.

Hinchey, M.G. and Bowen, J.P. (eds) (1995). *Applications of Formal Methods*. Prentice Hall.

Hoare, C.A.R. (1969). 'An Axiomatic Basis for Computer Programming', *Communications of the ACM*, Vol. 12, No. 10, 576–583.

Hoare, C.A.R. (1985). *Communicating Sequential Processes*. Prentice-Hall.

Holzmann, G. (1991). *Design and Validation of Computer Protocols*. Prentice Hall.

Holzmann, G. (1997). 'The Model Checker SPIN', *IEEE Transactions on Software Engineering*, Vol. 23, No. 5, May, 279–295.

Holzmann, G. (2003). *The Spin Model Checker: Primer and Reference Manual*. Addison-Wesley.

Hooks, I.A. and Farry, K.A. (2000). *Customer-Centered Requirements*. AMACOM.

Hopcroft, J.E., Ullman, J.D. (1979) *Introduction to Automata Theory, Languages, and Computation*, Addison-Wesley.

Hsia, P., Samuel, J., Gao, J., Kung, D., Toyoshima, Y. and Chen, C. (1994). 'Formal Approach to Scenario Analysis', *IEEE Software*, March, 33–41.

Huffman Hayes, J., Dekhtyar, A. and Osborne, J. (2003). 'Improving Requirements Tracing via Information Retrieval', *Proceedings of RE'03 – 11th IEEE Joint International Requirements Engineering Conference*, Monterey (CA), September, 138–150.

Hughes, J., King, V., Rodden, T. and Andersen, H. (1995). 'The Role of Ethnography in Interactive Systems Design', *ACM Interactions*, Vol. 2, No. 2, April, 56–65.

Hui, B., Laiskos, S. and Mylopoulos, J. (2003). 'Requirements Analysis for Customizable Software: A Goals Skills Preferences Framework', *Proceedings of RE'03 – 11th IEEE Joint International Requirements Engineering Conference*, Monterey (CA), September, 117–126.

Hull, M.E.C., Jackson, K. and Dick, A.J.J. (2002). *Requirements Engineering*. Springer-Verlag Practitioner Series.

Hunter, A. and Nuseibeh, B. (1998). 'Managing Inconsistent Specifications: Reasoning, Analysis and Action', *ACM Transactions on Software Engineering and Methodology*, Vol. 7, No. 4, October, 335–367.

Ibanez, M. and Rempp, H. (1996). *European User Survey Analysis*. Report USV_EUR 2.1, ESPITI Project, Deliverable D.05, European Software Institute & Forschungzentrum Karlsruhe, January.

IEEE (1998). Software Engineering Standards Committee, *IEEE Recommended Practice for Software Requirements Specifications*. ANSI/IEEE Std 830, October.

In, H., Boehm, B., Rodgers, T. and Deutsch, M. (2001). 'Applying WinWin to Quality Requirements: A Case Study', *Proceedings of 23rd International Conference on Software Engineering*, 555–564.

ITU (1996). *Message Sequence Charts*. Recommendation Z.120, International Telecommunication Union, Telecomm. Standardization Sector, November.

ITU (2002). *Specification and Description Language (SDL)*. Recommendation Z.100, International Telecommunication Union, Telecomm. Standardization Sector, August.

Jackson, D. (2006). *Software Abstractions: Logic, Language, and Analysis*. MIT Press.

Jackson, M. (1978). 'Information Systems: Modeling, Sequencing, and Transformation', *Proceedings of ICSE-3 – 3rd International Conference on Software Enginering,* Munich, 72–81.

Jackson, M. (1995a). *Software Requirements and Specifications: A Lexicon of Practice, Principles and Pejudices*. ACM Press/Addison-Wesley.

Jackson, M. (1995b). 'The World and the Machine', *Proceedings of ICSE'95 – 17th International Conference on Software Engineering*, ACM Press, 283–292.

Jackson, M. (2001). *Problem Frames: Analyzing and Structuring Software Development Problems*. ACM Press/Addison-Wesley.

Jackson, M. and Zave, P. (1993). 'Domain Descriptions', *Proceedings of RE'93 – 1st International IEEE Symposium on Requirements Engineering*, January, 56–64.

Jacobson, I., Booch, G. and Rumbaugh, J. (1999). *The Unified Software Development Process*. Addison-Wesley.

Jacobson, I., Christerson, M., Jonsson P. and Overgaard, G. (1993). *Object-Oriented Software Engineering: A Use Case Driven Approach*. ACM Press/Addison-Wesley.

Jaffe, M.S., Leveson, N., Heimdahl, M. and Melhart, B. (1991). 'Software Requirements Analysis for Real-Time Process-Control Systems', *IEEE Transactions on Software Engineering*, Vol. 17, No. 3, March, 241–258.

Jahanian, F. and Mok, A.K. (1986). 'Safety Analysis of Timing Properties in Real-Time Systems', *IEEE Transactions on Software Engineering*, Vol. 12, September, 890–904.

Jarke, M. and Kurki-Suonio, R. (eds) (1998). Special Issue on Scenario Management, *IEEE Transactions on Sofware Engineering*, December.

Jarke, M., Gallersdoerfer, R., Jeusfeld, M., Staudt, M. and Eherer, S. (1995). 'ConceptBase – A Deductive Object Base for Meta Data Management', *International Journal of Intelligent Information Systems*, Vol. 5, No. 3, 167–192.

Jeffords, R. and Heitmeyer, C. (1998). 'Automatic Generation of State Invariants from Requirements Specifications', *Proceedings of FSE-6 – 6th ACM SIGSOFT International Symposium on the Foundations of Software Engineering*, Lake Buena Vista, 56–69.

Johnson, P.M. (1994). 'An Instrumented Approach to Improving Software Quality through Formal Technical Review', *Proceedings of ICSE'94 – 16th International Conference on Software Engineering*, Sorrento.

Jones, A.J. and Sergot, M. (1993). 'On the Characterization of Law and Computer Systems: The Normative System Perspective', *in* J.C. Meyer and R.J. Wieringa (eds), *Deontic Logic in Computer Science: Normative System Specification*, John Wiley & Sons Ltd.

Jones, C.B. (1990). *Systematic Software Development Using VDM*. Second edition, Prentice Hall.

Jones, C.B. and Shaw, R.C. (eds) (1990). *Case Studies in Systematic Software Development*. Prentice Hall.

Jones, T.C. (1991). *Applied Software Measurement: Assuring Productivity and Quality*. McGraw-Hill.

Jones, T.C. (1994). *Assessment and Control of Software Risks*. Prentice Hall.

Jones, T.C. (1995). 'Software Challenges', *Computing Industry*, Vol. 28, No. 10, 102–103.

Jones, T.C. (1996). *Patterns of Software Systems Failure and Success*. International Thomson Computer Press.

Jones, T.C. (2003). 'Variations in Software Practices', *IEEE Software*, November, 23–27.

Joseph, M. (1996). *Real-Time Systems: Specification, Verification and Analysis*. Prentice Hall.

Kain, R. (1972). *Automata Theory: Machines and Languages*. McGraw-Hill.

Kaindl, H. (2000). 'A Design Process Based on a Model Combining Scenarios with Goals and Functions', *IEEE Transactions on Systems, Man and Cybernetics*, Vol. 30, No. 5, September, 537–551.

Kang, K.C., Cohen, S.G., Hess, J., Nowak, W. and Peterson, A. (1990). *Feature-Oriented Domain Analysis (FODA) Feasibility Study*. Technical Report CMU/SEI-90-TR-21, Software Engineering Institute, Carnegie-Mellon University.

Karlsson, J. and Ryan, K. (1997). 'A Cost-Value Approach to Prioritizing Requirements', *IEEE Software*, Vol. 14, No. 5, 67–74.

Katz, S., Richter, C.A. and The, K.S. (1987). 'PARIS: A System for Reusing Partially Interpreted Schemas', *Proceedings of ICSE-87 – 9th International Conference on Software Enginering*, Monterey, CA, March, 377–385.

Kawashima, H. (1971). 'Functional Specification of Call Processing by State Transition Diagrams', *IEEE Transactions on Communications*, Vol. 19, No. 5, October, 581–587.

Keck, D.O. and Kuehn, P.J (1998). 'The Feature and Service Interaction Problem in Telecommunication Systems: A Survey', *IEEE Transactions on Sofware Engineering*, Special Issue on Managing Feature Interactions in Telecommunication Software Systems, Vol. 24, No. 10, October, 779–796.

Keller, S.E., Kahn, L.G. and Panara, R.B. (1990). 'Specifying Software Quality Requirements with Metrics', in *Tutorial: System and Software Requirements Enginering*, R.H. Thayer and M. Dorfman (eds), IEEE Computer Society Press, 145–163.

Kelly, J., Sherif, J.S. and Hops, J. (1992). 'An Analysis of Defect Densities Found during Software Inspections', *Journal of Systems and Software*, Vol. 17, 111–117.

Kelly, T.P. and McDermid, J.A. (1997). 'Safety Case Construction and Reuse Using Patterns', *Proceedings of SAFECOMP'97 – 16th International Conference on Computer Safety, Reliability, and Security*, September.

Kelly, T.P. and Weaver, R. (2004). 'The Goal Structuring Notation – A Safety Argument Notation', *Proceedings of Dependable Systems and Networks 2004 Workshop on Assurance Cases*, July.

Kemmerer, R. (2003). 'Cybersecurity', *Proceedings of ICSE'03 – 25th International Conference on Software Engineering*, Portland, 705–715.

Kemmerer, R., Meadows, C. and Millen, J. (1994) 'Three systems for cryptographic protocol analysis', *Journal of Cryptology*, Vol. 7, No. 2, 79–130.

Kent, S., Maibaum, T. and Quirk, W. (1993). 'Formally Specifying Temporal Constraints and Error Recovery', *Proceedings of RE'93 – 1st International IEEE Symposium on Requirements Engineering*, January, 208–215.

Knight, J.C. (2002). 'Safety-Critical Systems: Challenges and Directions', Invited Mini-Tutorial, *Proceedings of ICSE'2002 – 24th International Conference on Software Engineering*, ACM Press, 547–550.

Kondo, Y. (1994). 'Kaoru Ishikawa: What He Thought and Achieved – A Basis for Further Research', *Quality Management Journal*, 86–91.

Konrad, S., Cheng, B. and Campbell, L. (2004). 'Object Analysis Patterns for Embedded Systems'. *IEEE Transactions on Software Engineering*, Vol. 30, No. 12, 970–992.

Kotonya, G. and Sommerville, I. (1997). *Requirements Engineering: Processes and Techniques*. John Wiley & Sons Ltd.

Kovitz, B.L. (1999). *Practical Software Requirements: A Manual of Content and Style*. Manning.

Koymans, R. (1992). *Specifying Message Passing and Time-Critical Systems with Temporal Logic*. LNCS 651, Springer-Verlag.

Kramer, J., Magee, J. and Sloman, M. (1983). 'CONIC: An Integrated Approach to Distributed Computer Control Systems', *IEE Proceedings*, Part E 130, Vol. 1, January, 1–10.

Kruger, I., Grosu, R., Scholz, P. and Broy, M. (1998). From MSCs to Statecharts, *Proceedings of IFIP Wg10.3/Wg10.5 International Workshop on Distributed and Parallel Embedded Systems*, F.J. Rammig (ed.), Kluwer, 61–71.

Ladkin, P. (1995) in *The Risks Digest*, P. Neumann (ed.), *ACM Software Engineering Notes*, 15.

Laitenberger, O. and DeBaud, J.-M. (2000). 'An Encompassing Lifecycle Centric Survey of Software Inspection', *Journal of Systems and Software*, Vol. 50, No. 1, 5–31.

Lamport, L. (1994). 'The Temporal Logic of Actions', *ACM Transactions on Programming Languages and Systems*, Vol. 16, No. 3, May, 872–923.

van Lamsweerde, A. (1991). 'Learning Machine Learning', in *Introducing a Logic Based Approach to Artificial Intelligence*, A. Thayse (ed.), Vol. 3, John Wiley & Sons Ltd, 263–356.

van Lamsweerde, A. (2000a). 'Formal Specification: a Roadmap', in *The Future of Software Engineering*, A. Finkelstein (ed.), ACM Press.

van Lamsweerde, A. (2000b). 'Requirements Engineering in the Year 00: A Research Perspective'. Invited Keynote Paper, *Proceedings of ICSE'2000 – 22nd International Conference on Software Engineering*, ACM Press, 5–19.

van Lamsweerde, A. (2001). 'Goal-Oriented Requirements Engineering: A Guided Tour', Invited Minitutorial, *Proceedings of RE'01 – 5th International Symposium on Requirements Engineering*, Toronto, August, 249–263.

van Lamsweerde, A. (2003). 'From System Goals to Software Architecture', in *Formal Methods for Software Architecture*, M. Bernardo & P. Inverardi (eds), LNCS 2804, Springer-Verlag.

van Lamsweerde, A. (2004a). 'Elaborating Security Requirements by Construction of Intentional Anti-Models', *Proceedings of ICSE'04 – 26th International Conference on Software Engineering*, Edinburgh, May, ACM-IEEE, 148–157.

van Lamsweerde, A. (2004b). 'Goal-Oriented Requirements Engineering: A Roundtrip from Research to Practice', Invited Keynote Paper, *Proceedings of RE'04 – 12th IEEE Joint International Requirements Engineering Conference*, Kyoto, September, 4–8.

van Lamsweerde, A. (2007). 'Engineering Requirements for System Reliability and Security', in *Software System Reliability and Security*, M. Broy, J. Grünbauer and C.A.R. Hoare (eds), NATO Security through Science Series – D: Information and Communicarion Security, Vol. 9. IOS Press, 196–238.

van Lamsweerde, A. and Letier, E. (1998). 'Integrating Obstacles in Goal-Driven Requirements Engineering', *Proceedings of ICSE-98 – 20th International Conference on Software Engineering*, Kyoto, April.

van Lamsweerde, A. and Letier, E. (2000). 'Handling Obstacles in Goal-Oriented Requirements Engineering', *IEEE Transactions on Software Engineering*, Special Issue on Exception Handling, Vol. 26, No. 10, October, 978–1005.

van Lamsweerde, A. and E. Letier, E. (2004). 'From Object Orientation to Goal Orientation: A Paradigm Shift for Requirements Engineering', in *Radical Innovations of Software and Systems Engineering*, LNCS 2491, Springer-Verlag.

van Lamsweerde, A. and Willemet, L. (1998). 'Inferring Declarative Requirements Specifications from Operational Scenarios', *IEEE Transactions on Software Engineering*, Special Issue on Scenario Management, Vol. 24, No. 12, December, 1089–1114.

van Lamsweerde, A., Darimont, R. and Letier, E. (1998). 'Managing Conflicts in Goal-Driven Requirements Engineering', *IEEE Transactions on Software Engineering*, Special Issue on Inconsistency Management in Software Development, Vol. 24, No. 11, November, 908–926.

van Lamsweerde, A., Darimont, R. and Massonet, P. (1993). *The Meeting Scheduler System: Preliminary Definition*. University of Louvain.

van Lamsweerde, A., Darimont, R. and Massonet, P. (1995). 'Goal-Directed Elaboration of Requirements for a Meeting Scheduler: Problems and Lessons Learnt', *Proceedings of RE'95 – 2nd International IEEE Symposium on Requirements Engineering*, March, 194–203.

van Lamsweerde, A., Delcourt, B., Delor, E., Schayes, M.C. and Champagne, R. (1988). 'Generic Lifecycle Support in the ALMA Environment', *IEEE Transactions on Software Engineering*, Special Issue on Software Environment Architectures, Vol. 14, No. 6, June, 720–741.

Lang, K.J., Pearlmutter, B.A. and Price, R.A. (1998). 'Results of the Abbadingo One DFA Learning Competition and a New Evidence-Driven State Merging Algorithm', in *Grammatical Inference*, Lecture Notes in Artificial Intelligence, No. 1433, Springer-Verlag, 1–12.

Lano, K. (1995). *Formal Object-Oriented Development*. Springer-Verlag.

Lano, K. (1996). *The B Language and Method: A Guide to Practical Formal Development*. Springer-Verlag.

Larsen, K.G., Petersson, P. and Yi, W. (1997). 'UPPAAL in a Nutshell', *International Journal on Software Tools for Technology Transfer*, Vol. 1, Springer-Verlag, 134–152.

LAS (1993). *Report of the Inquiry into the London Ambulance Service*, Communications Directorate, South West Thames Regional Authority, February. See also the London Ambulance System home page, http://hsn.lond-amb.sthames.nhs.uk/http.dir/service/organisation/featurs/info.html.

Lauesen, S. (2002). *Software Requirements: Styles and Techniques*. Addison-Wesley.

Ledru, Y. (1997). 'Specification and Animation of a Bank Transfer using KIDS/VDM', *Automated Software Engineering*, Vol. 4, No. 1, January, 33–51.

Lee, J. (1991). 'Extending the Potts and Bruns Model for Recording Design Rationale', *Proceedings of ICSE-13 – 13th International Conference on Software Engineering*, IEEE-ACM, 114–125.

Leffingwell, D. and Widrig, D. (2003). *Managing Software Requirements: A Use Case Approach*. Second edition, Addison-Wesley.

Lehman, M.M. (1980). 'On Understanding Laws, Evolution, and Conservation in the Large Program Lifecycle', *Journal of Systems and Software*, Vol. 1, No. 3, 213–221.

Lehman, M.M. and Belady, L.A. (1985). *Program Evolution: Processes of Software Change*. Academic Press.

Leite, J.C., Doorn, J.H., Hadad, G.D. and Kaplan, G.N. (2005). 'Scenario Inspections', *Requirements Engineering Journal*, Vol. 10, No. 1, 1–21.

Leite, J.C., Rossi, G., Balaguer, F., Maiorana, V., Kaplan, G., Hadad, G. and Oliveiros, A. (1997). 'Enhancing a Requirements Baseline with Scenarios', *Requirements Engineering Journal*, Vol. 2, No. 4, 184–198.

Lejk, M. and Deeks, D. (2002). *An Introduction to Systems Analysis Techniques*. Second edition, Addison-Wesley.

Lethbridge, T.C., Singer, J. and Forward, A. (2003). 'How Software Engineers Use Documentation: The State of the Practice', *IEEE Software*, November, 35–39.

Letier, E. (2001). 'Reasoning about Agents in Goal-Oriented Requirements Engineering'. Ph.D Thesis, University of Louvain, May.

Letier, E. and van Lamsweerde, A. (2002a). 'Agent-Based Tactics for Goal-Oriented Requirements Elaboration', *Proceedings of ICSE'02 – 24th International Conference on Software Engineering*, Orlando, IEEE Press.

Letier, E. and van Lamsweerde, A. (2002b). 'Deriving Operational Software Specifications from System Goals', *Proceedings of FSE'10 – 10th ACM Symposium on Foundations of Software Engineering*, Charleston, November.

Letier, E. and van Lamsweerde, A. (2004). 'Reasoning about Partial Goal Satisfaction for Requirements and Design Engineering', *Proceedings of FSE'04 – 12th ACM International Symposium on the Foundations of Software Engineering*, Newport Beach (CA), November, 53–62.

Letier, E., Kramer, J., Magee, J. and Uchitel, S. (2005). 'Monitoring and Control in Scenario-Based Requirements Analysis', *Proceedings of ICSE 2005 – 27th International Conference on Software Engineering*, St. Louis, May.

Leveson, N. (1995). *Safeware: System Safety and Computers*. Addison-Wesley.

Leveson, N. (2000). 'Intent Specifications', *IEEE Transactions on Software Engineering*, Vol. 26, No. 1, January.

Leveson, N. (2002). 'An Approach to Designing Safe Embedded Software', *Proceedings of EMSOFT 2002 – Embedded Software: 2nd International Conference*, Grenoble, October, LNCS 2491, Springer-Verlag, 15–29.

Leveson, N.G., Heimdahl, M.P. and Hildtreth, H. (1994). 'Requirements Specification for Process-Control Systems', *IEEE Transactions on Software Engineering*, Vol. 20, No. 9, September, 684–706.

Lions, J.-L. (1996). *Ariane 5 Flight 501 Failure: Report of the Inquiry Board*, July.

Liskov, B. and Zilles, S. (1975). 'Specification Techniques for Data Abstractions', *IEEE Transactions on Software Engineering*, Vol. 1, No. 1, March, 7–19.

Liu, L., Yu, E. and Mylopoulos, J. (2003). 'Security and Privacy Requirements Analysis within a Social Setting', *Proceedings of RE'03 – International Requirements Engineering Conference*, September.

Loucopoulos, P. and Karakostas, V. (1995). *System Requirements Engineering*. McGraw-Hill.

Loucopoulos, P. and Kavakli, E. (1995). 'Enterprise Modelling and the Teleological Approach to Requirements Engineering', *International Journal of Cooperative Information Systems*, Vol. 4, No. 1, 45–79.

Low, G.C. and Jeffery, R. (1990). 'Function Points in the Estimation and Evaluation of the Software Process', *IEEE Transactions on Software Engineering*, Vol. 16, No. 1, January, 64–71.

Lubars, M., Potts, C. and Richter, C. (1993). 'A Review of the State of the Practice In Requirements Modeling', *Proceedings of RE'93 – 1st International IEEE Symposium on Requirements Engineering*, San Diego, IEEE, 2–14.

Lutz, R.R. (1993). 'Analyzing Software Requirements Errors in Safety-Critical, Embedded Systems', *Proceedings of RE'93 – 1st International IEEE Symposium on Requirements Engineering*, San Diego, IEEE, 126–133.

Lutz, R.R. (1996). 'Targeting Safety-Related Errors During Software Requirements Analysis', *Journal of Systems and Software*, Vol. 34, No. 3, 223–230.

Lutz, R.R., Patterson-Hine, A., Nelson, S., Frost, C.R., Tal, D. and Harris, R. (2007). 'Using Obstacle Analysis to Identify Contingency Requirements on an Unpiloted Aerial Vehicle', *Requirements Engineering Journal*, Vol. 12, No. 1, 41–54.

Lyytinen, K. and Hirscheim, R. (1987). 'Information System Failures – A Survey and Classification of the Empirical Literature', *Oxford Survey of Information Technology*, Vol. 4, 257–309.

Macaulay, L.A. (1996). *Requirements Engineering*, Springer-Verlag Series on Applied Computing.

MacDonald, F. and Miller, J. (1999). 'A Comparison of Computer Support Systems for Software Inspections', *Automated Software Engineering*, Vol. 6, 291–313.

Maciaszek, L.A. (2001). *Requirements Analysis and System Design: Developing Information Systems with UML*. Pearson Education.

Magee, J. and Kramer, J. (2006). *Concurrency: State Models and Java Programs*. Second edition, John Wiley & Sons Ltd.

Magee, J., Dulay, N., Eisenbach, S. and Kramer, J. (1995). 'Specifying Distributed Software Architectures', *Proceedings of ESEC'95 – 5th European Software Engineering Conference*, Sitges, September, LNCS 989, Springer-Verlag, 137–153.

Magee, J., Pryce, N., Giannakopoulou, D. and Kramer, J. (2000). 'Graphical Animation of Behaviour Models', *Proceedings of ICSE'2000 – 22nd International Conference on Software Engineering*, Limerick, May, 499–508.

Maiden, N. and Rugg, G. (1996). 'ACRE: A Framework for Acquisition of Requirements', *Software Engineering Journal*, Vol. 11, No. 3, 183–192.

Maiden, N. and Sutcliffe, A. (1993). 'Exploiting Reusable Specifications Through Analogy', *Communications of the ACM*, Vol. 35, No. 4, 55–64.

Mäkinen, E. and Systä, T. (2001). 'MAS: An Interactive Synthesizer to Support Behavioural Modeling in UML', *Proceedings of ICSE 2001 International Conference on Software Engineering*, Toronto, Canada, May.

Mandrioli, D., Morasca, S. and Morzenti, A. (1995). 'Generating test cases for real-time systems from logic specifications', *ACM Transactions on Computer Systems*, Vol. 13, No. 4, November, 365–398.

Manna, Z. and Pnueli, A. (1992). *The Temporal Logic of Reactive and Concurrent Systems*, Springer-Verlag.

Manna, Z. and STeP Group (1996). 'STeP: Deductive-Algorithmic Verification of Reactive and Real-Time Systems', *Proceedings of CAV'96 – 8th International Conference on Computer-Aided Verification*, July, LNCS 1102, Springer-Verlag, 415–418.

Manna, Z. and Waldinger, R. (1993). *The Deductive Foundations of Computer Programming*. Addison-Wesley.

Marca, D. and Gowan, C. (1988). *SADT: Structured Analysis and Design Technique*. McGraw-Hill.

Massonet, P. and van Lamsweerde, A. (1997). 'Analogical Reuse of Requirements Frame-works', *Proceedings of RE-97 – 3rd International Symposium on Requirements Engineering*, Annapolis, 26–37.

McDermid, J.A. (1994). 'Support for Safety Cases and Safety Arguments Using SAM', *Reliability Engineering and System Safety*, Vol. 43, 111–127.

McMillan, K.L. (1993). *Symbolic Model Checking: An Approach to the State Explosion Problem*, Kluwer.

Meyer, B. (1985). 'On Formalism in Specifications', *IEEE Software*, Vol. 2, No. 1, January, 6–26.

Meyer, J.C. and Wieringa, R.J. (eds) (1993). *Deontic Logic in Computer Science: Normative System Specification*. John Wiley & Sons Ltd.

Miller, R. and Shanahan, M. (1999). 'The Event Calculus in Classical Logic – Alternative Axioma-tisations', *Linkoping Electronic Articles in Computer and Information Science*, Vol. 4, No. 16, 1–27.

Milner, R. (1989). *Communication and Concurrency*. Prentice-Hall.

Modugno, F., Leveson, N.G., Reese, J.D, Partridge, K. and Sandys, S.D. (1997). 'Integrated Safety Analysis of Requirements Specifications', *Proceedings of RE'97 – 3rd International IEEE Symposium on Requirements Engineering*, January, 148–159.

Moore, A.P., Klinker, J.E. and Mihelcik, D.M. (1999). 'How to Construct Formal Arguments that Persuade Certifiers', in M.G. Hinchey and J.P. Bowen (eds), *Industrial-Strength Formal Methods in Practice*. Springer-Verlag, FACIT Series, 285–314.

Morgan, C. (1990). *Programming from Specifications*. Prentice Hall.

Moriconi, M., Qian, X. and Riemenschneider, R. (1995). 'Correct Architecture Refinement', *IEEE Transactions on Software Engineering*, Vol. 21, No. 4, April, 356–372.

Morzenti, A., Mandrioli, D. and Ghezzi, C. (1992). 'A Model Parametric Real-Time Logic', *ACM Transactions on Programming Languages and Systems*, Vol. 14, No. 4, October, 521–573.

Moser, L., Ramakrishna, Y., Kutty, G., Melliar-Smith P.M. and Dillon, L. (1997). 'A Graphical Environment for the Design of Concurrent Real-Time Systems', *ACM Transactions on Software Engineering and Methodology*, Vol. 6, No. 1, January, 31–79.

Mostow, J. (1983). 'A Problem Solver for Making Advice Operational', *Proceedings of AAAI-83*, Morgan Kaufmann, 279–283.

Mostow, J. (1985). 'Towards Better Models of the Design Process', *AI Magazine*, Vol. 6, 44–57.

Mouratidis, H., and Giorgini, P. (2007). 'Secure Tropos: A Security-Oriented Extension of the TROPOS Methodology'. *International Journal of Software Engineering and Knowledge Engineering*, Vol. 17, No. 2, 285–309.

Munford, E. (1981). 'Participative Systems Design: Structure and Method', *Systems, Objectives, Solutions*, Vol. 1, North-Holland, 5–19.

Myers, G.J. (1979). *The Art of Software Testing*. John Wiley & Sons Ltd.

Mylopoulos, J. (1998). 'Information Modeling in the Time of the Revolution', Invited Review, *Information Systems*, Vol. 23, No. 3/4, 127–155.

Mylopoulos, J., Chung, L. and Nixon, B. (1992). 'Representing and Using Nonfunctional Requirements: A Process-Oriented Approach', *IEEE Transactions on Sofware. Engineering*, Vol. 18, No. 6, June, 483–497.

Mylopoulos, J., Chung, L. and Yu, E. (1999). 'From Object-Oriented to Goal-Oriented Requirements Analysis', *Communications of the ACM*, Vol. 42, No. 1, January, 31–37.

Mylopoulos, J., Chung, L., Liao, S., Wong, H. and Yu, E. (2001). 'Exploring Alternatives During Requirements Analysis', *IEEE Software*, Vol. 18, No. 1, January, 92–96.

Naur, P. (1969). 'Proofs of Algorithms by General Snapshots', *BIT*, Vol. 6, 310–316.

Nentwich, C., Emmerich, W., Finkelstein, A. and Ellmer, E. (2003). 'Flexible Consistency Checking', *ACM Transactions on Software Engineering and Methodology*, Vol. 12, No. 1, January, 28–63.

Neumann, P.G. (1995). *Computer Related Risks*. Addison-Wesley.

Nilsson, N.J. (1971). *Problem Solving Methods in Artificial Intelligence*. McGraw-Hill.

Niskier, C., Maibaum, T. and Schwabe, D. (1989). 'A Pluralistic Knowledge-Based Approach to Software Specification', *Proceedings of ESEC-89 – 2nd European Software Engineering Conference*, September, LNCS 387, 411–423.

Niu, J., Atlee, J.M. and Day, N. (2003). 'Template Semantics for Model-Based Notations', *IEEE Transactions on Software Engineering*, Vol. 29, No. 10, October, 866–882.

Nuseibeh, B. (1996). 'To Be and Not to Be: On Managing Inconsistency in Software Development', *Proceedings of IWSSD-8 – 8th International Workshop on Software Specification and Design*, Schloss Velen, 164–169.

Nuseibeh, B. (2001). 'Weaving Together Requirements and Architecture', *IEEE Computer*, Vol. 34, No. 3, March, 115–117.

Nuseibeh, B., Kramer, J. and Finkelstein, A. (1994). 'A Framework for Expressing the Relationships Between Multiple Views in Requirements Specifications', *IEEE Transactions on Software Engineering*, Vol. 20, No. 10, October, 760–773.

OMG (2006). 'Meta Object Factory', www.omg.org/docs/formal/06-01-01.pdf.

Oncinan J. and García, P. (1992) 'Inferring Regular Languages in Polynomial Update Time', in J.S. Marques, N. Pérez de la Blanca and P. Pina, (eds), *Pattern Recognition and Image Analysis*, Vol. 1, Series in Machine Perception and Artificial Intelligence, World Scientific, 49–61.

O'Neill, G. (1992). 'Automatic Translation of VDM into Standard ML Programs', *The Computer Journal*, Vol. 35, No. 6, March, 623–624.

Owre, S., Rushby, J. and Shankar, N. (1995). 'Formal Verification for Fault-Tolerant Architectures: Prolegomena to the Design of PVS', *IEEE Transactions on Software Engineering*, Vol. 21, No. 2, February, 107–125.

Paige, R., Brooke, P. and Ostroff, J. (2007). 'Metamodel-based Model Conformance and Multiview Consistency Checking', *ACM Transactions on Software Engineering and Methodology (TOSEM)*, Vol. 16, No. 3, July.

Palmer, J.D. (1997). 'Traceability', in *Software Requirements*, R.H. Thayer and M. Dorfman (eds), IEEE Press, 364–374.

Park, D.Y., Skakkebaek, J. and Dill, D.L. (1998). 'Static Analysis to Identify Invariants in RSML Specifications', *Proceedings of FTRTFT'98 – Formal Techniques for Real Time or Fault Tolerance*.

Parnas, D.L. (1972). 'On the Criteria to be Used in Decomposing Systems into Modules', *Communications of the ACM*, Vol. 15, No. 12, December.

Parnas, D.L. (1976). 'On the Design and Development of Program Families', *IEEE Transactions on Software Engineering*, Vol. 2, No. 1, March.

Parnas, D.L. (1979). 'Designing Software for Ease of Extension and Contraction', *IEEE Transactions on Software Engineering*, Vol. 5, No. 2, March.

Parnas, D.L. and J. Madey, J. (1995). 'Functional Documents for Computer Systems', *Science of Computer Programming*, Vol. 25, 41–61.

Parnas, D.L. and Weiss, D.M. (1985). 'Active Design Review: Principles and Practices', *Proceedings of ICSE'1985 – 8th International Conference on Software Engineering*.

Perry, D. and A. Wolf, A. (1992). 'Foundations for the Study of Software Architecture', *ACM Software Engineering Notes*, Vol. 17, No. 4, October, 40–52.

Peterson, J. (1977). 'Petri Nets', *ACM Computing Surveys*, Vol. 9, No. 3, September, 223–252.

Pfleeger, C. (1997). *Security in Computing*. Prentice Hall.

Pfleeger, S.L. (2001). *Software Engineering: Theory and Practice*. Second edition, Prentice Hall.

Pirotte, A. (1977). 'The Entity-Property-Association Model: An Information-Oriented Database Model, *Proceedings of ICS-77 – International Computing Symposium*, North-Holland.

Pnueli, A. (1977). 'The Temporal Logics of Programs', *Proceedings of 18th IEEE Symposium on Foundations of Computer Science*, 46–57.

Pohl, K. (1996). *Process-Centered Requirements Engineering*. John Wiley & Sons Ltd.

Pohl, K., Böckle, G. and van der Linden, F.J. (2005). *Software Product Line Engineering: Foundations, Principles, and Techniques*. Springer-Verlag.

Pollack, S. and Hicks, H. (1971). *Decision Tables: Theory and Practice*. John Wiley & Sons Ltd.

Ponsard, C., Massonet, P., Molderez, J.F., Rifaut, A. and van Lamsweerde, A. (2007). 'Early Verification and Validation of Mission-Critical Systems', *Formal Methods in System Design*, Vol. 30, No. 3, Springer, June, 233–247.

Ponsard, C., Massonet, P., Rifaut, A., Molderez, J.F., van Lamsweerde, A. and Tran Van, H. (2004). 'Early Verification and Validation of Mission-Critical Systems', *Proceedings of FMICS'04 – 9th International Workshop on Formal Methods for Industrial Critical Systems*, Linz (Austria), September.

Porter, A. and Johnson, P. (1997). 'Assessing Software Review Meetings: Results of a Comparative Analyis of Two Experimental Studies', *IEEE Transactions on Software Engineering*, Vol. 23, No. 3.

Porter, A., Votta, L.G. and Basili, V.R. (1995). 'Comparing Detection Methods for Software Requirements Inspections: A Replicated Experiment', *IEEE Transactions on Software Engineering*, Vol. 21, No. 6, 563–575.

Potts, C. (1995). 'Using Schematic Scenarios to Understand User Needs', *Proceedings of DIS'95 – ACM Symposium on Designing Interactive Systems: Processes, Practices and Techniques*, University of Michigan, August.

Potts, C. and Bruns, G. (1988). 'Recording the Reasons for Design Decisions', *Proceedings of ICSE'88 – 10th International Conference on Software Engineering*, Singapore, IEEE, CS Press.

Potts, C., Takahashi, K. and Anton, A.I. (1994). 'Inquiry-Based Requirements Analysis', *IEEE Software*, March, 21–32.

Potter, B., Sinclair, J. and Till, D. (1996). *An Introduction to Formal Specification and Z*. Prentice-Hall.

Prieditis, A. (ed.) (1988). *Analogica*. Pitman.

Pruitt, D.G. (1981). *Negotiation Behaviour*. Academic Press.

Queille, J. and Sifakis, J. (1982). 'Specification and Verification of Concurrent Systems in CAESAR', *Proceedings of 5th International Symposium on Programming*, LNCS 137.

Quillian, R. (1968). 'Semantic Memory'. in *Semantic Information Processing*, M. Minsky (ed.), MIT Press, 227–270.

Raiffa, H. (1982). *The Art and Science of Negotiation*. Harvard University Press.

Ramesh, B. (1998). 'Factors Influencing Requirements Traceability in Practice', *Communications of the ACM*, Vol. 41, No. 12, December, 37–44.

Ramesh, B. and Jarke, M. (2001). 'Towards Reference Models for Requirements Traceability', *IEEE Transactions on Software Engineering*, Vol. 27, No. 1, January, 58–92.

Rapanotti, L., Hall, J.G., Jackson, M. and Nuseibeh, B. (2004). 'Architecture-Driven Problem Decomposition', *Proceedings of RE'04, 12th IEEE Joint International Requirements Engineering Conference*, Kyoto, September.

Rasmussen, J. (1986). *Information Processing and Human-Machine Interaction: An Approach to Cognitive Engineering*. North-Holland.

Regnell, B., Kimbler, K. and Wesslen, A. (1995). 'Improving the Use Case Driven Approach to Requirements Engineering', *Proceedings of RE'95 – 2nd International Symposium on Requirements Engineering*, York, IEEE, 40–47.

Regnell, B., Runeson, P. and Thelin, T. (2000). 'Are the Perspectives Really Different? Further Experimentation on Scenario-Based Reading of Requirements', *Empirical Software Engineering*, Vol. 5, 331–356.

Reubenstein, H.B. and Waters, R.C. (1991). 'The Requirements Apprentice: Automated Assistance for Requirements Acquisition', *IEEE Transactions on Software Engineering*, Vol. 17, No. 3, March, 226–240.

Richardson, D.J., Leif Aha, S. and O'Malley, T.O. (1992). 'Specification-based test oracles for reactive systems', *Proceedings of ICSE'92 – International Conference on Software Engineering*, Melbourne, Australia, 11–15 May, ACM, 105–118.

Robertson, S. and Robertson, J. (1999). *Mastering the Requirements Process*. ACM Press/Addison-Wesley.

Robinson, W.N. (1989). 'Integrating Multiple Specifications Using Domain Goals', *Proceedings of IWSSD-5 – 5th International Workshop on Software Specification and Design*, IEEE, 219–225.

Robinson, W.N. (1990). 'Negotiation Behaviour During Requirement Specification', *Proceedings of ICSE12 – 12th International Conference on Software Engineering*, March, 268–276.

Robinson, W.N. (2006). 'A Requirements Monitoring Framework for Enterprise Systems', *Requirements Engineering Journal*, Vol. 11, No. 1, March, 17–41.

Robinson, W.N. and Volkov, S. (1997). 'A Meta-Model for Restructuring Stakeholder Requirements', *Proceedings of ICSE19 – 19th International Conference on Software Engineering*, Boston, May, 140–149.

Robinson, W.N., Pawlowski, S. and Volkov, S. (2003). 'Requirements Interaction Management', *ACM Computing Surveys*, Vol. 35, No. 2, June, 132–190.

Rolland, C. and Ben Achour, C. (1998). 'Guiding the Construction of Textual Use Case Specifications', *Data and Knowledge Engineering Journal*, Vol. 25, No. 1-2, March, 125–160.

Rolland, C., Souveyet, C. and Ben Achour, C. (1998). 'Guiding Goal Modeling Using Scenarios', *IEEE Transactions on Software Engineering*, Special Issue on Scenario Management, December, 1055–1071.

Roong-Ko, D. and Frankl, P.G. (1994). 'The ASTOOT approach to testing object-oriented programs', *ACM Transactions on Sofware Engineering and Methodology*, Vol. 3, No. 2, April, 101–130.

Ross, D.T and Schoman, K.E. (1977a). 'Structured Analysis for Requirements Definition', *IEEE Transactions on Software Engineering*, Vol. 3, No. 1, January, 6–15.

Ross, D.T. and Schoman, K.E. (1977b). 'Structured Analysis (SA): A Language for Communicating Ideas', *IEEE Transactions on Software Engineering*, Vol. 3, No. 1, January, 16–34.

Rubin, K.S. and Goldberg, A. (1992). 'Object Behaviour Analysis', *Communications of the ACM*, Vol. 35, No. 9, September, 48–62.

Rugg, G. and McGeorge, P. (1995). 'Laddering', *Expert Systems*, Vol. 12, 339–346.

Rugg, G. and McGeorge, P. (1997). 'The Sorting Techniques: A Tutorial Paper on Card Sorts, Picture Sorts, and Item Sorts', *Expert Systems*, Vol. 14, No. 2, 80–93.

Rumbaugh, J., Jacobson, I. and Booch, G. (1999). *The Unified Modeling Language Reference Manual*. Addison-Wesley Object Technology Series.

Rumbaugh, J., Blaha, M., Prmerlani, W., Eddy, F. and Lorensen, W. (1991). *Object-Oriented Modeling and Design*. Prentice-Hall.

Ryan, K. and Mathews, B. (1993). 'Matching Conceptual Graphs as an Aid to Requirements Reuse', *Proceedings of RE'93 – First IEEE International Symposium on Requirements Engineering*, San Diego, January, 112–120.

Saaltink, M. (1997). The Z/Eves System. *Proceedings of 10th International Conference of Z Users on the Z Formal Specification Notation,* LNCS 1212, Springer-Verlag, 72–85.

Saati, T.L. (1980). *The Analytic Hierarchy Process*. McGraw-Hill.

Schmid, R., Ryser, J., Berner, S., Glinz, M., Reutemann, R. and Fahr, E. (2000). *A Survey of Simulation Tools for Requirements Engineering*. Special Interest Group on RE, German Informatics Society (GI), August.

Schneider, S. (2001). *The B-Method: An Introduction*. Palgrave Cornerstones of Computing Series.

Schneier, B. (2000). *Secrets and Lies: Digital Security in a Networked World*. John Wiley & Sons Ltd.

Schobbens, P.Y., Heymans, P., Trigaux, J.C. and Bontemps, Y. (2006). 'Feature Diagrams: A Survey and a Formal Semantics', *Proceedings of RE'06 – 14th IEEE International Requirements Engineering Conference*, Minneapolis, September.

Sekerinski, E. and Sere, K. (eds) (1999). *Program Development by Refinement: Case Studies Using the B Method*. Springer-Verlag.

Shaw, M. and Garlan, D. (1996). *Software Architecture: Perspectives on an Emerging Discipline*. Prentice-Hall.

Shum, B. and Hammond, N. (1994). 'Argumentation-Based Design Rationale: What Use at What Cost?', *International Journal of Human-Computer Studies* Vol. 40, No. 4, April, 603–652.

Siddiqi, J., Morrey, I., Roast, C. and Ozcan, M. (1997). 'Towards Quality Requirements via Animated Formal Specifications', *Annals of Software Engineering*, Vol. 3.

Sindre, G. and Opdahl, A.L. (2005). 'Eliciting Security Requirements with Misuse Cases', *Requirements Engineering Journal*, Vol. 10, No. 1, 34–44.

Smith, J. and Smith, D. (1977). 'Database Abstractions: Aggregation and Generalization', *ACM Transactions on Database Systems*, Vol. 2, No. 2, 105–133.

Smith, R.L., Avrunin, G.S., Clarke, L.A. and Osterweil, L.J. (2002). 'PROPEL: An Approach Supporting Property Elucidation'. *Proceedings of ICSE'02: 24th International Conference on Software Engineering*, Orlando, IEEE Press, 11–21.

Sommerville, I. and Sawyer, P. (1997). *Requirements Engineering: A Good Practice Guide*. John Wiley & Sons Ltd.

Souquières, J. and Levy, N. (1993). 'Description of Specification Developments', *Proceedings of RE'93 – 1st IEEE Symposium on Requirements Engineering*, San Diego, 216–223.

Sowa, J.F. (1984). *Conceptual Structures: Information Processing in Mind and Machine*. Addison-Wesley.

Spanoudakis, G. and Finkelstein, A. (1997). 'Reconciling Requirements: A Method for Managing Interference, Inconsistency, and Conflict', *Annals of Software Engineering*, Vol. 3, 21, 433–457.

Spanoudakis, G., Finkelstein, A. and Till, D. (1999). 'Overlaps in Requirements Engineering', *Automated Software Engineering*, Vol. 6, No. 2, April, 171–198.

Spanoudakis, G., Zisman, A., Perez-Minana, E. and Krau, P. (2004). 'Rule-Based Generation of Requirements Traceability Relations', *Journal of Systems and Software*, Vol. 72, No. 2, 105–127.

Spivey, J.M. (1992). *The Z Notation: A Reference Manual*, Prentice Hall.

Standish Group (1995). *The Chaos Report*, http://www.standishgroup.com/sample_research/chaos.html.

Stepney, S., Coopere, D. and Woodcock, J. (1998). 'More Powerful Z Data Refinement: Pushing the State of the Art in Industrial Refinement', *Proceedings of ZUM'98*, LNCS 1493, Springer-Verlag, 284–307.

Suchman, L. (1987). *Plans and Situated Actions: the Problem of Human–Machine Communication*. Cambridge University Press.

Sutcliffe, A. (1997). 'A Technique Combination Approach to Requirements Engineering', *Proceedings of RE'97 – 3rd International Symposium on Requirements Engineering*, Anapolis, IEEE, 65–74.

Sutcliffe, A. (1998). 'Scenario-Based Requirements Analysis', *Requirements Engineering Journal* Vol. 3 No. 1, 48–65.

Sutcliffe, A. and Maiden, N. (1993). 'Bridging the Requirements Gap: Policies, Goals and Domains', *Proceedings of IWSSD-7 – 7th International Workshop on Software Specification and Design*, IEEE.

Sutcliffe, A. and Maiden, N. (1998). 'The Domain Theory for Requirements Engineering', *IEEE Transactions on Software Engineering*, Vol. 24, No. 3, March, 174–196.

Sutcliffe, A., Fickas, S. and Sohlberg, M.M. (2006). 'PC-RE: A Method for Personal and Contextual Requirements Engineering with Some Experience', *Requirements Engineering Journal*, March, 1–17.

Sutcliffe, A., Maiden, N.A., Minocha, S. and Manuel, D. (1998). 'Supporting Scenario-Based Requirements Engineering', *IEEE Transactions in Software Engineering*, Vol. 24, No. 12, December, 1072–1088.

Swartout, W.R. (1983). 'XPLAIN: A System for Creating and Explaining Expert Consulting Systems', *Artificial Intelligence*, Vol. 21, No. 3, September, 285–325.

Swartout, W.R. and Balzer, R. (1982). 'On the Inevitable Intertwining of Specification and Implementation', *Communications of the ACM*, Vol. 25, No. 7, July, 438–440.

Teichroew, D. and Hershey, E. (1977). 'PSL/PSA: A Computer-Aided Technique for Structured Documentation and Analysis of Infomation Processing Systems', *IEEE Transactions on Software Engineering*, Vol. 3, No. 1, 41–48.

Teichroew, D., Macasovic, P., Hershey, E.A. and Yamamoto, Y. (1980). 'Application of the Entity-Relationship Approach to Information Processing Systems Modelling', in P. Chen (ed.), *Entity-Relationship Approach to Systems Analysis and Design*, North-Holland.

Thayer, R. and Dorfman, M. (eds) (1990). *Systems and Software Requirements Engineering*. IEEE Computer Society Press.

Thompson, J.M., Heimdahl, M.E. and Miller, S.P. (1999). 'Specification-Based Prototyping for Embedded Systems', *Proceedings of ESEC/FSE'99*, Toulouse, ACM SIGSOFT, LNCS 1687, Springer-Verlag, 163–179.

Touretzky, D.S. (1986). *The Mathematics of Inheritance Systems*. Pitman/Morgan Kaufmann.

Tran Van, H., van Lamsweerde, A., Massonet, P. and Ponsard, C. (2004). 'Goal-Oriented Requirements Animation', *Proceedings of RE'04 – 12th IEEE Joint International Requirements Engineering Conference*, Kyoto, September, 218–228.

Turing, A. (1949). 'Checking a Large Routine', in *Report of a Conference on High-Speed Automatic Calculating Machines*, University Mathematical Laboratory, 67–9. Also in F. Morris and C. Jones (eds), *Annals of the History of Computing*, Vol. 6, IEEE, April 1984.

Turner, J.G. and McCluskey, T.L. (1994). *The Construction of Formal Specifications*. McGraw-Hill.

Uchitel, S., Kramer, J. and Magee, J. (2001). 'Detecting Implied Scenarios in Message Sequence Chart Specifications', *Proceedings of ESEC/FSE'01 – 9th European Software Engineering Conference*, Vienna, September.

Uchitel, S., Kramer, J. and Magee, J. (2003). 'Synthesis of Behaviour Models from Scenarios', *IEEE Transactions on Software Engineering*, Vol. 29, No. 2, 99–115.

Upchurch, L., Rugg, G. and B. Kitchenham (2001). 'Using Card Sorts to Elicit Web Page Quality Attributes', *IEEE Software*, Vol. 18, No. 4, 84–89.

US Department of Defense (1988). *Formal Investigation into the Circumstances Surrounding the Downing of IranAir Flight 655*, July.

Utting, M. (2006). *The Jaza Animator*. http://www.cs.waikato.ac.nz/~marku/jaza.

van der Aalst, W., ter Hofstede, A., Kiepuszewski, B. and Barros, A.P. (2003). 'Workflow Patterns', *Distributed and Parallel Databases*, Vol. 14, No. 1, 5–51.

Vicenti, W.G. (1993). *What Engineers Know and How They Know It: Analytical Studies from Aeronautical History*. Johns Hopkins University Press.

Viega, J. and McGraw, G. (2001). *Building Secure Software: How to Avoid Security Problems the Right Way*. Addison-Wesley.

Vincke, P. (1992). *Multicriteria Decision-Aid*, John Wiley & Sons Ltd.

Waldinger, R. (1977). 'Achieving Several Goals Simultaneously', in *Machine Intelligence*, Vol. 8, E. Elcock and D. Michie (eds), Ellis Horwood.

Ward, P.T. and Mellor, S.J. (1985). *Structured Development for Real-Time Systems*. Prentice-Hall.

Warmer, J. and Kleppe, A. (2003). *The Object Constraint Language: Getting Your Models Ready for MDA*. Addison-Wesley.

Wasserman, A. (1979). 'A Specification Method for Inteactive Information Systems', *Proceedings of SRS – Specification of Reliable Software*. IEEE, Catalog No. 79, CH1401-9C, 68–79.

Watkins, R. and Neal, M. (1994). 'Why and How of Requirements Tracing', *IEEE Software*, Vol. 11, No. 4, July, 104–106.

Weidenhaupt, K., Pohl, K., Jarke, M. and Haumer, P. (1998). 'Scenario Usage in System Development: A Report on Current Practice'. *IEEE Software*, March.

Weyuker, E., Goradia, T. and Singh, A. (1994). 'Automatically Generating Test Data from a Boolean Specification', *IEEE Transactions on Software Engineering*, Vol. 20, No. 5, May, 353–363.

Whitten, J.L. and Bentley, L.D. (1998). *Systems Analysis and Design Methods*, McGraw-Hill.

Whittle, J. and Schumann, J. (2000). 'Generating Statechart Designs from Scenarios', *Proceedings of ICSE'2000 – 22nd International Conference on Software Engineering*, Limerick, 314–323.

Wiels, V. and Easterbrook, S.M. (1999). 'Formal Modeling of Space Shuttle Software Change Requests using SCR', *Proceedings of RE'99 – 4th International Symposium on Requirements Engineering*, Limerick, IEEE, June.

Wieringa, R.J. (1996). *Requirements Engineering: Frameworks for Understanding*. John Wiley & Sons Ltd.

Wieringa, R.J. (2003). *Design Methods for Reactive Systems*. Morgan Kaufmann.

Wing, J.M. (1988). 'A Study of 12 Specifications of the Library Problem', *IEEE Software*, July, 66–76.

Wing, J.M. (1990). 'A Specifier's Introduction to Formal Methods', *IEEE Computer*, Vol. 23, No. 9, September.

Winter, V., Berg, R. and Ringland, J. (1999) 'Bay Area Rapid Transit District, Advance Automated Train Control System, Case Study Description'. Sandia National Labs, http://www.pst.informatik.uni-muenchen.de/dagstuhl.

Wood, J. and Silver, D. (1995). *Joint Application Development*. John Wiley & Sons Ltd.

Woodcock, J. and Davies, J. (1996). *Using Z: Specification, Refinement, and Proof*. Prentice Hall.

Yu, E.S.K. (1993). 'Modelling Organizations for Information Systems Requirements Engineering', *Proceedings of RE'93 – 1st International Symposium on Requirements Engineering*, 34–41.

Yu, E. (1997). 'Towards Modeling and Reasoning Support for Early-Phase Requirements Engineering', *Proceedings of RE-97 – 3rd International Symposium on Requirements Engineering*, Annapolis, 226–235.

Yu, E. and Mylopoulos, J. (1994). 'Understanding "why" in software process modeling, analysis, and design', *Proceedings of ICSE'94 – 16th International Conference on Software Engineering*, Sorrento, IEEE, 159–168.

Yue, K. (1987). 'What Does It Mean to Say that a Specification is Complete?', *Proceedings of IWSSD-4 – 4th International Workshop on Software Specification and Design*, Monterey.

Zaremski, A.M. and Wing, J. (1997). 'Specification Matching of Software Components', *ACM Transactions on Software Engineering and Methodology*, Vol. 6, No. 4, October, 333–369.

Zave, P. (1997). 'Classification of Research Efforts in Requirements Engineering', *ACM Computing Surveys*, Vol. 29, No. 4, 315–321.

Zave, P. and Jackson, M. (1993). 'Conjunction as Composition', *ACM Transactions on Software Engineering and Methodology*, Vol. 2, No. 4, October, 379–411.

Zave, P. and Jackson, M. (1996). 'Where Do Operations Come From? A Multiparadigm Specification Technique', *IEEE Transactions on Software Engineering*, Vol. 22, No. 7, July, 508–528.

Zave, P. and Jackson, M. (1997). 'Four Dark Corners of Requirements Engineering', *ACM Transactions on Software Engineering and Methodology*, Vol. 6, No. 1, 1–30.

Index

A

abnormal scenarios   69, 465–6, *Fig. 13.15*
abstract domains   74–6, *Fig. 2.4*
accuracy goals   270, 568, 572
accuracy requirements   22, 25–6
accuracy statements   22
Achieve goals   266–7, *Fig. 7.4*
  converse assertions   315–16, 621
  identification   474–5, *Fig. 13.20*
  obstruction patterns   617–18, *Fig. 18.12*
actigrams   133, *Fig. 4.6*
actions   456–9, *Fig. 13.8*
active observation   79
actors   30, 74, 136
agent behaviour   265, 431, 596–7
agent beliefs   403
agent concurrency   396, 424, 431–2
agent dependencies   274, 403–5, 432,
  Fig. 11.5
  see also dependency diagrams
agent diagrams   405–6, 411–13, *Fig. 11.6*
agent interfaces   398, 406–7, 414, *Fig. 11.7,*
  Fig. 11.13
agent knowledge   403, 618–19
agent meta-model   490–1, *Fig. 14.5*
agent models
  assignments   401
  building   411–15, 515–17
  interface with goal model 303, *Fig. II.1*
  purpose   395
  structural consistency   494–6

  use in RD   564, 565
  see also agent diagrams; context diagrams;
    dependency diagrams
agent orientation   278
agent substitution   350–1, *Fig. 9.11*
agent wishes   314, 402
agents
  capabilities   395, 396, 397–9, *Fig. 11.1*
  categories   396–7
  commitments   430–1
  decomposition   408–11, 453, *Fig. 11.10,*
    Fig. 13.5
  definition   260, 396–7
  features   397
  identification   411–12
  modelling   298, 384
  non-determinism   396, 431, 596
  as operation performers   401–2, 427,
    Fig. 11.4
  refinement   408–11, 453, *Fig. 11.10,*
    Fig. 13.5
  responsibilities   399, *Fig. 11.2*
aggregation
  agents   408
  objects   376–7, 386, *Fig. 10.9*
agile development   53–5
algebraic specification   167–72, 173
Alloy analyser   208
alternative goal refinements   304–5, *Fig. 8.8,*
  Fig. 8.9
  formal patterns   605, *Fig. 18.3*
  soft goal identification   313–14, *Fig. 8.16*

alternative options
   evaluation   14, 32, 105–7, 274, 517–18
   modelling   303–7
   product line projects   524
   qualitative assessment   106–7, 557–60
   quantitative assessment   107, 560–2
   soft goals and   268
   sources   87, 105, 557
alternative responsibility assignments   305,
    515–17
   evaluation   16–17, 306
   modelling   305–6, 401, *Fig. 8.10*
analogical reuse   541–4, *Fig. 16.2*
Analytic Hierarchy Process (AHP)   109–12
AND-refinement
   goals   297–300, *Fig. 8.2*, *Fig. 8.3*
   obstacles   341, *Fig. 9.3*
   obstruction propagation   342–3, *Fig. 9.5*
   vs OR-refinement   318–19, *Fig. 8.18*
AND/OR graphs   307–8
animations   198
anti-goals   552
   formal generation   618–22
   formal specification   591
   identification   554, 620–1
   refinement   621
architectural design   42–3, 566–7
architectural refinement patterns   572–4,
    Fig. 16.15, *Fig. 16.16*
architectural requirements   27, 570
arity
   associations   368
   relationships   131
artefact-driven elicitation techniques   62,
    64–76
   background study   64
   card sorts   66
   conceptual laddering   67
   data collection   65
   knowledge reuse   72–6
   prototypes   70–2
   questionnaires   65–6
   repertory grids   66
   storyboards/scenarios   67–70
associations   362, 363, 366–71
   arity   368
   of associations   379, *Fig. 10.11*
   constraint patterns   369–70
   controlled   398

derived   378
domain properties   370–1
   goals constraining   370–1
   identification   381
   instances   366–7, *Fig. 10.3*
   modelling   384–5, 386
   monitored   397
   multiplicities   368–71, *Fig. 10.4*, *Fig. 10.5*
   OR-associations   378–9, *Fig. 10.10*
   ordered   379, *Fig. 10.10*
   reflexive   368
   stability of   593
   vs relations   373
assumptions   19
   analysis   15–16
   definition   20, 264
atomic features   239
attackers   553, 554
attributes   131, 371–2
   controlled   398
   derived   378
   elementary   371
   modelling   384, 385
   monitored   397
   multiplicity   372, *Fig. 10.6*
   names   388
   as pointers   387, *Fig. 10.15*
   of relationships   131–2
   rigid   372, *Fig. 10.6*
   structured   371
auxiliary episodes   466
availability requirements   25

B

background study   64
behaviour meta-model   492–3, *Fig. 14.7*
behaviour models   449–50
   building   463–77, 521–4
   formal synthesis   627–35
   interface with goal model 303, *Fig. II.1*
   structural consistency   495–6
   use in RD   565
   see also scenarios; state machine models
behavioural goals   265–8, *Fig. 7.3*, *Fig. 7.4*
   coverage   303
   realizability   399–400
   satisfaction of   265
   scenarios and   276, 474–5, *Fig. 7.8*

binary associations   368
boundary conditions   88–9
    avoiding   92–3
    regression-based derivation   623–5
bounded model checkers   208
bounded SAT solvers   608–9, 610,
    Fig. 18.7
brainstorming   81
branching temporal logics   154
brownfield projects   40

C

capability instance declarations   398,
    406
card sorts   66
case studies   6–12
case-driven refinement patterns   322–5
causal links   592–3
change
    causes   224–5, 247, *Table 6.1*
    deferred   249
    documentation   223
    dynamic   249–51
    evaluation   248–9
    incorporation   249
    prioritization   247, 248
    types   221, *Table 6.1*
    see also requirements management
change anticipation   223–5
change control   246–9, *Fig. 6.16*
change management *see* requirements
    management
change requests   247
checklist-based reviewing   189
    defect-based checklists   191–2, *Table 5.1*
    domain-specific checklists   193
    language-based checklists   193–5
    quality-specific checklists   192–3
circularity checking   203
class behaviours
    in meta-model   492–3
    modelling   449, 454–63
class diagrams   144
    derivation   380–3, *Fig. 10.12*
    meta-model representation   487
commonality   524
    levels of   223, *Fig. 6.2*
commutativity axiom pattern   171

completeness   35, 335
completeness checking   203, 204–5
compliance requirements   27
component inspection   96
components   4–5, 566
composite features   239
composite state   459
composition   376, 386, *Fig. 10.9*
Computational Tree Logic (CTL)   154,
    208
concept-driven acquisition   66–7
conceptual laddering   67
conceptual objects
    agent monitoring/control   397–8
    definition   360–1
    features   364–6, *Fig. 10.2*
    identification   380–1
    modelling   359, 384, 385
    names   388
    types   362–3, *Fig. 10.1*
concern links   294, 303, 380
condition lists   467–9
condition tables   165–6, 203–5,
    Table 4.3
confidentiality goals   403, 619
confidentiality requirements   25
configuration management   47
conflict analysis   544–9, 622–7
conflict links   294, 308
conflict management   14–15, 90–3, 545,
    Fig. 3.1
conflict resolution   89, 92–3, 513–14,
    Fig. 15.10
conflicts
    causes   89
    documentation   91
    in goal models   271, 273–4, 301–2, 314,
        Fig. 8.7
    identification   32, 90–1, 512
    as source of change   225
    types   88–9
confusion obstacles   403
connectors   566
consistency checkers   244
consistency checks   203–4
consistency rules   88–9, 493–6
constraint analysis   15–16
content analysis   64
context diagrams   127–8, 130, *Fig. 4.2*

context diagrams *(continued)*
  agent interface view   406–7, 517, *Fig. 11.7,*
    Fig. 11.8, Fig. 15.13
  generation   413–15, *Fig. 11.14, Fig. 11.15*
contextual enquiry   81
contribution links   262
control links   397, 405
controlled variables   21, 469
countermeasures
  identification   99–101, 350–3, 556
  reuse   100
  run-time monitoring   99
  selection   101, 353
coverage links   303
cross referencing   237
customer-driven projects   40
cut-set trees   97, *Fig. 3.4*

D

data collection   65
data dependencies   34
data-flow architecture   568–70, *Fig. 16.11*
  quality refinement   571–4
  style refinement   570–1
dataflow diagrams (DFD)   134–6, *Fig. 4.8*
datagrams   133, *Fig. 4.7*
decision tables   122–3, 194, *Table 5.2*
decomposition-by-case pattern   322–3, 505,
    Fig. 8.21
Defect Detection Prevention (DDP)   102–5,
    Fig. 3.5
defects
  evaluation   189–90
  types   36–7, *Table 1.1*
deferred requirements   221
definitions   20, 593
dependency chains   404–5, 407
dependency diagrams   407–8
dependency links   228, 404, *Fig. 6.5*
derivation links   230–1, *Fig. 6.9*
  bi-directional nature   383, 441–2
  satisfaction arguments and   231–2, 541, *Fig.*
    6.10
  traceability   540
derived associations   378
derived attributes   378
descriptive statements   17, 264
desired behaviours   28

development requirements   27–8
diagrammatic notation   127–45
  activities and data   133–4
  conceptual structures   130–3
  information flows   134–6
  inspection checklists   194–5
  interaction   136–8
  stimuli and responses   142
  system behaviour   138–42
  system operations   136
  system scope   127–30
  view integration   142–4
diagrammatic visualisation   200
discriminators   376
dissatisfaction obstacles   338
distribution constraints   27
divergence   88–9, 301
  analysis   545–6
  formal patterns   627, *Fig. 18.13*
  formal resolution   625–7
  identification   548–9
  see also conflicts
divergence patterns   625, *Fig. 18.13*
divide-and-conquer pattern   324–5, *Fig. 8.24*
documentation   33, 43, 46, 119
  see also requirements document (RD)
domain knowledge   14
domain post-condition   426–7, *Fig. 12.3*
  formal specification   594
  required conditions   439–40
domain pre-condition   426–7, *Fig. 12.3*
  formal specification   594
  required conditions   439–40
domain properties
  definition   19, 264
  formal specification   592
  from obstacle analysis   338, *Fig. 9.2*
  modelling   298, 365–6, 370
  satisfaction arguments and   300, *Fig. 8.6*
domain understanding   30–1, 46, 61–2
  see also requirements elicitation
domain-specific visualisation   200
dynamic change   249–51

E

eager behaviour   431, 596–7
elementary attributes   371
entities   131, 362, 366

modelling   363, 384
entity-relationship diagrams   130–3, *Fig. 4.5*
entry/exit actions   457–9, *Fig. 13.10*
environment   5
environmental agents   410, 451
environmental operations   424
episodes   450, 453, *Fig. 13.4*
errors   36–7, *Table 1.2*
  cost   33, 48, 187
  impact   49–51, 187
  scale of problem   48
ethnographic studies   79–80
event notifications   457, *Fig. 13.9*
event tables   165, *Table 4.2*
event trace diagrams   136–8, *Fig. 4.10*
event-based specification   163–7, 173
  animation of   198
events   363
  internal/external   455
  modelling   384
  stimuli   466
evolutionary prototypes   71, 72
expectations
  definition   263, 264, 293
  formal specification   590
  in goal models   298
external events   455

F

fault trees   96–7, *Fig. 3.3, Fig. 3.4*
FAUST animator   198, 200, *Fig. 5.3*
feature diagrams   239–40, *Fig. 6.15*
features   23, 220
final sub-states   460, 462, *Fig. 13.14*
first-order predicate logic   148–50
first-order refinement patterns   607–8
first-order specification languages
   150–1
fit criterion   123–4, 296
flaws   37–8, *Table 1.3*
fluents   437–9, 632–3, *Fig. 12.9*
focus groups   80
formal specification   46, 127, 145–74
  algebraic   167–72
  event-based   163–7, 173
  first-order languages   150–1
  goal models   588–91
  history-based   151–5, 173

inspection checklists   195
  object models   592–3
  operation models   594–6
  state-based   155–63, 173
  strengths and limitations   173–5, 583, 603
  traceability management and   242–3, 246
formal verification   188, 202–11
four-variable model   21, *Fig. 1.4*
frame diagrams   129, *Fig. 4.4*
frame problem   160, 166, 597
free documentation   120–1
functional goals   269, *Fig. 7.5*
functional prototype   70
functional requirements   23, 28

G

gauge variables   561–2, *Fig. 16.8*
generalization
  modelling   387
  multiple   375
  see also specialization
generative semantics   166, 597
global templates   125–7, 194
glossary of terms   31, 89, 388
  from object model   359, 563
goal diagrams   293–4
  as AND/OR graphs   307–8
  class diagrams and   380–3, *Fig. 10.12*
goal meta-model   488–9, *Fig. 14.3*
goal models   293–4
  agent diagrams from   411–13
  annotations   294–6, *Fig. 8.1*
  building   309–27, 503–6, 507–10
  conflicts   301–2, *Fig. 8.7*
  context diagrams from   413–15
  interface with other views 293, 302–3,
   Fig. II.1
  obstacle diagrams and   340, *Fig. 9.4*
  product line projects   525, *Fig. 15.18*
  refinement graphs   297–300
  risk analysis on   273, 335
  scope   316–17
  structural consistency   494–5
  use in RD   564–5, 566
  see also goal diagrams
goal refinement   297–301
  features   308, *Fig. 8.12*
  formal methods   604–9

goal refinement *(continued)*
  refinement patterns   319–27
  satisfaction arguments and   272–3, 300,
    Fig. 7.6
  vs operation refinement   441
  see also alternative goal refinements
goal restoration   352
goal satisficing   268, 308
goal specification patterns   589–90,
    Fig. 17.1
goal substitution   350, *Fig. 9.11*
goal weakening   351–2, 514, 626–7,
    Fig. 15.10
goal-agent co-refinement   408–9, *Fig. 11.11*
goal-agent co-refinement pattern   410,
    Fig. 11.12
goal-oriented RE
  agent orientation compared   278
  definition   260
  object orientation compared   278
  top-down analysis and   279
goals
  ambiguities   319
  categories   265, 269–71, *Fig. 7.5*
  conflicts   271, 301–2
  definition   260, 293
  features   293, 294–6, *Fig. 8.1*
  formal specification   588–91
  granularity   262
  identification   270, 271, 275–6,
    309–16
  importance   272–5
  model checking   277–8
  obstructions *see* obstacles
  operations compared   317–18, *Fig. 8.17*
  realizability   399–401, *Fig. 11.3*
  satisfaction   231–2, *Fig. 6.10*
  scenarios and   276, 473–5, *Fig. 7.8*
  specification   295
  strengths and limitations   463, 464,
    Table 13.1
  types   265–9, *Fig. 7.2*
  unrealizability   400–1
  use cases and   277
greenfield projects   40
group sessions   80–1, 98
grouping rule   497
guard-introduction pattern   323–4, *Fig. 8.23*
  formal use   604–5, *Fig. 18.1*

guarded transitions   139–40, 456, 471,
    Fig. 13.7
guidewords   96–7

H

hazard obstacles   338
higher-order functions   172
history-based specification   151–5, 173
  animation of   198
hypotheses
  definition   264
  formal specification   592
  modelling   298
  satisfaction arguments and   300

I

i* diagrams   274, 404, 407–8, *Fig. 11.9*
IEEE Std-830 template   52, 125–6, 564–6,
    Fig. 4.1
in-house projects   41
inaccuracy obstacles   338
inconsistencies   87, 88–9
  see also conflicts
inconsistency management   88–93, 188
independence axiom pattern   171
information goals   270, 338
inheritance
  inhibiting   132, 375
  multiple   375
  transitions   459–60, 462
  see also specialization
inheritance conflict   375
initial sub-states   460, 462, *Fig. 13.14*
initializations   365, 366, 367
  formal specification   592
input variables   21
inspection reports   189, 190
inspections and reviews   187, 188–96,
    211
  checklists   191–5
  guidelines   190
  process   188–90, *Fig. 5.1*
installation constraints   27
instance behaviours
  in meta-model   492
  modelling   449, 450–4

integrity requirements   25
intentional specifications   277
intentional threats   552, 553–6
inter-view checks   538–9
inter-view consistency rules   142–4,
   493–6
   traceability and   242–3
interaction events   450, 451,
   468–9
interaction matrix   91
interface requirements   26
interleaving semantics   141, 596
internal events   455
interoperability requirements   26
interviews   77–9
intra-view rules   539–40
invariants   155

J

JAD (Joint Application Development)   80

K

knowledge acquisition   61, 62–3
knowledge reuse   72–6
   analogical reuse   541–4, *Fig. 16.2*
   domain-independent   72–4
   domain-specific   74–6
   process   72, 543–4
   and risk identification   98

L

labelled transition system   628–35
lazy behaviour   431, 596–7
lifelines   451
linear temporal logic (LTL)   151–4,
   584–91
   absolute time bounds   587–8
   model-checking   208
   relative time bounds   587
   state assertions   584–5
   temporal assertions   585–6
   variable-dependent time bounds   588
liveness property   207, 278
load analysis   540, *Fig. 16.1*
logic   146–51
   first-order predicate   148–50
   propositional   146–7

M

machine solution   4, *Fig. 1.1*
macro-events   454
Maintain goals   267–8, *Fig. 7.4*
   identification   315, 475
   obstruction patterns   617–18, *Fig. 18.11*
malevolent agents   397, 512
   see also threats
market studies   82
market-driven projects   40
message sequence charts (MSCs)   137, 629,
   631
meta-models   485–93
   definition   485
   domain level   486, *Fig. 14.1*
   instance level   486, *Fig. 14.1*
   meta level   485–6, *Fig. 14.1*
   reuse   73–4, *Fig. 2.3*
   role   486–7
   structure   487–8, *Fig. 14.2*
milestone-based dependencies   405
milestone-driven refinement pattern   321–2,
   405, 505, 513, *Fig. 8.19*
   formal use   604, *Fig. 18.1*
misinformation obstacles   338
mission-critical goals
   completeness   298, 337
   obstacle analysis   335
mission-critical systems
   change procedures   247
   importance of RE   49–51
   model checking   205
mock-ups   71
mode transition tables   164, *Table 4.1*
model checking   205–8, *Fig. 5.4*
   goals and   277–8
model checklists   540
model configurations   524, 525–8
model databases
   analogical reuse   541–4
   browsing   538
   query-based analysis   493,
      538–44
   structural consistency   538–40
   traceability management
      540–1
   view generation   540
model-driven elicitation   82

models
  requirements for 288–9
  role in RE 287–8
  see also individual models
monitored condition 467–8
monitored variables 21, 469
monitoring links 397, 405
multiplicity
  attributes 372, *Fig. 10.6*
  relationships 132

N

N-ary associations 368, *Fig. 10.4*
narratives 67
natural language
  in QA 212
  structured 121–7
  unrestricted 120–1
negative scenarios 68–9, 450
  obstacle coverage and 465
  as sequence diagrams 452, *Fig. 13.3*
negotiation 89–90
nested states 459
NFR framework 106–7, *Table 3.5*
non-functional goals 269, *Fig. 7.5*
non-functional requirements 24
  categories 24–8, *Fig. 1.5*
  functional overlap 28
non-functional statements *see* accuracy
    statements
non-rigid variables 454, 468
normal design projects 40
normal scenarios 69, 465–6, *Fig. 13.15*

O

object instances 360–2
object meta-model 489–90, *Fig. 14.4*
object models 359, 363–4
  annotations 364–6, *Fig. 10.2*
  building 380–8, 506, 510–11
  content 387–8, *Fig. 10.16*
  formal specification 592–3
  interface with goal model 303,
    Fig. II.1
  product line projects 525, *Fig. 15.19*
  structural consistency 494–5

use in RD 563, 565
  see also class diagrams
object orientation 278
objective identification 13–15
objects *see* conceptual objects
obligations 396, 402, 428, 430, 440
observation 79–80
obstacle analysis 314, 344–53, 512–15,
    Fig. 9.7, Fig. 15.9
obstacle diagrams 339–40, *Fig. 9.1*
  annotations 343, *Fig. 9.6*
obstacle mitigation 352, 513
obstacle models 339–43
  building 512
  interface with goal model 303, *Fig. II.1*
  see also obstacle diagrams
obstacle monitoring 349–50
obstacle prevention 351, *Fig. 9.11*
obstacle reduction 352
obstacle refinement
  AND-refinement 340, 341, *Fig. 9.3*
  OR-refinement 342–3, *Fig. 9.5*
  refinement patterns 349
obstacles
  categories 338
  completeness 337–8
  confusion 403
  definition 336–7
  evaluation 349
  features 343, *Fig. 9.6*
  formal generation 613–18
  formal specification 591
  in goal meta-model 488–9
  identification 344–9, 549–51
  resolution 349–53, 513
obstruction links 303
obstruction patterns 617–18
operation meta-model 491–2, *Fig. 14.6*
operation models
  building 437–42, 518–21
  completeness 433
  formal specification 594–6
  links to other models 303, 441–2, *Fig. II.1*
  purpose 421–2
  structural consistency 494–6
  use in RD 565
  see also operationalization diagrams; use
    case diagrams
operation performers 401–2, 427, *Fig. 11.4*

operational specifications 277
operationalization 277, 424, 427–34
  by multiple operations 430
  correctness 432–3
  formal checking 609–13
  formal specification 594–6
  of multiple goals 429
  satisfaction arguments and 432–4
  traceability and 434
operationalization diagrams 435, 442, *Fig. 12.6, Fig. 12.7*
operationalization links 294, 303, 424, 435
operationalization patterns 610–13
operations
  application 422–3, *Fig. 12.1*
  atomicity 423–4
  categories 424
  definition 422
  features 425
  formal specification 595–6
  generators 168–9
  goals compared 317–18, *Fig. 8.17*
  identification 437–9
  modifiers 159, 168
  obligations 396, 402, 428, 430, 440
  observers 159, 169
  permissions 396, 402, 428, 430, 440
  required conditions 427–9, *Fig. 12.4*
  scope 425–6, *Fig. 12.2*
  signature 422, 425, 430, 435, *Fig. 12.2*
OR-associations 378–9, *Fig. 10.10*
OR-refinement
  goals 274, *Fig. 7.7*
  obstacles 342–3, *Fig. 9.5*
  vs AND-refinement 318–19, *Fig. 8.18*
ordered associations 379, *Fig. 10.10*
output variables 21
outsourced projects 41
overspecification 38–9

P

packages 496–7, *Fig. 14.8*
passive observation 79
performance instance declaration 401, 406
performance links 405, 435
performance requirements 26
permissions 396, 402, 428, 430, 440
positive scenarios 68–9, 450, 463

and goal coverage 465
  notation 137
post-conditions 155
pre-conditions 155
preferred behaviours 29
Prefix Tree Acceptor (PTA) 629–34, *Fig. 18.15*
prescriptive statements 17, 264
prioritization *see* requirements prioritization
privacy requirements 25
probabilistic goals 269
problem diagrams 128–9, 130, *Fig. 4.3*
problem world 4, *Fig. 1.1*
process algebras 172
process-based reviewing 189, 190
process-related risks 94, 95
product-line projects 41, 524–8
product-related risks 94, 95, 335
project management 44
project types 40–2
property testers 633–4, *Fig. 18.19*
propositional logic 146–7
protocol analysis 79
prototyping 42, 70–2, 198, *Fig. 2.1*
pruning semantics 166, 597

Q

QFD (Quality Function Deployment) 80
qualitative labels 558–60
quality assurance
  requirements *see* requirements quality assurance
  software 43
quality requirements 24–6
questionnaires 65–6

R

R-net diagrams 142, *Fig. 4.14*
RAD (Rapid Application Development) 82
radical design projects 40
reachability graphs 207
real-time temporal logic 152–3, 584–91
refinement graphs/trees 297–300, 326–7, *Fig. 8.2*
  see also AND/OR graphs
refinement links 293–4, 297
  satisfaction arguments and 300, 432
  two way nature 299–300

refinement patterns
    common patterns   321–7
    completeness checking and   298, 319
    formal use   604–8, *Fig. 18.1*
    obstacle analysis   349
    reuse   320
reflexive associations   368
relations   373
relationships   131–2
reliability requirements   25
repertory grids   66
required conditions   427–9, *Fig. 12.4*
    consistency   429, 430
    domain conditions   439–40
    multiple   429–30
required post-condition   428
    on domain conditions   439–40
    formal specification   594–5
required pre-condition   428
    on domain conditions   439–40
    formal specification   594
required trigger condition   428
    on domain conditions   439–40
    formal specification   594
requirement taxonomies   24, 28–9, 72–3, *Fig
    .1.5*
requirements *see* software requirements; system
    requirements
requirements animation   187–8, 198, 211
    model extraction   199
    model simulation   199–200
    strengths and limitations   200–1
    visualisation   200, *Fig. 5.3*
requirements completeness   35, 335
requirements consolidation   33
requirements database   144
    conflicts in   91
    queries on   187, 196–7, 211
    see also model databases
requirements document (RD)   33
    changes   219, 220–2, *Table 6.1*
    defects   36–40, *Table 1.1*
    disciplined documentation   121–7
    errors   36–7, *Table 1.2*
    flaws   37–8, *Table 1.3*
    formal specification   127, 145–74
    free documentation   120–1
    model-driven generation   562–6
    qualities   35–6

quality assurance   187–8
semi-formal specification   127–45
structure   119, 124–7, 273
templates   125–6, 563–6, *Fig. 4.1*
traceability *see* traceability management
uses   42–4, 51–2, *Fig. 1.7*
requirements elicitation   31–2, 46
    artefact-driven techniques   62, 64–76
    combining techniques   81–2
    model-driven   82
    objectives   61
    stakeholder-driven techniques   62, 76–81
requirements engineering
    agile development and   53–5
    definition   3, 6
    dimensions   13–17, *Fig. 1.2*
    importance of   47–51
    obstacles to good practice   52–3
    other disciplines and   45–7
    process   34–5, 54, *Fig. 1.6*
    role   51–2
    software engineering and   45
    system design and   44–5
requirements evaluation   32–3, 46, 87–8
    QA and   188
    techniques   88–113
requirements evolution   47, 219–22
    documenting   225–46
    goals and   275
    time-space dimensions   220–1
    types and causes   221–2
    see also requirements management
requirements inspection checklists   191–5,
    494
requirements lifecycle   30–5
requirements management   220, 251
    change anticipation   223–5
    change control   246–9
    policy   251
    traceability management   225–46
requirements monitoring   249–51
requirements prioritization   32, 87, 108–13
    constraints   108
    value-cost comparison   109–12
requirements quality assurance   187–8
    animation based   187–8, 198–201
    database queries   196–7.87
    early analysis   212–13
    formal checks   188, 202–11

ideal process   212
inspection and reviews   187, 188–96
requirements specification   33, 43, 46, 119
requirements validation   33, 198
requirements verification   33, 202–12
resolution links   353, *Fig. 9.1*
responsibility assignments   16–17, 395
 alternative *see* alternative responsibility
   assignments
 features   308, *Fig. 8.12*
 goal realizability   399–401
 modelling   294, 412–13
 as source of change   225
responsibility instance declaration   399, 406
responsibility links   298, 303, 305, 405
reuse
 abstract domains   74–6, *Fig. 2.4*
 frame diagrams   129, *Fig. 4.4*
 meta-models   73–4, *Fig. 2.3*
 refinement patterns   319–27
 refinement trees   326–7
 requirement taxonomies   72–3
 see also knowledge reuse
review board   247–8
review meetings   63, 189, 190
reviews *see* inspections and reviews
revision links   229, *Fig. 6.7*
revisions   220–1, *Fig. 6.1*
rigid attributes   372, *Fig. 10.6*
risk analysis   88, 93–105
 on goal models   273, 335
 QA and   188
risk assessment   32, 98–9
risk assessment tables   98–9, *Table 3.2*
risk checklists   95
risk control   99–101
risk exposure   99
risk levels   98
risk management   95–101, 102–5, *Fig. 3.2*
risk trees   96–7, 613–18, *Fig. 3.3, Fig. 3.4*
risk-reduction leverage   101
risks
 definition   94, 335
 documentation   101–2
 identification   95–8
 as source of change   225
 types   94
RPNI   629–31
runtime monitoring   249–51, 349

S

SADT (Structured Analysis and Design
  Technique)   133–4, 242, *Fig. 4.6, Fig. 4.7*
safety goals   327, 338, *Fig. 8.28*
safety property   207, 278, 634
safety requirements   24
SAT solvers   608–9, 618
satisfaction arguments   22–3
 derivation links and   231–2, 541, *Fig. 6.10*
 from goal models   272–3, 300–1, *Fig. 7.6,*
   Fig. 8.5
 hypotheses and   505
 operationalization and   432–4
satisfaction goals   270, 338
 refinement trees   326–7, *Fig. 8.27*
scenarios   67–70
 conflict resolution   514, *Fig. 15.11*
 coverage   465–7
 goals and   276, 473–5, *Fig. 7.8*
 refinement   452–4
 risk identification   98
 as source of operations   439, *Fig. 12.10*
 state conditions and   467–9
 strengths and limitations   69–70, 463–4,
   Table 13.1
 types   68–9
 see also sequence diagrams
SCR (specification language)   163–6, 203–5
security goals   270, 572
 formal identification   620–1
 formal specification   618–20
 obstructions   338
 refinement trees   327, *Fig. 8.28*
 specification patterns   619–20
security requirements   25
semi-formal specification
 alternative option evaluation   557–62
 conflict analysis   544–9
 diagrammatic notations   127–45
 model database queries   538–44
 obstacle identification   549–51
 strengths and limitations   144–5, 174–5
 threat analysis   551–6
 traceability management and   242–3, 246
sequence diagrams   137, 144
 agent decomposition   453, *Fig. 13.5*
 episodes   453, *Fig. 13.4*
 scenario refinement   452–4

sequence diagrams *(continued)*
   scenario representation   450–4, *Fig. 13.1*
   state conditions   467–9, *Fig. 13.16*
   state diagrams from   469–73
shared phenomena   4
simulations   198
single-product project   41
SMV   208
snapshot state   454
soft goals   268–9
   conflicts   302
   formalization   589
   identification   305, 306, 313–14, *Fig. 8.16*
   satisfaction   268, 308
software agents
   refinement   410
   in sequence diagrams   451
software data architecture   567–8
software design   566–7
software engineering   45
software lifecycle   42–4, *Fig. 1.7*
software operations   424
software prototypes   70
software quality assurance   43
software requirements
   definition   19, 263, 411
   notation   21
   system requirements and   21–3
software-to-be   5
specialization   132, 373–6, *Fig. 10.7*
   modelling   386–7
   multiple   376, *Fig. 10.8*
specialization links   373, 374–5
specification *see* requirements specification
specification languages   119
   first order   150–1
   SCR   163–6, 203–5
   Z   156–62
   see also formal specification; semi-formal
      specification
specification patterns   155
specification-based traceability management
   242–3
SPIN   208
stability
   of associations   593
   levels of   223, *Fig. 6.2*
stakeholder-driven elicitation techniques   62,
   76–81, 82

group sessions   80–1
interviews   77–9
observation   79–80
uses   92, 100
stakeholders   30, 62–3
state assertions   584–5
state conditions   467–9
state diagrams   144, 455–63, *Fig. 13.6*
   actions   456–9, *Fig. 13.8*
   event notifications   457, *Fig. 13.9*
   from operation models   475–7, *Fig. 13.21*
   from sequence diagrams   469–73
   guarded transitions   456, *Fig. 13.7*
state machine diagrams   138–42, *Fig. 4.11*
state machine models   454
   from operationalized goals   475–7
   from sequence diagrams   469–73
   goal-driven synthesis   628
   model checking   205–7
   refinement   459–63
   scenario-driven synthesis   628–35
   strengths and limitations   464, *Table 13.1*
   see also state diagrams
state variables   265, 361, 397, 454
state-based specification   155–63, 173
   animation of   198, 199–200
   semantics   166
statecharts   141, *Fig. 4.13*
   see also state diagrams
statement templates   123–4, 193
statements
   goals and   264, *Fig. 7.1*
   local rules   121–4
   in object models   371
   overlapping   91–2
   scope   17–18, *Fig. 1.3*
   specification   119
   types   17–23
states   138–9, 454
   parallel decomposition   460–3, *Fig. 13.12*
   sequential decomposition   459–60, 462–3,
      Fig. 13.11
static semantics checking   203
stimuli events   466
stimulus-response goals   270
storyboards   67
structural consistency
   checks   538–40
   rules   493–6

structured attributes 371
structured interviews 77, 79
sub-states 459–63
synchrony hypothesis 166
syntax checking 202
system 4
system behaviour 265
  representation 138
  types 28–9
system boundary 17, 306, 317
system design 44–5
system model
  behavioural view 289
  building method 501–24, *Fig. 15.1*
  functional view 289
  integration mechanisms 485–97
  intentional view 289
  responsibility view 289
  semantic picture 434–5, 596–7, *Fig. 12.5*
  structural view 289
  views 289, *Fig. II.1*
  see also individual models
system proposal 31, 32, 61–2
system requirements 18–19, 263, 293, 411
  behaviours and 28–9
  deferred 221
  formal specification 590
  functional 23, 28
  non-functional 24–8
  notation 21
  software requirements and 21–3
system scope 274
  diagrammatic notation 127–30
system services 15–16
system state variables 361
system-as-is 5, 12–13
  modelling 294, 450, 503–6
system-to-be 5, 13
  modelling 294, 450, 507–24
systems-to-be-next 6, 219

T

tacit knowledge 63, 79
tasks 424
technology opportunities 14
temporal assertions 585–6
temporal logics 151
test data

from scenarios 201, 450, 463
  sources 123, 212
  specification 362
textual visualisation 200
theorem proving 208–11, 604
threat analysis 314, 512, 551–6
threat graphs 554–6, *Fig. 16.6*
threat models 552–3
threat trees 96, 553
threats 338, 552
throwaway prototypes 71, 72
top-down analysis 279
traceability databases 240–1
traceability graphs 235, *Fig. 6.12, Fig. 6.14*
traceability link generators 243–4
traceability links 226–33
  direction 226, *Fig. 6.3*
  ER model 232–3, *Fig. 6.11*
  identification 233–5, 275, 434
  maintenance 236–7
  types 228–31, *Fig. 6.4*
  uses 235–6
traceability lists 238, *Table 6.3*
traceability management 225–46, *Fig. 6.13*
  cost-benefit trade-off 233–5, 244–6
  goals and 275
  specification-based 242–3
  techniques 237–44
  using model databases 540–1
traceability matrices 237–9, *Table 6.2*
traceability model databases 241–2
traceability policy 233, 244, 246
traces 140, 141
tracking associations 382–3, *Fig. 10.13*
transition-based specification *see* event-based
  specification
transitions 139–40, 455–6
  guarded 139–40, 456, 471, *Fig. 13.7*
  inheritance 459–60, 462
trigger conditions 456
type checking 202–3

U

unacceptable behaviours 29
uncontrollability-driven refinement patterns
  326, *Fig. 8.26*
Unified Modelling Language (UML)
  use in RE 144, 289

Unified Modelling Language (UML) *(continued)*
  see also class diagrams; sequence diagrams;
    state diagrams; use case diagrams
unintentional threats   552
Unique Controller constraint   401
Unique Performer constraint   427
unmonitorability-driven refinement patterns
    325, *Fig. 8.25*
unrealizability-driven refinement patterns
    325–6, 382, 401
  formal use   606–7, *Fig. 18.4*
unstructured interviews   77
unuseability obstacles   338
use case diagrams   136, 144, 435–7, *Fig. 4.9,*
    Fig. 12.8
  generation   442, 521
use cases   277
use links   229–30, 541, *Fig. 6.8*
useability goals   338, 572
useability requirements   26
user interface prototype   70
user story   54

V

validation scenarios   198
value-cost comparison   109, *Fig. 3.6*
variant links   228–9, 239–40, *Fig. 6.6,*
    Fig. 6.15
variants   220–1, *Fig. 6.1*

  modelling   228–9, 239–40, *Fig. 6.15*
variations   525
versions   220–1, 306, *Fig. 6.1*
VOLERE template   126
vulnerability analysis   403, 405

W

walkthroughs   188
weighted matrices   107, 560–1, *Table 3.6,*
    Fig. 16.3
WHAT dimension   15–16
WHO dimension   16–17
WHY dimension   13–15
wish links   402

X

XlinkIt   244

Z

Z (specification language)   156–62
  combining schemas   161–2
  data schemas   156, 157–9
  initialization schemas   156, 158–9
  inspection checklist   195
  language checks   202–3
  operation schemas   156, 159–61
  traceability and   242